The Functional Approach
to Data Management

Springer
Berlin
Heidelberg
New York
Hong Kong
London
Milan
Paris
Tokyo

Peter M.D. Gray • Larry Kerschberg • Peter J.H. King •
Alexandra Poulovassilis (Eds.)

The Functional Approach to Data Management

Modeling, Analyzing and Integrating
Heterogeneous Data

Springer

Editors

Peter M.D. Gray
Department of Computing Science
University of Aberdeen
Aberdeen
UK

Larry Kerschberg
E-Center for E-Business and
Department of ISE
George Mason University
Fairfax, VA
USA

Peter J.H. King
Alexandra Poulovassilis
School of Computer Science and
Information Systems
Birkbeck College
University of London
London
UK

With 87 Figures and 8 Tables

Cataloging-in-Publication Data applied for

Bibliographic information published by Die Deutsche Bibliothek
Die Deutsche Bibliothek lists this publication in the Deutsche
Nationalbibliographie; detailed bibliographic data is available in
the Internet at <http://dnd.dd.de>

ACM Subject Classification (1998): H.2.5, H.2.3, D.1.1

ISBN   978-3-642-05575-1

Springer-Verlag Berlin Heidelberg New York
is a member of BertelsmannSpringer Science+Business Media GmbH
http://www.springer.de

© Springer-Verlag Berlin Heidelberg 2010
Printed in Germany

Cover Design: KünkelLopka, Heidelberg
Printed on acid-free paper   45/3142SR   – 5 4 3 2 1 0

Preface

The Functional Data Model and Functional Languages

The *functional data model* first appeared in the late 1970's with seminal work by Larry Kerschberg and by David Shipman. At the same time Peter Buneman was showing how it could be neatly combined with the newly developing interest in *functional languages* for computing and for specification. In this book we aim to show how those ideas have progressed and why the functional approach both to data models and to computing is now coming of age in the new era of the Semantic Web and distributed resources on the Internet.

Integrating Data from Heterogeneous Databases and in Bioinformatics

Shipman's work on integrating data from heterogeneous databases has been followed up by recent work on integrating widely distributed *bioinformatics databases* and heterogeneous *Internet-based resources*, as described in chapters in Section II. The crucial insight was that the functional abstraction creates a uniform way of viewing data, regardless of how it is actually stored. This may seem strange to programmers, who are used to manipulating data inside specific array or record structures in memory. However, when integrating data from many different sources, for compatibility with various application programs, it is important to hide these storage details and work at a higher conceptual level.

List Comprehensions, Monads and Monoids

From the computational point of view, the functional approach allows us to compose functions, and then to rewrite and transform functional expressions using the principle of referential transparency. A crucial construct is the *list comprehension* which allows one to specify many different kinds of computation with data and to apply mathematical principles in transforming it.

Section III of the book is devoted to the design, formal analysis, and optimization of functional database languages. It includes important refinements
of comprehensions, based on the mathematical structures of *monads* and
monoids. Applications of these principles appear throughout the book.

Associative Storage, Updates and Constraints

Functional abstractions fit very well with an Object–Attribute–Value view of
data. This is more flexible than an*n-ary* relational model and fits well with
semi-structured data, as others have shown. In Section I we see how it can
be implemented efficiently in *associative storage* and examine experimental
systems and novel query languages based on it. A related issue is how to
handle *updates* while preserving the correctness of transformations in their
presence. Several chapters in Section I describe novel approaches to this
problem, including the use of *constraints*.

Approaches to RDF Schema and E-Commerce

Most recently, with the development of the RDF and RDF Schema languages
for specifying resources on the Web, it has become possible to apply the
functional approach to Web resources. Section IV, the last section of the
book, describes recent work on capturing *RDF schema* information in functional form, so that the semantics of Web data can be put on a sounder
footing, so that data from different sources can be meaningfully integrated
and queried. This opens up an exciting new vision of *e-commerce* and web-
based applications, as described in the closing chapters of the book.

Tutorial Aspects

For those for whom the subject is very new, we have written a *tutorial
introductory chapter* assuming only basic knowledge of SQL and simple set-
theoretic notation. This should suffice to give the necessary background for
reading other chapters. It also includes a survey of the influential work which
laid the foundation for much that is described later in the book. Almost all
those active in this field have contributed chapters with detailed references,
so we hope that this book will become a *useful source book* for those working
in the field.

April 2003   *Peter M.D.Gray, Larry Kerschberg*
                                          Peter J H King, Alexandra Poulovassilis

Table of Contents

List of Contributors

S. Alexaki
Institute of Computer Science
FORTH
Vassilika Vouton
P.O. Box 1385,
GR 71110 HERAKLION,
Crete, Greece

J. Bailey
Department of Computer Science
University of Melbourne
MELBOURNE
Australia

P. Buneman
School of Informatics
University of Edinburgh
EDINBURGH EH8 9YL
U.K.

V. Christophides
Institute of Computer Science
FORTH
Vassilika Vouton
P.O. Box 1385,
GR 71110 HERAKLION,
Crete, Greece

S.B. Davidson
University of Pennsylvania
PHILADELPHIA,
Pennsylvania PA 19104
USA

S.M. Embury
Department of Computer Science
University of Manchester
Manchester M13 9PL
U.K.

L. Fegaras
University of Texas at Arlington
ARLINGTON
Texas TX 76019
USA

S. Flodin
Uppsala University
SE-751 05 UPPSALA
Sweden

P.M.D. Gray
Department of Computing Science
University of Aberdeen
King's College
ABERDEEN AB24 3UE
U.K.

T. Grust
Department of Computer
and Information Science
University of Konstanz
78457 KONSTANZ
Germany

K.Y. Hui
Department of Computing Science
University of Aberdeen
King's College
ABERDEEN AB24 3UE
U.K.

G. Karvounarakis
Institute of Computer Science
FORTH
Vassilika Vouton
P.O. Box 1385,
GR 71110 HERAKLION,
Crete, Greece

T. Katchaounov
Dept. of Information Technology
Uppsala University
Box 337
SE-751 05 UPPSALA
Sweden

G.J.L. Kemp
Department of Computing Science
Chalmers University of Technology
SE-412 96, Göteborg
Sweden

L. Kerschberg
E-Center for E-Business
Dept. of Information and Software
Engineering
George Mason University
FAIRFAX Virginia VA 22030-4444
USA

P.J.H. King
School of Computer Science
and Information Systems
Birkbeck College
University of London
LONDON WC1E 7HX
U.K.

A. Magkanaraki
Institute of Computer Science
FORTH
Vassilika Vouton
P.O. Box 1385,
GR 71110 HERAKLION,
Crete, Greece

P.F. Meredith
School of Computer Science
and Information Systems
Birkbeck College
University of London
LONDON WC1E 7HX
U.K.

K. Orsborn
Uppsala University
SE-751 05 UPPSALA
Sweden

N.W. Paton
Department of Computer Science
University of Manchester
MANCHESTER M13 9PL
U.K.

M. Peim
Department of Computer Science
University of Manchester
MANCHESTER M13 9PL
U.K.

D. Plexousakis
Institute of Computer Science
FORTH
Vassilika Vouton
P.O. Box 1385,
GR 71110 HERAKLION,
Crete, Greece

A. Poulovassilis
School of Computer Science
and Information Systems
Birkbeck College
University of London
LONDON WC1E 7HX
U.K.

A.D. Preece
Department of Computing Science
University of Aberdeen
King's College
ABERDEEN AB24 3UE
U.K.

T. Risch
Uppsala University
Box 337
SE-751 05 UPPSALA
Sweden

M. Scholl
INRIA-Rocquencourt
78153 Le Chesnay Cedex
France

V. Tannen
Department of Computer
and Information Science
University of Pennsylvania
PHILADELPHIA
Pennsylvania PA 19104-6389
USA

K. Tolle
Institute of Computer Science
FORTH
Vassilika Vouton
P.O. Box 1385,
GR 71110 HERAKLION,
Crete, Greece

L. Wong
Laboratories for Information
Technology
SINGAPORE 119613

J.P. Yoon
Center for Advanced Computer
Studies
University of Louisiana
LAFAYETTE
Louisiana LA 70504-4330
USA

1. Introduction to the Use of Functions in the Management of Data

Peter M.D. Gray[1], Peter J.H. King[2] and Alexandra Poulovassilis[2]

[1] Department of Computing Science, University of Aberdeen,
Aberdeen AB24 3UE, UK
email: pgray@csd.abdn.ac.uk
[2] School of Computer Science and Information Systems,
Birkbeck College, University of London,
London WC1E 7HX, UK
email: pjhk, ap@dcs.bbk.ac.uk

Summary.

This introductory chapter begins by arguing, by means of examples, that the basic idea of a function is quite straightforward and intuitive, when stripped of its mathematical jargon and notation. We further argue that it is particularly applicable to the management of data. We discuss the role and importance of data models and argue that, with modern computer technology, the functional data model has come of age. We then discuss the advantages of integrating database management software with functional programming and the scope this gives for providing flexible user interfaces and for calculation.

We then discuss the role and significance of the *list comprehension*, developed originally in the context of functional programming, but now seen in the wider context of performance optimisation and the integration of internet data. There follows an introduction to new research which is applying the functional approach to web data that is described by an RDF schema. Finally we present a survey of significant previous work and an extensive bibliography. Our aim is that this chapter will aid the reader in understanding the chapters that will follow.

1.1 Taking a Functional View

1.1.1 Why Use Functions?

In this introductory chapter and throughout this book the word *function* is used only in its mathematical sense of denoting a correspondence between one set of values or things and another. We avoid entirely the other meanings of this word, such as role or purpose, as in "My function in this organisation is to keep people happy."

When stripped of mathematical notation and jargon the basic idea of a function is readily understood by people with no special mathematical training and herein lies its attraction as a basis for data modelling and for database management software. A sales manager rings the Personnel Department to ask for the home telephone number of one of the newly recruited staff, Brian

Smith say. From our point of view, in giving the answer Personnel are evaluating a function. If we call this function home-no, then in the notation we will use we would specify it as

```
home-no :: employee -> telephone-no
```

which means that there is a mapping from the set of employees to a set of telephone numbers such that if we specify a particular employee then we can get the corresponding telephone number. In the case in point, we would say that Personnel are evaluating the function home-no with the argument Brian-Smith and would specify this evaluation as[1]

```
home-no Brian-Smith
```

The way in which Personnel do this and provide the answer is not material to our conceptual view of what is happening although we can readily imagine how it might be done with a desk-top computer, say, or with an old-style card index.

As another example, the chief executive of a retail chain asks for the current salary of the manager of their Birmingham store. In this case we have two functions involved which we could specify as

```
manager :: store -> employee
earns   :: employee -> salary
```

The first of these is evaluated for the Birmingham store to find the employee in question, and the second is then evaluated to provide the answer to the chief executive's query. We call this process the *composition of functions*, which in this case we would specify as

```
earns.manager Birmingham
```

Here, the names of the functions are written together and separated by a stop, the order of evaluation being from right to left[2]. With a computer system we would of course expect the evaluation of this composed function to appear as a single operation to the end user. Any number of functions may be composed in this way provided they are compatible, in the sense that the result of one must be a valid argument for the one immediately to its left, as in this example.

The most usual way of storing the sort of information we are describing with present-day computer systems is not as functions but in the form of

---

[1] In the notation we are using, we write the function name followed by the argument, as in this example. In some notations the argument is placed within brackets as is the convention in mathematics. We only use brackets where they are needed to make the meaning clear.

[2] In some programming language notations (e.g. Java) this would be written as Birmingham.manager.earns and would read from left to right, the interpretation being that Birmingham is "passed" to manager which then passes the employee who is the manager to earns which then determines the salary required.

records, a record being a collection of data items relating to some particular thing or entity. In the 1960s and into the 1970s this was the only practical way of holding significant volumes of information in computer systems due to the limitations of the hardware technology of those times. For many fairly straightforward applications this approach is logically adequate but for more sophisticated applications it can create difficulties and is not adequate; for a discussion of these matters see Kent [1.60].

As a result of research by IBM in the 1960s and early 1970s, an approach to database management was developed in which the user view of data stored in a system was as one or more simple tables, a record now being a row in a table and thus much simplified by contrast with other early systems. All the rows in a particular table are required to have the same kind of data items, those in a particular column being specified by the column heading.

This approach enabled the development of higher-level non-procedural languages to manage and specify operations on the data, notably the language SQL. The current mainstream database products, DB2, Informix, Sybase and Oracle, and for PCs, Access, are all implementations of this basic approach.

We note, however, that data organised in this tabular form could equally well be represented and stored in functional form rather than as records. We illustrate this representation with a simple example. A software house keeps data on its employees, one record for each employee, held in its database in the form of a table, the interpretation of which is: "each row represents an individual employee and the column entries for that employee give their identification number, name, job-title and current salary, respectively".

EMPLOYEE

emp-id	name	job-title	salary
1234	Paul	programmer	19,000
3456	Mary	programmer	22,000
5678	John	analyst	19,000
...	...	...	...

A functional view could specify this information as the three functions

```
called    :: emp-id -> name
works-as  :: emp-id -> job-title
earns     :: emp-id -> salary
```

with four sets of values — those for emp-id, name, job-title and salary.

Note that this approach is specifying information in smaller units, that is with a finer semantic granularity, than with the table where the unit of information is a row in a table. Thus, further information can readily be added such as the function

```
line-manager :: emp-id -> emp-id
```

A powerful argument for the functional approach, in addition to its greater flexibility, is that it facilitates the incremental development of systems. Note also the ease with which we can ask who is the line manager of a particular employee's line manager, by contrast with the record based approach, with

```
called.line-manager.line-manager 1234
```

If for some reason the data needs to be viewed in the form of the above table then it can readily be presented in this form by evaluating the 4-tuple

```
(x, called x, works-as x, earns x)
```

with x taking successively all the values of `emp-id`.

It is important to appreciate that the advantage of a functional approach is not confined to any particular syntax. One could use a point and click graphical interface to construct such a query which would then create an equivalent well-formed data structure. This structure could then be passed between different components in a distributed system and transformed for reuse on other platforms. This is the deep significance of working with functions in a web-based world, because composed functions are easy to map and transform. Later chapters will show how this can be done.

1.1.2 Single and Multi-Valued Functions

The most general form of direct correspondence between two sets of values is a binary relation over them, that is a set of pairs of values one from each domain. To take a specific example, consider a set of towns, T, and a set of retail chains, R. A relation P over these two sets can be used to specify which retailers have branches in which towns. Thus if the pair (r,t) is a member of the set P then this means that retailer r has a branch in town t. (In many data modelling methods this information would be termed a many–many relationship between the towns and the retail chains.)

Any such binary relation can be viewed as defining a function from one set of values to the powerset of the other. Thus, using the above example we would have a function from town to a set of retailers, which specifies for any particular town which retailers have branches in that town. This function we might write as

```
has-branch-of :: town -> {retailer}
```

and similarly the function

```
has-branch-in :: retailer -> {town}
```

which specifies for a particular retailer the towns in which it has branches.

We use the term *multi-valued function* to refer to a set-valued function of this form as being more expressive in our context. Such functions clearly occur in pairs and the detailed specification of one of them is sufficient to define the underlying relation. We refer to the other function as the *converse* of the one specified. Note that in general, although not in this specific example, evaluating a multi-valued function for a specific argument may give the empty set.

Some binary relations define what are naturally single-valued functions. Consider the relation marriage defined over a set of men and a set of women. This can be viewed as the function

```
wife :: man -> woman
```

and its converse

```
husband :: woman -> man
```

In this case both functions are single-valued and the converse function is the same as the mathematically defined inverse function.

In many cases a function can be single-valued but its converse be multi-valued. Clearly this is the case with the function **earns** used as illustration previously. An employee earns only one salary from a particular employer but that employer may pay the same salary to a number of employees.

1.1.3 Types and Function Definitions

Types are a way of classifying data items according to their representation and intended use. They may be specified by giving the possible values of the type explicitly, or by reference to the usual built-in types such as integer, string, etc. Defining new types based on the built-in types by renaming and giving a subrange can also be useful, for example a new type **age** defined as an integer between 0 and 120.

The definition of a function requires its type and one or more equations which specify how, for a particular value of its argument, the result is evaluated. For many functions these equations will be, in effect, an exhaustive list of the possible arguments with the corresponding results. In this case we say the function is *extensionally defined*. Thus, using the example of the previous section,

```
earns :: emp-id -> salary
```

the type of **earns** is **emp-id -> salary** and its definition would be completed by the set of equations

```
earns 1234 = 39000
earns 3456 = 52000
earns 5678 = 47000
       . . .
```

By contrast, the definition of some functions may be accomplished by a single equation which can be used in all cases. For example, a function giving the grossed-up amount for tax purposes for a UK resident on a UK equity dividend where the tax credit is 10% is given by

```
gross-value :: dividend -> gross
gross-value x = (10*x)/9
```

which says that for any dividend x, we calculate its gross value as one and one-ninth of the amount actually received. In this case we say that the function is defined *intentionally*.

We can also have functions which are defined partly intentionally and partly extensionally. To return again to the example in the previous section, suppose our staff are to be paid a bonus of 5% of their salary except for particular people who have an individually designated bonus. This could be achieved by defining the function

```
bonus :: emp-id -> amount
bonus 3456 = 5400
bonus 5678 = 3500
        ...
bonus x    = 0.05 * (salary x)
```

in which those for whom the bonus is specially designated are extensionally defined and all others are dealt with by the general equation. This can be regarded as specifying a *default rule* for calculating a value for all those for whom the result is not specifically stated.

Types are important in database languages, for a number of reasons. Firstly, they convey to users the meanings of functions, associated with their real-world semantics; for example, we know that the function **bonus** above associates an **amount** with each **emp-id**. Secondly, types allow automatic checking that expressions in the language are type-correct i.e. that only arguments of the appropriate type are passed to functions. *Static type-checking*, which happens at compile time rather than at run time, is particularly valuable as it allows erroneous code to be corrected by the programmer before attempting to execute it. Thirdly, the types of functions can be used for compile-time analysis and optimisation of the run-time behaviour of functions — some examples of such techniques are discussed in Section III of the book.

1.2 Data Modelling with Functions

1.2.1 Data Models: Their Role and Importance

Human speech and effective communication require named abstractions or generalisations, person, mammal, vehicle, bridge, child, etc., and the notion that these have specific instances which can be individually identified. Such abstractions, their instances and the connections between them provide in some sense a mental model of a relevant world within some context.

In a not dissimilar way, if we are to hold information in a computer which can be accessed and processed other than in a non-trival way, we need a model of what is held and a context in which it, and the results from its retrieval and processing, are meaningful. We call this the *data model* of the information held; and because we are now in a mechanistic environment, such a model requires a precise specification and representation.

The general recognition of the need for data models of this kind comes from database technology and can be dated from the publication of the influential ANSI/SPARC Report in 1975 [1.98]. Simple models were of course implicit in the earliest data processing systems of the 1950s with records held on tape, each record being there to represent something such as an employee, an insurance policy or an order, and the data items in the record being information about that thing.

As the use and role of data models developed, two modelling primitives became recognised and dominant, those of *aggregation* and *association*. Aggregation is the representation of an entity or thing by collecting together items of information about it, usually, but not necessarily, including one or more which will uniquely identify it. The collection itself represents the entity, and the individual items are its attributes or properties. If we use only this concept we are led to modelling using only the concept of a logical record, such as the *tabular model* briefly discussed in section 1.1.1[3].

With association we have a facility whereby associations between things are separately and explicitly represented and named. The fact that an employee works in a particular department, for example Accounts, would, using only aggregation, be recorded by including that department's name or other identifying characteristic within the employee's record, the meaning being implicit. Everything else would then be a matter of programming with records and using the connecting data items. When association is explicitly recognised, we specify the two things to be associated, in this case employee and department, and give the association a name, say `works-in`. It is a construct of the modelling method and recognised as such.

Data models have been proposed which use only association but a well-known and much-used model in which both concepts are used, known as the Entity/Relationship model, uses the concepts of entity, attribute and association. Each entity has a name and is represented as an aggregation of data items termed its attributes. Each association is also named and is represented by an aggregation of data items, at a minimum including data

---

[3] The tabular model we have described is of course known as the relational model within the database academic, research and development community. This terminology dates from the work of E.F. Codd in which the word "relation" is used in its mathematical sense which differs somewhat from its everyday use and meaning. This can cause misunderstanding and confusion outside the specialist community as exemplified by comments such as "Relational databases enable relations between things to be stored in a database" and "Databases store data in the form of tables", both of which have appeared in the technical press. "Tabular model" has the benefit both of being accurately descriptive for the layman, inferring that there are other models, but still being understood as meaning the relational model by the expert.

items sufficient in a particular association instance to identify the two entity instances it is between.

To illustrate how this approach to modelling proceeds consider a software house whose employees are assigned to work on the various projects it is undertaking. An employee is modelled as an entity as is a project (see Figure 1.1). The attributes specified for the employee entity will be those that relate only and directly to the employee, such as salary, home address, qualifications, date of joining the company, and so on. Similarly, those for the project entity will relate only to the project, such as the client's name, its commencing date, estimated completion date, and so on. The fact of an employee being assigned to a project will be modelled by a named association between the particular employee and the particular project, `assignment`, say. Its attributes will include items that identify the employee and the project concerned and others relating only to the assignment itself, like the date the assignment commenced, the number of hours per week the employee is allocated to this assignment, the role played in the project team, and so forth.

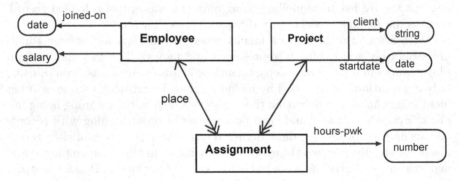

Fig. 1.1. This schema shows three entity classes.

1.2.2 Functional Data Models

A number of data models have been proposed based only on the concept of entity and function, with functions being used to represent both attributes and associations. Entities are of two kinds, those directly materialisable and of themselves providing information like a number, a character string, some text, a digital photograph, a sound fragment, video clip or fingerprint, all of which with current technology we can store in databases, and those which are concepts which do not have direct representation. Thus we can have an entity person for which we might well have name, date of birth, two digital photos, one full-face and one profile, their right thumbprint, and so on, all of which are materialisable entities relating to and providing information about the non-materialisable entity person.

The distinction between these two kinds of entity in data modelling has long been recognised and has been variously referred to by different authors as lexical and non-lexical, scalar and abstract, concrete and abstract, and value and entity. In this chapter and elsewhere in this book we use the terms *value entity* and *abstract entity* for this distinction or, more succinctly, *value* and *abstract* if the meaning is clear from the context. Remember that value has the broad meaning indicated above and thus a particular digital photograph is a "value" of the data type photo.

For the purposes of data modelling, all entities whether value or abstract are regarded as *atomic*, that is they have, in the context of the model, no internal structure. Entities are typed, and to construct a data model the abstract entity types will be named, usually with names from the application domain: person, vehicle, order, and so on. The value types of number, string and boolean are assumed to be augmented by types such as date, photo, thumbprint, etc., when relevant to the application area being modelled. Some value types will have their domains specified explicitly as a set (known as *enumerated types*) whereas the domains of the built-in types will be implicit in the usual way and the domains of types like photo and video-clip will be any which conform with the technical standard adopted.

Consider the abstract entity type person. The information we wish to specify about a person can be defined as functions as described in section 1.1 above. In data modelling, well-chosen names for the types and constructs are important in helping to make a particular model and its semantics understandable. A clear advantage with the functional approach is the added semantic richness possible as a result of having both function names and domain names available. Thus

```
earns :: employee -> salary
```

clearly expresses the semantics of the mapping to the salary domain; and the functions

```
date-of-birth    :: person -> date
date-of-marriage :: person -> date
date-of-death    :: person -> date
```

express the meanings of the various functions from **person** to **date** we might well have in a family history database. Here, of course, person is an abstract type and date is a value type.

Functions used to specify information about an abstract entity type may be single-valued, as above, or multi-valued. For example, we may record the relevant qualifications held by an employee with the multi-valued function

```
qualifications :: employee -> {string}
```

since an employee may have no, one or several qualifications. In the family history example, a person's children would be modelled by the function

```
children-of :: person -> {person}
```

and we could also have the function

    parents-of :: person -> {person}

which is the converse of `children-of`, as part of the model. Note that although we know that a person always has exactly two parents we nonetheless provide for the result being none, one or two, since with a family history database we would use the *open world assumption* (where we do not have complete knowledge of the problem domain), as opposed to the *closed world assumption*, where the information is assumed to be complete so that, for example, a person who cannot be found in the employee database is not an employee of the company.

In data modelling it has been found that a good practical diagramming method is of considerable value. Modelling with functions in the way we have described can be readily diagrammed using directed graphs in which labelled nodes represent the various types and labelled arcs the functions.

It should be noted that thus far we have illustrated only functions of a single variable in our discussions. Some authors, and in particular Shipman [1.86], have proposed the inclusion of functions of more than one variable in the functional approach to modelling. A function of two arguments, say, is in effect a function from the cartesian product of the two domains concerned. If the elements of this cartesian product are of sufficient semantic significance to be the argument of a function in the model then, it can be argued, they are of sufficient semantic significance to be regarded as entities in their own right. Moreover, if we are given an arbitrary relation (in the mathematical sense) over n domains we can always use it to define a function from any $n - 1$ of them to the other. But we know from relational database theory that arbitrary n-ary relations are not satisfactory and require normalisation. Thus if we allow in the model functions of more than one argument we will also need some criteria for deciding they are in some sense well formed, as with n-ary relations in the relational model. Since functions of more than one variable are unnecessary as a modelling construct we have a powerful case for invoking Occam's razor and not having them thus avoiding altogether these problems. This is not to say, however, that functions of two or more arguments are not of very considerable value when forming user views. We discuss this aspect further in section 1.3.3 below.

1.2.3 From Data Model to Operational System

A data modelling method can be used without any direct implementation of its constructs in the database management software to be used to create the operational system. This requires an agreed way of mapping the model constructs to the facilities provided by the database software product. Such is the case with the entity-elationship model. In SSADM [1.6] this process is known as proceeding from the logical to the physical data design. Where, however, the constructs of the model are directly implemented in the database software product, as with functional databases, this stage is not required.

In our discussion of data models thus far we have made no reference to the requirements for accessing and updating the database. In SSADM this is referred to as dialogue design and again there has to be a mapping to the access and update facilities of the database management system (DBMS). When we have the data model directly implemented, as with the functional model, then access and update facilities can be regarded as part of both the data model and the resulting DBMS.

1.3 Functional Databases and Functional Programming

We now give a brief overview of the main features of database programming interfaces implemented and proposed for DBMSs implementing the functional model of data. We consider first management of abstract entities, then query languages, and then updates and other features.

1.3.1 Abstract Entities: Their Representation and Management

The instances of an abstract entity are represented in most systems by internal tokens or surrogates which cannot meaningfully be displayed. One can think of such a surrogate as representing the entity itself, its uniqueness and persistence, as opposed to its attributes. In a DBMS, some way of creating, deleting and managing such surrogates is clearly needed.

The approach of Shipman's DAPLEX language [1.86] is to make only indirect reference to them. To create a new instance of an abstract entity Person, say, the language construct

    FOR A NEW Person BEGIN ... END

is used. Within the BEGIN ... END block, Person can now be used, not in the sense of a type but as a reference to the instance just created, for example by adding further equations to extensionally defined functions such as

    Name (Person) = "Paul"
    Occupation (Person) = "Programmer"

To add further information about an entity that already exists, it must first be identified using the construct

    FOR THE PERSON SUCH THAT Name (Person) = "Paul" BEGIN ... END

Again within the BEGIN ... END block, Person now is used to refer to the specific entity identified[4].

---

[4] Shipman also proposed the syntax FOR THE p IN PERSON SUCH THAT Name(p) = "Paul" which avoids confusing two different usages of Person and also allows one to distinguish two people by using two variable names, for example FOR EACH p2 IN PERSON SUCH THAT p2 <> p1.

A similar but more straightforward approach is adopted in the FDL language [1.77] and its further development, the Relief language [1.68]. Here, "session variables" are used, a session variable being an untyped variable which exists for the duration of the current login session and is implicitly declared on first use. It is denoted by a dollar sign followed by an alphanumeric string. Thus, in the syntax of Relief

```
$p = create Person.
```

assigns to the variable $p as its value the surrogate of the newly created instance of Person. The variable can now be used as in

```
def name $p       = "Paul";
def occupation $p = "Programmer".
```

There are two advantages in this approach, the first being that the reference to a particular entity instance is, unless there is reassignment to the particular session variable, available throughout a login session without the need to re-identify the entity instance if we again need to refer to it. The second is that we have uniformity of approach when more than one reference is required to distinct entities of the same type as in

```
$p = create Person;
$q = create Person;
def wife $p = $q.
```

With the "invisible surrogate" approach we have described, it is possible to have two or more distinct entities with the information stored about them being identical, although it may subsequently become different as a result of the addition of further information. However, it is widespread practice in data processing to introduce unique reference numbers even when not really necessary. An argument then asks why such reference numbers cannot be used instead of the invisible surrogates since they could then be displayed and could be useful. It would avoid the need in these cases for an identifying function such as

```
emp-id :: employee -> string
```

Updating the database for a new employee, for whom emp-id will have been separately assigned, would then proceed as:

```
$e            = create employee;
def emp-id $e = 1234.
```

However, such functions isomorphic with the surrogates have drawbacks. In addition to the function declaration, integrity constraints are required to ensure that the function is always defined and that all values are distinct. Moreover in some contexts it is more convenient to allow the system to generate the identifying numbers which may subsequently need to be changed.

A detailed discussion of these matters can be found in Ayres and King [1.7] who discuss a system for managing visible surrogates which can be supplied externally when a new entity instance is created or, in default of it being supplied externally, will be generated automatically by the system. In either case the visible surrogates can subsequently be changed. A log of all surrogate changes is kept. Old surrogates may not be reused and a reference to an old surrogate causes an error message which gives the new surrogate to which it was changed.

This approach has the advantage of clarity in terms of maintaining the extents of abstract entity types. Thus, if we have an abstract entity `person` declared, with an initially empty extent, three person instances could be added to its extent, with the visible surrogates shown:

```
person ::+ Robert, Peter, Paul;
```

To add a fourth surrogate but leaving the system to supply the surrogate requires

```
person ::+;
```

The extent will now consist of four entities with the visible surrogates:

```
{Robert, Peter, Paul, Person1}
```

After the two statements

```
person ::- Peter;
Person1 is now Anthony;
```

which deletes one entity and redesignates the surrogate for another, the extent will be

```
{Anthony, Robert, Paul}
```

This approach was implemented in the experimental system Hydra [1.8] and proved successful, although its practical use to date has been rather limited. Of importance is the fact that because of the method of implementation over a content-addressed triple store (see Chapter 2) there is no performance difference from using internally generated invisible surrogates. This would not be the case in implementations where the invisible surrogate contains an internal addressing component as is sometimes the case.

1.3.2 Querying Functional Databases

A functional database comprises sets of entities and functions defined over them, and these supply the basic primitives from which query languages for such databases are constructed. Additional functions are also provided for more powerful querying and in this section we briefly describe some of the extra query facilities provided by Hydra. A deeper discussion of some of these features is given in subsequent sections of this chapter.

As part of the system for the management of entity sets discussed in section 1.3.1 above, Hydra provides a function, `All`, which takes as its argument an abstract entity type or enumerated value type and gives as its result the current extent of that type. Thus if `person` is an abstract type, `All person` is the current set of instances of that type.

A second useful query construct is the *list comprehension* which we discuss in more detail in section 1.4. This together with the `All` function allows queries such as

```
[name x | x <- All person]
```

which causes the function `name` to be evaluated for every surrogate in the result of `All person` and the result to be presented as a list. Notice that while `All person` is a set and thus the order in which its members are provided is arbitrary, the result of the comprehension is not necessarily a set unless the function `name` has been constrained to be unique. The result is thus presented as a list in an order determined by the arbitrary ordering of `All person`.

There may be filtering out of values as in

```
[name x | x <- All person; job-title x = "analyst"]
```

which will provide only the names of those employees whose job title is "analyst". This query could equivalently have been written

```
[name x | x <- Conv job-title "analyst"]
```

where `Conv job-title` denotes the converse of the `job-title` function.

1.3.3 User Views in Functional Databases

Defining a user view of a database is an important way of providing a more convenient and readily usable view of the stored data for a particular application or activity. With an appropriate user view, queries against the database can be shorter and more easily written since transformations which would otherwise be common to many queries can be made part of the view.

Consider for example weighted points in a two-dimensional space, each point being represented by a pair of coordinates and an associated weight. The data model could be defined by

```
abstract point
x-coord :: point -> num
y-cood  :: point -> num
weight  :: point -> num
```

Suppose a particular application is much concerned with the distance between pairs of points. It would then clearly be useful to have a function to provide this directly as part of the user view. This can be achieved by including in the view specification the function definition

```
dist :: point  point -> num;
dist p1 p2 =  let x = (x-coord p1) - (x-coord p2)
              let y = (y-coord p1) - (y-coord p2)
              in sqrt (x*x+y*y);
```

If in a query the distance between two points a and b, say, is needed we can now simply write `dist a b`. This example shows the great virtue of the functional data model: that it can be extended by adding additional computed functions. It thus makes a significant advance over Codd's original tabular data model which provided extensibility through new types of tables, but did not provide for extending ways of computing derived values.

The syntax of the functional model allows us to call up normal mathematical functions (like `sqrt`) just as easily as data model functions (like `x-coord`) and to compose them into expressions, just as you would expect. The function definitions themselves together with the expressions can be sent across the Web for execution on remote servers. In this way they resemble Java servlets, but are more platform-independent.

1.3.4 Updating Functional Databases

The detailed information in a functional database is present in the various function definitions together with the type definitions and their extents. Updating thus, in the main, comprises making changes to these definitions.

Consider for example the function `earns` used in section 1.1.1. If a particular employee, say the one with `emp-id` 1234, receives a salary increase to 23,000, then this update is achieved by the equation

```
earns 1234 = 23000
```

replacing the equation

```
earns 1234 = 19000
```

If this employee also now has a specially designated bonus of 2500, say, then the equation

```
bonus 1234 = 2500
```

can be added to the earlier definition of the `bonus` function.

Update can also involve changing the data model. In terms of the functional database, such changes are equivalent to the deletion or addition of function definitions. Clearly if a function definition is deleted then the equations defining the mapping must also be deleted. Thus, again returning to the example of section 1.1, if the company decides to abandon paying bonuses then the update

```
delete bonus
```

brings the database into line with this change. If the data model is extended, for example by including the date on which an employee joined the company and also for those married women known by their married name, their maiden name, then the new function definitions

```
joined-on    :: emp-id -> date
maiden-name :: emp-id -> string
```

would be added.

Notice that these two functions have different semantics if there is no defining equation for a particular employee. In the case of joined-on it would mean that the date is not known (to the database) and this could be made explicit by adding the default equation

```
joined-on x = unknown
```

whereas in the case of maiden-name it may mean that it is not relevant for this particular employee (a man, for example), or that it is relevant but unknown. There are various ways of enabling this distinction to be made. One that has been successfully used in practice is to supply the value **not relevant** by default if there is no defining equation and to allow the **unknown** value to be explicitly encoded where required.

With regard to changing the extents of types discussed in section 1.3.1 above, consistency must be maintained between these extents and the occurrences of their values in the equations of function definitions; a specific value cannot occur in a function definition unless it is present in the type extent. Two approaches can be adopted to ensuring this. One is also to delete automatically all equations referring to a value when that value is deleted from its type extent. The other is not to permit a deletion from a type extent unless all such equations have already been deleted. There are good arguments for either approach, and a satisfactory compromise when systems are used directly by humans would be to give a warning that there are equations referring to a value about to be deleted and display them with the option either to proceed or to cancel.

1.3.5 The Integration of Functional Databases with Functional Programming

A DBMS provides a language for querying and updating a database, known as its query or data manipulation language. A well-known example is the various product-specific versions of SQL. Such languages do not in general provide a complete programming facility and are thus used in association with a general-purpose programming language, known as the host language. For example, SQL is often used in industry with C or Cobol as the host language.

With a functional database there are considerable advantages in it being fully integrated with a functional programming language such as ML[1.102],

Miranda[1.99] or Hope[1.41]. In this case functions which access the database will, in the context of programming, be usable in exactly the same way as functions defined for the purpose of programming. Moreover, further functions can be defined for the purpose of programming using both the database functions and those that have been defined in the language.

Suppose, for example, we have defined a function `average` which takes as its argument a list of numbers and produces their average as its result. Then the query

```
average [salary x | x <- All employee]
```

which uses `average` together with the database function `salary` gives the average salary paid by the company. If we have a database function `works-in`, which gives for a particular employee their department, then we could define a function to give the average salary for a particular department by

```
av-dept-sal :: dept -> num
av-dept-sal x = average [salary e | e <- Conv works-in x]
```

Here, `dept` is an enumerated type based on the built-in type `string`, and `Conv works-in` is the converse function of `works-in` and is thus a list of the employees working in department `x`. Then to obtain the average salary paid in the Accounts Department, say, we can use the query

```
av-dept-sal "Accounts"
```

To provide a list of all departments with the average salary paid in each we need only write

```
[(x, av-dept-sal x) | x <- All dept]
```

1.3.6 Referential transparency

A basic assumption of functional programming is that a function is defined by its value, that is to say by the mapping from one domain to another, from input to output; and that this mapping does not change during the execution of a program. This is the concept of *referential transparency*: that whenever a function is called with the same argument (input) it gives the same result (output). The assumption of referential transparency enables functional programs to be reasoned about mathematically so providing a tool to assist in ensuring the correctness of programs, enabling optimising transformations to take place on compilation, and facilitating the use of parallelism in program execution.

It is immediately clear that the *updating* of functions defining a functional database contradicts the basic assumption of referential transparency. In a functional database, the essence of a function is conveyed by its name and its type, with which is associated its real-world semantics, and not by its current mapping, which will change as a result of database updates. The function **earns** specifying a person's salary as used earlier is a case in point.

The partial loss of referential transparency due to updates does not, however, alter the other considerable advantages of functional programs: that they represent a high-level, non-procedural but executable specification of what is required, and enable programs to be created in a top-down fashion with local detail encapsulated within the specification of the functions to which these details relate. Moreover a functional program that does not involve updates but accesses a database in read-only mode will be referentially transparent. Even with updates there is what might be termed local referential transparency between such updates; thus some advantages can nonetheless be gained. This matter is discussed further in Chapters 3 and 4.

1.3.7 The lambda calculus

The functional database language FDL [1.75, 1.77, 1.76] unified a functional data model with functional programming. Like functional programming languages such as LISP, Scheme, ML, Miranda and Haskell, FDL is based on the λ *(lambda) calculus*.

The lambda calculus was invented in the 1930s by Alonzo Church as a notation for specifying functions. For example, the 2-argument function **g**

```
g x y = (x - 1) * (y - 2)
```

would be specified by the following *lambda abstraction*[5]:

```
lambda x. lambda y. * (- x 1) (- y 2)
```

Computation in the lambda calculus then consists of rewriting expressions by a series of transformations called *beta-reductions*. For example,

```
(lambda x. lambda y. * (- x 1) (- y 2))  5  6
```

beta-reduces to

```
(lambda y. * (- 5 1) (- y 2))  6
```

which beta-reduces to

```
* (- 5 1) (- 6 2)
```

which after three more reductions (for the two occurrences of - and the one occurrence of *) simplifies to 16, as we would expect for the value of **g 5 6**.

A lambda expression which cannot be further reduced is said to be in *normal form*. In general, there may be a choice of reduction steps to reach a normal form. For example, at this stage above:

```
(lambda y. * (- 5 1) (- y 2))  6
```

---

[5] By convention, all operators, even arithmetic ones, are written in prefix form in the lambda calculus.

We could have chosen first to simplify the inner expression (- 5 1) rather than the leftmost, outermost expression which is what we selected. Fortunately, all possible reduction sequences satisfy the so-called *Church–Rosser property*, namely that: *for all sequences of reduction steps that terminate in a normal form, these normal forms are the same (up to renaming of variables)*.

A sequence of reduction steps which reduces the leftmost, outermost expression whenever possible is termed a *normal order reduction*. This gives the best possible termination behaviour of a lambda expression, in that normal order reduction of an expression will terminate with a normal form if any reduction order does. Normal order reduction is also known as *lazy evaluation*.

1.4 Comprehensions - their Role and Significance

One common thread running through almost all the chapters in this book is the use of the functional programming concept of a *list comprehension* which deserves to be much more widely known. Some people may know it as a *set abstraction* [1.22] or as a *ZF-expression* [1.100]. Others may use Risch's terminology of a *calculus expression*. Buneman, Libkin, Suciu, Tannen and Wong [1.21] have generalised it for database use to include set and bag comprehensions. Wadler [1.101] has related it to the algebraic structure of monads.

The comprehension crosses the borders between the lambda calculus and the predicate calculus since functions, like predicates, can be used either as generators or as filters in collecting up sets of values. What is important is the mathematical theory worked out in connection with functional programming, which can be used in a variety of ways, for example to develop and prove correct new analysis and optimisation techniques for queries and database transactions. Some examples of this are discussed in Section III of the book.

The comprehension comes from ideas of mathematical set theory. It originated as a way of defining sets of values, starting from other well-defined sets and using some carefully chosen constructors and filters, so as to avoid the famous paradoxes of early set theory. The values in the sets could be tuples of basic values, which suits the relational model, or they could be object identifiers, which fits with ODMG object data models [1.25], or they could be tagged variant records which fit well with semi-structured data. They could even be sets, lists or bags defined by other comprehensions.

1.4.1 Comprehensions and SQL

Although comprehensions are very familiar to mathematicians, most people who use databases will be making use of SQL, and we shall assume basic familiarity with this. We shall now see how comprehensions have similar power to SQL.

Let us take a simple example, an SQL query to find the set of surnames of persons whose forename is "Jim":

```
SELECT   surname
FROM     person
WHERE    forename = "Jim"
```

Using a list comprehension[6] this can be written as:

```
[surname(p) | p <- person; f <- forename(p); f = "Jim"]
```

This denotes the list of values of the expression to the left of the vertical bar. This expression usually includes variables such as p which are instantiated by generators to the right of the vertical bar. We can, in fact, transliterate it as:

The set of values of the surname of p *such that* p *is in the set* person *and* f *is in the set* of forenames of p *and* f is equal to "Jim".

Thus, the vertical bar can be read as *such that* and the semicolons as conjunctions (*and*). The arrows act as *generators*, supplying alternative possible values, subject to restrictions by predicate terms to the right, acting as *filters*. Thus p is generated from the set of persons but is only chosen where the forename of p satisfies the test of equalling "Jim".

In the above syntax we have overloaded the arrow operator, so that if a function such as forename delivers a single value instead of a set then the arrow just assigns that single value to the variable on its left. Strictly, one should make a singleton set containing this value, and then extract it:

```
[surname(p) | p <- person; f <- [forename(p)]; f = "Jim"]
```

This wasteful operation would be compiled away to give this equivalent form:

```
[surname(p) | p <- person; forename(p) = "Jim"]
```

The term "list comprehension" is commonly used, but we should really distinguish between lists, sets and bags [1.21]. Thus comprehensions are usually represented internally as lists, but often the order is ignored, as in sets, and sometimes it is necessary to keep duplicates and form a bag, especially when totalling up the contents! Particular classes of operator used in comprehensions give rise to *monad comprehensions* and *monoid comprehensions* with valuable mathematical properties. These are described in Section III of this book, in chapters by Fegaras, Grust, and Buneman and Tannen.

Nested Generators and Nested Loops. Generators may just be based on finite sets (or subranges) of integers, and filters can also do calculations. For example, suppose we want the set of all right-angled triangles with whole-number sides less than 50. The comprehension for this neatly expresses the mathematical requirements:

---

[6] here, as in programming languages, the function parameters are bracketed

```
[(x,y,z) | x <- [1..50]; y <- [1..50]; z <- isqrt(x*x + y*y);
         z*z = x*x + y*y;   z <50]
```

Here for each value of x between 1 and 50, we explore all y values between 1 and 50, generate a value for the longest side z using a function to calculate the integer part of the square root, and then test that z is less than 50. The results are returned in the form of triples, such as (3,4,5). This is a typical use of functions in numerical calculation. It also introduces the subject of *nested loops*. Notice that when we use one generator to the right of another, we have to consider all values from the one in combination with all values from the other, which is just like using nested loops in an ordinary programming language.

Let us now consider a query involving nested generators, which corresponds to the use of joins in SQL, but we shall write it in the OQL object database query language [1.25]:

```
select x.name
from x in students, y in x.takes, z in y.taught_by
where z.rank = "full prof"
```

This gives the names of students who take courses taught by full professors. The equivalent comprehension is

```
[name(x) | x <- students; y <- takes(x); z <- taught_by(y);
          rank(z) = "full prof"]
```

In a programming language supporting assignment and for loops, we would write the computation using nested loops, which enables us to see more clearly the role of the generators:

```
result := [];
for x in students()
    for y in takes(x)
        for z in taught_by(y)
            if rank(z) = "full prof"
            then result := result ++ [name(x)];
```

Note that the variables are now treated as holding object identifiers. More significantly, each variable is only introduced once with an arrow, and this must come before it is used in a predicate or as a parameter of another generator. Apart from this, generators and predicates can be reordered without altering the value of the comprehension, since it behaves like a conjunction of booleans.

This reordering is made easier by using converse functions of the form f_inv (equivalent to Conv f used in section 1.3.2) which, like an inverted index, may enable one to move selections nearer to generators, so as to gain efficiency. For example, the following comprehension produces the same result more quickly by applying the filter on full professor much earlier:

```
[name(x) | z <- lecturers;  rank(z) = "full prof";
        y <- taught_by_inv(z); x <- takes_inv(y)]
```

This technique is widely used (see for example the chapters on AMOS II and Kleisli in this book). Note that it is not necessary for the end users themselves to use f_inv; this need only happen within the query optimiser module of the DBMS.

Representing Joins as Comprehensions. The example given above with nested loops may appear to require functions such as takes(x) with stored values that relate each student x to the set of object identifiers of courses that they take. However, this is only one way of representing the relationship. If, instead, we have a relational table takes(s:student; c:course) we would implement the generator y <- takes(x) as follows:

```
for x in students()
    for t in takes()
        if name(x) = s(t)
        then for z in taught_by(c(t)) ...
```

The corresponding list comprehension is:

```
[name(x) | x <- students; t <- takes; name(x) = s(t);
        z <-taught_by (c(t)); ...]
```

From considerations of efficiency, there need not be much difference between these implementations. If the implementor spots that they can use the index maintained on the table takes to locate directly those rows in column s containing the name of the student x, and thus satisfy the filter name(x) = s(t) following the generator for t, instead of naively iterating through all rows in the takes table and testing them, then performance will be similar.

However, this is to miss one of the great virtues of the functional approach. It is not necessary for the writer of the query to know how the data is stored. The abstraction y <- takes(x) is perfectly satisfactory. If the data turns out to be stored in relational tables with indexes, then the system itself can automatically perform the necessary transformations into the form shown above. The work of Kemp, Risch, Wong and others in the chapters that follow discusses techniques for doing this.

This is all backed by mathematical theory that goes right back to early papers by Burstall and Darlington [1.22] which were not then directed at databases. The great advantage over SQL is that comprehensions obey the ordinary mathematical rules of substitutivity and referential transparency. They are not confined by obscure syntax or legacy features in the language.

1.4.2 Data Independence

The fundamental advantage of list comprehensions as a database abstraction is that they preserve data independence in a very clean and simple way.

They do it by working entirely in terms of sets and functional relationships, regardless of how they are stored. This will seem strange to programmers who are used to carefully choosing between arrays of records or parallel arrays or linked lists or B-trees etc.

Database people realise that large collections of data may exist in different forms on different computers, and may need to change form by restructuring on a single computer. Thus it is necessary to do the translation from a list comprehension expressed against a conceptual schema into a specific storage schema at compile time (often close to run time). Likewise it may be necessary to send part of a query to a remote server, since data is increasingly distributed in different forms. Thus the list comprehension is a good choice for passing a complex computational request between computers, free from assumptions about data storage or whether functions are computed or based on stored values.

In order to show that list comprehensions can be more complex, consider another query which returns the codes of all courses that have some section taught by a senior lecturer:

```
[code(c) | c <- course;
           some([t | s <- sections(c); t <- lecturer(s);
                p <- position(t); p="SL"]) ]
```

Here, the inner comprehension depends on the variable c representing a course, which is bound by the outer comprehension. The function some is a predicate that tests whether its parameter (the inner comprehension) returns a non-empty list. It corresponds to the EXISTS predicate in SQL. In fact, the query can be translated into SQL automatically as discussed in the chapters by Kemp and Gray, and by Davidson and Wong.

We will now look at how comprehensions are used in a number of systems described in chapters in this book. There are slight variations in syntax and in emphasis, but all these systems can make use of mathematical results of comprehensions for transformation and optimisation. There are novel applications of comprehensions in many of the chapters in this book, and novel theoretical developments in Section III of the book.

1.4.3 Comprehensions in P/FDM and Constraints

P/FDM [1.48, 1.74], like AMOS [1.35], uses list comprehensions internally but provides an equivalent query language syntax which suits regular programmers. In P/FDM the above comprehension is rendered as

```
for each c in course such that
    some t in lecturer(sections(c)) has position(t)="SL"
        print(code(c));
```

This syntax is very close to Shipman's original DAPLEX language [1.86]. It is aimed at procedural programmers who are more used to nested loops as a way of collecting up values. Values can be collected into a stored set by using the **insert** function in place of the **print** function.

In P/FDM, the DAPLEX language was deliberately altered from its original specification so that its semantics could be defined by equivalent list comprehensions [1.32]. In particular, simple assignment operations, if present, could only take place within the innermost loop, and were implemented in such a way that the outcome did not depend on the ordering of the loops. Based on this, a very successful early optimiser was written [1.74].

Comprehensions in P/FDM are also used to describe the semantics of integrity constraints, representing invariants that must be held true under updates. For this purpose the nested loop syntax used in queries is adapted:

```
constrain each t in seniortutor
     each s in advisees(t)
          to have grade(s) > 60;
```

This constrains each person in the class **seniortutor** to have only advisees with grades over 60. It requires that the following list comprehension always computes an empty list:

```
[ t | t <- seniortutor; s <- advisees(t) ;
     not (grade(s) > 60)]
```

The constraint is equivalent to the following formula in predicate logic, where we see the correspondence between the generators and the nested quantifiers and also the similarity in use of conjunctions:

$$(\forall t)\ seniortutor(t)\ \Rightarrow\ ((\forall s,g)\ advisee(t,s) \land grade(s,g) \Rightarrow g > 60)$$

The comprehension is actually computing the set of members for which the constraint is false (technically the complement of the extension of the constraint predicate). The logic formula is defining the constraint predicate as an intention instead of an extension. This shows a fascinating connection between comprehensions and the predicate calculus, as well as the lambda calculus, and once more illustrates their versatility.

1.4.4 View Integration and Comprehensions in AMOS

In AMOS [1.35] the top-level language uses function application within an SQL-like syntax, for example:

```
create function sailing_children(person p) -> string as
     select name(c)
     from  person c
     where parent(c) = p and hobby(c) = 'sailing';
```

This is turned into a comprehension, treated as a *typed object calculus expression*. The types of all functions are known, and more specialised functions may be defined on object subtypes. Some functions may be defined as views on other databases accessed through mediators. In the comprehension form, such functions may easily be substituted because of referential transparency, leading to a longer conjunction with extra clauses. In this form it can be easily reordered and optimised, including removal of redundant runtime type checks and conversions. More details are given in [1.57] and in the later chapter by Risch in this book. Let us express the example above as a comprehension:

```
sailch(p) == [name(c) | c <- person; parent(c)=p;
                        hobby(c) = 'sailing']
```

Suppose information about hobby(c) was held in connection with sportsperson, a subclass of person with a surname attribute, and that we could express it thus:

```
hobby(c) == [recreation(x) | x <- sportsperson;
                             surname(x) = name(c)]
```

These comprehensions merge into the following which can be further simplified:

```
sailch(p) == [name(c) | c <- person; parent(c)=p;
                        x <- sportsperson;
                        surname(x) = name(c);
                        recreation(x) = 'sailing']
```

One feature to note is that Risch's internal form of comprehension does not explicitly distinguish the use of generators and just uses equality, as in a filter. This has the conceptual advantage that generators are not always a fixed role and some optimisations require one to reverse the role of filter and generator, but of course systems with explicit generators can also use rewrite rules to do this.

1.4.5 Comprehensions in Kleisli—Records, Lists and Mixed Types

In Kleisli [1.30, 1.103], comprehensions are written with a comma as separator for conjunctions in place of a semicolon. Also, the first time that a variable iterates over a set of values (in some generator), its name needs to be prefixed with a backslash. Subsequent uses of the unprefixed variable, either in filters or in generators, make use of these bindings. Lastly, record field names are prefixed by a #. Thus, our initial example would read:

```
{p.#surname | \p <- person, \f <- p.#forename, f = "Jim"}
```

If we wished to create a *list* comprehension or *bag* comprehension we would enclose the above expression in different brackets [... | ...] or {| ... | ...|} respectively. If then we need to enumerate a list, preserving its sorted order, we use the generator <---. Note that Kleisli's list comprehension constructor sorts its output, when it is of basic type, so we can extract items in sorted order from a set ORG by

```
\z <--- [u | \u <- ORG]
```

Kleisli has a tuple constructor that is very useful for creating records and labelling fields in results to give self-describing output. This can be passed back into generators of other comprehensions, thus giving it something of the closure property of the relational algebra but within a much richer type system. For example,

```
let Genpept == {(#uid: x.#uid, #detail: x) |
                \x <- aa-get-seqfg "PTP"}
in  {x.#detail.#title | \x <- Genpept, x.#uid = 12345}
```

Here Genpept is a set of *records* with two fields #uid and #detail. The fields are generated using a system-provided function aa-get-seqfg (abbreviated), with parameter "PTP" [7]. Genpept is then used in the following generator to extract a record with a specific uid. The chapter by Davidson and Wong in this book shows how Genpept can be written out to a relational database table and an index on it created, so as to avoid scanning the whole set of records for the one with uid=12345. This is a good example of an important optimisation considered earlier.

The CPL language used in Kleisli allows top-level commands rather like a batch file or a scripting language, so as to set off a sequence of calculations calling predefined functions with intermediate results passed through parameters (like Genpept above). The language is designed so that expressions may be type-checked dynamically against input files and the tags in their records and variant records. CPL is also very much designed for optimisation.

Thus the end user is basically confined to programming with comprehensions, while the full power of functional programming is reserved for the implementers, working in Standard ML. Rules expressed in Standard ML can then be used to pattern-match CPL structures and compute optimised or derived values. This is an elegant use of functional programming but note that it is not essential to use a functional language for optimising comprehensions; for example, P/FDM uses Prolog while AMOS uses a version of LISP. Any good list processing language will do but functional languages are, of course, better at type checking.

---

[7] Note that here the function *prefixes* the parameter, as normal, instead of *following* it as in record field selection.

1.4.6 Comprehensions in FDL and PFL

The functional database languages FDL [1.77] and PFL [1.79] incorporate list comprehensions as part of a more general, computationally complete, functional language based on the lambda calculus. In such languages, comprehensions can be formalised as successive applications of a function `flatmap`. This function is defined as follows (in the syntax of PFL), where the operator `++` concatenates two lists, `[]` is the empty list, and `(x:xs)` denotes a list with head `x` and tail `xs`:

```
flatmap f []     = []
flatmap f (x:xs) = (f x) ++ (flatmap f xs)
```

Thus we see that `flatmap` is a recursive function which takes a list-valued function `f` and a list and successively applies `f` to each element of the list, concatenating the resulting lists. The scheme for translating list comprehensions into successive applications of `flatmap` is as follows, where `e` and `e'` are arbitrary expressions, `p` is a variable or a tuple of variables, and `Q` is a sequence of generators or filters:

```
[e|]       = [e]
[e|e';Q]   = if e' then [e|Q] else []
[e|p<-e';Q] = flatmap (lambda p.[e|Q]) e'
```

Thus, for example, the following comprehension from earlier in this section:

```
[surname(p) | p <- person; f <- forename(p); f = "Jim"]
```

would translate into the following expression:

```
flatmap (lambda p.
            flatmap (lambda f.if f = "Jim"
                              then [surname(p)]
                              else [])
                    forename(p))
        person
```

The function `flatmap` is an example of a *higher-order* function, in that it takes another function as an argument (the parameter `f` in the case of `flatmap`).

`flatmap` is also an example of a *polymorphic* function, in that its type can be inferred to be `(a->[b])->[a]->[b]`, where `a` and `b` are *type variables* each of which can be replaced by *any* type. Thus, the definition of `flatmap` actually specifies a family of functions, one function for each possible instantiation of the type variables `a` and `b`. For example, in the above expression representing the comprehension `[surname(p) | p <- person; f <- forename(p); f = "Jim"]`, the first occurrence of `flatmap` has type

```
(Person->[String])->[Person]->[String]
```

while the second occurrence has type

(String->[String])->[String]->[String]

This kind of polymorphism is known as *parametric polymorphism* and is supported by most functional programming languages and by many functional database languages. The kind of polymorphism supported by object-oriented languages is *inclusion polymorphism*. This kind of polymorphism allows a property or method defined for one type of object to be also applicable to all suptypes of that type, and perhaps also to be *overriden* by a different definition for a subtype.

It is possible for languages, including functional languages, to support both kinds of polymorphism. DAPLEX and the languages derived from it support inclusion polymorphism but not parametric polymorphism. FDL incorporates a functional data model, similar to that of DAPLEX, and combines it with parametric polymorphism. However, FDL does not support subtypes and inclusion polymorphism.

PFL has a similar type system to FDL, but uses a class of functions called *selectors* which allow storage, querying and update of sets of values of the same type. Using comprehensions, further functions can be defined over selectors which are "invertible" in the sense that they simulate predicates as might be written in a logic language. To illustrate this feature of PFL, suppose the following selector stores information about people and their parents:

    parent :: (Person,Person) -> [(Person,Person)]

Thus, for example, the following queries respectively return Mary's parents, Joe's children, and the entire set of child/parent tuples[8]:

    parent (Mary,Any)
    parent (Any,Joe)
    parent (Any,Any)

Using **parent**, we can define a recursive derived function **ancestor** as follows:

    ancestor (x,y) = [(x,y) | (x,y) <- parent (x,y)] ++
                     [(x,y) | (x,z) <- ancestor (x,Any);
                              (z,y) <- ancestor (z,y)]

Note the syntactic similarity between the above definition and this Prolog predicate:

    ancestor(X,Y) :- parent(X,Y)
    ancestor(X,Y) :- ancestor(X,Z), ancestor(Z,Y)

---

[8] Here, the constant **Any** acts as a "wildcard" which matches any value. A selector function **f** when applied to an argument **a** returns the set of tuples matching **a**, in an arbitrary order.

We can now use the `ancestor` function to formulate several different queries, for example, to find Mary's ancestors, Anne's descendants, and the entire set of descendant/ancestor tuples:

```
ancestor (Mary,Any)
ancestor (Any,Anne)
ancestor (Any,Any)
```

It is also possible to define integrity constraints as derived functions over selectors, where a constraint f is deemed to be satisfied if f `Any` evaluates to the empty list. For example, the following two constraints state that everyone who is recorded as having parents has precisely two parents, and that noone can be their own ancestor:

```
twoParents x = [x | (x,y) <- parent (x,Any);
                     length (parent (x,Any)) != 2]
noSelfAnc  x = [x | (x,y) <- ancestor (x,Any); x = y]
```

Reddi discusses how such constraints can be checked efficiently after updates to the underlying selectors [1.82].

1.4.7 Comprehensions in Hydra

The power and generality of list comprehensions is well illustrated by their use in the functional database language Hydra [1.8]. The motivation for the design and development of Hydra came from considering the needs of non-standard database applications, in particular those of intelligence and investigative systems where information tends to be non-homogeneous and the existence of connections between specific entities and the form of such connections are often the object of queries. For example the question

```
What, if any, is the connection between John and 29 ?
```

corresponds in a functional context to asking what function or sequence of composed functions, if given the argument `John` returns the value `29`, to which the answer might be the function `age`.

Whilst the complete integration of a functional database language with functional programming was first achieved in FDL, this means that it only has the modelling power of the lambda calculus. However, the lambda calculus is a theory of anonymous functions whereas in a functional database we use named functions and the names carry semantics, as with the simple example `age` above. Thus, whilst remaining within the functional paradigm and including the power of FDL, Hydra goes beyond the power of the lambda calculus by having named functions which themselves can participate as objects of the computational process, and built-in higher-order functions to provide the base functions in such computations. For example, the built-in function `from` takes an abstract type as argument and returns a list of functions for which an instance of the type is a valid argument. Thus, the query

```
from person
```

is a query asking for all functions f with a type definition of the form f ::
person -> .... and might return the list

```
[name, aliases, age, modus-operandi, date-released]
```

Thus, the question "What do we know about N123?" is answered by the
query

```
[(f, f  N123) | f <- from person]
```

for which the result might be

```
[(name, Fred),(aliases, Benedict),(age, 37),
  (modus-operandi, catburglar),(date-released, 12/8/02)]
```

Notice that our query requires no change if functions have been added or
deleted in the database.

In FDL, all functions are treated uniformly whatever their purpose,
whereas in Hydra those functions which define the data model are designated
primary functions and all other functions designated as *secondary*. The various higher-order functions such as from above only take cognizance of the
primary functions. By restricting the primary functions to have only single
arguments, the database can then be viewed as a directed graph with the
nodes being entity instances, abstract or value, and the arc labels being the
names of primary functions. With its built-in set of higher-order functions
from which others can be defined, and their use within list comprehensions,
Hydra combines the query power of the lambda calculus with that of the
various graph query languages such as GraphDB [1.50] within the functional
paradigm.

1.5 The Functional Model and the RDF Data Model

1.5.1 Semantic Web Vision and RDFS

The *semantic web* vision is to enable rich machine processing of web information sources [1.17]. Most of the work done to date in realising this vision
has focused upon developing "web-friendly" representations for structured
data. Building on the XML standard, a number of proposals for expressing
data schemas have appeared, including RDF, RDFS and XML Schema [1.39].
These approaches support the representation and communication of entity–
relational information in web applications, for example allowing a set of instances of some entity type to be gathered from several structured web pages,
and transported for storage in a web-connected database.

RDF stands for Resource Description FrameWork Model, which was first accepted by W3C as a data model in February 1999[9]. A data interchange format is defined using XML syntax with tags starting <rdf: to encode *subject–predicate–object* triples. The *predicate* is just a function name, for example works-for, which occurs in the triple John works-for IBM.

Thus, RDF is not unlike the Entity-Relational data model in its use of Entity identifiers as *subject*, and Property or Relationship names as *predicate* in RDF triples. However, it also includes features of object data models in its use of object identifiers and subclasses. This makes it very similar to the Functional Data Model. We could represent facts such as the functional examples earlier as follows:

```
Paul instance-of Employee
Paul earns 20000
Paul name "Paul"
```

and such facts could be stored in a triple store (see Chapter 2). Here Paul, which would be a surrogate for an object, is represented by a URI (unique resource identifier) in RDF. By this means RDF can represent shared references to objects and form directed graphs; thus it gets away from the tree-like data structures of XML.

1.5.2 Storing Metadata in RDF

RDF triples can also be used to store metadata, by using the predicates *Class*, *subClassOf*, *Property*, *domain*, and *range* to make statements in the RDFS sublanguage. RDFS (RDF Schema) provides RDF with an object-oriented extensible type system, which again is serialisable in XML. Usually RDFS declarations provide entity and relationship and attribute names as well as function types (domain and range) which are then used in following RDF statements. An example is given below in Figure 1.3.

The next significant stage in the realisation of the semantic web lies in extending the basic data schema representations with information on how the data can and should be used. This information can take various forms, including logical axioms, rules, constraints, or even functional and procedural representations. For example, reference [1.56] shows how RDFS can be used to encode metadata for describing *schemas* (ontologies), *quantified constraints* for planning applications, and *structured data* for use in modelling Virtual Organisations. This data and metadata feeds into the *reasoning services* for the semantic web. Early work in this direction includes inference engines for large-scale ontologies [1.38, 1.52], mechanisms for representing and reasoning with business rules [1.84], and mobile constraint languages and constraint-solving frameworks [1.95, 1.46]. There is more on this in the review by Kerschberg (Chapter 15).

---

[9] http://www.w3.org/TR/REC-rdf-syntax

Another advantage of RDFS is its use from within Java as a convenient accessible metalanguage giving the types of structured data, including possible specialisations. When data is coming across the Web in many forms it is essential to have this type information easily available in memory. Thus the programmer does not have to invent their own form of object class for this metadata. They also have Java methods available to populate these classes from input in a widely used interchange format. One can contrast this with the convoluted methods for accessing some fairly basic relational database metadata in JDBC.

Lastly, because of the well-established use of XML, there are very reliable, widely used transport protocols, which is another plus for RDF/RDFS. For web sources, the *HTTP protocol* is very useful, particularly where there are firewalls. For remote agents running on different platforms *Linda* [1.44] is very useful in conjunction with remote procedure calls, while for Java platforms one can use *Servlet* technology.

1.5.3 Mapping a Functional Model to RDFS

The RDFS Data Model abstracts over relational storage, flat files and object-oriented storage, following the principle of data independence. Thus, it shares with the Functional Data Model the advantage of not tying one to any particular storage system. This is a great advantage to the programmer. The mapping to a particular knowledge source or data source can then take place separately through a wrapper. This makes it very much easier to integrate data from different sources, as is often required over the Web.

The following example [1.45], taken from Chapter 17, is part of a functional schema in P/FDM syntax showing the `pc` and `os` classes and the `memory` property in an application domain where components are put together to configure a workable PC. The corresponding entity–relationship diagram is shown in Figure 1.2:

```
declare os ->> entity
   ...
declare pc ->> entity
declare memory(pc) -> integer
declare has_os(pc) -> os
declare hard-disk(pc) ->> disk
   ...
```

The Functional Data Model is, of course, an extended ER model and it can be automatically mapped into an RDFS specification. The basic rules used when mapping the schema declarations to RDFS are as follows:

− a class *c* defined as an `entity` (declared as *c* `->>` `entity`) maps to an RDF resource of type `rdfs:Class` (where `rdfs` is the namespace prefix for the RDFS descriptions);

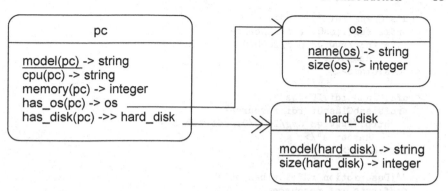

Fig. 1.2. This functional schema shows three entity classes. The single arrow means that each **pc** may have only one **os** installed. A double arrow means that a **pc** can have multiple **hard-disk**.

- a class c declared to be a subtype of another class s (declared as c ->> s) maps to an RDF resource of type `rdfs:Class`, with an `rdfs:subClassOf` property the value of which is the class named s;
- a function f declared on entities of class c, with result type r (declared as $f(c)$ -> r) maps to an RDF resource of type `rdf:Property` with an `rdfs:domain` of c and an `rdfs:range` of r.

A mapping program reads metadata from the database and *generates* the corresponding RDFS, as in Figure 1.3, making this knowledge web-accessible. Related work by Risch (Chapter 19) also shows how RDFS resources can be integrated and accessed by a functional query language.

Mapping a functional schema into RDFS has the advantage of making the domain model available to RDFS-ready software. On the other hand, some semantic information is lost. The cardinality of each attribute, for example, is not expressed in RDFS. Information on the *key* of each entity class is also omitted. However, this information could easily be added to an extra metadata class declared in RDFS, as described in Chapter 17.

1.5.4 Mobile Constraint Representation in RDFS

Although RDFS looks simple, it has all the essential features for mapping other data models or layering extra details, as intended in its design. It has been used to map data from P/FDM and constraints which are formulae of logic expressed in this model (section 1.4.3). Instead of just being restrictions on database state, such constraints can be considered as mobile problem specifications [1.45] to be moved across the Internet. Thus RDFS allows us to move both the data model description and the program specification, for remote compilation and execution on the target data!

```
<rdfs:Class rdf:ID="pc">
  <rdfs:subClassOf rdf:resource=
    "http://www.w3.org/2000/01/rdf-schema#
        Resource"/>
</rdfs:Class>

<rdfs:Class rdf:ID="os">
  <rdfs:subClassOf rdf:resource=
    "http://www.w3.org/2000/01/rdf-schema#
        Resource"/>
</rdfs:Class>

<rdf:Description rdf:ID="has_os">
  <rdf:type rdf:resource=
    "http://www.w3.org/1999/02/22-rdf-syntax-ns#
        Property"/>
  <rdfs:domain rdf:resource="#pc"/>
  <rdfs:range rdf:resource="#os"/>
</rdf:Description>
```

Fig. 1.3. RDFS (RDF Schema) representation of schema of Figure1.2.

The following is an example of a simple *design constraint* saying that: *the size of a hard disk must be big enough to accommodate the chosen operating system in every PC*:

```
constrain each p in pc
    to have size(has_os(p)) =< size(has_disk(p))
```

In practice, these human-readable constraints are compiled into an intermediate format, called *Constraint Interchange Format — CIF* (see Chapter 17). One very satisfying feature of CIF is that the RDF tags used make a clean separation between information about *logical formulae* with the usual connectives, and information about *expressions* denoting objects in the data model. Effectively, CIF gives another layer with richer semantic information, but it is able to use all the processing convenience of RDF and RDFS.

In summary, RDFS is able to carry all the basic information of a functional data model across the Web, with the priceless virtue of Data Independence, which allows it to be used with many different storage schemas. RDF is also able to express computations on the data or logical inference, usually through another layer of tags but so that the functions can be typechecked.

1.6 Functional Computation with Data on the Web

Much of the data on the Web, such as XML and RDF data, is *semi-structured*. Semi-structured data differs from structured data by not being constrained to conform to a schema that has been specified independently of the data.

Recent proposals have extended XML and RDF with additional formalisms for defining schemas such as DTDs, XML Schema, and RDFS, although conformance to a schema is not mandatory for XML or RDF data.

Semi-structured data can be represented as a *self-describing graph*. For example, [1.1] presents a general graph data model and discusses how this can be used to represent XML and RDF data, as well as, more generally, structured data such as relational and object-oriented data.

With their inherent support of recursion and complex data structures, functional languages are a natural formalism upon which to base languages for computing with semi-structured data. Many of the query languages proposed for semi-structured data have been partly motivated by the design of the OQL query language for object-oriented data [1.11, 1.12, 1.25]. OQL itself is a *functional language*. Its operators can be composed to an arbitrary level of nesting within a query provided the types of the operators are respected by the expressions passed to them — this is the property of *compositionality*. Moreover, any query evaluates to a single answer, irrespective of the order of evaluation of its subexpressions — this is the property of *referential transparency*.

These two properties are also true of many of the languages proposed for computing with semi-structured data, such as UnQL [1.18], YAT [1.27], Quilt [1.26] XQuery [1.104], RQL [1.58] and XDuce [1.55]. In particular, this means that analysis and optimisation techniques that have been developed for functional languages operating on structured data can also be adapted to such functional languages operating on semi-structured data. This issue is taken up again in some of the chapters in Section III of this book. The RQL query language is described in a chapter in Section IV. Here, we illustrate the family of functional query languages for XML by means of some examples in XQuery.

A normalisation process can be applied to XQuery expressions to transform them into a smaller *core language* — [1.104] gives details of the normalisation rules and the core language. Translating the larger XQuery language into the smaller core language has the advantage that effort can be directed into developing optimisation and analysis techniques for the core language and these techniques will then automatically extend to the full language. This includes techniques for analysing the type of an XQuery expression against an XML Schema and techniques for optimising an XQuery expression [1.88, 1.40]. Here, we illustrate the functional flavour of XQuery by means of some examples, and some of the techniques proposed for optimising XQuery expressions.

Suppose we have an XML document containing information about a set of products. For each product there is information about its name, category, price, and cost of shipping. The document is defined as follows in XML Schema:

```
<xsd:element name="products">
 <xsd:complexType>
    <xsd:sequence>
       <xsd:element name="product" minoccurs="0"
                       maxoccurs = "unbounded">
         <xsd:complexType>
            <xsd:attribute name="name" type="xsd:string"/>
            <xsd:attribute name="category" type="xsd:string"/>
            <xsd:attribute name="price" type="xsd:decimal"/>
            <xsd:attribute name="shipping" type="xsd:decimal"/>
         </xsd:complexType>
       </xsd:element>
    </xsd:sequence>
 </xsd:complexType>
</xsd:element>
```

The following query returns all products in the Toy category:

```
/products/product[@category = "Toy"]
```

or, equivalently, translating this XPath expression into a for–let–where–return expression:

Query 1

```
for    $prod in /products/product
where  $prod[@category = "Toy"]
return $prod
```

The following query returns the name and cost of each product, constructing a new element <answer> to hold this information for each product:

Query 2

```
for    $p in /products/product
return <answer> { $p/@name,
                 cost($p) }
       </answer>
```

Here, cost is a user-defined function that takes a product element as an argument and returns the total cost of this product, computed as the sum of its price and shipping attributes. This function can be defined as follows in the syntax of XQuery:

```
define function cost ($p as element product) as xsd:decimal {
     $p/@price + $p/@shipping
}
```

To write now a query which returns the name and cost of each product in the Toy category, we can nest Query 1 above within Query 2 (this is possible due to the properties of compositionality and referential transparency):

Query 3

```
for $p in (for    $prod in /products/product
           where  $prod[@category="Toy"]
           return $prod)
return <answer> { $p/@name,
                  cost($p) }
        </answer>
```

Some standard techniques can now be used to optimise this query, for example using some of the laws and equivalences discussed in [1.40]. Firstly, applying the *associative law* allows us to swap the order of the two for clauses, giving:

```
for    $prod  in /products/product
return for $p in (where  $prod[@category="Toy"]
                  return $prod)
       return <answer> { $p/@name,
                         cost($p) }
              </answer>
```

Expanding the where clause to the equivalent if ... then ... else clause gives:

```
for    $prod  in /products/product
return for $p in (if    $prod[@category="Toy"]
                  then  $prod
                  else  ())
       return <answer> { $p/@name,
                         cost($p) }
              </answer>
```

Since the if $prod[@category="Toy"] test only depends on the value of $prod, it can now be moved in front of the second for loop:

```
for    $prod  in /products/product
return if    $prod[@category="Toy"]
       then  for $p in $prod
             return <answer> { $p/@name,
                              cost($p) }
                    </answer>
       else  ()
```

In the for $p in $prod clause, $p can only take one value, the current value of $prod which has been set in the outer for loop. Thus it is possible to remove the for $p in $prod clause, and rename the variable $p to $prod within the answer element — this is the *left-unit monad law* from [1.40]:

```
for    $prod  in /products/product
return if     $prod[@category="Toy"]
       then   return <answer> { $prod/@name,
                                 cost($prod) }
              </answer>
       else  ()
```

Finally, replacing the if ... then ... else clause by the equivalent where clause gives the following query:

```
for    $prod  in /products/product
where  $prod[category="Toy"]
return <answer> { $prod/@name,
                  cost($prod) }
       </answer>
```

The net effect of this sequence of transformations is known as a *loop fusion* since what has happened is that the original two iterations (the first iteration over all products to construct the list of Toy products, and the second iteration over these to compute the cost of each such product) have been replaced by a single iteration which computes and returns the cost of each product found to be a Toy.

1.7 Review of Influential Work

1.7.1 The Functional Data Model

Functions provided an underlying formalism for data models from as early as Abrial's *access functions* for representing binary relationships between entities [1.2] and Florentin's *property functions* for representing the attributes of entities [1.43]

Kerschberg and Pacheco's *Functional Model of Data* [1.61] integrated these two uses for functions, modelling the universe of discourse by means of *entity sets* and *total functions*. Entity sets are represented by labelled nodes and functions by labelled arcs in a directed graph. The domain of each function is an entity set, while the range is either an entity set or the set, C, of character strings.

The main motivation for the Functional Model of Data was ease of conceptual modelling, and [1.61] showed how functional data models can be automatically transformed into relational and CODASYL data models for implementation within a DBMS.

The Functional Model of Data was further developed by Sibley and Kerschberg in [1.87]. In this development, the universe of discourse is again represented by labelled nodes and arcs. The arcs are again total functions, but the nodes are either entity sets or *value sets* (as opposed to a single set of character strings, C). A major motivation for this work was to derive a general, unifying conceptual data model which is independent of any particular DBMS. Such functional models could then be specialised into relational or CODASYL data models by the application of additional constraints.

At about the same time, Hammer and McLeod proposed the Semantic Data Model [1.51], also as a higher-level model than the data models supported by contemporary DBMS and better suited to conceptual modelling of an application domain. A key innovation of the Semantic Data Model was the recognition of the importance of *derived information*, and the model included derived entity attributes whose value is calculated from the values of stored attributes by means of a *derivation specification*.

Shipman used functions to represent both data and derived information in the very influential DAPLEX language [1.86].

1.7.2 DAPLEX

DAPLEX uses set-valued functions for representing real-world entity types, their attributes, and the relationships between them. Entity types may be either *scalar*, such as strings, integers and booleans, or *abstract*. For example, to declare the two abstract entity types Student and Course:

```
DECLARE Student( ) =>> ENTITY
DECLARE Course( )  =>> ENTITY
```

to declare that each Student and Course has a name:

```
DECLARE Name(Student) => STRING
DECLARE CName(Course) => STRING
```

and to declare the 'attendance' relationship between Student and Course:

```
DECLARE Attends(Student) =>> Course
```

In these declarations, the single-headed arrow signifies a single-valued function i.e. one returning a set consisting of precisely one element, while the double-headed arrow signifies a multi-valued function i.e. one returning a set which may contain any number of elements and possibly no elements at all. DAPLEX includes primitives for the definition of type hierarchies in which each type has at most one immediate supertype.

Functions such as those above which are introduced by the keyword DECLARE are termed *base* functions and are extensionally defined. It is possible to declare base functions of more than one argument, for example:

```
DECLARE Mark(Student,Course) => INTEGER
```

Intentionally defined functions are termed *derived* functions and are introduced by the keyword DEFINE, for example:

```
DEFINE StudentOfName(STRING) => INVERSE OF Name(Student)
DEFINE CourseOfName(STRING)  => INVERSE OF CName(Course)
DEFINE AverageMark(Student)  => AVERAGE (Mark(Student,Course)
                                    OVER Attends(Student))
DEFINE Fails(Student,Course) => Mark(Student,Course) < 40
```

The operator < is one of a number of built-in arithmetic and boolean operators, and AVERAGE is one of a number of built-in aggregation functions.

The operator INVERSE OF is built in and determines the converse of a single-argument base function over an abstract entity type. This allows one to model a bi-directional relationship, as in the ER model, by naming only one function.

Derived functions can be used to define *views*. For example, the following defines the function CourseNames which takes the name of a student and returns the names of the courses attended by the student of that name:

```
DEFINE CourseNames(Name AS STRING) =>>
           CName(Attends(THE StudentOfName(Name)))
```

In this definition, AS STRING indicates that Name is being used as an entity type rather than a function, while THE indicates that a single value is expected to result from the evaluation of StudentOfName.

DAPLEX queries are formulated by applying functions to arguments. There are also constructs for iteration (FOR, IN), quantification (THE, EACH, SOME), qualification (SUCH THAT) and output of results (PRINT), for example:

```
PRINT AverageMark(StudentOfName("John Smith"))


FOR EACH S IN Student SUCH THAT AverageMark(S) > 80
    PRINT Name(S)


FOR EACH X IN Student SUCH THAT
    SOME Y IN Attends(X) HAS Fails(X,Y)
        PRINT Name(X), CName(Y)
```

With regard to database updates, new abstract entities are created by means of the directive A NEW and values of base functions are assigned by means of the directive LET. For example, to create a new Student of name "Fred Jones" who attends the Biology and Biochemistry courses:

```
FOR A NEW Student
    BEGIN
        LET Name(Student) = "Fred Jones"
        LET Attends(Student) =
            { THE CourseOfName("Biology"),
              THE CourseOfName("Biochemistry") }
    END
```

Note here the use of CourseOfName("Biology") instead of just "Biology" as in a relational database. This is because variables in DAPLEX can denote actual *object identifiers* (as in Java, for example) whereas the analogous values in relational database columns will be *foreign key* values in order to identify the object. This is a big difference from the relational model and is common to most functional data models.

The value of a multi-valued function for a particular argument can be modified by using the built-in operators INCLUDE and EXCLUDE. For example, to modify the courses attended by Fred Jones to Physiology and Biochemistry:

```
FOR THE Student SUCH THAT Name(Student) = "Fred Jones"
  BEGIN
    EXCLUDE Attends(Student) = THE CourseOfName("Biology")
    INCLUDE Attends(Student) = THE CourseOfName("Physiology")
  END
```

It is possible to declare global semantic integrity constraints in DAPLEX, using the same syntax as for boolean-valued derived functions. For example, to enforce that all Students attend at least four courses:

```
DEFINE CONSTRAINT Number_of_courses(Student) =>
                  COUNT(Attends(Student)) > 3
```

A similar construct is used for defining "triggers" consisting of a sequence of commands to be executed when a particular precondition is satisfied by the database extension (note that these are condition–action rules rather than event–condition–action rules, as supported in present-day DBMSs). For example, to notify the user when the number of attendees of any course exceeds 15:

```
DEFINE AttendedBy(Course) =>> INVERSE OF Attends(Student)
DEFINE TRIGGER Overbooked(Course) =>
       COUNT(AttendedBy(Course)) > 15
       PRINT "Overbooked course ", CName(Course)
```

No full implementation of DAPLEX was undertaken. However, some later systems implemented large parts of the language and we describe them below.

The main achievement of DAPLEX was its integration of base functions, derived functions, views, and integrity constraints into a single functional framework. The main drawback of DAPLEX is that it is computationally incomplete and for general computation it requires either additional facilities for calling out to foreign functions, or embedding in a host programming language.

DAPLEX was used as a unifying query language in the MULTIBASE project [1.65]. MULTIBASE aimed to provide a single query language and a single integrated schema over multiple autonomous, heterogeneous, distributed databases. It was one of the earliest projects to address query processing over heterogeneous databases, and the first to use a functional data model and a functional query language for this purpose.

ADAPLEX. ADAPLEX [1.90] was an embedding of a subset of DAPLEX into the programming language ADA. The result is a language which has a functional model for querying stored data and a procedural model for computation. The data types of DAPLEX are reconciled with those of ADA by associating base functions with abstract entity types when these are declared, for example:

```
TYPE student IS ENTITY
     name    : string [1..30] ;
     age     : integer ;
     attends : SET OF course ;
  END ENTITY ;
```

Thus, the set of base functions associated with an entity type cannot be changed once the type has been declared. Also, derived functions are defined procedurally in ADA rather than in DAPLEX (this is an example of calling out to foreign functions).

EFDM. EFDM [1.62, 1.63, 1.64] extended DAPLEX with procedural computation, recursive functions over abstract types and scalar types, built-in metalevel functions for interrogating the meta data, and a construct

$$\text{PROGRAM } program\_name \text{ IS } command\_sequence$$

which can be used to store a sequence of EFDM staments in the database. The underlying database used persistent object storage techniques similar to current commercial object-oriented databases. As with DAPLEX, views are defined by means of derived functions which can be updated if suitable update procedures have been specified. Views operate on a new namespace and can be nested into a hierarchy. The facilities for semantic integrity constraints considerably extend those of DAPLEX, and EFDM was one of the earliest implementations.

P/FDM. P/FDM [1.48, 1.73, 1.74] integrated a functional data model with Prolog for general-purpose computation. In P/FDM, data is retrieved from the database by means of the built-in predicates *getentity(entity-type, key, instance-variable)* and *getfunctionval(function-name, argument-variable, value-variable)*. The first of these predicates requires that abstract entities be identifiable by unique, possibly compound, scalar keys. This is a feature first used in ADAPLEX and EFDM, though P/FDM extends it to allow composed (single-valued) functions, which aids in forming hierarchical keys.

P/FDM queries are written in DAPLEX and translated into Prolog for evaluation. From Prolog, calls are made to C functions to access the persistent entity storage. Prolog's `fail` predicate is used to backtrack over the predicate *getfunctionval* in order to instantiate its third argument (*value-variable* above) to each of the values of a multi-valued base function[10]. For example, assuming the following P/FDM declarations:

```
declare student ->> entity
declare name(student) -> string
key_of   student is name

declare course ->> entity
declare cname(course) -> string
key_of   course is cname

declare attends(student) ->> course
```

to print all the courses attended by Fred Jones, the DAPLEX query is:

```
FOR THE F IN STUDENT SUCH THAT name(F)="Fred Jones"
    FOR EACH C IN attends(F)
        PRINT(cname(C));
```

which generates the following Prolog:

```
getentity(student,'Fred Jones',F),
getfunctionval(attends,F,C),
getfunctionval(cname,C,N),
write(N),
fail;
true.
```

P/FDM was subsequently extended with constraints [1.33] and with alternative back-ends to remote databases [1.59], in the spirit of the original MULTIBASE system, and this is the version of the system which is described in Chapters 7 and 8 of this book.

1.7.3 FQL

At about the same time that Shipman was developing DAPLEX, Buneman and Frankel proposed the highly influential FQL functional query language [1.19]. A major motivation for this work was that it is in principle possible to combine arbitrary computable functions with stored database functions into a query language which is not limited to a predefined set of operators.

FQL was based on Backus's FP functional programming paradigm [1.9]. FP includes a built-in set of *functionals*, like higher-order functions, including function composition, ○ , and sequence construction, $\langle x_1, x_2, \ldots, x_n \rangle$. In addition to these, FQL provides the functionals !, * and ^.

---

[10] This gives much the same effect as lazy evaluation over suspended functions in a functional programming language.

Given an abstract entity type A, !A is a 0-argument function which returns a *stream* of all entities of type A. For example, given the abstract entity type COURSE, !COURSE returns a stream of all the entities of type COURSE.

Given any type A, *A is the type consisting of streams of entities of type A. For example, given the abstract entity types STUDENT and COURSE, the function

```
ATTENDS : STUDENT -> *COURSE
```

takes a STUDENT and returns a stream of the COURSEs attended by the STUDENT.

Given a function f:A → B, *f is the function of type *A → *B which takes as an argument a stream of entities of type A, a_1, a_2,... say, and returns the stream $f(a_1)$, $f(a_2)$, ... For example, given the function

```
CNAME : COURSE -> STRING
```

the query

```
!COURSE o *CNAME
```

returns the name of every COURSE.

Given a function f:A → B or f: A → *B, the function ^f:B → *A is the inverse (or converse) of f. For example, the following query returns the STUDENTs who attend the COURSES(s) of name Biology:

```
'Biology' o ^CNAME o *^ATTENDS
```

In a later version of FQL [1.69], the functionals ! and ^ are dropped. Inverse functions have explicit names and ! is replaced by an explicit *generator function* for each entity type. For example, the entity type COURSE induces the 0-ary generator function allCOURSE:->*COURSE.

As in EFDM, a set of built-in metalevel functions is provided. Thus, object-level querying and meta level querying can be carried out in the same functional syntax. FQL was intended for implementation over existing DBMSs and an abstract implementation based on the lazy evaluation of stream data was described. Also described was an implementation over a CODASYL DBMS [1.20, 1.69].

The main achievement of FQL was to demonstrate that functional programming in the style of FP can form the basis of a query language which adopts a single functional model both for representing real-world data and for computation.

In later publications [1.69, 1.70], FQL was extended with features from the functional programming language ML. In this version, function definition is simpler than in the variable-free FP-like syntax and new higher-order functions can be defined in addition to the built-in ones.

1.7.4 Functional Languages for Complex Object and Object-Oriented Databases

The work on DAPLEX and FQL was followed by the development of several functional languages for complex object and object-oriented databases.

The GENESIS query language [1.13] supported a functional data model and was intended as a front end for DBMSs supporting either a relational or nested relational data model.

The PROBE database system [1.31] supported the representation and manipulation of arbitrarily complex objects by means of a functional data model. This work inspired the Iris object-oriented database system, which used a LISP-like functional syntax [1.42]. Iris in turned influenced the development of the original AMOS system for active mediation of distributed data sources [1.35]. FAD [1.10] and FUGUE [1.53] also used functions as the underlying mechanism for modelling complex objects.

The O/SQL query language [1.14] was intended for use with object-oriented databases. It unified functional and relational modelling by extending SQL to include entities and functions. It included primitives for creation of entities, for assignment of base function values, and for updating multi-valued base functions. Derived functions were defined by means of a SELECT clause and queries had an SQL-like syntax.

The fundamental modelling concept of entity/object identifiers was accepted into the database mainstream in the late 1980s, and the move to using SQL-like syntax for querying such data models followed soon after. This resulted in query language proposals for object-oriented databases such as the very influential O2 query language and its successor, OQL [1.11, 1.12, 1.25]. For example, the DAPLEX query

```
FOR EACH S IN STUDENT
    SUCH THAT name(S)="Fred Jones"
        PRINT name(S), age(S);
```

is expressed as follows in OQL, basically by syntactic reordering of the query clauses and using path expressions rather than function application:

```
SELECT S.name, S.age
FROM   STUDENT S
WHERE  S.name="Fred Jones"
```

Unlike SQL, OQL is a functional language, and its operators can be composed to an arbitrary level of nesting within a query provided the query remains type-correct. Optimisation techniques for OQL that exploit its inherent functional nature are discussed in [1.28, 1.37, 1.36] and in the chapters by Fegaras and Grust in Section III of this book.

OQL has been influential in the development of the SQL3 standard and also the functional core of the XQuery language for XML. Thus optimisation techniques developed for OQL could also be applied to these languages, and this issue is raised in the chapters by Fegaras and Grust.

1.7.5 Functional Database Programming Languages

Database programming languages (DBPLs) combine the data definition and data manipulation facilities found in typical database query/update languages, with the general computational facilities of a programming language. Several functional DBPLs were developed from the mid 1980s which provided facilities for computing with complex objects by incorporating record types into their type system, for example [1.3, 1.4, 1.5, 1.23, 1.24, 1.66, 1.67, 1.71]. These languages made advances in type systems which integrate inclusion polymorphism and parametric polymorphism while still preserving static type-checking of programs.

In contrast to these languages, FDL [1.75, 1.77, 1.76] unified a *functional data model* with functional programming into a single DBPL. Unlike previous implementations of a functional data model, FDL is based on the lambda calculus and hence is computationally complete. Abstract entity types, termed *non-lexical types* in FDL, are populated dynamically by means of **create** and **delete** commands. Non-lexical values are hidden by displaying in lieu of any non-lexical a transient global variable of the form $x, where x is an alphanumeric identifier. For any non-lexical type, t, a zero-argument function All_t returns the current extent of t in the form of a list. These functions are non-deterministic with respect to the order in which non-lexicals are returned. For example, given a non-lexical type **person**, and the commands

```
create person $p1 $p2 $p3 $p4
delete $p2
```

the query All_person returns some permutation of the list [$p1, $p3, $p4].

Functions are specified incrementally by the insertion and deletion of equations. If the RHS of an equation is a list of constants, the user can specify that this be stored as a set, that is with no duplicates and in an arbitrary order. Such sets can then be updated by the insertion or removal of elements, similarly to multi-valued functions in DAPLEX.

We give some examples of FDL functions below: **salary** records the salaries of persons, where the default salary is 25000; **children** records people's children, where the default is no children; and **max** returns the maximum of a list of integers. In the equations defining **max**, [x] denotes a singleton list and [x|y] a list with head x and tail y:

```
salary : person -> integer
salary $p1 <= 40000
salary $p2 <= 60000
salary $p3 <= 55000
salary x    <= 25000

children : person -> (list person)
children $p1 <= set [$p2, $p3]
children x    <= []
```

```
max : (list integer) -> integer
max [x]   <= x
max [x|y] <= let z == max y in if (x > z) x z
```

FDL was one of the first database query languages to incorporate list comprehensions. For example, assuming also a function name : person -> string, the following query returns the names of those people who earn the maximal salary:

```
let max_sal = max [salary x | x <- All_person] in
    [name x | x <- All_person; (salary x) = max_sal]
```

Several subsequent functional language prototypes built on or extended FDL, such as GQL [1.72], Hydra [1.8] and Relief [1.68], and some of these were discussed earlier in this chapter, and are discussed again in Chapters 2 and 3.

PFL [1.89, 1.79] has similar functionality to FDL, but a different mechanism for storing and retrieving data. In particular, a class of extensionally defined updateable functions called *selectors* allow the storage and update of sets of tuples. Derived functions can be written over selectors which act as relational derivation rules. We gave some examples in section 1.4.6.

Later work on PFL extended it with constraints and automatic constraint enforcement [1.82], an update language [1.91], inclusion polymorphism [1.29], and event–condition–action (ECA) rules [1.83, 1.78]. The work on ECA rule analysis described by Bailey and Poulovassilis in Section III of this book arises in part from PFL's functionally specified ECA subsystem.

The work on extending PFL with inclusion polymorphism showed how it is possible to combine an entity-based data model with subtypes with the parametric polymorphism and higher-order functions found in most functional programming languages. The extended PFL described in [1.29] supports multiple inheritance and method overriding. The same approach could be adopted to extend languages like FDL, and its successors Hydra and Relief, to support inclusion polymorphism as well as parametric polymorphism.

1.7.6 Optimising Functional Query Languages

Functional query languages have several important properties which make them amenable to powerful query optimisation techniques, and these are issues which are taken up again in Section III of this book:

- a well-defined semantics, allowing formal reasoning about the properties of queries;
- referential transparency, allowing subexpressions of a query to be replaced by different expressions which have the same value but which can be evaluated more efficiently;

– natural support for collection types and aggregation operators, allowing earlier work on optimising relational languages to be placed on a sounder theoretical footing and to be extended with more powerful optimisation techniques for more expressive queries.

Motivated by the above advantages, several researchers began to research optimisation techniques for functional query languages from the late 1980s [1.96, 1.97, 1.34, 1.54, 1.74, 1.15, 1.16, 1.28].

Also in the early 1990s, Tannen, Buneman and Naqvi proposed *structural recursion over sets* as the basis for database query languages, a major motivating factor for this paradigm being its amenability to query optimisation [1.92]. They introduced a function, Φ, for folding a binary operator *op* into a finite set. Φ is defined as follows:

$$\Phi\ f\ op\ e\ \{\} = e$$
$$\Phi\ f\ op\ e\ \{x\} = f\ x$$
$$\Phi\ f\ op\ e\ (s_1 \cup s_2) = op\ (\Phi\ f\ op\ e\ s_1)\ (\Phi\ f\ op\ e\ s_2)$$

There are some restrictions on the permissible arguments *op* and *e* in order for an expression of the form $\Phi\ f\ op\ e\ s$ to be well-defined. In particular, in order for $\Phi\ f\ op\ e\ s$ to be well-defined for any set s, *op* must be commutative, associative and idempotent, and must have e as a left and right identity. Similar earlier operators to Φ were the "pump" operator of FAD [1.10] and the "hom" operator of Machiavelli [1.71]. Several equivalences involving Φ were derived in [1.92] and structural induction was used as the proof technique.

A similar folding operator can be specified for bags, by replacing $\{\}$ in the above definition by $\langle\rangle$ (denoting the empty bag), replacing $\{x\}$ by $\langle x\rangle$ (denoting a bag with one element x) and replacing $\cup$ by $\uplus$ (denoting bag union). Similarly, we can define a folding operator for lists, by replacing $\{\}$ in the above definition by $[\,]$ (the empty list), $\{x\}$ by $[x]$ (a list with one element x) and $\cup$ by $++$ (list append). In order for $\Phi\ f\ op\ e\ b$ to be well-defined for any bag b, *op* must be commutative and associative, and have e as a left and right identity. For $\Phi\ f\ op\ e\ l$ to be well-defined for any list l, *op* must be associative, and have e as a left and right identity.

Optimising folding operators over collection types, such as sets, bags and lists, has been the subject of much other work since the early 1990s. Collection types were formally defined by Wadler in [1.101], where their relationship with comprehensions was explored and several general equivalences were derived. Comprehensions are a restricted form of structural recursion where the operator *op* and value e are confined to be $\cup$ and $\{\}$ for the set collection type, $\uplus$ and $\langle\rangle$ for the bag collection type, and $++$ and $[\,]$ for the list collection type. For example, the expression `flatmap f` (recall `flatmap` defined in section 1.4.6) is equivalent to the expression Φ `f` (++) [].

Paton and Gray [1.74] translated DAPLEX queries into set comprehensions and discussed their optimisation. Trinder [1.96, 1.97] translated the relational calculus into list comprehensions and developed several equivalences. Sheard and Fegaras [1.85] investigated the optimisation of a folding operator over types that are sums-of-products (e.g. lists and trees), drawing together and generalising previous work in this area in the context of functional programming languages.

In [1.21], Buneman, Libkin, Suciu, Tannen and Wong argued that comprehensions are a better starting point for database query languages than the relational algebra, due to their greater expressiveness and closer affinity with non-relational data such as complex objects and semi-structured data. They described two flavours of structural recursion, *structural recursion on insert* (sri) and *structural recursion on union* (sru), which had also been explored in earlier papers [1.92, 1.94, 1.93]. The former views collections as being obtained by successive addition of a single element to an empty collection, while the latter views collections as being obtained by successively combining pairs of smaller collections (the folding function Φ discussed above undertakes sru).

In [1.21], a comprehensions-based query language called CPL is described. CPL lies at the heart of the Kleisli heterogeneous database integration system [1.30, 1.103] which is discussed in Chapter 6. The AMOS II system [1.57] (Chapter 9) also incorporates a functional query language within a heterogeneous database architecture. Chapter 14 by Buneman and Tannen is on theoretical foundations for the design of functional query languages and on the query optimisations that naturally arise.

Fegaras and Maier [1.37] used a comprehensions-based language to capture the main features of the OQL object-oriented query language. Grust *et al.* [1.49] discussed optimisation of this comprehension language and described how subqueries can be translated into algebraic expressions for more efficient evaluation. Fegaras [1.36] presented an algorithm for rewriting nested queries expressed in this language into an unnested form, thereby providing the opportunity for further optimisation. There are chapters by Fegaras and Grust in Section III of this book.

The UnQL language for semi-structured data is also based on structural recursion and hence is amenable to similar optimisation techniques. Examples include pushing selections into joins and fusing successive iterations over collections into one iteration (i.e. *loop fusion*) [1.18]. Structural recursion for tree and graph-structured data is discussed extensively by Abiteboul, Buneman and Suciu in [1.1]. They also point out that the computational model of XSLT is also one of structural recursion, and so optimisation techniques developed for structural recursion could also be applied to XSLT.

In contrast to the above work, Poulovassilis and Small [1.80] considered query optimisation for computationally complete functional DBPLs where non-terminating computations and infinite data structures may arise. In [1.81] this work was extended to a framework for optimising aggregation functions in such languages.

References

1.1 S. Abiteboul, P. Buneman, and D. Suciu. *Data on the Web*. Morgan Kaufmann, 2000.

1.2 J.R Abrial. Data Semantics. In J.W. Klimbie. and K.L. Koffeman, editors, *Data Base Management*. North Holland, 1974.

1.3 A. Albano, L. Cardelli, and R. Orsini. Galileo: A strongly-typed, interactive conceptual language. *ACM Transactions on Database Systems*, 10(2):230–260, 1985.

1.4 A. Albano, G. Ghelli, and R. Orsini. Objects for a database programming language. In *Proc. DBPL'91*, pages 236–253. Morgan Kaufmann, August 1991.

1.5 A. Albano, G. Ghelli, and R. Orsini. Fibonacci: A programming language for object databases. *VLDB Journal*, 4(3):403–444, 1995.

1.6 G. Ashworth and M. Goodland. *SSADM: A practical approach*. McGraw-Hill, 1990.

1.7 R. Ayres and P.J.H. King. Entities, functions and surrogates in functional database languages. In *Proc. Basque International Workshop on IT, BIWIT 95*, pages 226–237. IEEE Computer Society Press, 1995.

1.8 R. Ayres and P.J.H. King. Querying graph databases using a functional language extended with second order facilities. In *Proc. BNCOD'96, LNCS 1094*, pages 189–203, 1996.

1.9 J. Backus. Can programming be liberated from the Von Neumann Style? *Communications of the ACM*, 21(8):613–641, 1978.

1.10 F. Bancilhon, T. Briggs, S. Khoshafian, and P. Valduriez. FAD, a powerful and simple database language. In *Proc. VLDB'87*, pages 97–105, 1987.

1.11 F. Bancilhon, C. Delobel, and P.C. Kanellakis. *Building an Object-Oriented Database System, The Story of O2*. Morgan Kaufmann, 1992.

1.12 F. Bancilhon and G. Ferran. ODMG-93: The Object Database Standard. *IEEE Data Engineering Bulletin*, 17(4):3–14, 1994.

1.13 D.S. Batory, T.Y. Leung, and T.E. Wise Implementation concepts for an extensible data model and data language. *ACM Transactions on Database Systems*, 13(3):231–262, 1988.

1.14 D. Beech. A foundation of evolution from relational to object databases. In *Proc. EDBT'88, LNCS 303*, pages 251–270, 1988.

1.15 C. Beeri and Y. Kornatzky. Algebraic optimization of object-oriented query languages. In *Proc. ICDT'90, LNCS 470*, pages 72–88, 1990.

1.16 C. Beeri and T Milo. Functional and predicative programming in OODBs. In *Proc. ACM PODS'92*, pages 176–190, 1992.

1.17 Tim Berners-Lee, editor. *Weaving the Web*. Orion, 1999.

1.18 P. Buneman, S. Davidson, G. Hillebrand, and D. Suciu. A query language and optimisation techniques for unstructured data. In *Proc. ACM SIGMOD'96*, pages 505–516, 1996.

1.19 P. Buneman and R.E. Frankel. FQL - A Functional Query Language. In *Proc. ACM SIGMOD'79*, pages 52–58, 1979.

1.20 P. Buneman, R.E. Frankel, and R. Nikhil. An implementation technique for database query languages. *ACM Transactions on Database Systems*, 7(2):164–186, 1982.

1.21 P. Buneman, L. Libkin, D. Suciu, V. Tannen, and L. Wong. Comprehension syntax. *ACM SIGMOD Record*, 23(1):87–96, 1994.

1.22 R.M. Burstall and J. Darlington. A transformation system for developing recursive programs. *Journal of the ACM*, 24:44–67, 1977.

1.23 L. Cardelli. Amber. In G. Cousineau, P. Curien, and B. Robinet, editors, *Combinators and Functional Programming Languages, LNCS 242*, pages 21–47, Springer Verlag, 1985.

1.24 L. Cardelli and P. Wegner. On understanding types, data abstraction and polymorphism. *ACM Computing Surveys*, 17(4):471–523, 1985.

1.25 R.G.G. Cattell. *The Object Database Standard: ODMG-93, Release 1.2*. Morgan Kaufmann, 1996.

1.26 D.D. Chamberlin, J. Robie, and D. Florescu. Quilt: An XML Query Language for Heterogeneous Data Sources. In *Proc. WebDB (Selected Papers) 2000*, pages 1–25, 2000.

1.27 V. Christophides, S. Cluet, and J. Simeon. On Wrapping Query Languages and Efficient XML Integration. In *ACM SIGMOD 2000*, pages 141–152, 2000.

1.28 S. Cluet and C. Delobel. A general framework for the optimization of object-oriented queries. In *Proc. ACM SIGMOD'92*, pages 383–392, 1992.

1.29 S. Courtenage and A. Poulovassilis. Combining inheritance and parametric polymorphism in a functional database language. In *Proc. BNCOD'95, LNCS 940*, pages 24–46, 1995.

1.30 S.B. Davidson, G.C. Overton, V. Tannen, and L. Wong. BioKleisli : A digital library for biomedical researchers. *Int. Journal on Digital Libraries*, 1(1):36–53, 1997.

1.31 U. Dayal et al. Simplifying complex objects: The PROBE approach to modelling and querying them. In *Workshop on the Theory and Applications of Nested Relations and Complex Objects, Darmstadt*, page 17–37, 1987.

1.32 S.M. Embury. User Manual for P/FDM V.9.1. Technical Report, Dept. of Computing Science, University of Aberdeen, 1995. URL: http://www.csd.abdn.ac.uk/~pfdm/user_manual/user_manual.html

1.33 S.M. Embury, P.M.D. Gray, and N. Bassiliades. Constraint maintenance using generated methods in the P/FDM object-oriented database. In *Proc. Rules in Database Systems (RIDS'93)*, pages 364–381. Springer Verlag, 1993.

1.34 M. Erwig and U. Lipeck. A functional DBPL revealing high level optimizations. In *Proc. DBPL'91*, pages 306–321. Morgan Kaufmann, 1991.

1.35 G. Fahl, T. Risch, and M. Sköld. AMOS — an Architecture for Active Mediators. In *Proc. Workshop on Next Generation Information Technologies and Systems (NGITS'93), Haifa, Israel*, June 1993.

1.36 L. Fegaras. Query unnesting in object-oriented databases. In *Proc. ACM SIGMOD'98*, pages 49–60, 1998.

1.37 L. Fegaras and D. Maier. Towards an effective calculus for Object Query Languages. In *Proc. ACM SIGMOD'95*, pages 47–58, 1995.

1.38 Dieter Fensel, Jürgen Angele, Stefan Decker, Michael Erdmann, Hans-Peter Schnurr, Rudi Studer, and Andreas Witt. Lessons learned from applying AI to the Web. *International Journal of Cooperative Information Systems*, 9(4):361–382, 2000.

1.39 Dieter Fensel, Ora Lassila, Frank van Harmelen, Ian Horrocks, James Hendler, and Deborah L. McGuinness. The semantic web and its languages. *IEEE Intelligent Systems*, November/December 2000.

1.40 M.F. Fernandez, J. Simeon, and P. Wadler. A Semi-monad for Semi-structured Data. In *Proc. ICDT'01*, pages 263–300, 2001.

1.41 A.J. Field and P.G. Harrison. *Functional Programming*. Addison Wesley, 1998.

1.42 D.H. Fishman et al. Iris : An object-oriented database management system. *ACM Transactions on Office Information Systems*, 15(1):48–69, 1987.

1.43 J.J. Florentin. Consistency auditing of databases. *The Computer Journal*, 17(1):52–28, 1974.

1.44 David Gelernter and Nicholas Carriero. Coordination languages and their significance. *Communications of the ACM*, 35(2), 1992.

1.45 P.M.D. Gray, S.M. Embury, K. Hui, and G.J.L. Kemp. The evolving role of constraints in the functional data model. *Journal of Intelligent Information Systems*, 12:113–137, 1999.

1.46 P.M.D. Gray, K. Hui, and A.D. Preece. Finding and moving constraints in cyberspace. In *Intelligent Agents in Cyberspace*, pages 121–127. AAAI Press, 1999. Papers from the 1999 AAAI Spring Symposium Report SS-99-03.

1.47 Peter M. D. Gray, Kit-ying Hui, and Alun D. Preece. An expressive constraint language for semantic web applications. In A. Preece and D. O'Leary, editors, *E-Business and the Intelligent Web: Papers from the IJCAI-01 Workshop*, pages 46–53. AAAI Press, 2001.

1.48 P.M.D. Gray, D.S. Moffat, and N.W. Paton. A Prolog interface to a Functional Data Model database. In *Proc. EDBT'88, LNCS 303*, pages 34–48, 1988.

1.49 T. Grust, J. Kroger, D. Gluche, A. Heuer, and M. Scholl. Query evaluation in CROQUE - Calculus and Algebra coincide. In *Proc. BNCOD'97, LNCS 1271*, pages 84–100, 1997.

1.50 R.H. Guting. GraphDB: Modeling and Querying Graphs in Databases. In *Proc. VLDB'94*, pages 297–308, 1994.

1.51 M.M. Hammer and D.J. McLeod. The Semantic Data Model : A modelling mechanism for database applications. In *Proc. ACM SIGMOD'78*, pages 26–35, 1978.

1.52 Jeff Heflin and James Hendler. Dynamic ontologies on the web. In *Proc. 17th Nat. Conf. on Artificial Intelligence (AAAI-2000)*, pages 443–449, AAAI Press, 2000.

1.53 S. Heiler and S. Zdonik. Views, data abstraction and inheritance in the FUGUE data model. In *Advances in Object-Oriented Database Systems, LNCS 334*, pages 225–241, Springer-Verlag, 1988.

1.54 M.L. Heytens and R.S. Nikhil. List comprehensions in Agna, a parallel persistent object system. In *Proc. Functional Programming and Computer Architecture'91, LNCS 523*, pages 569–591, 1991.

1.55 H. Hosoya and B.C. Pierce. XDuce: A Typed XML Processing Language (Preliminary Report). In *Proc. WebDB (Selected Papers) 2000*, pages 226–244, 2000.

1.56 K. Hui, S. Chalmers, P.M.D. Gray, and A.D. Preece. Experience in using RDF in agent-mediated knowlege architectures. In *Agent Mediated Knowledge Management*, pages 82–89. AAAI Press, 2003. Papers from the 2003 AAAI Spring Symposium SS-03-01.

1.57 V. Josifovski and T. Risch. Functional query optimization over object-oriented views for data integration. *Journal of Intelligent Information Systems*, 12(2–3):165–190, 1999.

1.58 G. Karvounarakis, S. Alexaki, V. Christophides, D. Plexousakis, and M. Scholl. RQL: a declarative query language for RDF. In *Proc. WWW'2002*, pages 592–603, 2002.

1.59 G.J.L. Kemp, J. Dupont, and P.M.D. Gray. Using the functional data model to integrate distributed biological data sources. In *Proc. SSDBM'96*, pages 176–185, 1996.

1.60 W Kent. Limitations of record-based information models. *ACM Transactions on Database Systems*, 4(1):107–131, 1979.

1.61 L. Kerschberg and J.E.S. Pacheco. A Functional Data Base Model. Technical Report 2/76, Departmento de Informatica, Pontificia Universidade de Sao Vincente, Rio de Janeiro, 1976.

1.62 K.G. Kulkarni. Extended Functional Data Model - User Manual. Technical Report PPR-7-83, Edinburgh University, 1983.

1.63 K.G. Kulkarni and M.P. Atkinson. EFDM: Extended Functional Data Model. *The Computer Journal*, 29(1):38–46, 1986.

1.64 K.G. Kulkarni and M.P. Atkinson. Implementing an Extended Functional Data Model using PS-Algol. *Software Practice and Experience*, 17(3):171–185, 1987.

1.65 T. Landers and R.L. Rosenberg. An overview of Multibase. In *Proc. 2nd Int. Symp. on Distributed Databases*, pages 153–184. North-Holland, 1982.

1.66 M. Mannino, I.J. Choi, and D.S. Batory. The Object-Oriented Functional Data Language. *IEEE Transactions on Software Engineering*, 16(11):1258–1272, 1990.

1.67 F. Matthes and J.W. Schmidt. The type system of DBPL. In *Proc. DBPL'89*, pages 219–225. Morgan Kaufmann, 1989.

1.68 P. Meredith and P.J.H. King. Scoped referential transparency in a functional database language with updates. In *Proc. BNCOD'98, LNCS 1405*, pages 134–148, 1998.

1.69 R. Nikhil. An incremental, strongly-typed database language. PhD Thesis, University of Pennsylvania, 1984.

1.70 R. Nikhil. Practical polymorphism. In *Proc. Functional Programming and Computer Architecture'85, LNCS 201*, pages 319–333, 1985.

1.71 A. Ohori, P. Buneman, and V. Tannen. Database programming in Machiavelli - a polymorphic language with static type inference. In *Proc. ACM SIGMOD'89*, pages 46–57, 1989.

1.72 A. Papantonakis and P.J.H.K King. Syntax and semantics of GQL, a graphical query language. *Journal of Visual Languages and Computing*, 6(1):3–25, 1995.

1.73 N.W. Paton and P.D.M. Gray. Identification of database objects by key. In *Proc. 2nd Int. Workshop on Object-Oriented Database Systems, LNCS 334*, pages 280–285, Springer-Verlag, 1988.

1.74 N.W. Paton and P.M.D Gray. Optimising and executing Daplex queries using Prolog. *The Computer Journal*, 33(6):547–555, 1990.

1.75 A. Poulovassilis. FDL : An integration of the functional data model and the functional computational model. In *Proc. BNCOD'88*, pages 215–236. Cambridge Univ. Press., 1988.

1.76 A. Poulovassilis. The implementation of FDL, a functional database language. *The Computer Journal*, 35(2):119–128, 1992.

1.77 A. Poulovassilis and P.J.H. King. Extending the functional data model to computational completeness. In *Proc. Int. Conf. on Extending Database Technology (EDBT-90), LNCS 416*, pages 75–91, 1990.

1.78 A. Poulovassilis, S. Reddi, and C. Small. A formal semantics for an active functional DBPL. *Journal of Intelligent Information Systems*, 7(2):151–172, 1996.

1.79 A. Poulovassilis and C. Small. A functional programming approach to deductive databases. In *Proc. VLDB'91*, pages 491–500, 1991.

1.80 A. Poulovassilis and C. Small. Investigation of algebraic query optimisation for database programming languages. In *Proc. VLDB'94*, pages 415–426, 1994.

1.81 A Poulovassilis and C. Small. Formal foundations for optimising aggregation functions in database programming languages. In *Proc. DBPL'97, LNCS 1369*, pages 299–318, 1997.

1.82 S. Reddi. Integrity constraint enforcement in the functional database language PFL. In *Proc. BNCOD'93, LNCS 696*, pages 238–257, 1993.

1.83 S. Reddi, A. Poulovassilis, and C. Small. Extending a functional DBPL with ECA-rules. In *Proc. Rules in Database Systems (RIDS'95), LNCS 985*, pages 101–115. Springer-Verlag, 1995.

1.84 D. Reeves, B. Grosof, M. Wellman, and H. Chan. Toward a declarative language for negotiating executable contracts. In *Artificial Intelligence for Electronic Commerce: Papers from the AAAI-99 Workshop*, AAAI Press, 1999.

1.85 T. Sheard and L. Fegaras. A fold for all seasons. In *Proc. Functional Programming and Computer Architecture'93*, pages 233–242, 1993.

1.86 D.W. Shipman. The functional data model and the data language DAPLEX. *ACM Trans. on Database Systems*, 6(1):140–173, 1981.

1.87 E.H. Sibley and L. Kerschberg. Data architecture and data model considerations. In *Proc. AFIPS National Computer Conference*, pages 85–96, 1977.

1.88 J. Simeon and P. Wadler. The Essence of XML (Preliminary Version). In *Proc. FLOPS'02*, pages 21–46, 2002.

1.89 C. Small and A Poulovassilis. An overview of PFL. In *Proc. DBPL'91*, pages 96–110. Morgan Kaufmann, August 1991.

1.90 J.M Smith, S. Fox, and T. Landers. Adaplex rationale and reference manual. Technical Report CCA-83-08, Computer Corporation of America, 1983.

1.91 D.R. Sutton and C. Small. Extending functional database languages to update completeness. In *Proc. BNCOD'95, LNCS 940*, pages 47–63, 1995.

1.92 V. Tannen, P. Buneman, and S. Naqvi. Structural recursion as a query language. In *Proc. DBPL'91*, pages 9–19. Morgan Kaufmann, 1991.

1.93 V. Tannen, P. Buneman, and L. Wong. Naturally embedded query languages. In *Proc. ICDT'92*, pages 140–154, 1992.

1.94 V. Tannen and R. Subrahmanyam. Logical and computational aspects of programming with Sets/Bags/Lists. In *Proc. ICALP'91*, pages 60–75, 1991.

1.95 M. Torrens and B. Faltings. Smart clients: constraint satisfaction as a paradigm for scaleable intelligent information systems. In *Artificial Intelligence for Electronic Commerce: Papers from the AAAI-99 Workshop*, AAAI Press, 1999.

1.96 P. Trinder. A functional database. D.Phil. Thesis, Oxford University, 1989.

1.97 P Trinder. Comprehensions: a query notation for DBPLs. In *Proc. DBPL'91*, pages 55–68. Morgan Kaufmann, 1991.

1.98 D. Tsichritzis and A. Klug. *The ANSI/X3/SPARC DBMS Framework: Report of the Study Group on Database Management Systems*. AFIPS Press, 1977.

1.99 D.A. Turner. Miranda: a non-strict functional language with polymorphic types. In Jouannaud J.P., editor, *Functional Programming Languages and Computer Architectures*. Springer-Verlag, 1985.

1.100 D.A. Turner. The semantic elegance of applicative languages. In *Proc. Functional Programming and Computer Architecture'81*, pages 85–92, 1981.

1.101 P Wadler. Comprehending monads. In *Proc. ACM Conf. on Lisp and Functional Programming*, pages 61–78, 1990.

1.102 A. Wikstrom. *Functional Programming Using Standard ML*. Prentice Hall, 1987.

1.103 L. Wong. The functional guts of the Kleisli query system. In *Proc. ICFP 2000*, pages 1–10, 200.

1.104 World Wide Web Consortium. XQuery 1.0 and XPath 2.0 Formal Semantics. See http://www.w3.org/TR/query-semantics, November 2002. W3C Working Draft.

Section Editor's Preface

Introduction to Section I:
Advances in Information Modelling using a Functional Approach
by Peter King

This first section comprises four chapters, the first two of which deal directly with the further developemnt of general purpose database management systems based on a functional model of data. Chapters 2 and 5 are concerned with being able to represent semantic features important to two particular but significant application areas for which the special purpose products used at present are limiting since the facilities of a general purpose system are also needed. Chapters 3 and 4 address the problem of referential transparency, an important feature of functional programming *languages* which depends on the assumption that a function maps from input to output, i.e. from domain to range, but with no change in its state or environment and thus the same argument will *always* yield the same result. This assumption, of course, conflicts directly with the need for state change in functional database systems to provide for update. Chapters 2 and 3 take a functional view of the Associative Model of Data which really requires to be embedded in a general purpose functional programming language wheras chapters 4 and 5 use the model originally proposed by Shipman which does not.

Chapter 2 develops further the complete and seamless integration of functional programming with a functional database along the lines originally pioneered in FDL. It draws attention to the semantic limitations of systems based uniquely upon the lambda calculus and the need to extend the semantic range to take in the important areas of application which depend upon the need for highly flexible and incremental searching of labelled directed graphs as well as the normal query facilities. It shows how this can be achievd within the functional paradigm by making functions first class objects in the computation and by providing a small set of built in primitives both for querying the schema and for searching instance data. The use of these facilities in areas such as criminal intellidence analysis is then illustrated.

Chapter 5, by contrast, is concerned with with application in the specialist area of structural engineering known as finite element analysis and used for analysing the stresses in structures such as the pylons on which the grid's power cables are strung, bridges and oil rigs. The analysis results in large sets of linear equations, the solution of which is an area of classical numerical computation using matrices for which special purpose packages exist. The large quantities of data defining the FE analysis itself, the resulting matrices defining the equations for solution, and the results from the special purpose computational processes all need be held in the database. In their approach the authors of chapter 5 propose an extension to the type system to include matrices as a type and stress the importance of efficiency when computing with the converses of functions which they emphasise by designating such functions as *multi-directional functions*. They also aim to accomodate packages for the special numerical analysis methods developed for this work within the functional paradigm.

Chapters 3 and 4 both discuss the inherent conflict between referential transparency in functional programming languages and the requirement for database update although from a quite differeent perspective. After a relatively brief discussion of the problem the authors of chapter 3 define a set of language facilities using constructor functions which they consider to be necessary from a practical standpoint to achieve the updates for which there must be provision. They then analyse the consequences of what they have done in terms of the loss of refererential transparency which they consider necessary and inevitable to achieve a practically usable language and then show how that which remains can be identified and used beneficially.

The authors of chapter 4, by contrast, give an extensive and thorough discussion of previous work in the area of referential transparency, comparing and contrasting the various approaches. Their conclusion is to argue for a declarative approach to state change and they take a first step in this direction by implementing a version of DAPLEX which enables them to have a declarative description for the creation of sets of instances by specifying the constraints that new instances must satisfy which they then illustrate by example. Interestingly the authors of both chapters 3 and 4 are unanimous in dismissing the theoretically elegant formalism which apparently avoids any loss of referential transparency by modelling the database state explicitly and passing it around as a parameter as being quite impractical for real world software.

London, April 2003, *Peter J H King*

Table of Contents

2. A Functional Database Language for the Associative Model of Data

Peter J.H. King[1]

School of Computer Science and Information Systems,
Birkbeck College, University of London
email: pjhk@dcs.bbk.ac.uk

Summary.

The Associative Model of Data represents information, both schema and instance, in the form of a directed graph but with certain constraints on the labelling of nodes and edges, in our context termed arcs. Such a directed graph can readily be shown to be uniquely represented as a set of triples and thus held in some form of triple store repository. Many practical applications involve networks which can be represented as directed graphs and for which special purpose languages have been developed[2.10, 2.6, 2.5].

Previous work on FDL [2.9, 3.13] on which that described in this chapter builds, has shown that Shipman's functional data model can be integrated with a functional programming language to considerable advantage with the definitions of *all* the functions invoved, whether extensionally or intentionally defined or of mixed definition, being held in a triple store repository. This integration was an important advance but was soon discoverd to have limitations consequent upon its semantic power being equivalent only to that of the lambda calculus.

In this chapter we describe how we take a functional view of the associative model of data very similar to that of Shipman's approach if resricted to functions of a single variable, and integrate if with a functional programming language using a triple store repository just as with FDL. Then, by taking a somewhat more relaxed approach to typing than with conventional functional programming, by treating named functions as first class objects in the computation, and by defing a set of higher order functions, we show that the functional database/language paradigm can be extended to include the power of the graph query languages referred to above. We also show how this approach greatly facilitates working in areas where the schema is subject to continuous change and update, since useful queries can be made without any knowledge of the schema.

2.1 Introduction

A major concern in developing database management software for advanced applications is to capture as much of the semantics as possible of an application domain. The relational model has been shown to be limited in the capturing of such semantics, which has led to the development of graph-based data models as an alternative and better approach. In the next section we discuss one such data model, the Associative Data Model, in more detail giving it a precise specification and showing how it is best implemented.

A different and distinct development has been that of the functional data model which allows powerful query languages to be developed based on the use of functions [5.25]. The feasibility of using the functional style of programming as the basis for sophisticated database query languages has also been demonstrated [2.4]. This approach has been taken to its logical conclusioin with the complete integration of Shipman's functional data model with functional programming in FDL [2.9, 3.13], leading to a computationally complete, persistent database programming language. The advantage of such integration is that it provides a consistent and coherent language covering both retrieval of information from the database and the programming concerned with computation and the manipulation of the information as may be required by the particular application. Previous to this development the retrieval of information from the database was by means of one language (e.g. SQL), and the manipulation and computational aspects were carried out by some different language (e.g. C, Cobol, etc.) with the need to have mechanisms for them to cohabit in the sense of working with the same data, and reconciling their data types and programming styles: the so-called *impedance mismatch* problem.

Whilst a considerable advance, computational completeness is nevertheless still a somewhat limiting criterion to use in measuring the power of database programming languages. To say that a language is computationally complete is in effect to say that it has the same computational power as the lambda calculus. Yet the Lambda Calculus is a theory of anonymous functions whereas a functional database is a body of data held as named functions. Moreover the definition of these functions is dynamic — being modified by database updates and deletions — since the function definitions themselves constitute the database. The presence of function declarations which effectively define a schema for a database system means that there are queries which a user can reasonably make which have no counterpart in the Lambda Calculus. These include simple queries on the schema itself, such as:

What functions are defined on the type person?

and queries to retrieve the associations between values, for instance:

What connections are there, if any, between Angela and Edward?

These queries are essentially higher-order and are beyond the capability of languages based uniquely on the Lambda Calculus or on First-Order Logic. Thus the fact of a database programming language being computationally complete does not imply that it is possible to pose them.

It is clear, however, that with graph-based models of data such as the Associative Model it is, in principle, possible to answer such queries. Moreover the generality of access provided by the Triple Store [2.7, 3.8], over which FDL and other TriStarp Group experimental language software are implemented, means that the fundamental access mechanisms are available to allow such queries to be answered. In this chapter we show how the functional programming paradigm can be extended in a consistent and coherent way to enable such queries to be answered. This approach was first pioneered in the functional database programming language Hydra [2.1, 2.2], implemented over the same triple store software as that used for FDL.

An aspect of research into relational query languages which has some similarity to the provision of associational facilities is that of query inference. Typically this involves using a graphical schema of the database to infer queries either to fill in incomplete information or to correct errors in queries. The approach is to use tokens in the query to determine a spanning tree of the schema which can be used to generate a valid query. An example of such work is [2.11].

The more general availability of workstations from the late 1980s and the consequent possibility of using graphical interfaces to databases stimulated interest in graph-based data models that have a direct visual analogue. The graphical query language GraphLog [2.10, 2.6, 2.5] uses regular expressions as a means of specifying paths through a database whose nodes and arcs are then retrieved and presented to the user.

In Section 2.2 we introduce and discuss with examples *the Associative Model of Data*, and in Section 2.3 we specify how it can be used as the basis of a functional database system integrated with a functional programming language. In Section 2.4 we describe some higher-order built-in functions which make possible, within the functional paradigm, graph traversal and queries which have hitherto been the province of special-purpose languages. In Section 2.5 we discuss some conflicts between the established approach to typing in functional programming and the requirements of a functional database language for use with the Associative Model, and how we have resolved them. In Section 2.6 we give some examples of the use of the language. and in Section 2.7 we give some information on our experimental implementation. Finally, in Section 2.8 we summarise the approach, discuss its significance and further possible and required developments.

2.2 The Associative Model of Data

In Sections 1.2.1 and 1.2.2 we discussed the data modelling primitive *Association* and the two distinct forms of entity used in data modelling, which we termed *Abstract Entity* and *Value Entity*. The Associative Model of Data uses only these three concepts and represents information in the form of a directed graph or *digraph* . It is thus an application of the branch of discrete mathematics known as graph theory which thus provides a sound theoretical underpinning for the approach.

An example of such a representation of information as a digraph is shown in Figure 2.1. It comprises nodes and arcs (edges) with the arcs having direction as indicated by the arrowheads. Every node and arc is labelled and

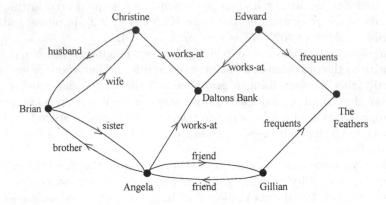

Fig. 2.1. A digraph model of some instance data

we require that all node labels be distinct. In this particular diagram each labelled node represents an entity instance and a labelled arc an association between the two entities which it connects. We can readily appreciate the information which Figure 2.1 represents: that Angela, Christine and Edward work at Daltons Bank; that Christine is married to Brian; that Brian and Angela are brother and sister; that Edward and Gillian both visit The Feathers pub from time to time; and that Angela and Gillian are friends. Note, however, the level of background understanding necessary to comprehend this information: what a pub is and that The Feathers is a particular one; what working at a place implies; the relationship of brother and sister; and so on.

It is clear that, layout apart, the requirement that every node label must be distinct implies that a digraph of the form shown in Figure 2.1 is uniquely represented by a set of triples of the form:

<node label, arc label, node label>

the order of the node labels within the triple giving the direction of the arc. In the case of Fig 2.1 this set clearly comprises nine triples. The equivalence of a digraph to a set of triples clearly points the way to a strategy for implementing database software using such models and was originally discussed by Frost[2.7].

Figure 2.1 represents what, in database terminology, is a model of some *instance data*. There is also the concept of *type* or *class*, and that one type can be a *sub-type* of another. We represent a type by a labelled node and use the special arc label *isa* which we overload to show either that an entity instance is a member of a type or that one type is a sub-type of another.

In Figure 2.2 we give a digraph of the schema information to which the instance information in Figure 1 conforms. It shows the entity types *Man*

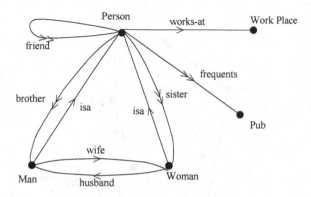

Fig. 2.2. A digraph model of the schema data

and *Woman* as sub-types of *Person* and the association types for the various association instances that appear in Figure 2.1. We could now combine the graphs of Figures 2.1 and 2.2 into a single digraph by connecting up each entity in Figure 2.1 to its type in Figure 2.2 using an *isa* arc. We show a fragment of such a combined graph in Figure 2.3.

Digraphs such as that of Figure 2.3 are particularly useful for tutorial and illustrative purposes. Conceptually this combined graph of both instance and schema information is important as a logical model or mental visualisation of how the information can be thought to exist within a computer system and thus how it might be accessed, retrieved and searched, particularly in investigative style applications such as criminal intelligence.

We have already observed that requiring every node label to be distinct means that a digraph modelling information can be represented as a set of triples. We now use this equivalence to specify the basic Associative Model of Data as a set of triples using BNF:

```
<entity instance>::=labelled node
<entity type>::=labelled node
<associator>::=labelled arc
<association instance>::=<entity instance><associator>
                                        <entity instance>
<association type>::=<entity type><associator><entity type>
<type specification>::=<entity instance> isa <entity type>
<sub-type specification>::=<entity type> isa <entity type>
<triple>::=<association instance>|<association type>|
               <type specification>|<sub-type specification>
```

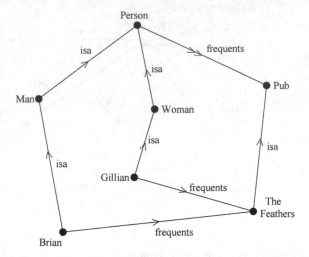

Fig. 2.3. A digraph model of both schema and instance data

We have the constraint that each node must have a distinct label. Further constraints are that the associators used in the association type definitions must be distinct, that no associator can be used in an association instance unless it has appeared in an association type definition and that every entity instance must have a type definition.

2.3 A Functional Language for the Associative Model

In this and the next four sections we descibe the main features of the experimental functional database language, Hydra , designed for the Associative Model. In this section we focus on the representation of the model in functional form and on its now conventional query and update facilities which are, in general, similar to those of FDL. We leave to the next section the associational facilities which make possible the sort of queries which go beyond what can be achieved with the lambda calculus, briefly disccussed in Section 2.1 above.

2.3.1 The Type System

The type system is similar to that of other standard functional languages except that a distinction is made between *atomic* types and *constructed* types. Atomic types are those which are used in the Associative Data Model, that is abstract entities and value entities. Constructed types are those which are used in the structuring of data — for example, lists. As in the standard functional languages, type polymorphism is supported, allowing the definition of polymorphic data types and higher-order functions.

New abstract entity types, such as *person* and *pub*, are introduced with the declaration:

    entity person, pub;

The approach of allowing visible surrogates described in Section 1.3.3 is supported, and the extents of these types managed as described there.

Constructed types are supported and may be polymorphic, with the standard functional programming types for representing multiple items and aggregates — *list* and *tuple* — built in. Lists are written using the format

    [1, 2, 3];

and tuples, which may be of any arity, are written as

    (1, 2);
    ("abc", True, 27);

Additional constructed types may be introduced by the user. For example, a recursive polymorphic tree type is defined by

    tree 'a ::= LEAF 'a | TREE (tree 'a) (tree 'a);

Polymorphic type variables are denoted by single lowercase letters preceded by a quote. All constructors must begin with an uppercase letter. An instance of an integer tree is then

    TREE (LEAF 1) (TREE (LEAF 3) (LEAF 5));

Once a constructed type has been defined it cannot be altered except by deletion and redefinition.

A novel feature of the type system is that it allows the specification of contexts in which mixed types may occur, such as within a list. This is achieved by having a special type, *any type*, which is effectively the union of all types. This approach and its rationale is discussed further in Section 2.5 below.

2.3.2 Primary and Secondary Functions

A main difference from earlier functional database languages is in making a clear distinction between those functions defined as a consequence of the data model, which we term *primary functions* , and those which are defined for the purpose of creating user views, for general computation and data manipulation. These we term *secondary functions* . The necessity for this distinction lies not in the first order facilities we are now describing but in the higher-order associational facilities which we describe in the next section.

Primary functions are declared by giving their name and type signature before any of their defining equations are entered. Their declaration is prefixed by the keyword *primary*. Examples, some of which are shown in the schema of Figure 2.2, are:

```
primary works-at    :: person -> work-place;
primary friend      :: person -> [person];
primary frequents   :: person -> [pub];
primary age         :: person -> integer;
primary address     :: person -> string;
```

The type signatures of primary functions must be consistent with the Associative Data Model. Hence primary functions must take an atomic parameter and return either an atomic value or a list of atomic values.

The motivation for secondary functions is to allow computational functions such as *sum* or *average* and higher-order or structure-manipulating functions such as *map*, *filter*, *reduce* and so on without compromising the Associative Model.

Secondary functions are declared in a similar way to primary functions except that their name and type signature is prefixed by the keyword *secondary*. They may, however, unlike primary functions take more than one argument[1] since they play no part in defining the schema and hence the structure of the database graph. For example

```
secondary map    :: ('a -> 'b) ['a] -> ['b];
secondary flatmap :: ('a -> ['b]) ['a] -> ['b];
```

the defining equations for which are

```
map f     []    = [];
map f (x:xs) = (f x):(map f xs);
flatmap f []    = [];
flatmap f (x:xs) = append (f x) (flatmap f xs);
```

The use of lists is well developed in functional programming and thus we use list-valued functions to represent the multivalued functions of the Associative Data Model, the ranges of which are in fact sets. Although the actual data held in the Triple Store is in set form and is thus unordered, when retrieved the data is presented as a list. However this order is arbitrary and may change as the result of updates. This issue is discussed further in Section 2.8.

---

[1] In functional programming a function of more than one argument can be regarded as a function of the elements of the cartesian product of its arguments as in the language Hope, or as a higher order function as in the language Miranda. The original version of Hydra adopted the latter approach for secondary functions whereas in the material presented here we adopt the former using the same notation as that used in FDL. We also imply the use of the same pattern matching strategy for both primary and secondary functions, i.e. *best fit*, and thus regard their defining equations as a set. Hydra, however, used this strategy only for primary functions and adopted the Miranda approach for secondary functions in which the defining equations are given as a list and pattern matching takes place sequentially. These are essentially matters of syntax and implementation detail and in no way effect the semantic power of the language.

Primary functions may be defined extensionally, intentionally, or partly extensionally and partly intentionally. Secondary functions may be used in the equations defining a primary function. For example, if we have the function declarations

```
primary salary  :: employee -> integer;
primary bonus   :: employee -> integer;
secondary min   :: integer integer -> integer;
```

and the equation

```
min x y = if x > y then y else x;
```

completing the definition of min, then whilst salary would be defined extensionally bonus might well be defined by the single equation:

```
bonus x = min 3000 (0.1*salary x);
```

meaning that the bonus for an employee is 10% of salary but subject to a maximum bonus of 3000. Likewise primary functions can be used in the definitions of secondary functions.

Updating, as with FDL, is carried out by a distinct set of commands which cannot be used within the context of the query language. Function definitions are updated by the deletion and insertion of equations or by the redefinition of the result when the argument of the updating equation is already present in the set of equations. The results for particular equations in the definition of a multi–valued function may be modified in the same way as the extents of abstract entities. Thus if we have the multi–valued function

```
friend  :: person -> [person]
```

and the defining equations include the equation

```
friend Susan = [Simon, Angela, Gillian];
```

then this could be modified to

```
friend Susan = [Angela, Gillian, Mary];
```

by means of the two update statements

```
friend Susan = - Simon;
friend Susan = + Mary;
```

For every primary function f of type a -> b or a -> [b] a converse function is automatically maintained which is denoted by ~f and is of type b -> [a]. For example, ~frequents will give for a particular pub a list of all the people who are recorded in the database as frequenting that pub; ~age would give for a particular integer a list of all the people who are recorded in the database as being of that particular age.

Of particular value in the context of a functional database are facilities for function composition. The Associative Data Model promotes a view of data in which data relationships between different entity classes are represented in terms of arcs or paths between those classes. It is important therefore that a path through the schema between two entity types (for example between *person* and *workplace*) to discover information such as

where the husband (or wife) of a particular person works

can be easily composed into a function to pose such a query. Simple function composition is represented by an infix dot so that the function corresponding to the above information request is

```
works-at.husband
```

This approach will not work with list-valued primary functions since the attempt to compose the single-valued function *age* with the list-valued function *friend*, for example, would result in an error. To overcome this problem we introduce two new composition operators. The first is used to combine single and list-valued functions, so that the expression:

```
age..friend Gillian;
```

returns a list of ages, one corresponding to each person recorded as being a friend of Gillian. Similarly, to combine two list-valued functions we can write

```
frequents...friend Gillian;
```

which will return a simple list of all the pubs frequented by the friends of Gillian. The definitions of these composition operators are:

```
f.g   x = f (g x)
f..g  x = map f (g x)
f...g x = flatmap f (g x)
```

2.4 Functions for Querying the Database Graph

In the previous section we described the basic features of a functional database language designed to work with an Associative Database. In this section we describe six built-in functions designed to provide for searching the directed graph which is the conceptual representation of the database.

These functions all carry out some form of schema-level interrogation using the types of the arguments they receive before retrieving the relevant data. They are designed to be usable in circumstances where the user may not have a detailed knowledge of the schema or may be unaware of recent updates to it. The syntax of these functions is:

```
like  <value> ;

to  <atomic value> ;
```

```
from  <atomic value> ;

link  <integer> <atomic value> <atomic value> ;

commonatts <entity> <entity> ;
```

with *trail* having the same syntax as *link*. We now discuss each in turn.

2.4.1 The Function *like*

Given a value, *like* determines its type and then retrieves all values of that type. Thus the query:

```
like Edward;
```

will retrieve all objects of type *person* (including *Edward*) and return the result as a list which will have the form

```
[Brian, Christine, . . , Edward . . .]
```

As well as being used for atomic values, *like* may also be used on functions, both primary and secondary. Hence

```
like salary;
```

will retrieve all functions of type

```
person -> integer
```

and return a result such as

```
[salary, bonus]
```

2.4.2 The Function *to*

The function *to* when passed a value returns a list of primary functions which produce a value of the same type as the parameter. Hence

```
to Edward;
```

might return the list of functions

```
[~works-at, ~frequents, ~friend]
```

There are two reasons why the functions are returned in converse form. The first is that a probable next step is to apply the functions to the value *Edward* and hence filter out those functions which do not actually return *Edward* from those that do. The second reason is that it gives greater uniformity of type since each function in the list is of the form

```
person -> [?]
```

where the question mark denotes a heteromorphic type (see Section 2.5).

2.4.3 The Function *from*

The function *from* retrieves all the primary functions which could take a given value as their argument. All functions returned are list-valued — single-valued functions are coerced to be list-valued through use of the built-in secondary function *ml* (make list). Hence the query

        from Edward;

returns the answer

        [ml.works-at, ml.salary, ml.bonus, frequents, friend]

The purpose of this coercion by the use of *ml* is to ensure that the result of distributing the argument *Edward* over the result will be a list of lists rather than a list of a mixture of lists and atomic values. This approach has been found to facilitate subsequent manipulation using the result.

2.4.4 The Functions *link* and *trail*

The function *link* returns a list of compositions of one or more primary functions which connect two values in the database, the result being presented in a form enabling it to be used in subsequent computations For example, if the database includes the instance level information shown in Figure 2.1

        link 3 Gillian Edward;

will return a list of the primary functions (or compositions of such functions) which connect *Gillian* and *Edward*. The result will be the list of two composed functions

        [frequents...~frequents, friend...works-at...~works-at]

since each of the these functions, when applied to the argument *Gillian* will return a list containing the value *Edward*. Had we posed the query in the other direction, that is

        link 3 Edward Gillian;

the result would have been

        [frequents...~frequents, works-at...~works-at...friend];

    The rationale for *link* taking a maximum length and two atomic values is that such graph searching clearly must be constrained to be practical. A variant of *link* is the function *trail* which, instead of composing the functions, returns them as a list together with the initial, last and intermediate nodes. It is designed to be used to provide information directly rather than for use in subsequent computations. Thus

        trail 3 Edward Gillian;

would return

```
[(Edward frequents The-Feathers ~frequents Gillian),
 (Edward works-at Daltons-Bank ~works-at Angela
                                  friend Gillian]
```

Notice how readily these two lists are close to the plain English

```
"Edward frequents The Feathers which is frequented
                                      by Gillian."
"Edward works at Daltons Bank as does Angela who is a
                                   friend of Gillian."
```

It is also straightforward to use *link* and *trail* in the definition of similar (secondary) functions of greater generality, e.g. to find the shortest path between two entities up to some maximum length, or paths up to some length but that either exclude or only contain certain specified associations (functions).

We note that the type of *link* is

```
link  :: integer 'a 'b -> [('a -> ['b)]
```

whereas that of *trail* is

```
trail :: integer 'a 'b -> [?]
```

The evaluation mechanism for these functions works by first inspecting the schema to find potential connections which do not exceed the specified length. These functions are then evaluated, with those functions which do not connect the two entities and those which contain loops being filtered out. Only paths which go through abstract entities are inspected to avoid finding trivial connections such as the fact that a friend of Edward has the same age as someone who also works at Daltons Bank. It should also be noted that these functions are restricted to paths involving only the instance data and take no account of paths which would involve typing information represented by the *isa* arcs in Figures 2.2 and 2.3 since it would not be useful to be told, for example, that Brian and Gillian are both persons.

2.4.5 The Function *commonatts*

The last of these functions we describe is *commonatts*. The constraining of *link* and *trail* to paths only traverse abstract entity nodes prevents a common attribute value of two entities being on a connecting path. The function *commonatts* is thus provided to discover which, if any, attribute value(s) two entities of the same type have in common. For example, the query,

```
commonatts Edward Angela;
```

will return the answer

```
[(age 30),(works-at Daltons-Bank)]
```

which is a list of attributes and their values which the two parameters have in common. Note that the second piece of information could have been discovered using trail whereas the first could not.

2.4.6 Querying the Schema Directly

The six functions presented above, which take instance data as parameters, work by accessing the schema and then using the results of the schema query. The results are either presented directly to the user, or filtered by inspecting the contents of the database. Given these facilities it is desirable to make them available as a mechanism for querying the schema directly, since in some circumstances the purpose of the query may be focussed on a type rather than a particular instance of that type. Moreover the facility to query the schema easily is of particular importance when the schema may frequently be modified and extended.

The approach used is to provide for *typed unknowns* which may be constructed from atomic types only. They are specified by prefixing the type name with a question mark. All the graph query functions except for *commonatts* will work with typed unknowns. Hence

        like ?person;

retrieves a list of all entities of type person in the database. The query

        from ?person;

retrieves all the attributes (the primary functions) defined for an entity of type person. In our example

        [ml.works-at, ml.age, ml.address, frequents, friend]

Similarly, the query

        to ?person;

retrieves all primary functions returning a value or list of values of type *person*, that is

        [~works-at, ~age, ~address, ~frequents, ~friend]

Finally the query

        link 3 ?person ?person;

retrieves all potential links of length not greater than 3 between two people.

2.5 Heteromorphism

As briefly discussed in Section 2.3.1 we provide for a heteromorphic type which is necessary in certain contexts for effective use of the higher-order graph traversal facilities. Consider a query such as

    from Edward;

which returns a list of functions such as

    [ml.salary, ml.bonus, frequents, friend]

the type of which cannot be expressed using the standard type system but which is to be used in subsequent computation and clearly has coherent meaning. Its type cannot be expressed because the members of this list are of three different types, these types being

    [person->[int], person->[pub], person -> [person]]

The most precise way to characterise the type of such a list is by using nested existential quantification, so that the type of the above list is

    [Exists 'a.(person->['a])]

However in the initial version of our language we adopted the simpler approach of using a single type variable which we denoted by a question mark to represent the *universal type* defined to be the union of all types. Thus the list

    ["abc", 1, [1]]

has type

    [?]

There are implications in this approach, both negative and positive, including

– type inference is no longer possible and the type signature must be entered for every function before any of its defining equations;
– type information on values must be present at run time;
– new kinds of functions and data become possible which are prevented by standard type systems.

One example of the third of the above points is that we can now record heteromorphic data using quite sensible functions which, with strict typing, cannot be used because they cannot be typed. Consider the function *owns* which has type

    owns :: person -> [?];

In effect *owns* takes an entity of type person and returns a list of things that the individual owns. The important point here is that these things need not necessarily all be of the same type; indeed it would be very surprising if they were. But with the *universal type*[2] we can now include in the function's definition equations such as

```
owns John =+ Car1, House9, Yacht3;
```

It can also be useful to have the argument of a function heteromorphic. Consider for example the function *heat-output* with type definition

```
heat_output :: ? -> int;
```

which recognises the fact that things of different type can generate heat. We can now enter defining equations such as

```
heat_output Photocopier1 = 2500;
heat_output Computer9    = 250;
heat_output Peter        = 100;
```

An interesting facility that becomes available and which we provide in our experimental implementation is to allow pattern-matching to work also on the type of the parameter so that we can have different default patterns for different parameter types. For example, the pattern

```
heat_output (x::person) = 90;
```

records a general default value applicable to objects of type *person* only.

2.6 The Resulting Query Langage

2.6.1 Queries

A query is a single expression to be evaluated and may include all the usual evaluation features available in functional programming, such as

```
1 + (7 * 6);
```

---

[2] A different approach is to provide for the union of types so forming type hierarchies in order to remain within the strict typing of the functional paradigm. Thus in the example we give we would need a type car-house-yacht to allow for a mixture from the three separate types car, house and yacht. This approach is not appropriate in the context of our target application domain since if the schema is subsequently updated to include the type horse, say, then a new equation or a variation to an existing equation such as owns Peter = + Dobbin; would not be accepted until a consequential new type, car-house-yacht-horse, had been created and the range type of owns modified accordingly. This would seem to be taking strict typing in the functional database context too far! It is worth noting that the approach we are adopting is essentially equivalent in the functional database context to allowing the type of a function to be determined by the system from its defining equations and modified as and when necessary.

To find out who we have recorded as working at Daltons Bank we would enter the expression

```
~works-at Daltons-Bank;
```

using the converse of the primary function *works-at*. To find out if we have the wife of Brian recorded we would simply use directly the primary function

```
wife Brian;
```

List abstractions may be used in the normal way in the construction of queries. Hence to print details recorded of the staff of Daltons Bank we might enter

```
[(x, age x, address x)| x <- ~works-at Daltons-Bank];
```

Note that to make the above three queries requires a knowledge of the schema in the conventional way. With the higher-order primitives we do not necessarily need this knowledge. This is of advantage when the schema itself is frequently the subject of update. More importantly, however, is that complex canned queries written for the user do not require modification when such updates take place. For example, if we simply want to know what is recorded about Angela we could write:

```
[(f,f Angela)|f<- from Angela]
```

since *from Angela* gives a list of all the primary functions currently defined on the entity type of which *Angela* is an instance (coerced to have the same type as described in Section reffrom) which are then successively applied to the argument Angela. If the instance information shown in Figure 2.1 were all that was recorded about Angela in the database, the result of the above query would be

```
[(brother Brian),(works-at Daltons-Bank),(friend Gillian)]
```

A complete knowledge of all the arcs, both *to* and *from* Angela, and the nodes, both value and abstract, to which they connect would be given by

```
[(f,f Angela)|f<- append from Angela to Angela]
```

We could, of course, have canned this query as a secondary function which could then be applied to anybody as

```
secondary all-about :: person -> [?];
all-about p = [(f, f p)|f<-
                        append from ?person to ?person]
```

and one could then have written

```
all-about Angela;
```

which the average detective would clearly prefer. Note particularly the immunity of this secondary function to schema changes.

With some knowledge of the schema we can be selective about the information returned. Thus to retrieve all the information recorded about people frequenting The Feathers, but ignoring their addresses, we could write

```
let attlist = (remove ml.address from ?person) in
  [(p,[(f,f p)|f<- attlist])|p<- ~frequents The Feathers];
```

with the secondary function *remove* defined in the obvious way.

2.6.2 Using the Query Facilities

We now illustrate how the query facilities might be used in an investigation and take, for illustration, a highly simplified example of a bank robbery. We assume that a special database has been set up for this investigation but with transparent connections to other similar databases. One aspect of the investigation might well involve trying to discover whether there is some connection between an employee of the bank and one or more known bank robbers since there are certain characteristics of the robbery which suggest some possible insider involvement. An essential part of any investigation is the gathering of possibly relevant information and this will be held in the database set up to support the investigation. In this context it is not possible to foresee all the kinds of information which may need to be recorded. Thus there will be an inital schema which is likely to be extended frequently.

Suppose the robbery took place at Daltons Bank which we can now think of as the central node in our database. Using function composition operators we find the results following particular paths from this node. To find all known employees of Daltons Bank we enter

```
~works-at Daltons-Bank;
```

To determine the pubs frequented by these employees we enter

```
frequents...~works-at Daltons-Bank;
```

and for those pubs which friends of the employees frequent

```
frequents...friend...~works-at Daltons-Bank;
```

Similarly, all the pub staff whom the friends of bank employees are likely to know can be obtained by

```
~works-at...frequents...friend...employee Daltons-Bank;
```

If a known bank robber, say *Bill*, has a brother who works as a pub barman then we can determine employees of the bank who might have met him with

```
[x | x <- ~works-at Daltons-Bank;
     y <- ~works-at...frequents x;
     y = (brother Bill)];
```

There is also a suspicion that there might be a connection between a particular employee *Gillian* and the known bank robber *Bill*, yet there is no indication of such a connection as a result of the above queries. Perhaps a wider search of the network is required, which coulld reveal an important connection. Thus we might try

```
link 6 Gillian Bill;
```

and also, for good measure,

```
[x | x <- ~works-at Daltons-Bank; (link 6 x Bill) != []];
```

to find out what other employees might have a connection. Note this query result will be a list of lists, one for each employee but with those employees for which the list is empty filtered out.

Direct links between entities are one kind of connection which are of interest. The other kind of connection is when entities share common attributes. For example, the fact that two people have the same age and attended the same school or were born in the same area and are about the same age suggests they might know each other. Hence, given the suspect *Bill* and an employee *Angela*, the query

```
commonatts Bill Angela
```

returning a list of common attributes such as

```
[(age 32), (born_in Aix_en_Provence)]
```

would at the least prompt some further action and inquiry.

Of course the solution to our toy problem, actually catching the bank robber and putting him (or her!) behind bars, lies outside the realm of database technology. But in the present day approach to the investigation of a serious crime a large team is likely to be involved and the very large amount of information collected must be properly managed. And some hidden crucial part that *will* point the way to the solution, must be discovered and extracted from the large mass, most of which in the end will prove to have been irrelevant. At the present time conventional relational technology is used with special purpose products interfacing to it. The functional approach to database management we describe here points, we believe, to a better way.

2.7 An experimental implementation

The experimental implementation of Hydra , which pioneered the graph searching language features described in this chapter, ran on a Sun workstation under Solaris. It comprised some 13,000 lines of C and used a software Triple Store as the underlying persistent storage mechanism, the same underlying storage mechanism as was used for the implementation of FDL. The implementation was lazy and uses a supercombinator approach [2.12].

Implementation of the primitives *to* and *from* is relatively simple involving a search of the schema for functions with the appropriate range or domain. The *link* primitive is more complicated. The evaluation proceeds by determining the types of the parameters and using the schema to construct possible paths through the database. Once a possible path has been found the database is accessed to determine if any instances of the path exist at the instance level. Instance level paths are inspected to ensure the absence of loops. If a potential path fails then backtracking takes place to evaluate the next potential solution.

An important aspect of the implementation is that these facilities are integrated into the graph reduction algorithm used for evaluation of standard functions. They are lazily evaluated so that a path is only retrieved when needed. Moreover the associational query facilities make use of the same heap. This close integration allows nesting of associational features within function bodies or other associational queries.

2.8 Summary and Discussion

This chapter describes work of the mid 1990s which takes forward the functional approach to database management by building on previous work that showed how Shipman's functional data model could be integrated with functional programming, and demonstrated the effectiveness of using a triple store as the basis for the underlying repository. Accepting that graph-based data models in general, and the Associative Data Model in particular, are more suited to advanced applications such as those which arise in criminal intelligence and other investigative work, we explored the development of appropriate tools for their management within a functional paradigm, the aim being to provide power equivalent to the specialised graph searching languages but within the context of a general purpose database management system.

It was soon clear that this could not be done within the context of languages equivalent in power to the lambda calculus, that functions cannot be anonymous and must be able to be treated as first class objects within computations and query evaluation. Previous functional languages such as EFDM, P/FDM and FDL have provided facilities for querying the schema but not within the query language and not with result objects that were immediately usable as part of the ongoing query process. Thus in FDL, for example, what was returned in response to the various schema query commands available were lists of strings, these being the names used for the various functions and types in the source code of the original declarations, only useful in the context of new code being created, and things like the current state of the instance data in the various sets of equations defining functions.

The important advance in the work described in this paper is to enable functions such as *all-about* defined in Section 2.6.1 above of be written and used together with functions like *trail* with no knowledge of the schema but only knowledge of some instance data. Indeed a longer term objective might be the creation of a system in which update of the schema might be on a par with that of the instance data and which can be meaningfully queried with only a general knowlege of the application domain.

It also became clear as the work progressed that the approach to typing in traditional functional programming was too limiting in our context and that new features were needed. Our approach to this latter problem has arguably been somewhat simplistic and could be said to amount to little more than switching off the typing system in certain contexts. However, it works! But a more sophisticated approach might be worth investigating. One possibility is to make the system more expressive with the introduction of true existential types. These could allow the types of associational primitives and the functions which use them to be more precisely characterised.

Priority needs to be given, however, to linking to some form of graphical interface which takes full advantage of the power of the functional paradigm, not so much in terms of formulating queries but in displaying the results of such queries to allow their significance fully to be appreciated. This approach would enable the results of a number queries to be built up in a window in graph form to show some particular part of the database of special relevance to, say, an investigation.

Current work is focussed on the integration of the facilities pioneered in Hydra with those of Relief discussed in the next chapter, and some of the facilities still only in the original FDL. The objective is to create a new functional database language for the Associative Data Model, with implementation over a content addressed triple store in which *all* information which persists is held; an objective achieved in the original FDL and still regarded as important.

Acknowledgements

The author would like to express his gratitude and indebtdness to Robert Ayres for the many enjoyable and interesting discussions on the subject matter of this chapter during his three years as a PhD student and his subsequent period as a Research Assistant in the TriStarp Group. Without him these ideas would never have been clarified in the way they have and brought to fruition in a most convincing experimental implementation, further information on which can be found in his thesis [2.3].

References

2.1 R. Ayres and P.J.H. King. Enhancing database query languages with associational facilities. *Ingenierie des Systemes d'Information*, 3(3):441–463, 1995.

2.2 R. Ayres and P.J.H. King. Querying graph databases using a functional language extended with second order facilities. In *Proc. BNCOD'96, LNCS 1094*, pages 189–203, 1996.

2.3 R. Ayres. Enhancing the Semantic Power of Functional Database Languages. PhD thesis, University of London, 1995.

2.4 P. Buneman, R.E. Frankel, and R. Nikhil. An implementation technique for database query languages. *ACM Transactions on Database Systems*, 7(2):164–186, 1982.

2.5 M.P. Consens, I.F. Cruz, and A.O. Mendelzon. Visualizing queries and querying visualizations. *ACM SIGMOD Record*, 21(1):39–46, 1992.

2.6 M.P. Consens and A.O. Mendelzon. Graphlog: a visual formalism for real life recursion. In *Proc. ACM PODS'90*, pages 404–416, 1990.

2.7 R.A. Frost. Binary relational storage structures. *The Computer Journal*, 28(5):359–67, 1985.

2.8 P.J.H. King, M. Derakhshan, A. Poulovassilis, and C. Small. TriStarp - an investigation into the Implementation and Exploitation of Binary Relational Storage Structures. In *Proc. BNCOD'90*, pages 64–84. Pitman, 1990.

2.9 P.J.H. King and A. Poulovassilis. FDL: a language which integrates database and functional programming. In *Proc. INFORSID'88, La Rochelle*, 1988.

2.10 A.O. Mendelzon and P.T. Wood. Finding regular simple paths in graph databases. In *Proc. VLDB'89*, pages 185–193, 1989.

2.11 A Motro. Constructing queries from tokens. In *Proc. ACM SIGMOD'86*, pages 120–131, 1986.

2.12 S.L. Peyton Jones. *The Implementation of Functional Programming Languages*. Prentice Hall, 1987.

2.13 A. Poulovassilis and P.J.H. King. Extending the functional data model to computational completeness. In *Proc. EDBT'90, LNCS 416*, pages 75–91, 1990.

2.14 D.W. Shipman. The functional data model and the data language DAPLEX. *ACM Trans. on Database Systems*, 6(1):140–173, 1981.

3. Scoped Referential Transparency in a Functional Database Language

Peter J.H. King and Paul F. Meredith

School of Computer Science and Information Systems, Birkbeck College, Malet Street, London WC1E 7HX, UK
email: {pjhk}@dcs.bbk.ac.uk

Summary.

This chapter first discusses the inherent conflict between referential transparency, an important property of functional programming languages, and the requirement for good updating facilities with functional databases which arises when we attempt their integration. This conflict has, in previous such integrations, simply been avoided by having the integration only for the purpose of querying and computing with the results of queries, but having a quite separate non-functional command style language for the purposes of update.

It then outlines an experimental language we have implemented, *Relief*, which integrates functional programming with a functional database and includes update facilities, simply accepting that there will be some loss of referential transparency. We then draw attention to the work of Gifford and Lucassen in the 1980s on the integration of functional and imperative programming languages and use their approach to analyse the loss of referential transparency in *Relief*.

This analysis shows that it is possible to identify regions or *scopes* within which there is local referential transparency and to which the parallelism and optimising techniques of functional programming and compiling can still be applied. These scopes can be readily identified provided all user-defined functions are specified as having an *effects class*, their being two such classes which we term *observer* and *procedure* which have been incorporated into the experimental language.

3.1 Introduction

An inherent conflict arises with functional languages in the database context between change of state on update and the concept of referential transparency. Passing the database itself as a parameter resolves the issue conceptually but is not a practical approach. Update by side-effect is efficient but necessarily implies some loss of referential transparency. Additionally side-effects are often incompatible with lazy evaluation since the occurrence and sequence of updates can become non-intuitive. Our approach is to accept that a change of database state will result in loss of global referential transparency but that referential transparency can be scoped so that areas of a program can be identified which retain the property. Equational reasoning and consequent optimisation and parallelism can then be applied within these scopes.

The work described in this chapter resulted from the use of FDL [3.11, 3.13] in practical contexts and the difficulties and awkwardness we found when updating. FDL does not provide facilities for updating. Updates are achieved through the use of a quite distinct command language. This language cannot be invoked from within FDL and neither can FDL be invoked from within the command language. Thus if we have a bulk update (a sequence of similar updates) where what has to be done in each case depends upon the current state of the database which has first to be established by means of an FDL query, the update cannot be achieved except by splitting it into two or more quite separate operations. A simple example is if we wish to add information concerning a number of people some of whom may be known to the database and others not. Instead of being able for each case to query whether the person is or is not known to the database and so choose between the two different command sequences required, we must first have a run against the database using FDL to discover those that are already known and then, using this information, split the bulk input data into two distinct runs, one for each case. If there are more than two different cases the process becomes yet more complex and cumbersome.

We therefore describe in this chapter an experimental variant of FDL which we called Relief. Relief is lazy and has been extended with functions to facilitate database update and the reading of files. These functions work by means of side-effects which are explicitly sequenced with an eager let expression and a derivative sequencing construct. There is, however, no change in the overall laziness of the graph reduction which we illustrate with an example update program which employs the lazy stream model. To redress the loss of global referential transparency an effects checker identifies referentially transparent regions or scopes.

3.2 The Entity–Function Model

The development of Relief was a contribution to the work of the TriStarp Group, initiated in 1984 to investigate the feasibility of database management systems which support the binary relational model both at the storage and the conceptual levels. A summary of the early work is given by King et al. [3.8]. Subsequently research focused on supporting the Group's entity–function model, a hybrid of the binary relational and functional data models [5.25, 3.1]. The relationships between entities are binary and are represented by (possibly) multivalued single argument functions. Entity types are classified into lexical and non-lexical as with the analysis methodology NIAM [3.17]. Members of lexical types have direct representation (e.g. the types string and integer) whereas those of non-lexical types are real or abstract objects without direct representation, for example persons, invoices, courses, etc.

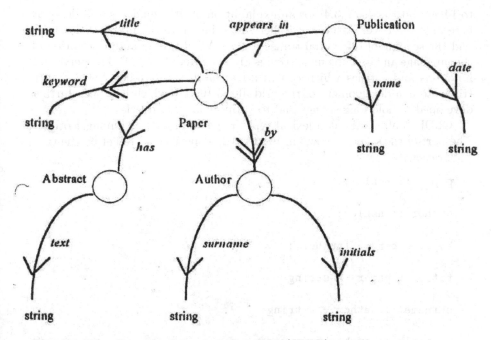

Fig. 3.1. The Computer Literature Database (CLDB)

Figure 3.1 shows a subschema of the Computer Literature Database (CLDB), a body of data comprising the title, author(s), source (where and when published), abstract and references for some 20,000 papers on computing and used for experimentation by the TriStarp Group. It is a simple illustration of the entity–function model. Non-lexical types are shown as circles with functions represented by arcs. A single-headed arrow represents a single-valued function and a double-headed arrow denotes a multivalued function. Thus a Paper has a single Abstract but may have one or several Authors. In this example, the lexical type "string" is used extensively in the ranges of the functions.

3.3 Defining a Database in Relief

Relief is an experimental variant of FDL, significant parts of the code of which were reused in its implementation. However, a completely new parser was written and the opportunity was taken to revise and improve the syntax to bring it more into line with theGroup's other experimental languages. The command language was of course abandoned. It has the usual features of a modern functional programming language such as polymorphic types, lazy evaluation, constructor functions and pattern matching. We refer the reader to Field and Harrison [3.4] for an explanation of these matters and describe here only the novel features of Relief which illustrate the updating facilities and the scoping of referential transparency. A full syntax and description of the language and its implementation is given in Meredith [3.9]. The persistent functions and entities which constitute a database in Relief are held in a triple store, a development of the grid file [3.10, 3.3] which had been further developed to hold long strings and to support interval queries.

CLDB contains the non-lexical types paper and author amongst others. The part of the schema shown in Figure 3.1 is specified in Relief by the type declarations

```
paper :: nonlex;

author :: nonlex;

by :: paper -> [author];

title :: paper -> string;

surname :: author -> string:

initials :: author -> string;
```

In order to facilitate easy navigation Relief automatically maintains a converse function for all functions whose domain is a non-lexical type, referred to by the prefix rev. For example, the converses of the functions surname and by are

```
rev_surname :: string -> [author];

rev_by :: author -> [ paper ];
```

As an example of their use consider the following list comprehension which retrieves the papers by authors with the surname "Meredith"

```
[ title p | a <- rev_surname "Meredith"];

p <- rev_by a] ;
```

3.4 The Four Update Functions of Relief

The extent of a database is defined and can be redefined by means of the functions create, destroy, define and delete. The function create takes a non-lexical type as an argument and returns a new entity of the specified type. For instance

```
create author
```

returns a new member of the type author. An attempt to print a non-lexical entity yields its type in angled brackets, thus: `<author>`. The extent of a non-lexical type can be queried with the `All` function which returns the members of the specified type, for example

```
All author ;
```

The function `destroy` causes an entity to be deleted from the extent of the specified non-lexical type. Thus to destroy the first element in the list of all authors

```
destroy author (head (All author));
```

In the functional programming paradigm it is required that every expression has a value and thus `destroy` returns the value `Done` which is the only value in the type `update`. Functions are incrementally defined using the function `def` which adds an equation to the database and returns the value `Done`. To illustrate this, we give an expression which creates an author entity, binds it to a scoped static variable a and then defines an equation for the author's initials. The binding is done with an eager form of the let expression, `e_let`, which is further explained in the next section. Thus:

```
e_let a = create author in (def initials a = "PF");
```

The left hand side of a function equation consists of the name of the function followed by one or more arguments, and the right hand side is an expression which is stored unevaluated. The arguments at definition time can be either patterns or a bound variable such as "a", in which case the value of the variable is used in the definition of the equation. The value of a function's application defaults to the constant "@" (denoting "undefined") if there is no equation which matches the function's arguments. The pattern matching in Relief uses the left-to-right best-fit algorithm developed by Poulovasillis [3.12].

The delete function `del` deletes an equation from the database and returns the value `Done`. The arguments of `del` identify the left hand side of the function equation for deletion, for example

```
e_let a = head(rev_surname "King") in
          (del initials a);
```

deletes the equation defining the initials of an author with the surname "King".

All four update functions are statically type checked, see Meredith [3.9] for details, and work at the object level. Thus their invocation needs to be sequenced which we discuss in the next section.

3.5 Sequencing the Updates

A new construct, the **eager let** (e_let) introduced above, sequences updates by employing call-by-value parameter substitution but within a general
scheme of lazy evaluation. We illustrate the eager let expression with an example in which an expression is evaluated before its use as the value of the
right hand side in an equation definition. The example assumes that people
have a unique name and the types of the functions `name` and `salary` are

```
name : person -> string;

salary : person -> integer;
```

The expression below defines the salary of Bill to be 5000 more than Fred's
current salary

```
e_let bill = head(rev_name "Bill") in

e_let fred = head(rev_name "Fred") in

e_let bills_salary = salary fred + 5000 in

            (def salary bill = bills_salary );
```

Thus the value of Bill's salary is stored as an integer and not a formula and
so a subsequent change to Fred's salary will not result in a change to Bill's
salary. The next example produces a sequence of updates to create an author
entity and define `surname` and `initials` before returning the new entity. Two
dummy variables, `dum1` and `dum2`, are used to bind with the values returned
by calls to the define function

```
e_let a = create author in

e_let dum1 = (def surname a = "Meredith") in

e_let dum2 = (def initials a = "PF")in a;
```

The overall evaluation scheme is still normal order reduction, the outermost
let being reduced before the innermost let and the body of each eager let
being evaluated lazily. The syntax of the eager let is not ideal because of
the need to specify binding patterns which are of no further interest as with
`dum1` amd `dum2` in the above example. Hence we have provided an explicit
sequencing construct in Relief which, although formally only equivalent to
the eager let, is much more succinct and convenient for programming. This
construct is written as a list of expressions separated by semicolons, enclosed
in curly brackets, and is optionally terminated by the keyword **puis** and a
following expression which gives a functional value for the entire sequence.
The expressions between the brackets are evaluated in their order, from left
to right. For example, the expression above can be written as the sequence

```
{ a = create author; (def surname a="Meredith");

    (def initials a = "PF") } puis a;
```

We refer to the keyword `puis` and its following expression as the `continuation`.
If it is omitted then a default value of `Done` is inferred for the sequence.

3.6 An Example – Updating the CLDB

We describe here a Relief program which processes a list of data constructors
representing the records in a file "TriStarp_papers" and updates that part
of the CLDB concerning authors and papers. Relief contains a `read_file`
function which can lazily convert a file of records into such a list [3.9]. The
elements of the list are members of the `paper_record` sum type which is
defined by the two constructors TITLE_REC and AUTHOR_REC. TITLE_REC has
a single string component, whereas AUTHOR_REC has two components: one for
the surname of the author and one for the initials:

```
paper_record :: sum;

TITLE_REC : string -> paper_record;

AUTHOR_REC : string string -> paper_record;
```

Our example will assume the following list of records as input:

```
[ (TITLE_REC "Scoped Referential Transparency in a Functional
Database Language with Updates"),
(AUTHOR_REC "Meredith" "PF"),
(AUTHOR_REC "King" "PJH"),
(TITLE_REC "TriStarp - An Investigation into the
% Implementation and
Exploitation of Binary Relational StorageStructures"),
(AUTHOR_REC "King" "PJH"), (AUTHOR_REC "Derakhshan" "M"),
(AUTHOR_REC "Poulovassilis" "A"), (AUTHOR_REC "Small" "C") ]}
```

The program to process the list consists of two functions: `cldbup`, which
creates the paper entities, and `add_authors`, which creates the author entities
and links them to the papers. Both functions operate recursively and process
records at the head of an input list before returning the remainder of the
list. For a list with a title record at its head, `cldbup` creates a paper, defines
its title and calls `add_authors` as specified by the first equation below. If the
head of the list is not a title record then the list is returned unaltered as given
by the second equation. This is an appropriate action when an unexpected or
unrecognised record is encountered. The third equation specifies that `cldbup`
returns the empty list when given the empty list. Thus `cldbup` will return

the empty list if all of the records in the file can be processed, otherwise it returns some remainder of the input list.

```
cldbup : [paper_record] -> [paper_record];

def cldbup ((TITLE_REC t) : xs) => {

p = create paper;

(def title p = t)

} puis cldbup (add_authors p xs);

def cldbup (h : t) = (h : t);

def cldbup [ ] = [ ];
```

The function add_authors recursively processes all the author records at the front of the list before returning the remainder of the list. The logic for processing a single author record is

- construct a list of authors with the specified surname and initials;
- if the list is empty create a new author, define their surname and initials, and bind them to the pattern "a" else bind the pattern to the head of the list of authors;
- if the list of authors for the specified paper is currently undefined, then define a list with the author "a" as its single member, otherwise add the author "a" to the existing list.

```
add_authors : paper [paper_record] -> [paper_record];

def add_authors p ((AUTHOR_REC s i) : xs) => {

auth_list = [ a1 | a1 <- rev_surname s;

            initials a1 == i ];

a = if auth_list == [ ] then

{a2 = create author;(def surname a2 = s);

(def initials a2 = i) } puis a2

else head auth_list fi;

e_let authors = by p in
```

```
if authors == @ then (def by p = [a])

else e_let new_authors = append authors [a]

in (def by p = new_authors)

fi

} puis add_authors p xs;

def add_authors p (h : t) => (h : t);

def add_authors p [ ] =>[ ];
```

The file of papers is then processed lazily by evaluating the following expression

```
cldbup (read_file paper_record "Tristarp_papers");
```

3.7 Scoping Referential Transparency

A defining property of languages which are purely functional is said to be *referential transparency* [3.7]. It is this property which allows functional languages to be declarative rather than imperative in nature. Put simply, referential transparency means that every instance of a particular variable has the same value within its scope of definition. This is the interpretation of variables in algebra and logic which allows the use of equational reasoning.

Although Relief is not a pure functional language it is possible to identify regions of referential transparency where the techniques used in functional programming, and by functional compilers, can still be applied. This follows from the fact that the concept of referential transparency is scoped by definition. In a purely functional language the scope is the environment or script in which an expression is evaluated. Referential transparency in Relief is scoped by the update operations which destroy reference. These regions of referential transparency can be statically identified by means of an *effects checker* which classifies the effect of an expression. Furthermore an effects checker is of use in concurrent systems since it identifies potential interference between expressions.

3.7.1 Gifford and Lucassen's Effects Checker

Effects checking was first described by Gifford and Lucassen [3.6] in connection with their research into the integration of imperative and functional languages. Gifford and Lucassen identify the following three kinds of effects of expressions:

- A: allocation and initialisation of mutable storage, for example the declaration of a variable or collection.
- R: reading a value from mutable storage.
- W: writing to mutable storage, that is assignment.

There are eight possible combinations of these three effects which form a lattice under the subset relation. These eight different combinations can be grouped into effect classes depending on the language requirement. Gifford and Lucassen were interested in identifying those parts of a program which could be *memoised* and were amenable to concurrent evaluation. Hence they produced an effect checking system which classified expressions into one of the following four effect classes:

```
{ W } { W,R } { W,A} { W,R,A } - PROCEDURE class

{ R } { R, A } - OBSERVER class

{ A } - FUNCTION class

{ } - PURE class
```

There is a total ordering of these effect classes in the sense that they form a hierarchy of effect properties. The effect properties of the four classes can be summarised as:

- PROCEDURE: expressions of this sublanguage can define variables, read mutable storage and write mutable values.
- OBSERVER: expressions of this sublanguage can define variables and read variables. They cannot perform assignments and cannot make use of expressions with the effect class PROCEDURE.
- FUNCTION: expressions of this sublanguage can define variables but they cannot read variables or change their value. FUNCTION expressions cannot make use of PROCEDURE or OBSERVER expressions.
- PURE: a pure function has no effects and cannot be affected by the evaluation of other expressions. It can neither define variables, nor read, nor write them. A PURE expression cannot make use of PROCEDURE, OBSERVER or FUNCTION expressions.

The only expressions which can interfere with concurrency are those in the effect class PROCEDURE and these can only interfere with other expressions in the PROCEDURE and OBSERVER effect classes. Thus the ability to identify expressions of these classes would be important in order to maximise concurrency in a multi-user system. In contrast PURE, FUNCTION and OBSERVER expressions do not interfere with each other and can be run concurrently. PURE expressions can be memoised and OBSERVER expressions can be memoised between updates. We now look at how effects checking is applied in Relief.

3.7.2 The Effects Checker in Relief

We begin by classifying the effect properties of constructs in Relief. Relief has no updateable variables in the usual sense but it does have extensible and updateable types, namely user-defined functions and non-lexical entities. Thus the Gifford and Lucassen concept of the allocation of mutable storage is equivalent to the declaration of such types. With regard to the initialisation of storage, a function declared in Relief has a default definition so that initially its application gives only the undefined value. The extent of a non-lexical type, accessed by the `All` metafunction, is initially the empty set. Type declarations, however, are commands and are not referentially transparent because they alter the database schema. Since they contain no subexpressions and cannot appear as subexpressions they are omitted from the effects checking.

With regard to updates, user-defined functions are updated by the **def** and **del** functions which define and delete equations in the definition of a function. The extents of non-lexical types are altered by the **create** and **destroy** functions. An expression which directly or indirectly calls any of these four functions has the (W) property. An expression which directly or indirectly applies a user-defined function or examines the extent of a non-lexical type has a value which is dependent on the state of the system. Such an expression has the (R) property. Since no expressions in Relief can have the (A) property it is sufficient to classify them as belonging to one of the following three effect classes:

```
{W } { W,R } - PROCEDURE class

{ R } - OBSERVER class

{ } - PURE class
```

Because Relief is a single-user sequential system we can say that an expression is referentially transparent if it makes no change to mutable storage under any condition. Thus an expression with the effect class OBSERVER or PURE is referentially transparent and has a value which is independent of the evaluation order of its subexpressions. The operational semantics of Relief allows the static scoping of referential transparency. Thus we arrive at the definition for the scope of referential transparency for an expression in Relief:

The scope of an expression's referential transparency in Relief is the maximal enclosing expression which has no (W) effects.

In a multi-user system, PURE and OBSERVER expressions can still be treated as referentially transparent if there is a locking mechanism to prevent expressions with effect class PROCEDURE from changing the function and entity types on which they depend.

Our approach differs from that of Gifford and Lucassen in that we regard the effect class of an expression as a property orthogonal to its type. We regard their approach of annotating each function type with its effect class as unnecessarily complex and giving no practical benefit. In our implementation an expression's effect class is inferred from its subexpressions in tandem with its type. Thus whilst performed in parallel effects checking and type checking are conceptually independent.

In Relief the programmer declares the effect class of a function from the outset and the compiler ensures that the declaration is not violated. The effect class of a user-defined function must be either PROCEDURE or OB-SERVER since it is an observer of its own mutable definition and hence possesses the (R) property. A user-defined function defaults to the effect class of OBSERVER, whereas an effect class of PROCEDURE is specified by preceding the function name with "proc". The following examples illustrate this. Firstly declaring a PROCEDURE whose application conditionally creates an author and defines their surname and initials:

```
proc create_author : string string -> update;

    def create_author sur init =

    if [ a | for a in rev_surname sur;

                              initials a == init ] == [
                              ]

    then { a = create author; (def surname a = sur);

    (def initials a = init) }

          else Done fi;
```

Secondly declaring an OBSERVER function which is dependent on other functions. This example defines a person's salary as the sum of their basic pay and their bonus:

```
salary : person -> integer;

def salary x = basic x + bonus x;
```

Finally declaring an OBSERVER function which is only dependent on its own definition. This example extracts the second component of a tuple:

```
sec_comp : (alpha1 ** alpha2) -> alpha2;

def sec_comp (x,y) = y;
```

The effects checker ensures that the declarations are not violated by checking that the effect class of each defining equation is less than or equal to the declared effect class of the function. The inference rules used in the effects checker are given by the pseudocode below. The effect class of a pattern is PURE and since this is the least value it can be ignored where some other expression is present.

The fundamental inference rule is the one for application. The effect class of an application is the maximum of the effect class of the function and the effect class of its argument. This means that effect inference is pessimistic since it assumes that if an expression contains a side-effect then that side-effect will take place. This is of course not necessarily true with lazy evaluation. We now give the algorithm for the function effect_chk which infers the effect class of an expression. The declared effect class of a user-defined function is retrieved by calling the function dec_effect. Thus the value of dec_effect(create_author) is PROCEDURE assuming the declaration of create_author above.

```
effect_chk(E) // effects checker

{

switch(E)

case (E1 E2) // application

case ( e_let p = E2 in E1 ) //eager let expression

case ( l_let p = E2 in E1 ) //lazy let expression

        e1 = effect_chk E1

        e2 = effect_chk E2

        return (max(e1, e2) )

case (\p. E) // lambda abstraction

        return ( effect_chk E)
```

```
case Qual //Qualifier in a list comprehension

        case ( for p in E) // generator

        case E // filter

                return ( effect_chk E)

case VAR v // a bound formal parameter, not

                        // updateable, hence PURE

case NONLEX n // a nonlexical entity

case CONFUN c // a data constructor

case ETYPE // a type as a parameter

case constant c // eg integer or string

        return (PURE)

case FUN f // a persistent function

        return(dec_effect(f))

case INFUN f // a built-in function

switch(f)

        case def f a1 .. an = rhs

        e = effect_chk (rhs)

        if e > dec_effect(f) then FAIL

        return(PROCEDURE)

                case del f a1 .. an

case create t

case destroy t
```

```
return(PROCEDURE)
```

```
OTHERWISE
```

```
return(PURE)
```

This algorithm can be modified to prohibit subexpressions with the effect class PROCEDURE from parts of the language. We suggest that this restriction might be applied to list comprehension qualifiers so that optimisations such as those published by Trinder [3.16] can be automatically performed.

3.8 Related Work

Ghelli et al. [3.5] have proposed an extension to list comprehension notation which provides update facilities for an object-oriented database language. The extension is achieved by adding a do qualifier which can perform actions on objects identified by earlier bindings in the list comprehension. They show that known optimisation techniques can be modified to operate in the presence of do qualifiers. Their technique, however, relies on the programmer restricting the use of side-effecting expressions to do qualifiers, there being no compile-time checking.

We briefly discuss three other approaches which promise efficient, functionally pure database update: linear types, monads and mutable abstract data types (MADTs). They are all efficient since they can guarantee a single-threaded store so that updates can be done in-place.

3.8.1 Linear Types

A linear object is an unshared, unaliased, singly referenced object and thus linear objects have the property that there is only one access path to them at any given time. A linear variable is a *use-once* variable which can only be bound to a linear object and must be dynamically referenced exactly once within its scope. Linear type checking systems have been designed which can statically check that linear variables are neither duplicated nor discarded. These systems have a theoretical foundation in linear logic whence they derive their name.

The motivation for having linear types in functional languages is to capture the notion of a resource that cannot or should not be shared, hence the linear variable. A linear type system does, however, allow for the explicit creation, copying and destruction of linear objects. Whenever a program creates a linear object it must also be responsible for its destruction. One advantage of this is that there is no need for garbage collection in a purely linear language. For functional programmers linear types offer a way, amongst other things, of guaranteeing safe in-place updates since a linear object can have only a single reference.

Purely linear languages, however, are very restrictive since functions must always pass-on their linear arguments, explicitly destroy them or return them even when they are not changed. The programs in these languages tend to be somewhat difficult to read due to their heavy use of multiple returned values. Another problem with languages which support linear types is that they must also deal with non-linear, that is shared, objects. This requires them to have a dual type checking system whereby most of the type inference rules have linear and non-linear counterparts. The programmer must be aware of the distinction between linear and non-linear values.

In the database context we want to treat database objects as linear when updating them but also to treat the same objects as shared when querying. However, an object cannot be both linear and non-linear at the same time. An interesting application of linear types to functional databases has been implemented by Sutton and Small [3.15] in their further development of PFL, a functional database language which uses a form of relation, called a selector, as its bulk data type. In the first version of PFL the incremental update of relations was achieved by means of the side-effecting functions `include` and `exclude`. A linear type checking system was introduced into PFL later on by changing these functions so that they took a linear relation name as an argument and returned the same relation name as a result. The type checking system worked by preventing the duplication or discarding of these relation names. Sutton and Small give examples of strict updating functions which show that the language is still update-complete within the constraints of this type checking. In order to reduce the number of parameters returned when querying they also allow a relation to be referred to by a nonlinear name. However, a relation's linear name and non-linear name cannot both appear within the same expression.

3.8.2 Monads

In-place update can also be guaranteed by wrapping up the state in a higher-order type which is accessed only by functions with the single-threaded property. The functions must support the creation, access and updating of the state within the type. Wadler has shown how monads can be used for this purpose [3.19]. Monads, a category-theoretic notion, are defined by a triple: the type constructor M, and the operations `unit` and `bind`. Monadic programming is an implicit environment-based approach to programming actions such as updating state and input/output. Actions on the environment have a special type which indicates what happens when the action is performed. The programmer composes actions with the two combinators `unit` and `bind`.

The monadic approach to handling state has both advantages and disadvantages when compared with the use of linear types. Its chief advantage is that it does not require a special type system beyond the usual Hindley–Milner one. Also, because monads handle state implicitly it is argued that this can make an underlying algorithm more apparent since there is less parameter passing. Their main disadvantage is that they require a centralised definition of state. Although this restriction might initially appear to fit nicely with the use of a single conceptual data model in databases, in practice, however, this lack of granularity would have performance and concurrency implications. A treatment of multiple stores with different types, such as relations in a relational database, requires the definition of many monads and monad morphisms in order to support operations involving the different types. It may also be that for databases a two-state monad is more appropriate in order to represent the current state and the state at the start of the transaction. This could then support the rollback operation. We consider these to be areas for further research.

Monads can also be defined in terms of **unit**, **map** and **join** operations which are a generalisation of the same operations which give the semantics of list comprehensions. Wadler has shown how the list comprehension notation can also be used to manipulate state monads [3.18], each qualifier becoming an action on the state. The resulting programs, however, look very procedural.

3.8.3 Mutable Abstract Data Types

Monads in themselves do not enforce linearity on the encapsulated state; their operations must be carefully designed in order to ensure this. The use of abstract data types which encapsulate state and linear access to it has been investigated by Chen and Hudak [3.2]. A **mutable abstract datatype** or MADT is any ADT whose rewrite semantics permit "destructive reuse" of one or more of its arguments while still retaining confluence in a general rewrite system. A MADT is an ADT whose axiomatisation possesses certain linearity properties. Chen and Hudak show how a number of MADTs can be automatically derived from such an ADT. Using an array as an example they give three ways of defining an appropriate MADT. These correspond to direct-style semantics, continuation passing style (CPS) and monadic semantics. A MADT is defined in terms of functions which generate, mutate and select state of a simple type.

Not only is the state hidden in a MADT but the linearity is too and so there is no need for the programs using MADTs to have a linear type system. It has been noted that programming in MADTs tends towards a continuation passing style no matter which form of MADT is used. MADTs are excellent at handling simple state but further research is required into handling bulk data types efficiently and into combining MADTs. Unlike monads there is no rigorous way of reasoning with a number of MADTs.

3.9 Conclusions

Whilst there is much promising research into handling state within functional languages the update problem in functional databases such as FDL remains problematical because the database is comprised of function definitions which must be both simple to apply and simple to update. The design of an un-complicated integrated language to handle both queries and updates in an efficient, purely functional manner is difficult. Whilst linear types could have been used it is our view that the result would have been less satisfactory and less programmer-friendly than the approach we have taken. The introduction of the four update functions described in Section 3.4, whilst not function-ally pure, has kept the language strongly data-model oriented. Also none of the approaches outlined in the section on related work have been used to address transaction handling which is a fundamental distinction between database programming and persistent programming. In contrast Relief does have a programmable transaction handling mechanism although this is not described here. (See [3.9] for details.)

Relief demonstrates that a functional interpreter based on graph reduction can be used to perform updates and that effects checking can scope referential transparency so that the usual functional optimisations can be used for queries and read-only subexpressions. The approach taken has allowed the benefits of lazy evaluation and static type checking to be retained. Updates are performed efficiently and the programmer does not have to learn a new type system. Whilst the eager let helps to make the sequencing of updates more explicit it is still necessary to understand the operational semantics of the pattern matcher when function arguments contain side-effects. Applicative order reduction would simplify these semantics but the lazy stream model used for file reading and the other advantages of lazy evaluation would be lost. Update by side-effect and effects checking are applicable to database systems supporting other data models.

Further work will centre on integrating Relief with the data model of Hydra [3.1] which distinguishes between navigable functions and non-navigable functions in a functional database. This may require the definition of further effect classes.

Acknowledgements

The authors would like to thank Alexandra Poulovassilis for her most helpful comments during the preparation of this account of our work. The second author would thank the EPSRC and IBM UK Labs Hursley for financial support during the work.

References

3.1 R. Ayres and P.J.H. King: Extending the Semantic Power of Functional Database query languages with Associational Facilities. In Actes du Xieme Congres INFORSID, pp301-320, Aix-en-Provence, France, May 1994.

3.2 Chih-Ping Chen and Paul Hudak: Rolling Your Own Mutable ADT - A connection between Linear Types and Monads. ACM Symposium on Principles of Programming Languages, January 1997.

3.3 M. Derakhshan: A Development of the Grid File for the Storage of Binary Relations. Ph.D. Thesis, Birkbeck College, University of London, 1989.

3.4 Anthony J. Field and Peter G. Harrison: Functional Programming. Addison-Wesley, 1988.

3.5 Giorgio Ghelli, Renzo Orsini, Alvaro Pereira Paz and Phil Trinder: Design of an Integrated Query and Manipulation Notation for Database Languages. Technical Report FIDE/92/41, University of Glasgow, 1992.

3.6 David K. Gifford and John M. Lucassen: Integrating Functional and Imperative Programming. In Proceedings of the ACM Conference on Lisp and Functional Programming, Cambridge, Massachusets, pp28-39, ACM, 1986.

3.7 Paul Hudak: Conception, Evolution, and Application of Functional Programming Languages. ACM Computing Surveys, Vol. 21, No. 3, September 1989, pp359-411.

3.8 Peter J.H. King, Mir Derakhshan, Alexandra Poulovassilis and Carol Small: TriStarp - An Investigation into the Implementation and Exploitation of Binary Relational Storage Structures. Proceedings of BNCOD-8, York, 1990.

3.9 P.F. Meredith: Extending a Lazy Functional Database Language with Updates. Ph.D. Thesis, Birkbeck College, University of London, 1999.

3.10 J. Nievergelt, H. Hinterberger and K.C. Sevcik: The Grid File: An Adaptable, Symmetric, Multikey File Structure. ACM TODS, Vol. 9(1):38-71, 1984.

3.11 A. Poulovassillis: FDL: An Integration of the Functional Data Model and the Functional Computational Model, Proceedings of BNCOD6, Cambridge University Press, pp215-236, 1988.

3.12 A. Poulovassilis: The Implementation of FDL, a Functional Database Language. The Computer Journal, Vol. 35, No. 2, 1992.

3.13 A. Poulovassilis and P. J. H. King: Extending the Functional Data Model to Computational Completeness. Proceedings of EDBT'90, pp75-91, Venice 1990. Springer-Verlag, LNCS 416.

3.14 David W. Shipman: The Functional Data Model and the Data Language DAPLEX. ACM TODS, Vol. 6, No. 1, March 1981, pp140-173.

3.15 David Sutton and Carol Small: Extending Functional Database Languages to Update Completeness. Proceedings of 13th BNCOD, pp47-63 Manchester, 1995. Springer-Verlag LNCS 940.

3.16 Phil Trinder: Comprehensions, a Query Notation for DBPLs. The 3rd International Workshop on DBPLs, "Bulk Types and Persistent Data". August 1991, Nafplion, Greece. Morgan Kaufmann.

3.17 G.M.A. Verheijen and J. Van Bekkum: NIAM: An Information Analysis Method. In "Information Systems Design Methodologies: A Comparative Review", T.W.Olle et al. (eds). North-Holland, 1982.

3.18 Philip Wadler: Comprehending Monads. ACM Conference on Lisp and Functional Programming, Nice, June 1990.

3.19 Philip Wadler: Monads for Functional Programming. In "Advanced Functional Programming", Proceedings of the Bastad Spring School, May 1995. LNCS 925

4. Functional Approaches to Constraint Handling and State Change

Suzanne M. Embury[1] and Peter M.D. Gray[2]

[1] Department of Computer Science, University of Manchester, Oxford Road, Manchester M13 9PL, UK
[2] Department of Computing Science, University of Aberdeen, Aberdeen AB24 3UE, UK

Summary.

Functional data languages have been shown to have many attractive features for the implementers of database management systems. Perhaps the most important of these is the property of referential transparency, which functional expressions possess and which makes them very easy to analyse, combine and transform. In this chapter, we discuss how referential transparency can be both a benefit and a stumbling block for the implementers of functional data languages. In particular, we show how referential transparency is compromised in the presence of certain forms of state change, and outline a number of solutions to this problem. We also show how referential transparency is a great advantage when implementing database facilities connected with state change, focusing in particular on the issue of semantic integrity.

4.1 Introduction

The attractions of functional data languages have resulted in the development of many functional database systems [4.20, 4.28, 4.5, 4.17, 4.29], and have even prompted the use of functional data languages for use with non-functional data models [4.1, 4.7, 4.22]. The advantages of the functional paradigm for data manipulation include:

- Programs are specified declaratively as referentially transparent expressions, which have a clean, well-understood semantics (the λ-calculus [4.21]) and are therefore easy to transform, optimise and reason about.
- Functional programs can be composed as easily as programs expressed in the relational calculus [4.15], but they are also able to express arbitrary, recursive calculations.
- Functional programs can be lazily evaluated [4.6], which not only allows the possibility of operating over infinite data structures, but can also avoid much redundant data retrieval when operating over large database sets.
- The standard "functionals" of functional programming (such as `map` and `filter` [4.36]) are very suitable for giving concise descriptions of computations over bulk data, such as large database sets.

For all these reasons, therefore, functional data languages offer a congenial environment in which to specify and evaluate data retrieval tasks. However, there is more to data manipulation than data retrieval; for a database management system to be useful, it must also provide facilities for updates. This causes problems for the designers of functional data languages, since the functional paradigm has no primitives for handling state change, nor even any implicit notion of a state itself. It is relatively easy to see how a form of state could be "grafted" onto a functional language, but it is much less easy to see how this can be done efficiently without also losing one of the most useful and important features of functional languages: namely, *referential transparency* [4.33]. Referential transparency is at the heart of most of the advantages listed above for functional data languages.

In this chapter, we describe some of the challenges that state change presents to the designers and implementers of functional data languages. We begin by outlining the range of solutions that have been proposed in the literature and their various characteristics (Section 4.2). We then look in more detail (Section 4.3) at one specific approach to incorporating update facilities into a functional data language (namely, Daplex [4.32]). This approach differs from other solutions, in that it allows the user to specify the state change required declaratively [4.10], rather than giving a declarative semantics to the standard (procedural) update operators.

However, it is also the case that the features of the functional paradigm can be helpful when implementing the components of a database that handle the various aspects of state change. For example, Trinder has described how referential transparency is of great value in simplifying the semantics of concurrent data access, and how the multiple versions maintained by many "functional" approaches to state change can help in guaranteeing transaction properties [4.37]. Similarly, in our own work on the efficient maintenance of semantic integrity constraints [4.11], we have found the ease with which functional expressions can be reasoned about and manipulated to be of great benefit. In Section 4.4, we describe in more detail why this is the case. Finally, Section 4.5 concludes.

4.2 Approaches to State Change in Functional Data Languages

There are two basic problems which must be overcome when including facilities for state change within a functional data language. One of these is the lack of any notion of "state" within the functional paradigm, and the consequent lack of any primitives for describing state change. Variables in functional languages are *placeholders* that stand for some value not known at compile time, rather than references to a mutable location in memory [4.6].

The second problem is that any naive attempt to introduce such a notion of state (especially in the implicit form in which state occurs in more traditional database programming languages) will destroy the referential transparency of the language. Amongst other things, referential transparency implies that the order of evaluation of an expression should have no effect on its final result. However, the meaning of a composite state change operation, such as:

$$x := x + 1; \ x := x * 2;$$

may result in a different value being assigned to x depending on which of the two assignments are executed first. Here, for simplicity, we have used a kind of state more common in programming languages in this example, but exactly the same loss of referential transparency is incurred by the introduction of the more complex forms of state needed to represent a database.

However, a DBMS which cannot support state change is clearly of limited value. Therefore, the implementers of systems based on functional data languages have been forced to find some way to allow update mechanisms to coexist with the constraints imposed by the functional paradigm. The approaches taken can be divided into those which attempt to introduce updates while remaining within the strictures of the functional paradigm, and those which relax some of the theoretical constraints.

The latter group of solutions have been most widely applied in implemented systems, but they are also perhaps the least interesting from a research point of view. We will therefore give only brief descriptions of them, before we look in more detail at those solutions which attempt to remain within the functional paradigm.

Functional Query Languages: Recognising the difficulties of handling updates in a functional way, and not wishing to compromise the clarity and conciseness of their languages in order to support state change, the developers of some systems (e.g. [4.8, 4.5]) have restricted the scope of their languages to handling database queries only. Update facilities are then assumed to be provided by a separate (non-functional) data manipulation language.

Embedded Update Commands in a Functional Language: An alternative to the aforementioned approach, and one which has perhaps been the most widely adopted, is to provide the user with a set of special update "functions" which are allowed to side-effect the database state [4.20, 4.17, 4.29, 4.12, 4.1]. The DBMS is able to detect when an expression makes use of one of these side-effecting functions, and it suppresses any transformations or inferences which assume referential transparency of such expression. In some of these systems (e.g. PFL [4.29] and ADAPLAN [4.12]) the DBMS provides a fixed set of low-level update functions, while others (e.g. IPL [4.1] and P/FDM [4.17]) allow users to define new update functions which they declare as causing side-effects at compile time.

Meredith and King have proposed a cleaner variant of this approach
which allows updates to the state[1] to be included within programs, by
providing a special construct which enforces eager evaluation of its arguments [4.24]. Effectively, the construct (called an "eager let") allows the
programmer to fence off parts of the program which cannot be treated
as referentially transparent. This is a good practical solution, but puts
a lot of responsibility onto the programmer to specify exactly when eager and lazy evaluation is required. However, the authors also describe
a means by which the referential transparency of a given expression can
be determined statically, through the use of an effects checker [4.23]

These two approaches both effectively restrict the benefits of referential transparency to pure queries. This is a pity, since many updates contain a significant data retrieval element and may also be amenable to optimisation, given
an appropriate underlying formalism [4.13]. Because of this, some authors
have attempted to find ways of incorporating update facilities into functional
data languages without stepping outside the functional paradigm. We will
now describe the major solution types that have been proposed.

4.2.1 Updates as Changes to an Explicit Database State

The most obvious way to provide a functional treatment of database updates is to model the database state explicitly within programs. Under this
approach, database "commands" are implemented as pure functions which
map an old database state into a new (updated) one [4.2]. For example,
the following function (defined in Miranda [4.36]) implements a very simple
DBMS:

```
dbms :: db -> [transaction] -> [response]

dbms db [] = [end_of_input]
dbms db (tx : rest)
    = output : dbms newdb rest
    where (output, newdb) = evaluate db trans
```

The evaluate function takes a database state and a transaction specification, and returns a new database state (newdb) formed by executing the
transaction against the given state, and any output message for the user
(output). Retrieval commands return the original database state unchanged
as the new state, and the data requested as the output message. A successful
update transaction, on the other hand, returns an updated version of the
original database and an empty output message. The dbms function, then,
executes each of the transactions in its input list in turn, using the resulting
database state from one execution as the input state for the next.

---

[1] In this approach, the state is actually modelled by the program environment, as
described later in this chapter.

This approach to handling updates is theoretically elegant and has some interesting properties [4.2, 4.37], but it is not of great practical use for the implementation of real database systems. One reason for this is the need continually to specify and pass around the explicit state, which can severely complicate the expression of both updates *and* queries. While end users can be protected from this to some extent through careful interface design, application developers and maintainers cannot.

A further problem with this approach is that it preserves referential transparency at the expense of maintaining multiple versions of the database state at any one time. This form of state change is known as *non-destructive update*, since a state (once brought into being) is never overwritten or destroyed. Clearly, storage of all these states can be very expensive, especially when real scale data volumes and transaction rates are considered. It is possible in some cases to reduce the storage overhead by sharing unchanged parts of consecutive states, but this can only be done effectively for certain bulk data types. Trinder has investigated the suitability of various bulk data types for supporting non-destructive update efficiently [4.37].

4.2.2 Updates as Changes to the Program Environment

A variation on the previously described approach is to view changes to data as *redefinitions* of the functions whose extensions define that data, that is as changes to the program environment [4.28, 4.23, 4.27]. Effectively, the program environment is being used as the state. This is directly analogous to the behaviour of standard functional programming languages, in which expressions are evaluated with respect to some "current environment" that may be modified by adding new function definitions or by redefining existing functions.

The advantage of this approach to updates over the non-destructive approach just described is that the program environment is used as an *implicit* state, and thus there is no need to pass explicit representations of the current database state back and forth between functions. However, as in the case of standard functional programming, referential transparency can only be guaranteed *in between* modifications to the environment. In other words, expressions evaluated against a single environment are referentially transparent; expressions which modify the environment may not be.

It is possible to get around this problem if we retain all previous versions of the program environment, and are careful always to evaluate expressions against the correct version. However, this severely complicates the system as a whole (including the querying facilities) and it suffers from the same practical implementation difficulties that dog non-destructive updates.

4.2.3 Updates Restricted to Linear Types

A third approach, proposed by Sutton and Small [4.35], has its basis in the observation that some complex updates are naturally referentially transparent, simply by virtue of the fact that the individual updates that they include cannot "interfere" with one another. For example, the following database update is naturally referentially transparent:

```
add(student, name, ''Fred''), delete(course, code, ''CS131'')
```

This update adds a new **student** record (with the **name** attribute set to the value "Fred") and deletes a **course** record. Provided that no cascaded updates will be triggered by these modifications, then the same database state will result from them, regardless of the order in which they are applied.

By contrast, the following complex update is not referentially transparent:

```
add(student, name, ''Fred''), delete(student, name, ''Fred'')
```

Assuming an empty initial database, this update might produce either a database state containing no students called "Fred" or a state containing a single student called "Fred", depending on the order in which the two updates are performed. Hence, it is not referentially transparent. A similar problem can occur when data retrieval commands are mixed with updates[2].

In fact, the property of an expression E which determines whether it will be referentially transparent in this way or not is that every updateable object (i.e. every persistent bulk data type) that appears within E must appear exactly once, *and* that any expression to which E is reducible must also contain exactly one occurrence of that object. In functional programming, such an object is said to be *linear*. Wadler has shown that it is possible to determine whether a functional program obeys these rules with respect to certain specified objects statically [4.39], through extension of the standard Hindley–Milner type system [4.25].

For any type-correct linear program, therefore, it is possible to implement updates destructively without loss of referential transparency. This sounds like the perfect solution to the functional update problem, but unfortunately this approach also has its problems. One of these is that we must accept a more complex type system, with considerably more complex rules regarding which programs are well-typed. These complications infect all parts of the language, so that all programs are affected whether they make updates or not. Sutton and Small have proposed a partial solution to this problem, whereby linear (i.e. updateable) objects also have a non-linear incarnation which can be used more simply [4.35]. However, the use of these non-linear

---

[2] For example, when a request to retrieve the names of all students is combined with an update to add a new student. The set of student names returned will depend on whether the retrieval command was evaluated before or after the update.

versions must be carefully controlled, so that, for example, it is not possible for the linear and non-linear version of an object to be referenced within the same expression.

A further limitation of this approach is that it is as yet unknown whether all useful updates can be expressed using linear types.

4.2.4 Updates as Changes to an Implicit State using Monads

One of the limitations of modelling state explicitly in functional languages is the complexity this adds to programs. Ideally, we would like to make use of an implicit state, but which appears to the functional language interpreter (or compiler) to be an explicit state. State monads [4.40] can be used to provide exactly this illusion, through the use of higher-order functions. An explicit state is present, but the programmer does not need continually to refer to it. Instead, special monadic operations are used to indicate the places where state is changed, and the sequencing of all state changes.

A state monad consists of a state transformer type constructor and two associated operations: *unit* and *bind*. The first of these, *unit*, is defined as

$$unit\ a = \lambda\ s\ .\ (a,\ s)$$

That is, it constructs a state transformer that converts a state into a (value, state) pair. The *bind* operation takes two state transforming functions as arguments (f and g) and produces a state transforming function which applies them in sequence:

$$bind\ f\ g = \lambda s1\ .\ g\ a\ s2$$
$$where\ (a,\ s2) = f\ s1$$

The programmer can then use these operations to construct complex updates that do not in themselves contain any references to explicit state variables.

Monads therefore provide us with a means of overcoming some of the more serious problems associated with the introduction of explicit state in functional data languages. However, they do not in themselves solve the efficiency problems that are entailed in non-destructive updates. Additional strictness conditions can be placed on state transformation functions that can guarantee linearity of update, and therefore allow efficient in-place updating of bulk data structures. However, the integration of the state and the programming language is far from complete, and some data manipulation operations are still difficult to express concisely [4.23].

4.2.5 Summary

It should be evident from this brief survey[3] that the main difficulties in incorporating state change into functional data languages are actually prac-

---

[3] A more complete survey of the various proposals for incorporating updates into functional data languages is given by Meredith [4.23].

tical rather than theoretical. The two major problems are: the difficulty of implementing non-destructive updates efficiently and the awkwardness of expressing updates (and queries) in the resulting language.

These are still open problems, although the issue of efficiency has so far received more attention than the issue of naturalness of expression. But, there is a third problem, which is very rarely mentioned. Although these four approaches can all be said to provide declarative support for update, in fact, what they really provide is a declarative semantics for what are otherwise procedural update operations. The implementer of the DBMS can take advantage of the declarativeness, but the user (or application programmer) who must formulate updates cannot. They must still describe in exact detail what state changes must be made, and exactly what order they must be made in.

In the next section of this chapter, we will outline an approach to state change that attempts to provide a truly declarative form of update for users and programmers.

4.3 A Declarative Approach to State Change

An ideal marriage of the declarative and the pragmatic approaches to supporting updates in FDLs would be a system which allowed users to describe their updates declaratively, and at as high a level as possible, and which then translated this specification into a sequence of low-level updates that would achieve the effect required. In this way, the user would state *what* their updates must achieve, rather than *how* to go about achieving it.

We have taken a first step towards this goal by implementing a version of the Daplex functional data language [4.17] which allows the declarative description of the creation of sets of instances. In this language, the user simply describes the constraints that the new instances must satisfy and the DBMS then uses these constraints, and any relevant domain constraints, to search for a sequence of updates that will satisfy the user's requirements [4.10].

In an early paper by Floyd [4.14], the addition of a non-deterministic *choice* construct to an otherwise deterministic language is proposed as a way of simplifying the expression of backtracking algorithms. Floyd also showed that ALGOL programs involving non-deterministic choice can be mechanically transformed into completely deterministic algorithms that use backtracking techniques to simulate the effects of the non-determinism. By this mechanism, Floyd provided a means by which the value of a variable could be specified declaratively, through the specification of a number of constraints which the intended value must satisfy.

Building on this idea, we extended the Daplex language with a new construct for describing object creations and the selection of values for their attributes non-deterministically. We call the extended version of the language *Angelic Daplex*, since the extra semantics are those of *angelic non-*

determinism [4.34]. The language is extended with just one new syntactic construct:

```
for a new <var> in <class> such that <predicate>
```

which can be read informally as describing the creation of a new instance of the class `<class>`, with its object identifier bound to the variable `<var>`, according to the constraints given in `<predicate>`[4]. The predicate consists of a conjunction of Boolean-valued expressions, such as equality comparisons and set-membership tests. These comparisons are expressed against the current database state, and may involve the comparison of attribute values with computed values or database sets generated using indexes or navigation. Constructs for expressing these kinds of predicate already exist in Daplex, so the only new piece of syntax required is that shown above for the "for a new" loop itself.

4.3.1 An Example Angelic Daplex Program

We will explain the semantics of this new syntactic construct informally through presentation of an example program based on a simple scheduling example. The following Angelic Daplex program describes an update which allocates a teacher and music lesson to a number of students, while ensuring that no student or teacher is required to attend more than one lesson at any one time:

```
for each s in student
    for a new ml in music_lesson such that
        pupil(ml) = s and
        teacher(ml) = any(t in music_teacher
            such that instrument(s) in instruments(t)) and
        day(ml) in freedays(teacher(ml)) and
        day(ml) in freedays(pupil(ml))
    print(name(s), "studies with", name(teacher(ml)), day(ml));
```

In the context of the "for a new" loop, the equality comparisons and set-membership tests on attribute values are interpreted non-deterministically, relative to the creation of the new instance. This is illustrated, for example, by the difference in the meaning of the "=" sign in the two loops of the above program. In the first loop (the deterministic "for each" loop), it represents a test for equality: does the value of the `pupil` attribute of the `music_lesson` instance equal the value of the variable `s`? In the second loop (the `for a new` loop), it is effectively an assignment: let the value of the `pupil` attribute of the newly created `music_lesson` equal the value of the variable `s`. Similarly, the keyword `in` usually indicates a test for set membership, but in the context

---

[4] I.e. the loop evaluates to the singleton set {`<var>`}

of a **for a new** loop it specifies a set of possible values for an attribute: let
the value of the **day** attribute of the newly created **music_lesson** take any
of the values returned by the **freedays** function. This is how we specify the
non-determinism; by "any of the values" here, we really mean "any of the
values that also satisfy the other constraints"[5].

What, then, is the meaning of the last component of the predicate

   day(ml) in freedays(pupil(ml))

which apparently specifies a second assignment to the **day** attribute? In fact,
since the attribute has already been assigned a value at this stage, we interpret this as an ordinary test, the effect of which is to check that the student
is not busy on the day of the lesson. Notice the similarity here with Prolog
instantiation: if both operands are defined then the expression is interpreted
as an ordinary comparison, otherwise the undefined operand takes on the
value of the defined one. Where there are several expressions involving the
same attribute (as in the case of the **day/1** attribute in our example) one
will represent a generator and the rest constraints on the attribute's value.
One of the advantages of a declarative specification is that any one of the expressions can be chosen as the generator without affecting the validity of the
resulting solution. So the compiler is free to choose one of the more restrictive
expressions for the generator, selecting for example equality comparisons over
set-membership tests, and thus cutting down on the backtracking required
to solve the problem.

We can now see that the **<predicate>** of a **for a new** loop can express
assignments, which initialise the state of the new object: domain specifications, which both define and reduce the search space; and constraints, which
give the conditions for success. It is from this last, this ability to specify
the properties that the completed objects must satisfy, that we gain the real
power: "the day should be chosen so that neither the pupil nor the teacher
is busy with something else". With the purely deterministic approach, how
could a valid day be selected, except when all the other allocations have been
made?

While the scope of the non-determinism introduced by a "for a new"
loop includes any other loops that are nested within it, it does not extend
to the actions part of the program. By the time we enter the second phase
of program execution, we expect either a complete solution to have been
created within the database or no updates to have been made at all. At this
stage, an arbitrary sequence of actions can be executed, which may include
further updates to the instances that were created during "loop" evaluation.
This allows us, for example, to create extra links between these instances and

---

[5] Note that this use of the set-membership operator is semantically equivalent to
the use of the aggregate function **any**, used in the description of the **teacher**
attribute's value, which selects a single element from its argument set (either
deterministically or non-deterministically according to the context).

existing data, or to update some status attribute noting that a solution has been found. Our example program here, however, simply displays the details of the solution that has been created, for example

```
Student J.S.B. allocated to Mrs. Mozart, thursday
Student C.P.E.B. allocated to Mrs. Mozart, tuesday
```

Thus, although several partial solutions may be created before a complete solution can be found, the user is only aware that the "infallible" non-deterministic program has invisibly avoided the problem allocations which involved some double-bookings for either pupils or teachers.

4.3.2 Non-Determinism and Functional Semantics

Non-deterministic operators of the kind described above are more typically found within logic-based programming languages, and have reached perhaps their highest development in constraint logic programming (CLP) languages [4.38]. However, there is no difficulty in incorporating this kind of non-deterministic construct into the semantics of a functional language [4.34]. The ZF-expression itself employs a non-deterministic approach to the specification of sets of values, since only members of the generating sets which satisfy the filter predicates are admitted to the final set of solutions.

That being said, the introduction of the new loop construct into Daplex has a further and more serious ramification for the semantics of the language. As we have seen, a Daplex program consists of zero or more loops, describing sets of database values, followed by a sequence of one or more actions, which are parametrised in terms of the loop values. For example, the semantics of the following Daplex program

```
for each s in student
    for each t in music_teacher(pupil_inv(s))
print(name(s), 'taught by', name(t));
```

can be described informally as follows: in the loops part of the program, a set of tuples ((s, t)) is generated, representing the loop values described by the loop sets. This is transformed into a set of tuples describing the values required by the actions ((name(s), 'taught by', name(t))). The sequence of actions is executed once for each tuple in the transformed set, with the appropriate value and variable substitutions being made.

The semantics of the declarative "loops" part can be given by the ZF-expression which specifies the equivalent set of tuples. The semantics of the "actions" part of the language can be given as a collection of functions mapping one database state to another. The semantics of a Daplex program, then, involving both loops and actions, is a function mapping an initial database state to a final database state, consisting of the composition of all the action functions parametrised by the set of values denoted by the loops part of the query[6].

From this we can see that the "loops" part of a Daplex query is completely declarative, and free of state change. Since the loops part of any Daplex program is evaluated in full before any of the actions are executed, it is separated semantically, as well as syntactically, from the non-declarative "actions" part. How, then, can we incorporate the "state changing", non-deterministic for a new loop within this framework?

In fact, no lack of declarativeness is implied by the new construct, since no updates are made until the complete set of variable values required for all the necessary updates have been made. Execution of a deterministic Daplex program involves two phases:

1. evaluation of the set of tuples described by the loops (a pure query), and
2. execution of the action sequence for each tuple previously identified.

In contrast, execution of an Angelic Daplex program consists of three phases:

1. evaluation of the sets of tuples described by the loops (still a pure query),
2. creation of the set of new objects identified during the previous phase as representing a "solution" to the constraint problem, and
3. execution of the action sequence for each tuple previously identified.

Thus we can see that no updates occur during the evaluation of the loops part of the query, which remains side-effect free and therefore referentially transparent.

What we have described above is the semantics of the language as it must appear to the user. There is, of course, no requirement on the implementer of such a language to adopt this execution approach, provided that the end result is the same. In fact, we have constructed two prototype compilers for the Angelic Daplex language, each of which takes a very different approach to the problem. One of these compiles the Angelic Daplex program into a Prolog program, which uses backtracking search to locate a satisfactory database state. The other uses a constraint logic programming language (CHIP [4.38]) as its search engine [4.10].

It is undoubtedly the case that the ease and flexibility with which functional programs can be manipulated was a major factor in simplifying the development of these two compilers. These same benefits (largely the result of referential transparency, as we have already said) can also be of great help in implementing other database functionality that is concerned with updates. In the next section, we will consider one example of such a functionality: semantic integrity constraints.

---

[6] A full definition of the semantics of the Daplex language can be found in [4.9].

4.4 Preserving Integrity Under State Change

Readers who are familiar with the literature on semantic integrity constraints in databases will be aware that the majority of proposals are based around either first-order logic or SQL. However, as we have seen above, there is no theoretical difficulty in using a functional language to express such constraints, and a number of projects have taken this approach. One of the earliest, for example, was the Extended Functional Data Model project [4.20], which used a variant of the functional data language Daplex [4.32] as the means to specify schemas, queries (on data and metadata), general-purpose computation, view definitions and integrity constraints — all within the same unifying language framework.

Other proposals for functional constraint languages include PRISM [4.31], ADAPLAN (the Applicative Data Programming Language) [4.12], PFL (Persistent Functional Language) [4.30] and CoLan [4.4]. The basic approach taken by these languages is that, rather than describing an integrity constraint directly, its semantics should be expressed as a query over the database, the results of which are the set of *violations* of the constraint. For example, if we have a constraint that all students must be aged 16 or over, we might express this functionally using the following set comprehension:

$$[s | s \leftarrow student; ages < 16]$$

The DBMS then has the task of ensuring that this set always evaluates to the empty set (i.e. that there are no violations present in the database). An integrity constraint mechanism can therefore be added to a DBMS with a functional data language very easily, since constraints now take the same form as queries.

In order to illustrate this point, we will present several examples of integrity constraints expressed in an extension of the Daplex language [4.11], as implemented in the P/FDM system [4.17]. This variant of Daplex already contained a rich variety of constructs for expressing Boolean conditions, so the extension to allow integrity constraints was straightforward, as far as the syntax of the language went. Most importantly, constructs for expressing *quantified expressions* were already available. For example, the following query requests the names of all research tutors who advise only students with good grades:

```
for each t in tutor such that status(t) = ''research'' and
        no s in advisees(t) has grade(s) =< 60
print(name(t));
```

We can easily reuse this syntax for Boolean conditions to express a constraint requiring that research tutors never advise students with poorer grades:

```
constrain each t in tutor such that status(t) = ''research''
so that no s in advisees(t) has grade(s) =< 60;
```

In the P/FDM system, queries (and, as we shall see shortly, constraints) are compiled into an intermediate format based on comprehensions[7]. For example, the semantics of the query given above is equivalent to the following list comprehension:

$$[name(t) \mid t \leftarrow tutor;$$
$$status(t) = \text{``}research\text{''};$$
$$[s \mid s \leftarrow advisees(t); grade(s) \leq 60] = []$$
$$]$$

In this notation, lists are described by expressions enclosed in square brackets. The term to the left of the vertical bar is a pattern which describes the form of each element of the list (in this case, a list of student instances). The expression to the right of the vertical bar consists of a sequence of generators (which supply values for variables) and tests (which specify constraints on those variables). Generator expressions take the form "$<var> \leftarrow <list>$" and describe the set of values over which the variable should iterate, while tests are formulated as Boolean expressions over the generated variables. Only combinations of variable values which fulfil the tests are used in instantiating the pattern, to produce the members of the final list.

The advantage of comprehensions as an intermediate language for queries is that they are very easy to analyse and manipulate, and they are therefore well suited to supporting query optimisation. For example, some very elegant results have been published regarding the use of monad comprehensions in query optimisation [4.18]. As we shall shortly see, these same advantages also make a functional intermediate language based on comprehensions very suitable for the kinds of manipulation that are required to convert integrity constraint expressions into code that will enforce them efficiently.

In P/FDM, therefore, we have adopted a comprehension-based intermediate format for the integrity constraint language. For example, the following constraint

```
constrain each t in tutor such that status(t) = ''research''
so that grade(t) > 3;
```

can be represented by the following functional expression [4.4]:

$$foldr\ and\ True\ [\ grade(t) > 3 \mid t \leftarrow tutor; status(t) = \text{``}research\text{''}]$$

Here, *foldr* is a standard combinator which takes an infix operator (in this case, logical conjunction), a starting value and a list of values, and produces a single value by "folding" the operator into the list values. So, for example, the following equality holds:

$$(foldr\ and\ True\ [a,\ b,\ c]) = (a\ and\ b\ and\ c\ and\ True)$$

---

[7] Also called *ZF-expressions* or Zermelo–Fraenkel set expressions.

We can also make use of existential quantifiers in constraints, as in the following (rather unrealistic) example, which states that every tutor must have some student who scores a mark of more than 70%:

```
constrain each t in tutor
so that some s in students(t) has marks(s) >= 70;
```

This is equivalent to the following (more complex) functional expression:

$$foldr\ and\ True\ [foldr\ or\ False\ [marks(s) \geq 70 \mid s \leftarrow students(t)]$$
$$\mid t \leftarrow tutor]$$

As these examples illustrate, functional expression of integrity constraints is straightforward, especially when some syntactic sugar (such as that provided by the Daplex language) can be offered, in order to make them more readable.

The ability to manipulate and transform functional expressions (especially those based on list comprehensions) is very valuable when those expressions represent database integrity constraints. It is relatively easy to implement an integrity constraint enforcement mechanism if one is not concerned about the efficiency of the implementation and the negative effect on the performance of database updates that will result. However, efficient enforcement of integrity constraints is significantly more challenging, and requires a great deal of compile-time analysis and transformation of constraint expressions. Both of these (i.e. analysis and transformation of expressions) are greatly facilitated by the use of a functional intermediate language.

The classic approach to the enforcement of integrity constraints was proposed by Nicolas [4.26]. He realised that, if one can assume that the database state satisfies all the integrity constraints immediately prior to an update operation, then it is only necessary to check those constraints which could be affected by that update. Thus, our earlier constraint about the ages of students, for example, cannot be violated by the addition of a new course to the database, and so need not be checked when this update occurs. Neither is it possible for any deletion, even of students or ages, to violate this constraint. In fact, it is only necessary to enforce this constraint whenever a new student is added to the database, or when a student's age is set or updated.

Nicolas also showed that it is sufficient to check a *simplified* form of the full constraint that tests for violation only within the subset of the data that is affected by the update. He also proposed that this simplified form could be generated at compile time by considering each of the updates that might violate the constraint in turn. For example, we know that the creation of a new student, S, with age A could violate the constraint presented at the start of this section, and we can use this information to evaluate it partially, so that: $[s \mid s \leftarrow [S]; ages < 16]$ becomes $[S \mid A < 16]$.

In other words, the update satisfies the full constraint if the new age value, A, satisfies the simplified constraint check. In fact, this simplified test can be made without requiring any retrieval from the database at all, which is certainly not the case with the unsimplified version of the constraint.

Nicolas originally proposed the notion of simplification in the context of constraints expressed as first-order logic conditions over relational databases. However, the basic principle is just as valid for constraints expressed in functional data languages [4.11]. Effectively, the compilation process for integrity constraints involves two steps:

1. Identification of all the update events that might possibly cause the constraint to be violated.
2. For each such update event, the constraint expression is simplified into an expression that checks validity of the constraint relative to that update, in as efficient a manner as possible.

Both these steps can be easily and naturally achieved when the constraints are represented functionally. For example, the identification of the events which may violate a constraint can be computed by structural induction over the constraint expression. For example, if the function *violEvents* takes a constraint expression and returns the set of events which may cause it to become false, then we can define the set of events which may violate a logical conjunction to be as follows:

(foldr and True list) = union (map (violEvents) list)

This expresses the idea that a logical conjunction can be made false by any update that might cause any of its component conjuncts to become false. By providing similar definitions for the other constructs in the constraint language, the set of violating events can be generated for arbitrary constraint expressions[8]. The clean semantics of a functional representation of constraints makes these definitions relatively straightforward to produce and check.

The second step (that of rewriting the constraint into its simplified form for each violating update) requires a form of partial evaluation of the integrity constraint condition. To do this, it is first necessary to match the condition expression with the schema elements affected by the update in question. The next step is to transform the expression under the assumption that the update has had a particular effect at the matched point, and to remove any computation that is made redundant by this assumption. Many of the matching and transformation steps inherent in this process are exactly the same as those used by a standard query optimiser. Therefore, all the arguments relating to the suitability of functional query languages for optimisation also apply to their suitability for the simplification of integrity constraints.

Although integrity constraints play their main role in the detection of invalid updates, they can also be used for the purposes of optimisation. This form of optimisation (known as *semantic query optimisation* or SQO [4.19]) incorporates integrity constraints as additional conditions in queries, in order to avoid attempts to retrieve data that cannot possibly exist in the database.

---

[8] In reality, of course, the situation is slightly more complicated than this. Full details of the procedure have been published elsewhere [4.11].

For example, if we have the constraint that no student may be aged less than 16, we can convert the following query:

$$[\,(s, name(s)) \mid s \leftarrow student; status(s) = \text{``}parttime\text{''} \vee age(s) < 15\,]$$

to this equivalent, but more efficient, version:

$$[\,(s, name(s)) \mid s \leftarrow student; status(s) = \text{``}parttime\text{''}\,]$$

This form of optimisation can also be applied to updates. For example, we have made use of SQO techniques in optimising the Angelic Daplex language described in Section 4.3. Since Angelic Daplex programs describe object creation in terms of constraints that the new objects must satisfy, each such program also implicitly includes all the integrity constraints that apply to those objects. A solution which satisfies the user's constraints, but which does not represent a valid update to the database, is no solution at all.

Rather than postpone checking of these integrity constraints until after the search for a "solution" is complete (which may require backtracking to find another solution), it is obviously much more efficient if they can be included in the original search. For example, suppose that, by law, no music lessons may be given on Wednesdays. This information would be modelled by adding the following integrity constraint to the database:

```
constrain no ml in music_lesson
to have day(l) = ''wednesday'';
```

which can then be automatically incorporated into the earlier example program to prevent any attempted allocations of music lessons on Wednesdays:

```
for each s in student
    for a new ml in music_lesson such that
        teacher(ml) = any(t in music_teacher
            such that instrument(s) in instruments(t)) and
        pupil(ml) = s and
        day(ml) in freedays(teacher(ml)) and
        day(ml) in freedays(pupil(ml)) and
        day(ml) <> ''wednesday''
print(name(s), "studies with", name(teacher(ml)), day(ml));
```

Having promoted the constraint in this way, it can be considered as a potential generator, along with the other constraints placed on the attribute's value.

Like other forms of optimisation, semantic query optimisation is facilitated by the use of a functional intermediate language, in which the necessary matching and transformation tasks are simplified. Since integrity constraints are represented internally in this same intermediate format as programs, the process of including them is basically one of deciding which constraints to incorporate, of eliminating the relevant quantifiers and of determining where within the original program they should be placed [4.16].

4.5 Conclusions

In this chapter, we have described some of the difficulties that the notion of state change, so essential to any practical data management technology, raises for the implementers and users of functional data languages. In particular, the key challenge is to find some means of modelling state that does not compromise the referential integrity of expressions that make use of it, *and* that retains the benefits of declarativeness, conciseness and clarity that the functional paradigm provides for data retrieval.

Several approaches have been suggested, ranging from the use of monads and linear types through to the exploitation of constraints and non-determinism to express updates declaratively, as seen in the Angelic Daplex language. However, each solution has different *pros* and *cons*, and it could be felt that none of the current approaches provides a completely satisfactory solution to the problem. This is therefore still an open research issue.

However, if state change presents a challenge for the functional paradigm, the reverse is most definitely not the case. The benefits of functional data languages are very much in evidence when they are used in the implementation of DBMS features to support updates. In this chapter, for example, we looked at how the use of a functional intermediate language can ease the development of efficient compilation techniques for integrity constraints. The expressiveness and ease of manipulation offered by the functional paradigm is an extremely powerful combination that has led many researchers to employ functional internal formats even in non-functional systems.

References

4.1 J. Annevelink. Database Programming Languages: a Functional Approach. In J. Clifford and R. King, editors, *SIGMOD 91 Conference*, pages 318–327, Denver, Colorado, May 1991. ACM Press.

4.2 G. Argo, J. Hughes, P. Trinder, J. Fairbairn, and J. Launchbury. Implementing Functional Databases. In Bancilhon and Buneman [4.3], chapter 10, pages 165–176.

4.3 F. Bancilhon and P. Buneman, editors. *Advances in Database Programming Languages*. Frontier Series. ACM Press, 1990.

4.4 N. Bassiliades and P.M.D Gray. CoLan: a Functional Constraint Language and Its Implementation. *Data and Knowledge Engineering*, 14:203–249, 1994.

4.5 D.S. Batory, T.Y. Leung, and T.E. Wise. Implementation Concepts for an Extensible Data Model and Data Language. *ACM Transactions on Database Systems*, 13(3):231–262, September 1988.

4.6 R. Bird and P. Wadler. *Introduction to Functional Programming*. Prentice Hall Series in Computer Science. Prentice Hall International, 1988.

4.7 O. Boucelma and J. Le Maitre. An Extensible Functional Query Language for an Object-Oriented Database System. In C. Delobel, M. Kifer, and Y. Masunaga, editors, *Second International Conference on Deductive and Object-Oriented Databases*, pages 567–581, Munich, December 1991. Springer-Verlag.

4.8 P. Buneman and R.E. Frankel. An Implementation Technique for Database Query Languages. *ACM Transactions on Database Systems*, 7(2):164–186, June 1982.

4.9 S.M. Embury. A Formal Semantics for the Daplex Language. Technical Report AUCS/TR9504, University of Aberdeen, Department of Computing Science, King's College, Aberdeen AB24 3UE, Scotland, October 1995. Accessible as http://www.csd.abdn.ac.uk/~pfdm/postscript/embury.1995b.ps.

4.10 S.M. Embury and P.M.D. Gray. Planning Complex Updates to Satisfy Constraint Rules Using a Constraint Logic Search Engine. In T. Sellis, editor, *Proc. of 2nd International Workshop on Rules in Database Systems (RIDS '95)*, LNCS 985, pages 230–244, Glyfada, Athens, Greece, September 1995. Springer-Verlag.

4.11 S.M. Embury and P.M.D. Gray. Compiling a Declarative, High-Level Language for Semantic Integrity Constraints. In R. Meersman and L. Mark, editors, *Proceedings of 6th IFIP TC-2 Working Conference on Data Semantics*, pages 188–226, Atlanta, USA, May 1997. Chapman and Hall.

4.12 M. Erwig and U.W. Lipeck. A Functional DBPL Revealing High Level Optimizations. In P. Kanellakis and J.W. Schmidt, editors, *Proceedings of 3rd International Workshop on Database Programming Languages – Bulk Types and Persistent Data*, pages 306–321, Nafplion, Greece, August 1991. Morgan Kaufmann.

4.13 L. Fegaras. Optimizing Queries with Object Updates. *Journal of Intelligent Information Systems*, 12(2–3):219–242, March 1999.

4.14 R.W. Floyd. Nondeterministic Algorithms. *Journal of the ACM*, 14(4):636–644, October 1967.

4.15 P.M.D. Gray. *Logic, Algebra and Databases*. Ellis Horwood Series in Computers and Their Applications. Ellis Horwood, 1984.

4.16 P.M.D. Gray, S.M. Embury, K.Y. Hui, and G.J.L. Kemp. The Evolving Role of Constraints in the Functional Data Model. *Journal of Intelligent Information Systems*, 12(2–3):113–137, 1999.

4.17 P.M.D. Gray, K.G. Kulkarni, and N.W. Paton. *Object-Oriented Databases: a Semantic Data Model Approach*. Prentice Hall Series in Computer Science. Prentice Hall International, 1992.

4.18 T. Grust, J. Kröger, D. Gluche, A. Heuer, and M.H. Scholl. Query Evaluation in CROQUE - Calculus and Algebra Coincide. In C. Small, P. Douglas, R.G. Johnson, P.J.H. King, and G.N. Martin, editors, *Advances in Databases: Proceedings of 17th British National Conference on Databases*, pages 84–100, London, UK, July 1997. Springer-Verlag.

4.19 J.J. King. *Query Optimisation by Semantic Reasoning*. UMI Research Press, 1984.

4.20 K.G. Kulkarni and M.P. Atkinson. EFDM: Extended Functional Data Model. *The Computer Journal*, 29(1):38–46, 1986.

4.21 P.J. Landin. A Lambda Calculus Approach. In L. Fox, editor, *Advances in Programming and Non-Numerical Computation*, Symposium Publications Division, chapter 5, pages 97–141. Pergamon Press, 1966.

4.22 F. Manola and U. Dayal. PDM: an Object-Oriented Data Model. In K. Dittrich and U. Dayal, editors, *International Workshop on Object-Oriented Database Systems*, pages 18–25, Pacific Grove, USA, September 1986. IEEE Computer Society Press.

4.23 P.F. Meredith. A Functional Programming Language which Integrates Queries and Updates for Managing an Entity-Function Database. PhD thesis, Birkbeck College, University of London, 1999.

4.24 P.F. Meredith and P.J.H. King. Scoped Referential Transparency in a Functional Database Language with Updates. In Suzanne M. Embury, N.J. Fiddian, W.A. Gray, and A.C. Jones, editors, *Advances in Databases: Proceedings of 16th British National Conference on Databases*, pages 134–148, Cardiff, Wales, July 1998. Springer-Verlag.

4.25 R. Milner. A Theory of Type Polymorphism in Programming. *Journal of Computer and System Sciences*, 17(3):348–375, December 1978.

4.26 J.-M. Nicolas. Logic for Improving Integrity Checking in Relational Databases. *Acta Informatica*, 18:227–253, 1982.

4.27 R.S. Nikhil. The Semantics of Update in a Functional Database Programming Language. In Bancilhon and Buneman [4.3], chapter 24, pages 403–421.

4.28 A. Poulovassilis and P. King. Extending the Functional Data Model to Computational Completeness. In C. Thanos F. Bancilhon and D. Tsichritzis, editors, *EDBT 90 Conference*, pages 75–91, Venice, March 1990. Springer Verlag.

4.29 A. Poulovassilis and C. Small. A Functional Programming Approach to Deductive Databases. In G. Lohman, A. Sernadas, and R. Camps, editors, *Proceedings of 17th International Conference on Very Large Databases*, pages 491–500, Barcelona, 1991. Morgan Kaufmann.

4.30 S. Reddi. Integrity Constraint Enforcement in the Functional Database Language PFL. In M. Worboys and A.F. Grundy, editors, *Proceedings of the 11th British National Conference on Databases*, pages 238–257, Keele, UK, July 1993. Springer-Verlag.

4.31 A. Shepherd and L. Kerschberg. PRISM: a Knowledge Based System for Semantic Integrity Specification and Enforcement in Database Systems. In B. Yormark, editor, *SIGMOD 84 Conference*, pages 307–315, Boston, 1984. ACM Press.

4.32 D.W. Shipman. The Functional Data Model and the Data Language DAPLEX. *ACM Transactions on Database Systems*, 6(1):140–173, March 1981.

4.33 H. Söndergaard and P. Sestoft. Referential Transparency, Definiteness and Unfoldability. *Acta Informatica*, 27(6):505–517, 1989.

4.34 H. Söndergaard and P. Sestoft. Non-Determinism in Functional Languages. *The Computer Journal*, 35(5):514–523, 1992.

4.35 David R. Sutton and Carol Small. Extending Functional Database Languages to Update Completeness. In Carole A. Goble and John A. Keane, editors, *Advances in Databases: Proceedings of 13th British National Conference on Databases*, LNCS 940, pages 47–63, Manchester, UK, July 1995. Springer.

4.36 S.J. Thompson. *Miranda: the Craft of Functional Programming*. Addison-Wesley, 1995.

4.37 P.W. Trinder. A Functional Database. PhD thesis, University of Oxford, 1989.

4.38 P. Van Hentenryck. *Constraint Satisfaction in Logic Programming*. MIT Press, 1989.

4.39 P. Wadler. Linear Types can Change the World! In M. Broy and C. Jones, editors, *Programming Concepts and Methods*. North-Holland, 1990.

4.40 P. Wadler. Monads for Functional Programming. In Johan Jeuring and Erik Meijer, editors, *First International Spring School on Advanced Functional Programming Techniques*, LNCS 925, pages 24–52, Bastad, Sweden, May 1995. Springer-Verlag.

5. Representing Matrices Using Multi-Directional Foreign Functions

Kjell Orsborn, Tore Risch, and Staffan Flodin

Dept. of Information Technology, Uppsala University,Uppsala, Sweden
email: {kjell.orsborn,tore.risch}@it.uu.se

Summary.

New application areas for database technology such as computer-aided design and analysis systems require a semantically rich data model, high performance, extensibility, and application oriented queries. We have built a system for finite element analysis using a functional database management system to represent multiple matrix representations. The Functional Data Model is well suited for managing the data complexity and representation needs of such applications. Our application domain needs multiple customized numerical data representations, user-defined (foreign) functions, multiply inherited types, and overloading of multi-argument functions. Type inheritance and overloading require the support for late binding of function calls in queries. Furthermore, queries may use functions as relationships, which means that the system needs to process inverses of both tabulated and foreign functions, *multi-directional functions*. It is shown how to model matrix algebra operators using multi-directional foreign functions and how to process queries to these functions.

5.1 Introduction

As the usage of database techniques will increase in scientific and engineering disciplines the requirements on analysis capabilities will grow. This work provides analysis capabilities in a database environment to support the needs of such applications. Scientific and engineering applications are computationally intensive applications and the idea is to provide numerical analysis capabilities within the database environment to support their processing needs.

By providing in the DBMS both application-oriented data structures and the corresponding implementations of relevant operations, it is possible to both store and process the data in the DBMS. In this way data transportation between application and database can be minimized. Furthermore, the embedding of local databases within applications can provide powerful new techniques for developing advanced applications.

For example, we would like to store numerical matrices in the database, not just the array data structure. This makes it possible to perform operations on matrices, producing new or modified matrices, in contrast to only accessing the physical array data structure. By having matrix types in the database it is possible to extend the query language with operations on matrices to form an algebra for the matrix domain that can be used in application modeling. It is furthermore possible to introduce special query optimization methods for numerical data processing. This includes, forexample, decisions for selecting suitable data representations, solution methods, and processing locations.

We have built a system [5.19, 5.20, 5.21] for finite element analysis (FEA) storing numerical data in the functional DBMS Amos II [5.22] (see chapter 10 of this book). The performance requirements on numerical data access in an FEA model are very high, and several special methods have been developed for efficient representation of, for example, matrices used in FEA where different methods are useful depending on the context. For instance, a fundamental component in an FEA system is an equation solving subsystem that can solve linear equation systems such as $K \times a = f$ where a is sought while K and f are known. Special representation methods and special equation solving methods must be applied depending on the properties and representations of the matrices. To get good performance in queries involving matrix operators, various matrix data representations and function definitions are stored in the database and the functions are executed in the database server. Special optimization methods and cost formulas have been developed for the matrix domain operators.

Views in our functional data model are represented as functions defined in terms of queries containing functions from the domain, e.g. for matrix algebra. In our query language, AmosQL [5.22], such functions are called *derived functions* and are expressed by side-effect-free queries. This provides a high abstraction level which is problem oriented and reusable. Query optimization techniques are used to optimize queries involving derived functions.

In simple object-oriented models the method invocation is based on the *message-passing* paradigm where methods are connected to the receiver of the message. The message-passing style of method invocation restricts the way in which relations between objects can be expressed [5.1].

In order to model a computational domain such as the matrix domain it is desirable to also support functions with more than one argument, corresponding to *multi-methods* [5.1] in object-oriented languages. This provides a natural way to represent, for example, matrix operators applied on various kinds of matrix representations. In Section 5.3 we show how matrix operators are modeled as multi-argument overloaded functions in our application.

High-level declarative queries with function calls do not specify exactly how a function is to be invoked in the query. We will show that *multi-directional foreign functions* [5.16] are needed in the database query language for efficient processing of queries involving inverses of functions. A function in the database query language is multi-directional if, for an arbitrary function invocation $m(x) = y$, it is possible to retrieve those arguments x that are mapped by the function m to a particular result, y. Multi-directional functions can furthermore have more than one argument. This ability provides a declarative and flexible query language where the user does not have to specify explicitly how a function should be called.

```
DECLARE m1 AS SymmetricMatrix;
DECLARE m2 AS ColumnMatrix;

SELECT x FROM ColumnMatrix x WHERE x IN f() AND m1 * x = m2;
```

Fig. 5.1. A sample query exemplifying a multi-directional method.

To exemplify a multi-directional function, consider the AmosQL query in Figure 5.1 that retrieves those matrices stored in function f() which, when multiplied by the matrix bound to the variable m1, equals the matrix bound to the variable m2. This query is a declarative specification of the retrieval of the matrix x from the result set of the function hf() where x solves the equation system m1 * x = m2 (m1 and m2 are assumed given). It is the task of the query optimizer to find an efficient execution strategy for the declarative specification, e.g. by using the inverse of the * method (matrix multiplication) that solves the equation system to get a value for x. The alternative execution strategy without multi-directional foreign functions is to go through all matrices in f() and multiply them with m1 to compare the result with m2. The first strategy clearly scales substantially better when f() contains large sets of matrices.

To extend the search space of a query optimizer it must be able to inspect the definitions of all referenced views. In our case this means that the definitions of derived functions are revealed to the optimizer, which can then in-line them before queries are fully optimized, a process called *revelation* [5.7]. With revelation the query optimizer is allowed to break encapsulation while the user still cannot access encapsulated data.

The combination of inheritance in the type hierarchy and function overriding results in the requirement of having to select at run time which resolvent to apply, i.e. *late binding*.

A function which is late bound obstructs global optimization since the resolvent cannot be selected until *run time*. This may cause indexes, function inverses, and other properties that are important to achieve good performance to be hidden from the optimizer inside function definitions and remain unused during execution. Thus, late bound functions may cause severe performance degradation if special query processing techniques are not applied. This is why providing a solution that enables optimization of late bound functions is an important issue in the context of a database [5.7].

A special problem is the combination of late bound functions and multi-directional functions. This problem is addressed in [5.9] where late bound function calls are represented by a special object algebra operator, DTR, in the execution plan. The DTR operator is defined in terms of the *possible resolvents*, i.e. the resolvents eligible for execution at run time. Each resolvent is optimized with respect to the enclosing query plan. The cost model and selectivity prediction of the DTR operator is defined in terms of the costs and selectivities of the possible (inverse) resolvents. The single argument DTR approach in [5.9] has been generalized to handle multi-directional functions with arbitrary arity [5.10].

Below it is shown, by using excerpts from our matrix domain, that using a functional data model with multi-directional functions results in a system where complex applications can be modeled easily compared to modeling within a pure object-oriented data model. We furthermore show how such queries are translated into an algebraic representation for evaluation.

5.2 Functional Database Representations

In this section we first give a short introduction to the data model we use. Then properties of multi-directional functions are discussed followed by an overview of the issues related to late binding.

5.2.1 The Functional Data Model

The Functional Data Model of Amos II [5.22] and its query language AmosQL is based on DAPLEX [5.25] with object-oriented extensions. The data model includes *stored functions* and *derived functions*. Stored functions store properties of objects and correspond to attributes in the relational model and the object-oriented model. Derived functions are used to derive through queries new properties which are not explicitly stored in the database. A derived function is defined by a query and corresponds to a view in the relational model and to a function (method) in the object-oriented model. In addition to stored and derived functions Amos II also has *foreign functions* which are defined using an auxiliary programming language such as Java, Lisp, or C and then introduced into the query language [5.16]. In Fig. 5.1 the overloaded operator * over type ColumnMatrix is implemented by foreign functions. The only way to access properties of objects is through functions, thus functions provide *encapsulation* of the objects in the database.

5.2.2 Multi-Directional Functions

Multi-directional functions are functions which may be called with several different configurations of bound or unbound arguments and results, called *binding-patterns*. The query compiler must be capable of generating an optimal execution plan choosing among the possible binding-patterns for each multi-directional function. Sometimes such an execution plan may not exist and the query processor must then report the query as being unexecutable.

To denote which binding-pattern a function is called with, the arguments, a_i, and result, r, are annotated with b or f, meaning *bound* or *free*, as a_i^b or a_i^f if a_i is bound or free, respectively. In the optimal execution plan for the query in Figure 5.1 the function * is called with its second argument unbound

```
CREATE FUNCTION times(SymmetricMatrix x, ColumnMatrix y) ->
                ColumnMatrix r AS
                MULTIDIRECTIONAL
                "bbf" FOREIGN "MatrixMultiplication"
                     COST "MultCost",
                "bfb" FOREIGN "GaussDecomposition"
                     COST "GaussCost";
```

Fig. 5.2. Definition of a multi-directional foreign function

and with the first argument and the result bound. Thus, the call to ∗ in that example will be denoted as $x^b \times y^f \to r^b$.

Recall the three types of functions in the Amos II data model: stored, foreign, and derived functions as decribed in a chapter 10. Stored functions are made multi-directional by having the system automatically derive access plans for all binding-pattern configurations. Derived functions are made multi-directional by accessing their definitions and finding efficient execution plans for binding-patterns when needed. For multi-directional foreign functions the programmer has to explicitly assign each binding-pattern configuration an implementation, as illustrated in Figure. 5.2.

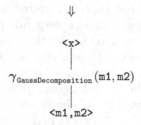

SELECT x FROM ColumnMatrix x WHERE m1 ∗ x = m2;

$$\Downarrow$$

$$<x>$$
$$|$$
$$\gamma_{\text{GaussDecomposition}}(m1, m2)$$
$$|$$
$$<m1,m2>$$

Fig. 5.3. Multi-directional function execution.

Figure 5.3 illustrates a very simple AmosQL query and its translation to object algebra. Notice that the terms following the FROM clause denote declarations of typed variables universally quantified over type extents [5.22]. This is different from OQL [5.6] where they denote collections and SQL where they denote tables.

In Figure 5.2 the function times (implementing ∗) is defined for two arguments and made multi-directional by defining which implementation to use for a certain binding-pattern. For $times(a^b, b^f) \to r^b$ (implementing $x^b \times y^f \to r^b$) the foreign function definition GaussDecomposition implements times, while MatrixMultiplication will be used for $times(a^b, b^b) \to r^f$. The functions GaussDecomposition and MatrixMultiplication are implemented in a conventional programming language such as C++. The implementer also provides optional cost functions, `MultCost` and `GaussCost`, which are applied by the query optimizer to compute both selectivities and costs.

The query compiler translates the AmosQL query into an internal algebra expression. Figure 5.3 gives an example of a query with a multidirectional function and the corresponding algebra tree. Here the query interpreter must use $times(a^b, b^f) \rightarrow r^b$ which is a multi-directional foreign function as shown in Figure 5.2. The chosen implementation of `times`, i.e. `GaussDecomposition`, depends on the types of `m1` and `m2`. It will be called by the `apply` algebra operator, γ, which takes as input a tuple of objects and applies the subscripted function (here `GaussDecomposition`) to get the result.

5.2.3 Function Overloading and Late Binding

In Amos II's data model types are organized in a hierarchy with inheritance where subtypes inherit properties from their supertypes. *Overloading* allows the function name to denote several variants, called *resolvents*. Resolvents are uniquely named by annotating the function name with the type of the arguments and result. The naming convention chosen in Amos II (and in this chapter) is: `t1.t2.....tn.m -> tr` for a function m whose argument types are `t1,t2,...,tn` and result type is `tr`.

When names are overloaded within the transitive closure of a subtype–supertype relationship that name is said to be *overridden*.

In our functional model an instance of type t is also an instance of all supertypes of that type, i.e. *inclusion polymorphism* [5.4]. Thus, any reference declared to denote objects of a particular type, t, may denote objects of type t or any subtype, t_{sub}, of that type. This is called *substitutability*. As a consequence of substitutability and overriding, functions may be required to be *late bound*.

For multi-argument functions the criterion for late binding is similar to that for pure object-oriented methods with the difference that for multi-argument functions, *tuple types* are considered instead of single types. Multi-argument functions enhance the expressive power of the data model but the type checker must include algorithms for type resolution of tuple types [5.1] and for handling ambiguities [5.2].

In Amos II the query compiler resolves which function calls require late binding. Whenever late binding is required a special operator, DTR [5.9], is inserted into the calculus expression. The optimizer translates each DTR call into the special algebra operator γ_{DTR} which, among a set of possible resolvents, selects the subplan to execute according to the types of its arguments. This will be illustrated below. If the call does not require late binding it is substituted either by its body, if a stored or derived function is called, or by a function application if a foreign function is called.

Special execution subplans are generated for the possible resolvents of the specific binding-patterns that are used in the execution plan. Thus available indexes will be utilized or other useful optimization will be performed on the possible resolvents. If any of the possible resolvents are unexecutable the enclosing DTR will also be unexecutable. The cost and selectivity of the DTR operator is calculated based on the costs and selectivities of the possible resolvents as their maximum cost and minimum selectivity, respectively. Hence, DTR is used by a cost-based optimizer [5.12] to find an efficient execution strategy.

5.3 Representing Matrices using Functions

We shall investigate how to represent matrices and their operators using our semantic functional data model, and how to process queries over these representations.

5.3.1 Matrix Algebraic Concepts

Some matrix algebraic concepts are introduced where the notation mainly follows that of Golub and van Loan [5.11]. The vector space of all m-by-n matrices is denoted by the m-by-n scalar field $S^{m \times n}$, where normally $S \in R$, the set of real numbers. However, due to computational requirements it might be necessary to extend the types of matrix representations such that S belongs to one of Z (the set of integers), R_f (the set of 4-byte reals), and R_d (the set of 8-byte reals). This means that matrices can have integer, float, and double representations. This must covered in the definition of matrix operations for allowing matrix expressions mixing matrix types. This distinction is omitted in the subsequent presentation of matrix concepts.

Thus, for a matrix $\mathbf{A}$ we have

$$\mathbf{A} \in S^{m \times n} \Leftrightarrow \mathbf{A} = (a_{ij}) = \begin{pmatrix} a_{11} & \cdots & a_{1n} \\ \vdots & \ddots & \vdots \\ a_{m1} & \cdots & a_{mn} \end{pmatrix}, \text{ where } a_{ij} \in S . \qquad (5.1)$$

Here, a_{ij} represents the element of $\mathbf{A}$ at row i and column j.

Basic algebraic operations of matrices can now be introduced. The conventional approach introduces matrix algebraic operations as functions that take matrices as arguments and produce new or altered matrices. Here, a somewhat different approach will be applied. Since the query language AmosQL allows the definition of multi-directional functions, it is possible to define operations on matrices as relationships that are isomorphic to the corresponding

mathematical expressions. In Golub and van Loan[5.11], operations are represented by the $a \rightarrow b$ notation, where the arrow associates to a one-directional
function application. In the present context, this notation is replaced by the
$a \leftrightarrow b$ notation that is more associated to bi-directional or multi-directional
relationships. However, it should be noted that this notation does not imply
that the relationship exists, or is defined, for every direction that corresponds
to combinations of matrix types.

Hence, the basic operations on matrices include:

- **addition**: $S^{m \times n} \times S^{m \times n} \leftrightarrow S^{m \times n}$, where $\mathbf{A} + \mathbf{B} = \mathbf{C}$ with the elements
  $a_{ij} + b_{ij} = c_{ij}$
- **subtraction**: $S^{m \times n} \times S^{m \times n} \leftrightarrow S^{m \times n}$, where $\mathbf{A} - \mathbf{B} = \mathbf{C}$ with the elements
  $a_{ij} - b_{ij} = c_{ij}$
- **multiplication**: $S^{m \times r} \times S^{r \times n} \leftrightarrow S^{m \times n}$, where $\mathbf{A} \times \mathbf{B} = \mathbf{C}$ with the
  elements $a_{ij} \cdot b_{ij} = c_{ij}$
- **transposition**: $S^{m \times n} \leftrightarrow S^{n \times m}$, where $\mathbf{A}^T = \mathbf{B}$ with the elements $a_{ij} = b_{ji}$.

We should note that the matrix concept defined above covers general
m-by-n matrices. By making restrictions on this definition it is possible to
define specialized categories of matrices that form subspaces of the vector
space $S^{m \times n}$. For instance, we can define:

- $S^{m \times n}$, representing the general **rectangular** matrix, $\mathbf{A}_{rect}$.
- $S^{m \times m}$, representing a **square** matrix, $\mathbf{A}_{square}$, with the same number of
  rows and columns.
- $S^{m \times m}$, a square matrix with the additional constraint $s_{ij} = s_{ji}$ that represents a **symmetric** matrix, $\mathbf{A}_{symm}$.
- $S^{m \times m}$, a symmetric matrix with the additional constraint $s_{ij} = 0$ for $i \neq j$
  that represents a **diagonal** matrix, $\mathbf{A}_{diag}$.
- $S^{m \times m}$, a matrix with the same number of rows and columns with the
  additional constraint $s_{ij} = 0$ for $i > j$ and that represents an **upper
  triangular** matrix, $\mathbf{A}_{uptri}$.
- $S^{m \times m}$, an upper triangular matrix with the additional constraint $s_{ij} = 1$
  for $i = j$ that represents an **upper unit triangular** matrix, $\mathbf{A}_{uputri}$.
- $S^{m \times m}$, a matrix with the same number of rows and columns with the additional constraint $s_{ij} = 0$ for $i < j$ and that represents a **lower triangular**
  matrix, $\mathbf{A}_{lowtri}$.
- $S^{m \times m}$, an lower triangular matrix with the additional constraint $s_{ij} = 1$
  for $i = j$ that represents a **lower unit triangular** matrix, $\mathbf{A}_{lowutri}$.
- $S^{m \times 1}$, a rectangular matrix with one column representing a **column** matrix, $\mathbf{a}$ or $\mathbf{A}_{col}$.
- $S^{1 \times m}$, a rectangular matrix with one row representing a **row** matrix type,
  $\mathbf{a}$ or $\mathbf{A}_{row}$.

With these additional categories of matrices, the previous list of matrix
operations can also be specialized further taking the additional categories

into account. This is exemplified in Eqs. 5.2a–5.2r for the case of matrix multiplication of rectangular matrices where index sizes and symmetries have been used to identify different combinations

$$\mathbf{A}_{rect} \times \mathbf{B}_{rect} = \mathbf{C}_{rect} \tag{5.2a}$$

$$\mathbf{A}_{rect} \times \mathbf{B}_{square} = \mathbf{C}_{rect} \tag{5.2b}$$

$$\mathbf{A}_{square} \times \mathbf{B}_{rect} = \mathbf{C}_{rect} \tag{5.2c}$$

$$\mathbf{A}_{symm} \times \mathbf{B}_{rect} = \mathbf{C}_{rect} \tag{5.2d}$$

$$\mathbf{A}_{square} \times \mathbf{B}_{col} = \mathbf{C}_{col} \tag{5.2e}$$

$$\mathbf{A}_{symm} \times \mathbf{B}_{col} = \mathbf{C}_{col} \tag{5.2f}$$

$$\mathbf{A}_{lowtri} \times \mathbf{B}_{col} = \mathbf{C}_{col} \tag{5.2g}$$

$$\mathbf{A}_{uptri} \times \mathbf{B}_{col} = \mathbf{C}_{col} \tag{5.2h}$$

$$\mathbf{A}_{lowtri} \times \mathbf{B}_{uptri} = \mathbf{C}_{square} \tag{5.2i}$$

$$\mathbf{A}_{diag} \times \mathbf{B}_{col} = \mathbf{C}_{col} \tag{5.2j}$$

$$\mathbf{A}_{diag} \times \mathbf{B}_{uptri} = \mathbf{C}_{uptri} \tag{5.2k}$$

$$\mathbf{A}_{col} \times \mathbf{B}_{row} = \mathbf{C}_{rect} \tag{5.2l}$$

$$\mathbf{A}_{rect} \times \mathbf{B}_{rect} = \mathbf{C}_{square} \tag{5.2m}$$

$$\mathbf{A}_{square} \times \mathbf{B}_{square} = \mathbf{C}_{square} \tag{5.2n}$$

$$\mathbf{A}_{col} \times \mathbf{B}_{row} = \mathbf{C}_{square} \tag{5.2o}$$

$$\mathbf{A}_{rect} \times \mathbf{B}_{col} = \mathbf{C}_{col} \tag{5.2p}$$

$$\mathbf{A}_{row} \times \mathbf{B}_{rect} = \mathbf{C}_{row} \tag{5.2q}$$

$$\mathbf{A}_{row} \times \mathbf{B}_{square} = \mathbf{C}_{row} \tag{5.2r}$$

Hence, the resulting matrix category of multiplying two (rectangular) matrices is dependent on the sizes of the outer indexes of the argument matrices. By interpreting the matrix spaces as subcategories of the rectangular matrix category we get relationships between argument matrix categories and the result argument category for the matrix multiplication operator. By considering other matrix characteristics, such as symmetry and singularity, further specializations of these relationships can be established.

Furthermore, in applications like FEA, it is common to use specialized and more compact physical representations [5.14, 5.5] of matrices in contrast to *full* regular matrix representations. These types of compressed representations include, for example, skyline matrix (or profile matrix) representations where consecutive zero-valued elements above the skyline are left out and the matrix is usually represented by matrix columns in a one-dimensional array. This is an example of a compact representation where the matrix structure is static, i.e. it is not allowed to change. Additional static representations along the same theme exist. There are also dynamic matrix representations where the storage structure is allowed to change. These representation types are usually referred to as sparse matrix representations and are typically implemented by some linked-list data structure. The categorizations and their usage in establishing the multiplication operator as relationships among different categories that are exemplified above can be further extended to establish relationships between combinations of other matrix categories and representations as well as for different operators.

To sum up this section, three principles have been presented that can divide the matrix concept into different categories, namely:

− mathematically related matrix categories based on the general matrix concept and its characteristics that further restrict this concept to subcategories;
− the data types integer, float, and double used for representing and implementing numerical matrices;
− various physical representation schemes for representing and implementing matrices such as regular, skyline, or sparse. A database implementation that covers regular and skyline representations is presented in [5.21].

The reason for defining several matrix categories is the potential ability to take advantage of the knowledge about specific categories in representing numerical data and applying numerical analysis methods. This concerns the possibilities of applying efficient storage and processing techniques. So far it is possible to use:

− a priori information to determine matrix categories appropriate for a specific problem;
− information about matrix categories related by a specific operator to determine the appropriate operator and correct result (or argument) category;
− information about matrix characteristics, i.e. properties that are not distinguished by separate categories, to determine correct operator result (or argument) to efficiently direct subsequent matrix representations and operations.

This type of information has been used to establish the matrix type structure in Figure 5.4 together with the set of mathematical operations that will be discussed below.

5.3.2 Queries for Solving Linear Equations

A fundamental component in an FEA system is a linear equation solving sub-system. To model an equation solving system we define a type hierarchy of matrix types as illustrated in Figure 5.4. Furthermore, the matrix multiplication operator, ×, is defined as functions on this matrix type hierarchy for several combinations of arguments. Equations 5.2a–5.2r illustrate how each variant of the multiplication function takes various matrix types as arguments.

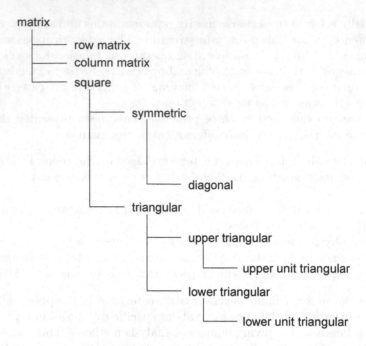

Fig. 5.4. A matrix type hierarchy for linear matrix algebra

The functions for multiplication are used to specify linear equation systems as matrix multiplications as $\mathbf{K} \times \mathbf{a} = \mathbf{f}$, where $\mathbf{a}$ is sought while $\mathbf{K}$ and $\mathbf{f}$ are known. Special representation methods and special equation solving methods have been developed that are dependent on the properties of the matrices. In our system, the function `times` (= infix operator *) is overloaded on both its arguments and has different implementations depending on the type (and thus representations) of the matrices used in its arguments. For example, when $\mathbf{K}$ is a symmetric matrix, i.e. corresponding to the case in Eq. 5.2f, it can be solved by a method that explores the symmetric properties of the first argument. One such method, $\mathbf{LDL}^T$ decomposition [5.11] outlined in Eq. 5.3, substitutes the equation system with several equivalent equation systems that are simpler to solve. According to Eq. 5.3 the lefthand equation can be transformed into a set of simpler equations on the righthand side:

$$\mathbf{K}^b \times \mathbf{a}^f = \mathbf{f}^b \longrightarrow \left\{ \begin{array}{c} \mathbf{K}^b = (\mathbf{U}^T)^f \times \mathbf{D}^f \times \mathbf{U}^f \\ \mathbf{U}^b \times \mathbf{a}^f = \mathbf{x}^b \\ \mathbf{D}^b \times \mathbf{x}^f = \mathbf{y}^b \\ (\mathbf{U}^T)^b \times \mathbf{y}^f = \mathbf{f}^b \end{array} \right. \qquad (5.3)$$

The linear equation system is solved by starting with the factorization, $\mathbf{K} = \mathbf{U}^T \times \mathbf{D} \times \mathbf{U}$, that transforms $\mathbf{K}$ into the three matrices $\mathbf{U}^T$, $\mathbf{D}$, and $\mathbf{U}$.

Then the upper triangular equation system $\mathbf{U}^T \times \mathbf{y} = \mathbf{f}$ is solved to get $\mathbf{y}$. The diagonal equation system $\mathbf{D} \times \mathbf{x} = \mathbf{y}$ is then solved to get $\mathbf{x}$, and finally the solution of the lower triangular equation system $\mathbf{U} \times \mathbf{a} = \mathbf{x}$ gets $\mathbf{a}$. If the equation on the other hand corresponds to Eq. 5.2e, the symmetry of $\mathbf{K}$ cannot be exploited and some other method to solve it must be applied, e.g. Gauss decomposition.

The rationale for having these different overloaded matrix multiplication functions is efficiency and reusability, the former because mathematical properties of the more specialized matrix types can be considered when implementing multiplication operators for them. Furthermore, specialized physical representations have been developed for many of the matrix types, e.g. to suppress zeros or symmetric elements, and the matrix operators are defined in terms of these representations. The more specialized operators will in general have lower execution costs than the more general ones. The overloading provides reusability because every multiplication operator may be used in different contexts. To illustrate this consider the example in Figure 5.5 over the type hierarchy in Figure 5.4 and the multiplication operators from Eqs. 5.2a–5.2r.

In this example a query is stated that solves an equation system by taking one square and one column matrix as arguments and calculating the solution by using the multiplication function. Depending on the type of the arguments the appropriate function from the type hierarchy below `SquareMatrix` will be selected at run time, i.e. late binding. Also note that here the multiplication function (∗) is overloaded and used with the first argument and the result bound and the second argument unbound. This is only possible when multi-directional functions are supported by the system. With multi-directional functions the equation system in Figure 5.5 can be written as $\mathbf{K} \times \mathbf{a} = \mathbf{f}$ which is a more declarative and reusable form than if separate functions were needed for matrix multiplication and equation solving, respectively. It is also a more optimizable form since the optimizer can find ways to execute the statement which would be hidden if the user explicitly had stated in which direction the ∗ function is executed.

```
DECLARE K AS SymmetricMatrix;
DECLARE f AS ColumnMatrix;

SELECT a FROM ColumnMatrix a WHERE K * a = f;
```

Fig. 5.5. A simple query illustrating function overloading

The implementer can often define different implementations of the `times` (∗) operation depending on whether an argument or the result is unknown. For the case in Eq. 5.2e, where a square matrix is multiplied with a column matrix resulting in another column matrix, two variants are required. The first variant does matrix multiplication when both arguments are known and the result is unknown. When the first argument and the result are known and the second argument is unknown, the `times` (*) operation will perform equation solving using Gauss decomposition. There are also two variants for symmetric matrices, Eq. 5.2f; the difference is that instead of using Gauss decomposition when the second argument is unknown, the more efficient $\mathbf{LDL}^T$ decomposition algorithm is used.

Late binding relieves the user from having to decide when any of the more specialized multiplication operators can be used since the system will do this at run time. Thus, the general matrix multiplication at run-time will be selected as the most specialised variant possible, e.g. a variant corresponding to Eq. 5.2f when the first argument is a symmetric matrix. Note that the types of all arguments participate in type resolution to select which resolvents of the multiplication operator to use from all the possible multiplication operators in Eqs. 5.2a–5.2r. Contrast this with a pure object-oriented data model without multi-argument functions where the system cannot select the correct resolvent when the type of argument other than the first one has to be considered. This imposes restrictions on how object relations can be expressed in a pure object-oriented data model. In some models, e.g. C++, the types of all arguments are used to select theresolvent if the function is early bound but not when it is late bound. Thus, the introduction of an overriding function may become problematic.

Our example shows that multi-directional functions are useful to support the modeling of complex applications. A system that supports both late binding and multi-directional multi-argument functions offers the programmer a flexible and powerful modeling tool. The challenge is then to provide query processing techniques to support these features. This will be addressed next.

5.4 Processing Queries with Multi-Directional Functions

We will show through an example how queries with multi-directional functions are processed in Amos II for a subset of the functions corresponding to Eqs. 5.2a–5.2r. Figure 5.6 gives the function definitions in AmosQL that are needed for modeling equation solving using the method of $\mathbf{LDL}^T$ decomposition according to Eq. 5.3.

The multi-directional foreign function `times` is overloaded and defined differently depending on the shape and representation of the matrices. It is multi-directional to transparently handle both matrix multiplication and equation solving in queries. The primitive matrix operations are implemented as a set of foreign functions in some programming language (here C). For symmetric matrices the multiplication is implemented by the foreign function `SymmetricMult` while equation solving uses the $\mathbf{LDL}$ method above, as specified by the derived function named (`SymmetricSolve`).

```
CREATE FUNCTION factorise(SymmetricMatrix K) ->
                <DiagonalMatrix D, UpUTriMatrix U> AS
                FOREIGN "Factorise";

CREATE FUNCTION transpose(UpUTriMatrix U) -> LowUTriMatrix L AS
                FOREIGN "Transpose";

CREATE FUNCTION times(LowUTriMatrix L, ColumnMatrix y) ->
                ColumnMatrix f AS
                MULTIDIRECTIONAL "bbf" FOREIGN "LowUTriMult",
                                "bfb" FOREIGN "LowUTriSolve";

CREATE FUNCTION times(DiagonalMatrix D, ColumnMatrix x) ->
                ColumnMatrix y AS
                MULTIDIRECTIONAL "bbf" FOREIGN "DiagonalMult",
                                "bfb" FOREIGN "DiagonalSolve";

CREATE FUNCTION times(UpUTriMatrix U, ColumnMatrix a) ->
                ColumnMatrix x AS
                MULTIDIRECTIONAL "bbf" FOREIGN "UpUTriMult",
                                "bfb" FOREIGN "UpUTriSolve";

CREATE FUNCTION times(SymmetricMatrix K, ColumnMatrix a) ->
                ColumnMatrix f AS
                MULTIDIRECTIONAL "bbf" FOREIGN "SymmetricMult",
                                "bfb" DERIVED "SymmetricSolve";

CREATE FUNCTION SymmetricSolve(SymmetricMatrix K,ColumnMatrix f) ->
                ColumnMatrix AS SELECT a
                FROM UpUTriMatrix U,DiagonalMatrix D,
                     ColumnMatrix x,ColumnMatrix y
                WHERE factorise(K) = <U,D> AND
                      transpose(U) * y = f AND
                      D * x = y AND
                      U * a = x;
```

Fig. 5.6. Multi-directional function definitions.

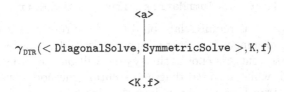

Fig. 5.7. The top-level query algebra tree for the query in Figure 5.5.

The query optimizer translates the query into an optimized execution plan represented as an algebra tree in Figure 5.7. During the translation to the algebra the optimizer will apply type resolution methods to avoid late binding in the execution plan when possible. In cases where late binding is required the execution plan may call subplans.

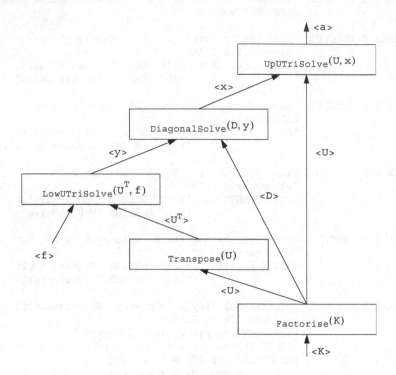

Fig. 5.8. Algebra graph showing the execution order for the transformed matrix expression.

In the example query of Fig. 5.5 there are two possible resolvents of the name `times`:

1. `DiagonalMatrix.ColumnMatrix.times`→`ColumnMatrix`
2. `SymmetricMatrix.ColumnMatrix.times`→`ColumnMatrix`

The example thus requires late binding where resolvent 2 will be chosen when the first argument is a `SymmetricMatrix` and 1 will be chosen otherwise. When resolvent 2 is chosen the system will be solved using the $\mathbf{LDL}^{T}$ decomposition, while a trivial diagonal solution method is used for case 1. The optimizer translates the query into the algebra tree in Figure 5.7, where the algebra operator γ_{DTR} implements late binding. At run time it selects the subplan to apply on its arguments K and f based on their types. In the example there are two subplans, `DiagonalSolve` and `SymmetricSolve`.

DiagonalSolve is implemented as a foreign function in C shown in Figure 5.6, while SymmetricSolve references the subplan performing the $\mathbf{LDL}^T$ decomposition in Figure 5.8.

The subplan in Figure 5.8 has K and f as input parameters (tuples) and produces a as the result tuple. The K parameter is input to the application of the foreign function Factorise that does the $\mathbf{LDL}^T$ factorization producing the output tuple <D,U>. The U part is projected as the argument of the functions Transpose and UpUTriSolve (the projection operator is omitted for clarity), while the projection of D is the argument to DiagonalSolve. The application of LowUTriSolve has the arguments f and the result of Transpose(U), i.e. $\mathbf{U}^T$. Analogous applications are made for DiagonalSolve and UpUTriSolve to produce the result tuple <a>.

5.5 Related Work

Object-oriented database management systems (OODBMSs) are often motivated by advanced applications such as systems for the management of scientific and engineering data [5.27, 5.3, 5.12]. In our case, a functional data model is shown to be even better suited for managing the complexity of the data in such applications.

Modeling matrix computations using the object-oriented paradigm has been addressed in, for example, [5.23, 5.24]. In [5.15, 5.18] algebras for primitive matrix operations are proposed. None of those papers address late binding, multi-methods, or multi-directional functions. We have shown the benefits of having these features when modeling complex applications.

OODBMSs have been the subject of extensive research during the last decade, e.g. [5.3, 5.27]. Several object-oriented query languages [5.6, 5.8, 5.17] have been proposed. However, queries with multi-directional functions have not been used in OODBMSs.

Multi-argument functions require generalized type resolution methods compared to the type resolution of pure object-oriented methods [5.2, 5.1]. In the database context the issue is not mainly fast type resolution when looking up methods but rather optimizing queries with expanded function definitions (views) in order to detect hidden search paths and multi-directional function inverses [5.9].

In the area of constraint programming [5.13] the user specifies *constraints* and then a constraint solver works out the best way to interpret them. Multi-directional foreign functions are a form of constraints compiled using a cost-based query optimizer for scalability over large data sets (large sets of matrices in the case presented here)

Advanced applications, such as our FEA application, require domain-dependent data representations of matrices and an extensible object-relational query optimizer [5.26] to efficiently process queries over these representations.

For accessing domain-specific physical representations we have extended the technique of multi-directional foreign functions described in [5.16].

In [5.9] the optimization of queries with multi-directional late bound functions in a pure object-oriented model is addressed and the DTR operator is defined and proven to be efficient. Here that approach is generalized to multi-argument foreign functions [5.10].

5.6 Summary and future work

Domain-oriented data representations are needed when representing and querying data for numerical applications using a database system, e.g. to store matrices. To avoid unnecessary data transformations and transmissions, it is important that the query language can be extended with domain-oriented operators, e.g. for matrix calculus. For high-level application modeling and querying of, e.g., matrix operators multi-directional functions are required.

Although multi-argument functions require generalized type checking and query processing, the benefits gained as increased naturalness and modeling power of the data model are important for many applications, including ours.

It was shown how multi-directional and overloaded functions can be utilized by the query optimizer to scale the execution of queries over large sets of matrices. This is a new area for query optimization techniques.

The system must support optimization of queries with late binding for multi-directional functions in order for the proposed query optimization methods to be applicable. In our approach each late bound function in a query is substituted with a DTR calculus operator which is defined in terms of the resolvents eligible for execution. Each DTR call is then translated to the algebra operator γ_{DTR} that chooses among eligible subplans according to the types of its arguments. Local query execution plans are generated at each application of γ_{DTR} and optimized for the specific binding-patterns that will be used at run-time, as illustrated in our examples.

Further interesting optimization techniques to be investigated include the identification of common subexpressions among the possible resolvents, query rewrite techniques for multi-directional functions, and transformations of DTR expressions.

References

5.1 R. Agrawal, L.G. DeMichiel, B.G. Lindsay: Static Type Checking of Multi-Methods. *OOPSLA Conf.*, 113-128, 1991.

5.2 E. Amiel, E. Dujardin: Supporting Explicit Disambiguation of Multi-Methods. *ECOOP Conf.*, 1996.

5.3 E. Bertino, M. Negri, G. Pelagatti, L. Sbattella: Object-Oriented Query Languages: The Notion and the Issues. *IEEE Transactions on Knowledge and Data Engineering*, 4(3), 223-237, June 1992.

5.4 L. Cardelli, P. Wegner: On Understanding Types, Data Abstraction, and Polymorphism. *ACM Computing Surveys*, 17(4), 471-522, 1985.

5.5 G.F. Carey, J.T. Oden: *Finite Elements: Computational Aspects*, Prentice Hall, Vol. 3, Texas Finite Element Series, 1984.

5.6 R.G.G. Cattell (ed.): *The Object Database Standard: ODMG 2.0*. Morgan Kaufmann, 1997.

5.7 S. Daniels, G. Graefe, T. Keller, D. Maier, D. Schmidt, B. Vance: Query Optimization in Revelation, an Overview. *IEEE Data Engineering Bulletin*, 14(2), 58-62, June 1992.

5.8 A. Eisenberg, J. Melton: SQL:1999, formerly known as SQL 3. *SIGMOD Record*, 28(1), 131-138, 1999.

5.9 S. Flodin, T. Risch: Processing Object-Oriented Queries with Invertible Late Bound Functions. *21st Conf. on Very Large Databases (VLDB'95)*, 335-344, 1995.

5.10 S. Flodin: Efficient Management of Object-Oriented Queries with Late Bound Functions. Licentiate Thesis 538, Dept. of Computer and Inf. Science, Linköping Univ., Feb. 1996.

5.11 G.H. Golub, C.F. van Loan: *Matrix Computations 3rd ed.*, John Hopkins Univ. Press, 1996.

5.12 G. Graefe: Query Evaluation Techniques for Large Databases. *ACM Computing Surveys*, 25(2), 73-170, June 1993.

5.13 P. van Hentenryck: Constraint Programming for Combinatorial Search Problems. *ACM Computing Surveys*, 28(4), 1996.

5.14 J.T.H. Hughes: *The Finite Element Method: Linear Static and Dynamic Finite Element Analysis*, Prentice Hall International, 1987.

5.15 L. Libkin, R. Machlin, L. Wong: A Query Language for Multidimensional Arrays: Design, Implementation and Optimization Techniques. *ACM SIGMOD conf.*, 228-239, June 1996.

5.16 W. Litwin, T. Risch: Main Memory Oriented Optimization of OO Queries using Typed Datalog with Foreign Predicates. *IEEE Transactions on Knowledge and Data Engineering*, 4(6), 517-528, 1992.

5.17 P. Lyngbaek: *OSQL: A Language for Object Databases*, Technical Report, HP Labs, HPL-DTD-91-4, 1991.

5.18 A.P. Marathe, K. Salem: A Language for Manipulating Arrays. *VLDB Conf.*, 323-334, 1997.

5.19 K. Orsborn: Applying Next Generation Object-Oriented DBMS to Finite Element Analysis. In W. Litwin, T. Risch (eds.): *Int. Conf. on Applications of Databases (ADB'94)*, Springer, 215-233, 1994.

5.20 K. Orsborn, T. Risch: Next Generation of O-O Database Techniques in Finite Element Analysis. *3rd Int. Conf. on Computational Structures Technology (CST96)*, Budapest, Hungary, August 1996.

5.21 K.Orsborn: On Extensible and Object-Relational Database Technology for Finite Element Analysis Applications. PhD Thesis 452, Linköping University, October 1996.

5.22 T. Risch, V. Josifovski, T. Katchaounov: Functional Data Integration in a Distributed Mediator System. In P. Gray (ed.): *The Functional Approache to Data Management*, Springer, 2003.

5.23 T.J. Ross, L.R. Wagner, G.F. Luger: Object-Oriented Programming for Scientific Codes. II: Examples in C++. *Journal of Computing in Civil Engineering*, 6, 497-514, 1992.

5.24 S.P. Scholz: Elements of an Object-Oriented FEM++ Program in C++. *Computers & Structures*, 43, 517-529, 1992.

5.25 D. Shipman: The Functional Data Model and the Data Language DAPLEX. *ACM Transactions on Database Systems*, 6(1), 140-173, 1981.

5.26 M. Stonebraker, P. Brown: *Object-Relational DBMSs: Tracking the Next Great Wave*. Morgan Kaufmann, 1999.

5.27 D.D. Straube, M.T. Özsu: Query Optimization and Execution Plan Generation in Object-Oriented Data Management Systems. *IEEE Transactions on Knowledge and Data Engineering*, 7(2), 210-227, 1995.

Section Editor's Preface

Introduction to Section II:
Advances in Information Integration and Interoperability
by Peter Gray

This section focuses on the very real advantages that the Functional Model and functional approaches bring to data integration. Four of the chapters take examples from Bioinformatics. This is because biomolecular structure data arises naturally in a very distributed fashion, with data being generated in laboratories world wide. It is also an area where a basic ontology of protein structure is shared by most protein scientists, even if it is not written down!

Thus there is a great demand for tools to collate and compare this data, despite the fact that it often arises in different storage formats with subtle variants of ontology. Because of this, there is a need to write the same query adapted for different forms of data, and to optimise it for bulk data access. This a common theme, and related theoretical work on optimisation is described in section III.

The MultiBase project in 1979-83 (see Chapter 1) which developed the earliest Functional Data Model, did it because of the need to fuse data from heterogeneous database platforms, which then included Codasyl and IMS! The platforms have changed, but the principles are the same, and the development of the Internet has created even more need for their application.

Chapter 6 describes a system (Kleisli) built on the mathematical work of Buneman and Tannen (as summarised in chapter 14). This is now in use commercially. In particular it shows how once the data is in a functional form, then complex queries, which arise quite often, can be formulated using List Comprehensions (see Chapter 1). These comprehensions can also call out to functions written in the functional programming language SML (Standard ML). In order to answer these queries it is necessary to do certain functional transformations and optimisations. These are described in detail.

Chapter 7 describes developments in the original FDM data model used in MultiBase, and its Daplex Language. The extended P/FDM system has been implemented in Prolog, which was one of the earliest garbage-collected languages apart from Lisp, and is very good for program transformation by pattern matching. Complex queries are translated into a List Comprehension form, which is independent of data storage. A variety of wrappers are then implemented, which serve to transform the Comprehensions for execution on different platforms.

Similarly to chapter 6, this allows the construction of a Federated Information Infrastructure, where data is held autonomously on different nodes which can evolve but also subscribe to a shared data model, for exchanging data they are willing to export. The chapter is mainly concerned with the development of such a data model. It shows how Derived Relationships can be represented as functions, and computed on demand instead of being stored redundantly.

Chapter 8 explains how the functional transformations are used in the P/FDM system of chapter 7. It describes how rewrite rules, easily implemented in Prolog, can be used to do important practical optimisations, which arise when building wrappers to connect to new database platforms. The architecture is that of an intelligent Mediator system, also used in distributed AI.

Chapter 9 also describes a Mediator system, based on the AmosII system, a distributed mediator system using the functional data model which implements a relationally complete functional query language AmosQL, with similarities to OQL. This time it is not applied to bioinformatics, but to a number of different mediators, acting as intelligent data servers, which interact. Data servers can maintain Derived Types, as a kind of view, and complex queries can access combinations of data from different types efficiently, through some very elegant optimisations. Once again, this is a use of Comprehensions, as described in chapter 1.

Chapter 10 brings us into the world of Description Logics, as used to describe complex ontologies and classification hierarchies. This shows yet another elegant use of the Monoid Comprehension Calculus of Fegaras, described in section III. The application is to data maintained under Tambis, a classification system and interface developed for objects in Bioinformatics. The Tambis processing architecture is described. What is particularly interesting is the combination of object database query processing techniques with description logics, which are more normally used for metadata queries. Thus the query optimisation rules makes use of reasoning over the DL ontology.

Table of Contents

6. The Kleisli Approach to Data Transformation and Integration

Susan B. Davidson[1] and Limsoon Wong[2]

[1] University of Pennsylvania, Philadelphia, PA 19104, USA
   email: susan@central.cis.upenn.edu
[2] Laboratories for Information Technology, Singapore 119613
   email: limsoon@lit.org.sg

Summary.
   Kleisli is a data transformation and integration system that can be used for any application where the data is typed, and has proven especially useful for bioinformatics applications. It extends the conventional flat relational data model supported by the query language SQL to a complex object data model supported by the collection programming language CPL. It also opens up the closed nature of commercial relational data management systems to an easily extensible system that performs complex transformations on autonomous data sources that are heterogeneous and geographically dispersed. This chapter describes some implementation details and example applications of Kleisli.

6.1 Introduction

The Kleisli system [6.12, 6.32, 6.33] is an advanced broad-scale integration technology that has proven very useful in the bioinformatics arena. Many bioinformatics problems require access to data sources that are large, highly heterogeneous and complex, constantly evolving, and geographically dispersed. Solutions to these problems usually involve many steps and require information to be passed smoothly (and usually transformed) between the steps. Kleisli is designed to handle these requirements directly by providing a high-level query language, CPL, that can be used to express complicated transformations across multiple data sources in a clear and simple way[1].

Many key ideas in the Kleisli system are influenced by functional programming research, as well as database query language research. Its high-level query language CPL is a functional programming language that has a built-in notion of "bulk" data types suitable for database programming and has many built-in operations required for modern bioinformatics. Kleisli is itself implemented on top of the functional programming language Standard ML of New Jersey (SML). Even the data format that Kleisli uses to exchange information with the external world is derived from ideas in type inference.

This chapter provides an overview of the Kleisli system, a summary of its impact on query language theory, a description of its SML-based implementation, a description of its handling of relational databases, as well as some

---

[1] A nested relational version of SQL, called sSQL, was recently developed by GeneticXchange Inc. as a second query language supported by Kleisli.

sample applications in the biomedical arena. The organization of the chapter
is as follows. Section 6.2 offers an overview of the architecture, data model,
and query language (CPL) of Kleisli. Section 6.3 is a discussion of Kleisli's
type system and self-describing data exchange format and their impact on
data integration in a dynamic heterogeneous environment. Section 6.4 describes how monads give rise to Kleisli's internal abstract representation of
queries and simple optimization rules. Section 6.5 explains how higher-order
functions give rise to a simple implementation of Kleisli's powerful optimizer.
Section 6.6 gives details on Kleisli's optimization with respect to the most
important class of external data sources, viz. relational databases. Section
6.7 discusses the impact of Kleisli on bioinformatics data integration. In particular, the first Kleisli query written for this purpose is reproduced here to
illustrate the smoothness of Kleisli's interface to relational and non-relational
bioinformatics sources and to show its optimizations. Section 6.8 shows how
to use Kleisli to turn a flat relational database system into a complex object
store to warehouse complex biological data. Section 6.9 demonstrates the use
of Kleisli to access multiple external data sources and external data analysis
functions for querying protein patents. Finally, Section 6.10 uses a clinical
database to demonstrate Kleisli's ability to perform "window" queries. Such
queries are very clumsy to write in SQL, since the data must first be segmented and then each segment is analyzed separately.

6.2 Quick Tour of Kleisli

We provide here the complex object data model of Kleisli, and the high-level
query language supported by Kleisli called CPL (the Collection Programming
Language). Let us begin with the architecture of the system, as depicted in
Figure 6.1 below.

Kleisli is extensible in several ways. It can be used to support other high-
level query languages by replacing the CPL module. Kleisli can also be used to
support many different types of external data sources by adding new drivers,
which forward Kleisli's requests to these sources and translate their replies
into Kleisli's exchange format. The version of Kleisli that is marketed by
GeneticXchange Inc. (www.geneticXchange.com) contains over 60 drivers for
many popular bioinformatics systems, including Sybase, Oracle, Entrez [6.25],
WU-BLAST2 [6.1], Gapped BLAST [6.3], ACEDB [6.31], etc. The optimizer
of Kleisli can also be customized by different rules and strategies.

When a query is submitted to Kleisli, it is first processed by the CPL
Module which translates it into an equivalent expression in the abstract calculus NRC. NRC is based on that described in [6.7], and is chosen as the
internal query representation because it is easy to manipulate and amenable
to machine analysis. The NRC expression is then analyzed by the Type Module to infer the most general valid type for the expression, and is passed to
the Optimizer Module. Once optimized, the NRC expression is then compiled

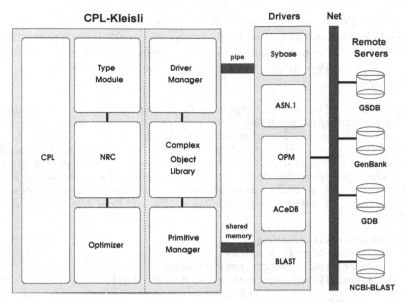

Fig. 6.1. Kleisli architecture showing CPL Modules and Drivers

by the NRC Module into calls to the Complex Object Library. The resulting compiled code is then executed, accessing drivers and external primitives as needed through pipes or shared memory. The Driver and Primitive Managers keep information on external sources and primitives and the wrapper/interface routines. The Complex Object Library contains routines for manipulating complex objects such as codes for set intersection and codes for set iteration.

The data model underlying Kleisli is a complex object type system that goes beyond the "sets of records" or "flat relations" type system of relational databases [6.11]. It allows arbitrarily nested records, sets, lists, bags, and variants. A variant is also called a tagged union type, and represents a type that is "either this or that". The collection or "bulk" types—sets, bags, and lists—are homogeneous. In order to mix objects of different types in a set, bag, or list, it is necessary to inject these objects into a variant type.

The simultaneous availability of sets, bags, and lists in Kleisli deserves some comments. In a relational database, the sole bulk data type is the set. Having only one bulk data type presents at least two problems in real-life applications. Firstly, the particular bulk data type may not be a natural model of real data. Secondly, the particular bulk data type may not be an efficient model of real data. For example, if we are restricted to the flat relational data model, the GenPept report in Example 6.2.1 below must necessarily be split into many separate tables in order to be losslessly stored in a relational database. The resulting multi-table representation of the GenPept report is conceptually unnatural and operationally inefficient. A person querying the resulting data must pay the mental overhead of understanding both the original GenPept report and its badly fragmented multi-table representation. They may also have to pay the performance overhead of having to reassemble the original GenPept report from its fragmented multi-table representation to answer queries.

Example 6.2.1. The GenPept report is the format chosen by the US National Center for Biotechnology Information to present amino acid sequence information. While an amino acid sequence is a string of letters, certain regions and positions of the string are of special biological interest, such as binding sites, domains, and so on. The feature table of a GenPept report is the part of the GenPept report that documents the positions of these regions of special biological interest, as well as annotations or comments on these regions. The following type represents the feature table of a GenPept report from Entrez [6.25].

```
(#uid:num, #title:string,
  #accession:string, #feature:{(
     #name:string, #start:num, #end:num,
     #anno:[(#anno_name:string, #descr:string)])})
```

It is an interesting type because one of its fields (#feature) is a set of records, one of whose fields (#anno) is in turn a list of records. More precisely, it is a record with four fields #uid, #title, #accession, and #feature. The first three of these store values of types num, string, and string respectively. The #uid field uniquely identifies the GenPept report. The #feature field is a set of records, which together form the feature table of the corresponding GenPept report. Each of these records has four fields #name, #start, #end, and #anno. The first three of these have types string, num, and num respectively. They represent the name, start position, and end position of a particular feature in the feature table. The #anno field is a list of records. Each of these records has two fields #anno_name and #descr, both of type string. These records together represent all annotations on the corresponding feature.

In general, the types are freely formed by the syntax:

$$t ::= \text{num} \mid \text{string} \mid \text{bool} \mid \{t\} \mid \{|t|\} \mid [t]$$
$$\mid (l_1 : t_1, \dots l_n : t_n) \mid <l_1 : t_1, \dots l_n : t_n>$$

Here num, string, and bool are the base types. The other types are constructors and build new types from existing types. The types $\{t\}$, $\{|t|\}$, and $[t]$ respectively construct set, bag, and list types from type t. The type $(l_1 : t_1, \dots l_n : t_n)$ constructs record types from types $t_1, \dots t_n$. The type $<l_1 : t_1, \dots l_n : t_n>$ constructs variant types from types $t_1, \dots t_n$. The flat relations of relational databases are basically sets of records, where each field of the records is a base type; in other words, relational databases have no bags, no lists, no variants, no nested sets, and no nested records. Values of these types can be explicitly constructed in CPL as follows, assuming the e's are values of appropriate types: $(l_1 : e_1, \ldots l_n : e_n)$ for records; $<l : e>$ for variants; $\{e_1,$ $\ldots e_n\}$ for sets; $\{|e_1, \ldots e_n|\}$ for bags; and $[e_1, \ldots e_n]$ for lists.

Example 6.2.2. The feature table of GenPept report 131470, a tyrosine phosphatase 1C sequence, is shown below.

```
(#uid:131470, #accession:"131470",
  #title:"... (PTP-1C)...", #feature:{(
  #name:"source", #start:0, #end:594, #anno:[
  (#anno_name:"organism", #descr:"Mus musculus"),
  (#anno_name:"db_xref", #descr:"taxon:10090")]),
  ...})
```

The particular feature displayed above goes from amino acid 0 to amino acid 594, which is actually the entire sequence, and has two annotations. The first annotation indicates that this amino acid sequence is derived from mouse DNA sequence. The second is a cross reference to the US National Center for Biotechnology Information taxonomy database.

The schemas and structures of all popular bioinformatics databases, flat files, and software are easily mapped into this data model. At the high end of data structure complexity are Entrez [6.25] and ACEDB [6.31], which contain deeply nested mixtures of sets, bags, lists, records, and variants. At the low end of data structure complexity are the relational database systems [6.11] such as Sybase and Oracle, which contain flat sets of records. Currently, Kleisli gives access to over 60 of these and other bioinformatics sources. The reason for this ease of mapping bioinformatics sources to Kleisli's data model is that they are all inherently composed of combinations of sets, bags, lists, records, and variants. We can directly and naturally map sets to sets, bags to bags, lists to lists, records to records, and variants to variants into Kleisli's data model, without having to make any (type) declaration beforehand.

We now come to CPL, the primary query language of Kleisli. An interesting feature of the syntax of CPL is the use of the comprehension syntax discussed in Chapter 1 [6.6, 6.30]. An example of a typical comprehension in CPL syntax is `{x * x | \x <- S, odd(x)}`, which returns a set consisting of the squares of all odd numbers in the set S. This is similar to the notation found in functional languages, the main difference being that the binding occurrence of x is indicated by preceding it with a backslash, and that the expression returns a set rather than a list. As in functional languages, `\x <- S` is called a "generator", and `odd(x)` is called a "filter". Rather than giving the complete syntax, we illustrate CPL by a few examples on a set of feature tables DB.

Example 6.2.3. The query below extracts the titles and features of those elements of DB whose titles contain `tyrosine` *as a substring.*

```
{ (#title: x.#title, #feature: x.#feature)
| \x <- DB, x.#title string-islike "%tyrosine%" };
```

This query is a simple project–select query. A project–select query is a query that operates on one (flat) relation or set. Thus the transformation that such a query can perform is limited to selecting some elements of the relation and extracting or projecting some fields from these elements. Except for the fact that the source data and the result may not be in first normal form, these queries can be expressed in a relational query language. However, CPL can perform more complex restructurings such as nesting and unnesting not found in common relational database languages like SQL, as shown in the following examples.

Example 6.2.4. The following query flattens DB *completely. The syntax* \a <--- f.#anno *has similar meaning to* \x <- DB, *but works on lists instead of sets. Thus it binds* a *to each item in the list* f.#anno.

```
{(#title:x.#title, #feature:f.#name, #start:f.#start, #end:f.#end,
   #anno-name:a.#anno_name, #anno-descr:a.#descr)
 | \x <- DB, \f <- x.#feature, \a <--- f.#anno};
```

Example 6.2.5. This query demonstrates how to do nesting in CPL. The subquery DB' *is the restructuring of* DB *by pairing each entry with its source organism. The subquery* ORG *then extracts all organism names. The main query groups entries in* DB' *by organism names. It also sorts the output list by alphabetical order of organism names, i.e.* [u | \u <- ORG] *converts the set* ORG *into a duplicate-free sorted list.*

```
let \DB' == {(#entry:x, #organism:a.#descr)
             | \x <- DB, \f <- x.#feature, \a <--- f.#anno,
               a.#anno_name = "organism"} in
let \ORG == {y.#organism | \y <- DB'}
in [(#organism:z, #entries:{v.#entry | \v <- DB', v.#organism = z})
    | \z <--- [u | \u <- ORG]];
```

The inspiration for CPL came from [6.28] where structural recursion was presented as a query language. However, structural recursion has two difficulties. The first is that not every syntactically correct structural recursion program is logically well defined [6.29]. The second is that structural recursion has too much expressive power because it can express queries that require exponential time and space.

In the context of databases, which are typically very large, programs (queries) are usually restricted to those which are "practical" in the sense that they are in a low complexity class such as LOGSPACE, PTIME, or TC^0. In fact, one may even want to prevent any query that has worse than $O(n \cdot \log n)$ complexity, unless one is confident that the query optimizer has a high probability of optimizing the query to no more than $O(n \cdot \log n)$ complexity. Database query languages such as SQL are therefore designed in such a way that joins are easily recognized, since joins are the only operations in a typical database query language that require $O(n^2)$ complexity if evaluated naively.

Thus Tannen and Buneman suggested a natural restriction on structural recursion to reduce its expressive power and to guarantee its well-definedness. Their restriction cuts structural recursion down to homomorphisms on the commutative idempotent monoid of sets, revealing a telling correspondence to monads [6.30]. A nested relational calculus, which is denoted here by $\mathcal{NRC}$, was then designed around this restriction [6.7]. $\mathcal{NRC}$ is essentially the simply-typed lambda calculus extended by a construct for building records, a construct for decomposing records by field selection, a construct for building sets, a construct for decomposing sets by means of the restriction on structural recursion. Specifically, the construct for decomposing sets is $\bigcup\{e_1 \mid x \in e_2\}$, which forms a set by taking the big union of $e_1[o/x]$ over each o in the set e_2. $\mathcal{NRC}$ (suitably extended) is implemented by the NRC Module of Kleisli and is the abstract counterpart of CPL, á la Wadler's equations relating monads and comprehensions[6.30].

The expressive power of $\mathcal{NRC}$ and its extensions are studied in [6.26, 6.13, 6.17, 6.7, 6.27]. The impact of these and other theoretical results on the design of CPL and Kleisli is that CPL adopts $\mathcal{NRC}(\mathbb{Q}, +, \cdot, -, \div, \sum, \leq^{\mathbb{Q}}, =)$ as its core, while allowing for full-fledged recursion and other operators to be imported easily as needed into the system. $\mathcal{NRC}(\mathbb{Q}, +, \cdot, -, \div, \sum, \leq^{\mathbb{Q}}, =)$ captures all standard nested relational queries in a high-level manner that is easy for automated optimizer analysis. It is also easy to translate a more user-friendly surface syntax such as the comprehension syntax or the SQL select-from-where syntax into $\mathcal{NRC}(\mathbb{Q}, +, \cdot, -, \div, \sum, \leq^{\mathbb{Q}}, =)$. It is thus a very suitable core.

6.3 Type Inference and Self-Describing Exchange Format

In a dynamic heterogeneous environment such as that of bioinformatics, many different database and software systems are used. They often do not have anything that can be thought of as an explicit database schema. Further compounding the problem is that research biologists demand flexible access and queries in ad hoc combinations. Thus, a query system that aims to be a general integration mechanism in such an environment must satisfy four conditions. First, it must not count on the availability of schemas. It must be able to compile any query submitted based solely on the structure of that query. Second, it must have a data model that the external database and software systems can easily translate to, without doing a lot of type declarations. Third, it must shield existing queries from evolution of the external sources as much as possible. For example, an extra field appearing in an external database table must not necessitate the recompilation or rewriting of existing queries over that data source. Fourth, it must have a data exchange format that is straightforward to use, so that it does not demand too much programming effort or contortion to capture the variety of structures of output from external databases and software.

Three of these requirements are addressed by features of CPL's type system. CPL has polymorphic record types that allow, for example,

```
\R => {x.#name | \x <- R, x.#salary > 1000}
```

which defines a function that returns names of people in R earning more than a thousand dollars. This function is applicable to any R that has at least the #name and the #salary fields, thus allowing the input source some freedom to evolve. CPL also has variant types that allow, for example, the value:

```
{ <#name: "John">, <#zip-code: 119613> }
```

This set contains objects of very different structures: a string carrying a #name tag and a number carrying a #zip-code tag. This feature is particularly useful in handling ASN.1-formatted [6.16] data from Entrez, one of the most important and most complex sources of DNA sequences, as it contains a profusion of variant types.

In addition, CPL does not require any type to be declared at all. The type and meaning of any CPL program can always be completely inferred from its structure without the use of any schema or type declaration. This makes it possible to logically plug in any data source without doing any form of schema declaration, at a small acceptable risk of run-time errors if the inferred type and the actual structure are not compatible. This is an important feature because most of our data sources do not have explicit schemas, while a few have extremely large schemas that take many pages to write down—for example, the ASN.1 schema of Entrez [6.20]—making it impractical to have any form of declaration.

We now come to the fourth requirement. A data exchange format is an agreement on how to lay out data in a data stream or message when the data is exchanged between two systems. In our case, it is the format for exchanging data between Kleisli and all the bioinformatics sources. The data exchange format of Kleisli corresponds one-to-one to Kleisli's data model. It provides for records, variants, sets, bags, and lists; and it allows these data types to be freely composed. In fact, the data exchange format completely adopts the syntax of value construction in CPL, as described in the previous section. Recall that CPL programs contain no type declaration. A CPL compiler has to figure out if a CPL program has a principle typing scheme. This kind of type inference is possible because every construct in CPL has an unambiguous most general type. In particular, the value construction syntax is such that it is possible to inspect only the first several symbols to figure out local type constraints on the corresponding value, as each value constructor is unambiguous. For example, if a {| bracket is seen, it is immediately clear that it is a bag; and if a (bracket is seen, it is immediately clear that it is a record. Thus, by adopting the value construction syntax of CPL as the data exchange format, the latter becomes self-describing.

A self-describing exchange format is one in which there is no need to define in advance the structure of the objects being exchanged. That is, there is no fixed schema and no type declaration. In a sense, each object being exchanged carries its own description. A self-describing format has the important property that, no matter how complex the object being exchanged is, it can be easily parsed and reconstructed without any schema information. To understand this advantage, one should look at the ISO ASN.1 standard [6.16] open systems interconnection. It is not easy to exchange ASN.1 objects because before we can parse any ASN.1 object, we need to parse the schema that describes its structure first—making it necessary to write two complicated parsers instead of one simple parser.

6.4 Kleisli Triples and Abstract Syntax

Let us now consider the restricted form of structural recursion which corresponds to the presentation of monads by Kleisli [6.30, 6.7]. It is the combinator $ext(\cdot)(\cdot)$ obeying the following three equations:

$$ext(f)\{\} = \{\}$$
$$ext(f)\{o\} = f(o)$$
$$ext(f)(A \cup B) = ext(f)(A) \ \cup \ ext(f)(B)$$

Thus, $ext(f)(R)$ is equivalent to the $\bigcup\{f(x) \mid x \in R\}$ construct of $\mathcal{NRC}$. The direct correspondence in CPL is: $\texttt{ext}\{e_1 \mid \texttt{\textbackslash x <- } e_2 \}$, which is interpreted as $ext(f)(e_2)$, where $f(x) = c_1$. This combinator is a key operator in the Complex Object Library of Kleisli and is at the heart of the NRC, the abstract representation of queries in the implementation of CPL. It earns its central position in the Kleisli system because it offers tremendous practical and theoretical convenience.

Its practical convenience is best seen in the issue of abstract syntax in the implementation of a database query language. The abstract syntax is the internal representation of a query and is usually manipulated by code generators; the better abstract synax is the one that is easier to analyse. It must not be confused with the surface syntax, which is what the usual database programmer programs in; the better surface syntax is the one that is easier to read. It is worth contrasting the **ext** construct to the comprehension syntax here. With regard to surface syntax, CPL adopts the comprehension syntax because it is easier to read than the **ext** construct. For example, the Cartesian product is expressed using the comprehension syntax as

```
{(x, y) | \x <- R, \y <- S}
```

In contrast, it is expressed using the **ext** construct as

```
ext{ext{{(x,y)} | \y <- S} | \x <- R}
```

which is more convoluted. However, the advantage of the comprehension syntax more or less ends here. With regard to abstract syntax, the situation is exactly the opposite! Comprehensions are easy for the human programmer to read and understand. However, they are in fact extremely inconvenient for automatic analysis and thus a poor candidate as an abstract representation of queries. This difference is illustrated below by a pair of contrasting examples in implementing optimization rules.

A well-known optimization rule is vertical loop fusion [6.15], which corresponds to the physical notion of getting rid of intermediate data and the logical notion of quantifier elimination. Such an optimization on queries in the comprehension syntax can be expressed informally as

$$\{e \mid G_1, \ldots G_n, \backslash x \text{ <- } \{e' \mid H_1, \ldots H_m\}, J_1, \ldots J_k\}$$
$$\rightsquigarrow \{e[e'/x] \mid G_1, \ldots G_n, H_1, \ldots H_m, J_1[e'/x], \ldots J_k[e'/x]\}$$

Such a rule in comprehension form is very simple to grasp. Basically the intermediate set built by the comprehension $\{e' \mid H_1, \ldots H_m\}$ has been eliminated, in favour of generating the x on the fly. In practice it is quite messy to implement the rule above. In writing that rule, the informal "..." denotes any number of generators or filters in a comprehension. When it comes to actually implementing it, a nasty traversal routine must be written to skip over the non-applicable G_i in order to locate the applicable $\backslash x$ <- $\{e' \mid H_1, \ldots H_m\}$ and J_i.

Let us now consider the ext construct. As pointed out by Wadler [6.30], any comprehension can be translated into this contruct. Its effect on the optimization rule for vertical loop fusion is dramatic. This optimization is now expressed as

$$\text{ext}\{e_1 \mid \backslash x \text{ <- } \text{ext}\{e_2 \mid \backslash y \text{ <- } e_3\}\}$$
$$\rightsquigarrow \text{ext}\{ \text{ext}\{e_1 \mid \backslash x \text{ <- } e_2\} \mid \backslash y \text{ <- } e_3\}$$

The informal and troublesome "..." no longer appears. Such a rule can be coded up straightforwardly in almost any implementation language. A similar simplification is also observed in proofs using structural induction. For comprehension syntax, when one comes to the case for comprehension, one must introduce a secondary induction proof based on the number of generators and filters in the comprehension, whereas the ext construct does not give rise to such complication. A related saving, pointed out to us by Wadler, is that comprehensions require two kinds of terms, expressions and qualifiers, whereas the ext formulation requires only one kind of term, expressions.

In order to illustrate this point more concretely, it is necessary to introduce some detail from the implementation of the Kleisli system. Recall from the introductory section that Kleisli is implemented on top of the Standard ML of New Jersey (SML). The type SYN of SML objects that represent queries in Kleisli is declared in the NRC Module mentioned in Section 6.2. The data constructors that are relevant to our discussion are:

```
type VAR = int              (* Variables, represented by int *)
type SVR = int              (* Server connections, rep. by int*)
type CO = ...               (* Rep. of complex objects *)
datatype SYN = ...
| EmptySet                  (* { }                        *)
| SngSet of SYN             (* { E }                      *)
| UnionSet of SYN * SYN     (* E1 {+} E2                  *)
| ExtSet of SYN * VAR * SYN (* ext{ E1 | \x <- E2 }  *)
| IfThenElse of SYN * SYN * SYN (* if E1 then E2 else E3 *)
| Read of SVR * real * SYN  (* process E using S, the real
        is the request priority assigned by optimizer *)
| Variable VAR              (* x *)
| Binary (CO * CO -> CO) * SYN * SYN (* Construct for caching
        static objects. This allows the optimizer to insert
        some codes for doing dynamic optimization *)
```

All SML objects that represent optimization rules in Kleisli are functions and they have type RULE:

```
type RULE = SYN -> SYN option
```

If an optimization rule r can be successfully applied to rewrite an expression e to an expression e', then $r(e) = \text{SOME}(e')$. If it cannot be successfully applied, then $r(e) = \text{NONE}$.

Example 6.4.1. We return to the rule on vertical loop fusion. As promised earlier, we have a very simple implementation:

```
fun Vertfusion(ExtSet(E1,x,ExtSet(E2,y,E3))) =
        SOME(ExtSet(ExtSet(E1,x E2),y,E3))
  | Vertfusion _ = NONE
```

6.5 Higher-Order Functions and Optimization

Another idea that we have exploited in implementing Kleisli is the use of higher-order functions. There are many advantages and conveniences of higher-order functions, besides allowing the expression of better algorithms as discussed in [6.27]. We use the implementation of the Kleisli Query Optimizer Module for illustration here. The optimizer consists of an extensible number of phases. Each phase is associated with a rulebase and a rule application strategy. A large number of rule application strategies are supported. The more familiar ones include BottomUpOnce, which applies rules to rewrite an expression tree from leaves to root in a single pass; TopDownOnce, which applies rules to rewrite an expression tree from root to leaves in a single pass; MaxOnce, which applies rules to the largest indices in a single pass; and so on, together with their multi-pass versions.

By exploiting higher-order functions, all of these rule application strategies can be decomposed into a "traversal" component that is common to all strategies and a very simple "control" component that is special for each strategy. In short, higher-order functions can generate all these strategies extremely simply, resulting in a very small optimizer core. To give some ideas on how this is done, some SML code fragments from the optimizer module mentioned in Section 6.2 are presented below.

The "traversal" component is higher-order and is shared by all strategies:

```
val Decompose: (SYN -> SYN) -> SYN -> SYN
```

Recall that SYN is the type of SML object that represents query expressions. The Decompose function accepts a rewrite rule r and a query expression Q. Then it applies r to all immediate subtrees of Q to rewrite these immediate subtrees. Note that it does not touch the root of Q and it does not traverse Q—it just non-recursively rewrites immediate subtrees using r. It is therefore very straightforward and looks like this:

```
fun Decompose r (SngSet N) = SngSet(r N)
| Decompose r (UnionSet(N,M)) = UnionSet(r N, r M)
| Decompose r (ExtSet(N,x,M)) = ExtSet(r N, x, r M)
| ...
```

A rule application strategy S is a function having the following type:

```
val S: RULEDB -> SYN -> SYN
```

The precise definition of the type RULEDB is not important to our discussion at this point and is deferred until later. Such a function takes in a rule base R and a query expression Q and optimizes it to a new query expression Q' by applying rules in R according to the strategy S.

Let Pick: RULEDB -> RULE be an SML function that takes a rule base R and a query Q and returns NONE if no rule is applicable, and SOME(Q') if some rule in R can be applied to rewrite Q to Q'. Then the "control" components of all the strategies mentioned earlier can be generated easily.

Example 6.5.1. The MaxOnce *strategy applies rules to maximal subtrees. It starts trying the rules on the root of the query expression. If no rule can be applied, it moves down one level along all paths and tries again. But as soon as a rule can be applied along a path, it stops at that level for that path. In other words, it applies each rule at most once along each path from the root to the leaves. Here is its "control" component:*

```
fun MaxOnce RDB Qry = case Pick RDB Qry
    of SOME ImprovedQry => ImprovedQry
    | NONE => Decompose (MaxOnce RDB) Qry
```

Example 6.5.2. The BottomUpOnce *strategy applies rules in a leaves-to-root pass. It tries to rewrite each node at most once as it moves towards the root of the query expression. Here is its "control" component:*

```
fun BottomUpOnce RDB Qry =
  let fun Pass SubQry =
        let val BetterSubQry = Decompose Pass SubQry
        in case Pick RDB BetterSubQry
             of SOME EvenBetterSubQry => EvenBetterSubQry
              | NONE => BetterSubQry end
  in Pass Qry end
```

Let us now present an interesting class of rules that require the use of multiple rule application strategies. The scope of rules like the vertical loop fusion in the previous section is over the entire query. In contrast, this class of rules has two parts. The inner part is "context sensitive" and its scope is limited to certain components of the query. The outer part scopes over the entire query to identify contexts where the inner part can be applied. The two parts of the rule can be applied using completely different strategies.

A rule base RDB is represented in our system as an SML record of type

```
type RULEDB = {
  DoTrace: bool ref,
  Trace: (rulename -> SYN -> SYN -> unit) ref,
  Rules: (rulename * RULE) list ref }
```

The `Rules` field of RDB stores the list of rules in RDB together with their names. The `Trace` field of RDB stores a function f that is to be used for tracing the usage of the rules in RDB. The `DoTrace` field of RDB stores a flag to indicate whether tracing is to be done. If tracing is indicated, then whenever a rule of name N in RDB is applied successfully to transform a query Q to Q', the trace function is invoked as $f\ N\ Q\ Q'$ to record a trace. Normally, this simply means a message like "Q is rewritten to Q' using the rule N" is printed. However, the trace function f is allowed to carry out considerably more complicated activities.

It is possible to exploit trace functions to achieve sophisticated transformations in a simple way. An example is the rule that rewrites if e_1 then ... e_1 ... else e_3 to if e_1 then ... true ... else e_3. The inner part of this rule rewrites e_1 to true. The outer part of this rule identifies the context and scope of the inner part of this rule: limited to the **then**-branch. This example is very intuitive to a human being. In the **then**-branch of a conditional, all subexpressions that are identical to the test predicate of the conditional must eventually evaluate to true. However, such a rule is not so straightforward to express to a machine. The informal "..." are again in the way. Fortunately, rules of this kind are straightforward to implement in our system.

Example 6.5.3. The if-then-else absorption rule is expressed by the `AbsorbThen` *rule below. The rule has three clauses. The first clause says that the rule should not be applied to an* `IfThenElse` *whose test predicate is already a Boolean constant, because it would lead to non-termination otherwise. The second clause says that the rule should be applied to all other forms of*

IfThenElse. *The third clause says that the rule is not applicable in any other situation.*

```
fun AbsorbThen (IfThenElse(Bool _,_,_)) = NONE
  | AbsorbThen (IfThenElse(E1,E2,E3)) =
    let fun Then E = if SyntaxTools.Equiv E1 E
          then SOME(Bool true) else NONE
    in case ContextSensitive Then TopDownOnce E2
        of SOME E2' => IfThenElse(E1,E2',E3)
         | NONE => NONE end
  | AbsorbThen _ = NONE
```

The second clause is the meat of the implementation. The inner part of the rewrite if e_1 then ... e_1 ... else e_3 to if e_1 then ... true ... else e_3 is captured by the function **Then** *which rewrites any e identical to e_1 to* **true.** *This function is then supplied as the rule to be applied using the TopDownOnce strategy within the scope of the* **then**-*branch ... e_1 ... using the* **ContextSensitive** *rule generator given below.*

```
fun ContextSensitive Rule Strategy Qry =
let val Changed = ref false     (* Set if Rule is applied *)
    val RDB = {                 (* Context-sensitive rule base *)
      DoTrace = ref true,
      Trace = ref (fn _ => fn _ => fn _ => Changed := true)
      Rules = ref [("", Rule)]}
    val OptimizedQry= Strategy RDB Qry (* Apply Rule using Strategy.*)
in if !Changed then SOME OptimizedQry else NONE end
```

This **ContextSensitive** *rule generator is reused for many other context-sensitive optimization rules, such as the rule for migrating projections to external relational database systems.*

6.6 Optimization of Queries on Relational Databases

Relational database systems are the most powerful data sources that Kleisli interfaces to. These database systems are themselves equipped with the ability to perform sophisticated transformations expressed in SQL. A good optimizer should aim to migrate as many operations in Kleisli to these systems as possible. There are four main optimizations that are useful in this context: the migration of projections, selections, and joins on a single database; and the migration of joins across two databases. The Kleisli optimizer has four different rules to exploit these four opportunities. We show them below.

Let us begin with the rule for migrating projections. A special case of this rule is to rewrite {x.#name | \x <- process "select * from T x where 1 = 1" using A} to { x.#name | \x <- process "select name =x.name from T x where 1 = 1" using A}, assuming A connects to an SQL database. In the original query, the entire table T has to be retrieved. In the rewritten query, only one column of that table has to be retrieved. More generally, if x is from a relational database system and every use of x is in the context of a field projection x.#*l*, these projections can be "pushed" to the relational database so that unused fields are not retrieved and transferred.

Example 6.6.1. The rule for migrating projections to a relational database is implemented by MigrateProj *below. The rule requires a function* FullyProjected x N *that traverses an expression* N *to determine whether* x *is always used within* N *in the context of a field projection and to determine what fields are being projected; it returns* NONE *if* x *is not always used in such a context; otherwise, it returns* SOME L, *where the list* L *contains all the fields being projected. This function is implemented in a simple way using the* ContextSensitive *rule generator from Example 6.5.3.*

```
fun FullyProjected x N =
let val (Count, Projs) = (ref 0, ref [])
   fun FindProjs (Variable y) = (if x=y then inc Count else ();NONE)
   | FindProjs (Proj (L, Variable y)) =
         (if x = y then Projs := L :: (!Projs) else (); NONE)
   | FindProjs _ = NONE
in ContextSensitive FindProjs BottomUpOnce N;
   if length (!Projs) = !Count then SOME (!Projs) else NONE
end
```

Recall from Section 6.4 that process M using S *is represented in the NRC Module as a* SYN *object* Read(S, p, M), *where* p *is a priority to be assigned by Kleisli. The* MigrateProj *rule is defined below. The function* SQL.PushProj *is one of the many support routines available in the current release of Kleisli that handle manipulation of SQL queries and other* SYN *abstract syntax objects.*

```
fun MigrateProj (ExtSet (N, x, Read (S, p, String M))) =
  if Annotations.IsSQL S      (* does S connect to SQL server? *)
  then case FullyProjected x N (* is x always in a projection? *)
     of SOME Projs => SOME (
          ExtSet (N, x, Read (S, p, String (SQL.PushProj Projs M))))
     | NONE => NONE
  else NONE
| MigrateProj _ = NONE
```

Second is the rule for migrating selections. A special case is to rewrite {x | \x <- process "select * from EMP e where 1 = 1" using A, x.#name = "peter"} to {x | \x <- process "select * from EMP e where e.name = 'peter'" using A}. In the original query, the entire table EMP has to be retrieved from the relational database A so that Kleisli can filter for Peter's record. In the rewritten query, the record for Peter is retrieved directly without retrieving any other records. More generally, if x is from a relational database and there are some equality tests x.#$l_1 = c$, then we should push as many of these tests to the database as possible.

Example 6.6.2. The rule for migrating selections to a relational database is implemented by MigrateSelect *below. It requires a function* FlattenTests Ok N *that traverses a tower of if–then–elses in N to extract equality tests satisfying the check Ok for migration; it returns a triple* (Pve, Nve, N'), *where Pve is a list of tests to be "and-ed" together, Nve is a list of tests to be negated and "and-ed" together, and N' is the remaining (transformed) unflattenable part of the tower; it satisfies* if $(\bigwedge Pve) \wedge \neg(\bigvee Nve)$ then N' else $\{\} = N$. *This function is implemented in a simple way as follows:*

```
fun FlattenTests Ok (IfThenElse (C, N, EmptySet)) =
    let val (Pve, Nve, N') = FlattenTests Ok N
    in if Ok C then (C::Pve, Nve, N')
        else (Pve, Nve, IfThenElse (C, N', EmptySet)) end
  | FlattenTests Ok (IfThenElse (C, EmptySet, M)) =
    let val (Pve, Nve, M') = FlattenTests Ok M
    in if Ok C then (Pve, C::Nve, M')
        else (Pve, Nve, IfThenElse (C, EmptySet, M')) end
  | FlattenTests Ok (ExtSet (N, x, M)) =
    let val (Pve, Nve, N') = FlattenTests Ok N
    in (Pve, Nve, ExtSet (N', x, M)) end
  | FlattenTests Ok N = ([], [], N)
```

The MigrateSelect *rule is defined below. The function* SQL.PushTest *is one of the many support routines available in the current release of Kleisli that handle manipulation of SQL queries and other* SYN *abstract syntax objects. The function call* SQLDict.ExtractLONG S C *uses the catalog of the relational database S to determine which of the fields in the output of the SQL query C are BLOB-like; a BLOB-like field is usually a very large string where equality test on it is not supported by the underlying database S. The function* CanPushTest *uses the output of* SQLDict.ExtractLONG *to produce a function to test if an expression is an equality test that can be migrated.*

```
fun MigrateSelect (ExtSet (N, x, Read (S, p, String M))) =
    if Annotations.IsSQL S        (* is S a relational db? *)
    then
      let (* can't migrate tests on BLOB-like fields *)
          val Forbidden = SQLDict.ExtractLONG S((!SQL.Mk) M)
          val Hash = IntHashTable.mkTable (1, Error.Goofed "Oops!")
          val _ = IntHashTable.insert Hash (x, Forbidden)
          val (Pve, Nve, N') = FlattenTests (CheckPushTest Hash) N
          (* convert lists Pve and Nve to tower of if-then-else *)
          val Pve = CvtTest S Pve
          val Nve = CvtTest S Nve
      in if (null Pve) andalso (null Nve)
          then NONE
          else SOME (ExtSet (N', x,
            Read (S, p, String (SQL.PushTest Pve Nve x M)))) end
    else NONE
  | PushSelect _ = NONE
```

Third is the rule for migrating joins. A special case of this rule is to rewrite

```
{y.#mgr | \x <- process "select * from EMP e where 1 = 1"
using A,
\y <- process "select * from DEP where 1 = 1"
using
x.#name = "peter", y.#name = x.#dep}
to
{ y.#mgr | \x <- process "select dept: e.dept
from EMP e, DEPT d where
e.name = 'peter' and d.name = e.dept"
using A }.
```

In the original query, the entire table EMP has to be retrieved once and the
entire table DEPT has to be retrieved n times, where n is the cardinality of
EMP. In other words, $n+1$ requests have to be made on the relational database
A. In the rewritten query, only one request is made on the relational database
A to retrieve the record in the join of EMP and DEPT matching Peter. More
generally, if x and y are from the same relational database and are always
used in the context of a field projection and there are some equality tests
$x.\#l_1 = y.\#l_2$, then this is a join that we should push to that database. The
advantages are that only one request is made, instead of $n+1$; only matching
records in the joins are retrieved, instead of entire tables; and the underlying
relational database system now also has more context information to perform
a better optimization.

*Example 6.6.3. The rule for migrating joins to a relational database is im-
plemented by* MigrateJoin *below. The function* SQL.PushJoin *is one of the
many support routines available in the current release of Kleisli that handle
manipulation of SQL queries and other* SYN *abstract syntax objects.*

```
fun MigrateJoin (ExtSet (N, x, Read (S, p, String M))) =
    if Annotations.IsSQL S        (* is S a SQL server? *)
    then case FullyProjected x N (* is x always in a projection? *)
      of SOME ProjO =>            (* ProjO are projs on outer reln *)
      let (* can't migrate tests on BLOB-like fields *)
          val Forbidden = SQLDict.ExtractLONG S ((!SQL.Mk) M)
          val Hash = IntHashTable.mkTable (10, Error.Goofed "Oops!")
          val _ = IntHashTable.insert Hash (x, Forbidden)
          (* PO, NO are tests on outer reln that can be migrated.
             N' is what's left after migration *)
          val (PO, NO, N') = FlattenTests (CheckPushTest Hash) N
      in case CheckJoin Hash x S N'
          of SOME (PI, NI, ProjI, ExtSet(U,v,Read(_,_,String W))) =>
            (* W is the inner relation of the join.
               PI, NI are tests on W that can be migrated.
               ProjI are projections on W.
               U is what's left after migration *)
            SOME (ExtSet (Rename x v U, x, Read (S, p, String (
            SQL.PushJoin x v ProjO ProjI (PO @ PI) (NO @ NI) M W))))
          | _ => NONE end
      | NONE => NONE
    else NONE
  | MigrateJoin _ = NONE
```

Most of the work is done by the function CheckJoin Hash S N', *which traverses* N' *to look for a subexpression that uses the same database* S *to be the inner relation of the join. If such a relation exists, it returns* SOME(PI, NI, ProjI, ExtSet (U,v,Read(S,q,String W))) *such that the set* W *can be used as the inner relation of the join, the join condition is* $(\bigwedge PI) \wedge \neg (\bigvee NI)$, ProjI *stores the projections in which the inner join variable* v *occurs, and* U *is an expression corresponding to the remaining operations that cannot be migrated.*

Fourth is the migration of selections across two relational databases. An example is the following rewrite of { y.#mgr | \x <- process "select * from EMP e where 1 = 1" using A, \y <- process "select * from DEPT d where 1 = 1" using B, x.#name = "peter", y.#name = x.#dept} to {y.#mgr | \x <- process "select dept: e.dept from EMP e where e.name = 'peter'" using A, \y <- process "select mgr: d.mgr from DEPT d where d.name ='" ^ x.#dept ^ "'" using B}. Here A and B are two different relational databases, so we cannot use MigrateSelect to push the test x.#dept = y.#name to B. The reason is that B, being a database different from A, has no access to the value of each instance of x.#dept. To enable such a migration, the value of each instance of x.#dept must be passed dynamically to B, as shown in the rewritten query above where x.#dept is dynamically concatenated into the SQL query select mgr: d.mgr from DEPT d where d.name = to be passed to B. Note that, in general, x does not need to come from a relational database and we simply need to look for equality tests involving the variable of the inner relation that we can migrate.

Example 6.6.4. The rule for migrating selections dynamically across two relational databases is implemented by MigrateSelectDyn *below. The function* SQL.PushTestDyn *is one of the many support routines available in the current release of Kleisli that handle manipulation of SQL queries and other* SYN *abstract syntax objects.*

```
fun MigrateSelectDyn (ExtSet (N, x, Read (S, p, String M))) =
  if Annotations.IsSQL S           (* is S a relational db? *)
  then
    let (* Vars are free variables in N *)
        val Vars = SyntaxTools.FV N
        (* can't migrate BLOB-like fields *)
        val Forbidden =  SQLDict.ExtractLONG S ((!SQL.Mk) M)
        val Hash = IntHashTable.mkTable (1, Error.Goofed "Oops!")
        val _ = IntHashTable.insert Hash (x, Forbidden)
        fun Ins y = IntHashTable.insert Hash (y, fn _ => false)
        val _ = IntSet.app(fn y => if y=x then () else Ins y) Vars
        (* Vars' are free variables of the entire expression.
           If there is a x.#1 = y.#1' for any y in Vars' inside N,
           then we may have something to migrate! *)
        val Vars' = IntSet.difference (Vars, IntSet.singleton x)
```

```
        (* Pve, Nve are tests that can be migrated dynamically.
           N' is what's left. *)
        val (Pve, Nve, N') = FlattenTests (fn N =>
          (CheckPushTest Hash N) andalso
          (IntSet.member(SyntaxTools.FV N, x))) N
  in if null Pve andalso null Nve
     then NONE
     else SOME (ExtSet (N', x, Read (S, p, Binary (fn (X,Y)=>
       COString.Mk (SQL.PushTestDyn Pve Nve Vars' x
       (COString.Km X) (CvtTestCO S Y)), String M, Record (
       Record.MkTuple (map Variable (IntSet.listItems Vars')))))))
  end
else NONE
| PushSelectDyn _ = NONE
```

The use of the `Binary` *(f, E, V) construct above is notable. When the Kleisli engine encounters this construct, it effectively executes $f(E, V)$ using the values of E and V at that point. In our example, E happens to be the original SQL query, V happens to store the values on which equality tests are to be performed, and f dynamically pushes V to E!*

Besides the four rules above, there is also a rule for reordering joins on two relational databases. While we do not provide here the implementation of the reordering rule in Kleisli, let us use an example to explain this optimization. Consider the join

```
{y.#mgr | \x <- process "select * from EMP e where 1 = 1"
using A,
\y <- process "select * from DEPT d where 1 = 1"
using B,
y.#name = x.#dept }.
```

We could optimize it as

```
{y.#mgr | \x <- process "select dept: e.dept from EMP e
where 1 = 1"
using A,
\y <- process "select mgr: d.mgr from DEPT d
where d.name = '" ^ x.#dept ^ '"
using B}.
```

But we could also optimize it as

```
{y.#mgr | \y <- process "select mgr: d.mgr, name: d.name
from DEPT d where 1 = 1" using B,
\x <- process "select 1 from EMP e
where e.dept ='" ^ y.#name ^ "'"
using A}.
```

Assume that there is an index on the name field of `DEPT`; then the first optimization is good, because for each `x.#dept`, the cost of looking up the corresponding manager in `DEPT` from B would be $\log n$ where n is the cardinality of `DEPT`. However, if such an index does not exist, that cost would be n

instead of $\log n$. In such a case, if an index happens to exist for the dept field of EMP in A, the second optimization would have been much better. More generally, in a nested loop, the order should be swapped if the outer relation is larger than the inner relation and there is an index on the selected field of the outer relation which has good selectivity.

6.7 A DOE "Impossible" Query

Having seen the optimizations for queries that involve relational database sources, we now show a sample bioinformatics query that benefits significantly from these optimizations. In fact, it is the very first bioinformatics query implemented in Kleisli in 1994 [6.12], and was one of the so-called "impossible" queries of a US Department of Energy Bioinformatics Summit Report (www.gdb.org/Dan/DOE/whitepaper/contents.html). The query was to find for each gene located on a particular cytogenetic band of a particular human chromosome as many of its non-human homologs as possible. Basically, the query means that for each gene in a particular position in the human genome, find DNA sequences from non-human organisms that are similar to it.

In 1994, the main database containing cytogenetic band information was the GDB [6.22], which was a Sybase relational database. In order to find homologs, the actual DNA sequences were needed and the ability to compare them was also needed. Unfortunately, that database did not keep actual DNA sequences. The actual DNA sequences were kept in another database called GenBank [6.8]. At the time, access to GenBank was provided through the ASN.1 version of Entrez [6.25], which was an extremely complicated retrieval system. Entrez also kept precomputed homologs of GenBank sequences.

So this query needed the integration of GDB (a relational database located in Baltimore) and Entrez (a non-relational "database" located in Bethesda). The query first extracted the names of genes on the desired cytogenetic band from GDB, and then accessed Entrez for homologs of these genes. Finally, these homologs were filtered to retain the non-human ones. This query was considered "impossible" as there was at that time no system that could work across the bioinformatics sources involved due to their heterogeneity, complexity, and geographical locations. Given the complexity of this query, the CPL query given in [6.12] was remarkably short. Since then Kleisli has been used to power many bioinformatics applications [6.4, 6.10, 6.9, etc.].

Example 6.7.1. The query mentioned is shown below.[2]

---

[2] Those who have read [6.12] will notice that the use of SQL encoded in strings—which is typical of JDBC-like interfaces and is very error prone—in the original implementation [6.12] has completely vanished. This is because the current version of Kleisli has made significant advancements in interfacing with relational databases.

```
sybase-add (#name:"gdb", ...);
readfile locus from "locus_cyto_location" using gdb-read;
readfile eref from "object_genbank_eref" using gdb-read;
{(#accn: g.#genbank_ref, #nonhuman-homologs: H)
| \c <- locus, c.#chrom_num = "22",
  \g <- eref, g.#object_id = c.#locus_id,
  \H == { u
  | \u <- na-get-homolog-summary(g.#genbank_ref),
    not(u.#title string-islike "%Human%"),
    not(u.#title string-islike "%H.sapien%")},
  not (H = { })}
```

The first three lines connect to GDB and map two tables in GDB to Kleisli.
After that, these two tables could be referenced within Kleisli as if they
were two locally defined sets, locus and eref. The next nine lines extract
from these tables the accession numbers of genes on Chromosome 22, use
the Entrez function na-get-homolog-summary to obtain their homologs, and
filter these homologs for non-human ones.

Besides the obvious smoothness of integration of the two data sources,
this query is also remarkably efficient. On the surface, it seems to fetch the
locus table in its entirety once and the eref table in its entirety n times from
GDB, as a naive evaluation of the comprehension would be two nested loops
iterating over these two tables. Fortunately, in reality, the Kleisli optimizer
is able to migrate the join, selection, and projections on these two tables into
a single efficient access to GDB using the optimizing rules from Section 6.6.
Furthermore, the accesses to Entrez are also automatically made concurrent.

Since the query above, Kleisli and its components have been used in a
number of bioinformatics projects such as GAIA at the University of Pennsylvania (www.cis.upenn.edu/gaia2), TAMBIS at the University of Manchester [6.4], and FIMM at Kent Ridge Digital Labs [6.24]. It has also been
used in constructing databases in pharmaceutical/biotechnology companies
such as SmithKline Beecham, Schering-Plough, GlaxoWellcome, Genomics
Collaborative, Signature Biosciences, etc. Kleisli is also the backbone of GeneticXchange Inc. (www.geneticxchange.com).

6.8 Warehousing of GenPept Reports

Besides the ability to query, assemble, and transform data from remote heterogeneous sources, it is also important to be able to conveniently warehouse
the data locally. The reasons to create local warehouses are several: (1) it
increases efficiency; (2) it increases availabilty; (3) it reduces risk of unin-
tended "denial of service" attacks on the original sources; and (4) it allows
more careful data cleansing that cannot be done on the fly.

The warehouse should be efficient to query and easy to update. Equally
important in the biology arena is that the warehouse should model the data

in a conceptually natural form. Although a relational database system is efficient for querying and easy to update, its native data model of flat tables forces us to unnaturally and unnecessarily fragment our data in order to fit our data into third normal form.

Kleisli does not have its own native database management system. Instead, Kleisli has the ability to turn many kinds of database systems into an updateable store conforming to its complex object data model. In particular, Kleisli can use flat relational database management systems such as Sybase, Oracle, MySQL, etc., to be its updateable complex object store. It can even use all of these systems simultaneously!

We illustrate this power of Kleisli using the example of GenPept reports. Kleisli provides several functions to access GenPept reports remotely from Entrez [6.25]: **aa-get-uid-general**, which retrieves unique identifiers of GenPept reports matching a search string; **aa-get-seqfeat-general**, which retrieves GenPept reports matching a search string; **aa-get-seqfeat-by-uid**, which retrieves the GenPept report corresponding to a given unique identifier; and so on. The National Center for Biotechnology Information imposes a quota on how many times a foreign user can access Entrez in a day. Thus, it would be prudent and desirable if we incrementally "warehouse" GenPept reports into a local database.

Example 6.8.1. Create a warehouse of GenPept reports. Initialize it to reports on protein tyrosine phosphatases.

```
! connect to our Oracle database system
oracle-cplobj-add (#name: "db", ...);
! create a table to store GenPept reports
db-mktable (
    #table: "genpept", #schema: (#uid: "NUMBER", #detail: "LONG"));
! initialize it with PTP data
writefile
    {(#uid: x.#uid, #detail: x) | \x <- aa-get-seqfeat-general "PTP"}
to "genpept" using db-write;
! index the uid field for fast access
db-mkindex (
    #table: "genpept", #index: "genpeptindex", #schema: "uid");
! let's use it now to see the title of report 131470
readfile GenPept from "genpept" using db-read;
{ x.#detail.#title | \x <- GenPept, x.#uid = 131470};
```

In this example, a table **genpept** is created in our Oracle database system. This table has two columns, **uid** for recording the unique identifier and **detail** for recording the GenPept report. A LONG data type is used for the **detail** column of this table. However, recall from Example 6.2.2 that each GenPept report is a highly nested complex object. There is therefore a "mismatch" between LONG (which is essentially a big uninterpreted string) and the complex structure of a GenPept report. This mismatch is resolved by Kleisli which automatically performs the appropriate encoding and decoding. Thus, as far as the Kleisli user is concerned, **x.#detail** has the type of GenPept report as given in Example 6.2.1. So they can ask for the title of a report as straightforwardly as x.#detail.#title.

Normally, when the daily quota for accessing Entrez is exhausted, the function aa-get-seqfeat-by-uid returns the empty set. However, it is possible to configure Kleisli so that a testable "null" value is returned instead. Then it would be useful to regularly examine the local warehouse to update "null" values to their proper GenPept records.

Example 6.8.2. A query to check for "null" values in the local warehouse and to replace them with proper GenPept reports. This query should be run regularly whenever new Entrez quota becomes available[3].

```
oracle-cplobj-add (#name: "db", ...);
readfile GenPept from "genpept" using db-read;
{ db-update (#table: "genpept",
    #selector: (#uid: y.#uid), #replacement: (#detail: y))
| \x <- GenPept, x.#detail = null,
  \y <- aa-get-seqfeat-by-uid (x.#uid)};
```

It would also be convenient to provide a function my-aa-get-seqfeat-by-uid that looks up the local warehouse for GenPept reports first, instead of going straight to Entrez. It would be even more useful if it also automatically updates the warehouse if it ever needs to fetch new reports from Entrez.

Example 6.8.3. Implement a "memoized" form of aa-get-seqfeat-by-uid. It uses the before (E, f) function of Kleisli which makes sure that the expression E is first evaluated to some value v and then evaluates and returns f(v). Also implement a "memoized" version of aa-get-seqfeat-general.

```
oracle-cplobj-add (#name: "db", ...);
readfile GenPept from "genpept" using db-read;
primitive my-aa-get-seqfeat-by-uid == \u =>
  { x.#detail | \x <- GenPept, x.#uid = u} before (\X =>
    if X = { }
    then ! the desired GenPept report was never fetched
        { x | \x <- aa-get-seqfeat-by-uid (u),
           _ <- db-insert (#table: "genpept",
                     #replacement: (#uid:x.#uid, #detail: x)) }
    else if X = { null }
    then ! quota ran out last time we tried to fetch
        { x | \x <- aa-get-seqfeat-by-uid (u),
           _ <- db-update (#table:"genpept",
                    #selector: (#uid: x.#uid),
                    #replacement:(#detail: x))}
    else X);
primitive my-aa-get-seqfeat-general == \s =>
  { x | \u <- aa-get-uid-general (s),
        \x <- my-aa-get-seqfeat-by-uid (u) };
```

---

[3] The oracle-cplobj-add ... and the readfile GenPept ... part are not needed if the local warehouse is currently connected.

6.9 A Protein Patent Query

In this section, we demonstrate Kleisli in the context of querying protein patents. We use Kleisli to tie together the following sources to answer queries on protein patents that are considerably more demanding than simple free-text search: (1) the protein section of the Entrez system at the National Center for Biotechnology Information [6.25]; (2) the BLAST sequence homology service at the the National Center for Biotechnology Information [6.2]; (3) the WU-BLAST2 sequence homology software from Washington University [6.1]; (4) the Isite system at the US Patent and Trademark Office (http://patents.uspto.gov); and (5) the structural classification of protein database SCOP at Cambridge MRC Laboratory of Molecular Biology [6.19].

Consider a pharmaceutical company that has a large choice of protein sequences to work on (i.e. to determine their functions.) A criterion for selection is patent potential. A process involving many data sources and steps is required, as depicted in Figure 6.2 below.

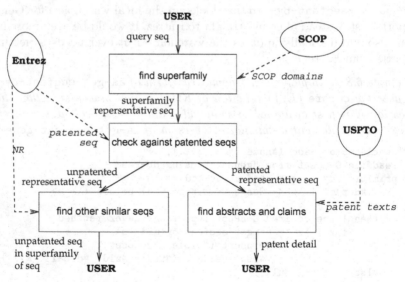

Fig. 6.2. Steps in Patenting Process

At the initial stage, we know only the amino acid sequence of these sequences and very little else. A question at this point would be: which of the sequences have already been patented? Existing patent search systems are IR systems that rely on English words. These systems suffer from the dichotomy of recall vs precision [6.14]: they either return only the highly relevant information at the expense of missing out a large portion of it, or return most of the highly relevant information at the expense of also returning a lot of irrelevent information. So using the standard interface to patent search systems is laborious and not always fruitful. Furthermore, at this early search, we do not even have an English word to use for searching—we have only the actual amino acid sequences! Thus, we need more reliable technology for comparing our protein sequences to those sequences already patented.

There are, however, two things in our favour. First, protein patents are generally based on protein function *and* primary sequence structure (i.e. the linear string of 20 letters in the amino sequence.) Second, tools that can reliably identify homology at the primary sequence structure level are available [6.23, 6.5]. Therefore, if patented protein sequences can be extracted from some database and prepared in a form suitable for such tools to operate on, we will have a means to reliably identify which of our sequences have not yet been patented. We obtain the patented sequences from the protein section of Entrez [6.25]. These are "warehoused" locally for greater efficiency. We then use WU-BLAST2 [6.1] for comparing our sequences against this warehouse for primary sequence structure homology.

After the unpatented protein sequences have been identified, the second question at this point is: which ones of these have the potential for wider patent claims? To understand this question it is necessary to recognize that protein patents are generally granted on a sequence *and* its function. While we do not know the functions of our proteins, because we have not done work on them yet, we know that proteins of the same evolutionary origin tend to have similar functions even if they differ significantly in their primary structure [6.18]. Using the terminology of SCOP, these proteins are in the same superfamily [6.19]. So one way to identify protein sequences that have the potential for wider patent claims is to find those having large number of unpatented sequences in the same families. Homology searching algorithms based on primary structure are generally not sufficiently sensitive to detect the majority of sequences in a typical superfamily [6.23], as the primary structures of distant members of the family are likely to have mutated significantly. So we need tools for homology at the tertiary structure level.

No reliable automatic tools for this purpose exist at this moment, because structural similarity at the tertiary level does not necessarily imply similarity in function. Nevertheless, reliable manually constructed databases of superfamilies exist. A very nice one is the SCOP database [6.19]. Therefore, if we screen our unpatented sequences against SCOP, we can pull out other *representative* sequences in their superfamilies and check which ones have already been patented, thus identifying superfamilies with good potential. We use WU-BLAST2 for the screening. After unpatented representatives of superfamilies have been found, it is still necessary to use them to fish out the rest of the unpatented members of superfamilies. This step can be accomplished by using BLAST [6.2] to remotely compare the representatives against the huge non-redundant protein database (NR) curated at the National Center for Biotechnology Information.

Having found these potentially good protein sequences, we are ready to work on them and hopefully patent our results. We thus need to ask the third question: what are the relevant prior arts? Retrieving the texts of patented sequences in the same superfamilies as our proteins would be very helpful here. This step is complementary to the previous step and can be carried out using exactly the same technology.

Example 6.9.1. We describe the query to find unpatented sequences in the same superfamily of a user-supplied protein sequence, as it is the most complicated of the three questions we mentioned. The program is shown below.

```
webblast-blastp(#name: "nr-blast", #db: "nr", #level: 2); ! line 1
localblast-blastp(#name:"patent-blast",#db:"patent-aa/blast/fasta");
localblast-blastp(#name: "scop-blast", #db: "scop-aa/blast/fasta")
seqindex-scanseq(#name:"scop-index",#index:"scop-aa/seqindex",
    #level:1);
scop-add "scop";                                            ! line 5
readfile scop-summary from "scop-aa/data/summary" using stdin;
primitive scop-accn2uid ==(set-index'(#accession,scop-summary)).#eq;
materialize "scop-accn2uid";
{(#title: z.#title, #accession: z.#accession, #uid: z.#uid,
    #class:i.#desc.#cl, #fold:i.#desc.#cf, #superfamily:i.#desc.#sf,
    #family:i.#desc.#fa, #protein:i.#desc.#dm, #species:i.#desc.#sp,
    #scop-pscore: x.#pscore, #nr-pscore: z.#p-n)          ! line 12
| \x <- process SEQ using scop-blast, x.#pscore <= PSCORE-SCOP,
    \i <- process <#sidinfo: x.#accession> using scop,
    \sf <- process <#numsid: i.#type.#sf> using scop,
    \sfuid <- scop-accn2uid (sf),                        ! line 16
    \y <- process <#get: sfuid.#uid> using scop-index,
    {} = { x | \x <- process y.#seq using patent-blast,
            x.#pscore <= PSCORE-PATENT },
    \z <- process y.#seq using nr-blast, z.#p-n <= PSCORE-NR };
```

As several data sources are used, we must first connect to them. We establish a connection **nr-blast** to BLAST at the National Center for Biotechnology Information for searching its NR database (line 1). The concurrency level of this connection is set to 2 for more efficient parallel access. We establish a connection **patent-blast** to WU-BLAST2 for searching against our local warehouse of patented proteins (line 2). We establish a connection **scop-blast** to WU-BLAST2 for searching against our local warehouse of SCOP representative sequences (line 3). We establish a connection **scop-index** to the index of SCOP representative sequences (line 4). Both warehouses and the index were constructed previously using Kleisli. We establish a connection **scop** to the SCOP classification database (line 5). These different connections to SCOP are needed because the SCOP database (line 5) contains only names and classification but not the actual representative sequences. We keep our sequences using a proprietary sequence indexing technology SeqIndex [6.21]. This index (line 4) allows us to quickly retrieve a sequence given an identifier or a pattern. Unfortunately, WU-BLAST2 requires the sequences to be stored in a different format. Hence we need the third connection to SCOP (line 3). We must also deal with one more problem: the identifiers used by SCOP (lines 3, 5) are different from the identifiers used by SeqIndex (line 4). We thus need a map between these identifiers, which is captured in the relation `scop-summary` (line 6). For fast access we create a memory-resident index `scop-accn2uid` to map SCOP identifiers to SeqIndex identifiers (lines 7–8).

After setting up connections to various data sources as described above, we are ready to issue our query to retrieve information about unpatented sequences in the same superfamily as our protein sequence `SEQ`. The information returned includes title, accession, unique identifer, and classification of these sequences (lines 9–11). Also returned with each unpatented protein sequence is its *pscore* with respect to SCOP and NR (line 12). The pscore is a reliable estimate of the corresponding sequence being a false positive, given by BLAST and WU-BLAST2 [6.2, 6.1]. For example, if BLAST returns a hit with a pscore of 0.001 to your sequence, then there is a one in a thousand chance of the hit being a fluke.

Let us step through the body of the program. Given the user sequence `SEQ`, we compare it against representative sequences in SCOP; we keep only those hits x whose pscore is within the error threshold `PSCORE-SCOP` (line 13). Since each hit x is good, the superfamily of x can be taken as the superfamily of the input sequence `SEQ`. We find the superfamily of x by simply asking SCOP to return us the SCOP classification i of x (line 14). The name and identifier of x's superfamily are stored in the `#desc.#sf` and `#type.#sf` fields of i respectively. Next, we need to fish out all representatives of that family from SCOP. SCOP gives us their SCOP identifiers `sf` (line 15). We convert these identifiers into unique identifiers `sfuid` in the SeqIndex where the sequences are kept (line 16). The SeqIndex is then accessed to give us the actual representative sequences y (line 17). Each representative sequence y is compared against patented sequences. We retain those that have no hits within the error threshold `PSCORE-PATENT` (line 18). These are representatives of our superfamily that are dissimilar to every patented sequence. We compare them against the NR database to fish out all sequences z that are similar to them within the error threshold `PSCORE-NR` (line 19). These are all the desired unpatented sequences in our superfamily.

Although the details of this process may seem confusing and it requires knowledge of the biomedical data resources available, it should be clear that a high-level technology such as Kleisli [6.32, 6.33, 6.12] greatly simplifies the process of developing interesting integrated systems. Furthermore, the Kleisli/CPL programs that access multiple distributed databases and software are clear and concise, easily written and easilty modifiable. The ability to return information on protein patents as shown above goes well beyond the reach of existing patent information servers based on standard IR systems.

6.10 A Clinical Data Query

We discuss one last example application of Kleisli; this time, in the context of querying clinical data. Clinical data usually involves historical records of patient visits. Queries over such data often involve the concept of "window", which is difficult to express using SQL.

We illustrate this point using a clinical database of Hepatitis-B patients. The database has a table BLD_IMG of type {(#patient: string, #date: num, #ALT: num, ...}[4]. Each time a patient's ALT level is measured, a new record is added to this table. One typical query of this data might be: "Find patients who have been tracked for at least 300 days and whose ALT level is always between 70 and 200 units." Such a query is easily expressed in SQL using the GROUP-BY and HAVING constructs and the aggregate functions MIN and MAX. However, another typical query might be: "Find patients whose ALT levels have stayed between 70 and 200 units for a period of at least 300 days." This query is problematic for SQL.

The challenges posed by the second query are the following. First, the records must be grouped by patients. Second, the records in each group must be sorted in chronological order. Third, the sorted records in each group must be segmented into subgroups such that within each subgroup either all ALT levels are between 70 and 200 units or all ALT levels are outside this range; futhermore, the date span of each subgroup must not overlap another subgroup. Fourth, the records of a patient are returned if they have a subgroup that spans at least 300 days and all ALT levels in that subgroup are between 70 and 200 units. The first, second, and fourth steps are straightforward in SQL. Unfortunately, the third step is not easily do-able in SQL.

This query is also not easily expressible in the Kleisli system using just the core calculus $\mathcal{NRC}(\mathbb{Q}, +, \cdot, -, \div, \sum, \leq^{\mathbb{Q}}, =)$. However, after a combinator for structural recursion [6.28] is imported into Kleisli, the query becomes straightforward. The combinator is list-sri, which corresponds to the fold operation in functional programming languages.

Example 6.10.1. We can define a function split *in terms of* list-sri *so that* split (d, c) S *returns a list* $[(x_1, Y_1), \ldots (x_n, Y_n)]$ *such that* $Y_1, \ldots Y_n$ *is* S *sorted chronologically;* $x_1, \ldots x_n$ *alternate between true and false; and* $c(y_j) = x_i$ *for each* $y_j \in Y_i$. *In the implementation below,* s2l *converts a set into a list and* list-gensort *sorts a list using a given ordering.*

```
primitive split == (\date, \check) =>
   (list-sri ((\x, \y) =>
      if y = []
      then [ (x.check, [x]) ]
      else if y.list-head.#1 = x.check
```

---

[4] As we do not want to complicate our discussion with arithmetic on dates, we treat the value of the date attribute in our patient database as an integer corresponding to the number of days passed since a particular fixed time point.

```
         then (y.list-head.#1, x +] y.list-head.#2) +] y.list-tail
         else (x.check, [x]) +] y, [])) o
     (list-gensort ((\x, \y) => x.date > y.date)) o s21;
```

Then the query *"Find patients whose ALT levels have stayed between 70 and 200 units for a period of at least 300 days"* can be defined as follows:

```
! access the hepatitis-B database on Oracle
oracle-cplobj-add (#name: "hepB", ...);
readfile BLD_IMG from "BLD_IMG" using hepB-read;
! define the ''window'' based on ALT level
primitive window == split(#date,\x =>(x.#ALT>70)
                    andalso (x.#ALT<=200));
! compute the answer
{p | \k <- set-unique { x.#patient | \x <- BLD_IMG },
    \P == { y | \y <- BLD_IMG, y.#patient = k },
    {()} = { () | \g <--- window (P), g.#1,
    (g.#2.list-rev.list-head.#date - g.#2.list-head.#date)>=300},
    \p <- P };
```

This implementation also shows the seamless integration of the operation of Kleisli, such as the use of *"window"*, with that of a relational database.

6.11 Conclusion

The Kleisli system and its high-level query language CPL embody many advances that have been made in database query languages and in functional programming. It represents a substantial deployment of functional programming in an industrial strength prototype that has had a significant impact on data integration in bioinformatics. Indeed, since the early Kleisli prototype was applied to bioinformatics, it has been used to efficiently solve many data integration problems in bioinformatics. To date, thanks to the use of CPL, we do not know of another system that can express general bioinformatics queries as succinctly as Kleisli.

There are several key ideas behind the success of the system. The first is its use of a complex object data model where sets, bags, lists, records, and variants can be flexibly combined. The second is its use of a high-level query language (CPL) which allows these objects to be easily manipulated. The third is its use of a self-describing data exchange format, which serves as a simple conduit to external data sources. The fourth is its query optimizer, which is capable of many powerful optimizations. The last-but-not-least reason behind the success of the system is the choice of SML as its implementation platform, which enables a remarkably compact implementation consisting of about 45,000 lines of code in SML. We have no doubt that without this robust platform of functional programming, it would have demanded much more effort to implement Kleisli.

Acknowledgements

We would like to end this paper by acknowledging the contributions to Kleisli by our colleagues. The first prototype of Kleisli/CPL was designed and implemented in 1994, while Wong was at the University of Pennsylvania. Peter Buneman, Val Tannen, Leonid Libkin, and Dan Suciu contributed to the query language theory and foundational issues of CPL. Chris Overton introduced us to problems in bioinformatics. Kyle Hart helped us in applying Kleisli to address the first bioinformatic integration problem ever solved by Kleisli. Wong redesigned and reimplemented the entire system in 1995, when he returned to Singapore. The new system, which is in production use in the pharmaceutical industry, has many new implementation ideas, has much higher performance, is much more robust, and has much better support for bioinformatics. Desai Narasimhalu supported its development in Singapore. Oliver Wu, Jing Chen, and Jiren Wang added much to its bioinformatics support under funding from the Singapore Economic Development Board. Finally, S. Subbiah took Kleisli to the market—Kleisli is now available commercially from GeneticXchange Inc (www.geneticxchange.com).

References

6.1 S. F. Altschul and W. Gish. (1996): Local alignment statistics. *Method. Enzymol.* **266**, 460–480.

6.2 S. F. Altschul et al. (1990): Basic local alignment search tool. *JMB* **215**, 403–410.

6.3 S. F. Altschul et al. (1997): Gapped BLAST and PSI-BLAST: A new generation of protein database search programs. *NAR* **25**, 3389–3402.

6.4 P. G. Baker et al. (1998): TAMBIS—transparent access to multiple bioinformatics information sources. *ISMB* **6**, 25–34.

6.5 G. J. Barton and M.J.E. Sternberg. (1987): Evaluation and improvements in the automatic alignment of protein sequences. *Prot. Eng.* **1**, 89–94.

6.6 P. Buneman et al. (1994): Comprehension syntax. *SIGMOD Record* **23**, 87–96.

6.7 P. Buneman et al. (1995): Principles of programming with complex objects and collection types. *TCS* **149**, 3–48.

6.8 C. Burks et al. (1992): GenBank. *NAR*, **20 Supplement**, 2065–2069.

6.9 J. Chen et al. (1998) Using Kleisli to bring out features in BLASTP results. *GIW* **9**, 102–111.

6.10 J. Chen et al. (1998): A protein patent query system powered by Kleisli. In *Proc. ACM SIGMOD Int. Conf. on Management of Data*, pages 593–595.

6.11 E. F. Codd. (1970): A relational model for large shared data bank. *CACM* **13**, 377–387.

6.12 S. Davidson et al. (1996): BioKleisli: A digital library for biomedical researchers. *Int. J. Digital Libr.* **1**, 36–53.

6.13 G. Dong et al. (1997): Local properties of query languages. *ICDT* **6**, 140–154.

6.14 W. B. Frakes and R. Baeza-Yates. (1992): *Information Retrieval: Data Structures and Algorithms*. Prentice Hall.

6.15 A. Goldberg and R. Paige. (1984): Stream processing. In *Proc. ACM Symp. on LISP and Functional Programming*, pages 53–62.

6.16 ISO. (1987): *Standard 8824. Information Processing Systems. Open Systems Interconnection. Specification of Abstraction Syntax Notation One (ASN.1)*.

6.17 L. Libkin and L. Wong. (1997): Query languages for bags and aggregate functions. *JCSS* **55**, 241–272.

6.18 H. Lodish et al. (1995): *Molecular Cell Biology*. W. H. Freeman.

6.19 A. Murzin et al. (1995): SCOP: A structural classification of protein database for the investigation of sequences and structures. *JMB* **247**, 536–540.

6.20 National Center for Biotechnology Information, National Library of Medicine, Bethesda, MD. (1992): *NCBI ASN.1 Specification*. Revision 2.0.

6.21 B. C. Ooi et al. (2002): Fast filter-and-refine algorithms for subsequence selection. In *Proc. Int. Data Engineering and Applications Symp.*, IEEE Computer Society, 243–255.

6.22 P. Pearson et al. (1992): The GDB human genome data base anno 1992. *NAR* **20**, 2201–2206.

6.23 W. R. Pearson. (1995): Comparison of methods for searching protein sequence databases. *Prot. Sci.* **4**, 1145–1160.

6.24 C. Schoenbach et al. (2002): FIMM, a database of functional molecular immunology—Update 2001. *NAR* **30**, 226–229.

6.25 G. D. Schuler et al. (1996): Entrez: Molecular biology database and retrieval system. *Method. Enzymol.* **266**, 141–162.

6.26 D. Suciu. (1997): Bounded fixpoints for complex objects. *TCS* **176**, 283–328.

6.27 D. Suciu and L. Wong. (1995): On two forms of structural recursion. *ICDT* **5**, 111–124.

6.28 V. Tannen et al. (1991): Structural recursion as a query language. *DBPL* **3**, 9–19.

6.29 V. Tannen and R. Subrahmanyam. (1991): Logical and computational aspects of programming with Sets/Bags/Lists. *ICALP* **18**, 60–75.

6.30 P. Wadler. (1992): Comprehending monads. *Math. Struct. Comp. Sci.* **2**, 461–493.

6.31 S. Walsh et al. (1998): ACEDB: A database for genome information. *Method. Biochem. Anal.* **39**, 299–318.

6.32 L. Wong. (2000): The functional guts of the Kleisli query system. *ICFP* **5**, 1–10.

6.33 L. Wong. (2000): Kleisli, a functional query system. *JFP* **10**, 19–56.

7. An Expressive Functional Data Model and Query Language for Bioinformatics Data Integration

Peter M.D. Gray[1] and Graham J.L. Kemp[2]

[1] Department of Computing Science, University of Aberdeen,
King's College, Aberdeen, AB24 3UE, UK
email: pgray@csd.abdn.ac.uk

[2] Department of Computing Science, Chalmers University of Technology,
SE-412 96, Göteborg, Sweden
email: kemp@cs.chalmers.se

Summary.

We argue the need for a *federated information infrastructure* that is perceived by users to be functionally integrated, yet maintaining its autonomy. There are various ways to do this, but the crucial issue is the provision of a common semantics and a shared data model. For this purpose we have adapted the Functional Data Model[1] and the Daplex language (originally designed for heterogeneous multi-database work) and developed a graphic user interface for it. We show how the model's ability to compose functions makes it able to combine computed data with stored data. This makes it especially suitable for bioinformatics queries involving derived data and we give examples from *antibodies*. We also describe a view mechanism for creating *derived relationships* as functions which adapt objects to a given application program, in order to simplify a shared data model.

7.1 Introduction – Multi-Database Integration

Bioinformatics data sets have grown remarkably in size and variety. From small early collections of sequences and protein structures compiled and distributed by individual scientists or labs, these activities are now often undertaken by major institutions and consortia such as the European Bioinformatics Institute (EBI), National Center for Biotechnology Information (NCBI) and the Research Collaboratory for Structural Bioinformatics (RCSB), who are devoted to this purpose. Data on protein structure and genome sequences and is now mirrored at various sites worldwide, and are cross-referenced with each other and with new data sets such as expression data, biological pathways, molecular interactions and single nucleotide polymorphisms.

As time goes on even more types of database will appear. The challenge is to integrate them in a flexible way that allows their continued expansion with local autonomy in updating, yet also allows us to automate a search for

---

[1] URL: http://www.csd.abdn.ac.uk/~pfdm

answers to queries over the whole collection of databases. This is the problem addressed by multi-database architectures.

Early computing science research concentrated on distributed database systems that were tightly coupled together and accessible through a shared data model (sometimes known as a global schema) [8.32]. Each of the participating databases exports a view of its tables or data that conforms to the shared data model, so that queries can be expressed using a common set of names for properties and relationships regardless of the database. The queries are then translated so that they are actually run against the local data using local names, and in the reverse direction, results can be scaled to take account of a change of measurement units or character codes.

One advantage of this is that the local query language can take advantage of indexing techniques that are locally available. Also the existing update programs can continue to run, using the local names and storage structures and indexes. If instead the data was to be copied into some homogeneous format on a central computer, a great deal of work would be needed to rewrite the update programs. Another possibility is for the data to be updated locally and periodically copied across to a central form, but then there is a delay in getting up-to-date information. Thus, the technical challenge of distributed systems is to write programs with the intelligence required to split queries apart into subqueries to be sent to separate local databases, each translated into a local query language, and then to combine all the results that are returned. Great advances have been made in optimising plans for efficient distributed execution (see other chapters in this Section).

The snag with commercial distributed databases has been in the over-tight coupling between the centralised data model and the individual databases, which made them very similar in structure. This was done partly for performance and partly in order to guarantee consistency of updates of pieces of linked data. Thus this model has tended to be used within large companies such as banks, but not across autonomous sites. Further the implementations made the shared data model very inflexible, so that when local databases evolved and added extra tables in different representations there was nowhere for this to be held in the shared model, and thus much of the extra information was not shared. Indeed, some observers became very pessimistic about global schema integration, and rejected it as impractical and requiring too much strong central management [7.3].

These pessimistic views began to change with the enormous success of the World Wide Web, which has shown that loosely coupled systems with only local updates can be remarkably flexible and effective. In this case users have been very willing to adjust their exported data to conform to a common syntax for marked up documents (HTML) and a common protocol for exchanging messages (HTTP). The question is whether scientists with information to exchange will go one step further and use a shared data model, because the problem with WWW is that the information is now exchanged largely in natural language which computers can transport but not understand! Thus it is much harder for computers to process answers from autonomous web sites and be sure that the questions asked were interpreted consistently at each site!

The spectrum of choices for data integration is summarised in Figure 7.1 taken from [7.21]. At the top we have tight-coupling options which, as we have seen, are too restrictive. At the bottom we have an agreement solely on syntax, which corresponds roughly to the use of HTML. In order to get the desired federated information infrastructure we believe, with Robbins, that we do not require the adoption of a common hardware platform or vendor DBMS, but we do need a "shared data model across participating sites".

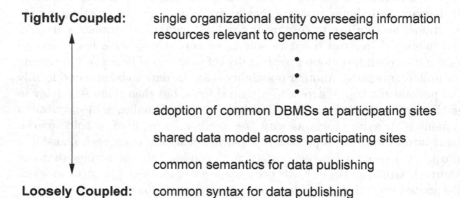

Tightly Coupled: single organizational entity overseeing information resources relevant to genome research

adoption of common DBMSs at participating sites

shared data model across participating sites

common semantics for data publishing

Loosely Coupled: common syntax for data publishing

Fig. 7.1. Spectrum of ways of coupling databases (taken from [7.21] with permission).

7.2 The Challenge of a Shared Data Model

The challenge of a shared data model (or object model) is considerable. In commercial data processing systems the model is presented as an Entity-Relationship (ER diagram). This diagramming technique has now been adapted to object-oriented systems, using the UML Class Diagram notation [7.22]. It is highly abstract in that it represents the names of entity classes and subclasses (in boxes or ovals), and of relationships between them (using thin lines), but it does not represent individual entity instances. Thus a box may be labelled to represent the whole class *protein* but not an instance such as *bovine beta-trypsin*. It also shows the cardinality of relationships – how few or how many entity instances can be related by the relationship to a given instance. This is shown by asterisks or a *crow's-foot* at each end of the relationship line, and it makes clear whether the relationship is optional (0..1) or mandatory (1..*).etc.

In object-oriented programming the diagrams are called object models. They have been adapted to show the methods (parametrised procedures) that are permitted to operate on the entities. They also show specialised subclasses (joined by a thick line) which can inherit behaviour defined by methods on the superclass. Beginners, unfortunately, tend to overuse subclasses instead of using them in combination with relationships. This is not surprising as there is still much to be understood about this process [7.7].

The effort and experience needed to make a data model or object model that will stand the test of time is considerable. Recently there has been a substantial project at the EBI (see *http://industry.ebi.ac.uk/applab/*) to make an object model in reusable sections for various kinds of genome sequence database, including the procedures that will work on the stored objects.

7.2.1 BRIDGE Protein Structure Data Model

Figure 7.2 shows a shared data model for protein structures developed as part of the EC-funded BRIDGE project [7.11, 7.6]. It looks deceptively simple as a finished article, but in fact it evolved through many versions and much debate. Such debates are likely to recur for the following reasons:

- People are too used to the way of naming or listing information in their own local database, and can't conceive of another more general way of doing it which adapts easily to suit other sites.
- Programmers have difficulty working at the abstract level of an ER diagram and tend to think in terms of familiar storage structures such as arrays or lists instead of recognising them as different ways to represent a one-to-many relationship.
- Object-oriented programmers are so keen to reuse the *behaviour* defined in some methods that they make otherwise unrelated entity classes into subclasses of a shared superclass despite a lack of biological or structural *raison d'être*.
- Some items can be easily computed from other items, and vice versa, so it is not clear which should be stored and which computed. If the computing takes a long time, then maybe both should be stored.

There can also be genuine scientific debate, especially where knowledge of the entities being modelled is evolving. For example, early work on backbone structure only recognised two kinds of backbone structure—alpha helix and beta strand. We debated whether to introduce some alternative classes of helix (a pi helix or a three-ten helix) which are known from observation but often so short as to be meaningless, and decided to reject them.

This is where we have to distinguish between storage of the data and storage of an *interpretation* of the data! The helices and strands are a useful widely shared interpretation, but they are really in the eye of the beholder! It may even be necessary to store an alternative interpretation according to

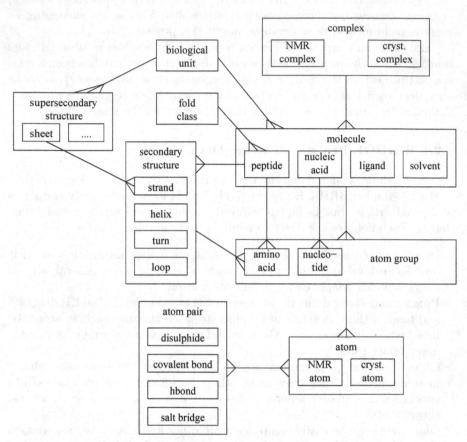

Fig. 7.2. Database schema for macromolecular structure. Each rectangle represents a class with certain properties or attributes. Relationships between classes (associations in a UML Class Diagram) are indicated by connecting lines. Some lines have *crow's feet* at the end, indicating a multi-valued relationship. A class can be specialised into subclasses which are like the parent superclass, but have extra attributes or relationships which only apply to the subclass. For example, *strand* is a subclass of *secondary structure* which is related to a *sheet*. It is shown as a rectangle within that for its superclass.

another theory! What one wants to avoid doing is generating a combinatorial explosion of interpretations according to varying assumptions! In this case it is better to wait until theory has advanced and the interpretation is better understood before attempting to store it.

7.3 Evolution of the Model

Even when a model has been designed it is essential that it can evolve, with matching updates to stored data where needed to store rearranged information or extra information. This was recognised early on in database research and it was understood that the conceptual schema which formally describes the data model could evolve, but that exported views could be used to hide this, where needed, for example to give a consistent interface to legacy application programs. It was also understood that the underlying storage representation (which is chosen to give efficient access or update performance or some compromise) might well change without changing the data model. This is allowed by the principle of data independence. However, some users with home-made database systems break this principle in a shortsighted search for extra performance. They then find they have a totally inflexible data model tied to one particular storage representation, with a suite of programs that gets impossible to maintain! History shows that this should be avoided at all costs! It is one reason why good relational databases, which understood this, have lasted so well.

The easiest changes to make in an evolving model are those involving the addition of an extra named attribute to an existing entity class, or the introduction of a new entity class together with its properties (attributes). One can also introduce new relationships between existing entity classes. This commonly happens as science progresses and for example a new kind of experiment is introduced with measurements that need to be related back to existing entities such as proteins or brain regions. It is also possible to replace a stored attribute by a rule or procedure that computes it from some more primitive properties. This can happen when observations which were thought to be independent turn out not to be.

Another useful mechanism is to introduce a new subclass which is a specialisation of an existing class, as in the case of the *pi helix* mentioned earlier. The instances of the subclass (technically a subtype) will have all the attributes of the existing entity class, and be counted as identifiable members of it, but they will also have extra attributes or relationships which are only meaningful for that subclass. All these forms of evolution are easily supported in a functional data model.

7.4 Why Not Use Web Storage?

At this point, it may be useful to discuss why, since much sequence data is held in self-describing files with tag names for fields at the start of each line, this interchange format cannot be used as a data model. After all, it is very similar to XML! The answer is that the syntax descriptions (DTD) for XML are overly prescriptive on the ordering of fields, and are not easy to extend. Thus we should consider these files as the load files for the database, not the database itself! Thus the data in a database may have been loaded from a number of different file formats, on different occasions. What matters is not the format used, but that it conforms to an integrated data model that is extensible.

Despite the shortcomings of web pages for storing data *per se*, there is no doubt that web browsers are a good way to view the results of structured database searches, and that they are becoming a universal end-user interface. Thus a better way forward is to hold the basic data in a structured database according to a data model, and to provide interfaces that generate web pages on demand in order to browse the data. It is even possible to give the illusion of querying the generated pages for selected results, whilst the actual results are produced by generated database queries run on the underlying data. This is increasingly common, using the PHP sublanguage from within Java.

7.5 P/FDM Multi-Database System

In our current work, we are using the P/FDM database management system [8.10], which is based on a powerful shared data model (FDM) [8.33], to provide access to data held in different physical formats and at different sites [7.15]. The FDM and its query language, Daplex, arose originally from the MULTIBASE project [8.25] which was an early project in integrating distributed heterogeneous database systems. Another feature of FDM is that both stored and derived data are accessed in a uniform way, through functions (hence the name functional data model). This flexibility allows us to derive data through calls to remote databases.

We continue to improve and extend the FDM because of its solid theoretical foundation and amazing adaptability [8.8]. Its data manipulation language (Daplex) strongly influenced early OODBMS such as IRIS. In fact our current version of Daplex is very similar to the ODMG language OQL [7.2] both in syntactic structure and in how it handles and passes object identifiers as values. It is recursively defined and strongly typed (see http://www.csd.abdn.ac.uk/~pfdm/).

Our main use of this database has been to support three-dimensional structural analysis and protein modelling [7.14], and we have extended our initial general protein structure database to enable specialised techniques to be developed for modelling antibodies [8.21, 7.20]. A strong semantic data model like the FDM provides data independence, and we have experimented with several alternative physical storage formats, including hash files and relational tables [8.20].

Since this model uses object identifiers it is also potentially useful for federated access both to the newer ODMG object databases and to hybrid object-relational databases. These latter have the advantage of storing many special data types such as images and sound, possibly in huge volumes, which can be cross-referenced from the usual relational tables of numerical and character data [7.1].

Our first prototype federated system [7.15] (since superseded by the P/FDM Mediator, see next chapter) accessed biological databanks held at the EBI. These databanks consist of formatted flat files, and a system called the sequence retrieval system (SRS) maintains cross-references between related entries in different databanks held as indexes in separate tables. SRS also provides a command line interface which supports simple data selection requests. Our prototype system used a description of the EBI databanks which mapped these onto entities, relationships and attributes in an FDM schema. Queries submitted by the user were analysed and partitioned automatically into parts which refer to data held locally and data held at the EBI. Code generators constructed data access requests to retrieve those data values from the local databases and SRS code was produced and sent to the EBI for execution. This process is illustrated in Figure 7.3, which shows in detail the steps in processing a query that relates structural data in a local antibody database and data held at the EBI.

7.6 Combining Calculation and Searching in an Antibody Database

While well suited to particular categories of protein structure queries, relational systems have limitations. For example, complex calculation involving distances and angles cannot be combined easily with data retrieval, so queries can only use values which are explicitly stored in the database.

To get round these problems, programmers can use database calls from Perl or ODBC/JDBC calls from C/Java to retrieve relational tuples into a program, where a small calculation takes place. Instead, in a functional language, both calculation and data access are uniformly expressed in a clean *compositional* fashion. This makes it much easier for an optimiser, as discussed in other chapters, to rearrange the calculation, even using parallel processors or a remote host. This is the true significance of the functional approach.

In the work presented here, we have integrated antibody structure and sequence data to develop a system tailored to antibody analysis and modelling. We give this example in detail in order to illustrate the usefulness and

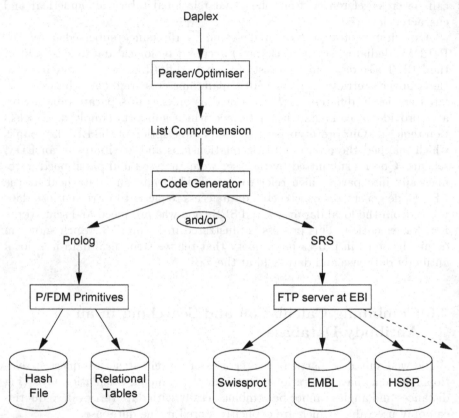

Fig. 7.3. A Daplex query may be translated into a Prolog query to access data held locally or SRS code to access data at EBI. However, some Daplex queries will need to access both local and remote data and so will be translated into a combination of Prolog and SRS code.

```
      * *        * *                    ** **        *  **
... SSLSASLGDRVTISCRASQ------DISNHLNWYQQKPDGTVKLLIYY ...
... AIMSASPGEKVTMTCSASS-------SVSYMHWYQQKSGTSPKRWIYD ...
... SSLAVSVGEKVTMSCQSSQSLLYNSNQKNFLAWYQQKPGQSPKLLIYW ...
... SSLSASVGGRVTITCRASQ------GISNNLNWYQQKPGKTPKLLIYA ...
... LSLPVSLGDQASISCRSSQSLVHS-NGNTYLHWYLQKPGQSPKLLIYK ...
```

Fig. 7.4. Extract from a multiple alignment showing parts of five protein sequences. Asterisks mark the 11 of the 48 alignment positions at which all five proteins have the same residue. Hyphens represent gaps which have been introduced artificially to improve the alignment by increasing the number of matches found elsewhere.

extensibility of calling out from P/FDM to computed functions, which can be in different compiled languages.

7.6.1 Antibody Sequences

We find a real need for this combination of data access and calculation in the study of *antibodies*. These are large proteins produced on demand by the immune response system. Normally they consist of four chains of amino acid residues – two long chains of around 400 residues (referred to as *heavy* chains) and two shorter chains of around 220 residues (referred to as *light* chains). Several thousand antibody sequences have been determined experimentally. These have been collected and organised by Kabat et al. [7.13]. We have taken sequence data from this collection (which we will refer to as "Kabat data bank") and loaded this into our object-oriented database in accordance with the schema shown in the lower part of Figure 7.5. A fuller Daplex definition of this schema is given in [8.21]. In the Kabat data bank, the sequences are organised in "groups" with strong similarities. We currently store sequences in 34 of these groups, storing on average around 100 sequences for each group.

Within each group, Kabat et al. [7.13] have identified positions at which a particular residue, or residues with similar chemical properties, invariably or very frequently occur. These positions can be grouped together into contiguous blocks referred to as framework regions. In addition to these relatively conserved regions there are others where there is no apparent "preference" and any residue type is found. These are sometimes described as the "hypervariable" regions. The entity class called kabat_group_region is used to record the extents of these regions, and the familiar codes used to refer to them. These groups and regions are well known to scientists working in this field.

When the sequences are entered into the Kabat data bank, they are compared with one another, and aligned to give the best match. An extract from such a multiple alignment is shown in Figure 7.4. Since the sequences will sometimes differ in length, it is often necessary to introduce artificial breaks in the string of characters representing a sequence to maximise the number of residue matches with other sequences and thereby achieve the best possible alignment (differences in the sequence lengths are expected to have arisen through evolution, and "gaps" correspond to insertions and deletions in the genetic material). While it may be useful to know what residue is, say, the 40th in a chain it is generally more useful to know what kind of residue is at, say, position 45 in the multiple alignment. There is one kabat_group_position entity instance per multiple alignment position (i.e. alignment column) within each subgroup and both the well-known Kabat data bank code for each position and the ordinal number of this position within a multiple alignment (contiguous numbers, starting at one) are recorded as attributes of this class.

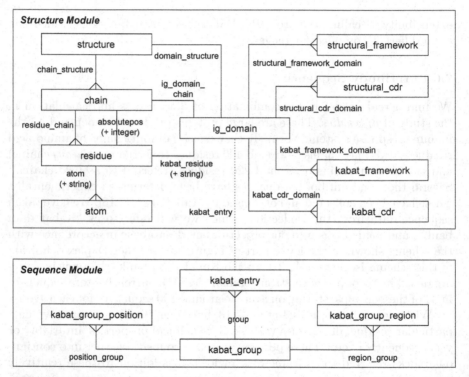

Fig. 7.5. Schema diagram. Object classes are represented by rectangular boxes. One-to-many relationships are shown as lines fanning out into a crow's-foot. The dotted line represents an optional (partial) relationship between structural information and sequence information held on the same antibody in different database modules.

7.7 Antibody Data Searches

Antibodies are able to bind foreign bodies like viruses and toxins, which are called *antigens*. A VL domain from a light chain usually lies beside a VH domain from a heavy chain in such a way that each contributes three loops to form a surface patch that is directly involved in binding the antigen. Structural studies of variable domains [7.4] [7.5] have shown that these loops can adopt very different conformations from one antibody structure to another, while the framework of strands remains relatively conserved. These structurally variable regions roughly correspond to the hypervariable regions in sequences listed by Kabat et al., but the endpoints are often different. These regions, whether sequence-based or structure-based, are commonly referred to as the complementarity determining regions (CDRs), and it is these that normally establish direct contact with the antigen. It is they that give an antibody its specificity, and so sequence modifications to an antibody in these regions may result in a molecule that binds with higher or lower affinity, or even binds to a different antigen.

We have designed a database (Figure 7.5) to hold both structural CDRs and framework regions (established by Chothia and Lesk [7.4]) and sequence-based CDRs and framework regions (established by Kabat et al. [7.13]). These are stored in the **structural** and **sequence** modules of the database respectively, and linked by the relationship **kabat_entry**.

7.7.1 Antibody Structure Searches

The following examples use the schema of the structure module (Figure 7.5). They are representative of actual structural queries, and demonstrate how calculation is combined with data retrieval. Example queries on the sequence module are given in the next chapter.

Arrangements of Strands within an Immunoglobulin Domain. The database can be used to examine spatial relationships between strands within a domain. Looking at the three-dimensional structure of the antibody with PDB code 7FAB, we observe that the valine residue at Kabat position 33 and the alanine residue at position 71 in the light chain are in different sheets but are adjacent in space with their side chains directed towards each other. We may speculate that the separation between the two sheets at this point may be related to the kinds of residues at these positions. The following Daplex query examines all VL domains and prints the PDB code, the names of residues at (Kabat) positions 33 and 71 and the computed distance between their Cβ atoms. Note the use of functions with two arguments, such as kabat_residue(d, "33"), to denote "the residue in object d at position 3":

```
for each d in ig_domain such that
   domain_type(d) = "variable" and chain_type(d) = "light"
print(protein_code(d),
   name(kabat_residue(d, "33")),
   name(kabat_residue(d, "71")),
   distance(atom(kabat_residue(d, "33"), "CB"),
```

```
atom(kabat_residue(d, "71"), "CB")));
```

We find that when the residue at Kabat position 33 is valine, which has a small branched side chain, or methionine, which has an unbranched side chain, then the separation is between 4.15 and 4.56 angstroms. However, when leucine, which has a larger branched side chain, is at position 33 we find the separation between the Cβ atoms to be greater in all cases. In all of the VL structures in the database that have leucine at position 33, a large aromatic residue is present at position 71. The two other structures that have an aromatic residue at position 71 have a methionine residue at position 33, and their separation is small.

The function *distance* calculates the distance between the two atoms given as its arguments. It would be impractical to store the distance between all pairs of atoms in the database, so it is vital that quantities can be calculated when needed.

Orientation of Complementarity Determining Regions. Another example query showing the use of functions in calculation concerns the orientation of the CDR binding regions introduced earlier. Chothia and Lesk [7.4] and Chothia et al. [7.5] have made careful studies of these regions, and have identified groups of variable domains whose CDRs have similar conformations. They observe that in a particular class of VL domains (called Vλ domains), the first five residues of the L1 region have a similar conformation, and that the side chain of the isoleucine residue at the fifth position in the L1 region points inwards towards the centre of the domain. We can query the database to investigate this observation.

First we must devise a way to express "side chain pointing inwards". The first bond in the side chain connects the alpha-carbon (Cα) atom to the beta-carbon (Cβ), and the direction of this bond can be used as the direction of the side chain. Now, VL domains have a disulphide bond connecting the cysteine residues at Kabat positions 23 and 88. Visual inspection of any one of the known VL domain structures shows this disulphide bridge to be located in the middle of the VL domain, between the two β-sheets. Therefore, the angle defined by the Cβ of the fifth residue in the L1 loop, the Cα of that residue and the Cα of residue 23 will be acute if the fifth residue in the L1 loop is directed towards the centre of the VL domain. A function called *angle* takes three atoms as its arguments and returns the angle (in degrees) defined by their centres. This function calls out to a routine written in C to calculate this value. The following query finds all L1 regions from Vλ domains and prints their PDB code, the names of the residues at the relevant positions and the calculated angle:

```
for each c in structural_cdr such that name(c) = "L1"
   for the d in structural_cdr_domain(c) such that
       chain_class(d) = "lambda"
     for the r1 in residue(c,5)
```

```
        for the r2 in kabat_residue(d,"23")
    print(protein_code(d), name(r1), name(r2),
        angle(atom(r1,"CB"), atom(r1,"CA"), atom(r2,"CA")));
```

The results for this query are as follows:

```
1FB4 ILE CYS 19.3
2FB4 ILE CYS 19.3
2RHE ILE CYS 18.8
3FAB ILE CYS 16.6
7FAB ILE CYS 15.8
8FAB ASN CYS 116.2
```

The first five results support the observations made by Chothia and Lesk [7.4]. The structure 8FAB has been determined since that earlier study. It has a very different L1 conformation and its fifth residue is an outward-pointing asparagine rather than an inward-pointing isoleucine.

7.7.2 Graphic Editor for Queries using the Data Model

In order to help protein scientists to use our database, we have developed an interactive query-builder [8.7] that has at its centre a graphical representation of the database schema. Figure 7.6 shows a screenshot of this Java application in use with the schema for Figure 7.5. Users construct queries by clicking on entity classes and relationships in the schema diagram and constraining the values of attributes selected from menus. As this is done, fragments of Daplex text are automatically generated, and the query is built up in the query editor window shown, with hyperlinks back to the schema diagram. Note that the temporary empty rectangular boxes will expand on clicking to give a separate expression editor window where the user fills in values from menus to replace them. Any line of the query can be modified at any time, and highlightable parts can be deleted.

Once complete, the query is submitted to the database via a CORBA interface [8.22]. Results satisfying the selection criteria are displayed in a table in a separate result window. A particularly novel feature of the interface is a *copy-and-drop* facility (Figure 7.7) which enables the user to select and copy data values from the result window and merge them into the original query automatically in the appropriate place, to produce a more selective query.

This differs from other interfaces in that it explicitly encourages the user to understand the textual version of the query as it is built up and evolves, by relating it back to the schema through hyperlinks, and also to values from tabulated intermediate results. We believe this is necessary for complex scientific queries.

180   Peter Gray et al.

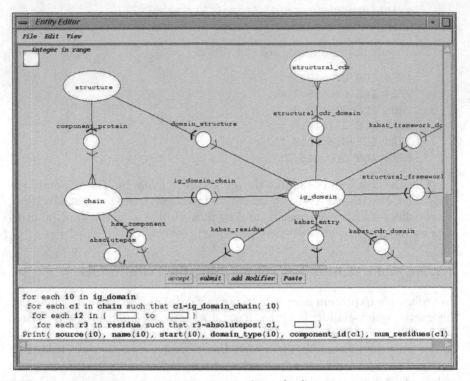

Fig. 7.6. Visual Navigator query interface (from [8.7]).

name(i0)	subgroup(i0)	resolution(s1)
VL	kappa-V	2.8
VH	III	1.9
VL	lambda-I	1.9
VH	III(B)	2.6
VL	kappa-VI	2.6

Fig. 7.7. Visual Navigator "copy-and-drop" facility to modify the query to select in future for particular values appearing in the results as highlighted. Generates simple combinations of *and* and *or* depending on whether values are in
the same row or same column. This example adds such that .. (name(i0)="VH"
and resolution(s1)=1.9) or (name(i0)="VL" and resolution(s1)=2.6) to the
query.

7.8 Compositionality of Derived Collection Views

This is another example of the extensibility and conceptual clarity of the functional approach. It has allowed us to extend the P/FDM semantic data model to include a complex form of derived data, without generating a combinatorial explosion of specialised classes. It also provided an easy extension to the query language allowing one to compute over derived views.

In our work with scientific databases we have found the need to adapt external method code to calculate with sets of stored data values from the database at a chosen level of aggregation, in an is-part-of hierarchy. In the course of doing this we have found the need for a kind of view over collections of objects at various such levels of aggregation. This *collection view* is distinguished by a particular kind of transitivity (or inheritance) based on the abstract is-part-of relationship. At first sight it fits the usual kind of subtype inheritance used in databases, but this turns out not to be so.

Consider another more familiar hierarchy of geographic entities at various levels, representing spatial regions. Each region encloses a collection of non-overlapping regions at the next level. For example, we could have countries enclosing their states, within which are their related districts each containing their related towns. On an ER diagram these correspond to distinct entity classes joined together by a hierarchy of one-to-many relationships. Suppose we want a view that gives us all the towns in a state, in order to compute demographic statistics or the economic profile of a state. This relationship between a state and its towns is a derived one, implied by the transitivity of existing relationships.

Unlike normal views, where we derive a class containing new non-persistent objects, here we are deriving a relationship to sets of existing objects (towns in this example). We wish to avoid storing these derived relationships persistently, since they are based on transitivity, with many possible combinations that can quickly be derived at run time.

The real value of this is in a clear conceptual separation of this kind of derived relationship in an ER diagram, even when the corresponding functions are implemented in an ad hoc fashion as interfaces to Java or C++. It is useful where the data is structured around part–whole relationships, with various levels of repeated subunits, which is not uncommon.

7.9 Protein Structure: Motivation for Collection Views

The idea of collection views presented in this chapter was motivated by our participation in schema design for the BRIDGE project, as described in section 7.2.1. An extract from this schema diagram (Figure 7.2) is shown on the left side of Figure 7.8. We needed to interface entity classes in this figure to functions/methods shown on the right that calculate aggregate values, such

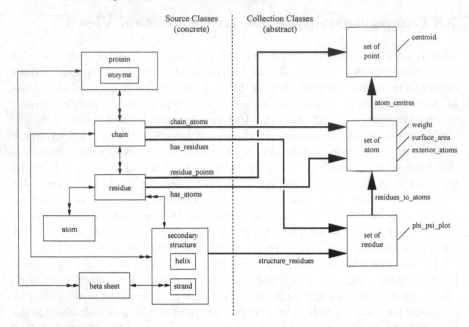

Fig. 7.8. Extract from the protein structure database. Thick arrows represent *adapter functions* which populate collection classes, shown as the boxes they point to. Thin arrows represent relationships named in the schema. Nested boxes represent specialised subtypes of the enclosing box.

as `weight` or the position of the `centroid`, from sets of instances of these entity classes.

Consider an example of how this could be introduced into a well-structured object query language such as OQL. We can imagine a query in OQL style to select certain residues based on `weight`, which needs an interface, as described below, from the `weight` calculation function to a selected set of atoms.

```
select  r.name
from    residue r
where   weight(r) > 20.0
```

Here `weight` does not apply directly to `residue`, which needs adapting via the adapter function `has_atoms` (labelled thick arrow in Figure 7.8) to generate a set of atoms to which `weight` can be applied individually.

We started by using just two kinds of relationship in the schema: subclass–superclass relationships (e.g. an `enzyme` *is-a* `protein`) and named relationships, such as those between classes `chain` and `protein`, and between classes `residue` and `chain`. Subclass–superclass relationships could be used to inherit key definitions, attributes and methods, but other named relationships were not used to provide inheritance. We now explain how we found the need for a third sort of relationship, representing an adapter as shown by the thick arrows in Figure 7.8.

From the object-oriented viewpoint, one of the most significant aspects is that the same set of objects may be viewed at different levels of abstraction, ignoring differences of detail that are important at lower levels. Thus a helix object may be viewed as an ordered sequence of residues (ignoring 3-D coordinates) which may in turn be viewed as a set of residues (unordered) which can be viewed as a merged set of atoms with some derived property (weight, surface area). However, it is also meaningful to ask for the weight of a chain, or the weight of an individual residue. In designing the schema, we wanted to capture the notion of kinds of protein fragment to which functions such as weight or surface area could be applied. Therefore, our early schema diagrams included classes like *set-of-residue* and *set-of-atom*, but we tried to make these just like other stored entity classes, and in order to inherit functions defined on these classes we found ourselves overusing *is-a* inheritance arrows. This confused the schema diagram. It was also inappropriate since it was only *behaviour*, and not *structure*, that we wanted to inherit from classes like *set-of-atom*.

We can see that the view hierarchy on the right of Figure 7.8 is not a simple *is-a* hierarchy inheriting structure, because the means of identifying instances changes as we proceed through the hierarchy, since we are looking at sets of very different objects. By contrast, in an *is-a* hierarchy of stored objects, the means of identifying instances is the same at all levels and all specialised classes inherit the key definition defined at the top of that hierarchy. For example, a *student* instance is completely identified by virtue of being a person, in the same way as a more specialised *undergraduate student*.

Thus, while our early schema diagrams showed classes like *chain* and *residue* related by an *is-a* relationship to *set-of-atom*, these classes were not in fact related in that way. This led us to clarify the schema diagram by considering collection view inheritance as if in "another dimension", joined by thick arrows to view classes on the right of Figure 7.8. This replaces a combinatorial explosion of subtype inheritance arrows.

Thus we consider a *collection view* to be a kind of adapter or coercion mechanism that takes any object of a given class or type and derives on demand a collection of objects of an adapted type, so as to fit a desired tool or method. It thus presents a consistent interface to a method which is possibly legacy code, adapting it to an evolving collection of objects as described in Section 7.3. Each such "view" is basically a derived relationship, without the privacy aspects of a subschema.

It is important to realise that collection views are transitory and computed on demand in order to provide a set of objects with an appropriate interface to one or more utility methods (such as `phi-psi-plot`). They may look like persistent classes (which also have methods) on a schema diagram, but they do not persist. It is possible to enlarge the definition of the view by adding extra functions to compute other derived properties; this is a form of schema evolution. However, it is not possible for a view class to have *stored* properties, because it is just an abstract class defining an interface. Further, if you compute a collection of residue objects forming a `set-of-residue`, it cannot contain any new residue objects.

7.10 Schema Definitions for Collection Views

A collection view can be defined on any of the concrete classes or subclasses described in the database schema, or on another collection view. It takes any object of the given class or view type and derives on demand a collection of objects of an adapted type, so as to fit a desired tool or method. It may return a set of concrete instances declared in the database schema, or else a set of primitive values or tuples of such values (such as `point(x,y,z)`).

We have implemented this scheme on the P/FDM object database by adapting and generalising the system code (written in Prolog) that handles inheritance. Because P/FDM represents relationships as functions, which may be stored or derived, it is easy to represent *adapter functions* (shown by thick arrows in Figure 7.8) directly as P/FDM functions. In order to do this we identify the adapter functions F by introducing extra schema declarations with the keyword `using`:

> `using F, an Atype can be viewed as a set of Btype`

Example declarations are given in Figure 7.9. In one example we are able to use an existing stored relationship called *has_residues* as an adapter function, relating a protein chain to its many residues. In the general case an adapter function would be defined as a stored method, written in Daplex or in Prolog (possibly with callouts to C).

7.10.1 Composition of Adapter Functions

There is a kind of transitivity between adapter functions that allows us to compose them. Many people will look on this as a kind of *view inheritance*, so that a method defined on a more abstract view is applicable to an object belonging to a view lower down in the hierarchy. Thus for example the method `centroid` can be applied to a set of points, but it can also be applied to a set of residues, or even to a helix further down the hierarchy of thick arrows.

In order to implement this, we use the adapters to perform what in programming language theory is a coercion or *type cast*, for example where
$\quad$ `y := sqrt(2)` is coerced to `y := sqrt(float(2))`

Thus if `h` is a variable holding an instance of type helix then `centroid(h)` really stands for (see Figure 7.8):
$\quad$ `centroid(atom_centres(residues_to_atoms(structure_residues(h))))`

Schema Extract

```
declare chain ->> entity            % Class definition
declare chain_id(chain) -> string    % Function definition
declare num_residues(chain) -> integer
define has_residues(chain) ->> residue   % Adapter function

declare residue ->> entity
declare position(residue) -> integer
declare name(residue) -> string
define has_atoms(residue) ->> atom

declare atom ->> entity

define weight(set of atom) -> integer    % Function defined on a set
```

View Declarations

```
using has_residues, a chain can be viewed as a set of residue

using has_atoms, a residue can be viewed as a set of atom

using atom_centres, a set of atom can be viewed as a set of point
```

Queries

```
for each c in chain such that
    weight(c) >= 1000 and weight(c) =< 2000
print(protein_name(chain_protein(c)), weight(c));

print(chain_id(any c in chain such that weight(c) > 1000));

for each h in helix such that surface_area(h) > 1000
print(chain_id(structure_chain(h)), surface_area(h));

for each c in chain
print(average(over r in has_residues(c) of weight(r)));
```

Extract from Typescript

```
| ?- daplex.
|: for the c in chain such that protein_code(chain_protein(c)) = "1CRN"
|:    for each r in has_residues(c)
|:    print(name(r), weight(r));

ASN 23.6
ALA 15.4
GLY 12.0      % more result values have been omitted

|: for each c in chain
|: print(chain_id(c), weight(c));

A 1006.2      % more result values have been omitted
```

Fig. 7.9. Collection Views and example queries on them.

Here `atom_centres` is an adapter function defined on a derived class `set-of-atom`, delivering an object of class `set-of-point`. This and other various adapter functions shown in Figure 7.8 are thus composed together as required into a derived relationship which will then construct a set of objects to which `centroid` is applicable.

Where only a single coercion is needed, we can determine it from a knowledge of the source and destination classes, since we allow at most one adapter function (or arrow) between any two classes. However, where arrows form a path, there may be alternative paths, and we explain how to resolve this in [7.10]. Note that adapter functions are often multi-valued (i.e. deliver a set or bag) and that two such functions can be composed and will deliver a single flattened set as a result. This is in accordance with Shipman's original Functional Data Model, because if instead they delivered a set of sets then it would not fit the next adapter function.

7.11 Conclusions

We have seen the value of a functional data model schema for describing types of related bioinformatics data, while allowing it to be held in a variety of forms on remote machines and integrated on demand. The Daplex query language allows us to do computations over objects in the schema diagram, as in a UML class diagram. It neatly combines calculation and data access, avoiding the awkward mismatch with relational databases. Further, it enables us to define collection views through composition of adapter functions in the schema. This composition is done to meet the requirements of a type coercion. Thus it is not necessary to name the composed function or declare it on a schema diagram, which is what saves one from an explosion of such functions. This also allows the schema to evolve while continuing to provide a consistent interface to the application, by changing the adapter functions. This is the proper role of a schema in supporting views.

References

7.1 P. Brown and M.L. Stonebraker. BigSur: A System for the Management of Earth Science Data. In *Proc. 21st International Conference on Very Large Data Bases VLDB'95*, pages 720–728, 1995.

7.2 R.G.G. Cattell, editor. *The Object Database Standard: ODMG 2.0*. Morgan Kaufmann, 1997.

7.3 D.N. Chorafas and H. Steinmann. *Solutions for Networked Databases*. Academic Press, 1993.

7.4 C. Chothia and A.M. Lesk. Canonical structures for the hypervariable regions of immunoglobulins. *J.Mol.Biol.*, 196:901–917, 1987.

7.5 C. Chothia, A.M. Lesk, A. Tramontano, et al. Conformations of immunoglobulin hypervariable regions. *Nature*, 342:877–883, 1989.

7.6 S.M. Embury and P.M.D. Gray. The Declarative Expression of Semantic Integrity in a Database of Protein Structure. In A. Illaramendi and O. Díaz, editors, *Data Management Systems: Proceedings of the Basque International Workshop on Information Technology (BIWIT 95)*, pages 216–224, San Sebastían, Spain, July 1995. IEEE Computer Society Press.

7.7 E. Gamma, R. Helm, R. Johnson, and J. Vlissides. *Design Patterns*. Addison-Wesley, 1994.

7.8 I. Gil, P.M.D. Gray, and G.J.L Kemp. A Visual Interface and Navigator for the P/FDM Object Database. In N.W. Paton and T Griffiths, editors, *Proceedings of User Interfaces to Data Intensive Systems (UIDIS'99)*, pages 54–63. IEEE Computer Society Press, 1999.

7.9 P.M.D. Gray, S.M. Embury, K.Y. Hui, and G.J.L. Kemp. The Evolving Role of Constraints in the Functional Data Model. *Journal of Intelligent Information Systems*, 12:113–137, 1999.

7.10 P.M.D. Gray, G.J.L. Kemp, P. Brunschwig, and S.M.Embury. Collection Views: Dynamically Composed Views which Inherit Behaviour. In B. Lings and K. Jeffery, editors, *Advances in Databases, Proc. BNCOD17*, pages 102–121. (LNCS 1832). Springer-Verlag, 2000.

7.11 P.M.D. Gray, G.J.L. Kemp, C.J. Rawlings, N.P. Brown, C. Sander, J.M. Thornton, C.M. Orengo, S.J. Wodak, and J. Richelle. Macromolecular Structure Information and Databases. *Trends in Biochemical Sciences*, 21:251–256, 1996.

7.12 P.M.D. Gray, K.G. Kulkarni, and N.W. Paton. *Object-Oriented Databases: a Semantic Data Model Approach*. Prentice Hall Series in Computer Science. Prentice Hall International, 1992.

7.13 E.A. Kabat, T.T. Wu, H.M. Perry, K.S. Gottesman, and C. Foeller. *Sequences of proteins of immunological interest*, 5th edition Public Health Service, NIH, Washington D.C., 1992.

7.14 G.J.L. Kemp. Protein Modelling: a Design Application of an Object-Oriented Database. In J. Gero, editor, *Proc. 1st International Conference on Artificial Intelligence in Design*, pages 387–406. Butterworth–Heinemann, 1991.

7.15 G.J.L. Kemp, J. Dupont, and P.M.D. Gray. Using the Functional Data Model to Integrate Distributed Biological Data Sources. In P. Svensson and J.C. French, editors, *Proc. Eighth International Conference on Scientific and Statistical Database Management*, pages 176–185. IEEE Computer Society Press, 1996.

7.16 G.J.L. Kemp, J.J. Iriarte, and P.M.D. Gray. Efficient Access to FDM Objects Stored in a Relational Database. In D.S. Bowers, editor, *Directions in Databases: Proc. Twelfth British National Conference on Databases (BNCOD 12)*, pages 170–186. Springer-Verlag, 1994.

7.17 G.J.L. Kemp, Z. Jiao, P.M.D. Gray, and J.E. Fothergill. Combining Computation with Database Access in Biomolecular Computing. In W. Litwin and T. Risch, editors, *Applications of Databases: Proceedings of the First International Conference*, pages 317–335. Springer-Verlag, 1994.

7.18 G.J.L. Kemp, C.J. Robertson, P.M.D. Gray, and N. Angelopoulos. CORBA and XML: Design Choices for Database Federations. In B. Lings and K. Jeffery, editors, *Proceedings of the Seventeenth British National Conference on Databases*, pages 191–208. Springer-Verlag, 2000.

7.19 T. Landers and R. L. Rosenberg. An Overview of MULTIBASE. In H.-J. Schneider, editor, *Distributed Data Bases*. North-Holland, 1982.

7.20 D.W. Ritchie and G.J.L. Kemp. Modeling Antibody Side Chain Conformations Using Heuristic Database Search. In T. Gaasterland, P. Karp, K. Karplus, C. Ouzounis, C. Sander, and A. Valencia, editors, *Proceedings of the Fifth International Conference on Intelligent Systems for Molecular Biology*, pages 237–240. AAAI Press, 1997.

7.21 R.J. Robbins. BioInformatics: Essential Infrastructure for Global Biology. *J. Comp. Biol.*, 3:465–478, 1996.

7.22 J. Rumbaugh, M. Blaha, and W. Premerlani. *Object-oriented Modelling and Design*. Prentice Hall, 1991.

7.23 A.P. Sheth and J.A. Larson. Federated Database Systems for Managing Distributed, Heterogeneous and Autonomous databases. *ACM Computing Surveys*, 22:183–236, 1990.

7.24 D.W. Shipman.   The Functional Data Model and the Data Language DAPLEX. *ACM Transactions on Database Systems*, 6(1):140–173, 1981.

8. Optimisation Strategies for Functional Queries in a Distributed Environment

Graham J.L. Kemp[1], Peter M.D. Gray[2], and Suzanne M. Embury[3]

[1] Department of Computing Science, Chalmers University of Technology,
SE-412 96, Göteborg, Sweden
email: kemp@cs.chalmers.se
[2] Department of Computing Science, University of Aberdeen,
King's College, Aberdeen AB24 3UE, UK
email: pgray@csd.abdn.ac.uk
[3] Department of Computer Science, University of Manchester,
Oxford Road, Manchester M13 9PL, UK
email: embury@cs.man.ac.uk

Summary.
 In this chapter we describe the architecture of two distributed systems based on the Functional Data Model (FDM): the P/FDM database management system and the P/FDM mediator. These systems are closely related to one another and they share several source modules. In describing these systems we shall focus on their modular design, and the different kinds of optimisation that can be performed when processing queries and constraints. Both systems make use of an internal intermediate code for queries and constraints that is based on ZF-expressions. We describe how different query processing strategies can be adopted to improve performance when using different kinds of storage module. In describing the architecture of the P/FDM mediator we explain and how modules from the Daplex compiler have been reused in the P/FDM mediator's own architecture, and the different kinds of optimisation that can be performed when processing queries that will be executed in a federated system.

8.1 The P/FDM Database Management System

P/FDM is a database management system that has been designed primarily for use with scientific applications [8.10]. It is an implementation of Shipman's Functional Data Model [8.33], which has been extended to include some features of the object-oriented data model. Databases defined using this model are accessed and updated using a small set of primitive operations that are implemented as Prolog procedures and that are embedded into a full Prolog language system, giving users all the power of Prolog as a database programming language. In addition to the Prolog interface, several higher-level interfaces to P/FDM have been defined. The principal interface is a compiler for the Daplex data definition and manipulation language as introduced in Chapter 1. Daplex is a high-level declarative language that uses function composition to express database navigation concisely but clearly.

The initial prototype P/FDM database management system was implemented by Norman Paton in the late 1980s. Subsequently, the system has been rewritten and extended in a series of research projects. However, two of the early design decisions have remained throughout and have facilitated the system's evolution. The first was the choice of Prolog as the main implementation language. Prolog has several advantages over procedural languages for implementing a database management system in a research environment. For a start, parsers for data definition and manipulation languages (DDLs and DMLs) can be implemented conveniently using Prolog's grammar rule syntax. But of greater importance is the ease with which queries can be manipulated and processed by code that uses Prolog's pattern matching capabilities. The second design choice was to compile Daplex queries into a simple internal intermediate code ("ICode") for subsequent processing [8.8, 8.3].

In section 8.1.1 we describe the format of P/FDM's ICode, and the design of P/FDM's Daplex compiler is described in section 8.1.2. The syntax and usage of rewrite rules in P/FDM is shown in section 8.1.3. Sections 8.1.4 and 8.1.5 demonstrate how we can take advantage of different physical storage formats in order to improve query performance. An example of semantic query optimisation using rewrite rules with our antibody database is given in section 8.1.6.

8.1.1 ICode: Intermediate Code Format

The intermediate code format used in P/FDM is based on ZF-notation, or *list comprehensions*, as described in Chapter 1. In this notation, a set is described by a pattern giving the form of the elements of the set, and a declarative specification of what values are set members. For example, the set of third-year students is described by the ZF-expression:

```
[ s | s <- student; year(s) = 3 ]
```

So our example set specification consists of a single generator, assigning student instances to the variable s, and a single restriction, filtering out those student instances whose **year** attribute evaluates to something other than the value 3. The Daplex compiler uses a very similar form to this for representing sets. For example, the Daplex set described by:

```
s in student such that year(s) = 3
```

is represented internally by the pattern [var(1)] and the ICode list:

```
[ generate(student, var(1)),
  restrict(year, [student], [var(1)], var(2)),
  expression(=, var(2), 3) ]
```

The **generate/2** term takes a class name and a variable, and corresponds to the ZF-expression generator construct. The restriction "**year(s) = 3**" is represented by the remaining two constructs. The set description would then be translated into the following fragment of Prolog:

```
( getentity(student, V1),
  getfnval(year, [V1], V2),
  V2 = 3 )
```

Here, `getentity/2` is the primitive provided for enumeration of class instances, with the result variable (`V1`) being bound to successive instance
identifiers on backtracking. Similarly, `getfnval/3` takes a function name,
a list of argument values and a result variable, and attempts to apply the
function to produce the result. Thus, this fragment of Prolog, when executed,
will bind the variable `V1` to all **student** instances for which the **year** function
evaluates to 3, one by one, on backtracking.

8.1.2 Modular Daplex Compiler

The Daplex compiler has been designed with reuse and extensibility in mind
[8.3]. It is based around the pipeline architecture traditionally used for compilers and language processors, consisting of a lexical analyser followed by a
parser, an optimiser and a (Prolog) code generator.

The Daplex compiler has several modular components, some of which are
shown later in Figure 8.1. The Daplex text of a query is first converted to
a stream of lexical tokens, and is then parsed to produce a parse tree. In
addition to validating the syntax of the query, the parser also checks that
it is consistent with the database's schema. In a second pass, the parse tree
is converted into ICode. Then the four modules described below are used to
improve the original ICode. Each of these modules takes ICode as its input
and produces ICode as its output.

- The *simplifier*'s role is to produce shorter, more elegant, and more consistent ICode, mainly through removing redundant variables and expressions
  (e.g. if the ICode contains an expression equating two variables, then that
  expression can be eliminated, provided that all references to one variable
  are replaced by references to the other), and flattening out nested expressions where this doesn't change the meaning of the query.
- The rule-based *rewriter* matches expressions in the query with patterns
  present on the lefthand side of rewrite rules, and replaces these with the
  righthand side of the rewrite rule, after making appropriate variable substitutions (see section 8.1.3).
- The *optimiser* [8.14, 8.15] performs generic query optimisations.
- The *reordering module* reorders expressions in the ICode to ensure that all
  variable dependencies are observed.

Typically, queries are improved by first invoking the simplifier, and then
the rewriter to perform semantic optimisations. Simplifying the original
ICode prior to rewriting makes the rewriter's task much easier because it
reduces the number and complexity of patterns to be recognised.

Rewrite rules can be used to perform *semantic query optimisation* (see section 8.1.6). This capability is important since graphical interfaces (e.g. [8.7]) make it easy for users to express inefficient queries which cannot always be optimised using general purpose query optimisation strategies. This is because transforming the original query to a more efficient one may require domain knowledge, e.g. two or more alternative navigation paths may exist between distantly related object classes but domain knowledge is needed to recognise that these are indeed equivalent.

After all user-defined rewrites have been applied, the resulting ICode is passed to the optimiser so that generic optimisations (using built-in generic rewrite rules that were written directly in Prolog) can be applied, and the costs of alternative execution paths can be estimated. The ICode produced by the optimiser is passed once more to the simplifier to streamline the ICode before this is passed to the reordering module.

We have been able to reuse many of the modules within our compiler. This is due in large part to the use of ZF-expressions as the format by which intermediate code fragments are communicated. Unlike most intermediate code formats (such as three place codes, or reverse polish notation, which are designed for ease of code generation), our intermediate code format retains most of the source code semantics explicitly, making regeneration of the original source program relatively easy. We also benefit in a DBMS context, in that all important metadata generated during the compilation process is retained in an easily accessible persistent form for use by later invocations of the compiler modules, or by other system components. This is a completely different philosophy from that underlying the construction of standard programming language compilers, in which symbol tables and other internal structures are designed for use by just one process (the compiler) in the course of a single invocation.

Another prime advantage of the ZF-expression format is the ease with which it can be analysed and manipulated by another Prolog module. This is obviously seen in the optimiser submodules, which use Prolog's searching and pattern matching abilities to look for known patterns in the code fragment to be optimised.

Perhaps the most significant feature of the ZF-expression notation is its ability to be fragmented into smaller expression components of well-defined type which are still meaningful in their own right. It is this feature which makes ZF-expressions such a suitable notation for the representation of constraints (see Chapter 4) as *mobile* fragments of knowledge, which can be communicated independently or combined with other knowledge fragments [8.8]. This shows that ZF-expressions facilitate the transmission of knowledge between the modules of an otherwise monolithic piece of software.

8.1.3 Rewrite Rules in P/FDM

Our user-defined rewrite rules are expressed in a syntax that is designed to be easier to read and maintain than the Prolog that underpins it. We have also used this system to rewrite constraints, which have a very similar syntax [8.8]. To introduce this syntax, we shall first consider a transformation that is described by Jiao [8.14, 8.15]. Jiao did some optimisation work regarding existentially quantified expressions in P/FDM, focusing on semantic query optimisation and on rewrites using key values of entity classes. Consider the following query:

```
for each u in undergrad such that
    some c1 in takes(u) has code(c1) = 'C_331'
print(forename(u), surname(u));
```

Based on a schema declaration that `code(X)` is the uniquely valued key used to identify courses and thus that there can be at most one such course that is taken, we can rewrite this to work more efficiently as:

```
for the u in takes_inv(the c2 in course such that
    code(c2) = 'C_331')
print(forename(u), surname(u));
```

The improved speed comes from reordering the query so that it can use an index on `code` for direct access followed by a system-maintained inverse of the `takes` function, instead of by iteration. This example shows how we are able to use the principle of referential transparency to replace one expression by an equivalent one.

This particular transformation can be expressed directly as a rewrite rule:

```
with common s in string
rewrite     u in undergrad such that
            some c1 in takes(u) has code(c1) = s
into        takes_inv(the c2 in course
                such that code(c2) = s);
```

This rule is compiled into two expressions with certain parameters in common:

```
u <- undergrad;
Exists [ c1 | c1 <- takes(u); code(c1) = s ]

u <- takes_inv( [ c2 | c2 <- course; code(c2) = s ] )
```

There may be one or more **common** variables which stand for common expressions denoting atomic values (strings, integers, reals, booleans) or entity values (object identifiers). Note that the variable names chosen (u, c1, etc.) have no significance.

Rewrite rules are stored internally in P/FDM as Prolog term structures. Rewriting is done by pattern matching to find whether the left hand side of any rewrite rule is present as a sub-expression. If a match is found, the sub-expression is replaced by the righthand side of the rewrite rule with appropriate variable substitutions. This process is repeated until no more rewrites can be done, and assumes stratified rules as in most such systems.

Note that the rules are Horn Clause rules based on unification and substitution, working top-down, rather than the bottom-up rules, as used for example in [8.29] where rules have righthand side actions that change the state of various flags. The Horn Clause rules are thus much easier to maintain because they depend on equivalences rather than on side-effects.

The Prolog implementation of this rewrite [8.15] matches a wider variety of expressions. Our rule syntax is easier to read than Prolog, but does not have its matching power. However, recent extensions to the Daplex compiler enable more generic rewrites to be expressed declaratively using a high-level syntax [8.19], making it easier to add new query optimisation strategies to the mediator.

8.1.4 Using Relational Storage with P/FDM

Our decision to use the Functional Data Model does not dictate the choice of physical data model. We have often used hash files to store internal instance identifiers and function values. However, in accordance with the principle of physical data independence, alternative storage modules can be substituted without application programs or user queries having to be changed.

As an example of this, we have experimented with relational storage modules, using an external relational database management system to provide persistent storage for the entity instances and function values used by a client P/FDM process [8.20]. By writing new versions of the primitive data access and manipulation operations (such as `getentity` and `getfnval`) that used SQL statements to perform the requested task, we were able to make use of the Daplex compiler without modification. However, this could result in many small SQL queries being sent to the relational database server as the Prolog code is executed. A much better approach has been to add an SQL code generator, DAPSTRA [8.20], that takes ICode as its input and generates a single equivalent SQL query that is executed once on the server. If this is not possible, then the compiler "backtracks" and uses the original Prolog code generator instead.

Performance for simple searches is close to that obtained by using SQL directly, i.e. the time to generate the SQL is not significant. The main efficiency improvement in translating simple ZF-expressions to a single SQL statement comes from two sources: it avoids the overhead of parsing and moving many "penny packet" queries to the server, and it saves sending back unfiltered results which are then mostly rejected by the client.

8.1.5 Antibody Sequence Searches

The value of data independence in P/FDM is also illustrated in our experience with antibody structure and sequence data [8.21] as introduced in the preceding chapter. A query against the sequence data typically tries to find sequences with particular characteristics, e.g. certain residues at particular positions, and then prints additional information about these sequences, or prints the number of such sequences found. Recalling that each residue type can be represented by a single letter, the one-letter code for the residue at a particular Kabat position in a sequence can be found using the function *residue_code*. Values for this function are not stored directly, but are derived by mapping to the appropriate position in the sequence when this function is called. This function takes a kabat_entry object and a (usually numeric) string representing a Kabat position code as its arguments and retrieves the one-letter code of the residue at the requested position.

As an example, the following Daplex query finds the entry codes for all light chain sequences that have a valine residue (code "V") at Kabat position 33 and an alanine (code "A") residue at Kabat position 71:

```
for each e in kabat_entry such that
    chain_type(group(e)) = "light" and
    residue_code(e, "33") = "V" and
    residue_code(e, "71") = "A"
print(entry_code(e));
```

This query is optimised and translated to Prolog code that processes the query by first iterating over all kabat_group objects, and testing these to see whether their chain type is "light". For those that are, the related kabat_entry objects are retrieved. For each candidate kabat_entry object, the sequence is retrieved and the function residue_code retrieves the one letter code of the residues at the requested positions. Each time the function residue_code is called, the sequence of the kabat_entry given as an argument must be retrieved from disc (or disc buffer). The sequence is then converted to a list of characters, which is passed to another Prolog predicate that processes the list recursively to find the position in the list corresponding to the given Kabat position.

This approach can answer all queries expressed in Daplex, but performance is disappointing – many of the queries relating to the sequence data are slow compared with answering these queries simply by searching flat files using standard string searching techniques or UNIX commands. However, formulating UNIX scripts to answer these queries is awkward and the scripts are devoid of any biological meaning.

To get efficient performance for these queries while continuing to express queries in Daplex with reference to the biochemical concepts described in the database schema, a program was written that attempts to generate a

UNIX script from a Daplex query automatically. The idea is to recognise ZF-expressions for queries that perform a straightforward sequence search, and to translate these to a UNIX command that performs the same operation on the flat files of sequences.

The ZF-expression for the Daplex query shown above is as follows:

[f | a ← kabat_entry; b ← group(a); c ← chain_type(b); c = 'light';
    d ← residue_code(a,'33'); d = 'V'; e ← residue_code(a,'71'); e = 'A';
    f ← entry_code(a)]

The qualifiers on the first line (generating values for variables a, b and c, and testing c) recognise that the file containing light chain sequences should be searched. The second line of qualifiers (generating and testing values for d and e) defines the pattern that will constrain the search. The final line shows how the result will be generated, and is translated to a UNIX command that can extract the entry code from lines matching the search criteria. This translation is implemented easily in Prolog since items in the list of qualifiers can be matched with template queries using Prolog's unification mechanism. A variation on this kind of query is to count the number of sequences satisfying a particular pattern. These queries can also be translated to UNIX scripts.

We accept that schema-specific optimisations like this are rather ad hoc. However, each optimising transformation implemented can deal with a class of queries, and is not restricted to answering only one particular query, retrieving a particular set of data values. Further, each class of query optimised in this way is one identified as important to the users, thus a small number of ad hoc optimisations can improve processing of many user queries since the sequence-based queries have a similar form.

The ability to introduce optimisations like these is a benefit of having data independence and being able to hide the storage implementation details from users and user applications. All of the optimisations are done below the level of the conceptual schema. The point is that from the outset arbitrary queries can be formulated and answered using the system's standard data access operations. As particular kinds of query are identified as important, useful, and amenable to being optimised by using alternative (or additional) data representations, then this can be done. Users don't lose the investment made in developing and storing queries prior to the optimisation strategies being implemented – pre-existing Daplex code will be able to take advantage of later processing improvements, since optimisation is done using the ICode version of queries to which all Daplex queries are first translated.

The UNIX scripts operate on flat files that contain a copy of the sequences stored in the database. This requires extra storage space, but we believe this to be a worthwhile trade-off for improved performance for common sequence queries. Having an alternative stored version of the data may make schema changes more difficult – again a reason for first using standard P/FDM system facilities while experiments with prototype schemata are carried out.

Only when we have established a schema to be successful for all applications initially envisaged, and we believe that it is sufficiently well structured to cope with future needs, do we turn our attention to optimising frequently asked queries. Also note that sequence data never changes unless there has been an error. Hence there is no problem of updating duplicate copies.

8.1.6 Using rewrite rules to optimise antibody queries

We can use the generic rules that flatten nested quantifiers in combination with other domain specific rules, such as those that use indexes. For example, in our database of antibody proteins [8.21] we model the sequence of amino acid residues forming a protein chain in several ways. Thus we can find a residue at a given position in any chain either (i) by iterating over residues in each chain and checking pos(r)=N, or (ii) by a function giving direct access to any residue at position N of a chain by r=absolutepos(chain,N). Rewrite rules are used to replace iteration over residues by direct access thus:

```
with common i in integer
rewrite      r in residue such that pos(r) = i
into         absolutepos(chain,i);
```

We can then transform the following nested query:

```
for each c in structural_cdr such that
    name(c) = "L1"
    and some r in residue has
            name(r) = "CYS"
            and c in structural_cdr_domain_inv(
                    ig_domain_chain_inv(
                    residue_chain(r)))
            and pos(r) = start(c)
    print(protein_code(domain_structure(
        structural_cdr_domain(c))));
```

as if it was written:

```
for each c in structural_cdr such that
    name(c) = "L1"
    and some r in absolutepos(chain,start(c)) has
            name(r) = "CYS"
            and c in structural_cdr_domain_inv(
                    ig_domain_chain_inv(
                    residue_chain(r)))
    print(protein_code(domain_structure(
        structural_cdr_domain(c))));
```

If instead of the test pos(r)=start(c) we have:

```
pos(r) in {start(c) to end(c)}
```

then we could use the following rule to eliminate the existential quantifier:

```
with common r in residue, st in integer, fin in integer
rewrite    some i in {st to fin} has pos(r) = i
into       pos(r) >= st  and  pos(r) =< fin
```

8.2 The P/FDM Mediator

Developments in our ability to integrate and analyse data held in existing heterogeneous data resources can lead to an increase in our understanding of biological function at all levels. However, correlating data from different data resources is still difficult. To address this, we have developed a federated architecture and *mediator* to integrate access to heterogeneous, distributed biological databases [8.17, 8.18]. Robbins [8.31] and Karp [8.16] have also advocated a federated multi-database approach. Like Robbins, we believe that we do not need to adopt a common hardware platform or vendor DBMS, but we do need a "shared data model across participating sites". Our approach does not require that the participating sites use the same data model. Rather, it is sufficient for the mediator to hold descriptions of the participating sites that are expressed in a common data model — in our system the Functional Data Model is used for this purpose.

Transforming queries for efficient execution is particularly important in federated database systems since a more efficient execution plan can require many fewer data requests to be sent to the component databases. Also, it is important to do as much as possible of the selection and processing close to where the data is stored, thereby making best use of facilities provided by the federation's component DBMSs.

In section 8.2.2 we shall address the problem of processing complex queries including quantifiers, which have to be executed against different databases in an expanding heterogeneous federation. This is done by transforming queries within a mediator for global query improvement, and within wrappers to make best use of the query processing capabilities of external databases. Our approach is based on pattern matching and query rewriting. We shall give further examples of our language for expressing rewrite rules declaratively, and demonstrate the use and flexibility of such rules in improving query performance for existentially quantified subqueries. Before studying these important functional transformations we need to understand the mediator architecture and where mappings take place between the different schemas.

8.2.1 Mediator Architecture

A vital task performed by the mediator is to map between the mediator's conceptual schema (which we call C_M) and the conceptual schemas of each of the external resources in the federation (which we call C_R) [8.17].

C_M, which we also refer to as the federation's integration schema, is expressed using the Functional Data Model. Queries can be expressed against this schema using Daplex, helped by a graphical interface.

The conceptual schema of each external resource, C_R, describes the logical structure of the data contained in that resource. If the resource is a relational database then this will include information about table names and column names, and type information about stored values. With SRS [8.4], it is the databank names and field names. These systems also provide a mechanism for querying the data resource in terms of the table|class|databank names and column|tag|attribute|field names that are presented in the conceptual schema.

To make it easier to translate queries expressed against schema C_M into queries that are expressed against schema C_R, we create an external schema for each of the federation's resource (we call this schema E_R). Each E_R schema is expressed using the Functional Data Model. We design the E_R schema so that it matches the structure of a particular external resource as closely as possible. C_M, E_R and C_R are the central three layers in a five-level schema [8.17] architecture similar to that described by Sheth and Larson [8.32].

The architecture of the P/FDM mediator is shown in Figure 8.1. The mediator incorporates most of the modules from the Daplex compiler described in Section 8.1.2 and the following additional modules:

Condition compiler: This module reads declarative statements about the conditions that must hold between data items in different external data resources in order that these values can be mapped onto the integration schema.

ICode rewriter: The original ICode is expanded in this step by applying mapping functions that transform references to the integration schema into references to the federation's component databases. Essentially the same rewriter that was mentioned in section 8.1.2 is used here, but with a different set of rewrite rules. These rewrite rules enhance the ICode by adding tags to indicate the actual data sources that contain particular entity classes and attribute values. Thus, the ICode rewriter transforms the query expressed against the C_M into a query expressed against the E_R of one or more external databases.

Query splitter: In a simple situation where all the data is in a single database, a single code generator is used to transform the ICode into executable code. If the data is spread across different databases in the federation then the P/FDM mediator must split the ICode into fragments, and each fragment must be translated into code that can be executed by a particular

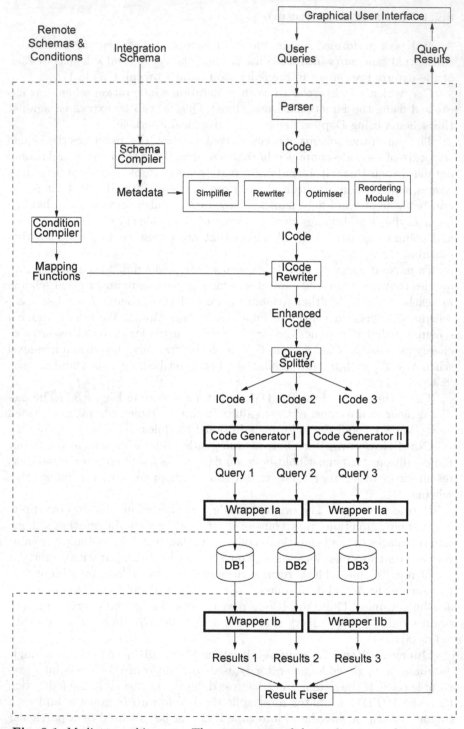

Fig. 8.1. Mediator architecture. The components of the mediator are shown inside the dashed line. Dark borders enclose domain-specific code.

component database. The query splitter identifies which external databases hold data referred to by parts of an integrated query by inspecting the metadata. Adjacent query elements referring to the same database are grouped together into "chunks". Query "chunks" are shuffled and variable dependencies are checked to produce alternative execution plans. A generic description of costs is used to select a good schedule/sequence of instructions for accessing the remote databases. The crucial idea is to move selective filter operations in the query down into the appropriate chunks so that they can be applied early and efficiently using local search facilities as registered with the mediator.

Code generators: Each ICode chunk is sent to one of several code generators. These translate ICode into queries that are executable by the remote databases, transforming query fragments from E_R to C_R. New code generators can be linked into the mediator at run time.

Wrappers: These deal with communication with the external data resources. They consist of two parts: code responsible for sending queries to remote resources, and code that receives and parses the results returned from the remote resources. Wrappers for new resources can be linked into the mediator at run time. Note that a wrapper can only make use of whatever querying facilities are provided by the federation's component databases. Thus, the mediator's conceptual model (C_M) will only be able to map onto those data values that are identified in the remote resource's conceptual model (C_R). Thus, queries involving concepts like *gene* and *chromosome* in C_M can only be transformed into queries that run against a remote resource if that resource exports these concepts.

Result fuser: The result fuser provides a synchronisation layer, combining results retrieved from external databases so that the rest of the query can proceed smoothly. It interacts tightly with the wrappers.

When a new external resource is added to the federation, the contents of that resource must be described in terms of entities, attributes and relationships — the basic concepts in the FDM. For example, entity classes and attributes are used to describe the tables and columns in a relational database, the classes and tags in an ACEDB database, and the databanks and fields accessed by SRS. The integration schema has to be extended to include concepts in the new resource, and mapping functions to be used by the ICode rewriter must be generated. Since the mediator has a modular architecture in which query transformation is done in stages, the only new software components that might have to be written are code generators and wrappers — the components shown with dark borders in Figure 8.1. All other components within the mediator are generic. However, the federation administrator might want to add declarative rewrite rules that can be used by the rewriter to improve the performance of queries involving the new resource.

In our architecture, as shown in Figure 8.1, the code generators produce code in a different query language or constraint language that can be used directly at the knowledge source. This can be crucial for efficiency, by allowing one to move selection predicates closer to the knowledge source in a form that is capable of using local indexes etc. This can have a very big effect with database queries, because it saves bringing many "penny packets" of data back through the interface, only to be filtered and rejected on the far side [8.20].

8.2.2 Optimising Quantified Subqueries for Execution on a Remote AMOSQL Server

We are interested in the problem of processing complex queries including quantifiers (*some, all*) which have to be executed against different databases. This is an important issue because such queries often involve a lot of iteration, resulting in inefficient execution plans that require many "penny packet" data requests to be sent to the component databases. Therefore, we are investigating how to transform these queries for efficient execution in a growing network of sites accessed through a mediator. These transformations are done at two levels. First, the mediator uses rewrite rules to recognise structural patterns in the entire query that can be replaced with equivalent expressions that require fewer database accesses. Second, after global improvements have been made to the query and it has been split into subqueries destined for remote sites, the wrappers apply further rewrite rules that are based on classical equivalences to convert a subquery into an alternative form. Local optimisers are often very poor at this for quantified queries, and just use the structure of the query as given. Thus, our mediator architecture incorporates rewrite rules to recognise particular logical structures in the query and casts them in a form that suits the strategy of the remote optimiser.

The existing papers on optimising and evaluating queries with quantified expressions date mostly from the early 1980s and assume relational storage on a single processor. Claußen et al. [8.2] deal with a semantic data model like FDM, but again the context is fast execution on a single processor or high-performance parallel processor. Instead, we focus on adapting the early techniques for reuse in distributed object-based systems, which may include a mix of platforms.

Rewrite Rules for Transforming Quantified Subqueries. Consider the following example which prints the names of undergraduates who take at least one course that satisfies the boolean function **pred** and whose level is the same as the undergraduate's year of study:

```
for each u in undergrad such that
    some c1 in course such that
        pred(c1) has level(c1) = year(u)
print(forename(u), surname(u));
```

Suppose that the information on **course** is maintained on the remote database at site 2, while information on **undergrad** is held at site 1. The straightforward way to execute it is to iterate over undergrads on one site and send across one at a time to be used to execute the inner loop (possibly even with recompilation). However, we want to split the work up sensibly between two sites and not send many "penny packet" queries that attract a relatively large communications overhead. Therefore, we can rewrite this query to generate an inner query whose results are calculated once only and then sent back to the first site thus:

```
with common u in undergrad
rewrite      some c1 in course such that pred(c1)
                 has level(c1) = year(u)
into         year(u) in level(c2 in course
                             such that pred(c2));
```

Note that the rewritten expression denotes a predicate and that the common expression denotes an **undergrad** entity. Effectively this produces a query executed once only on site 2:

```
print(level(c1 in course such that pred(c1)))
```

with result, for example, $\{1,4\}$. This result is then incorporated into the follow-on query on site 1:

```
for each u1 in undergrad such that
    year(u1) in {1,4}
print(forename(u), surname(u));
```

This follow-on query does not have the overheads of executing an inner loop on another machine across the network. Further, this technique extends by generalisation to more than two sites.

Transforming Quantified Subqueries in Wrappers. We have been testing our strategy in a federated database system, coupling P/FDM [8.10] to other databases as external data sources, including AMOS II [8.30]. This enables us to gain experience with SQL3 for an object relational database.

When AMOS II is an external data source in the federation, ZF-expressions will be translated to AMOSQL, the language of AMOS II. The semantics of quantified expressions are equivalent in the two systems and the translation from ZF-expressions to AMOSQL is largely very straightforward. The main difference [8.34] lies in that AMOS II supports multiple inheritance, which can only be approximated in Daplex. A similar difference, of course, exists between C++ and Java. Daplex does allow an object to be an instance of more than one subtype, but requires the choice of subtype in a specific query to be made in the query by means of a cast operation (thus the required method definition can be bound at compile time). Daplex also supports a number of arithmetic functions, and a constructor for lists of constants. If these rather unusual constructs are avoided, then queries are easily translated, as our implementation shows.

When AMOS II executes a generated query it starts by compiling it, producing a query plan in a form of set expressions similar to ZF-expressions. However, the AMOSQL compiler in the version of AMOS II we were using at that time did not traverse subqueries during this compilation phase.

This meant that after the compilation phase, during the evaluation of the global query, the compiler would be called to compile the inner quantified query for each member retrieved from iteration over outer sets. This resulted in a large overhead in execution time, making it very important to minimise the nesting of quantified expressions so as to reduce calls on the compiler during execution. We did this conveniently by incorporating a final phase of rewriting that is target specific, as part of the mediator. This architecture conveniently accommodates known restrictions on remote DBMS optimisers, which may be given expressions they are not used to! Such expressions are a common side-effect of query transformation and mapping between heterogeneous systems. Thus the extra rewriting phase is very important in practical applications.

Unnesting Nested Quantified Expressions. Fortunately, nested existentially quantified expressions can be unnested without altering the semantics. Thus we start with a ZF-expression containing nested quantifiers such as:

```
[ name(u1) | u1 <- undergrad;
             Exists [ c | c <- takes(u1); level(c) > 3;
                          Exists [ u2 | u2 <- enrolled(c);
                                        age(u2) < 19] ]]
```

This returns the name of all the undergrads taking at least one course with level above 3 having at least one enrolled undergrad of age below 19. This expression translates straightforwardly into a nested AMOSQL query. However, the ZF-expression form makes it easy to spot and remove a level of nesting thus:

```
[ name(u1) | u1 <- undergrad;
             Exists [ c | c <- takes(u1); level(c) > 3;
                          u2 <- enrolled(c); age(u2)<19]]
```

Here we make use of the fact that extra variables introduced by a generator in the body of a ZF-expression are effectively existentially quantified, since if the generator produces no values or they are all filtered out by the following predicate, then the whole expression evaluates to an empty set. We can formalise this by a rewrite rule as follows:

```
Exists [ x | x <- generator; P(x);
             Exists [ y | y <- h(x); Q(x,y) ] ] =
Exists [ x | x <- generator; P(x);
             y <- h(x); Q(x,y) ]
```

Here P and Q represent any boolean expression which involves x (or y). Currently these rules are implemented directly in Prolog [8.34], since this has a more general ability to pattern-match expressions in ICode, than that provided in our rewrite rule language.

The rewritten, semantically equivalent, AMOSQL query is:

```
SELECT name(u1)
FROM    undergrad u1
WHERE   some(
   SELECT c
   FROM    course c, undergrad u2
   WHERE   c = takes(u1)
   AND     level(c) > 3
   AND     u2 = enrolled(c)
   AND     age(u2) < 19
);
```

The real gain in execution time is due to the fact that the number of subqueries that must be evaluated is reduced. In the nested original query there will be $O(\#(undergrad) \cdot \#(course))$ subquery evaluations. Applying the same kind of reasoning on the rewritten query yields $\#(undergrad)$ subquery evaluations, which means a reduction from quadratic to linear time.

Note that we depend on the AMOSQL optimiser to use the join predicates and selections concealed within P and Q to avoid a simplistic iteration over the Cartesian product of x(course) and y(undergrad), otherwise the rule could actually worsen performance for a very selective P. This shows the importance of knowledge about the remote query evaluation.

8.3 Related Work

Related work in the bioinformatics field includes the TAMBIS system [8.28] (also Chapter 10) which writes query plans in CPL (the Collection Programming Language) [8.1]. CPL is a comprehension-based language in which the *generators* are calls to library functions that request data from specific databases according to specific criteria. Plans in TAMBIS are based on following a classification hierarchy, whereas our plans are oriented towards ad hoc SQL3-like queries. However, the overall approach is similar in using a high-level intermediate code translated through wrappers.

The Kleisli system [8.35] (also Chapter 6) is a sophisticated system for querying and data integration over heterogeneous databases, with impressive applications in bioinformatics. It pioneered the application of the CPL comprehension language. It has recently been rewritten in standard ML, a functional language, and so uses functions to implement rewrite rules in the optimiser. These functions are currently built into the optimiser but are extensible by the implementers. They work directly on their internal monad composition form of queries, which plays a similar role to our ICode. By contrast our rule syntax endeavours to make rules both writable and readable by end users (domain specialists), hiding the complexity of ICode. Our rules work within a unification paradigm, whereas theirs can be executed under various alternative control regimes. Their rules do have the advantage of being more generic than ours, but pay a price in readability. They also use rewrite rules to generate SQL code, including joins and selections to be executed remotely, by successive transformations on a null SQL query. However, they do not give any rules for improving existential queries. Currently we generate a rewritten ICode query which is then translated directly into the target language inside a wrapper. Since some of our rules are specific to particular wrappers, corresponding to their ones customised to SQL, the approaches are effectively similar; only a closer comparison can tell which is more easily maintainable.

Another related project is DiscoveryLink [8.11]. The architecture of the DiscoveryLink system is similar to that presented here. While we use the FDM, DiscoveryLink uses the relational data model, and all of the databases accessed via DiscoveryLink must present an SQL interface.

Methods to optimise the query processing of nested queries in relational databases, including queries with an existentially quantified subquery, have been thoroughly investigated. Kim suggested an unnesting method in 1982 [8.23]. Strictly speaking, this method dealt with nested queries in general and not specifically with quantified expressions. It was later improved by Ganski and Wong [8.6], who also showed how to rewrite some expressions for evaluation using aggregation functions such as the COUNT operator. Further improvements came from Muralikrishna [8.26] and Freytag [8.5].

In 1983, Jarke and Koch [8.13] described a set of transformations based on logical identities to evaluate quantified expressions more efficiently in limited memory. Although their work concentrated on an algorithm for efficiently evaluating nested quantified queries by successive operations on an intermediate relation, their mathematical transformations are useful nowadays in a distributed setting.

The 1997 paper by Claußen et al. [8.2] is closely related to our work. It states:
"Our discussion focuses on modern data models which use set-valued attributes to represent M:N-relationships — such as in the object-oriented model or the object relational model. In such a data model queries with universal quantification can usually be formulated in a much more natural way than in a flat relational model."

These remarks also apply to the FDM, since it is a modern semantic data model based on entities with subtypes, much like objects with inheritance. These examples use a Daplex syntax adapted from Shipman's original and bear out the readability of quantified queries expressed with set-valued attributes as functions. We should also remember that Dayal's original optimisation work was done with heterogeneous distributed databases on the Multibase project [8.25] for which the FDM was designed.

8.4 Discussion and Conclusions

We have discussed the role of rewrite rules in transforming quantified queries for execution on heterogeneous databases. We advocate the use of the FDM with a high-level language including quantifiers that does not tie us to either relational or object storage. This was indeed the motivation of the original Multibase project [8.25], which was way ahead of its time.

The functional approach is important because it enables us to apply well-tried mathematical equivalences to complex queries in order to adapt them to the characteristics of the remote database. These rules depend on substitution of equivalent expressions and unification of variables, and do not involve bottom-up production rules with side-effects. Thus we believe this approach to be extensible and scalable, and we are testing it in a mediator in use for a bioinformatics application, which has so far worked with simpler queries [8.22]. We are making the usual assumptions that the rules form an acyclic graph; rules that give rise to cycles should be identified and rejected.

We have shown how the rewrite rules provide a great deal of flexibility. They can implement the logical rules given by Jarke and Koch [8.13]. They can implement many forms of rewrites based on data semantics as in King [8.24]. They can spot opportunities to replace iteration by indexed search, possibly of a materialised view. They can implement flattening and unnesting transformations that save wasting time compiling subqueries in AMOSQL. We believe they can be similarly adapted to features of other DBMSs. Most importantly, we can perform rewrites that change the relative workload between two processors in a distributed query. Finally, we can combine all these rewrites, since applying some of them will then enable others to take place. Thus we can deal with many combinations without having to foresee them and code them individually.

The rules prepare the way for the Optimiser and the Query Splitter. The original Optimiser performs generic query optimisations. Its philosophy is to use heuristics to improve queries. It examines alternative execution plans and, although it uses a simple cost model, it is successful in avoiding inefficient strategies, and it often selects the most effective approach [8.27, 8.15].

The Query Splitter attempts to group together query elements into chunks that can be sent as single units to the external data resources, thus providing the remote system with as much information as possible in order to give it greater scope for optimising the subquery. This enables us to make good use of the optimisation capabilities of the external resources.

There is still scope for introducing adaptive query processing techniques to improve the execution plans as execution proceeds and as results are returned to the mediator [8.12], but this has not yet been done in our prototype system.

Our simple but powerful rewrite language includes FOL quantifiers and allows a very general form of parametrisation, which suits unification in Prolog. There is, admittedly, a trade-off between readability and degree of abstract parametrisation. Rules that refer to very domain-specific situations involving specific named attributes are much easier to read and understand, which is what we want. One way to extend this could be to include carefully formatted specific instances of abstract rules as comments, for ease of understanding. Another problem is that users could make rules more general than intended by not putting enough checks in the where-clause of a rule. This is a direction for future work involving cross-checks with metadata.

Quantified queries are an important target for optimisation in a federated system because they usually involve a lot of iteration, possibly on a remote database. Rewrite rules enable us to spot cases where the iteration can all be done on one database, or replaced by faster indexed searches, with greatly improved performance. They also allow us to have rewrites in more than one phase, with a final phase for rules specific to a target DBMS. This leads us to a uniform optimisation framework within which we can cope with an expanding network of remote data sources with different characteristics. This is essential in an Internet environment, where data sources continue to appear, using different data management systems [8.9].

Acknowledgements

The prototype P/FDM Mediator described in this chapter was implemented by Nicos Angelopoulos. This work was supported by a grant from the BBSRC/EPSRC Joint Programme in Bioinformatics (Grant Ref. 1/BIF06716).

References

8.1 P. Buneman, S.B. Davidson, K. Hart, G.C. Overton, and L. Wong. A Data Transformation System for Biological Data Sources. In U. Dayal, P.M.D. Gray, and S. Nishio, editors, *VLDB'95, Proceedings of 21th International Conference on Very Large Data Bases*, pages 158–169. Morgan Kaufmann, 1995.

8.2 J. Claußen, A. Kemper, G. Moerkotte, and K. Peithner. Optimizing queries with universal quantification in object-oriented and object-relational databases. In M. Jarke, M.J. Carey, K.R. Dittrich, F.H. Lochovsky, P. Loucopoulos, and M.A. Jeusfeld, editors, *VLDB'97, Proceedings of 23rd International Conference on Very Large Data Bases, Athens, Greece*, pages 286–295. Morgan Kaufmann, 1997.

8.3 S.M. Embury and P.M.D Gray. A Modular Compiler Architecture for a Data Manipulation Language. In *Proceedings of 14th British National Conference on Databases (BNCOD 14)*, Edinburgh, Scotland, July 1996, pages 170–188. Springer-Verlag.

8.4 T. Etzold and P. Argos. SRS an indexing and retrieval tool for flat file data libraries. *CABIOS*, 9:49–57, 1993.

8.5   J.C. Freytag. A Rule-Based View of Query Optimization. In U. Dayal and
      I. Traiger, editors, *Proceedings of the ACM SIGMOD 87 Conference*, pages
      173–180. ACM Press, 1987.
8.6   R.A. Ganski and H.K.T. Wong. Optimization of Nested SQL Queries Revis-
      ited. In U. Dayal and I.L. Traiger, editors, *Proceedings of the ACM SIGMOD
      87 Conference*, pages 23–33. ACM Press, 1987.
8.7   I. Gil, P.M.D. Gray, and G.J.L Kemp. A Visual Interface and Navigator
      for the P/FDM Object Database. In N.W. Paton and T Griffiths, editors,
      Proceedings of User Interfaces to Data Intensive Systems (UIDIS'99), pages
      54–63. IEEE Computer Society Press, 1999.
8.8   P.M.D. Gray, S.M. Embury, K.Y. Hui, and G.J.L. Kemp. The Evolving Role of
      Constraints in the Functional Data Model. *Journal of Intelligent Information
      Systems*, 12:113–137, 1999.
8.9   P.M.D. Gray, P.J.H. King, and L. Kerschberg. Guest Editor Introduction:
      Functional Approach to Intelligent Information Systems. *Journal of Intelligent
      Information Systems*, 12:107–111, 1999.
8.10 P.M.D. Gray, K.G. Kulkarni, and N.W. Paton. *Object-Oriented Databases: a
      Semantic Data Model Approach*. Prentice Hall Series in Computer Science.
      Prentice Hall International, 1992.
8.11 L.M. Haas, P. Kodali, J.E. Rice, P.M. Schwarz, and W.C. Swope. Integrating
      Life Sciences Data — With a Little Garlic. In *Proceedings IEEE International
      Symposium on Bio-Informatics and Biomedical Engineering*, pages 5–12. IEEE
      Computer Society Press, 2000.
8.12 Z.G. Ives, D. Florescu, M. Friedman, A.Y. Levy, and D.S. Weld. An adap-
      tive query execution system for data integration. In A. Delis, C. Faloutsos,
      and S. Ghandeharizadeh, editors, *SIGMOD 1999, Proceedings of the ACM
      SIGMOD Conference*, pages 299–310. ACM Press, 1999.
8.13 M. Jarke and J. Koch. Range nesting: A fast method to evaluate quantified
      queries. In D. J. DeWitt and G. Gardarin, editors, *SIGMOD'83, Proceedings
      of Annual Meeting, San Jose, California*, pages 196–206. ACM Press, 1983.
8.14 Z. Jiao. *Optimisation Studies in a Prolog Object-Oriented Database*. PhD
      thesis, University of Aberdeen, Department of Computing Science, November
      1992.
8.15 Z. Jiao and P.M.D. Gray. Optimisation of Methods in a Navigational Query
      Language. In C. Delobel, M. Kifer, and Y. Masunaga, editors, *Second Interna-
      tional Conference on Deductive and Object-Oriented Databases*, pages 22–42.
      Springer-Verlag, 1991.
8.16 P.D. Karp. A Vision of DB Interoperation. Meeting on the Interconnection
      of Molecular Biology Databases, 1995.
8.17 G.J.L. Kemp, N. Angelopoulos, and P.M.D. Gray. A Schema-based Approach
      to Building a Bioinformatics Database Federation. In *Proceedings IEEE In-
      ternational Symposium on Bio-Informatics and Biomedical Engineering*, pages
      13–20. IEEE Computer Society Press, 2000.
8.18 G.J.L. Kemp, N. Angelopoulos, and P.M.D. Gray. Architecture of a Mediator
      for a Bioinformatics Database Federation. *IEEE Transactions on Information
      Technology in Biomedicine*, 6:116–122, 2002.
8.19 G.J.L. Kemp, P.M.D. Gray, and A.R. Sjöstedt. Rewrite Rules for Quantified
      Subqueries in a Federated Database. In L. Kerschberg and M. Kafatos, editors,
      *Proceedings Thirteenth International Conference on Scientific and Statistical
      Database Management*, pages 134–143. IEEE Computer Society Press, 2001.
8.20 G.J.L. Kemp, J.J. Iriarte, and P.M.D. Gray. Efficient Access to FDM Ob-
      jects Stored in a Relational Database. In D.S. Bowers, editor, *Directions*

in Databases: Proceedings of the Twelfth British National Conference on Databases, pages 170–186. Springer-Verlag, 1994.

8.21 G.J.L. Kemp, Z. Jiao, P.M.D. Gray, and J.E. Fothergill. Combining Computation with Database Access in Biomolecular Computing. In W. Litwin and T. Risch, editors, *Applications of Databases: Proceedings of the First International Conference*, pages 317–335. Springer-Verlag, 1994.

8.22 G.J.L. Kemp, C.J. Robertson, P.M.D. Gray, and N. Angelopoulos. CORBA and XML: Design Choices for Database Federations. In B. Lings and K. Jeffery, editors, *Proceedings of the Seventeenth British National Conference on Databases*, pages 191–208. Springer-Verlag, 2000.

8.23 W. Kim. On Optimizing an SQL-like Nested Query. *ACM Transactions on Database Systems*, 7:443–469, 1982.

8.24 J.J. King. *Query Optimisation by Semantic Reasoning*. UMI Research Press, 1984.

8.25 T. Landers and R. L. Rosenberg. An Overview of MULTIBASE. In H.-J. Schneider, editor, *Distributed Data Bases*. North-Holland, 1982.

8.26 M. Muralikrishna. Improved Unnesting Algorithms for Join Aggregate SQL Queries. In L. Yuan, editor, *18th International Conference on Very Large Data Bases, August 23-27, 1992, Vancouver, Canada, Proceedings*, pages 91–102. Morgan Kaufmann, 1992.

8.27 N.W. Paton and P.M.D. Gray. Optimising and Executing Daplex Queries Using Prolog. *The Computer Journal*, 33:547–555, 1990.

8.28 N.W. Paton, R. Stevens, P. Baker, C.A. Goble, S. Bechhofer, and A. Brass. Query Processing in the TAMBIS Bioinformatics Source Integration System. In *11th International Conference on Scientific and Statistical Database Management, Proceedings*, pages 138–147. IEEE Computer Society Press, 1999.

8.29 H. Pirahesh, J.M. Hellerstein, and W. Hasan. Extensible/Rule Based Query Rewrite Optimization in Starburst. In M. Stonebraker, editor, *Proceedings of the 1992 ACM SIGMOD International Conference*, pages 39–48. ACM Press, 1992.

8.30 T. Risch, V. Josifovski, and T. Katchaounov. AMOS II Concepts. Available at http://www.dis.uu.se/~udbl/amos/ doc/amos_concepts.html, November 1999.

8.31 R. J. Robbins. Bioinformatics: Essential Infrastructure for Global Biology. *Journal of Computational Biolology*, 3:465–478, 1996.

8.32 A.P. Sheth and J.A. Larson. Federated database systems for managing distributed, heterogeneous and autonomous databases. *ACM Computing Surveys*, 22:183–236, 1990.

8.33 D.W. Shipman. The Functional Data Model and the Data Language DAPLEX. *ACM Transactions on Database Systems*, 6(1):140–173, 1981.

8.34 Sjöstedt, A.R. *Using AMOS II as Data Source for P/FDM and Rewriting Quantified AMOSQL Queries*. Project Report, Department of Computing Science, University of Aberdeen, 2000.

8.35 L. Wong. Kleisli, a Functional Query System. *Journal of Functional Programming*, 10(1):19–56, 2000.

9. Functional Data Integration in a Distributed Mediator System

Tore Risch[1], Vanja Josifovski[2], and Timour Katchaounov[1]

[1] Dept. of Information Technology, Uppsala University, Uppsala, Sweden
email: Tore.Risch@dis.uu.se
[2] IBM Almaden Research Institute, San Jose, USA

Summary.

Amos II (Active Mediator Object System) is a distributed mediator system that uses a functional data model and has a relationally complete functional query language, AmosQL. Through its distributed multi-database facilities many autonomous and distributed Amos II peers can interoperate. Functional multi-database queries and views can be defined where external data sources of different kinds are translated through Amos II and reconciled through its functional mediation primitives. Each mediator peer provides a number of transparent functional views of data reconciled from other mediator peers, wrapped data sources, and data stored in Amos II itself. The composition of mediator peers in terms of other peers provides a way to scale the data integration process by composing mediation modules. The Amos II data manager and query processor are extensible so that new application oriented data types and operators can be added to AmosQL, implemented in some external programming language (Java, C, or Lisp). The extensibility allows wrapping data representations specialized for different application areas in mediator peers. The functional data model provides very powerful query and data integration primitives which require advanced query optimization.

9.1 Introduction

The mediator/wrapper approach, originally proposed by [9.42], has been used for integrating heterogeneous data in several projects, e.g. [9.16, 9.41, 9.14, 9.5]. Most mediator systems integrate data through a central mediator server accessing one or several data sources through a number of "wrapper" interfaces that translate data to a common data model (CDM). However, one of the original goals for mediator architectures [9.42] was that mediators should be relatively simple distributed software modules that transparently encode domain-specific knowledge about data and share abstractions of that data with higher layers of mediators or applications. Larger networks of mediators would then be defined through these primitive mediators by composing new mediators in terms of other mediators and data sources. The core of Amos II is an open, light-weight, and extensible database management system (DBMS) with a functional data model. Each Amos II server contains all the traditional database facilities, such as a storage manager, a recovery manager, a transaction manager, and a functional query language named

AmosQL. The system can be used as a single-user database or as a multi-user server to applications and to other Amos II peers.

9.1.1 Distribution

Amos II is a distributed mediator system where several mediator peers communicate over the Internet. Each mediator peer appears as a virtual functional database layer having data abstractions and a functional query language. Functional views provide transparent access to data sources from clients and other mediator peers. Conflicts and overlaps between similar real-world entities being modeled differently in different data sources are reconciled through the mediation primitives [9.18, 9.17] of the multi-mediator query language AmosQL. The mediation services allow transparent access to similar data structures represented differently in different data sources. Applications access data from distributed data sources through queries to views in some mediator peer.

Logical composition of mediators is achieved when *multi-database views* in mediators are defined in terms of views, tables, and functions in other mediators or data sources. The multi-database views make the mediator peers appear to the user as a single virtual database. Amos II mediators are composable since a mediator peer can regard other mediator peers as data sources.

9.1.2 Wrappers

In order to access data from external data sources Amos II mediators may contain one or several *wrappers* which process data from different kinds of external data sources, e.g. ODBC-based access to relational databases [9.11, 9.4], access to XML files [9.28], CAD systems [9.25], or Internet search engines [9.22]. A wrapper is a program module in Amos II having specialized facilities for query processing and translation of data from a particular class of external data sources. It contains both interfaces to external data sources and knowledge of how to efficiently translate and process queries involving accesses to a class of external data sources. In particular, external Amos II peers known to a mediator are also regarded as external data sources and there is a special wrapper for accessing other Amos II peers. However, among the Amos II peers special query optimization methods are used that take into account the distribution, capabilities, costs, etc., of the different peers [9.20].

9.1.3 The Name Server

Every mediator peer must belong to a group of mediator peers. The mediator peers in a group are described through a meta-schema stored in a mediator server called *name server*. The mediator peers are autonomous and there is no central schema in the name server. The name server contains only some general meta-information such as the locations and names of the peers in the group while each mediator peer has its own schema describing its local data and data sources. The information in the name server is managed without explicit operator intervention; its content is managed through messages from the mediator peers. To avoid a bottleneck, mediator peers usually communicate directly without involving the name server; it is normally involved only when a connection to some new mediator peer is established.

9.1.4 AmosQL

AmosQL is a functional language having its roots in the functional query languages OSQL [9.31] and DAPLEX [9.37] with extensions of mediation primitives [9.18, 9.17], multi-directional foreign functions [9.29], late binding [9.13], active rules [9.38], etc. Queries are specified using the select–from–where construct as in SQL. AmosQL furthermore has aggregation operators, nested subqueries, disjunctive queries, quantifiers, and is relationally complete.

9.1.5 Query Optimization

The declarative multi-database query language AmosQL requires queries to be optimized before execution. The query compiler translates AmosQL statements first into *object calculus* and then into *object algebra* expressions. The object calculus is expressed in an internal simple logic based language called ObjectLog [9.29], which is an object-oriented dialect of Datalog. As part of the translation into object algebra programs, many optimizations are applied on AmosQL expressions relying on its functional and multi-database properties. During the optimization steps, the object calculus expressions are re-written into equivalent but more efficient expressions. For distributed multi-database queries a multi-database query decomposer [9.20] distributes each object calculus query into local queries executed in the different distributed Amos II peers and data sources. For better performance, the decomposed query plans are rebalanced over the distributed Amos II peers [9.17]. A cost-based optimizer on each site translates the local queries into procedural execution plans in the object algebra, based on statistical estimates of the cost to execute each generated query execution plan expressed in the object algebra. A query interpreter finally interprets the optimized algebra to produce the result of a query.

9.1.6 Multi-Directional Foreign Functions

The query optimizer is extensible through a generalized foreign function mechanism, *multi-directional foreign functions*. It gives transparent access from AmosQL to special purpose data structures such as internal Amos II meta-data representations or user defined storage structures. The mechanism allows the programmer to implement query language operators in an external language (Java, C, or Lisp) and to associate costs and selectivity estimates with different user-defined access paths. The architecture relies on extensible optimization of such foreign function calls [9.29]. They are important both for accessing external query processors [9.4] and for integrating customized data representations from data sources.

9.1.7 Organization

Next the distributed mediator architecture of Amos II is described. Then the functional data model used in Amos II is described along with its functional query language followed by a description of how the basic functional data model is extended with data integration primitives. After that there is an overview of the distributed multi-mediator query processing. Finally, related work is discussed followed by a summary.

9.2 Distributed Mediation

Groups of distributed Amos II peers can interoperate over a network using TCP/IP. This is illustrated by Figure 9.1 where an application accesses data from two distributed data sources through three distributed mediator peers. The thick lines indicate communication between peers where the arrows indicate peers acting as servers.

The *name server* is a mediator peer storing names, locations, and other general data about the mediators in a group. As illustrated by the dashed lines, mediators in a group communicate with the name server to register themselves in the group or obtain information about other peers.

The figure furthermore illustrates that several layers of mediator peers can call other mediator peers. Notice, however, that the communication topology is dynamic and any peer can communicate directly with any other peer or data source in a group. It is up to the distributed mediator query optimizer to automatically come up with the optimal communication topology between the peers for a given query. The query optimizers of the peers can furthermore exchange both data and schema information in order to produce an optimized distributed execution plan.

In the figure, the uppermost mediator defines mediating functional views integrating data from them. The views include facilities for semantic reconciliation of data retrieved from the two lower mediators.

The two lower mediators translate data from a wrapped relational database and a web server, respectively. They have knowledge of how to translate AmosQL queries to SQL [9.11] through JDBC and, for the web server, to web service requests.

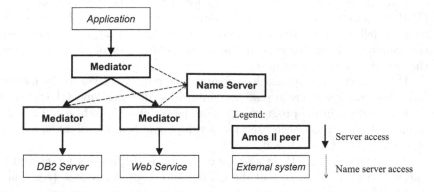

Fig. 9.1. Distributed mediator communication

When an Amos II system is started, it initially assumes stand-alone single-user mode of operation in which no communication with other Amos II systems can be done. The stand-alone system can join a group by issuing a *registration* command to the name server of the group. Another system command makes the mediator a peer that accepts incoming commands from other peers in the group.

In order to access data from external data sources Amos II mediators may contain one or several *wrappers* to interface and process data from external data sources. A wrapper is a program module in a mediator having specialized facilities for query processing and translation of data from a particular kind of external data sources. It contains interfaces to external data repositories to obtain both meta-data (schema definitions) and data. It also includes data source specific rewrite rules to efficiently translate and process queries involving accesses to a particular kind of external data source. More specifically the wrappers perform the following functions:

– *Schema importation* translates schema information from the sources into a set of Amos II types and functions.
– *Query translation* translates internal calculus representations of AmosQL queries into equivalent API calls or query language expressions executable by the source.
– *Source statistics computation* estimates costs and selectivities for API calls or query expressions to a data source.
– *Proxy OID generation* executes in the source query expressions or API calls to construct *proxy OIDs* describing source data.
– *OID verification* executes in the source query expressions or API calls to verify the validity of involved proxy OIDs, in case they have become invalid between different query requests.

Once a wrapper has been defined for a particular kind of source, e.g. ODBC or a web service, the system knows how to process any AmosQL query or view definition for all such sources. When integrating a new instance of the source the mediator administrator can define a set of views in AmosQL that provide abstractions of it.

Different types of applications require different interfaces to the mediator layer. For example, there are call level interfaces allowing AmosQL statements to be embedded in the programming languages Java, C, and Lisp. The call-in interface for Java has been used for developing a Java-based multi-database object browser, GOOVI [9.6].

The Amos II kernel can also be extended with plug-ins for customized query optimization, fusion of data, and data representations (e.g. matrix data). Often specialized algorithms are needed for operating on data from a particular application domain. Through the plug-in features of Amos II , domain-oriented algorithms can easily be included in the system and made available as new query language functions in AmosQL. It is furthermore possible to add new query transformation rules (rewrite rules) for optimizing queries over the new domain.

9.3 Functional Data Model

The data model of Amos II is an extension of the Daplex [9.37] functional data model. The basic concepts of the data model are *objects, types,* and *functions.*

9.3.1 Objects

Objects model all entities in the database. The system is reflective is the sense that everything in Amos II is represented as objects managed by the system, both system and user-defined objects. There are two main kinds of representations of objects: *literals* and *surrogates.* The surrogates have associated object identifiers (OIDs), which are explicitly created and deleted by the user or the system. Examples of surrogates are objects representing real-world entities such as persons, meta-objects such as functions, or even Amos II mediators as meta-mediator objects.

The literal objects are self-described system-maintained objects which do not have explicit OIDs. Examples of literal objects are numbers and strings. Literal objects can also be *collections*, representing collections of other objects. The system-supported collections are *bags* (unordered sets with duplicates) and *vectors* (order-preserving collections). Literals are automatically deleted by an incremental garbage collector when they are no longer referenced in the database.

9.3.2 Types

Objects are classified into *types* making each object an *instance* of one or several types. The set of all instances of a type is called the *extent* of the type. The types are organized in a multiple inheritance, supertype/subtype hierarchy. If an object is an instance of a type, then it is also an instance of all the supertypes of that type; conversely, the extent of a type is a subset of all extents of the supertypes of that type (extent-subset semantics). For example, if the type `Student` is a subtype of type `Person`, the extent of type `Student` is also a subset of the extent of type `Person`. The extent of a type which is multiple inherited from other types is a subset of the intersection of its supertypes' extents.

There are two kinds of types, *stored* and *derived* types. Derived types are used mainly for data reconciliation and are described in the next section. Stored types are defined and stored in an Amos II peer through the `create type` statement, e.g.:

```
create type Person;
create type Student under Person;
create type Teacher under Person;
create type TA under Student, Teacher;
```

The above statements extend the database schema with four new types. A `TA` object is both a `Student` and a `Teacher`. The extent of type `Person` is the union of all objects of types `Person`, `Student`, `Teacher`, and `TA`. The extent of type `TA` is the intersection of the extents of types `Teacher` and `Student`.

All objects in the database are typed, including meta-objects such as those representing the types themselves. The meta-objects representing types are also stored types and instances of the meta-type named `Type`. In the example the extent of the type named `Type` is the meta-objects representing the types named `TA`, `Teacher`, `Student`, and `Person`.

The root in the type hierarchy is the system type named `Object`. The system type `Userobject` is the root of all user-defined types and the extent of type `Userobject` contains all user-defined objects in the database.

The major root types in the type hierarchy are illustrated by the *function diagram* on Figure 9.2 where ovals denote types, thin arrows denote functions, thick arrows denote type inheritance, and literal function result types are omitted for readability. The type `Datasource` and its subtypes and functions are explained later in section 9.4.2.

Every object has an associated *type set*, which is the set of those types that the object is an instance of. Every object also has one *most specific type* which is the type specified when the object is created. The full type set includes the most specific type and all types above the type in the type hierarchy. For example, objects of type `TA` have the most specific type named `TA` while its full type set is {`TA`, `Teacher`, `Student`, `Person`, `Userobject`, `Object`}.

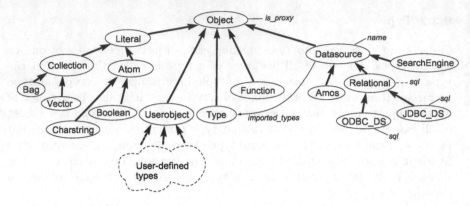

Fig. 9.2. System type hierarchy

The type set of an object can dynamically change during the lifetime of the object through AmosQL statements that change the most specific type of an object. The reason for such facilities is because the *role* of an object may change during the lifetime of the database. For example, a TA might become a student for a while and then a teacher.

9.3.3 Functions

Functions model the semantics (meaning) of objects. They model properties of objects, computations over objects, and relationships between objects. They furthermore are basic primitives in functional queries and views. Functions are instances of the system type `Function`.

A function consists of two parts, the *signature* and the *implementation*.

The *signature* defines the types, and optional names, of the argument(s) and the result of a function. For example, the signature of the function modeling the attribute `name` of type `Person` would have the signature:

    name(Person)->Charstring

Functions can be defined to take any number of arguments, e.g. the arithmetic addition function implementing the infix operator "+" has the signature:

    plus(Number,Number)->Number

The *implementation* specifies how to compute the result of a function given a tuple of argument values. For example, the function `plus` computes the result by adding the two arguments, and `name` obtains the name of a person by accessing the database. The implementation of a function is normally non-procedural, i.e. a function only computes result values for given arguments and does not have any side-effects. The exception is *database procedures* defined through procedural AmosQL statements.

Furthermore, Amos II functions are often *multi-directional*, meaning that the system is able to inversely compute one or several argument values if (some part of) the expected result value is known [9.29]. Inverses of multi-directional functions can be used in database queries and are important for specifying general queries with function calls over the database. For example, the following query, which finds the age of the person named "Tore", uses the inverse of function **name** to avoid iterating over the entire extent of type **Person**:

```
select age(p) from Person p where name(p)='Tore';
```

Depending on their implementation the basic functions can be classified into *stored*, *derived*, and *foreign* functions. In addition, there are *database procedures* with side-effects and *proxy* functions for multi-mediator access as explained later.

- *Stored functions* represent properties of objects (attributes) locally stored in an Amos II database. Stored functions correspond to attributes in object-oriented databases and tables in relational databases.
- *Derived functions* are functions defined in terms of functional queries over other Amos II functions. Derived functions cannot have side effects and the query optimizer is applied when they are defined. Derived functions correspond to side-effect free methods in object-oriented models and views in relational databases. AmosQL has an SQL-like *select* statement for defining derived functions and ad hoc queries.
- *Foreign functions* provide the low-level interfaces for wrapping external systems from Amos II. For example, data structures stored in external storage managers can be manipulated through foreign functions. Foreign functions can also be defined for updating external data structures, but foreign functions to be used in queries must be side-effect free.
  Foreign functions correspond to methods in object-oriented databases. Amos II furthermore provides a possibility to associate several implementations of inverses of a given foreign function, *multi-directional foreign functions*, which informs the query optimizer that there are several access paths implemented for the function. To help the query processor, each associated access path implementation may have associated cost and selectivity functions. The multi-directional foreign functions provide access to external storage structures similar to data "blades", "cartridges", or "extenders" in object-relational databases.
- *Database procedures* are functions defined using a procedural sublanguage of AmosQL. They correspond to methods with side-effects in object-oriented models and constructors. A common usage is for defining constructors of objects along with associated properties.

Amos II functions can furthermore be *overloaded*, meaning that they can have different implementations, called *resolvents*, depending on the type(s) of their argument(s). For example, the salary may be computed differently for types `Student` and `Teacher`. Resolvents can be any of the basic function types[1]. Amos II's query compiler chooses the resolvent based on the types of the argument(s), but not the result.

The *extent* of a function is a set of tuples mapping its arguments and its results. For example, the extent of the function defined as

```
create function name(Person)-> Charstring as stored;
```

is a set of tuples $< P_i, N_i >$ where P_i are objects of type `Person` and N_i are their corresponding names. The extent of a stored function is stored in the database and the extent of a derived function is defined by its query. The extents are accessed in database queries.

The structure of the data associated with types is defined through a set of function definitions. For example:

```
create function name(Person) -> Charstring as stored;
create function birthyear(Person) -> Integer as stored;

create function hobbies(Person) -> Bag of Charstring
                                   as stored;
create function name(Course) -> Charstring as stored;

create function teaches(Teacher) -> Bag of Course
                                    as stored;
create function enrolled(Student) -> Bag of Course
                                     as stored;
create function instructors(Course c) -> Bag of Teacher t
    as
    select t
    where teaches(t) = c; /* Inverse of teaches */
```

The above stored function and type definitions can be illustrated with the function diagram of Figure 9.3.

The function `name` is overloaded on types `Person` and `Course`. The function `instructors` is a derived function that uses the inverse of function `teaches`. The functions `hobbies`, `teaches`, and `enrolled` return sets of values. If `Bag of` is declared for the value of a stored function it means that the result of the function is a bag (multiset)[2], otherwise it is an atomic value.

Functions (attributes) are inherited so the above statement will make objects of type `Teacher` have the attributes `name`, `birthyear`, `hobbies`, and `teaches`.

We notice here that single argument Amos II *functions* are similar to *relationships* and *attributes* in the entity–relationship (ER) model and that

---

[1] A resolvent cannot be overloaded itself, though.

[2] DAPLEX uses the notation `->>` for sets.

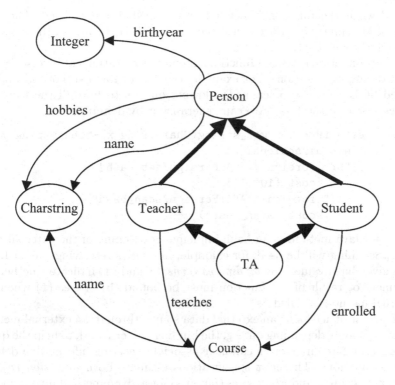

Fig. 9.3. Function diagram

Amos II *types* are similar to ER *entities*. The main difference between an Amos II function and an ER relationship is that Amos II functions have a logical *direction* from the argument to the result, while ER entities are direction neutral. Notice that Amos II functions normally are invertible and thus can be used in the inverse direction too. The main difference between Amos II types and the entities in the basic ER model is that Amos II types can be inherited.

Multi-Directional Foreign Functions

As a very simple example of a multi-directional foreign function, assume we have an external disk-based hash table on strings to be accessed from Amos II. We can then implement it as follows:

```
create function get_string(Charstring x)-> Charstring r
    as foreign "JAVA:Foreign/get_hash";
```

Here the foreign function get_string is implemented as a Java method get_hash of the public Java class Foreign. The Java code is dynamically loaded when the function is defined or the mediator initialized. The Java Virtual Machine is interfaced with the Amos II kernel through the Java Native Interface to C.

Multi-directional foreign functions include declarations of inverse foreign function implementations. For example, our hash table can not only be accessed by keys but also scanned, allowing queries to find all the keys and values stored in the table. We can generalize it by defining:

```
create function get_string(Charstring x)->Charstring y
as multidirectional
    ("bf" foreign "JAVA:Foreign/get_hash"
        cost {100,1})
    ("ff" foreign "JAVA:Foreign/scan_hash"
        cost "scan_cost");
```

Here, the Java method scan_hash implements scanning of the external hash table. Scanning will be used, for example, in queries retrieving the hash key for a given hash value. The *binding patterns*, bf and ff, indicate whether the argument or result of the function must be bound (b) or free (f) when the external method is called.

The cost of accessing an external data source through an external method can vary heavily depending on, e.g. the binding pattern, and, to help the query optimizer, a foreign function can have associated costing information defined as user functions. The cost specifications estimate both *execution costs* in internal cost units and *result sizes* (fanouts) for a given method invocation. In the example, the cost specifications are constant for get_hash and computed through the Amos II function scan_cost for scan_hash.

The basis for the multi-directional foreign function was developed in [9.29], where the mechanisms are further described.

9.3.4 Queries

General queries are formulated through the select statement with format:

```
select <result>
from   <type extents>
where  <condition>
```

For example:

```
select name(p), birthyear(p)
from   Person p
where  birthyear(p) > 1970;
```

The above query will retrieve a tuple of the names and birth years of all persons in the database born after 1970.

In general the semantics of an AmosQL query is as follows:

1. Form the cartesian product of the *type extents*.
2. Restrict the cartesian product by the *condition*.
3. For each possible variable binding to tuple elements in the restricted cartesian product, evaluate the result expressions to form a result tuple.
4. Result tuples containing NIL are not included in the result set; queries are *null intolerant*.

It would be very inefficient to directly use the above semantics to execute a query. It is therefore necessary for the system to do extensive query optimization to transform the query into an efficient execution strategy. Actually, unlike in SQL, AmosQL permits formulation of queries accessing indefinite extents and such queries are not executable at all without query optimization. For example, the previous query could also have been formulated as:

```
select nm, b
from Person P, Charstring nm, Integer b
where b = birthyear(p) and
      nm = name(p) and
      b > 1970;
```

In this case, the cartesian product of all persons, integers, and strings is infinite so the above query is not executable without query optimization.

Some functions may not have a fully computable extent, e.g. arithmetic functions have an infinitely large extent. Queries over infinite extents are not executable, e.g. the system will refuse to execute this query:

```
select x+1 from Number x;
```

9.4 Functional Mediation

For supporting multi-database queries, the basic data model is extended with *proxy* objects, types, and functions. Any object, including meta-objects, can be defined by Amos II as a proxy object by associating with it a property describing its source. The proxy objects allow data and meta-data to be transparently exchanged between mediator peers.

On top of this, reconciliation of conflicting data is supported through regular stored and derived functions and through *derived types* (DTs) [9.18, 9.19] that define types through declarative multi-database queries.

9.4.1 Proxy Objects

The distributed mediator architecture requires the exchange of objects and meta-data between mediator peers and data sources. To support multi-database queries and views, the basic concepts of objects, types, and functions are generalized to include also *proxy objects*, *proxy types*, and *proxy functions*:

– *Proxy objects* in a mediator peer are local OIDs having associated descriptions of corresponding objects stored in other mediators or data sources. They provide a general mechanism to define references to remote objects.
– *Proxy types* in a mediator peer describe types represented in other mediators or data sources. The proxy objects are instances of some proxy types and the extent of a proxy type is a set of proxy objects.
– Analogously, *proxy functions* in a mediator peer describe functions in other mediators or sources.

The proxy objects, types, and functions are implicitly created by the system in the mediator where the user makes a multi-database query, e.g.:

```
select name(p) from Personnel@Tb p;
```

This query retrieves the names of all persons in a data source named **Tb**. It causes the system to internally generate a proxy type for **Personnel@Tb** in the mediator server where the query is issued, M. It will also create a proxy function **name** in M representing the function **name** in **Tb**. In this query it is not necessary or desirable to create any proxy instances of type **Personel@Tb** in M since the query is not retrieving their identities. The multi-database query optimizer will here make such an optimization.

Proxy objects can be used in combination with local objects. This allows for general multi-database queries over several mediator peers. The result of such queries may be literals (as in the example), proxy objects, or local objects. The system stores internally information about the origin of each proxy object so it can be identified properly. Each local OID has a locally unique OID number and two proxy objects are considered equal if they represent objects created in the same mediator or source with equal OID numbers.

Proxy types can be used in function definitions as any other type. In the example one can define a derived function of the persons located in a certain location:

```
create function personnel_in(Charstring l) -> Personnel@Tb
    as select p from Personnel@Tb p
        where  location(p) = l;
```

In this case the local function **personnel_in** will return those instances of the proxy type for **Personnel** in the mediator named **Tb** for which it holds that the value of function **location** in **Tb** returns l. The function can be used in local queries and function definitions, and as proxy functions in multi-database queries from other mediator peers.

Multi-database queries and functions are compiled and optimized through a distributed query decomposition process fully described in [9.20] and summarized later. Notice again that there is no central mediator schema and the compilation and execution of multi-database queries is made by exchanging data and meta-data with the accessed mediator servers. If some schema of a mediator server is modified, the multi-database functions accessing that mediator server become invalid and must be recompiled.

9.4.2 Data Source Modeling

Information about different data sources is represented explicitly in the Amos II data model through the system type `Datasource` and its subtypes (Figure 9.2). Some subtypes of `Datasource` represent generic kinds of data sources that share common properties, such as the types `Relational` and `SearchEngine` [9.22] representing the common properties of all RDBMSs and all Internet search engines, respectively. Other subtypes of `Datasource` like `ODBC_DS` and `JDBC_DS` represent specific kinds of sources, such as ODBC and JDBC drivers. In particular the system type `Amos` represents other Amos II peers. Instances of these types represent individual data sources. All types under `Datasource` are collectively called the *datasource types*.

Since wrappers and their corresponding datasource types interact tightly, every wrapper module installs its corresponding types and functions whenever initialized. This reflexive design promotes code and data reuse and provides transparent management of information about data sources via the Amos II query language.

Each datasource type instance has a unique name and a set of imported types. Some of the (more specific) subtypes have defined a set of low-level access functions. For example, the type `Relational` has the function `sql` that accepts any relational data source instance, a parametrized SQL query, and its parameters. Since there is no generic way to access all relational data sources this function only defines an interface. On the other hand the type `ODBC_DS` overloads this function with an implementation that can submit a parametrized query to an ODBC source. These functions can be used in low-level mediator queries, which roughly corresponds to the *pass-through* mode defined in the SQL-MED standard [9.32]. However, normally the low-level data access functions are not used directly by the users. Instead queries that refer to external sources are rewritten by the wrapper modules in terms of these functions. In addition datasource types may include other functions, such as source address, user names, and passwords.

9.4.3 Reconciliation

Proxy objects provide a general way to query and exchange data between mediators and sources. However, reconciliation requires types defined in terms of data in different mediators. For this, the basic system is extended with *derived types* (DTs), which are types defined in terms of queries defining their extents. These *extent queries* may access both local and proxy objects.

Data integration by DTs is performed by building a hierarchy of DTs based on local types and types imported from other data sources. The traditional inheritance mechanism, where the corresponding instances of an object in the super/subtypes are identified by the same OID, is extended with declarative query specification of the correspondence between the instances of the derived super/subtypes. Integration by sub/supertyping is related to the mechanisms in some other systems such as the integrated views and column adding in the Pegasus system [9.9], but is better suited for use in an object-oriented environment.

The extents of derived subtypes are defined through queries restricting the intersection of the extents of the constituent supertypes. For example:

```
create derived type CSD_emp under Personnel p
    where location(p)=''CSD'';
```

This statement creates a DT CSD_emp whose extent contains those persons who work in the CSD department. When a DT is queried the system will implicitly create those of its instance OIDs necessary to execute the query.

An important purpose of DTs is to define types as views that reconcile differences between types in different mediator servers. For example, the type Personnel might be defined in mediator Tb while Ta has a corresponding type Faculty. The following statement executed in a third mediator, M, defines a DT Emp in M representing those employees who work both in Ta and Tb:

```
create derived type Emp
    under Faculty@Ta f, Personnel@Tb p
    where ssn(f)=id_to_ssn(id(p))
```

Here the where clause identifies how to match equivalent proxy objects from both sources. The function ssn uniquely identifies faculty members in Ta, while the function id in Tb identifies personnel by employee numbers. A (foreign) function id_to_ssn in M translates employee numbers to SSNs.

The system internally maintains the information necessary to map between OIDs of a DT and its supertypes.

An important issue in designing object views is the placement of the DTs in the type hierarchy. Mixing freely the DTs and ordinary types in a type hierarchy can lead to semantically inconsistent hierarchies [9.24]. In order to provide the user with powerful modeling capabilities along with a semantically consistent inheritance hierarchy, the ordinary types and DTs in Amos II are placed in a single type hierarchy where it is not allowed to have an ordinary type as a subtype of a DT. This rule preserves the extent–subset semantics for all types in the hierarchy. If DTs were allowed to be supertypes of ordinary types, due to the declarative specification of the DTs, it would not have been possible to guarantee that each instance of the ordinary type has a corresponding instance in its supertypes [9.24].

The DT instances are derived from the instances of their supertypes according to an extent query specified in the DT definition. DT instances are assigned OIDs by the system, which allows their use in locally stored functions defined over the DTs in the same way as over the ordinary types. A selective OID generation for the DT instances is used to avoid performance and storage overhead.

The concept of DTs and its use for data integration is fully described in [9.18]. The regular DTs, defined by subtyping through queries of their supertypes, provide means for mediation based on operators such as join, selection, and projection. However, these do not suffice for integration of sources having overlapping data. When integrating data from different mediator servers it is often the case that the same entity appears either in one of the mediators or in both. For example, if one wants to combine employees from different departments, some employees will only work in one of the departments while others will work in both of them.

For this type of integration requirements the Amos II system features a special kind of DTs called *Integration Union Types* (IUTs) defined as supertypes of other types through queries. IUTs are used to model unions of real-world entities represented by overlapping type extents. Informally, while the regular DTs represent restrictions and intersections of extents of other types, the IUTs represent reconciled unions of (possibly overlapping) data in one or more mediator server or data sources. The example in Figure 9.4 illustrates the features and the applications of the IUTs.

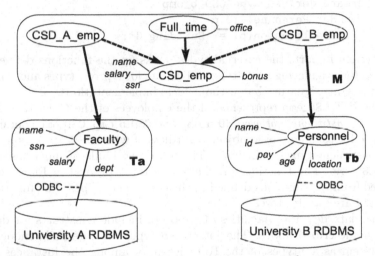

Fig. 9.4. An object-oriented view for the computer science department.

In this example, a computer science department (CSD) is formed out of the faculty members of two universities named *A* and *B*. The CSD administration needs to set up a database of the faculty members of the new department in terms of the databases of the two universities. The faculty members of CSD can be employed by either one of the universities. There are also faculty members employed by both universities. The full-time members of a department are assigned an office in the department.

In Figure 9.4 the mediators are represented by rectangles; the ovals in the rectangles represent types, and the solid lines represent inheritance relationships between the types. The two mediators Ta and Tb provide Amos II views of the relational databases *University A DB* and *University B DB*. In mediator Ta there is a type Faculty and in mediator Tb a type Personnel.

The relational databases are accessed through an ODBC wrapper in Ta and Tb that translates AmosQL queries into ODBC calls. The ODBC wrapper interface translates AmosQL queries over objects represented in relations into calls to a foreign function executing SQL statements [9.4]. The translation process is based on partitioning general queries into subqueries only using the capabilities of the data source, as fully explained in [9.20].

A third mediator M is set up in the CSD to provide the integrated view. Here, the semantically equivalent types CSD_A_emp and CSD_B_emp are defined as derived subtypes of types in Ta and Tb:

```
create derived type CSD_a_emp
  under Faculty@Ta f
  where dept(f) = 'CSD';

create derived type CSD_b_emp
  under Personnel@Tb p
  where location(p) = 'Building G';
```

The system imports the external types, looks up the functions defined over them in the originating mediators, and defines local proxy types and functions with the same signature but without local implementations.

The IUT CSD_emp represents all the employees of the CSD. It is defined over the *constituent subtypes* CSD_a_emp and CSD_b_emp. CSD_emp contains one instance for each employee object regardless of whether it appears in one of the constituent types or in both. There are two kinds of functions defined over CSD_emp. The functions on the left of the type oval in Figure 9.4 are derived from the functions defined in the constituent types. The functions on the right are locally stored.

The data definition facilities of AmosQL include constructs for defining IUTs as described above. The integrated types are internally modeled by the system as subtypes of the IUT. Equality among the instances of the integrated types is established based on a set of key attributes. IUTs can also have locally stored attributes, and attributes reconciled from the integrated types. See [9.19] for details.

The type CSD_emp is defined as follows:

```
CREATE INTEGRATION TYPE CSD_emp
  KEYS ssn Integer;
  SUPERTYPE OF
    CSD_A_emp ae: ssn = ssn(ae);
    CSD_B_emp be: ssn = id_to_ssn(id(be));
  FUNCTIONS
    CASE ae
      name = name(ae);
```

```
        salary = pay(ae);
      CASE be
        name = name(be);
        salary = salary(be);
      CASE ae, be
        salary = pay(ae) + salary(be);
    PROPERTIES
        bonus Integer;
  END;
```

For each of the constituent subtypes, a KEYS clause is specified. The instances of different constituent types having the same key values will map into a single IUT instance. The key expressions can contain calls to any function.

The FUNCTIONS clause defines the reconciled functions of CSD_emp, derived from functions over the constituent subtypes. For different subsets of the constituent subtypes, a reconciled function of an IUT can have different implementations specified by the CASE clauses. For example, the definition of CSD_emp specifies that the salary function is calculated as the salary of the faculty member at the university to which it belongs. In the case when s/he is employed by both universities, the salary is the sum of the two salaries. When the same function is defined for more than one case, the most specific case applies. Finally, the PROPERTIES clause defines the stored function bonus over the IUT CSD_emp.

The IUTs can be subtyped by DTs. In Figure 9.4, the 2 type Full_Time is defined as a subtype of the CSD_emp type, representing the instances for which the salary exceeds a certain number (50000). The locally stored function office stores information about the offices of the full-time CSD employees. The type Full_Time and its property office have the following definitions:

```
    create derived type Full_Time under CSD_emp e
                            where salary(e)>50000;
    create function office(Full_Time)->Charstring
        as stored;
```

9.5 Query Processing

The description of type hierarchies and semantic heterogeneity using declarative multi-database functions is very powerful. However, a naive implementation of the framework could be very inefficient, and there are many opportunities for the extensive query optimization needed for distributed mediation.

The query processor of Amos II, illustrated by Figure 9.5, consists of three main components. The core component of the query processor is the *local query compiler* that optimizes queries accessing local data in a mediator. The

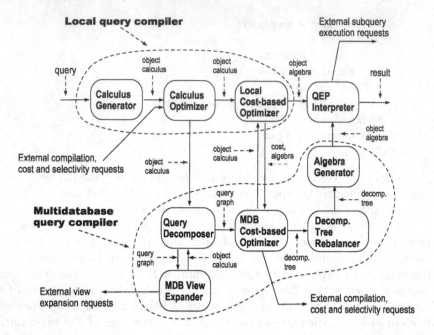

Fig. 9.5. Query processing in Amos II

Multi-database Query Compiler MQC, allows Amos II mediators to process queries that also access other mediator peers and data sources. Both compilers generate query execution plans (*QEPs*) in terms of an *object algebra* that is interpreted by the *QEP interpreter* component. The following two sections describe in more detail the subcomponents of the local and the multi-database query compilers.

9.5.1 Local Query Processing

To illustrate the query compilation of single-site queries we use the sample ad hoc query:

```
select p, name(parent(p))
  from person p
  where hobby(p) = 'sailing';
```

The first query compilation step, *calculus generation*, translates the parsed AmosQL query tree into an *object calculus* representation called ObjectLog [9.29]. The object calculus is a declarative representation of the original query and is an extension of Datalog with objects, types, overloading, and multi-directional foreign functions.

The calculus generator translates the example query into this expression:

$\{ p, nm \mid$
$\quad p = Person_{nil \to Person}() \ \land$
$\quad pa = parent_{Person \to Person}(p) \ \land$
$\quad nm = name_{Person \to Charstring}(pa) \ \land$
$\quad 'sailing' = hobby_{Person \to Charstring}(p) \}$

The first predicate in the expression is inserted by the system to assert the type of the variable p. This *type check predicate* defines that the variable p is bound to one of the objects returned by the *extent function* for type **Person**, $Person()$, which returns all the instances (the extent) of its type. The variables nm and pa are generated by the system. Notice that the functions in the predicates are annotated with their type signatures, to allow for overloading of function symbols over the argument types.

The *calculus optimizer* of the query optimizer first transforms the unoptimized calculus expression to reduce the number of predicates, e.g. by exploring properties of type definitions. In the example, it removes the type check predicate:

$\{ p, nm \mid$
$\quad pa = parent_{Person \to Person}(p) \ \land$
$\quad nm = name_{Person \to Charstring}(pa) \ \land$
$\quad 'sailing' = hobby_{Person \to Charstring}(p) \}$

This transformation is correct because p is used in a stored function (**parent** or **hobby**) with argument or result of type **Person**. The referential integrity system constrains instances of stored functions to be of correct types [9.29].

The *local cost-based optimizer* will use cost-based optimization to produce an executable object algebra plan from the transformed query calculus expression. The system has a built-in cost model for local data and built-in algebra operators. Basically the cost-based optimizer generates a number of execution plans, applies the cost model on each of them, and chooses the cheapest for execution. The system has the options of using dynamic programming, hill climbing, or random search to find an execution plan with minimal cost. Users can instruct the system to choose a particular strategy.

The optimizer is furthermore extensible whereby new algebra operators are defined using the multi-directional foreign functions, which also provide the basic mechanisms for interactions between mediator peers in distributed execution plans.

The *query execution plan interpreter* will finally interpret the execution plan to yield the result of the query.

9.5.2 Queries over Derived Types

Queries over DTs are expanded by system-inserted predicates performing the DT system support tasks [9.18]. These tasks are divided into three mechanisms: (i) providing consistency of queries over DTs so that the extent–subset semantics is followed; (ii) generation of OIDs for those DT instances needed to execute the query; and (iii) validation of the DT instances with assigned OIDs so that DT instances satisfy the constraints of the DT definitions. The system generates derived function definitions to perform these tasks. During the calculus optimization the query is analyzed and, where needed, the appropriate function definitions are added to the query. A selective OID generation mechanism avoids overhead by generating OIDs only for those derived objects that are either needed during the execution of a query, or have associated local data in the mediator database.

The functions specifying the view support tasks often have overlapping parts. Reference [9.18] demonstrates how calculus-based query optimization can be used to remove redundant computations introduced from the overlap among the system-inserted expressions, and between the system-inserted and user-specified parts of the query.

Each IUT is mapped by the calculus optimizer to a hierarchy of system-generated DTs, called *auxiliary types* [9.19]. The auxiliary types represent disjoint parts of the outerjoin needed for this type of data integration. The reconciliation of the attributes of the integrated types is modeled by a set of overloaded derived functions generated by the system from the specification in the IUT definition. Several novel query processing and optimization techniques are developed for efficiently processing the queries containing overloaded functions over the auxiliary types, as described in [9.19].

9.5.3 Multi-database Query Processing

The *Multi-database Query Compiler (MQC)* [9.20, 9.17] is invoked whenever a query is posed over data from more than one mediator peer. The goal of the MQC is to explore the space of possible distributed execution plans and choose a "reasonably" cheap one. As the local query compiler, the MQC uses a combination of heuristic and dynamic programming strategies to produce a set of distributed object algebra plans.

The distributed nature of Amos II mediators requires a query processing framework that allows cooperation of a number of autonomous mediator peers. The MQC interacts with the local optimizer as well as with the query optimizers of the other mediator peers involved in the query via requests to estimate costs and selectivities of subqueries, requests to expand the view definitions of remote views, and requests to compile subqueries in remote mediator peers. The generated local execution plan interacts with the execution plans produced by the other mediator peers.

The details of the MQC are described in [9.20]. Here we will overview its main subcomponents:

– The *query decomposer* identifies fragments of a multi-database query, *subqueries*, where each subquery can be processed by a single data source. The decomposer takes as input an object calculus query and produces a *query graph* with nodes representing subqueries assigned to an execution site and arcs representing variables connecting the subqueries. The benefit of decomposition is twofold. First, complex computations in subqueries can be pushed to the data sources to avoid expensive communication and to utilize the processing capabilities of the sources. Second, the multi-database query optimization cost is reduced by the partitioning of the input query into several smaller subqueries.

Query decomposition is performed in two steps:

1. *Predicate grouping* collects predicates executable at only one data source and groups them together into one or more subqueries. The grouping process uses a heuristic where cross-products are avoided by placing predicates without common variables in separate subqueries.

2. *Site assignment* uses a cost-based heuristics to place those predicates that can be executed at more than one site (e.g. θ-joins), eventually replicates some of the predicates in the subqueries to improve the selectivity of subqueries, and finally assigns execution sites to the subqueries.

- The *multi-database view expander* expands remote views directly or indirectly referenced in queries. This may lead to significant improvement in the query plan quality because there may be many redundancies in large compositions of multi-database views.

The multi-database view expander traverses the query graph to send expansion requests for the subqueries. In this way, all predicates defined in the same database are expanded in a single request. This approach allows the remote site to perform calculus simplifications of the expanded and merged predicate definitions as a whole and then return the transformed subquery. However, when there are many mediator layers it is not always beneficial to fully expand all view definitions, as shown in [9.21]. The multi-database view expander therefore uses a heuristic to choose the most promising views for expansion, a technique called *controlled view expansion*. After all subqueries in the query graph have been view expanded the query decomposer is called again for predicate regrouping.

- The *multi-database (MDB) query optimizer* decides on the order of execution of the predicates in the query graph nodes, and on the direction of the data shipping between the peers. Execution plans for distributed queries in Amos II are represented by *decomposition trees*. Each node in a decomposition tree describes a join cycle through a client mediator (i.e. the mediator where the query is issued). In a cycle, first intermediate results are shipped to the site where they are used. Then a subquery is executed at that site using the shipped data as input, and the result is shipped back to the mediator. Finally, one or more post-processing subqueries are performed at the client mediator. The result of a cycle is always materialized in the mediator. A sequence of cycles can represent any execution plan. As the space of all execution plans is exponential to the number of subqueries in the input query graph, we examine only the space of left-deep decomposition trees using a dynamic programming approach. To evaluate the costs and selectivities of the subqueries the multi-database optimizer sends compilation requests for the subqueries both to the local optimizer and to the query compilers of the remote mediators.

- The *decomposition tree rebalancer* transforms the initial left-deep decomposition tree into a bushy one. To prevent all the data flowing through the client mediator, the decomposition tree rebalancer uses a heuristic that selects pairs of adjacent nodes in the decomposition tree, merges the selected nodes into one new node, and sends the merged node to the two mediators corresponding to the original nodes for recompilation. From the merged nodes, each of the two mediators generate different decomposition subtrees and the cheaper one is chosen. In this way, the input decomposition tree is rebalanced from a left-deep tree into a bushy one. The overall execution plan resulting from the tree rebalancing can contain plans where the data is shipped directly from one remote mediator to another, eliminating the bottleneck of shipping all data through a single mediator. See [9.17] for details.
- The *object algebra generator* translates a decomposition tree into a set of inter-calling local object algebra plans.

9.6 Related Work

Amos II is related to research in the areas of data integration, object views, distributed databases, and general query processing. There has been several projects on intergration of data in a multi-database environment [9.5, 9.8, 9.10, 9.12, 9.14, 9.16, 9.23, 9.27, 9.30, 9.40, 9.41]. The integration facilities of Amos II are based on work in the area of object-oriented views [9.1, 9.3, 9.15, 9.26, 9.33, 9.35, 9.36, 9.39].

Most of the mediator frameworks reported in the literature (e.g. [9.16, 9.41, 9.14]) propose centralized query compilation and execution coordination. In [9.9] it is indicated that a distributed mediation framework is a promising research direction, but to the best of our knowledge no results in this area are reported. Some recent commercial data integration products, such as IBM's Federated DB2, also provide centralized mediation features.

In the DIOM project [9.30] a framework for integration of relational data sources is presented where the operations can be executed either in the mediator or in a data source. The compilation process in DIOM is centrally performed, and there is no clear distinction between the data sources and the mediators in the optimization framework.

The Multiview [9.35] object-oriented view system provides multiple inheritance and a capacity-augmented view mechanism implemented with a technique called Object Slicing [9.26] using OID coercion in an inheritance hierarchy. However, it assumes active view maintenance and does not elaborate on the consequences of using this technique for integration of data in autonomous and dislocated repositories. Furthermore, it is not implemented using declarative functions for the description of the view functionality.

One of the few research reports describing the use of functional view mechanisms for data integration is the Multibase system [9.8]. It is also based on a derivative of the DAPLEX data model and does reconciliation similar to the IUTs in this chapter. An important difference between Multibase and Amos II is that the data model used in Multibase does not contain the object-oriented concept of OIDs and inheritance. The query optimization and meta-modeling methods in Amos II are also more elaborate than in Multibase.

The UNISQL [9.23] system also provides views for database integration. The virtual classes (corresponding to the DTs) are organized in a separate class hierarchy. However, the virtual class instances inherit the OIDs from the corresponding instances in the ordinary classes, which prohibits definition of stored functions over virtual classes defined by multiple inheritance as in Amos II. There is no integration mechanism corresponding to the IUTs.

Reference [9.34] gives a good overview of distributed databases and query processing. As opposed to the distributed databases, where there is a centralized repository containing meta-data about the whole system, the architecture described in this paper consists of autonomous systems, each storing only locally relevant meta-data.

One of the most thorough attempts to tackle the query optimization problem in distributed databases was done within the System R* project [9.7] where, unlike Amos II, an exhaustive, cost-based, and centrally performed query optimization is made to find the optimal plan. Another classic distributed database system is SDD-1 [9.2] which used a hill-climbing heuristic like the query decomposer in Amos II.

9.7 Summary

We have given an overview of the Amos II mediator system where groups of distributed mediator peers are used to integrate data from different sources. Each mediator in a group has DBMS facilities for query compilation and exchange of data and meta-data with other mediator peers. Derived functions can be defined where data from several mediator peers is abstracted, transformed, and reconciled. Wrappers are defined by interfacing Amos II systems with external systems through its multi-directional foreign function interface. Amos II can furthermore be embedded in applications and used as stand-alone databases. The chapter gave an overview of Amos II's architecture with references to other published papers on the system for details.

We described the Functional Data Model and query language forming the basis for data integration in Amos II. The distributed multi-mediator query decomposition strategies used were summarized.

The mediator peers are autonomous without any central schema. A special mediator, the name server, keeps track of what mediator peers are members of a group. The name servers can be queried for the location of mediator peers in a group. Meta-queries to each mediator peer can be posed to investigate the structure of its schema.

Some unique features of Amos II are:

- A distributed mediator architecture where query plans are distributed over several communicating mediator peers.
- Using declarative functional queries to model reconciled functional views spanning multiple mediator peers.
- Query processing and optimization techniques for queries to reconcile views involving function overloading, late binding, and type-aware query rewrites.

The Amos II system is fully implemented and can be downloaded from http://user.it.uu.se/~udbl/amos. Amos II runs under Windows and Unix.

Acknowledgements

The following persons have contributed to the development of the Amos II kernel: Gustav Fahl, Staffan Flodin, Jörn Gebhardt, Martin Hansson, Vanja Josifovski, Jonas Karlsson, Timour Katchaounov, Milena Koparanova, Salah-Eddine Machani, Joakim Näs, Kjell Orsborn, Tore Risch, Martin Sköld, and Magnus Werner.

References

9.1 S. Abiteboul, A. Bonner: Objects and Views. *ACM Int. Conf. on Management of Data (SIGMOD'91)*, 238-247, 1991.

9.2 P. Bernstein, N. Goodman, E. Wong, C. Reeve, J. Rothnie Jr.: Query Processing in a System for Distributed Databases (SDD-1). *ACM Transactions on Database Systems (TODS)*, 6(4), 602-625, 1981.

9.3 E. Bertino: A View Mechanism for Object-Oriented Databases. *3rd Int. Conf. on Extending Database Technology (EDBT'92)*, 136-151, 1992.

9.4 S. Brandani: Multi-database Access from Amos II using ODBC. *Linköping Electronic Press*, 3(19), Dec., 1998, http://www.ep.liu.se/ea/cis/1998/019/.

9.5 O. Bukhres, A. Elmagarmid (eds.): *Object-Oriented Multidatabase Systems*. Prentice Hall, 1996.

9.6 K. Cassel and T. Risch: An Object-Oriented Multi-Mediator Browser. *2nd International Workshop on User Interfaces to Data Intensive Systems*, Zurich, Switzerland, 2001.

9.7 D. Daniels, P. Selinger, L. Haas, B. Lindsay, C. Mohan, A. Walker, P.F. Wilms: An Introduction to Distributed Query Compilation in R*. *2nd Int. Symp. on Distributed Data Bases*, 291-309, 1982.

9.8 U. Dayal, H-Y. Hwang: View Definition and Generalization for Database Integration in a Multidatabase System. *IEEE Transactions on Software Engineering*, 10(6), 628-645, 1984.

9.9 W. Du, M. Shan: Query Processing in Pegasus, In O. Bukhres, A. Elmagarmid (eds.): *Object-Oriented Multidatabase Systems*. Prentice Hall, 449-471, 1996.

9.10 C. Evrendilek, A. Dogac, S. Nural, F. Ozcan: Multidatabase Query Optimization. *Distributed and Parallel Databases*, 5(1), 77-114, 1997.

9.11 G. Fahl, T. Risch: Query Processing over Object Views of Relational Data. *The VLDB Journal*, 6(4), 261-281, 1997.

9.12 D. Fang, S. Ghandeharizadeh, D. McLeod, A. Si: The Design, Implementation, and Evaluation of an Object-Based Sharing Mechanism for Federated Database System. *9th Int. Conf. on Data Engineering (ICDE'93)*, IEEE, 467-475, 1993.

9.13 S. Flodin, T. Risch: Processing Object-Oriented Queries with Invertible Late Bound Functions. *21st Conf. on Very Large Databases (VLDB'95)*, 335-344, 1995

9.14 H. Garcia-Molina, Y. Papakonstantinou, D. Quass, A. Rajaraman, Y.Sagiv, J. Ullman, V. Vassalos, J. Widom: The TSIMMIS Approach to Mediation: Data Models and Languages. *Journal of Intelligent Information Systems*, 8(2), 117-132, 1997.

9.15 S. Heiler, S. Zdonik: Object views: Extending the Vision. *6th Int. Conf. on Data Engineering (ICDE'90)*, IEEE, 86-93, 1990.

9.16 V. Josifovski, P. Schwarz, L. Haas, and E. Lin: Garlic: A New Flavor of Federated Query Processing for DB2, *ACM SIGMOD Conf.*, 2002.

9.17 V. Josifovski, T. Katchaounov, T. Risch: Optimizing Queries in Distributed and Composable Mediators. *4th Conf. on Cooperative Information Systems (CoopIS'99)*, 291-302, 1999.

9.18 V. Josifovski, T. Risch: Functional Query Optimization over Object-Oriented Views for Data Integration. *Journal of Intelligent Information Systems* 12(2-3), 165-190, 1999.

9.19 V. Josifovski, T. Risch: Integrating Heterogeneous Overlapping Databases through Object-Oriented Transformations. *25th Conf. on Very Large Databases (VLDB'99)*, 435-446, 1999.

9.20 V.Josifovski and T.Risch: Query Decomposition for a Distributed Object-Oriented Mediator System. *Distributed and Parallel Databases*, 11(3), 307-336, 2002.

9.21 T. Katchaounov, V. Josifovski, T. Risch: Distributed View Expansion in Object-Oriented Mediators, *5th Int. Conf. on Cooperative Information Systems (CoopIS'00), Eilat, Israel*, LNCS 1901, Springer Verlag, 2000.

9.22 T. Katchaounov, T. Risch, and S. Zürcher: Object-Oriented Mediator Queries to Internet Search Engines, *Int. Workshop on Efficient Web-based Information Systems (EWIS)*, Montpellier, France, 2002.

9.23 W. Kelley, S. Gala, W. Kim, T. Reyes, B. Graham: Schema Architecture of the UNISQL/M Multidatabase System. In W. Kim (ed.): *Modern Database Systems - The Object Model, Interoperability, and Beyond*, ACM Press, 621-648, 1995.

9.24 W. Kim and W. Kelley: On View Support in Object-Oriented Database Systems, In W. Kim (ed.), *Modern Database Systems - The Object Model, Interoperability, and Beyond*, ACM Press, 1995.

9.25 M.Koparanova and T.Risch: Completing CAD Data Queries for Visualization, *Int. Database Engineering and Applications Symp. (IDEAS 2002) Edmonton, Canada*, 2002.

9.26 H. Kuno, Y. Ra, E. Rundensteiner: *The Object-Slicing Technique: A Flexible Object Representation and Its Evaluation*. Univ. of Michigan Tech. Report CSE-TR-241-95, 1995.

9.27 E-P. Lim, S-Y. Hwang, J. Srivastava, D. Clements, M. Ganesh: Myriad: Design and Implementation of a Federated Database System. *Software - Practice and Experience*, John Wiley & Sons, 25(5), 533-562, 1995.

9.28 H. Lin, T. Risch, and T. Katchaounov: Adaptive data mediation over XML data. In special issue on Web Information Systems Applications of *Journal of Applied System Studies*, 3(2), 2002.

9.29 W. Litwin, T. Risch: Main Memory Oriented Optimization of OO Queries using Typed Datalog with Foreign Predicates. *IEEE Transactions on Knowledge and Data Engineering*, 4(6), 517-528, 1992.

9.30 L. Liu, C. Pu: An Adaptive Object-Oriented Approach to Integration and Access of Heterogeneous Information Sources. *Distributed and Parallel Databases*, 5(2), 167-205, 1997.

9.31 P. Lyngbaek: *OSQL: A Language for Object Databases*, Tech. Report, HP Labs, HPL-DTD-91-4, 1991.

9.32 J. Melton, J. Michels, V. Josifovski, K. Kulkarni, P. Schwarz, and K. Zeidenstein: SQL and Management of External Data, *SIGMOD Record*, 30(1), 70-77, March 2001.

9.33 A. Motro: Superviews: Virtual Integration of Multiple Databases. *IEEE Transactions on Software Engineering*, 13(7), 785-798, 1987.

9.34 M.T. Özsu, P. Valduriez: *Principles of Distributed Database Systems*, Prentice Hall, 1999.

9.35 E. Rundensteiner, H. Kuno, Y. Ra, V. Crestana-Taube, M. Jones, P. Marron: The MultiView project: Object-Oriented View Technology and Applications, *ACM Int. Conf. on Management of Data (SIGMOD'96)*, 555, 1996.

9.36 M. Scholl, C. Laasch, M. Tresch: Updatable Views in Object-Oriented Databases. *2nd Deductive and Object-Oriented Databases Conf. (DOOD91)*, 189-207, 1991.

9.37 D. Shipman: The Functional Data Model and the Data Language DAPLEX. *ACM Transactions on Database Systems*, 6(1), 140-173, 1981.

9.38 M. Sköld, T. Risch: Using Partial Differencing for Efficient Monitoring of Deferred Complex Rule Conditions. *12th Int. Conf. on Data Engineering (ICDE'96)*, IEEE, 392-401, 1996.

9.39 C. Souza dos Santos, S. Abiteboul, C. Delobel: Virtual Schemas and Bases. *Int. Conf. on Extending Database Technology (EDBT'92)*, 81-94, 1994.

9.40 S. Subramananian, S. Venkataraman: Cost-Based Optimization of Decision Support Queries using Transient Views. *ACM Int. Conf. on Management of Data (SIGMOD'98)*, 319-330, 1998.

9.41 A. Tomasic, L. Raschid, P. Valduriez: Scaling Access to Heterogeneous Data Sources with DISCO. *IEEE Transactions on Knowledge and Data Engineering*, 10(5), 808-823, 1998.

9.42 G. Wiederhold: Mediators in the Architecture of Future Information Systems. *IEEE Computer*, 25(3), 38-49, 1992.

10. Applying Functional Languages in Knowledge-Based Information Integration Systems

Martin Peim[1], Norman W. Paton[1], and Enrico Franconi[2]

[1] Department of Computer Science, University of Manchester, Oxford Road, Manchester M13 9PL, UK
   email: (mpeim,norm)@cs.man.ac.uk
[2] Faculty of Computer Science, Free University of Bolzano, Piazza Domenicani 3, 39100 Bolzano, Italy
   email: franconi@inf.unibz.it

Summary.

Knowledge-based information integration systems exploit rich descriptions of domain knowledge to support query formulation, source reconciliation or query optimisation. A characteristic shared by most such systems is that at some stage during query compilation, a query is translated from an expression over the knowledge base into one phrased in terms of the data models of the (possibly wrapped) sources that are being integrated. Individual proposals differ (i) in the knowledge model used; (ii) in the source model and language used; (iii) in the nature of the rewriting required from the knowledge model to the source model; and (iv) in the role of the source model and language. This chapter discusses some of the alternative options and describes in some detail a knowledge-based query processor, in which: (i) the knowledge model is an expressive Description Logic; (ii) the source model is an object model and the source language is the monoid comprehension calculus; (iii) the rewriting involved is query expansion, in a global-as-view approach to schema integration; and (iv) the source language is used for query normalisation and semantic optimisation, but not for direct evaluation. The approach thus illustrates one role that a language with functional underpinnings can play in a knowledge-based integration system, and provides a context for the comparison of alternative functional source languages and roles for those languages.

10.1 Introduction

The provision of systems for integrating diverse computational and information resources occupies a significant portion of research in computer systems. Integration infrastructures provide different levels of abstraction to developers. For example, Grid middleware [10.13] provides reasonably direct access to the physical computational resources being accessed. By contrast, the services provided by J2EE [10.12] typically hide certain of the lower-level details of, for example, data representations and protocols that may be visible to Grid application developers. At a still higher level of abstraction, distributed data management facilities, such as those supported by distributed query processors [10.20], provide high-level declarative access to distributed information resources. Towards the top of the current layers of abstraction are knowledge-based information integration systems, in which even the details of logical data models are hidden from users.

In general, where there are n levels of abstraction over the underlying computational resources, developers of platforms at level i need only concern themselves directly with the facilities provided by level $i-1$ in the stack. This chapter is concerned principally with the relationship between knowledge-based information integration systems and the level of logically-wrapped sources over which they traditionally sit. Information is typically modelled at the knowledge level using a formal conceptual model that is both expressive and amenable to automated reasoning. Logically-wrapped sources generally support one or other of the standard data model paradigms (relational, semi-structured or object-oriented), over which some form of declarative query language is supported.

What benefits do knowledge-based information integration systems offer? The following are commonly cited:

1. Users interact with a conceptual view of the domain, and thus are able to phrase requests over richer models that can both guide the user in the phrasing of suitable questions and detect certain inconsistencies in user queries [10.15, 10.3].
2. The provision of declarative modelling and associated reasoning facilities can be used (i) to make explicit relationships between the sources being integrated, and to allow these relationships to be described in a declarative way [10.21]; (ii) to detect inconsistencies between the sources being integrated [10.4]; and (iii) to perform semantic query optimisation involving requests over the knowledge model [10.16].

Knowledge-based query processing systems have been used with different source-wrapping models and different languages over these models. The most prominent proposals for the use of functional languages for source integration have typically: (i) used the functional language as the user-level query language; (ii) operated over semi-structured or object-oriented data models; (iii) provided global-as-view schema integration; and (iv) provided consistent access to local stores and remote sources.

Each of these points will now be discussed for some representative functional data integration systems. K2 [10.9] is a source integration system for bioinformatics descended from Kleisli. It has the following features: (i) its query language is the object query language OQL, although it acts over a complex-value model, and has a comprehension-based semantics; (ii) it acts over a model with recursive type constructors for sets, bags, lists, tuple and tagged unions; (iii) it views external sources as collections of functions that return hierarchical source records, and places little direct emphasis on the creation of a global schema; and (iv) queries can range over remote resources and local stores in the form of the GUS data warehouse.

AMOS II [10.26], a generic mediator system, has the following features: (i) its query language is a functional language with the select-from-where syntax of SQL; (ii) it acts over an object model, with type extensions designed to ease model integration; (iii) there is no particular emphasis on the development of a global schema, but functions can be used to hide source details of specific sources; and (iv) the system is associated with local main-memory database facilities as well as being able to access remote resources.

Unlike K2 and AMOS II, P/FDM [10.19] was originally developed as a centralised database, the query processor of which was extended to support calls to remote data sources. In terms of its features: (i) its query language is Daplex [10.27], but with semantics based on comprehensions; (ii) its data model is the associated Functional Data Model [10.27], in essence, a compact object model; (iii) external resources become part of a P/FDM integration schema implemented through external functions; and (iv) queries can range over the local database and the remote stores.

In essence, any system such as the above could be used as a source model and language in a knowledge-based query processing system. Indeed, in the original TAMBIS (Transparent Access to Multiple Biological Information Sources) [10.15], Kleisli is used to wrap sources and to evaluate queries. In this approach, query optimisation is carried out within TAMBIS [10.23], and the generated query over Kleisli is essentially an ordered execution plan over the functions representing the wrapped sources. Kleisli was chosen as the source wrapping and query execution layer for TAMBIS because it provided significant numbers of source wrappers, it supported the hierarchical structures of the wrapped sources in a natural manner, and it provided a convenient language for expressing execution plans over the sources. Section 10.4 describes a successor to the original TAMBIS system in which sources are wrapped using the ODMG object model, and knowledge-based queries are mapped into the monoid comprehension calculus for optimisation. Before that, a review is given of knowledge-based query processing systems, focusing on the relationship between queries over the knowledge model and queries over the individual sources.

10.2 Knowledge-Based Query Processing

Knowledge-based query processing generally involves a query phrased over a conceptual model being mapped into an equivalent request over the corresponding source model. The nature of this mapping depends crucially on the way in which the relationship between entities in the conceptual model and entities in the source model is described. There are two principal approaches, known as *global-as-view* and *local as view* [10.29].

In the *global-as-view* approach, the entities of the global model are defined as views over the (local) source model. For example, assume that there are two sources *DB1* and *DB2*, such that: *DB1* contains the table *Used-CarForSale(Reg,Price)* and *DB2* contains the table *CarForSale(Reg)*. Let's also assume that every car in *DB2* is new. The global model might contain the tables *CarForSale(Reg)*, *UsedCar(Reg)*, *Price(Reg,Price)*, and *Desirable-Car(Reg)*. The source and global models may then be related by views such as:

```
CarForSale(c) <- DB2:CarForSale(Reg).
CarForSale(c) <- DB1:UsedCarForSale(Reg,_).

UsedCar(r) <- DB1:UsedCarForSale(r,_).

DesirableCar(r) <- DB1:UsedCarForSale(r,p), p > 10000.
DesirableCar(r) <- DB2:CarForSale(r).

Price(c,p) <- DB1:UsedCarForSale(r,p).
```

In the example, the views are defined such that the values for the tables in the global model can be derived from the tables in the source models. In this approach, identifying the instances of *DesirableCar* in the global model simply involves evaluating the views used in the definition of *DesirableCar*. The views are a direct means of obtaining instances for concepts.

In the *local-as-view* approach, the views are defined the other way around, as illustrated below:

```
DB2:CarForSale(r) <- CarForSale(r), not UsedCar(r).
DB1:UsedCarForSale(r,p) <- CarForSale(r), UsedCar(r), Price(r,p).
```

In this case, the views essentially represent declarative statements about the contents of the sources, rather than providing direct ways of computing the values for the tables in the global model. As such, an initial *rewriting* step is required during query processing to convert a query over the global model into a query expressed only in terms of the local models. It is argued that the *local-as-view* approach is more declarative and more maintainable than *global-as-view*, but it imposes certain restrictions on the expressiveness of the languages that can be used for view definition.

Table 10.2 summarises the properties of several representative distributed query processing systems. In the table, the following acronyms are used: DL – Description Logic; GAV – Global as view; LAV – Local as view. The approach described in this chapter is represented as *TAMBIS-II* in the table.

One important way of classifying the proposals in Table 10.2 is according to the *Rewriting* approach adopted, in that the way the sources are related to the global model and the implementation technologies deployed are significantly affected by this aspect. TAMBIS-II adopts the global-as-view approach to relating the knowledge model to the source model, as this has allowed us to exploit a powerful DL for ontology description and querying, as well as easing the implementation.

Proposal	Knowledge Model	Source Model/ Language	Rewriting	Source Role
DWQ [10.5]	DLR DL	Relational/ Datalog	LAV	Not Implemented
Information Manifold [10.21]	Relational	Relational/ Datalog	LAV	Classical Query Opt/Eval
Observer [10.22]	CLASSIC DL	Relational/ Algebra	GAV	Classical Query Opt/Eval
PICSEL [10.14]	CARIN DL,	Relational/ Datalog	GAV/ LAV	Evaluated Directly
SIMS [10.1]	LOOP DL	Relational Algebra	GAV	Distributed Query Opt
TAMBIS-I [10.23]	GRAIL DL	Complex Value/ CPL	GAV	Direct Evaluation
TAMBIS-II [10.25]	$\mathcal{ALCQI}$ DL	Object/ Monoid Calculus	GAV	Semantic Optimisation

Table 10.1. Summary of knowledge-based query processing systems

Another important point for this chapter is the *Source Role*. In TAMBIS-II the source language, the monoid calculus, is subject to many optimisation steps before queries are evaluated. This has partly been to allow the reuse of an existing query optimisation infrastructure, but the monoid calculus has also been a conducive framework for capturing the semantics of and expressing transformations over query plans.

10.3 Technical Context

10.3.1 Description Logics

The knowledge model in TAMBIS-II is represented using the $\mathcal{ALCQI}$ [10.7] Description Logic (DL). In essence, a DL provides a collection of logical connectives for describing the structural properties of the concepts in a domain. The selection of $\mathcal{ALCQI}$ for TAMBIS-II is motivated by the existence of an efficient reasoning engine (the FaCT system [10.18]), and by the fact that $\mathcal{ALCQI}$ is sufficiently expressive to capture—in a provably correct way—standard conceptual data modelling formalisms such as entity–relationship and object-oriented models [10.6]. Note, however that certain kinds of constraints involving concrete data types (for example, arithmetic or string expressions) cannot be expressed in $\mathcal{ALCQI}$. This restriction helps to minimise the algorithmic complexity of reasoning over $\mathcal{ALCQI}$.

The basic types of a DL are *concepts* and *roles*. A concept expression is a description gathering the common properties among a collection of individuals; from a logical point of view it is a unary predicate ranging over the

$$C, D \rightarrow A \mid$$
$$\top \mid \qquad\qquad \top^{\mathcal{I}} = \Delta^{\mathcal{I}}$$
$$\bot \mid \qquad\qquad \bot^{\mathcal{I}} = \emptyset$$
$$\neg C \mid \qquad\qquad (\neg C)^{\mathcal{I}} = \Delta^{\mathcal{I}} \setminus C^{\mathcal{I}}$$
$$C \sqcap D \mid \qquad\qquad (C \sqcap D)^{\mathcal{I}} = C^{\mathcal{I}} \cap D^{\mathcal{I}}$$
$$C \sqcup D \mid \qquad\qquad (C \sqcup D)^{\mathcal{I}} = C^{\mathcal{I}} \cup D^{\mathcal{I}}$$
$$\forall R.C \mid \qquad\qquad (\forall R.C)^{\mathcal{I}} = \{i \in \Delta^{\mathcal{I}} \mid \forall j.\, R^{\mathcal{I}}(i,j) \Rightarrow C^{\mathcal{I}}(j)\}$$
$$\exists R.C \mid \qquad\qquad (\exists R.C)^{\mathcal{I}} = \{i \in \Delta^{\mathcal{I}} \mid \exists j.\, R^{\mathcal{I}}(i,j) \wedge C^{\mathcal{I}}(j)\}$$
$$\exists^{\geq n} R.C \mid \qquad (\exists^{\geq n} R.C)^{\mathcal{I}} = \{i \in \Delta^{\mathcal{I}} \mid \sharp\{j \in \Delta^{\mathcal{I}} \mid R^{\mathcal{I}}(i,j) \wedge C^{\mathcal{I}}(j)\} \geq n\}$$
$$\exists^{\leq n} R.C \qquad (\exists^{\leq n} R.C)^{\mathcal{I}} = \{i \in \Delta^{\mathcal{I}} \mid \sharp\{j \in \Delta^{\mathcal{I}} \mid R^{\mathcal{I}}(i,j) \wedge C^{\mathcal{I}}(j)\} \leq n\}$$
$$R \rightarrow P \mid$$
$$R^{-} \qquad\qquad (R^{-})^{\mathcal{I}} = \{(i,j) \in \Delta^{\mathcal{I}} \times \Delta^{\mathcal{I}} \mid R^{\mathcal{I}}(j,i)\}$$

Fig. 10.1. Syntax of $\mathcal{ALCQI}$ concept expressions (C, D) and role expressions (R), and their semantics under an interpretation $\mathcal{I}$. A is an atomic concept name and P is an atomic role name.

domain of individuals. Interrelationships between these individuals are represented by means of role expressions (which are interpreted as binary relations over the domain of individuals). We present here only a brief summary of the syntax and semantics of $\mathcal{ALCQI}$.

$\mathcal{ALCQI}$ has a rich combination of constructors, including full boolean operators, qualified number restrictions, inverse roles and inclusion assertions of a general form. Its syntax rules at the left hand side of Figure 10.1 define valid concept and role expressions whose semantics is shown at the right hand side of Figure 10.1.

The semantics of $\mathcal{ALCQI}$ is given in terms of an interpretation $\mathcal{I} = (\Delta^{\mathcal{I}}, \cdot^{\mathcal{I}})$ consisting of a set $\Delta^{\mathcal{I}}$ of individuals (the *domain* of $\mathcal{I}$) and a function $\cdot^{\mathcal{I}}$ (the *interpretation function* of $\mathcal{I}$). Every concept is interpreted as a subset of $\Delta^{\mathcal{I}}$ and every role as a subset of $\Delta^{\mathcal{I}} \times \Delta^{\mathcal{I}}$. A knowledge base (or ontology) is a finite set Σ of axioms of the form $C \sqsubseteq D$, involving concept expressions C, D; we write $C \doteq D$ as a shortcut for both $C \sqsubseteq D$ and $D \sqsubseteq C$. An interpretation $\mathcal{I}$ satisfies $C \sqsubseteq D$ if and only if the interpretation of C is included in the interpretation of D, i.e., $C^{\mathcal{I}} \subseteq D^{\mathcal{I}}$; it is said that C is subsumed (or contained) by D. An interpretation $\mathcal{I}$ is a *model* of an ontology Σ iff every axiom of Σ is satisfied by $\mathcal{I}$. If Σ has a model, then it is *satisfiable* (or *consistent*). Σ *logically implies* an axiom $C \sqsubseteq D$ (written $\Sigma \models C \sqsubseteq D$) if $C \sqsubseteq D$ is satisfied by every model of Σ; in this case we say that C is *contained* in D under the ontology Σ.

10.3.2 The Monoid Comprehension Calculus

The source language to which DL queries are translated is the Monoid Comprehension Calculus of Fegaras and Maier [10.11]. The calculus provides a uniform notation for collection types such as lists, bags and sets, based on the observation that the operations of set and bag union and list concatenation are *monoid* operations (that is, they are associative and have an identity element). Monoids for collection types are known as *collection monoids*. Operations like conjunctions and disjunctions on booleans and integer addition over collections can also be expressed in terms of so-called *primitive monoids*. A monoid comprehension has the form:

$$\otimes\{e \mid q_1, \ldots, q_n\} \tag{10.1}$$

The symbol $\otimes$ is a monoid operator, and determines the type of the comprehension. The expression e is called the *head* of the comprehension. Each q_i is a *qualifier*, which can be either a *generator* of the form $v \leftarrow e'$, where v is a variable and e' is a collection-valued expression, or a *filter* of the form p, where p is a predicate (a boolean-valued expression). Each variable v is assigned a type T, and the type of the head of the corresponding collection monoid e' must be a subtype of T. We will usually omit the variable type from our notation, except where it needs to be emphasised. If q_i is a generator for the variable v, then the head expression e and the q_j for $j > i$ can contain free occurrences of v. The value of the expression (10.1) is determined as follows. All possible sets of assignments of values to the generator variables from the corresponding domain expressions are considered. For each assignment which satisfies all the filter predicates, the value of the head e is computed and the results are combined using the monoid operation $\otimes$ (since the monoids used in our system are all commutative, we don't need to worry about the order in which the head values are computed).

The identity, or zero, element of the monoid whose operation is $\otimes$ is denoted by $\mathcal{Z}_\otimes$.

The primitive monoids used in examples below are:

- The logical-and monoid $\wedge$. This is a simple monoid whose underlying type is boolean. The monoid operation is boolean conjunction and $\mathcal{Z}_\wedge = \textbf{true}$.
- The plus-monoid $+$. This is also a simple monoid whose underlying type is integer. The monoid operation is integer addition and $\mathcal{Z}_+ = 0$. The plus-monoid is used in examples in the form $+\{1 \mid \bar{s}\}$, to compute cardinalities of sets. The result of this expression is the number of distinct assignments to the generator variables in $\bar{s}$ which satisfy all the filters.

An important feature of the monoid comprehension calculus is its inherent extensibility, in that new monoids can be added to the calculus. This extensibility is exploited in TAMBIS-II through the introduction of the *match-union* monoid described below.

A single individual belonging to the extension of a DL concept or query may be represented by several database instances (with distinct OIDs), possibly coming from different sources. Thus, a query may have alternative answers if more than one choice of database instance is available for some of the relevant individuals. In order to support the reconstruction of a unique individual object from the sparse information coming from the same or different sources, we introduce a new boolean-valued operator $match(x, y)$ which returns **true** if the database instances x and y represent the same individual.

This $match(\_, \_)$ operator is really a collection of operators $match_{S_1, S_2}(\_, \_)$, one for each pair of source databases S_1, S_2 (we can also divide it according to different object types returned by each source). We require that $match()$ defines an equivalence relation—that is, it must be reflexive, symmetric and transitive. We also assume that distinct elements from the same source are intended to represent distinct individuals, so that if x and y come from the same source S, $match_{S,S}(x, y)$ reduces to $x = y$. The $match()$ operator extends to tuples of objects in the obvious way. It can be interpreted as a simple equality test for domain values like integers and strings.

At the physical level, the implementation of $match()$ for any given pair of sources may consist of a function which performs a comparison between certain key attributes of the objects concerned. Alternatively, if the two source classes do not have a common key, it might be necessary to use a binary table to associate the corresponding elements.

An answer to a query, then, is a set S of object references, such that

$$\text{for all } x, y \in S, \; match(x, y) = \textbf{false} \text{ unless } x = y \tag{10.2}$$

Such sets are referred to as *match-sets*—they are still sets (rather than bags) even if we regard $match()$ as equality.

In order to capture query answers as match-sets, comprehensions are written in terms of a collection monoid whose merge operation $\oplus$ (read as *match-union*) is like the set union operation but preserves the uniqueness condition (10.2). So, if S_1 and S_2 satisfy (10.2) then $S_1 \oplus S_2$ may be any set $W \subseteq S_1 \cup S_2$ of object references, such that for each $x \in S_1 \cup S_2$ there is precisely one $w \in W$ such that $match(x, w) = \textbf{true}$. For those elements of S_1 which match some element of S_2, we can choose which element to include in $S_1 \oplus S_2$. This choice can be made by the system on the basis of user preference or cost estimation or, if we have no preference, by taking the representative for S_1 whenever possible.

10.4 The TAMBIS-II Query Processor

This section gives an overview of the components that participate in the query processing framework described in more detail later in the chapter, which are illustrated in Figure 10.2.

The example ontology used in this chapter is in Figure 10.3.

Queries are formulated over the ontology in a query language which is itself a DL. The system translates such high-level user queries into queries over the definitions at the object layer. The translation process can be broken down into several phases:

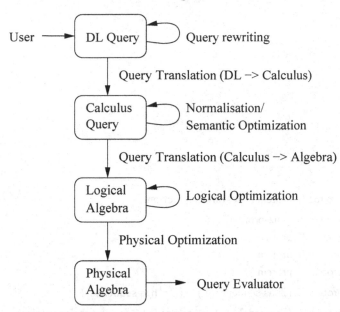

Fig. 10.2. The principal components of the TAMBIS-II query processor.

- The *query rewriting* phase comprises a simple expansion algorithm to rewrite the query as an expression containing only ground terms; this is based on a global-as-view approach. Any ground term which appears in the rewritten query must be mapped to a set of source extents in the Ontology-to-Object-Model (OOM) mapping.
- The *query translation* phase translates the rewritten query into an expression in the Monoid Comprehension Calculus described in section 10.3.2. The Calculus is used in [10.11] as an intermediate form for an optimiser for the ODMG object query language OQL [10.8]. The translation process works in a compositional fashion, using the OOM mapping to translate DL terms, and handling logical connectives using a set of rules illustrated in section 10.4.3.
- The *semantic optimisation* phase takes the (possibly deeply nested) calculus expression generated by the query translation algorithm and performs simplifying transformations on it. The ontology is used at this stage to improve the calculus expression by identifying redundant generators (potential iterations) over source extents.
- The *calculus-to-algebra translation* phase. From this point on, the translation system is an adaptation of Fegaras' OQL optimiser. The calculus expression is translated into an expression in a logical query algebra based on the nested–relational algebra. The translation rules are quite general and do not depend on source-specific information.

$$\text{enzyme} \sqsubseteq \text{protein} \sqcap \exists\text{catalyses.reaction} \tag{10.3}$$

$$\text{enzyme} \doteq \exists\text{enz-protein}^-.\top \tag{10.4}$$

$$\exists\text{catalyses}.\top \sqsubseteq \text{protein} \tag{10.5}$$

$$\text{sp-protein} \sqsubseteq \text{protein} \tag{10.6}$$

$$\text{pir-protein} \sqsubseteq \text{protein} \tag{10.7}$$

$$\text{protein} \sqsubseteq (\exists\text{has-sequence}.\top) \sqcap (\exists^{\leq 1}\text{has-sequence}.\top) \tag{10.8}$$

$$\text{sp-protein} \sqsubseteq (\exists\text{sp-acc}.\top) \sqcap (\exists^{\leq 1}\text{sp-acc}.\top) \sqcap (\forall\text{has-species.species}) \tag{10.9}$$

$$\text{pir-protein} \sqsubseteq (\exists\text{pir-acc}.\top) \sqcap (\exists^{\leq 1}\text{pir-acc}.\top) \sqcap (\forall\text{cited-in.reference}) \tag{10.10}$$

$$\text{species} \sqsubseteq (\exists\text{common-name}.\top) \sqcap (\exists^{\leq 1}\text{common-name}.\top) \tag{10.11}$$

$$\sqcap (\exists\text{latin-name}.\top) \sqcap (\exists^{\leq 1}\text{latin-name}.\top)$$

$$\text{mammal} \sqsubseteq \text{species} \tag{10.12}$$

$$\text{reference} \sqsubseteq (\exists\text{has-author}.\top) \sqcap (\exists\text{has-journal}.\top) \sqcap (\exists^{\leq 1}\text{has-journal}.\top) \tag{10.13}$$

$$\sqcap (\exists\text{has-year}.\top) \sqcap (\exists^{\leq 1}\text{has-year}.\top)$$

$$\text{enz-entry} \sqsubseteq (\exists\text{enz-protein}.\top) \sqcap (\forall\text{enz-protein.sp-protein}) \tag{10.14}$$

$$\sqcap (\exists\text{enz-reaction}.\top)$$

$$\text{journal} \doteq \exists\text{has-journal}^-.\top \tag{10.15}$$

$$\text{top-journal} \sqsubseteq \text{journal} \tag{10.16}$$

Fig. 10.3. The example ontology.

– The *logical and physical optimisation* phases are essentially those presented in [10.11]. Firstly, a calculus expression is translated to a corresponding expression in a logical algebra. This logical algebra is then subject to heuristic optimisation by a logical optimiser, and then the logical algebra operators are replaced by operators in a physical algebra during physical optimisation. For example, at the logical stage alternative join orders are generated, and at the physical stage the optimiser decides to implement the join operation by a nested-loop join, a hash-join or a bind-join. For lack of space, the logical and physical optimisers are not described further in this chapter.

The above infrastructure can potentially sit on top of different implementation platforms; in the case of TAMBIS-II, the target back-end is the distributed query processor for the Grid described in [10.28].

10.4.1 Query Rewriting

The query rewriting task can be phrased in general terms as follows. Given a query Q, an ontology, and a set of view definitions that characterise the actual source data, reformulate the query into an expression, the *rewriting*, that refers only to the views, and provides the answer to Q. In our case, the view definitions correspond to the classes and relationships of the object wrapped sources.

In this chapter we will consider only the simplistic case of the logical vocabulary being a subset of the conceptual DL vocabulary. We call these concepts and roles *ground*. Moreover, we restrict our attention to top-level *class queries*, which are themselves DL concept expressions. Concept expressions which are to be treated as queries are rewritten into equivalent concept expressions involving only the ground concept names.

The simplest rewriting system we can use is a stratified system with a straightforward expansion algorithm. In a stratified system, a distinguished subset of the DL axioms, called the *expansion axioms*, is used for query rewriting. The expansion axioms are all of the form $A \doteq C$, where A is an atomic concept (a concept name) and C is a concept expression. The set of definitions in the expansion axioms is required to be acyclic, or *stratified*. Furthermore, each concept name which can appear in a query and is not represented by a source database must be defined in an expansion axiom. Also, the names used on the right-hand sides of definitions must all be queryable. The rewriting process is then a simple matter of expanding definitions of non-ground concepts until only ground ones are left. This expansion process is guaranteed to terminate and to produce a grounded query equivalent to the original one.

Once a query has been rewritten into a an equivalent query containing only ground terms, it is important to check that the query is *safe* [10.10]. Essentially, a query (or concept) is considered safe if answering that query does not involve looking up information not referred to in the query. This is crucial to restrict the scope of a query. Our translation scheme in section 10.4.3 only produces translations for safe queries. For example, the query $\forall R.C$ is unsafe because answering it involves, among other things, finding all individuals with no R fillers, and this information is not available from extents for R and C.

Let Q be a concept expression which has been expanded (so it contains only ground concept names) and rewritten into *negation normal form*[1]. Then Q is safe if it has the form $\bot$, A (where A is a ground concept), $\exists R.C$ or $\exists^{\geq n} R.C$ (provided $n \geq 1$). It is unsafe if it has the form $\top$, $\neg A$, $\forall R.C$ or $\exists^{\leq n} R.C$. A conjunction is safe if and only if at least one of its conjuncts is safe. A disjunction is safe if and only if all of its disjuncts are safe. Note that, under this definition, a concept expression is safe if and only if its negation is unsafe.

10.4.2 Relating the Knowledge Model to the Source Model

The query translator takes a DL query and translates it into a calculus expression over an object model representing the sources.

The source databases are presented to the rest of the system by software wrappers in such a way that they can be seen as forming an object database, conforming to the ODMG data model [10.8]. From an implementation point of view, this is a practical choice because of its compatibility with CORBA and the fact the model is associated with well understood query processing techniques [10.11]. The structure of the objects returned by the wrappers is given by a schema in the ODMG's Object Definition Language (ODL).

Each ground term in the ontology is viewed as a named persistent set of database objects. This set may be an extent over an ODL class or a set of values of some simple type like String. For the sake of brevity, we will refer to all such named collections as *source extents*. So that we can use the DL reasoner to assist in query optimisation (as described in section 10.5), we require that each source name be represented by a name in the knowledge base, and we record any information about containment between sources in the ontology.

Figure 10.4 shows the wrapper class definitions for the domain represented by the ontology in Figure 10.3. For example, the interface Protein represents protein data from the sources SwissProt and PIR, which are represented by the classes SP_Protein and PIR_Protein.

The attribute SPAccessionNumber in the source class SP_Protein corresponds to the accession number of a SwissProt entry. It is a unique identifier for the entry. The species attribute contains the set of species in which

---

[1] By pushing negations inwards in the usual way, one can rewrite any $\mathcal{ALCQI}$ concept expression into an equivalent expression in *negation normal form* or NNF, where negations only appear in front of concept names.

```
interface Protein {
  attribute String sequence;
}
class SP_Protein (extent sp_proteins)
  extends Protein {
    attribute String SPAccessionNumber;
    attribute Set<Species> species;
    attribute String sequence;
}
class PIR_Protein (extent pir_proteins)
  extends Protein {
    attribute String PirAccessionNumber;
    attribute Set<Reference> references;
    attribute String sequence;
}
class Species (extent species) {
  attribute String common_name;
  attribute String latin_name;
}
class Reference (extent references) {
  attribute Set<String> authors;
  attribute String title;
  attribute String journal;
  attribute String year;
}
class EnzEntry (extent enz_entries) {
  attribute String enz_id;
  attribute Set<SP_Protein> enz_proteins;
  attribute Set<String> reactions;
  attribute Set<String> cofactors;
}
class Enz_catalyses_class (extent enz_catalyses) {
  attribute SP_Protein base;
  attribute String filler;
}
Set<Species> mammals
Set<String> top_journals
```

Fig. 10.4. Declarations of source classes.

the protein can be found. Finally, **sequence** is a string representation of the protein's amino acid sequence.

Like SwissProt, PIR also identifies its protein entries with an accession number (see **PIR_Protein**). Note that PIR accession numbers are not the same as SwissProt accession numbers, so the attributes must be given different names and correspond to different roles at the DL level. The **references** attribute is a set of descriptions of references to the protein in the scientific literature. As with **SP_Entry**, the string **sequence** represents the amino acid sequence.

The OOM mapping describes how ground DL concepts and roles relate to object model classes and relationships. For the example application, Ta-

Concept	Source extents
protein	sp_proteins
	pir_proteins
sp-protein	sp_proteins
pir-protein	pir_proteins
enz-entry	enz_entries
species	species
reference	references
top-journal	top_journals
mammal	mammals

Table 10.2. Concept to source mapping for biological example

Role	Attribute	Cardinality
sp-acc	SPAccessionNumber	Single
pir-acc	PirAccessionNumber	Single
has-species	species	Multiple
has-sequence	sequence	Single
cited-in	references	Multiple
common-name	common_name	Single
latin-name	latin_name	Single
has-author	authors	Multiple
has-title	title	Single
has-journal	journal	Single
has-year	year	Single
enz-id	enz_id	Single
enz-protein	enz_proteins	Multiple
enz-reaction	reactions	Multiple
cofactor	cofactors	Multiple

Table 10.3. Attribute role mappings for biological example

ble 10.2 gives the mapping between DL concepts and source extents, and Table 10.3 shows the mapping of DL roles to class attributes.

In addition to the attribute roles, the model contains a single enumerated role, **catalyses**, which represents the relationship between an enzyme and the reaction it catalyses. This role is mapped to the extent **enz_catalyses** of Figure 10.4, which is implemented as part of the wrapper on the Enzyme database.

DL roles are divided into *enumerated roles*, which are represented by the OOM mapping directly as sets of pairs, and *attribute roles*, which are represented as attributes of the base objects. An enumerated role R is represented by a set of source extents. Each of these is an extent e over a class of the form

```
class  C (extent e){
    attribute  T₁  base;
    attribute  T₂  filler;
}
```

The attribute names *base* and *filler* are used to refer to the first and second components of the binary relation represented by R. We say that e has type $T_1 \times T_2$.

An attribute role R is represented by an attribute name a_R. The attribute may be defined in several classes, and may have a different value type in each. For example, the fillers for a role like has-name may be simple strings in most classes, but structured objects (for example, botanical names of plants) in others. An attribute role can be either *single-valued* or *multiple-valued*. We require that a single-valued attribute role be represented by an attribute whose value type is a simple class name in each class which supports it, and that a multiple-valued attribute role be represented by an attribute whose value type is $\mathsf{Set}(T)$ for some class name T.

In order to answer all queries involving quantification over an attribute role, and not just those where we can prove that the objects in question support the appropriate attribute, we need to be able to iterate over the domain of the role. So, for each attribute role R, we must have a set of domains $\{D_i\}$, where each D_i is an extent over some type T_i which supports a_R. We require that there is some class T which supports the attribute a_R such that each T_i is a subclass of T. Then any union over some of the D_i will have a type which supports a_R.

10.4.3 Translating $\mathcal{ALCQI}$ Queries to Monoid Comprehensions

The rules given in this section illustrate how to translate a safe $\mathcal{ALCQI}$ concept expression C into an expression E in the monoid comprehension calculus. Extensions of the translation to handle partially unsafe queries are considered in the technical report [10.24]. The rules constitute a compositional syntax-directed translation scheme.

The expression E is a collection monoid comprehension using the monoid operation $\oplus$ described in section 10.3.2. If the element type of this comprehension (the type of its head expression) is T we will say that E is a translation of C having type T. The full translation rules for safe queries are described in [10.25], and illustrated below.

The Empty Concept. The unsatisfiable concept $\bot$ is translated by the empty $\oplus$-monoid $\mathcal{Z}_\oplus$.

Atomic Terms. To translate a ground atomic concept (a concept name) A we consult the OOM mapping to find the set of database extent names which represent A. Each extent name has a type (a class name) T_i and refers to a set S_i of object references of type T_i. Let T be the most specific superclass of the T_i. Then $\bigoplus_i S_i$ is a translation of A having type T. If more than one source is available for an atomic concept, the system is free to decide whether to use all of them or some subset chosen according to user preference or cost estimates.

For instance, in our example application the concept protein is mapped to the source extents sp_proteins and pir_proteins, and so it has three possible translations: sp_proteins (of type SP_Protein), pir_proteins (of type PIR_Protein) and sp_proteins $\oplus$ pir_proteins (of type Protein).

Conjunctions. If C and D are safe concepts with translations C' and D' of type $T_{C'}$ and $T_{D'}$ then $C \sqcap D$ can be translated to either of the following, with types $T_{C'}$ and $T_{D'}$ respectively:

$$\oplus\{c \mid c \leftarrow C', d \leftarrow D', match(c, d)\} \tag{10.17}$$

$$\oplus\{d \mid c \leftarrow C', d \leftarrow D', match(c, d)\} \tag{10.18}$$

If we don't want to commit to choosing all our answers from one of C' and D' and we have a choice function $choose(x, y)$ which selects one of x and y according to some unspecified criteria, we can make a third translation with the type T which is the most specific superclass of T_1 and T_2:

$$\oplus\{choose(c, d) \mid c \leftarrow C', d \leftarrow D', match(c, d)\} \tag{10.19}$$

Disjunctions. If C, D are safe concepts with translations C' and D' of type $T_{C'}$ and $T_{D'}$, let T be the most specific superclass of $T_{C'}$ and $T_{D'}$. Then

$$(\oplus\{c \mid c : T \leftarrow C'\}) \oplus (\oplus\{d \mid d : T \leftarrow D'\}) \tag{10.20}$$

is a translation of $C \sqcup D$ of type T. Note the use of type specifiers for the variables c and d to emphasise that we are assigning subclass references to superclass reference variables. That is, we just take the $\oplus$ merge of C' and D' but interpret the references as having type T.

For example, if we had more than two protein sources, a user might want to specify two of them by a forming a (sub-)query such as sp-protein $\oplus$ pir-protein. This translates to

$$\begin{aligned} (\oplus\{c \mid c : \texttt{Protein} \leftarrow \texttt{sp-protein}\}) \\ \oplus (\oplus\{d \mid d : \texttt{Protein} \leftarrow \texttt{pir-protein}\}), \end{aligned} \tag{10.21}$$

of type Protein.

Existentially Quantified and At-Least Formulae.. Existentially quantified formulae and at-least formulae are closely related, since $\exists R.C$ is equivalent to $\exists^{\geq 1} R.C$; they are handled together here. Furthermore, inverses of enumerated roles (for example, in $\exists R^-.C$) can be handled similarly, by exchanging the roles of base and filler. The complete mappings are provided in [10.25].

Example. As an example of the query translation process, consider the query

$$\text{protein} \sqcap \exists\text{cited-in.}(\exists\text{has-journal.top-journal}) \tag{10.22}$$

which asks for all proteins referred to in important journals. To translate this query, we first translate the subquery,

$$\exists\text{has-journal.top-journal} \tag{10.23}$$

As shown in Table 10.3, the role has-journal is a single-valued attribute role. It is mapped to the attribute journal, which is supported by the class extent references. The concept top-journal is mapped to the extent top_journals, as described in Table 10.2. With renaming of variables, the translation is

$$\oplus\{r_1 \mid r_1 \leftarrow \textbf{references}, t \leftarrow \textbf{top\_journals},$$
$$match(r_1.\textbf{journal}, t)\} \tag{10.24}$$

Proceeding in this way we obtain the monoid comprehension:

$$\oplus\{p_2 \mid p_2 \leftarrow \textbf{sp\_proteins} \oplus \textbf{pir\_proteins},$$
$$p_3 \leftarrow \oplus\{p_1 \mid p_1 \leftarrow \textbf{pir\_proteins},$$
$$r_2 \leftarrow p_1.\textbf{references},$$
$$r_3 \leftarrow \oplus\{r_1 \mid r_1 \leftarrow \textbf{references},$$
$$t \leftarrow \textbf{top\_journals}, \tag{10.25}$$
$$match(r_1.\textbf{journal}, t)\},$$
$$match(r_2, r_3)\},$$
$$match(p_2, p_3)\},$$

supposing that the system decides to use both sources for the concept protein. This rather unwieldy form can be considerably simplified by the methods of section 10.5.

10.5 Optimisation

For the most part, the optimisation of the queries that result from the translation process described in section 10.4.3 follows that of Fegaras's optimiser [10.11]. Following translation, a normalisation algorithm rewrites the comprehension into a normal form. The normalisation rules are given in section 10.5.1. In an extension to Fegaras's normalisation algorithm, certain optimisations are made during the normalisation process to remove unnecessary iterations or generators. Unlike [10.17]—where both the constraints introduced by the ODL schema and the OQL queries are translated into a

$$\langle A_1 = e_1, \ldots, A_n = e_n \rangle.A_i \longrightarrow e_i \tag{10.26}$$

$$\otimes\{e \mid \bar{q}, v \leftarrow \mathcal{Z}_\oslash, \bar{s}\} \longrightarrow \mathcal{Z}_\otimes \tag{10.27}$$

$$\odot\{e \mid \bar{q}, v \leftarrow e_1 \oplus e_2, \bar{s}\} \longrightarrow (\odot\{e \mid \bar{q}, v \leftarrow e_1, \bar{s}\}) \tag{10.28}$$
$$\odot (\odot\{e \mid \bar{q}, v \leftarrow e_2, \bar{s}\})$$

$$+\{e \mid \bar{q}, v \leftarrow e_1 \oplus e_2, \bar{s}\} \longrightarrow (+\{e \mid \bar{q}, v \leftarrow e_1, \bar{s}\})$$
$$+ (+\{e \mid \bar{q}, v \leftarrow e_2, \tag{10.29}$$
$$\wedge\{\neg match(v, w) \mid w \leftarrow e_1\}, \bar{s}\})$$

$$\otimes\{e \mid \bar{q}, \vee\{pred \mid \bar{r}\}, \bar{s}\} \longrightarrow \otimes\{e \mid \bar{q}, \bar{r}, pred, \bar{s}\} \tag{10.30}$$

$$\otimes\{e \mid \bar{q}, v \leftarrow \oplus\{e' \mid \bar{r}\}, \bar{s}\} \longrightarrow \otimes\{e[e'/v] \mid \bar{q}, \bar{r}, \bar{s}[e'/v]\} \tag{10.31}$$

$$*\{*\{e \mid \bar{r}\} \mid \bar{s}\} \longrightarrow *\{e \mid \bar{s}, \bar{r}\}, \tag{10.32}$$

Fig. 10.5. Normalisation rules for the calculus.

Datalog program, and semantic optimisation is performed by adding extra conditions or "residues" coming from the integrity constraints to the query optimiser—and unlike [10.2]—where the system computes the complete explicit semantic expansion of the original query—we base the semantic optimisations on *oracle* calls to the DL reasoner from the standard (Fegaras) OQL optimiser. These calls check containment between subqueries given the semantic information specified in the ontology. The optimisation rules are given in section 10.5.2.

10.5.1 Normalisation

The first stage of Fegaras' optimiser [10.11] is a normalisation process which does some unnesting of nested comprehensions. The process results in a canonical form which is (in our case) a $\oplus$-merge of comprehensions of the form

$$\oplus\{e \mid v_1 \leftarrow path_1, \ldots, v_n \leftarrow path_n, pred\}, \tag{10.33}$$

where each $path_i$ is a database extent name or an expression of the form $v.a_1 \ldots a_n$, where v is a bound variable and the a_i are attribute names. Note that the head e and the predicate $pred$ may still contain nested comprehensions, though these will also be in canonical form. The normalisation rules needed to convert the comprehension expressions produced by the algorithm in section 10.4.3 are given in Figure 10.5. In the figure, $\otimes$ and $\oslash$ may be any of the monoid operations $\oplus$, $\vee$, $\wedge$ or $+$, $*$ may be $\vee$, $\wedge$ or $+$, and $\odot$ may be $\oplus$, $\wedge$ or $\vee$. The notation $e[e'/v]$ denotes the result of substituting e' for the free occurrences of v in e. Further details on the normalisation of the monoid calculus can be obtained from [10.11].

$$\oplus\{e \mid \bar{q}, v \leftarrow X, \bar{r}, w \leftarrow Y, \bar{s}, match(v, w) \wedge p\}$$
$$\longrightarrow \oplus\{e[v/w] \mid \bar{q}, v \leftarrow X, \bar{r}, \bar{s}[v/w], p[v/w]\}, \quad \text{if } X \sqsubseteq Y \quad (10.34)$$

$$\oplus\{e \mid \bar{q}, v \leftarrow X, \bar{r}, w \leftarrow Y, \bar{s}, match(v, w) \wedge p\}$$
$$\longrightarrow \oplus\{e[v/w] \mid \bar{q}, v \leftarrow Y, \bar{r}, \bar{s}[v/w], p[v/w]\}, \quad \text{if } Y \sqsubseteq X \quad (10.35)$$

$$\oplus\{e \mid \bar{q}, v \leftarrow X, \bar{r}, w \leftarrow Y, \bar{s}, match(v, w) \wedge p\} \longrightarrow \emptyset, \quad \text{if } X \sqcap Y \doteq \bot \quad (10.36)$$

$$\oplus\{e \mid \bar{q}, x \leftarrow X \oplus Z, \bar{r}, p\} \longrightarrow \oplus\{e \mid \bar{q}, x \leftarrow X, \bar{r}, p\},$$
$$\text{if } can\text{-}restrict(x, X, p, concat(q, r)) \quad (10.37)$$

Fig. 10.6. Semantic optimisation rules for the calculus.

10.5.2 Semantic Optimisation

The translations given in section 10.4.3 are applicable to any concept expression. However, in certain circumstances more efficient translations can be produced by exploiting knowledge about the types returned by translations of subexpressions and the containment relationships stored within the ontology.

For example, the concept $C \sqcap \exists R.D$ (where R is a multiple-valued attribute role, C is translated as C' and D as D') is translated to a monoid comprehension which, after normalisation (ignoring for the moment the fact that C' and D_R may be $\oplus$-unions), looks like

$$\oplus\{c \mid c \leftarrow C', x \leftarrow D_R, f \leftarrow x.a_R, d \leftarrow D',$$
$$match(c, x), match(f, d)\} \quad (10.38)$$

However, if the type of C' is such that the elements can be guaranteed to be in D_R, the iteration over x can be dispensed with. In this case, each instantiation of the variable c has its own set $c.a_R$ of R-fillers and the query can be answered by the comprehension

$$\oplus\{c \mid c \leftarrow C', f \leftarrow c.a_R, d \leftarrow D', match(f, d)\} \quad (10.39)$$

The optimisation rules (10.34) and (10.35) in Figure 10.6 achieve the required simplification.

Similarly, if a comprehension has two generators whose variables are supposed to match but whose domains are known to be incompatible from the ontology, then the comprehension is empty. This is captured by rule (10.36) in Figure 10.6.

Another optimisation can be applied to a comprehension C that contains a generator of the form $x \leftarrow X \oplus Z$. If the predicate of C implies matches between x and other variables, then it may be that the intersection of the ranges of those variables is contained in X. In that case we can restrict x to range only over X. The formalisation of this rule (rule (10.37) in Figure 10.6) refers to the predicate *can-restrict* defined as follows. Let x be a variable, X a union of extents, p a predicate and $\bar{r}$ a sequence of generators. Let $\{y_i\}$ be the set of expressions which are related to x by $match()$ conjuncts in p, not including x itself. The y_i are the elements (excluding x) of the connected component of the graph defined by the $match()$ conjuncts in p. Each y_i is either a variable or a path expression of the form $z.a_1 \ldots a_n$ where z is a variable and the a_j are attributes. So each y_i has a type which corresponds to a DL concept Y_i. Let X' be the DL concept corresponding to X. Then *can-restrict*$(x, X, p, \bar{q})$ is true if $(\prod_i Y_i) \sqsubseteq X'$ (which we can find out from the DL classifier) and false otherwise.

10.5.3 Optimisation Example

As an example of query simplification, we can consider the translation (10.25) of query (10.22) from section 10.4.3. This form immediately admits a simplification by rule (10.37), since the type of p_3 is PIR_Protein which corresponds to the concept pir_protein so that the sp_proteins summand in the domain of p_2 can be eliminated. Normalisation then yields

$$
\begin{aligned}
\oplus \{ p_2 \mid p_2 \leftarrow \; &\texttt{pir\_proteins}, p_1 \leftarrow \texttt{pir\_proteins}, \\
&r_2 \leftarrow p_1.\texttt{references}, r_1 \leftarrow \texttt{references}, \\
&t \leftarrow \texttt{top\_journals}, match(r_1.\texttt{journal}, t) \wedge \\
&match(r_2, r_1) \wedge match(p_2, p_1) \}
\end{aligned}
\tag{10.40}
$$

Two applications of rule (10.34) then eliminate the variables p_1 and r_1, leaving the form

$$
\begin{aligned}
\oplus \{ p_2 \mid p_2 \leftarrow \; &\texttt{pir\_proteins}, r_2 \leftarrow p_2.\texttt{references}, \\
&t \leftarrow \texttt{top\_journals}, match(r_2.\texttt{journal}, t) \}
\end{aligned}
\tag{10.41}
$$

Note that the $match()$ comparison which remains is between values of type String and so it will be evaluated by a simple equality test.

10.6 Conclusions

Knowledge-based query processing promises to provide effective, high-level facilities for integrating and querying disparate information resources. This chapter has described one such approach, in which a DL is mapped into the monoid calculus for optimisation and evaluation. Key distinctive features of the approach are: (i) the use of the expressive $\mathcal{ALCQI}$ DL; (ii) the adoption of the stratified approach to query rewriting; (iii) the use of the monoid calculus, extended with the *match-union* monoid, for capturing the semantics of multiple-source queries; and (iv) the semantic optimisation of the calculus queries using optimisation rules that exploit reasoning over the DL ontology.

Acknowledgements

This work has been funded by the EPSRC Distributed Information Management programme, whose support we are pleased to acknowledge. The work has also benefited from discussions with our colleagues Carole Goble, Ian Horrocks and Robert Stephens.

References

10.1   Y. Arens, C. A. Knoblock, and W.-M. Shen. Query reformulation for dynamic information integration. *Journal of Intelligent Information Systems*, 6(2/3):99–130, 1996.

10.2   S. Bergamaschi, D. Beneventano, C. Sartori, and M. Vincini. ODBQOPTIMIZER: A tool for semantic query optimization in OODB. In *Proc. of the Thirteenth International Conference on Data Engineering (ICDE'97)*, page 578, 1997.

10.3   P. Bresciani, M. Nori, and N. Pedot. A knowledge based paradigm for querying databases. In *Proc. 11th DEXA Conference*, pages 794–804. Springer-Verlag, 2000.

10.4   D. Calvanese, G. D. Giacomo, M. Lenzerini, D. Nardi, and R. Rosati. Information integration: Conceptual modelling and reasoning support. In *Proc. COOPIS*, pages 280–291, 1998.

10.5   D. Calvanese, G. D. Giacomo, M. Lenzerini, D. Nardi, and R. Rosati. Data integration in data warehousing. *Int. J. Cooperative Information Systems*, 10(3):237–271, 2001.

10.6   D. Calvanese, M. Lenzerini, and D. Nardi. Description logics for conceptual data modeling. In J. Chomicki and G. Saake, editors, *Logics for Databases and Information Systems*, pages 229–263. Kluwer, 1998.

10.7   D. Calvanese, M. Lenzerini, and D. Nardi. Unifying class-based representation formalisms. *Journal of Artificial Intelligence Research*, 11:199–240, 1999.

10.8   R. G. G. Cattell, D. K. Barry, M. Berler, J. Eastman, D. Jordan, C. Russell, O. Schadow, T. Stanienda, and F. Velez, editors. *The Object Data Standard: ODMG 3.0*. Morgan Kaufmann, 2000.

10.9   S. B. Davidson, J. Crabtree, B. P. Brunk, J. Schug, V. Tannen, G. C. Overton, and C. J. Stoeckert. K2/Kleisli and GUS: Experiments in integrated access to genomic data sources. *IBM Systems Journal*, 40(2):512–531, 2001.

10.10 P. T. Devanbu. Translating description logics to information server queries. In *Proc. of the Second International Conference on Information and Knowledge Management (CIKM'93)*, pages 256–263, 1993.

10.11 L. Fegaras and D. Maier. Optimizing object queries using an effective calculus. *ACM Transactions on Database Systems*, 25(4):457–516, 2001.

10.12 D. Flanagan and J. Farley, editors. *Java Enterprise in a Nutshell.* O'Reilly, 1999.

10.13 I. Foster, C. Kesselman, and S. Tuecke. The anatomy of the Grid: Enabling scalable virtual organizations. *Int. Journal of Supercomputer Applications,* 15(3), 2001.

10.14 F. Goasdoue, V. Lattes, and M.-C. Rousset. The use of CARIN language and algorithms for information integration: the Picsel system. *International Journal on Cooperative Information Systems,* 9(4):383–401, 2000.

10.15 C. A. Goble, R. Stevens, G. Ng, S. Bechhofer, N. W. Paton, P. G. Baker, M. Peim, and A. Brass. Transparent access to multiple bioinformatics information sources. *IBM Systems Journal,* 40(2):534–551, 2001.

10.16 A. Goni, A. Illarramendi, and E. Mena. Semantic query optimisation and data caching for a multidatabase system. In O. Diaz and A. Illarramendi, editors, *Proc. 2nd BIWIT,* pages 60–71. IEEE Press, 1995.

10.17 J. Grant, J. Gryz, J. Minker, and L. Raschid. Semantic query optimization for object databases. In *Proc. of the Thirteenth International Conference on Data Engineering (ICDE'97),* pages 444–453, 1997.

10.18 I. Horrocks. FaCT and iFaCT. In *Proc. of the International Workshop on Description Logics (DL'99),* pages 133–135, 1999.

10.19 G. J. L. Kemp and P. M. D. Gray. Using the functional data model to integrate distributed biological data sources. In P. Svensson and J. C. French, editors, *Proc. SSDBM,* pages 176–185. IEEE Press, 1996.

10.20 D. Kossmann. The state of the art in distributed query processing. *ACM Computing Surveys,* 32(4):422–469, 2000.

10.21 A. Y. Levy, D. Srivastava, and T. Kirk. Data model and query evaluation in global information systems. *Journal of Intelligent Information Systems,* 5:121–143, 1995.

10.22 E. Mena, A. Illarramendi, V. Kashyap, and A. P. Sheth. OBSERVER: An approach for query processing in global information systems based on interoperation across pre-existing ontologies. *Distributed and Parallel Databases,* 8(2):223–271, 2000.

10.23 N. W. Paton, R. Stevens, P. Baker, C. A. Goble, S. Bechhofer, and A. Brass. Query processing in the TAMBIS bioinformatics source integration system. In *Proc. SSDBM,* pages 138–147. IEEE Press, 1999.

10.24 M. Peim, E. Franconi, N. W. Paton, and C. A. Goble. Query processing with description logic ontologies over object-wrapped databases. Technical Report, Dept. of Computer Science, University of Manchester, UK, 2001.

10.25 M. Peim, E. Franconi, N. W. Paton, and C. A. Goble. Query processing with description logic ontologies over object-wrapped databases. In *Proc. 14th Int. Conf. on Scientific and Statistical Databases (SSDBM).* IEEE Press, 27–36, 2002.

10.26 T. Risch and V. Josifovski. Distributed data integration by object-oriented mediator servers. *Concurrency and Computation: Practice and Experience,* 13:933–953, 2001.

10.27 D. W. Shipman. The Functional Data Model and the Data Language DAPLEX. *ACM Transactions on Database Systems,* 6(1):140–173, 1981. Also in [10.30], pages 95-111.

10.28 J. Smith, A. Gounaris, P. Watson, N. W. Paton, A. A. A. Fernandes, and R. Sakellariou. Distributed query processing on the Grid. In *Proc. 3rd Int. Workshop on Grid Computing.* Springer-Verlag, 2002.

10.29 J. D. Ullman. Information integration using logical views. In *Proc. ICDT,* pages 19–40. Springer-Verlag, 1997.

10.30 S. B. Zdonik and D. Maier, editors. *Readings in Object-Oriented Database Systems*. Morgan Kaufmann, 1990.

Section Editor's Preface

Introduction to Section III:
Advances in Analysis and Optimisation using a Functional Approach
by Alexandra Poulovassilis

This section of the book discusses the benefits that a functional approach can bring to the development of analysis and optimisation techniques for data manipulation languages.

The topic of Chapter 11 is event–condition–action rules. Event–condition–action (ECA) rules turn databases from being "passive" into being "active", by allowing a timely response to the occurrence of specified events on the database. They localise this reactive functionality into one set of rules, allowing easier and more reliable management and evolution of this aspect of an application. However, the interactions between ECA rules can be difficult to predict, since the action part of a rule may cause an event which triggers one or more other rules, which in turn may trigger further rules, and so on, potentially causing an infinite cascading of rules. Thus, there has been much research on developing techniques for analysing the behaviour of ECA rules, mostly in the context of relational databases, but also for object-oriented databases.

Chapter 11 shows that if a functional approach is adopted for specifying the rule execution model of an active DBMS, then *abstract interpretation* can be used as a sound basis for developing analysis techniques for ECA rules. This abstract interpretation framework models the execution of ECA rules on real databases by means of an "abstract" execution of the rules on a simpler, approximate, representation of the database. The framework provides a small set of criteria for establishing the correctness of any particular approximation technique. The approach is general and can be used for analysing ECA rules over relational, object-oriented, and indeed semi-structured data. The chapter gives examples of all three cases, in particular using a recent ECA rule language for XML to illustrate application of the approach to semi-structured data.

A more general conclusion from this chapter is that, if the rule execution model of an ECA system is specified in a functional form, then this allows techniques developed for analysing and optimising functional programs to be applied in this particular context, since the rule execution model is just a functional program. Abstract interpretation is one such technique, and the chapter concludes by pointing to other recent work by the authors which uses another technique from programming languages, namely *partial evaluation*, for optimising the execution of ECA rules.

Chapters 12 — 14 discuss optimisation techniques for database queries. Database queries are characterised by their potential to access and manipulate very large volumes of data. Generally, it is possible to write a database query in many different ways, each giving the same results but possibly having very different performance characteristics. Thus, a major area of research in DBMSs over the past thirty years has been in the development of effective optimisation techniques for database queries, allowing different equivalent forms of a query to be automatically generated and their relative costs to be estimated. The bulk of this work has been in the context of SQL queries on relational databases, but more recently there has also been considerable work on optimising queries over object-oriented and semi-structured data.

Chapters 12 — 14 show how designing query languages which are functional and are based on a very small number of core constructs, allows a principled approach to the development of query optimisation techniques which can apply to a broad variety of data, including relational, object-oriented and semi-structured data.

Chapter 12 explores a query language construct known as the *monad comprehension* which captures the essential features of practical query languages such as SQL and OQL. The chapter describes how monad comprehensions provide a single formalism for proving the correctness of many optimisations that have been developed for specific query languages and specific language constructs. The chapter then shows how XPath expressions can also be translated into monad comprehension syntax, and how this representation can then be used to prove a number of equivalences for XPath expressions.

Chapter 13 discusses a similar query formalism, the *monoid comprehension calculus*, for representing the essential features of OQL queries. It discusses query processing and query optimisation in the Lambda-DB DBMS, in which OQL queries are first translated into the monoid comprehension calculus for optimisation, and then into a nested-relational algebra for further optimisation and translation into an execution plan. The chapter shows how using the monoid comprehension calculus as an intermediate query formalism allows nested queries to be unnested so that they can subsequently be translated into more efficient execution plans. The chapter also describes how XML data can be stored in the Lambda-DB DBMS and can be queried using a language called XML-OQL, which is an extension of OQL. Queries expressed in XML-OQL are also translated into the monoid comprehension calculus, and are optimised and evaluated in the same way as OQL queries.

Chapter 14 concludes the section by bringing together many of the strands on the design and optimisation of functional query languages that have been discussed in earlier chapters of the book. Written by two of the pioneers of the field, the chapter starts with a short review of the development of relational query languages and then develops a generalisation of the relational algebra to more complex types than just "flat" tables. This generalisation is based on *structural recursion* and it allows a natural extension of query optimisation techniques previously developed for the relational algebra to a much richer query language and set of data types, including the complex objects handled by object-oriented languages, and semi-structured data. Along the way, the authors summarise the theoretical connections between structural recursion, collections, monads, monoids, and comprehensions.

Much work has also been done on optimising queries over distributed, heterogeneous data sources. Taking a functional approach brings similar advantages as for centralised, homogeneous data, and the chapters in Section II of the book include descriptions of query optimisers lying at the heart of several functional data integration systems.

Table of Contents

11. Analysis of Functional Active Databases

James Bailey[1] and Alexandra Poulovassilis[2]

[1] Department of Computer Science, University of Melbourne,
Melbourne, Australia
email: jbailey@cs.mu.oz.au
[2] School of Computer Science and Information Systems,
Birkbeck College, University of London, London WC1E 7HX, U.K.
email: ap@dcs.bbk.ac.uk

Summary.

Active databases are capable of reacting automatically to state changes without user intervention by supporting *event–condition–action* (ECA) rules of the form "on *event* if *condition* do *action*". However, it is recognised that the lack of sufficiently powerful analysis techniques for ECA rules is still an impediment to the wider use of active database technology.

In this chapter we discuss how *abstract interpretation* is a promising analysis technique for ECA rules. A major feature of our approach is its generality: it can be applied to any active DBMS whose rule execution semantics have been specified as a function that takes an initial database and an initial list of rule actions to be executed, and returns the resulting database when there are no more actions left to execute.

We give an example of such functional semantics in this chapter and then specify an abstract version of these semantics, operating on abstract databases. In our framework, a specific analysis technique is modelled by defining a specific abstraction for real databases, and we describe some abstractions. We also discuss how the correctness of a particular abstraction can be formally proved, how our framework can be used for analysing both instance-oriented and set-oriented rules, and how it can also be applied to analysing ECA rules on XML databases.

11.1 Introduction

Active databases are capable of reacting automatically to state changes without user intervention by supporting *event–condition–action* (ECA) rules of the form "on *event* if *condition* do *action*". ECA rules are also known as *triggers* and they are supported in some form by all the major DBMS products. Comprehensive accounts of the active database field can be found in [11.31, 11.27].

The potential benefits of active databases are numerous. Rather than application code having to explicitly query the database at predefined intervals in order to find out if particular events have occurred, ECA rules allow a timely response to critical events. They also allow reactive functionality to be defined and managed within the DBMS rather than being encoded in diverse programs. This enhances the modularity and maintainability of applications. Also, ECA rules are amenable to powerful analysis and optimisation techniques which cannot be applied if the same functionality is dispersed throughout the application code.

ECA rules provide a unifying approach to many advanced database features, including constraint enforcement, incremental view materialisation, provision of audit trails, and maintenance of database statistics. However, when several ECA rules have been defined within an active database, the execution dependencies between them can be complex and it can be difficult to predict their behaviour. It is recognised that the lack of sufficiently powerful analysis techniques for ECA rules is still an impediment to their wider deployment in database applications [11.22, 11.14].

As a contribution to this area, we have developed a framework for ECA rule analysis in functional active databases which is based on *abstract interpretation* [11.1, 11.17]. By *functional active database* we mean one whose ECA rule execution semantics have been specified in a purely functional metalanguage as a function that takes an initial database and an initial list of actions to be executed, and returns the resulting database when there are no more actions left to execute. We give an example of such semantics in Section 11.2 of this chapter.

Abstract interpretation is a semantics-based method for static analysis of program behaviour. The basic idea is to infer and collect information about a program's run-time properties and its operational aspects. Once the program's semantics have been captured formally, a variety of analyses can be derived as abstractions of these semantics.

An important analysis question for ECA rules is that of termination, where a rule set is *terminating* if for any initial database and initial transaction each ECA rule will fire a finite number of times during the execution of the transaction. This problem is undecidable even for relatively simple rule languages [11.5] and so work on termination analysis has focused on developing conservative techniques for detecting terminating rule sets.

One precursor to the work we describe here was the ECA subsystem of the PFL functional DBMS [11.30, 11.28]. The rule execution semantics of this ECA subsystem were specified in a functional metalanguage, namely PFL itself. This brought about several advantages: the formal semantics were a robust basis for implementing the ECA subsystem; they were executable and hence allowed us to experiment with the design of the ECA subsystem before investing effort in implementation; and, being specified in PFL itself, the semantics were relatively easily understood by PFL users. In this chapter we illustrate a further significant advantage of such functional specifications of ECA rule execution semantics, namely that they can be used as a basis for developing powerful analysis techniques for ECA rules, and moreover for proving the correctness of such techniques.

The other precursor to the work we describe here is earlier work on using abstract interpretation for termination analysis [11.3, 11.4]. However, this was for a simple variable-based language, supporting variable assignment rather than database updates. Also, this earlier treatment was described somewhat informally and in an imperative language context.

Several other static analysis techniques have been developed for guaranteeing that a given set of ECA rules definitely terminates, and we will be reviewing some of them in Section 11.7. However, in many cases it is not clear whether a method developed for a particular rule language and rule execution semantics would be correct if applied to a different language or execution semantics. It may also not be clear whether there is a general strategy for proving the correctness of a method and understanding the trade-offs made in its design.

Abstract interpretation has proven to be a useful tool in the analysis of imperative, functional and logic programs [11.1, 11.17, 11.25, 11.26]. In this chapter we show how it can be used as a general, formal tool for developing techniques for analysing ECA rule behaviour.

We first specify in Section 11.2 our ECA rule execution semantics as a function that takes a database state and an initial list of actions to be executed, and returns the resulting database state when there are no more actions left to execute. We next specify in Section 11.3 an abstract version of these rule execution semantics, operating on abstract databases.

In our framework, a specific analysis technique is modelled by defining a specific abstraction for real databases, and we describe some abstractions in Section 11.5. The correctness of a particular abstraction is established by proving a set of generic requirements, which we give in Section 11.4. Our framework can be used both statically, i.e. at rule definition time, and dynamically, during rule execution. The formal nature of the framework allows a smooth adoption of previous work on query satisfiability, incremental evaluation techniques, and approximation techniques. In Section 11.6, we discuss how our framework can be used for analysing instance-oriented as well as set-oriented rules. We give an overview of other approaches to ECA rule analysis in Section 11.7. We finally describe how our framework can also be applied to analysing ECA rules on XML databases in Section 11.8.

11.2 The Rule Execution Semantics

Our ECA rule execution semantics are expressed as a function, *execSched*, which takes as input a *database* and a *schedule*. The schedule consists of a sequence of actions which are to be executed on the database. The execution of an action may cause events to occur. These may cause further rules to fire, modifying the schedule with new sub-sequences of actions. The execution continues until the schedule becomes empty.

In our semantics we assume that for each type of event E detectable by the database there are two system-defined database objects: *has_occurred_E* and *change_E*. The former is non-empty if event E occurred during the execution of the last action, and it contains information about the occurrences of event

E, e.g. the time at which they occurred and which transaction caused them to occur. *change_E* contains information about the changes that occurrences of event E made to user-defined database objects during the execution of the last action.

For example, in a typical active relational database there may be for each user-defined relation R a set of six system-defined relations:

- *has_occurred_insertion_R*, which would be non-empty if one or more INSERT statements on relation R occurred during the execution of the last action;
- *change_insertion_R*, which would contain the set of new tuples inserted into relation R during the execution of the last action;
- *has_occurred_deletion_R*, which would be non-empty if one or more DELE- TE statements on relation R occurred during the execution of the last action;
- *change_deletion_R*, which would contain the set of tuples deleted from R during the execution of the last action;
- *has_occurred_update_R*, which would be non-empty if one or more UP- DATE statements on relation R occurred during the execution of the last action; and
- *change_update_R*, which would contain a set of pairs (*old_tuple,new_tuple*) for each tuple of R which was updated during the execution of the last action.

Similarly, in a typical active object-oriented database there may be classes *has_occurred_M* and *change_M* for each method M whose invocation is detectable as an event by the database. *has_occurred_M* would be non-empty if method M was invoked during the execution of the last action. *change_M* would contain information about changes made to user-defined database objects by invocations of method M during the last action.

The event part of an ECA rule is either *has_occurred_E* or *change_E*, for some event E. The identifiers *has_occurred_E* and *change_E* may also occur within the rule's condition and action parts.

The rule is said to be *triggered* if its event part is non-empty. Allowing either *has_occurred_E* or *change_E* to appear as rule events means that both "syntactic" and "semantic" triggering of rules are supported within our framework: syntactic triggering happens if the rule's event query is *has_occurred_E* and instances of event E occur; semantic triggering happens if the rule's event query is *change_E* and instances of event E occur and make changes to the database.

The condition part of the rule is a boolean-valued query. The rule's *event–condition query* is the conjunction of its event and condition parts, where an event part is deemed to be *True* if it is non-empty and *False* otherwise. The rule *fires* if it is triggered and its condition evaluates to *True*, i.e. if its overall event–condition query evaluates to *True*.

A rule has a list of one or more *actions*. A rule also has a *coupling mode*, which may be either *Immediate* or *Deferred*. With Immediate coupling mode, if the rule fires then its actions are prefixed to the current schedule, while with Deferred coupling mode, they are suffixed. If multiple rules with the same coupling mode fire, then the actions of higher-priority rules precede those of lower-priority ones on the schedule. We thus assume that there is a total ordering imposed on the set of ECA rules as, for example, in the SQL3 trigger standard [11.23]. We also assume that all rules have the same *binding mode*, whereby any occurrences of *has_occurred* and *change* identifiers appearing in the rule's actions are bound to the database state in which the rule's event–condition query was evaluated.

Our rule execution semantics can be enriched to handle a greater variety of coupling modes and binding modes, but here we confine ourselves to this subset and focus on the use of abstract interpretation for rule analysis. A detailed description of the coupling and binding possibilities for active rules can be found in [11.27].

We specify our rule execution semantics as a recursive function *execSched* (see below) which takes a database and schedule, and repeatedly executes the action at the head of the schedule, updating the schedule with the actions of rules that fire along the way. If *execSched* terminates, it outputs the final database and the final, empty, schedule.

In this specification, ∘ denotes function composition, [] the empty list, $(x : y)$ a list with head x and tail y, and $++$ is the list append operator. We also assume the following standard function for "left folding" a binary function f into a list:

```
foldl f a []    = a
foldl f a (x:xs) = foldl f (f x a) xs
```

A schedule is a list of *updates*:

```
Schedule = List (Update)
```

where each update is a 4-tuple consisting of a rule action and the values of the rule's event and condition queries at the time that the action was placed on the schedule:

```
Update = (Value, Value, Value, Action)
```

In particular, if E is the event that triggers the rule, i.e. the rule's event part is either *has_occurred_E* or *change_E*, then the first component of the 4-tuple is the value of *has_occurred_E*, the second component is the value of *change_E*, and the third component is the value of the rule's condition query, all of these at the time that the rule's actions were placed on the schedule.

The parameter u passed to the function *exec* is an update, i.e. a 4-tuple $(oc, ch, cond, a)$. *exec* $(oc, ch, cond, a)$ *db* replaces any *has_occurred* or *change* identifiers occurring within action a by the value of these identifiers at the time that the rule was scheduled, i.e. by the parameters oc or ch, respectively.

exec then executes action *a* on the current database *db* and returns the new database, including the updated *change* and *has_occurred* objects[1].

We assume that ECA rules are identified by unique identifiers of type *RuleId*. If *E* is the event that triggers rule *r*, then *has_occurred r* returns the query *has_occurred_E*, *change r* returns the query *change_E*, *condition r* returns the rule's condition query, *actions r* its list of actions, and *mode r* its coupling mode. The function *ecq* returns the rule's combined event–condition query.

The function *triggers* takes a rule action, and returns a list comprising the identifiers of the rules that may be triggered by that action, in decreasing order of the rules' priority. We assume here that *triggers* performs a syntactic analysis of rule actions and rule events, and that it is conservative in the sense that if *triggers a* does not return a rule identifier, then there is no database state in which execution of action *a* can trigger that rule. Clearly, the most naive *triggers* function would return all rule identifiers.

The function *schedRules* applies the function *schedRule* to each rule that may be triggered by *a*, in decreasing order of the rules' priority. *schedRule* determines whether a given rule fires by invoking the *eval* function to evaluate the rule's event–condition query with respect to the current database. If so, the function *updateSched* is called to update either the schedule's prefix or its suffix, depending on the rule's coupling mode:

```
execSched : (DBState,Schedule) -> (DBState,Schedule)
execSched (db,[]) = (db,[])
execSched (db,u:s) =
    execSched o schedRules (exec u db, u:s)

schedRules : (DBState,Schedule) -> (DBState,Schedule)
schedRules (db,(oc,ch,cond,a):s) =
    let (db,pre,suf) =
        foldl schedRule (db,[],[]) (triggers a)
    in  (db,pre++s++suf)

schedRule : RuleId -> (DBState,Schedule,Schedule) ->
                      (DBState,Schedule,Schedule)
```

---

[1] Before making this update, *exec* first checks that the rule's event and condition queries — namely, the parameter *oc* or *ch* and the parameter *cond* — were *True* at the time the rule was scheduled. For the real rule execution semantics this will trivially be the case since only the actions of such rules are placed onto the schedule. But in order to show the correctness of the abstract semantics, we allow the concrete executions that they represent to place on the schedule the actions of rules whose event or condition query may be *False*. The concrete rule execution must ensure that such "null actions" have no effect on the database or on the subsequent rule firings. We take up this point again in the footnote in Section 11.4 below.

```
schedRule i (db,pre,suf) =
    if (eval (ecq r) db) = False
    then (db,pre,suf)
    else updateSched (eval (has_occurred r) db,
                      eval (change r) db,
                      eval (condition r) db,
                      actions r,mode r,pre,suf)

updateSched (oc,ch,cond,actions,Immediate,pre,suf) =
    (db,pre ++ [(oc,ch,cond,a) | a <- actions], suf)

updateSched (oc,ch,cond,actions,Deferred, pre,suf) =
    (db,pre, suf ++ [(oc,ch,cond,a) | a <- actions])
```

Example 1. Assume a relational active database and two ECA rules both with Immediate coupling mode:

Rule 1: on *change_insertion_R* if $(R \cap S) \times (R \cap T)$ do *delete R T*

Rule 2: on *change_deletion_R* if *true* do *insert R (S − T)*

Only an *insert* or *delete* statement on R can trigger one of the above rules.

Suppose first that a transaction executes an *insert* statement *insert R e*, for some expression e. This update is represented by an initial single-ton schedule $[(Unknown, Unknown, Unknown, insert\ R\ e)]$ being passed to *execSched*. *exec* will execute the action *insert R e* on the database. If this results in one or more new tuples being inserted into R, then Rule 1 will be triggered. If its condition is true, then *execSched* will be invoked recursively with the new schedule $[(oc, ch, True, delete\ R\ T)]$ where oc and ch are respectively the current values of *has_occurred_insertion_R* and *change_insertion_R* (second invocation of *execSched*). *exec* will execute the action *delete R T*, which will result in $(R \cap T)$ being deleted from R. Thus Rule 2 will be triggered, and its condition is trivially true. The schedule becomes $[(oc, ch, True, insert\ R\ (S − T))]$ where oc and ch are respectively the current values of *has_occurred_deletion_R* and *change_deletion_R* (third invocation of *execSched*). *exec* will execute the action *insert R (S − T)*. If this results in new tuples being inserted into R then Rule 1 will be triggered again. At this point, though, Rule 1's condition is *False* because $R \cap T = \emptyset$. The schedule becomes empty and *execSched* terminates (at the fourth invocation of *execSched*).

Suppose now that a transaction executes a *delete* statement *delete R e*, for some expression e. This update is represented by an initial singleton schedule $(Unknown, Unknown, Unknown, delete\ R\ e)$ being passed to *execSched*. *exec* will execute this action on the database. If this results in one or more tuples being deleted, then Rule 2 will be triggered. Its condition is true, and so *execSched* will be invoked recursively with the new schedule $[(oc, ch, True, insert\ R\ (S - T)]$, where oc and ch are the current values of *has_occurred_deletion_R* and *change_deletion_R*. Execution then proceeds as above and it is easy to see that *execSched* will terminate after at most five invocations. ∎

11.2.1 Discussion

The above rule execution semantics encompass the functionality of statement-level AFTER triggers in the SQL3 standard [11.23]. SQL3 uses syntactic triggering, so the event parts of its triggers are captured by our *has_occurred* objects. In SQL3, rule conditions are evaluated against the database state that the action will be executed on, rather than the database state in which the rule was triggered. This different binding mode can be captured in our semantics by syntactically modifying each rule so that its condition is encoded with each of its actions and its condition part becomes just *True*. In this way, the actions of any triggered rule will be placed on the schedule by *updateSched* and it is *exec* that will determine whether any give action will actually be applied to the database.

Our semantics also encompass semantic triggering and Deferred rule coupling, which are not supported in SQL3.

The above semantics do not encompass SQL3's BEFORE triggers but could easily be extended to allow these, and the analysis techniques that we describe here would also apply to such rules.

The above semantics assume that all ECA rules are *set-oriented* as opposed to *instance-oriented*. When a set-oriented rule is triggered by some event E and is then scheduled for execution, one copy of its actions is placed on the schedule, each action being tupled up with the current values of the *has_occurred_E* and *change_E* objects. SQL3's statement-level triggers are set-oriented.

When an instance-oriented rule is triggered by some event E, one copy of its actions is placed on the schedule for each $c \in change\_E$ for which the rule's condition evaluates to *True*. SQL3's row-level triggers are instance-oriented. Our semantics and analysis techniques can be extended to instance-oriented rules and we discuss how in Section 11.6 below.

Finally, the above semantics assume that there is a total ordering imposed on the set of ECA rules, as in SQL3. It would be straightforward to extend our semantics to allow multiple rules of equal priority: if multiple rules of the same priority were to fire, then their actions would be placed on the schedule in an arbitrary order. It is generally assumed with such rules that they are well-defined, in the sense that the same final database state will result when rule execution terminates irrespective of the order in which such rules are scheduled. A rule set that satisfies this property is termed *confluent* and several techniques have been developed for detecting confluent rule sets [11.2], including using abstract interpretation [11.6].

11.3 The Abstract Execution Semantics

The abstract counterpart to *execSched* is *execSched**, given below. This is identical to *execSched* except that it operates on abstract databases and abstract schedules, and that at the "leaves" of the computation the functions *eval* and *exec* are replaced by their abstract counterparts *eval** and *exec**. We distinguish abstract types and functions from their concrete counterparts by suffixing their names with a "*".

An abstract database consists of a set of identifiers and an abstract value associated with each identifier. Generally, these abstract values will be drawn from different domains for different abstractions.

An abstract schedule is a list of abstract updates:

```
Schedule* = List (Update*)
```

Each abstract update is a 4-tuple, consisting of a rule action, and the abstract values of the rule's event and condition queries at the time that the rule fired:

```
Update* = (Value*, Value*, Value*, Action)
```

An abstract database approximates a number of real databases and an abstract schedule a number of real schedules. These possible concretisations are given by a *concretisation function*, *conc*. This *conc* function depends on the specific abstraction and is generally different for different abstractions. We will be seeing some examples in Section 11.5 below.

Rules, queries and actions are syntactic objects which are common to both the concrete and the abstract semantics. The functions *triggers*, *has_occurred*, *change*, *condition*, *ecq*, *actions*, *mode* and *updateSched* are thus the same in both semantics.

```
execSched* : (DBState*,Schedule*) -> (DBState*,Schedule*)
execSched* (db*,[]) = (db*,[])
execSched* (db*,u*:s*) =
    execSched* o schedRules* (exec* u* db*, u*:s*)

schedRules* : (DBState*,Schedule*) -> (DBState*,Schedule*)
schedRules* (db*,(oc*,ch*,cond*,a):s*) =
    let (db*,pre*,suf*) =
        foldl schedRule* (db*,[],[]) (triggers a)
    in  (db*,pre* ++ s* ++ suf*)

schedRule* : RuleId -> (DBState*,Schedule*,Schedule*) ->
                       (DBState*,Schedule*,Schedule*)
```

```
schedRule* i (db*,pre*,suf*) =
    if (eval* (ecq r) db*) = False
    then (db*,pre*,suf*)
    else updateSched (eval* (has_occurred r) db*,
                      eval* (change r) db*,
                      eval* (condition r) db*,
                      actions r,mode r,pre*,suf*)
```

Note that in general there is no guarantee that $execSched^*$ will terminate and so a criterion is needed for halting it. A simple way is to choose a priori a bound on the number of recursive calls of $execSched^*$. Increasing this bound allows more precision and can be balanced against the time available for undertaking the analysis.

An alternative strategy for halting $execSched^*$ is to maintain a history of the $(db^*, head\ s^*)$ arguments passed to $execSched^*$ and to halt if a repeating argument is detected, since in such a case we know that $execSched^*$ would continue to process the same sequence of rules *ad infinitum*.

Before looking at some specific abstractions, we consider first the issue of the correctness of the abstract semantics.

11.4 Correctness of the Abstract Semantics

Suppose the following two conditions hold for any event–condition query q, abstract update u^*, and abstract database db^*:

$$conc\ (exec^*\ u^*\ db^*) \supseteq \{exec\ u\ db \mid (u, db) \in conc\ (u^*, db^*)\} \qquad (11.1)$$

$$eval^*\ q\ db^* = False \Rightarrow (\forall db \in conc\ db^*\ .\ eval\ q\ db = False) \qquad (11.2)$$

Condition (11.1) states that the abstract database created by an abstract update $exec^*\ u^*\ db^*$ represents all the databases that could be created by $exec\ u\ db$ for any concretisation of (u, db) of (u^*, db^*) (and possibly other databases as well).

Condition (11.2) states that if an event–condition query evaluates to *False* with respect to an abstract database db^*, then it evaluates to *False* with respect to all concretisations db of db^*.

In combination, these two conditions imply that (a) the abstract database at each iteration of $execSched^*$ represents a superset of the set of concrete databases that may arise at the same iteration of $execSched$, and that (b) the set of rules firing at any iteration of $execSched^*$ is a superset of the set of rules that may fire at the same iteration of $execSched^2$.

---

[2] There is a subtlety here in that the formal proof of (a) and (b) (given in [11.7]) requires that all the concrete executions proceed "in step" with the abstract execution, with the same set of rule actions being scheduled at each step. In reality real rule executions will cause different combinations of rules to fire. However,

Thus, if a particular abstraction satisfies (11.1) and (11.2) above, then the abstract execution from any initial abstract state (db^*, s^*) represents a *superset* of the set of real executions from the set of real initial states $(db, s) \in conc\ (db^*, s^*)$. Thus the abstraction is *safe* (i.e. conservative) for all properties P such that if P holds for a set of real executions S then it must also hold for each subset of S. Examples of such properties are the following:

- **Termination**: If $execSched^*\ (db^*, s^*)$ terminates, then so must all $execSched\ (db, s)$ such that $(db, s) \in conc\ (db^*, s^*)$.
- **Rule Not Fired**: If a rule r does not fire during the execution of $execSched^*\ (db^*, s^*)$, then it cannot fire during the execution of any $execSched\ (db, s)$ such that $(db, s) \in conc\ (db^*, s^*)$.
- **Rule Sequence Not Fired**: If rules $r_1, \ldots, r_n$ do not fire in this sequence during the execution of $execSched^*\ (db^*, s^*)$, then this sequence of rules cannot fire during the execution of any $execSched\ (db, s)$ such that $(db, s) \in conc\ (db^*, s^*)$.

An abstraction may additionally satisfy the following pair of stronger conditions:

$$conc\ (exec^*\ u^*\ db^*) = \{exec\ u\ db \mid (u, db) \in conc\ (u^*, db^*)\} \qquad (11.3)$$

$$eval^*\ q\ db^* = False \Leftrightarrow (\forall db \in conc\ db^* . eval\ q\ db = False) \qquad (11.4)$$

In this case the abstract execution represents exactly the set of real executions from each pair $(db, s) \in conc\ (db^*, s^*)$ and the abstraction is both safe and also *precise*.

Additional properties can be analysed with a precise abstraction. In particular, for any property P as above, if $\neg P$ holds for $execSched^*\ (db^*, s^*)$ then $\neg P$ must hold for some $execSched\ (db, s)$ such that $(db, s) \in conc\ (db^*, s^*)$. Examples of $\neg P$ are the following:

- **Non-termination**: If some iteration of $execSched^*\ (db^*, s^*)$ encounters the same abstract database and same abstract schedule as an earlier iteration, then $execSched^*$ will fail to terminate. With a precise abstraction this means that some $execSched\ (db, s)$ such that $(db, s) \in conc\ (db^*, s^*)$ will also pass twice through the same concrete database and concrete update at the head of the schedule and hence will also fail to terminate.
- **Rule Fired**: If a rule r fires during the execution of $execSched^*\ (db^*, s^*)$, then it must fire during the execution of some $execSched\ (db, s)$ such that $(db, s) \in conc\ (db^*, s^*)$.
- **Rule Sequence Fired**: If rules $r_1, \ldots, r_n$ fire in this sequence during the execution of $execSched^*\ (db^*, s^*)$, then this same sequence of rules must

---

as discussed in the footnote in Section 11.2, we can "pad out" real schedules with the actions of rules which have not in fact fired and such actions will have no effect on the database state or on subsequent rule firings. Such "padded out" schedules arising from the concretisation of abstract schedules are thus semantically equivalent to non-padded-out real schedules.

fire during the execution of some *execSched* (db, s) such that $(db, s) \in$ *conc* (db^*, s^*).

11.4.1 Discussion

The information provided directly by *execSched** is for concretisations of the initial abstract database and initial abstract schedule. A broader question is: does the analysis property hold for *any* initial database and initial finite schedule?

To capture all possible initial databases we can use as the initial abstract database the "least informative" element of *DBState**: let us denote it by db_0^*. This abstract database maps each database object *Obj* to an abstract value Obj_0 which concretises to all possible valid real values for *Obj*.

To capture all possible initial finite schedules, let us consider first properties P as above, i.e. such that if P holds for a set of real executions S then it must also hold for each subset of S. Let us also suppose first that all rules have Immediate coupling mode.

In this case, it is sufficient to run execSched* on each possible singleton schedule $[(Unknown, Unknown, Unknown, a)]$ *for each action a that may trigger one or more rules in the rule set.*

Properties P as above hold for all initial finite schedules if they hold for all such singleton schedules. To see why this is, consider any initial finite abstract schedule

$$s^* = [u_1^*, u_2^*, \ldots, u_n^*]$$

Running *execSched** (db_0^*, s^*) would result in the following sequence of abstract updates being applied to db_0^*, where each T_i is the (possibly empty) sequence of abstract updates arising from the execution of rules that have fired as a result of executing u_i^*:

$$u_1^*, T_1, u_2^*, T_2, \ldots, u_n^*, T_n$$

If P holds for *execSched** $(db_0^*, [u_i^*])$ then it must hold for T_i, since db_0^* is the least informative abstract database state and hence *execSched** $(db_0^*, [u_i^*])$ represents a superset of the set of real executions represented by T_i.

Thus, if P holds for all *execSched** $(db_0^*, [u_1^*])$, ..., *execSched** $(db_0^*, [u_n^*])$ it must hold for all $T_1, \ldots, T_n$, and thus must hold for *execSched** (db_0^*, s^*). Thus P must hold for all *execSched* (db, s) such that $(db, s) \in$ *conc* (db_0^*, s^*).

Finally, for any initial finite abstract schedule $[u_1^*, u_2^*, \ldots, u_n^*]$, it is sufficient to run *execSched** $(db_0^*, [u_i^*])$ only for those updates u_i^* whose action may trigger one or more rules, since for all other updates u_j^* we know that T_j will be empty. Moreover, the behaviour of any such update $u_i^* = (oc^*, ch^*, cond^*, a)$ is encompassed by running *execSched** $(db_0^*, [(Unknown, Unknown, Unknown, a)])$ since these *Unknown* truth values for the initial event and condition queries incorporate the possible truth values of oc^*, ch^* and $cond^*$.

Let us consider now the case where some rules may have Deferred coupling mode. In this case, the execution of each u_i^* may result both in an "immediate" sub-transaction such as T_i above which is scheduled immediately after u_i^* and also in a "deferred" sub-transaction which is appended to the current schedule. The abstract database state that deferred sub-transactions encounter during the execution of $execSched^*$ (db_0^*, s^*) may thus be different from the abstract database state that they encounter during the execution of each individual $execSched^*$ $(db_0^*, [u_i^*])$. Thus, for a safe analysis, the abstract database state must be reinitialised to db_0^* at the start of each deferred sub-transaction.

Let $execSched^{*m}$ be $execSched^*$ modified so as to reinitialise the abstract database state to db_0^* at the start of each deferred sub-transaction. Then, properties P as above hold for all initial finite schedules if they hold for all singleton schedules with the modified abstract semantics $execSched^{*m}$.

For properties $\neg P$ and precise abstractions, it is not sufficient to execute $execSched^*$ on singleton schedules. For example, a rule set may in general be non-terminating for some singleton schedule $[u_i^*]$ but for the specific databases that will arise as a result of first executing the schedule $[u_1^*, \ldots, u_{i-1}^*]$ it may actually always terminate. Similarly, a rule or rule sequence may in general fire during the execution of $[u_i^*]$ but for the specific databases that will arise as a result of first executing $[u_1^*, \ldots, u_{i-1}^*]$ the rule or rule sequence may actually never fire.

Hence, such properties can only be analysed for concretisations of a *specific* abstract schedule. This can none-the-less be useful in a *dynamic* setting, where there is indeed a specific current schedule that we wish to analyse. This is the setting in [11.9], where we discuss dynamic termination analysis of ECA rules. We refer the reader to this paper for further discussion of dynamic ECA rule analysis and how our abstract interpretation approach compares with other approaches.

As a final remark, we note that $execSched^*$ as defined above assumes that the ECA rules are totally ordered. If this is not the case and at some point multiple rules of the same priority fire, then the abstract execution would need to branch into a separate execution pathway for each possible permutation of these rules. We specified such branching semantics in [11.6] and we refer the reader to that paper for details. We consider an example of a branching abstract execution in Section 11.6 below.

11.5 Some Abstractions

In [11.7], we discussed the use of abstract interpretation for rule termination analysis and we identified three specific abstractions. Here we review again these abstractions, and note that they can be used more generally for analysing other rule properties, as discussed above.

The first abstraction we presented in [11.7] is precise for rule languages for which query satisfiability is decidable. This abstraction maintains an abstract database state consisting of an expression for each database object. These expressions are expanded by $exec^*$ as rule actions are applied to them. Satisfiability of a rule's event–condition query determines whether the rule may fire in the current abstract database state. Thus, $eval^*$ is a query satisfiability test which, if satisfiability is decidable for the particular rule language, will return either $True$ or $False$.

If satisfiability is not decidable, $eval^*$ may in addition return $Unknown$. In this case we get a safe but non-precise abstraction. This is because an $Unknown$ truth value for an event–condition query is treated in the same way as $True$ by $execSched^*$, i.e. if it is not known whether a rule would fire, the abstract semantics assume that it *will* fire in some real execution whereas it may in fact not fire in any real execution.

Example 2. Consider again the rules of Example 1. The following is a trace of the abstract execution with an initial singleton schedule consisting of the action $insert\ R\ ?$. Here, "?" is an unused identifier denoting the set of tuples being inserted into R. As with the other database objects, its initial abstract value is $?_0$ which concretises to all possible valid real values. We do not show it below as it cannot be changed by any of the rules. "Iteration i" means the ith invocation of $execSched^*$. For simplicity we show only the actions on the schedule, not the abstract values of the event and condition queries:

Iteration	Abstract database state			Schedule
	R	S	T	
1	R_0	S_0	T_0	$[insert\ R\ ?]$
2	$R_0 \cup ?_0$	S_0	T_0	$[delete\ R\ T]$
3	$(R_0 \cup ?_0) - T_0$	S_0	T_0	$[insert\ R\ (S-T)]$
4	$((R_0 \cup ?_0) - T_0) \cup (S_0 - T_0)$	S_0	T_0	$[]$

At iteration 1, Rule 1 is triggered because the expression $?-R$ is satisfiable and tuples may indeed have been inserted into R. The condition of Rule 1 is also satisfiable, and so the action of Rule 1 is placed on the schedule. After $delete\ R\ T$ is applied to R at iteration 2, Rule 2 is triggered because the expression $R \cap T$, which we term Rule 1's *delta query*, is satisfiable at this stage and so tuples may indeed have been deleted from R. The condition of Rule 2 is trivially true, and so its action is placed on the schedule. After the update $insert\ R\ (S-T)$ is applied to R at iteration 3, Rule 1 is triggered because Rule 2's delta query, $(S-T)-R$, is satisfiable at this stage and so tuples may indeed have been inserted into R. However, the condition of Rule 1 now expands to $(((R_0 \cup ?_0) - T_0) \cup (S_0 - T_0) \cap S_0) \times (((R_0 \cup ?_0) - T_0) \cup (S_0 - T_0) \cap T_0)$, which is not satisfiable because the second argument of this cartesian product is not satisfiable. The schedule thus becomes empty and $execSched^*$ terminates at iteration 4.

Similarly, the following is a trace of the abstract execution with an initial singleton schedule consisting of the action $delete\ R\ ?$, and we see that this terminates at iteration 5 (we do not show the abstract values of S and T as these are again S_0 and T_0 throughout):

Iter.	R	Schedule
1	R_0	$[delete\ R\ ?]$
2	$R_0 - ?_0$	$[insert\ R\ (S - T)]$
3	$(R_0 - ?_0) \cup (S_0 - T_0)$	$[delete\ R\ T]$
4	$((R_0 - ?_0) \cup (S_0 - T_0)) - T_0$	$[insert\ R\ (S - T)]$
5	$(((R_0 - ?_0) \cup (S_0 - T_0)) - T_0) \cup (S_0 - T_0)$	$[]$

Thus, we can conclude that this rule set is definitely a terminating one.

■

Testing satisfiability is generally expensive, and the second and third abstractions we presented in [11.7] undertake a cheaper and less precise analysis by maintaining in the abstract database only the truth values of specific queries, and not the entire history of updates that have have been applied to the database objects. Both these abstractions are safe. They are also precise provided $eval^*$ returns only $True$ or $False$, not if $eval^*$ returns $Unknown$.

With the second abstraction, the abstract database consists of an identifier corresponding to each event query and each condition query in the rule set. These identifiers are assigned values from the two-valued domain $\{False, Unknown\}$. $conc(db^*)$ returns all databases db satisfying the following conditions:

- the values assigned to database objects in db are consistent with the abstract values assigned to the event and condition queries in db^*;
- if the abstract value of an event–condition query, q, is $False$ then its concrete value must also be $False$, i.e.

$$eval^*\ q\ db^* = False \Rightarrow eval\ q\ db = False$$

Given an event-condition query q and abstract database db^*, $eval^*\ q\ db^*$ looks up in db^* the current truth value of the event query and the condition query and returns their logical conjunction.

$exec^*\ (oc^*, ch^*, c^*, a)\ db^*$ updates the abstract database as follows. It first sets the values of all event queries that may be affected by a to $Unknown$ and the values of all other event queries to $False$. It then uses a function $infer\_cond\ q\ a$ to infer a new abstract value for each condition query q. This returns:

- $Unknown$ if the condition may be true after the action executes;
- $False$ if the condition can never be true after the action executes.

A method such as the propagation algorithm described in [11.13] can be used to determine the effect of actions on conditions.

Example 3. Consider again the rules of Example 1. The following is a trace of the abstract execution with an initial singleton schedule consisting of the action *insert R ?*, where e_i denotes the event query of rule i and c_i the condition query of rule i:

Iteration	Abstract database state				Schedule
	e_1	c_1	e_2	c_2	
1	U	U	U	U	$[insert\ R\ ?]$
2	U	U	F	U	$[delete\ R\ T]$
3	F	F	U	U	$[insert\ R\ (S-T)]$
4	U	U	F	U	$[delete\ R\ T]$

At iteration 3, Rule 1's condition becomes *False*, since its action will always falsify $R \cap T$. At iteration 4 the execution of Rule 2's action makes Rule 1's condition *Unknown* again because only the overall truth values of conditions are recorded, so *infer_cond* cannot make use of the fact that $R \cap T$ was previously *False*. The fourth state is thus a repetition of the second, so *execSched** is halted and possible rule non-termination is concluded. ∎

Example 4. Suppose now we change the condition of Rule 1 to be just $R \cap T$. Then the following is a trace of the abstract execution with an initial singleton schedule consisting of the action *insert R ?*:

Iteration	Abstract database state				Schedule
	e_1	c_1	e_2	c_2	
1	U	U	U	U	$[insert\ R\ ?]$
2	U	U	F	U	$[delete\ R\ T]$
3	F	F	U	U	$[insert\ R\ (S-T)]$
4	U	F	F	U	$[]$

Now Rule 2's action can no longer alter the truth value of Rule 1's condition and *execSched** terminates at iteration 4, since Rule 1's condition is *False*.

Similarly, the following is a trace of the abstract execution with an initial singleton schedule consisting of the action *delete R ?*:

Iteration	Abstract database state				Schedule
	e_1	c_1	e_2	c_2	
1	U	U	U	U	$[delete\ R\ ?]$
2	F	U	U	U	$[insert\ R\ (S-T)]$
3	U	U	F	U	$[delete\ R\ T]$
4	F	F	U	U	$[insert\ R\ (S-T)]$
5	U	F	F	U	$[]$

Again *execSched** terminates. Thus, this cheaper analysis can be used to conclude that the modified rule set is a terminating one. ■

The above function *infer_cond* uses only the syntax of conditions and actions to deduce new values for the event and condition queries. The third abstraction we describe in [11.7] incorporates a more refined inferencing method which makes use of information about the previous values of queries. Its increased precision is reflected by the inclusion of the value $True$ in the abstract domain, as well as $Unknown$ and $False$.

This abstraction assumes that for each rule action a_i there is a set of events $E_1, \ldots, E_n$ which the execution of a_i may cause to occur, and that for each such E_j we can write a query, $q\_a_i\_E_j$, which defines the value of $change\_E_j$ resulting from action a. We term these queries the actions' *delta queries*. For example, in a relational setting, an action *insert R q* can cause only event *insertion_R* to occur and the delta query is $q - R$; similarly, an action *delete R q* can cause only event *deletion_R* to occur and the delta query is $R \cap q$; updates to relations are a bit more complex, but the same principle applies.

With this abstraction, the abstract database again consists of an identifier corresponding to each event and condition query in the rule set. However, there is now also an identifier corresponding to each delta query. These identifiers are assigned values from the three-valued domain $\{True, False, Unknown\}$ in the abstract database.

For this abstraction, $conc(db^*)$ consists of all the databases db satisfying the following conditions:

− the values assigned to database objects in db are consistent with the abstract values assigned to the event, condition and delta queries in db^*;
− if the abstract value of an event–condition query, q, is $False$ then its concrete value must also be $False$, i.e.

$$eval^* \ q \ db^* = False \ \Rightarrow \ eval \ q \ db = False$$

− if the abstract value of an event–condition query, q, is $True$ then its concrete value must also also $True$, i.e.

$$eval^* \ q \ db^* = True \ \Rightarrow \ eval \ q \ db = True$$

Given an event–condition query q and abstract database db^*, $eval^* \ q \ db^*$ again looks up in db^* the current truth values of the event query and the condition query and returns their logical conjunction.

$exec^* \ a^* \ db^*$ updates the query values in the abstract database by using incremental propagation techniques which perform query rewriting to determine if updates can have an effect on an expression [11.29, 11.18]. We refer the reader to [11.7, 11.9] for full details of our inferencing method.

This third abstraction is again not powerful enough to detect termination of the original rule set from Example 1. But it can detect more cases of termination than our second abstraction because it can make use of more precise information about the abstract database state by distinguishing between *True* and *Unknown* query values. We give an example that uses this third abstraction in Section 11.6 below.

Distinguishing between *True* and *Unknown* query values also gives more precision in a dynamic setting by allowing the current real database state to be described more accurately. In [11.9], we describe the practical use of this third abstraction for dynamic analysis of rule termination. In [11.8], we describe how it can also be used for optimising ECA rule execution, both in a static and in a dynamic setting.

11.6 Handling Instance-Oriented Rules

So far we have assumed that all rules are set-oriented ones. Our rule execution semantics and analysis techniques can be extended to apply also to instance-oriented rules and we now discuss how.

The concrete semantics, *execSched*, are easily extended to also allow for instance-oriented rules. If some rule r has fired and it is an instance-oriented rule then for each action a of r, *updateSched* places onto the schedule a list of updates $[(oc, \{c_1\}, cond, a)], [(oc, \{c_2\}, cond, a)], \ldots$ where oc is the current value of *has_occurred* r, $\{c_1, c_2, \ldots\}$ the current value of *change* r and *cond* the current value of *condition* r.

The c_i are placed onto the schedule in an arbitrary order since it is usually assumed that, if used, instance-oriented rules are well-defined in the sense that the same final database state will result when rule execution terminates irrespective of the order in which individual changes arising from instance-level rules are scheduled.

A condition guaranteeing this is that for all pairs c_i, c_j, the queries that are evaluated during $execSched(db, [(oc, \{c_i\}, cond, a)])$ are independent of the database updates that take place during $execSched(db, [(oc, \{c_j\}, cond, a)])$. Techniques for analysing independence of queries from updates can be used to determine whether this is the case for a given set of rules [11.24].

The question is how should *execSched** be modified to analyse instance-oriented rules, and in particular how many copies of each rule action should be placed onto the abstract schedule? Assuming the above condition holds, then it is sufficient to place just one copy of the rule action onto the abstract schedule, i.e. *execSched** remains exactly the same as for set-oriented rules. *execSched** will represent by one abstract execution pathway the multiple independent execution paths that can occur when instance-oriented rules are present.

Example 5. This example is motivated by one given in [11.16]. An object-oriented active database contains a class *Account* which has attributes *overdraft*, *rate*, *capacity* and *type*. There are four instance-oriented ECA rules, all with Immediate coupling mode. Rules 2 and 3 have the same priority, as have Rules 1 and 4. Rule 1 can trigger Rules 2 and 3, Rule 2 can trigger Rules 1 and 4, and Rules 3 and 4 do not trigger any other rule.

In Rule 1, the event $update(Account.overdraft)$ is synonymous with our earlier terminology $has\_occurred\_update\_of\_Account.overdraft$, and this is syntactic triggering. The same applies to the other rules. In Rule 1, the $changed$ object is synonymous with our terminology $change\_update\_of-$ $\_Account.overdraft$. Since the rule is an instance-level one, we assume here that $changed$ returns a single $Account$ object to which the update has been applied. A similar syntax is used in the other rules.

Rule 1: on $update(Account.overdraft)$
      if $changed.rate = 8$
      do $update(changed.capacity, 6000)$

Rule 2: on $update(Account.capacity)$
      if $changed.rate = 4$
      do $update(changed.overdraft, 20)$

Rule 3: on $update(Account.capacity)$
      if $changed.type = stocks\_account$
      do $update(changed.rate, 4)$

Rule 4: on $update(Account.overdraft)$
      if $changed.type = standard\_account$
      do $update(changed.rate, 8)$

Two kinds of actions can trigger this rule set:

$update(Account.overdraft, ?)$ and $update(Account.capacity, ?)$

Let us consider first an initial singleton abstract schedule consisting of the action $a_0 = update(Account.overdraft, ?)$.

We give below the abstract execution trace, assuming the third abstraction from the previous section. We do not show the delta query values as these are all $True$ throughout the execution (because in this rule language $update$ actions are always deemed to happen, irrespective of whether they change the actual value of the attribute).

At iteration 2, the abstract execution branches because both Rules 1 and 4 are triggered and we need to consider both orders in which their actions may be scheduled for execution — traces $2^1 - 5^1$ and $2^2 - 5^2$ in the table below.

At iteration 2^1, c_1 must be true since a_1 has just been placed on the schedule. Thus c_2 must be false. So although a_1 triggers both Rules 2 and 3, only a_3 is placed on the schedule. c_3 is unknown at this point, so in a real execution a_3 may or may not occur, depending on whether the object has $type = stocks\_account$. So at iteration 4^1, the values of c_1 and c_2 have become unknown again. a_3 triggers no rules, so a_4 has come to the head of the schedule at iteration 4^1. a_4 triggers no rules, and this execution branch terminates at iteration 5^1.

At iteration 2^2, c_1 is again true and c_2 false. Execution of a_4 does not change these values and triggers no rules. Thus at iteration 3^2, a_1 has come to the head of the schedule. Execution of a_1 triggers both Rules 2 and 3, but because c_2 is false only a_3 is placed on the schedule. This execution branch thus terminates at iteration 5^2.

Iteration	Abstract database state								Schedule
	e_1	c_1	e_2	c_2	e_3	c_3	e_4	c_4	
1	F	U	F	U	F	U	F	U	$[a_0]$
2^1	T	T	F	F	F	U	T	U	$[a_1, a_4]$
3^1	F	T	T	F	T	U	F	U	$[a_3, a_4]$
4^1	F	U	F	U	F	U	F	U	$[a_4]$
5^1	F	U	F	U	F	U	F	U	$[]$
2^2	T	T	F	F	F	U	T	U	$[a_4, a_1]$
3^2	F	T	F	F	F	U	F	U	$[a_1]$
4^2	F	T	T	F	T	U	F	U	$[a_3]$
5^2	F	U	F	U	F	U	F	U	$[]$

Similarly, this is the abstract execution trace with an initial abstract schedule consisting of the action $a_0 = update(Account.capacity, ?)$. At iteration 3^2 the abstract execution branches a second time, into $4^{2,1}$ and $4^{2,2}$, depending on the order that a_1 and a_4 are scheduled after a_2 executes. We notice that these states are exactly the same as 2^1 and 2^2 above, and so these two branches would proceed exactly as $2^1 - 5^1$ and $2^2 - 5^2$ above.

Iteration	Abstract database state								Schedule
	e_1	c_1	e_2	c_2	e_3	c_3	e_4	c_4	
1	F	U	F	U	F	U	F	U	$[a_0]$
2^1	F	F	T	T	T	U	F	U	$[a_2, a_3]$
3^1	T	F	F	T	F	U	T	U	$[a_4, a_3]$
4^1	F	U	F	U	F	U	F	U	$[a_3]$
5^1	F	U	F	U	F	U	F	U	$[]$
2^2	F	F	T	T	T	U	F	U	$[a_3, a_2]$
3^2	F	U	F	U	F	U	F	U	$[a_2]$
$4^{2,1}$	T	T	F	F	F	U	T	U	$[a_1, a_4]$
$4^{2,2}$	T	T	F	F	F	U	T	U	$[a_4, a_1]$

Thus, we can conclude that this rule set is a terminating one. ∎

11.7 Other Approaches to ECA Rule Analysis

Many previous methods for ECA rule analysis have been based on analysing the triggering and activation relationships between pairs of rules. In these approaches, a rule r_i *may trigger* a rule r_j if execution of the action of r_i may generate an event which causes the event part of r_j to become *True*. A rule r_i *may activate* another rule r_j if r_j's condition may be changed from *False* to *True* after the execution of r_i's action. A rule r_i *may activate* itself if its condition may be *True* after the execution of its action.

A *triggering graph* [11.2] represents each rule as a vertex, and there is a directed arc from a vertex r_i to a vertex r_j if r_i *may trigger* r_j. Acyclicity of the triggering graph implies definite termination of rule execution. Triggering graphs can also be used for deriving rule reachability information. An *activation graph* [11.13] also represents rules as vertices. In this case there is a directed arc from a vertex r_i to a vertex r_j if r_i *may activate* r_j. Acyclicity of this graph also implies definite termination of rule execution.

Previous methods of ECA rule analysis have often been closely linked to specific rule languages. In contrast, the abstract interpretation framework that we have described here does not assume any particular rule language. Moreover, our rule execution semantics can simulate most standard features of active database systems and research prototypes.

The method in [11.21] used satisfiability tests between pairs of rules to refine triggering graphs. This can be interpreted as a less sophisticated version of the first abstraction we described in Section 11.5. For example, in Example 1, if we only considered the relationships between pairs of rules, we would derive the information that Rules 1 and 2 can cause each other to fire. By itself, this information does not allow us to make any conclusions about the rules' termination behaviour. However, we showed in Example 1 that by doing satisfiability testing on accumulated "history" expressions, we can conclude that this rule set is indeed a terminating one.

The second abstraction we described in Section 11.5 does focus on pairwise relationships between rules and so is similar to graph-based analysis techniques based on triggering and activation relationships between rules [11.2, 11.13, 11.12, 11.21, 11.15]. Our abstraction is not identical to these, however, since in their pure form graph-based techniques do not "execute" the rule set and so have no notion of control flow. This can cause loss of precision for rule sets where the order of execution prohibits certain activation states of conditions. Extensions to these techniques are certainly possible to recognise such situations, but they do not arise naturally from the specifications of the techniques themselves.

Couchot gives in [11.16] a detailed review of the main methods for rule termination analysis and discusses their limitations in capturing control flow. He proposes an extension of the Refined Triggering Graph method for object-oriented databases [11.21], and this extension can detect definite termination of the rule set in Example 5. In this chapter, we have shown how our abstract interpretation can also be used to effectively analyse such rule sets, due to its inherent incorporation of control flow information, and moreover our abstract interpretation framework achieves this in a language-independent setting.

11.8 Analysing XML ECA Rules

We conclude this chapter by describing how our framework can also be applied to analysing ECA rules on XML databases. In [11.10, 11.11] we describe an ECA rule language for XML which uses the XPath and XQuery languages to specify events, conditions and actions.

The event part of an ECA rule in this language is an expression of the form

INSERT e

or

DELETE e

where e is an XPath expression which evaluates to a set of nodes. The rule is triggered if this set of nodes includes any node in a new subdocument in the case of an insertion, or in a deleted subdocument in the case of a deletion. We note that this is semantic triggering, i.e. rules are triggered only if changes occur to the database.

Thus, using our earlier terminology, there is an identifier $change\_INS\text{-}ERT\_e$ for each event of the form INSERT e appearing in the rule set, and an identifier $change\_DELETE\_e$, for each event of the form DELETE e appearing in the rule set. Since only semantic triggering is supported in this rule language, we can ignore the $has\_occurred$ identifiers.

A system-defined variable, $delta, is available for use within the condition and action parts of the rule. Its set of instantiations is the set of new or deleted nodes returned by e. Thus, $delta is synonymous with the $change$ identifier corresponding to the rule's event part.

The condition part of an ECA rule is either the constant TRUE, or one or more XPath expressions connected by the boolean connectives **and, or, not**. This condition is evaluated on each XML document in the database which has been changed by an event of the form specified in the rule's event part. If the condition references the $delta variable, it is evaluated once for each instantiation of $delta — this is instance-oriented triggering. Otherwise, the condition is evaluated just once for each document — set-oriented triggering.

The action part of an ECA rule is a sequence of one or more actions:

$action_1; \ldots; action_n$

These actions are executed on each XML document which has been changed by an event of the form specified in the rule's event part and for which the rule's condition query evaluates to *True*. An ECA rule fires if this set of documents is non-empty.

Each *action_i* above is an expression of the form

```
INSERT  r  BELOW  e
```

or

```
DELETE  e
```

where *r* is an XQuery expression and *e* an XPath expression[3].

In an `INSERT` action, the expression *e* specifies the set of nodes immediately below which new subdocument(s) will be inserted. These sub-documents are specified by the expression *r*.

If there is no occurrence of `$delta` in *e* or *r*, the action is executed at most once on each document each time the rule fires (set-oriented triggering). If there is an occurrence of `$delta` in *e* or *r*, the action is executed once for each possible instantiation of `$delta` for which the rule's condition query evaluates to *True* (instance-oriented triggering).

In a `DELETE` action, the expression *e* specifies the set of nodes which will be deleted (together with their subdocuments). Again, *e* may reference `$delta` and both set-oriented and instance-oriented triggering are possible.

11.8.1 Analysing Rule Behaviour

In [11.10, 11.11] we describe techniques for inferring triggering and activation relationships between pairs of our XML ECA rules (with the techniques described in [11.11] superceding those in the earlier paper [11.10]). As with the inferencing techniques that we used in the second and third abstractions of Section 11.5, these techniques for inferring triggering and activation relationships between XML ECA rules can be "plugged into" our abstract interpretation framework in order to analyse such rules. To illustrate, consider the following pair of rules:

```
Rule 1: on INSERT /a/*
        if /a/b and /a/c
        do DELETE /a/b

Rule 2: on DELETE /a/*
        if TRUE
        do INSERT <c/> BELOW /a
```

Let the abstract database state consist of a truth value *False* or *Unknown* for each rule's event query and also for each XPath expression appearing

---

[3] This is a slight simplification of the syntax of actions and we refer the reader to [11.11] for the full syntax.

within the rules' condition parts. Consider first a singleton schedule consisting of the action $a_0 =$ INSERT ? BELOW /a.

A trace of the abstract execution is as follows, where for $i = 1, 2$, e_i and a_i respectively denote the event query and action of rule i, $c_{1,1}$ is the first conjunct of Rule 1's condition and $c_{1,2}$ the second conjunct of Rule 1's condition. Rule 2's condition is trivially $True$ throughout so we don't show it:

Iteration	e_1	$c_{1,1}$	$c_{1,2}$	e_2	Schedule
1	U	U	U	U	$[a_0]$
2	U	U	U	F	$[a_1]$
3	F	F	U	U	$[a_2]$
4	U	F	U	F	$[]$

Abstract execution of a_1 at iteration 2 causes $c_{1,1}$ to become $False$, using the analysis techniques from [11.11]. After the execution of a_2 at iteration 3, $c_{1,1}$ remains $False$ because a_2 cannot alter it. The falsity of c_1 means that Rule 1 cannot fire at this point and the abstract execution terminates.

Similarly, given an initial singleton schedule consisting of the action $a_0 =$ DELETE /a/?, a trace of the abstract execution of the rules is as follows:

Iteration	e_1	$c_{1,1}$	$c_{1,2}$	e_2	Schedule
1	U	U	U	U	$[a_0]$
2	F	U	U	U	$[a_2]$
3	U	U	U	F	$[a_1]$
4	F	F	U	U	$[a_2]$
5	U	F	U	F	$[]$

This time, execution of a_1 at iteration 3 causes $c_{1,1}$ to become $False$. Again it remains $False$ at iteration 4, and so Rule 1 cannot fire at this point. Overall, we therefore conclude that this is a terminating rule set.

11.9 Concluding Remarks

ECA rules have the potential to improve the robustness and maintainability of database applications by abstracting common reactive functionality and placing it under the management of the DBMS. However, it is recognised that the lack of sufficiently powerful analysis techniques for ECA rules is still an impediment to their wider use. Our recent work has shown that abstract interpretation is a promising analysis technique for ECA rules and can readily be deployed within practical rule analysis tools.

A major feature of our abstract interpretation approach is its generality: it can be applied to any active DBMS whose rule execution semantics have been specified as a function that takes an initial database and an initial list of rule actions to be executed, and returns the resulting database when there are no more actions left to execute. Different abstraction methods can be employed within our framework, and the correctness of a particular method is established by proving a small set of generic requirements. The framework can be used both statically and dynamically.

In other recent work [11.8] we have also been investigating applying both abstract interpretation and *partial evaluation* [11.20, 11.19] to functional rule execution semantics in order to derive a number of rule optimisations. In particular, we use abstract rule execution from the current abstract database state in order to infer information about possible sequences of rule actions that will be executed in the future. Partial evaluation is then applied to the rule execution semantics in order to produced a specialised version for each of these possible sequences of actions. This gives the opportunity to optimise rule execution for each particular sequence of actions, e.g. by abstracting common subqueries from the set of event–condition queries that will be evaluated.

References

11.1 S. Abramsky and C. Hankin, editors. *Abstract Interpretation of Declarative Languages*. Ellis Horwood, 1987.
11.2 A. Aiken, J. Widom, and J. M. Hellerstein. Static analysis techniques for predicting the behavior of active database rules. *ACM TODS*, 20(1):3–41, 1995.
11.3 J. Bailey. On the foundations of termination analysis of active database Rules. PhD thesis, Department of Computer Science, University of Melbourne, September 1997.
11.4 J. Bailey, L. Crnogorac, K. Ramamohanarao, and H. Søndergaard. Abstract interpretation of active rules and its use in termination analysis. In *Proc. ICDT'97, LNCS 1186*, pages 188–202, Delphi, Greece, 1997.
11.5 J. Bailey, G. Dong, and K. Ramamohanarao. Decidability and undecidability results for the termination problem of active database rules. In *Proc. ACM PODS'98*, pages 264–273, Seattle, Washington, 1998.
11.6 J. Bailey and A. Poulovassilis. Abstract interpretation for termination analysis in functional active databases. *Journal of Intelligent Information Systems*, 12(2/3):243–273, 1999.
11.7 J. Bailey and A. Poulovassilis. An abstract interpretation framework for termination analysis of active rules. In *Proc. 7th Int. Workshop on Database Programming Languages (DBPL-7), LNCS 1949*, pages 249–266, Scotland, 1999.
11.8 J. Bailey, A. Poulovassilis, and C. Courtenage. Optimising active database rules by partial evaluation and abstract interpretation. In *Proc. 8th Int. Workshop on Database Programming Languages (DBPL-8), LNCS 2397*, pages 300–317, Rome, 2001.
11.9 J. Bailey, A. Poulovassilis, and P. Newson. A dynamic approach to termination analysis for active database rules. In *Proc. 1st Int. Conf. on Computational Logic (DOOD'2000 stream), LNCS 1861*, pages 1106–1120, London, 2000.

11.10 J. Bailey, A. Poulovassilis, and P.T. Wood. Analysis and optimisation of event-condition-action rules on XML. *Computer Networks*, 39(3):239–259, 2002.

11.11 J. Bailey, A. Poulovassilis, and P.T. Wood. An event-condition-action language for XML. In *Proc. WWW 2002*, pages 486–495, Hawaii, 2002.

11.12 E. Baralis, S. Ceri, and S. Paraboschi. Compile-time and runtime analysis of active behaviors. *IEEE Transactions on Knowledge and Data Engineering*, 10(3):353–370, 1998.

11.13 E. Baralis and J. Widom. An algebraic approach to rule analysis in expert database systems. In *Proc. VLDB'94*, pages 475–486, Santiago, Chile, 1994.

11.14 S. Ceri, R. Cochrane, and J. Widom. Practical applications of triggers and constraints: Success and lingering issues. In *Proc. VLDB'2000*, pages 254–262, Cairo, 2000.

11.15 S. Ceri and P. Fraternalli. *Designing Database Applications with Objects and Rules: The IDEA Methodology*. Addison-Wesley, 1997.

11.16 A. Couchot. Improving the refined triggering graph method for active rules termination analysis. In *Proc. BNCOD 2002, LNCS 2405*, pages 114–133, Sheffield, 2002.

11.17 P. Cousot and R. Cousot. Abstract interpretation frameworks. *Journal of Logic Programming*, 13(2&3):103–179, 1992.

11.18 T. Griffin, L. Libkin, and H. Trickey. A correction to "Incremental recomputation of active relational expressions" by Qian and Wiederhold. *IEEE Transactions on Knowledge and Data Engineering*, 9(3):508–511, 1997.

11.19 N. Jones. An introduction to partial evaluation. *ACM Computing Surveys*, 28(3):480–503, 1996.

11.20 N. Jones, C. Gomard, and P. Sestoft. *Partial Evaluation and Automatic Program Generation*. Prentice Hall, 1993.

11.21 A. Karadimce and S. Urban. Refined triggering graphs: A logic based approach to termination analysis in an active object-oriented database. In *Proc. ICDE'96*, pages 384–391, New Orleans, 1996.

11.22 A. Kotz-Dittrich and E. Simon. Active database systems: Expectations, commercial experience and beyond. In Paton [11.27], pages 367–404.

11.23 K. Kulkarni, N. Mattos, and R. Cochrane. Active database features in SQL3. In Paton [11.27], pages 197–219.

11.24 A. Levy and Y. Sagiv. Queries independent of updates. In *Proc. 19th Int. Conf. on Very Large Databases*, pages 171–181, Dublin, Ireland, 1993.

11.25 K. Marriott, H. Søndergaard, and N.D. Jones. Denotational abstract interpretation of logic programs. *ACM Transactions on Programming Languages and Systems*, 16(3):607–648, 1994.

11.26 F. Nielson, H.R. Nielson, and C. Hankin. *Principles of Program Analysis*. Springer-Verlag, 1999.

11.27 N. Paton, editor. *Active Rules in Database Systems*. Springer-Verlag, 1999.

11.28 A. Poulovassilis, S. Reddi, and C. Small. A formal semantics for an active functional DBPL. *Journal of Intelligent Information Systems*, 7(2):151–172, 1996.

11.29 X. Qian and G. Wiederhold. Incremental recomputation of active relational expressions. *IEEE Transactions on Knowledge and Data Engineering*, 3(3):337–341, 1991.

11.30 S. Reddi, A. Poulovassilis, and C. Small. Extending a functional DBPL with ECA-rules. In *Proc. 2nd Int. Workshop on Rules in Database Systems (RIDS'95), LNCS 985*, pages 101–115, Athens, 1995.

11.31 J. Widom and S. Ceri. *Active Database Systems*. Morgan-Kaufmann, 1995.

12. Monad Comprehensions: A Versatile Representation for Queries

Torsten Grust

University of Konstanz, Department of Computer and Information
Science, 78457 Konstanz, Germany
email: Torsten.Grust@uni-konstanz.de

Summary.

This chapter is an exploration of the possibilities that open up if we consistently adopt a style of database query and collection processing which allows us to look *inside* collections and thus enables us to play with atomic constructors instead of the monolithic collection values they build.

This comprehension of values goes well together with a completely functional style of query formulation: queries map between the constructors of different collection types. It turns out that a single uniform type of mapping, the *catamorphism*, is sufficient to embrace the functionality of today's database query languages, like SQL, OQL, but also XPath. *Monad comprehensions* provide just the right amount of syntactic sugar to express these mappings in a style that is similar to relational calculus (but goes beyond its expressiveness).

The major portion of this chapter, however, demonstrates how monad comprehensions enable a succinct yet deep understanding of database queries. We will revisit a number of problems in the advanced query processing domain to see how monad comprehensions can (a) provide remarkably concise proofs of correctness for earlier work, (b) clarify and then broaden the applicability of existing query optimisation techniques, and (c) enable query transformations which otherwise require extensive sets of rewriting rules.

12.1 A Functional Seed

In line with the major theme of this book, we perceive query translation and transformation as a *functional programming activity*. Superficially, this concerns a number of notational conventions we will adopt. More deeply, we note that we generate query results solely through the side-effect-free construction of values from simpler constituents and that functional composition will be the predominant way of forming complex queries. Referential transparency is the key to transformational programming and equational reasoning.

Relatively few components are needed in our initial query language core. We grow this language through *function definitions* of the form

$$f \equiv e$$

where e is an expression built from components we have already introduced. The functions f so defined will get more complex as we go on until we are ready to give the meaning of SQL, OQL [12.4], or XPath [12.1] query clauses such as `select-from-where`, `exists-in`, `flatten`, or path expressions.

12.1.1 Notation, Types, and Values

If you are familiar with notational conventions of functional programming languages such as Haskell [12.14] you will feel at home right away. Figure 12.1 introduces the core expression forms e and their notation.

$$
\begin{array}{lll}
e & ::= & c & \text{constants} \\
& | & v & \text{variables} \\
& | & \lambda p \rightarrow e & \text{lambda abstraction} \\
& | & v \equiv e & \text{(recursive) function definition} \\
& | & (e,e) & \text{pair former} \\
& | & e\,e & \text{function application} \\
& | & \textbf{case } p \textbf{ of } e \rightarrow e | \ldots | e \rightarrow e & \text{case (pattern matching)} \\
& | & e \uparrow e & \text{insertion constructor} \\
& | & [\,] \mid \{\!|\,|\!\} \mid \{\} & \text{empty list, empty bag, empty set} \\
& | & e \; op \; e & \text{infix operator } (op = \texttt{+,*,=,<,>,} \ldots) \\
p & ::= & c & \text{constants} \\
& | & v & \text{variable binding} \\
& | & (p,p) & \text{pair pattern} \\
& | & p \uparrow p & \text{collection pattern}
\end{array}
$$

Fig. 12.1. Core language syntax. The *insertion constructor* ↑ will be introduced in Section 12.1.2.

We assume the presence of a *prelude*, i.e. a library of basic function definitions which makes working with the core language somewhat less tedious, e.g. $\mathsf{id} \equiv \lambda x \rightarrow x$, $\mathsf{fst} \equiv \lambda(v_1, v_2) \rightarrow v_1$ (and corresponding snd). The function definition $f \equiv \lambda x \rightarrow e$ may also be written as $f\,x \equiv e$. The core is *strongly* and *statically typed*. This means that any value —including functions— has a unique type which we can deduce from its definition alone. We write $e :: t$ to indicate that value e has type t. The application of a function to wrongly typed arguments is bound to fail. Figure 12.2 summarizes the types t we will encounter. Some values are *polymorphic*, i.e., their type includes type variables which (consistently) assume specific types when the value is used. The left projection fst has the polymorphic type $\forall \alpha\beta . \alpha \times \beta \rightarrow \alpha$ and can thus be applied to pairs of arbitrarily typed constituents. (The type quantifier $\forall \alpha$ indicates that α may indeed be instantiated by any type; we assume its implicit presence whenever polymorphic types are used.)

$$
\begin{array}{llll}
t & ::= & \mathbb{N} \mid \mathbb{B} \mid \mathbb{S} \mid \dots & \text{atomic (numeric, boolean, string, \dots)} \\
& \mid & v & \text{variables } (\alpha, \beta, \gamma, \dots) \\
& \mid & t \to t & \text{functions} \\
& \mid & t \times t & \text{pairs} \\
& \mid & [t] \mid \{\!\{t\}\!\} \mid \{t\} & \text{list (bag, set) type constructor}
\end{array}
$$

Fig. 12.2. Core language types.

We draw constants from a pool of domains of atomic types that we choose according to the actual query language we need to represent: if the query language supports numeric constants and arithmetic on these, we incorporate numeric type $\mathbb{N}$ and operations on it in the core language. If the query language supports dates, e.g. values of the form Oct 8 2002, we incorporate an atomic Date type or choose an *implementation type* such as $\mathbb{N} \times \mathbb{N} \times \mathbb{N}$ (which represents the month, day, year constituents of a date value via three numbers) or simply $\mathbb{S}$ (a character string using an appropriate date format).

12.1.2 Constructing Collections

Remember that we are growing this language for a specific purpose: to represent database query languages. So, where a typical functional language would offer *lists* only, the core supports the *collection types bags* (multi-sets) and *sets* as well. Again, this is a means to properly reflect the type system of the query language: SQL primarily operates on bags, while OQL includes clauses that operate on all three collection types.

Starting from an empty collection ([], $\{\!\{\}\!\}$, or {}), we can *insert* elements one by one using constructor ↑ to construct a more complex collection value.

To aid compact notation, we define the *insertion constructor* ↑ as overloaded, i.e. the type of its second argument determines its behaviour. Let $x :: \alpha$. Then:

$$
x \uparrow xs = \begin{cases}
[x] +\!\!+ xs & \text{if } xs :: [\alpha] \\
\{\!\{x\}\!\} \uplus xs & \text{if } xs :: \{\!\{\alpha\}\!\} \\
\{x\} \cup xs & \text{if } xs :: \{\alpha\} \\
\text{type error} & \text{otherwise}
\end{cases}
$$

(+\!+ denotes list concatenation, while $\uplus$ is bag union respecting multiplicity of elements.) Note that *insertion order* is only relevant if ↑ constructs lists (in this case, ↑ is also widely known as *cons*). Insertion of *duplicates* is respected if ↑ constructs lists or bags. Set insertion ↑ :: $\alpha \times \{\alpha\} \to \{\alpha\}$ disregards both order and duplicates, i.e. the constructor is commutative and idempotent[1].

---

[1] As the type of constructor ↑ suggests, we are actually talking of *left-commutativity* $y \uparrow x \uparrow xs = x \uparrow y \uparrow xs$ and/or *left-idempotence* $x \uparrow x \uparrow xs = x \uparrow xs$. Note that element type α in the set case requires a notion of equality, = :: $\alpha \times \alpha \to \mathbb{B}$, to decide if a duplicate has been inserted into a set.

We assume that $\uparrow$ is right-associative so that $x_0 \uparrow x_1 \uparrow \ldots x_n \uparrow \{\!|\,|\!\}$ corresponds to the following parse tree, which we also term the the *spine* of the collection:

$$
\begin{array}{c}
x_0 \!\!\diagup^{\uparrow}\!\!\searrow \uparrow \\
\qquad x_1 \!\!\diagup \quad \diagdown \cdots \\
\qquad\qquad\qquad x_n \!\!\diagup^{\uparrow}\!\!\searrow \{\!|\,|\!\}
\end{array}
$$

We will also write this expression as $\{\!| \, x_0, x_1, \ldots, x_n \, |\!\}$.

12.2 Spine Transformers

Programming with collections in our core language consequently means writing programs that create, transform, and analyse spines. To provide a taste of the resulting programming style, here is a function that computes the maximum element of a given collection of numbers assuming that the prelude contains a definition $\mathtt{max}\,(x,y) \equiv \mathtt{case}\, x < y\, \mathtt{of}\, \mathtt{true} \rightarrow y\,|\, \mathtt{false} \rightarrow x$:

```
maximum :: {|N|}→ N
maximum xs ≡ case xs of {||}     → -∞
                       | x ↑ xs' → max (x,maximum xs')
```

There are two things to note here:

1. As indicated in the introduction to this chapter, we are analysing and building collection values on the basis of their constructors.
2. The two **case** branches exactly correspond with the two principal forms a collection value can take: empty (here: $\{\!|\,|\!\}$) or constructed ($x \uparrow xs'$). In the latter branch, **maximum** cuts off x and recurses on xs'.

The second observation is particularly interesting for our forthcoming discussion. It effectively states that **maximum** acts like a *spine transformer*:

$$
\mathtt{maximum}
\left(
\begin{array}{c}
x_0 \!\!\diagup^{\uparrow}\!\!\searrow \uparrow \\
\quad x_1 \!\!\diagup\quad\diagdown \cdots \\
\qquad\qquad x_n \!\!\diagup^{\uparrow}\!\!\searrow \{\!|\,|\!\}
\end{array}
\right)
=
\begin{array}{c}
x_0 \!\!\diagup^{\mathtt{max}}\!\!\searrow \mathtt{max} \\
\quad x_1 \!\!\diagup\quad\diagdown \cdots \\
\qquad\qquad x_n \!\!\diagup^{\mathtt{max}}\!\!\searrow -\infty
\end{array}
$$

In other words, **maximum** performs its computation solely through *consistent replacement of constructors*.

This pattern of computation seems to be rather rigid but in fact it is far from that: the expressive power of these spine transformers is sufficient to embrace almost all computations expressible by current database query languages. We will thus adopt spine transformers as *the* basic query building block.

12.2.1 Catamorphisms

To stress this idea of deriving a recursive computation from the recursive structure of the input collection, let us undertake a generalisation step. Given a collection $[a]$ (or $\{\!| a |\!\}$, $\{a\}$) and values $z :: \beta$, $\otimes :: \alpha \times \beta \to \beta$ we define the overloaded mix–fix operator $(\!|\ |\!)$ as

$$(\!| z; \otimes |\!) :: \beta \times (\alpha \times \beta \to \beta) \to [a] \to \beta$$
$$(\!| z; \otimes |\!)\, xs \equiv \mathbf{case}\, xs\, \mathbf{of}\, []\quad \to z$$
$$\qquad\qquad\qquad\qquad |\ x \uparrow xs' \to x \otimes ((\!| z; \otimes |\!)\, xs')$$

Pictorially, $(\!| z; \otimes |\!)$ is the spine transformer

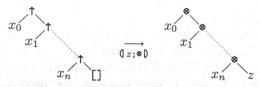

and we can immediately see that we could have defined $\mathtt{maximum} \equiv (\!| -\infty; \mathtt{max} |\!)$. When applied to lists, the operator $(\!|\ |\!)$ is known as $\mathtt{foldr}$ or $\mathtt{reduce}$, especially in the functional programming community. In more general collection programming settings, $(\!|\ |\!)$ is also known as *sri* (structural recursion on insert) [12.2, 12.21].

We can give an algebraic account of the nature of $(\!|\ |\!)$. Observe that $(\!| z; \otimes |\!)$ is a solution to the equations below which effectively say that the unknown h is a *homomorphism* from monoid $([], \uparrow)$ to monoid $(z, \otimes)$:

$$h\ [] = z \tag{12.1a}$$
$$h\ (x \uparrow xs) = x \otimes h\, xs \tag{12.1b}$$

It can be shown—based on the fact that $([], \uparrow)$ is the *term* or *initial algebra* of lists built using these two constructors—that $(\!| z; \otimes |\!)$ is the *unique* solution to these equations, completely determined by z and $\otimes$ [12.16]. Homomorphisms of initial algebras have been dubbed *catamorphisms* [12.17] and this is the terminology we will adopt.

Caveat: Equation (12.1b) suggests that operator $\otimes$ of the target algebra must *not* be completely arbitrary: $\otimes$ needs to have the same algebraic properties as $\uparrow$: associativity, left-commutativity (if $\uparrow :: \alpha \times \{\!| a |\!\} \to \{\!| a |\!\}$ or $\uparrow :: \alpha \times \{a\} \to \{a\}$), or left-idempotence (if $\uparrow :: \alpha \times \{a\} \to \{a\}$).

Catamorphisms are a versatile tool. A number of useful collection processing functions turn out to be catamorphisms:

$$
\begin{aligned}
\text{maximum} &\equiv (\!\!|-\infty;\texttt{max}|\!\!) \\
\text{minimum} &\equiv (\!\!|+\infty;\texttt{min}|\!\!) \\
\text{or} &\equiv (\!\!|\texttt{false};\vee|\!\!) \\
\text{and} &\equiv (\!\!|\texttt{true};\wedge|\!\!) \\
xs \oplus ys &\equiv (\!\!|\,ys;\uparrow|\!\!)\,xs \\
\text{first} &\equiv (\!\!|0;\texttt{fst}|\!\!) \\
\texttt{list\_map}\,f &\equiv (\!\!|\,[]\,;\lambda(x,xs)\to(f\,x)\uparrow xs\,|\!\!) \\
\texttt{flatten} &\equiv (\!\!|\,[]\,;\oplus|\!\!)
\end{aligned}
$$

Note that infix operator $\oplus$ is overloaded and behaves like $+\!\!+$, $\uplus$, or $\cup$ depending on the type of its arguments. As given, `list_map` is well-defined on lists only. The same is true for function `first`: `fst` is neither left-commutative nor left-idempotent, an expression of the fact that there is no notion of a first element in a bag or set.

12.2.2 Catamorphism Fusion

A query translator and optimizer based on the core language we have defined so far would more closely resemble a *program transformation system* than a traditional query optimizer. To ensure that the system can operate completely unguided and without the need for *Eureka steps*—transformation steps not immediately motivated by the goal the overall transformation strives for—we need to be restrictive in the program forms we may admit.

Catamorphisms represent this restricted form of computation and in our case, simplicity enables optimisation.

Reconsider `list_map`. We can turn this function into a generic `map` catamorphism if we make its implicit use of the list constructors [] and $\uparrow :: \alpha \times [\alpha] \to [\alpha]$ explicit and thus define

$$
\texttt{map}\ n\ c\ f \equiv (\!\!|\,n;\lambda(x,xs)\to c\,(f\,x,xs)\,|\!\!) \tag{12.2}
$$

Now, `list_map` $f \equiv$ `map` [] ($\uparrow$) f, `set_map` $f \equiv$ `map` {} ($\uparrow$) f, and `bag_map` $f \equiv$ `map` $(\!|\ |\!)$ ($\uparrow$) f.

Apart from this generalisation, factoring the constructors out of a catamorphism opens up an important optimisation opportunity: we can "reach inside" a catamorphism and influence the constructor replacement it performs. This is all we need to formulate a simple yet effective *catamorphism fusion law*. Let `cata` denote any catamorphism with constructors factored out as above; then

$$
(\!\!|\,z;\otimes|\!\!)\cdot\texttt{cata}\,n\,c = \texttt{cata}\,z\,\otimes \tag{12.3}
$$

Note that while the left hand side walks the spine twice, the righthand side computes the same result in a single spine traversal. With catamorphisms being the basic program building blocks, a typical program form will be catamorphism compositions. These composition chains can be shortened and simplified using law (12.3). The two-step catamorphism chain below decides if there is *any* element in the input satisfying p. Catamorphism fusion merges the steps and yields a general-purpose existential quantifier `exists` p:

$$\text{exists}\, p \;\equiv\; \text{or} \cdot \text{map}\, \{\} \uparrow p \;=\; \text{map false} \vee p \qquad (12.4)$$

Law (12.3) is known as *cheap deforestation* [12.9] or the *acid rain theorem* [12.22]. Its correctness obviously depends on `cata` being well-behaved: `cata` is *required* to exclusively use the supplied constructors c and n to build its result. Perhaps surprisingly, one can formulate a prerequisite that restricts the *type* of `cata` to ensure this behaviour (parametricity of `cata` [12.23]).

12.3 Monad Comprehensions

We have seen that catamorphisms represent a form of computation restrictive enough to enable mechanical program optimisations, yet expressive enough to provide a useful target for query translation.

However, we need to make sure that query translation actually yields nothing but compositions of catamorphisms. This is what we turn to now.

To achieve this goal, we grow our language once more to include the expressions of the *monad comprehension calculus* [12.24, 12.25] whose syntactic forms closely resemble the well-known relational calculus. The calculus is a good candidate to serve as a translation target for user-level query syntax [12.3]. Its semantics can be explained in terms of catamorphisms, thus completing the desired query translation framework:

$$Query\ syntax \rightarrow monad\ comprehension\ calculus \rightarrow catamorphisms. (12.5)$$

Figure 12.3 displays the syntactic sugar *mc* introduced by the monad comprehension calculus.

mc	$::=$	e	core language (Figure 12.1)
	$\mid$	$[mc \mid qs]\ \mid\!\{ mc \mid qs \}\!\mid\ \{mc \mid qs\}$	monad comprehension
qs	$::=$	ε	empty
	$\mid$	q	qualifier
	$\mid$	qs, qs	qualifiers
q	$::=$	$v \leftarrow mc$	generator
	$\mid$	mc	filter

Fig. 12.3. Syntax of the monad comprehension calculus

We obtain a relational calculus-style sublanguage that can succinctly express computations over lists, bags, and sets (actually over any *monad*—we will shortly come to this). The general syntactic form is

$$[e \mid q_0, \dots, q_n] \qquad (12.6)$$

Informally, the semantics of this comprehension are as follows: starting with *qualifier* q_0, a *generator* $q_i = v_i \leftarrow e_i$ sequentially binds v_i to the elements of its *range* e_i. This binding is propagated through the list of qualifiers $q_{i+1}, \ldots, q_n$. *Filters* are qualifiers of type $\mathbb{B}$ (boolean). A binding is discarded if a filter evaluates to `false` under it. The *head* expression e is evaluated for those bindings that satisfy all the filters, and the resulting values are collected to form the final result list.

Here is how we can define `bag_map` f and `flatten`:

$$\texttt{bag\_map}\, f\, xs \;\equiv\; \{\!|\, f\, x \mid x \leftarrow xs \,|\!\}$$
$$\texttt{flatten}\, xss \;\equiv\; \{\, x \mid xs \leftarrow xss, x \leftarrow xs \,\}$$

SQL and OQL queries, like the following *semi-join* between relations r and s, may now be understood as yet more syntactic sugar (we will encounter many more examples in the sequel):

```
select r
  from r,s   ≡   {| v₁ | v₁ ← r, v₂ ← s, p |}
 where p
```

Note that the grammar in Figure 12.3 allows for arbitrary nesting of monad comprehensions. The occurrence of a comprehension as generator range, filter, or head will allows us to express the diverse forms of query nesting found in user-level query languages [12.10, 12.12].

Figure 12.4 gives the translation scheme in the core language for the monad comprehension calculus.

$$\llbracket\, e \mid \,\rrbracket \;\equiv\; \texttt{unit}\; e \tag{12.7a}$$
$$\llbracket\, e \mid v \leftarrow e' :: \llbracket\, \alpha \,\rrbracket \,\rrbracket \;\equiv\; \texttt{mmap}\,(\lambda v \rightarrow e)\; e' \tag{12.7b}$$
$$\llbracket\, e \mid v \leftarrow e' :: [\alpha] \,\rrbracket \;\equiv\; \texttt{mmap}\; \texttt{id}\,(\llbracket\, e \mid v \leftarrow e' \,\rrbracket) \tag{12.7c}$$
$$\llbracket\, e \mid v \leftarrow e' :: \{\!|\, \alpha \,|\!\} \,\rrbracket \;\equiv\; \texttt{mmap}\; \texttt{id}\,(\{\!|\, e \mid v \leftarrow e' \,|\!\}) \tag{12.7d}$$
$$\llbracket\, e \mid v \leftarrow e' :: \{\alpha\} \,\rrbracket \;\equiv\; \texttt{mmap}\; \texttt{id}\,(\{\, e \mid v \leftarrow e' \,\}) \tag{12.7e}$$
$$\llbracket\, e \mid e' :: \mathbb{B} \,\rrbracket \;\equiv\; \texttt{case}\; e'\; \texttt{of}\; \texttt{true} \rightarrow \texttt{unit}\; e \mid \texttt{false} \rightarrow \texttt{zero} \tag{12.7f}$$
$$\llbracket\, e \mid qs, qs' \,\rrbracket \;\equiv\; \texttt{join}\,(\llbracket\, \llbracket\, e \mid qs' \,\rrbracket \mid qs \,\rrbracket) \tag{12.7g}$$

$$\texttt{zero} \equiv \llbracket\,\rrbracket$$
$$\texttt{unit}\; e \equiv \llbracket\, e \,\rrbracket$$
$$\texttt{mmap} \equiv \texttt{map}\,\llbracket\,\rrbracket\,(\uparrow)$$
$$\texttt{join} \equiv \langle\!|\, \llbracket\,\rrbracket ; \oplus \,|\!\rangle$$

Fig. 12.4. Monad comprehension semantics.

This translation scheme is based on the so-called *Wadler identities* which were originally developed to explain the semantics of list comprehensions. The scheme of Figure 12.4, however, is applicable to bag and set comprehensions as well (simply consistently replace all occurrences of $[\![$, $]\!]$ by $[$,$]$ or $\langle\!|$, $|\!\rangle$ or $\{$,$\}$, respectively).

These translation rules, to be applied top-down, reduce a monad comprehension step by step until we are left with an equivalent core language expression. Definition (12.7g) breaks a complex qualifier list down to a single generator or filter. Note how (12.7c, 12.7d, 12.7e) examine the type of the generator range to temporarily switch to a list, bag, or set comprehension. The results are then coerced using `mmap id` which effectively enables us to mix and match comprehensions over different collection types. (Coercion is not completely arbitrary since the well-definedness condition for catamorphisms of Section 12.2.2 applies. This restriction is rather natural, however, as it forbids non-well-founded coercions like the conversion of a set into a list.)

Monad comprehensions provide quite powerful syntactic sugar and will save us from juggling with complex catamorphism chains. Consider, for example, the translation of `filter p` (which evaluates predicate p against the elements of the argument list):

$$
\begin{aligned}
\texttt{filter}\,p\,xs \;\; &\equiv\;\; [\,x \mid x \leftarrow xs, p\,x\,] \\
&=\;\; \texttt{join}\,([\,[x \mid p\,x] \mid x \leftarrow xs]) \\
&=\;\; (\texttt{join} \cdot \texttt{mmap}\,(\lambda x \to [x \mid p\,x]))\;xs \\
&=\;\; \texttt{map}\,[]\; \oplus\, (\lambda x \to [x \mid p\,x])\;xs \\
&=\;\; \texttt{map}\,[]\; \oplus\, (\lambda x \to \texttt{case}\,p\,x\,\texttt{of}\,\texttt{true} \to [x]\,|\,\texttt{false} \to [])\;xs
\end{aligned}
$$

Interestingly, comprehensions are just the "syntactic shadow" of a deeper, categorical concept: *monads* [12.24]. Comprehension syntax can be sensibly defined for any type constructor $[\![\,\alpha\,]\!]$ with operations `mmap`, `zero`, `unit`, `join` obeying the laws of a *monad with zero* which—for our collection constructors—are as follows:

$$
\begin{aligned}
\texttt{join} \cdot \texttt{unit} &= \texttt{id} & \text{(12.8a)} \\
\texttt{join} \cdot \texttt{mmap}\,\texttt{unit} &= \texttt{id} & \text{(12.8b)} \\
\texttt{join} \cdot \texttt{join} &= \texttt{join} \cdot \texttt{mmap}\,\texttt{join} & \text{(12.8c)} \\
\texttt{join} \cdot \texttt{zero} &= \texttt{zero} & \text{(12.8d)} \\
\texttt{join} \cdot \texttt{mmap}\,\texttt{zero} &= \texttt{zero} & \text{(12.8e)}
\end{aligned}
$$

With the definitions given in Figure 12.4, lists, bags, and sets are easily verified to be monad instances. Monads are a remarkably general concept that has been widely used by the functional programming community to study, among others, I/O, stateful computation, and exception handling [12.19]. Monad comprehensions have even found their way into mainstream functional programming languages[2]. We will meet other monads in the upcoming sections.

More importantly, though, we can exercise a large number of query transformations and optimisation exclusively in comprehension syntax.

12.4 Type Conversion Saves Work

Perhaps the principal decision in solving a problem is the choice of language in which we represent both the problem and its possible solutions. Choosing the "right" language can turn the concealed or difficult into the obvious or simple. This section exemplifies one such situation and we argue that the functional language we have constructed so far provides an efficient framework to reason about queries.

Some constructs introduced in recent SQL dialects (being liberal, we count OQL as such) have no immediate counterpart in the traditional relational algebra. Among these, for example, are *type conversion* or *extraction* operators like OQL's `element`: the query `element` e tests if e evaluates to a singleton collection and, if so, returns the singleton element (tuple, object, ...) itself. Otherwise, an exception is raised. SQL 3 introduces so-called *row subqueries* which exhibit the same behaviour. The type of such an operator is $[\![\alpha]\!] \to \alpha$.

Different placements of a type conversion operator in a query may have dramatic effects on the query plan's quality. Early execution of type conversion can lead to removal of joins or even query unnesting. Consider the OQL query below (we use the convention that a query expression like $f\, x\, y$ denotes a query f containing free variables x, y, i.e. f is a function of x, y):

```
element (select f x y
         from xs as x, ys as y)
```

Computing the join between xs and ys is wasted work as we are throwing the result away should the join (unexpectedly) contain more than one element (in which case the query raises an exception). A *type conversion aware* optimizer could emit the equivalent

```
f (element xs) (element ys)
```

The join is gone as is the danger of doing unnecessary work. Pushing down type conversion has a perilous nature, though:

- The above rewrite does not preserve equivalence if we compute with sets (`select distinct...`): function f might not be one-to-one. If, for example, we have $f\, x\, y \equiv c$, then the query

---

[2] Haskell [12.14] being the primary example here, although monad comprehensions come in the disguise of Haskell's `do`-notation these days.

```
element (select distinct f x y
                from xs as x, ys as y)
```

effectively computes `element` $\{c\} = c$ for arbitrary non-empty collections xs and ys, while the rewritten query will raise an exception should xs or ys contain more than one element.

- We must not push type conversion beyond a selection: the selection might select exactly one element (selection on a key) and thus satisfy `element` while pushing down `element` beyond the selection might lead to an application of `element` to a collection of cardinality greater than one and thus raise an exception instead.

How do we safely obtain the optimized query? This is where our functional query language jumps in. First off, note that we can represent `element` as

$$\text{element} \equiv \text{snd} \cdot (\!(z;\otimes)\!)$$
$$\text{with} \qquad z \equiv (\text{true}, \bot)$$
$$x \otimes (c,e) \equiv \text{case } c \text{ of true} \;\to\; (\text{false}, x)$$
$$\mid \text{false} \to \bot$$

Evaluating the *bottom* symbol $\bot$ yields an error and is our way of modeling the exception we might need to raise. Function `element` interacts with the collection monads list and bag (but not set) in the following ways:

$$\text{element} \cdot \text{mmap } f = f \cdot \text{element} \tag{12.9a}$$
$$\text{element} \cdot \text{unit} = \text{id} \tag{12.9b}$$
$$\text{element} \cdot \text{join} = \text{element} \cdot \text{element} \tag{12.9c}$$

This characterizes `element` as a *monad morphism* [12.24] from the list and bag monads to the *identity monad* (which is defined through the identity type constructor $\text{Id } \alpha = \alpha$ plus $\text{mmap } f\,e = f\,e$, $\text{join} = \text{unit} = \text{id}$). We can exploit the morphism laws to propagate `element` through the monad operations and implement type conversion pushdown this way. For the example query the rewrite derives the exact simplification we were after:

$$\text{element (select } f\,x\,y$$
$$\text{from } xs \text{ as } x, ys \text{ as } y)$$
$$= \text{element} \; (\!(f\,x\,y \mid x \leftarrow xs, y \leftarrow ys)\!)$$
$$= (\text{element} \cdot \text{join}) \; (\!(\!(f\,x\,y \mid y \leftarrow ys)\!) \mid x \leftarrow xs)\!)$$
$$= (\text{element} \cdot \text{join} \cdot \text{mmap}) \; (\lambda x \to \text{mmap } (\lambda y \to f\,x\,y)\, ys)\, xs$$
$$= (\text{element} \cdot \text{element} \cdot \text{mmap}) \; (\lambda x \to \text{mmap } (\lambda y \to f\,x\,y)\, ys)\, xs$$
$$= \text{element} \; ((\lambda x \to \text{mmap } (\lambda y \to f\,x\,y)\, ys) \,(\text{element } xs))$$
$$= (\text{element} \cdot \text{mmap}) \; (\lambda y \to f\,(\text{element } xs)\, y)\, ys$$
$$= (\lambda y \to f\,(\text{element } xs)\, y) \,(\text{element } ys)$$
$$= f\,(\text{element } xs) \,(\text{element } ys)$$

The morphism laws push the type conversion down as far as possible but not beyond filters since these are mapped into **case** expressions (see Eq. 12.7f) for which none of the morphism laws apply.

Early type conversion can indeed save a lot and even reduce the nesting depth of queries. As a another example, consider the following OQL query (note the nesting in the **select** clause):

$$\texttt{element} \, (\texttt{select} \, (\texttt{select} \, f\,x\,y$$
$$\texttt{from} \, ys \, \texttt{as} \, y)$$
$$\texttt{from} \, xs \, \texttt{as} \, x)$$
$$= \texttt{element} \, (\!\{\!\{ f\,x\,y \mid y \leftarrow ys \,\}\!\} \mid x \leftarrow xs \,\}\!\})$$

Type conversion pushdown converts the above into a query of the form $\{\!\{ f\,(\texttt{element} \, xs) \, y \mid y \leftarrow ys \,\}\!\}$ which simply maps f over collection ys instead of creating a nested bag of bags like the original query did.

To wrap up: Wadler [12.24] observed that the action of a monad morphism on a monad comprehension may more concisely described by way of the comprehension syntax itself. Space constraints force us to skip the details here, but the resulting rewriting steps are remarkably simple and thus especially suited for inclusion in a rule-based query optimizer [12.10].

12.5 Unravelling Deeply Nested Queries

Comprehensions may be nested within each other and a translator for a source query language that supports nesting can make good use of this: a nested user-level query may be mapped rather straightforwardly into a nested comprehension (see the example query at the end of the last section). However, deriving anything but a nested-loops execution plan from a deeply nested query is a hard task and a widely recognized challenge in the query optimisation community. We are really better off trying *unnest* a nested query before we process it further.

The monad comprehension calculus provides particularly efficient yet simple hooks to attack this problem:

- Different types of query nesting lead to similar nested forms of monad comprehensions. Rather than maintaining and identifying a number of special nesting cases —this route has been taken by numerous approaches, notably Kim's original and follow-up work [12.15, 12.8] on classifying nested SQL queries— we can concentrate on unnesting the relatively few comprehension forms.
- Much of the unnesting work can, once more, be achieved by application of a small number of syntactic rewriting laws, the *normalisation rules* (12.10a–12.10d below).

The normalisation rules exclusively operate on the monad comprehension syntax level. As before, we use generic monad comprehensions to introduce the rules and you can obtain the specific variants through a consistent replacement of $[\![,]\!]_n$ by $[,]$ or $\{\!|, |\!\}$ or $\{,\}$, respectively:

$$[\![\, e \mid qs, v \leftarrow [\![\,]\!]_2, qs'\,]\!]_1 = [\![\,]\!]_1 \tag{12.10a}$$

$$[\![\, e \mid qs, v \leftarrow [\![\, e'\,]\!]_2, qs'\,]\!]_1 = [\![\, e[e'/v] \mid qs, qs'[e'/v]\,]\!]_1 \tag{12.10b}$$

$$[\![\, e \mid qs, v \leftarrow [\![\, e' \mid qs''\,]\!]_2, qs'\,]\!]_1 = [\![\, e[e'/v] \mid qs, qs'', qs'[e'/v]\,]\!]_1 \tag{12.10c}$$

$$\{e \mid qs, \mathbf{or}\ [\![\, e' \mid qs''\,]\!], qs'\} = \{e \mid qs, qs'', e', qs'\} \tag{12.10d}$$

(Expression $e[e'/v]$ denotes e with all free occurrences of v replaced by e'.)

The rules form a confluent and terminating set of rewriting rules which is our main incentive for referring to them as *normalisation rules*.

Normalisation gives an unnesting procedure that is *complete* in the sense that an exhaustive application of the rules leads to a query in which all semantically sound unnestings have been performed [12.7]. In the set monad, this may go as far as

$$\{e \mid v_1 \leftarrow e_1, v_2 \leftarrow e_2, \ldots, v_n \leftarrow e_n, p\}$$

with all e_i being atomic expressions with respect to monad comprehension syntax, i.e. the e_i are references to database entry points (relations, class extents) or constants. Nested queries may only occur in the comprehension head e or filter p (to see that we really end up with a single filter p, note that we can always "push back" a filter in the qualifier list and that two adjacent filters p_1, p_2 may be merged to give $p_1 \wedge p_2$).

Unnesting disentangles queries and makes operands of formerly inner queries accessible in the outer enclosing comprehension. This, in turn, provides new possibilities for further rewritings and optimisations. We will see many applications of unnesting in the sequel.

Comprehension syntax provides a rather poor variety of syntactical forms, but in the early stages of query translation this is more of a virtue than a shortcoming. Monad comprehensions extract and emphasize the *structural* gist of a query rather than stressing the diversity of query constructs. It is this uniformity that facilitates query analysis like the completeness result for comprehension normalisation we have just mentioned. This can lead to new insights and simplifications, which is the next point we make.

In [12.20], Steenhagen, Apers, and Blanken analysed a class of SQL-like queries which exhibit correlated nesting in the **where**-clause, more specifically:

$$
\begin{array}{ll}
\texttt{select distinct } f\,x & \\
\qquad \texttt{from } xs \texttt{ as } x \quad \texttt{with} \quad z = \left(\begin{array}{l} \texttt{select } g\,x\,y \\ \qquad \texttt{from } ys \texttt{ as } y \\ \qquad \texttt{where } q\,x\,y \end{array} \right) \\
\qquad \texttt{where } p\,x\,z &
\end{array}
$$

The question is, can queries of this class be rewritten into *flat join queries* of the form select distinct $f\,x$

$\qquad$ from xs as x, ys as y
$\qquad$ where $q\,x\,y$
$\qquad$ and $p'\,x\,(g\,x\,y)$

Queries for which such a replacement predicate p' cannot be found have to be processed either (a) using a nested-loops strategy, or (b) by grouping. Whether we can derive a flat join query is, obviously, dependent on the nature of the yet unspecified predicate p.

Steenhagen et. al. state the following theorem — reproduced here using our functional language — which provides a partial answer to the question:

> *Whenever $p\,x\,z$ can be rewritten into* or $[\![p'\,x\,v \mid v \leftarrow z]\!]$ *(i.e., p is an existential quantification w.r.t. some p') the original query may be evaluated by a flat join.*

The monad comprehension normalisation rules provide an elegant proof of this theorem:

$\qquad$ select distinct $f\,x$
$\qquad\qquad$ from xs as x
$\qquad\qquad$ where $p\,x\,z$

$$= \{f\,x \mid x \leftarrow xs, p\,x\,z\}$$
$$= \{f\,x \mid x \leftarrow xs, \text{or } [\![p'\,x\,v \mid v \leftarrow z]\!]\}$$
$$= \{f\,x \mid x \leftarrow xs, v \leftarrow z, p'\,x\,v\}$$
$$= \{f\,x \mid x \leftarrow xs, v \leftarrow \{\!\lvert g\,x\,y \mid y \leftarrow ys, q\,x\,y \rvert\!\}, p'\,x\,v\}$$
$$= \{f\,x \mid x \leftarrow xs, y \leftarrow ys, q\,x\,y, p'\,x\,(g\,x\,y)\}$$

Observe that the normalisation result is the monad comprehension equivalent of the unnested SQL query.

But we can say even more and strengthen the statement of the theorem (thus answering an open question that has been put by Steenhagen et. al. in [12.20]):

> *If p is not rewriteable into an existential quantification like above, then we can conclude—based on the completeness of comprehensions normalisation—that unnesting will in fact be impossible.*

Kim's fundamental work [12.15] on the unnesting of SQL queries may largely be understood in terms of normalisation if queries are interpreted in the monad comprehension calculus. We additionally gain insight into questions on the validity of these unnesting strategies in the context of complex data models featuring collection constructors other than the set constructor.

Monad comprehension normalisation readily unnests queries of Kim's *type J*, i.e. SQL queries of the form

$$Q \quad \equiv \quad \text{select distinct } f\, x$$
$$\text{from } xs \text{ as } x$$
$$\text{where } p\, x \text{ in } (\text{select } g\, y$$
$$\text{from } ys \text{ as } y$$
$$\text{where } q\, x\, y)$$

Note that predicate q refers to query variable x so that the outer and nested query blocks are correlated. (The SQL predicate in is translated into an existential quantifier.) The derivation of the normal form for this query effectively yields Kim's *canonical 2-relation query*:

$$Q = \{f\, x \mid x \leftarrow xs, \text{or } [\![p\, x = v \mid v \leftarrow [\![g\, y \mid y \leftarrow ys, q\, x\, y]\!]]\!] \}$$
$$= \{f\, x \mid x \leftarrow xs, \text{or } [\![p\, x = g\, y \mid y \leftarrow ys, q\, x\, y]\!] \}$$
$$= \{f\, x \mid x \leftarrow xs, y \leftarrow ys, q\, x\, y, p\, x = g\, y \}$$

We can see that Kim's *type J* unnesting is sound only if the outer query block is evaluated in the set monad. No such restriction, though, is necessary for the inner block—an immediate consequence of the well-definedness conditions for monad comprehension coercion (see Section 12.3).

12.6 Parallelizing Group-By Queries

The database back-ends of decision support or data mining systems frequently face SQL queries of the following general type (termed *group queries* in [12.5]):

$$Q\, f\, g\, a\, xs \quad \equiv \quad \text{select } f\, x, a\, (g\, x)$$
$$\text{from } xs \text{ as } x$$
$$\text{group by } f\, x$$

Group queries extract a particular dimension or feature—described by function f—from given base data xs and then pair each data point $f\, x$ in this dimension with aggregated data $a\, (g\, x)$ associated with that point; a may be instantiated by any of the SQL aggregate functions, e.g. sum or max.

Here is query Q expressed in the monad comprehension calculus (the group by introduces nesting in the outer comprehension's head):

$$Q\, f\, g\, a\, xs \quad \equiv \quad \{(f\, x, (agg\, a)\, \{\!| g\, y \mid y \leftarrow xs, f\, y = f\, x |\!\}) \mid x \leftarrow xs\}$$

Helper function agg translates SQL aggregates into their implementing catamorphisms, *e.g.*, agg sum $= (\!| 0; + |\!)$ and agg max $=$ maximum.

We are essentially stuck with the inherent nesting. Normalisation is of no use in this case (the query is in normal form already). Chatziantoniou and Ross [12.5] thus propose to take a different three-step route to process this type of query:

1. Separate the data points in dimension f of xs in a preprocessing step, i.e., *partition* input xs with respect to f.

2. Evaluate a simplified variant Q' of Q on each partition. In particular, Q' does not need to take care of grouping. Let ps denote one partition of xs, then we have

$$Q' \ g \ a \ ps \quad \equiv \quad \texttt{select} \ a \ (g \ x)$$
$$\texttt{from} \ ps \ \texttt{as} \ x$$

or, equivalently,

$$Q' \ g \ a \ ps \quad \equiv \quad (agg \ a) \, \{\!| \ g \ y \ | \ y \leftarrow ps \ |\!\}$$

3. Finally, merge the results obtained in step 2 to form the query response.

This strategy clearly shows its benefit in step 2: first, since xs has been split into disjoint partitions during the preprocessing step, we may execute Q' on the different partitions in parallel. Second, there is a chance of processing the Q' in main memory should the partitions ps fit. Measurements reported in [12.5] show the performance gains in terms of time and I/O cost to compensate for the effort spent in the partitioning and joining stages.

In [12.5], classical relational algebra is the target language for the translation of group queries. This choice of query representation introduces subtleties. Relational algebra lacks canonical forms to express the grouping and aggregation found in Q. The authors thus propose to understand Q as a *syntactical* query class: the membership of a specific query in this class and thus the applicability of the partitioning strategy is decided by the inspection of the SQL parse tree for that query.

Relational algebra also fails to provide idioms that could express the preprocessing, i.e. partitioning, step of the strategy. To remedy this situation, Chatziantoniou and Ross add attributes to the nodes of query graphs to indicate which partition is represented by a specific node.

Finally, the core stage 2 of the strategy has no equivalent at the target language level as well. Classical relational algebra is unable to express the iteration (or parallel application) inherent to this phase. The authors implement this step *on top* of the relational database back-end and thus outside the relational domain.

Facing this mix of query representations (SQL syntax, query graphs, relational algebra, procedural iteration), it is considerably hard to assess the correctness of this parallel processing strategy for query class Q.

Reasoning in the monad comprehension calculus can significantly simplify the matter. Once expressed in our functional query representation language, we can construct a correctness proof for the strategy which is basically built from the unfolding of definitions and normalisation steps. Let us proceed by filling the two gaps (partitioning and iteration) that relational algebra has left open.

First, partitioning the base data collection xs with respect to a function f is expressible as follows (note that we require type β to allow equality tests):

$$\text{partition} :: (\alpha \to \beta) \to [\![\alpha]\!] \to \{(\beta, [\![\alpha]\!])\}$$
$$\text{partition } f \ xs \equiv \{(f \ x, [\![y \mid y \leftarrow xs, f \ x = f \ y]\!]) \mid x \leftarrow xs\}$$

which builds a set of disjunct partitions such that all elements inside one partition agree on feature f with the latter attached to its associated partition. We have, for example,

$$\text{partition odd } [1 \ldots 5] \quad = \quad \{(\text{true}, [1,3,5]), (\text{false}, [2,4])\}$$

Second, recall that iteration forms a core building block of our functional language by means of map; map f also adequately encodes parallel application of f to the elements of its argument. See, for example, the work of Hill [12.13] in which a complete theory of *data-parallel programming* is developed on top of map.

With the definition of Q' given earlier, we can compose the phases and express the complete parallel grouping plan as

$$(\text{map } \{\} \ (\uparrow) \ (\lambda(z, ps) \to (z, Q' \ g \ a \ ps)) \cdot \text{partition } f) \ xs$$

We can now derive a purely calculational proof of the correctness of the parallel grouping idea through a sequence of simple rewriting steps: unfold the definitions of Q', partition, and map, then apply monad comprehension normalisation to finally obtain $Q \ f \ g \ a \ xs$, the original group query:

$$(\text{map } \{\} \ (\uparrow) \ (\lambda(z, ps) \to (z, Q' \ g \ a \ ps)) \cdot \text{partition } f) \ xs$$

$$\underset{(\cdot)}{=} \quad (\text{map } \{\} \ (\uparrow) \ (\lambda(z, ps) \to (z, Q' \ g \ a \ ps)) \ (\text{partition } f \ xs)$$

$$\underset{\text{partition}}{=} \quad (\text{map } \{\} \ (\uparrow) \ (\lambda(z, ps) \to (z, Q' \ g \ a \ ps)) \\ \{(f \ x, \{\!|y \mid y \leftarrow xs, f \ x = f \ y|\!\}) \mid x \leftarrow xs\}$$

$$\underset{Q'}{=} \quad (\text{map } \{\} \ (\uparrow) \ (\lambda(z, ps) \to (z, (agg \ a) \{\!|g \ y' \mid y' \leftarrow ps|\!\})) \\ \{(f \ x, \{\!|y \mid y \leftarrow xs, f \ x = f \ y|\!\}) \mid x \leftarrow xs\}$$

$$\underset{\text{map}}{=} \quad \{(\lambda(z, ps) \to (z, (agg \ a) \{\!|g \ y' \mid y' \leftarrow ps|\!\})) \ v \mid \\ v \leftarrow \{(f \ x, \{\!|y \mid y \leftarrow xs, f \ x = f \ y|\!\}) \mid x \leftarrow xs\}\}$$

$$\underset{12.10c}{=} \quad \{(f \ x, (agg \ a) \{\!|g \ y' \mid y' \leftarrow \{\!|y \mid y \leftarrow xs, f \ x = f \ y|\!\}|\!\}) \mid x \leftarrow xs\}$$

$$\underset{12.10c}{=} \quad \{(f \ x, (agg \ a) \{\!|g \ y \mid y \leftarrow xs, f \ x = f \ y|\!\}) \mid x \leftarrow xs\}$$

$$= \quad Q \ f \ g \ a \ xs$$

12.7 A Purely Functional View of XPath

Monad comprehensions can serve as an effective "semantical back-end" for other than SQL-style languages. To make this point and to conclude the chapter let us take a closer look at how monad comprehensions can provide a useful interpretation of XPath path expressions [12.1].

XML syntax provides an unlimited number of *tree dialects*: data (*document content*) is structured using properly nested opening <t> and matching closing tags </t>.

XPath provides operators to describe *path traversals* over such tree-shaped data structures. Starting from a *context node*, an XPath path expression traverses its input document via a sequence of *steps*. A step's *axis*, e.g. ancestor, descendant, with the obvious semantics) indicates which tree nodes are reachable from the context node, a step's *node test* ::t filters these nodes to retain those with tag name t only[3]. These new nodes are then interpreted as context nodes for subsequent steps, and so forth.

In XPath syntax, the steps of a path p are syntactically separated by slashes /; a path originating in the document's root node starts with a leading slash: /p. In addition to node tests, XPath provides path predicates q which may be evaluated against p's set of result nodes: p[q]. Predicates have existential semantics: a node c qualifies if path q starting from context node c evaluates to a non-empty set of nodes.

We can capture the XPath semantics by a translation function xpath p c which yields a monad comprehension that computes the node set returned by path p starting from context node c. Function xpath is defined by structural recursion over the XPath syntax:

$$
\begin{aligned}
\text{xpath}\,(/p)\,c &\equiv \text{xpath}\,p\,(\text{root}\,c) \\
\text{xpath}\,(p_1/p_2)\,c &\equiv \{n' \mid n \leftarrow \text{xpath}\,p_1\,c, n' \leftarrow \text{xpath}\,p_2\,n\} \\
\text{xpath}\,(p[q])\,c &\equiv \{n \mid n \leftarrow \text{xpath}\,p\,c, \text{or}\,\{\text{true} \mid n' \leftarrow \text{xpath}\,q\,n\}\} \\
\text{xpath}\,(a{::}t)\,c &\equiv \text{step}\,(a{::}t)\,c
\end{aligned}
$$

The primitive root c evaluates to the root of the document that includes node c. Function step does the actual evaluation of a step from a given context node. We will shortly come back to its implementation.

As given, function xpath fails to reflect one important detail of XPath: nodes resulting from path evaluation are returned in *document order*. The XML document order ≪ orders the nodes of a document according to a preorder traversal of the document tree. A complete XPath translation would thus read (sidoaed · xpath) p c where sidoaed[4] (*sort in document order and eliminate duplicates*) orders a node set according to ≪.

---

[3] For brevity, we omit XPath features like the *, node(), or text() node tests.

[4] The particular name sidoaed has been borrowed from an XQuery tutorial by Peter Fankhauser and Phil Wadler [12.6].

Note that `sidoaed` is a catamorphism itself. Let `iidoaed` (n, ns) (*insert in document order and eliminate duplicates*) denote the function that inserts node n into node list ns with respect to $\ll$ if n is not an element of ns (by straightforward recursion over ns). We then have

```
sidoaed :: [[X]] → [X]
sidoaed ≡ ([];iidoaed)
```

with `X` being the implementation type for XML nodes (see below). Note that `sidoaed` is well-defined over any collection type since `iidoaed` is left-idempotent and left-commutative.

(We could even go a step further and integrate document order more tightly into our model. To this end, observe that

$$
\begin{aligned}
\texttt{zero} &\equiv [] \\
\texttt{unit } n &\equiv [n] \\
\texttt{mmap} &\equiv \texttt{map } [] \ (\uparrow) \\
\texttt{join} &\equiv ([];\oplus) \qquad \text{with } xs \oplus ys \equiv (ys;\texttt{iidoaed}) \ xs
\end{aligned}
$$

yields a monad of *node sequences in document order* and its associated notion of node sequence comprehensions—see Figure 12.4.)

To illustrate, the XPath expression `/child::a[child::b]` is translated as follows (where c denotes the context node):

$$
\begin{aligned}
&\texttt{sidoaed } (\texttt{xpath } (\texttt{/child::a[child::b]}) \ c) \\
&= \texttt{sidoaed } (\texttt{xpath } (\texttt{child::a[child::b]}) \ (\texttt{root } c)) \\
&= \texttt{sidoaed } (\{n \mid n \leftarrow \texttt{xpath } (\texttt{child::a}) \ (\texttt{root } c), \\
&\qquad\qquad\qquad \texttt{or } \{\texttt{true} \mid n' \leftarrow \texttt{xpath } (\texttt{child::b}) \ n\}\}) \\
&= \texttt{sidoaed } (\{n \mid n \leftarrow \texttt{step } (\texttt{child::a}) \ (\texttt{root } c), n' \leftarrow \texttt{step } (\texttt{child::b}) \ n\})
\end{aligned}
$$

Note how the second step depends on the context nodes n computed in the first step.

Thanks to the comprehension semantics for path expressions we are in a position to find concise proofs for a number of useful XPath equivalences. As an example, consider *predicate flattening*:

$$
\begin{aligned}
&\texttt{xpath } (p[p_1 [p_2]]) \ c \\
&= \{n \mid n \leftarrow \texttt{xpath } p \ c, \texttt{or } \{\texttt{true} \mid n' \leftarrow \texttt{xpath } (p_1 [p_2]) \ n\}\} \\
&= \{n \mid n \leftarrow \texttt{xpath } p \ c, \texttt{or } \{\texttt{true} \mid n' \leftarrow \{v \mid v \leftarrow \texttt{xpath } p_1 \ n, \\
&\qquad\qquad\qquad\qquad\qquad\qquad\qquad \texttt{or } \{\texttt{true} \mid v' \leftarrow \texttt{xpath } p_2 \ v\}\}\}\} \\
&= \{n \mid n \leftarrow \texttt{xpath } p \ c, \texttt{or } \{\texttt{true} \mid n' \leftarrow \{v \mid v \leftarrow \texttt{xpath } p_1 \ n, v' \leftarrow \texttt{xpath } p_2 \ v\}\}\} \\
&= \{n \mid n \leftarrow \texttt{xpath } p \ c, \texttt{or } \{\texttt{true} \mid n' \leftarrow \texttt{xpath } (p_1/p_2) \ n\}\} \\
&= \texttt{xpath } (p[p_1/p_2]) \ c
\end{aligned}
$$

The more explicit we are in explaining the XPath semantics, the more opportunities for optimisation are created. Since XPath axes are defined with respect to document order and tag inclusion, let us make these notions explicit.

We choose a specific implementation type for an XML node, namely $X = (\$,(\mathbb{N},\mathbb{N}))$. While the first component will store the node's tag name as a string, the pair of numbers represents its *preorder* and *postorder* traversal rank, respectively. The ranks are sufficient to encode document order as well as to characterize the major XPath axes [12.11]. Figure 12.5 displays an XML document instance, its associated document tree as well as its internal representation, the set doc of X values. Intuitively, the preorder rank of a node represents the position of its opening tag relative to the positions of the opening tags of all other nodes in the document. An equivalent observation applies to the postorder rank and the node's closing tag. Obviously, then,

$$v' \text{ is a descendant of } v$$
$$\Leftrightarrow$$
$$\mathsf{pre}\ v < \mathsf{pre}\ v' \wedge \mathsf{post}\ v' < \mathsf{post}\ v\ ,$$

i.e. the tags of v embrace those of v'. The other major XPath axes ancestor, preceding, and following may be understood in terms of preorder and postorder ranks, too.

```
<a>                 root
  <b><c/></b>
  <d>
    <e/><f/>
  </d>
</a>
```

$doc = \{\ (\text{"a"},(1,6)),(\text{"b"},(2,2)),$
$(\text{"c"},(3,1)),(\text{"d"},(4,5)),$
$(\text{"e"},(5,3)),(\text{"f"},(6,4))\ \}$

$root\ c = (\text{"root"},(0,7))$

Fig. 12.5. XML document and its *preorder/postorder* encoding

Given the following function definitions:

$$
\begin{aligned}
\mathsf{tag}\ (t,(pre,post)) &\equiv t \\
\mathsf{pre}\ (t,(pre,post)) &\equiv pre \\
\mathsf{post}\ (t,(pre,post)) &\equiv post \\
n_1 \ll n_2 &\equiv (\mathsf{pre}\ n_1) < (\mathsf{pre}\ n_2)
\end{aligned}
$$

we can encode XPath step evaluation as follows:

$$\mathsf{step}\ (\mathsf{descendant}::t)\ c \equiv \{n \mid n \leftarrow \mathsf{doc}, c \ll n, \mathsf{post}\ n < \mathsf{post}\ c, \mathsf{tag}\ n = t\}$$
$$\mathsf{step}\ (\mathsf{following}::t)\ c\ \equiv \{n \mid n \leftarrow \mathsf{doc}, c \ll n, \mathsf{post}\ c < \mathsf{post}\ n, \mathsf{tag}\ n = t\}$$
$$\mathsf{step}\ (\mathsf{preceding}::t)\ c\ \equiv \{n \mid n \leftarrow \mathsf{doc}, n \ll c, \mathsf{post}\ c < \mathsf{post}\ n, \mathsf{tag}\ n = t\}$$
$$\mathsf{step}\ (\mathsf{ancestor}::t)\ c\ \ \equiv \{n \mid n \leftarrow \mathsf{doc}, n \ll c, \mathsf{post}\ n < \mathsf{post}\ c, \mathsf{tag}\ n = t\}$$

Now, given the XML instance of Figure 12.5, it is easy to verify that our monad comprehension semantics and the XPath semantics are indeed the same. We have, for example:

$$\text{xpath} \, (\text{/descendant::d[preceding::b]}) \, c \;\; = \;\; \{(\texttt{"d"},(4,5))\}$$

Note that the choice of context node c is immaterial here since the path expression is absolute, effectively having the document root node as the context node.

If you look at the definitions for the **preceding** and **ancestor** axes you will notice that both axes select nodes n that are *before* context node c in document order. Axes of this kind are referred to as *reverse axes*.

Reverse axes pose a problem for so-called *streaming XPath processors*. XPath engines of this type try to perform a single preorder traversal, e.g. by receiving the events of a SAX parser) over the input document to evaluate a given path expression. The big win is that only very limited memory space is necessary to perform the evaluation: a streaming XPath processor can, in principle, operate on XML documents of arbitrary size.

To evaluate a reverse axis step in such a setup is problematic because the XPath processor would need temporary space to remember *past* SAX events. To restore the modest memory requirements we thus need to get rid of the reverse axes. Such an approach is indeed possible and discussed in [12.18]. The authors present a number of XPath equivalences, e.g.

$$\text{/descendant::}t\text{/preceding::}t' \; = \; \text{/descendant::}t'\text{[following::}t\text{]}$$

(note that the right-hand side trades a reverse axis for a forward axis and a step for a predicate, respectively).

A proof for this equality naturally depends on the path expression semantics as well as the semantics of the XPath axes themselves. As we have defined both semantics in terms of monad comprehensions, we can carry out the actual proof solely by means of equational reasoning, which is typical for a purely functional query representation. We first map the right-hand side XPath expression into its monad comprehension equivalent, and then exhaustively apply the monad comprehension normalisation rules 12.10a–12.10d. For our current example, the normal form is reached after two normalisation steps (see below). Applied to the left-hand side of the above equation, mapping and normalisation (not shown here) yield an identical monad comprehension, which validates the equality.

$$\text{xpath} \, (\text{/descendant::}t'\text{[following::}t\text{]}) \, c$$
$$\underset{\text{xpath}}{=} \;\; \text{xpath} \, (\text{descendant::}t'\text{[following::}t\text{]}) \, (\text{root } c)$$

$$\underset{\text{xpath}}{=} \{n \mid n \leftarrow \text{xpath}\,(\text{descendant}::t')\,(\text{root}\ c),$$
$$\text{or}\ \{\text{true} \mid n' \leftarrow \text{xpath}\,(\text{following}::t)\ n\}\}$$

$$\underset{\text{xpath}}{=} \{n \mid n \leftarrow \text{step}\,(\text{descendant}::t')\,(\text{root}\ c),$$
$$\text{or}\ \{\text{true} \mid n' \leftarrow \text{step}\,(\text{following}::t)\ n\}\}$$

$$\underset{\text{step}}{=} \{n \mid n \leftarrow \{v \mid v \leftarrow \text{doc},(\text{root}\ c) \ll v, \text{post}\ v < \text{post}\,(\text{root}\ c), \text{tag}\ v = t'\},$$
$$\text{or}\ \{\text{true} \mid n' \leftarrow \{v' \mid v' \leftarrow \text{doc}, n \ll v', \text{post}\ n < \text{post}\ v',$$
$$\text{tag}\ v' = t\}\}\}$$

$$\underset{12.10c}{=} \{v \mid v \leftarrow \text{doc},(\text{root}\ c) \ll v, \text{post}\ v < \text{post}\,(\text{root}\ c), \text{tag}\ v = t',$$
$$\text{or}\ \{\text{true} \mid v' \leftarrow \text{doc}, v \ll v', \text{post}\ v < \text{post}\ v', \text{tag}\ v' = t\}\}$$

$$\underset{12.10d}{=} \{v \mid v \leftarrow \text{doc},(\text{root}\ c) \ll v, \text{post}\ v < \text{post}\,(\text{root}\ c), \text{tag}\ v = t',$$
$$v' \leftarrow \text{doc}, v \ll v', \text{post}\ v < \text{post}\ v', \text{tag}\ v' = t\}$$

$$= \{v \mid v \leftarrow \text{doc}, \text{tag}\ v = t', v' \leftarrow \text{doc}, v \ll v', \text{post}\ v < \text{post}\ v', \text{tag}\ v' = t\}$$

To understand the last rewriting step above, note that $(\text{root}\ c) \ll v$ and post $v <$ post $(\text{root}\ c)$ for arbitrary nodes c, v of the same document (also see Figure 12.5).

We observe that the resulting normalised monad comprehension describes the same computation as the following SQL query:

```
select v
  from doc v, doc v'
 where tag v = t' and tag v' = t
   and v ≪ v' and post v < post v'
```

More generally, an XPath expression consisting of n steps or predicates yields an n-ary join of the relation doc of $\mathbf{X}$ values with itself. The structural aspects of a path expression, implicitly given by the XPath axes, as well as name tests are mapped into a simple conjunctive predicate against this intermediary n-ary self-join result.

Although this XPath evaluation scheme may appear rather simplistic, it offers a number of—sometimes non-obvious—optimization hooks, especially if the scheme is used in a set-oriented manner [12.11] i.e. when a path expression is evaluated for a *context node set*, not just a single context node c as discussed here.

12.8 Conclusion

In this chapter we have used monads in the role that sets play in the relational calculus. A key feature of the monad notion is that it comes with just enough internal structure necessary to interpret a query calculus. The resulting monad comprehension calculus is limitted with respect to the variety of syntactic forms it offers but this ultimately leads to a form of query representation that stresses the core structure inherent to a query.

We have seen that a monad comprehension $[\![\, f\ x\ |\ x \leftarrow xs\,]\!]$ can describe a variety of query constructs, e.g. parallel application of f to the elements of xs, iteration, duplicate elimination, aggregation, or a quantifier ranging over xs, depending on the actual choice of monad we are evaluating the comprehension in. This uniformity has enabled us to spot useful and sometimes unexpected dualities between query constructs, e.g. the close connection of the class of flat join queries and existential quantification discussed in Section 12.5.

The terseness of the calculus additionally has a positive impact on the size of the rule sets necessary to express complex query rewrites, most notably monad comprehension normalisation.

This chapter has aimed to show that monad comprehensions provide an ideal framework in which the interaction of a diversity of query representation and optimisation techniques may be studied. We have found this purely functional representation of queries based on catamorphisms and monads to cover, simplify, and generalize many of the proposed views of classical database query languages as well as the more recent XML languages such as like XPath.

References

12.1 Anders Berglund, Scott Boag, Don Chamberlin, Mary F. Fernandez, Michael Kay, Jonathan Robie, and Jérôme Siméon. XML Path Language (XPath) 2.0. Technical Report W3C Working Draft, Version 2.0, World Wide Web Consortium, December 2001. http://www.w3.org/TR/xpath20/.

12.2 Val Breazu-Tannen, Peter Buneman, and Limsoon Wong. Naturally Embedded Query Languages. In *Proc. of the International Conference on Database Theory (ICDT)*, pages 140–154, Berlin, Germany, October 1992.

12.3 Peter Buneman, Leonid Libkin, Dan Suciu, Val Tannen, and Limsoon Wong. Comprehension Syntax. *ACM SIGMOD Record*, 23:87–96, March 1994.

12.4 Rick G. Cattell and Douglas K. Barry, editors. *The Object Database Standard: ODMG 2.0*. Morgan Kaufmann, 1997.

12.5 Damianos Chatziantoniou and Kenneth A. Ross. Groupwise Processing of Relational Queries. In *Proceedings of the 23rd Internatinal Conference on Very Large Data Bases (VLDB)*, pages 476–485, Athens, Greece, August 1997.

12.6 Peter Fankhauser and Philip Wadler. XQuery Tutorial. *XML 2001*, Orlando, Florida, USA, December 2001.

12.7 Leonidas Fegaras and David Maier. Optimizing Object Queries Using an Effective Calculus. *ACM Transactions on Database Systems*, 25(4):457–516, 2000.

12.8 Richard A. Ganski and Harry K. T. Wong. Optimization of Nested SQL Queries Revisited. In *Proceedings of the ACM SIGMOD International Conference on Management of Data*, pages 23–33, San Francisco, USA, 1987.

12.9 Andrew J. Gill, John Launchbury, and Simon L. Peyton Jones. A Short Cut to Deforestation. In *Proceedings of the ACM Conference on Functional Programming and Computer Architecture (FPCA)*, pages 223–232, Copenhagen, Denmark, April 1993.

12.10 Torsten Grust. Comprehending Queries. PhD thesis, University of Konstanz, September 1999. Available at `http://www.ub.uni-konstanz.de/kops/volltexte/1999/312/312_1.pdf`.

12.11 Torsten Grust. Accelerating XPath Location Steps. In *Proceedings of the 21st International ACM SIGMOD Conference on Management of Data*, pages 109–120, Madison, Wisconsin, USA, June 2002.

12.12 Torsten Grust and Marc H. Scholl. How to Comprehend Queries Functionally. *Journal of Intelligent Information Systems*, 12(2/3):191–218, March 1999. Special Issue on Functional Approach to Intelligent Information Systems.

12.13 Jonathan M.D. Hill. Data-Parallel Lazy Functional Programming. PhD thesis, University of London, Queen Mary and Westfield College, September 1994.

12.14 John Hughes and Simon L. Peyton Jones (editors). Haskell 98: A Non-strict, Purely Functional Language. `http://haskell.org/definition/`, February 1999.

12.15 Won Kim. On Optimizing an SQL-like Nested Query. *ACM Transactions on Database Systems*, 7(3):443–469, September 1982.

12.16 Joachim Lambek. A Fixpoint Theorem for Complete Categories. *Mathematische Zeitschrift*, 103:151–161, 1968.

12.17 Erik Meijer, Marten M. Fokkinga, and Ross Paterson. Functional Programming with Bananas, Lenses, Envelopes and Barbed Wire. In *Procedings of the ACM Conference on Functional Programming and Computer Architecture (FPCA)*, number 523 in Lecture Notes in Computer Science (LNCS), pages 124–144, Cambridge, USA, 1991. Springer Verlag.

12.18 Dan Olteanu, Holger Meuss, Tim Furche, and François Bry. Symmetry in XPath. Technical Report PMS-FB-2001-16, Institute of Computer Science, University of Munich, Germany, October 2001.

12.19 Simon Peyton-Jones. Tackling the Awkward Squad: Monadic Input/Output, Concurrency, Exceptions, and Foreign-Language Calls in Haskell. In Tony Hoare, Manfred Broy, and Ralf Steinbruggen, editors, *Engineering Theories of Software Construction*, pages 47–96. IOS Press, 2001.

12.20 Hennie J. Steenhagen, Peter M.G. Apers, and Henk M. Blanken. Optimization of Nested Queries in a Complex Object Model. In *Proceedings of the 4th Interntional Conference on Extending Database Technology (EDBT)*, pages 337–350, Cambridge, UK, March 1994.

12.21 Dan Suciu and Limsoon Wong. On Two Forms of Strutural Recursion. In Georg Gottlob and Moshe Y. Vardi, editors, *Proceedings of the 5th International Conference on Database Theory (ICDT)*, number 893 in Lecture Notes in Computer Science (LNCS), pages 111–124, Prague, Czech Republic, January 1995. Springer Verlag.

12.22 Akihiko Takano and Erik Meijer. Shortcut Deforestation in Calculational Form. In *Proceedings of the ACM Conference on Functional Programming and Computer Architecture (FPCA)*, pages 306–313, La Jolla, USA, June 1995. ACM Press.

12.23 Philip Wadler. Theorems for Free! In *Proceedings of the 4th International Conference on Functional Programming and Computer Architecture (FPCA)*, London, England, September 1989.

12.24 Philip Wadler. Comprehending Monads. In *Conference on Lisp and Functional Programming*, pages 61–78, June 1990.

12.25 Limsoon Wong. Querying Nested Collections. PhD thesis, University of Pennsylvania, Philadelphia, August 1994.

13. Query Processing and Optimization in λ-DB

Leonidas Fegaras

University of Texas at Arlington, CSE, Arlington, TX, USA
email: fegaras@cse.uta.edu

Summary.

The advent of web databases and XML has sprouted a new interest in object-oriented database technology for storing and manipulating semi-structured data. Still lacking from object-oriented databases is a suitable framework for query processing and optimization that meets the performance requirements of these applications. We present an effective framework with a solid theoretical basis for optimizing query languages. Our calculus, called the monoid comprehension calculus, captures most features of ODMG OQL and is a good basis for expressing various optimization algorithms concisely. As a realistic domain to demonstrate the effectiveness of our framework, we have chosen the domain of XML query processing. We present a framework for storing XML data and for translating XML queries into OQL queries. Instead of inventing yet another semi-structured algebra for expressing our translations, the target of our transformation rules is OQL code, which is optimized without any fundamental extension to the existing optimization framework.

13.1 Introduction

Relational database systems suffer from the impedance mismatch problem since their data manipulation languages are based on a different type system and on a different processing paradigm from current application programming languages. In addition, relational databases have a limited modeling power, especially in representing ordered sequences and hierarchical data in a straightforward way. Complex data, such as XML data, needs to be normalized into flat tables, which may cause entities to be split over multiple tables and artificial keys to be introduced when modeling nested sets and hierarchical data. Furthermore, SQL has a limited processing power, especially in its ability to construct complex and nested query results on the fly, such as XML data, and to group-by and aggregate over complex expressions, used in many forms of OLAP queries.

Even though the interest in object-oriented dataBases (OODBs) has gradually declined in the last decade, there is a new interest in using OODBs for storing and manipulating XML data [13.16], because of the new focus of database research towards web databases and XML. XML schema descriptions may contain nested elements in many levels, and thus they closely resemble nested collections of elements, directly supported by current OODBs, rather than flat relational tables. Furthermore, hierarchical data is more naturally mapped to nested objects than to flat relations, while navigations along XML paths are more easily expressible in terms of OODB path expressions than in terms of joins. In addition, the query language of the ODMG standard for OODBs, OQL [13.6], already provides the functionality for performing very complex operations on XML data, such as string pattern matching, sorting, grouping, aggregation, universal quantification, and random access of XML subelements, which are essential for any realistic XML query language.

Even though OODBs provide powerful data abstractions and modeling facilities, they usually lack a suitable framework for query processing and optimization. There are many aspects to the OODB query optimization problem that can benefit from the already proven relational query-optimization technology. However, many key features of OODB languages present new and difficult problems not adequately addressed by this technology. These features include object identity, methods, encapsulation, subtype hierarchy, user-defined type constructors, large multimedia objects, multiple collection types, arbitrary nesting of collections, and nesting of query expressions.

We present an effective framework with a solid theoretical basis for optimizing OQL. OQL queries in our framework are translated into a calculus format that serves as an intermediate form, and then are translated into a version of the nested–relational algebra. We use both a calculus and an algebra as intermediate forms because the calculus closely resembles current OODB languages and is easy to put into canonical form, while the algebra is lower-level and can be directly translated into the execution algorithms supported by database systems.

Our calculus is called the *monoid comprehension calculus* [13.17]. It can capture most features of OQL and is a good basis for expressing various optimization algorithms concisely. It is based on monoids, a general template for a data type, which can capture most collection and aggregate operators currently in use for relational and object-oriented databases. Monoid comprehensions give us a uniform way to express queries that simultaneously deal with more than one collection type and also naturally compose in a way that mirrors the allowable query nesting in OQL.

We will show that the monoid calculus is amenable to efficient optimization and evaluation. We focus on a very important optimization problem, query unnesting (sometimes called query decorrelation), and present a practical, effective, and general solution [13.18, 13.15]. Our method generalizes many unnesting techniques proposed in the literature. Our framework is capable of removing any form of query nesting in our calculus using a simple and efficient algorithm. The simplicity of our method is due to the use of the monoid comprehension calculus as an intermediate form for OODB queries. The monoid comprehension calculus treats operations over multiple collection types, aggregates, and quantifiers in a similar way, resulting in a uniform way of unnesting queries, regardless of their type of nesting. Our unnesting algorithm is compositional, that is, the translation of an embedded query does not depend on the context in which it is embedded; instead, each subquery is translated independently, and all translations are composed to form the final unnested query.

Based on our theoretical framework, we have built a prototype OODB management system, called λ-DB [13.19]. Our system can handle most ODL declarations and can process most OQL query forms. As the name λ-DB suggests, the framework and the implementation of our system is based on the functional programming paradigm. In particular, our monoid comprehension calculus is influenced by Haskell's list comprehensions [13.30], and our normalization algorithm is reminiscent of the *loop fusion* and *deforestation* (elimination of intermediate data structures) techniques used for functional programming languages [13.31]. Furthermore, our stream-based evaluation engine has a higher-order, purely functional interface, even though it is implemented on top of a procedural, high-performance storage manager (SHORE [13.5]).

As a realistic domain to demonstrate the effectiveness of our system, we have chosen the domain of XML query processing. We present a framework for storing XML data in λ-DB and for translating XML queries into OQL queries. This framework does not require any fundamental change to the query optimizer and evaluator of an OODB system, since XML queries are translated into OQL code after type checking but before optimization. For XML data manipulation, we have designed a new XML query language, called XML-OQL [13.16], which is basically a small set of syntactic extensions to OQL. Our query language resembles current related proposals, such as XQuery [13.7] and Quilt [13.8], but is more uniformly integrated with OQL and has precise semantics. We describe a mapping of XML data to OODB objects using a fixed ODMG ODL schema, in the same spirit as the core interface proposed for the XML Document Object Model (DOM) [13.32]. We then present a method for translating XML queries into ODMG OQL queries over that fixed schema. Instead of inventing yet another algebra or calculus for expressing our semantic transformations, the target of our transformations is OQL, which not only has precise semantics in the form of object algebras and calculi, but has also been the focus of various optimization techniques, such as path indexing, path materialization, and query decorrelation. These optimizations can now be used to speed up XML queries.

Our translation schemes from XML-OQL queries to plain OQL code are purely compositional. Even though compositional translations are easy to express and verify on paper, the produced translations may contain many levels of nested queries, which can be overwhelmingly slow if they are interpreted as is. Hence, essential to the success of our framework is an OODB system that can support our translations effectively. λ-DB is a good choice for implementing this framework, because, unlike commercial systems, λ-DB performs complete query unnesting, which is essential for the performance requirements of the framework.

This chapter is organized as follows. Section 13.2 describes the monoid comprehension calculus, the algebra, and the transformation rules for translating OODB queries into the algebra and for unnesting nested queries. Section 13.3 reports on a novel stream-based query execution engine for our algebra, which is purely functional. Finally, Section 13.4 presents a framework for storing XML data into our system and for translating XML queries into OQL queries.

13.2 The Theoretical Framework

In this section, we present an effective framework for optimizing OODB query languages, which is the basis of the λ-DB query optimizer. We first define a calculus, called the *monoid comprehension calculus*, that captures operations involving multiple collection types in declarative form. In a way, monoid comprehensions resemble the tuple relational calculus, but here query variables may range over multiple collection types, while the output of the comprehension may be of a yet different collection type. For example, the following monoid comprehension

$$\cup\{ (a, b) \mathbin{[\![} a \leftarrow [1, 2, 3],\ b \leftarrow \{\!\{4, 5\}\!\} \}$$

joins the list $[1, 2, 3]$ with the bag $\{\!\{4, 5\}\!\}$ and returns the following set (it is a set because the comprehension is tagged by $\cup$, which indicates how the results are accumulated to form the output):

$$\{(1, 4), (1, 5), (2, 4), (2, 5), (3, 4), (3, 5)\}$$

Another example is

$$+\{ a \mathbin{[\![} a \leftarrow [1, 2, 3],\ a \geq 2 \}$$

which returns 5, the sum of all list elements greater than or equal to 2, because it uses the function + to add the integer results.

We then describe a version of the nested–relational algebra that supports aggregation, quantification, and the handling of null values (using outer-joins and outer-unnests). The semantics of these operations is given in terms of the monoid calculus. Finally, we present transformation rules for translating OODB queries into the algebra and for unnesting nested queries.

13.2.1 The Calculus

The monoid calculus is based on the concept of *monoids* from abstract algebra. A monoid of type T is a pair $(\oplus, \mathcal{Z}_\oplus)$. $\oplus$ is an associative function of type $T \times T \to T$ (i.e., a binary function that takes two values of type T and returns a value of type T), called the *accumulator* or the *merge* function of this monoid. $\mathcal{Z}_\oplus$ of type T is called the *zero* element of the monoid and is the left and right identity of $\oplus$. That is, the zero element satisfies $\mathcal{Z}_\oplus \oplus x = x \oplus \mathcal{Z}_\oplus = x$, for every x. Examples of monoids include $(\cup, \{\})$ for sets, $(\uplus, \{\!\!\{\}\!\!\})$ for bags, $(+\!\!+, [\,])$ for lists, $(+, 0)$, $(*, 1)$, and $(max, 0)$ for integers, and $(\vee, \text{false})$ and $(\wedge, \text{true})$ for booleans. The monoids for integers and booleans are called *primitive monoids* because they construct values of a primitive type. The set, bag, and list monoids are called *collection monoids*. Each collection monoid $(\oplus, \mathcal{Z}_\oplus)$ requires the additional definition of a *unit function*, $\mathcal{U}_\oplus$, which, along with merge and zero, allows us the construction of all possible values of this type. For example, the unit function for the set monoid is $\lambda x. \{x\}$, which takes a value x as input and constructs the singleton set $\{x\}$ as output. The unit function of a primitive monoid is the identity function $\lambda x. x$. All but the list monoid are commutative, i.e., they satisfy $x \oplus y = y \oplus x$ for every x and y. In addition, some of them ($\cup$, $\wedge$, $\vee$, and max) are idempotent, i.e., they satisfy $x \oplus x = x$ for every x.

A *monoid comprehension* over the monoid $\oplus$ takes the form $\oplus\{ e \,\|\, \bar{r} \}$. Expression e is called the *head* of the comprehension. Each term r_i in the term sequence $\bar{r} = r_1, \ldots, r_n$, for $n \geq 0$, is called a *qualifier*, and is either a *generator* of the form $v \leftarrow e'$, where v is a *range variable* and e' is an expression (the generator domain) that constructs a collection, or a *filter p*, where p is a boolean predicate.

For any monoid $\oplus$ and for any collection monoid $\otimes$, a monoid comprehension is defined by the following reduction rules:

$$\oplus\{ e \,\|\, \} \to \mathcal{U}_\oplus(e) \tag{13.1}$$

$$\oplus\{ e \,\|\, \text{false}, \bar{r} \} \to \mathcal{Z}_\oplus \tag{13.2}$$

$$\oplus\{ e \,\|\, \text{true}, \bar{r} \} \to \oplus\{ e \,\|\, \bar{r} \} \tag{13.3}$$

$$\oplus\{ e \,\|\, v \leftarrow \mathcal{Z}_\otimes, \bar{r} \} \to \mathcal{Z}_\oplus \tag{13.4}$$

$$\oplus\{ e \,\|\, v \leftarrow \mathcal{U}_\otimes(e'), \bar{r} \} \to \mathbf{let}\, v = e' \,\mathbf{in}\, \oplus\{ e \,\|\, \bar{r} \} \tag{13.5}$$

$$\oplus\{ e \,\|\, v \leftarrow (e_1 \otimes e_2), \bar{r} \} \to (\oplus\{ e \,\|\, v \leftarrow e_1, \bar{r} \}) \oplus (\oplus\{ e \,\|\, v \leftarrow e_2, \bar{r} \}) \tag{13.6}$$

Rules (13.2) and (13.3) reduce a comprehension in which the leftmost qualifier is a filter, while Rules (13.4) through (13.6) reduce a comprehension in which the leftmost qualifier is a generator. The let-statement in (13.5) binds v to e' and uses this binding in every free occurrence of v in $\oplus\{ e \,\|\, \bar{r} \}$.

The calculus has a semantic well-formedness requirement that a comprehension be over an idempotent or commutative monoid if any of its generators are over idempotent or commutative monoids. For example, $+\!\!+\{ x \,\|\, x \leftarrow \{1, 2\} \}$ is not a valid monoid comprehension, since it maps a set monoid (which is both commutative and idempotent) to a list monoid (which is neither commutative nor idempotent), while $+\!\!+\{ x \,\|\, x \leftarrow \{\!\!\{1, 2\}\!\!\} \}$ is valid (since both ⊎ and + are commutative). This requirement can be easily checked during compile time.

When restricted to sets, monoid comprehensions are equivalent to set monad comprehensions [13.4], which capture precisely the nested relational algebra [13.17]. Most OQL expressions have a direct translation into the monoid calculus. For example, the OQL query

> **select distinct** hotel.price
> **from** hotel **in** (**select** h **from** c **in** Cities, h **in** c.hotels
>   **where** c.name = "Arlington")
> **where exists** r **in** hotel.rooms: r.bed_num = 3
>   **and** hotel.name **in** (**select** t.name **from** s **in** States, t **in** s.attractions
>   **where** s.name = "Texas");

finds the prices of hotels in Arlington that have rooms with three beds and are also tourist attractions in Texas. This query is translated into the following comprehension:

> ∪{ hotel.price
>   ‖ hotel ← ∪{ h ‖ c ← Cities, h ← c.hotels, c.name= "Arlington" },
>   ∨{ r.bed_num=3 ‖ r ← hotel.rooms },
>   ∨{ e=hotel.name ‖ e ← ∪{ t.name ‖ s ← States, t ← s.attractions,
>   s.name= "Texas" } } }

We use the shorthand $x \equiv u$ to represent the binding of the variable x with the value u. The meaning of this construct is given by the following reduction:

$$\oplus\{\, e \parallel \bar{r}, x \equiv u, \bar{s} \,\} \longrightarrow \oplus\{\, e[u/x] \parallel \bar{r}, \bar{s}[u/x] \,\} \tag{13.7}$$

where $e[u/x]$ is the expression e with u substituted for all the free occurrences of x (i.e., $e[u/x]$ is equivalent to **let** $x = u$ **in** e).

The monoid calculus can be put into a canonical form by an efficient rewrite algorithm, called the *normalization algorithm*, described below. The evaluation of these canonical forms generally produces fewer intermediate data structures than the initial unnormalized programs. Moreover, the normalization algorithm improves program performance in many cases. It generalizes many optimization techniques already used in relational algebra, such as fusing two selections into one selection. The following are the most important rules of the normalization algorithm:

$$\oplus\{\, e \parallel \bar{q}, v \leftarrow \cup\{\, e' \parallel \bar{r} \,\}, \bar{s} \,\} \longrightarrow \oplus\{\, e \parallel \bar{q}, \bar{r}, v \equiv e', \bar{s} \,\} \tag{13.8}$$

$$\oplus\{\, e \parallel \bar{q}, \vee\{\, pred \parallel \bar{r} \,\}, \bar{s} \,\} \longrightarrow \oplus\{\, e \parallel \bar{q}, \bar{r}, pred, \bar{s} \,\} \tag{13.9}$$
$$\text{(for idempotent monoid } \oplus)$$

The soundness of the normalization rules can be proved using the definition of the monoid comprehension [13.18]. Rule (13.8) flattens a comprehension that contains a generator whose domain is another comprehension (it may require variable renaming to avoid name conflicts). Rule (13.9) unnests an existential quantification.

For example, the previous OQL query is normalized into

$$\cup\{ \text{ h.price } \| \text{ c} \leftarrow \text{Cities, h} \leftarrow \text{c.hotels, r} \leftarrow \text{h.rooms,}$$
$$\text{s} \leftarrow \text{States, t} \leftarrow \text{s.attractions, c.name}= \text{"Arlington",}$$
$$\text{r.bed\_num}=3, \text{ s.name}= \text{"Texas", t.name}=\text{h.name } \}$$

by applying Rule (13.8) to unnest the two inner set comprehensions and Rule (13.9) to unnest the two existential quantifications, and by moving the four predicates to the end of the comprehension.

13.2.2 The Monoid Algebra

The reduction rules (13.1) through (13.6), which define a comprehension, imply a nested-loop evaluation: for each domain value of the outer generator, the rest of the comprehension is evaluated (Rule (13.5)). But we can do better than that in most cases. Research in relational query optimization has already addressed the related problem of efficiently evaluating join queries by considering different join orders, different access paths to data, and different join algorithms [13.27]. To effectively adapt this technology to handle comprehensions, comprehensions must be expressed in terms of algebraic operators, which, eventually, will be mapped into physical execution algorithms, like those found in database systems (e.g., merge join, hash join, etc.). We present a framework for translating terms in our calculus into efficient algorithms. This translation is done in stages. Queries in our framework are first translated into monoid comprehensions, which serve as an intermediate form, and then are translated into a version of the nested relational algebra that supports aggregation, quantification, outer-joins, and outer-unnests. At the end, the algebraic terms are translated into execution plans. This algebra is called the *monoid algebra*. We use both a calculus and an algebra as intermediate forms because the calculus closely resembles current OODB languages and is easy to normalize, while the algebra is lower-level and can be directly translated into the execution algorithms supported by database systems.

The algebraic bulk operators along with their semantics are given in Figure 13.1. The inputs and output of each operator are streams, which are captured as lists of tuples. Tuples are constructed using the comma operator, which is associative with zero, (). That is, $((x,y),z) = (x,(y,z)) = (x,y,z)$ and $(x,()) = ((),x) = x$. For a tuple v, the ith element is v_i. This unconventional definition of tuples is motivated by the need to preserve the associativity of joins, $X \bowtie (Y \bowtie Z) = (X \bowtie Y) \bowtie Z$, and for validating transformation rules. There are other non-bulk operators, such as boolean comparisons, which are not listed here. Selection (σ), projection (π), merging ($\cup$), and join ($\bowtie$) are similar to their relational algebra counterparts (although they are based on lists rather than sets), while unnest (μ) and nest (Γ) are based on the nested relational algebra. The unnest operator, μ, applies a

$$X \bowtie_p Y = \uplus \{\, (v,w) \parallel v \leftarrow X,\, w \leftarrow Y,\, p(v,w) \,\} \tag{13.10}$$

$$X \cup Y = X \uplus Y \tag{13.11}$$

$$\sigma_p(X) = \uplus \{\, v \parallel v \leftarrow X,\, p(v) \,\} \tag{13.12}$$

$$\pi_{k_1,\dots,k_m}(X) = \uplus \{\, (v_{k_1},\dots,v_{k_m}) \parallel v \leftarrow X \,\} \tag{13.13}$$

$$\mu_p^{path}(X) = \uplus \{\, (v,w) \parallel v \leftarrow X,\, w \leftarrow path(v),\, p(v,w) \,\} \tag{13.14}$$

$$\Delta_p^{\oplus,h}(X) = \oplus \{\, h(v) \parallel v \leftarrow X,\, p(v) \,\} \tag{13.15}$$

$$\Gamma_p^{\oplus,h,g}(X) = \uplus \{\, (g(v), \oplus \{\, h(w) \parallel w \leftarrow X,\, g(v) = g(w),\, p(w) \,\}) \parallel v \leftarrow X \,\} \tag{13.16}$$

Fig. 13.1. Semantics of the monoid algebra.

path expression *path* to each element v of the input, yielding a set of elements w, and then concatenates each derived element w to v and sends it to the output. The reduce operator, Δ, is used in producing the final result of a query/subquery, such as in aggregations and existential/universal quantifications. It applies the function h to each input element that satisfies the predicate p, puts the results into a set, and applies the binary function $\oplus$ (a monoid) to the resulting set, reducing the elements in pairs. For example, the OQL universal quantification **for all** v **in** X: v.A > 5 can be captured by the Δ operator, with $\oplus = \wedge$ and $h(v) = v.A > 5$ (i.e. $h = \lambda v.\, v.A > 5$). The nest operator, Γ, groups the element of the input by the function g so that any two elements v and w in a group satisfy $g(v) = g(w)$. After groups are formed, for each group, the nest operator sends one tuple to the output that contains the group-by values (which are the same for every group element) and the reduction of each group by $\Delta^{\oplus,h}$. Finally, even though selections and projections can be expressed as reductions, for convenience, they are treated as separate operations.

The above algebraic operators have sufficient expressive power to capture any OQL query [13.18]. However, our query unnesting algorithm (described in the next section) requires the introduction of outer-unnests and outer-joins to relate the data between the inner and outer queries of a nested query before the group-by operator reconstructs the result of the nested query. The outer-join, $\Rightarrow\!\bowtie$, is defined as follows:

$$X \Rightarrow\!\bowtie_p Y = \uplus \{\, (v,w) \parallel v \leftarrow X,\, w \leftarrow \textbf{if } \wedge \{\, \neg p(v,w') \parallel w' \leftarrow Y \,\}$$
$$\textbf{then } [\text{NULL}]$$
$$\textbf{else } \uplus \{\, w' \parallel w' \leftarrow Y,\, p(v,w') \,\} \,\}$$

It is a left outer-join between X and Y using the join predicate p. The domain of the second generator (the generator of w) is always non-empty. If Y is empty or there are no elements that can be joined with v (this condition is tested by the universal quantification, $\wedge$), then the domain is the singleton value [NULL], i.e., w becomes null. Otherwise each qualified element w of Y is joined with v. The outer-unnest operator, $\nrightarrow\mu_p^{path}(X)$, is defined as follows:

$$\nrightarrow\mu_p^{path}(X) = +\!\!+\!\{\,(v',w) \mathbin{\|} v \leftarrow X,$$
$$w \leftarrow \textbf{if } \wedge\{\,\neg p(v,w') \mathbin{\|} v \neq \text{NULL},\ w' \leftarrow path(v)\,\}$$
$$\textbf{then } [\text{NULL}]$$
$$\textbf{else } +\!\!+\!\{\,w' \mathbin{\|} w' \leftarrow path(v),\ p(v,w')\,\}\,\}$$

It is similar to $\mu_p^{path}(X)$, but if $x.path$ is empty for $x \in X$ or $p(x,y)$ is false for all $y \in x.path$, then the pair (x, NULL) appears in the output.

13.2.3 Algebraic Optimization

After OQL queries have been translated to monoid comprehensions, they are converted to algebraic forms and are optimized. There are many proposals on OODB query optimization. Some of them are focused on handling nested collections [13.26, 13.14], others on converting path expressions into joins [13.22, 13.11], and others on unnesting nested queries [13.12, 13.13, 13.10, 13.29] (also known as query decorrelation). Nested queries appear more often in OODB queries than in relational queries, because OODB query languages allow complex expressions at any point in a query. In addition, OODB types are allowed to have attributes with collection values (i.e., nested collections), which lead naturally to nested queries. Current OODB systems typically evaluate nested queries in a nested-loop fashion, which does not leave many opportunities for optimization. Most unnesting techniques for OODB queries are actually based on similar techniques for relational queries [13.23, 13.20, 13.25]. For all but the trivial nested queries, these techniques require the use of outer-joins, to prevent loss of data, and grouping, to accumulate the data and to remove the null values introduced by the outer-joins.

If considered in isolation, query unnesting itself does not result in performance improvement. Instead, it makes possible other optimizations that would not be possible otherwise. More specifically, without unnesting, the only choice of evaluating nested queries is a naive nested-loop method: for each step of the outer query, all the steps of the inner query need to be executed. Query unnesting promotes all the operators of the inner query into the operators of the outer query. This operator mixing allows other optimization techniques to take place, such as the rearrangement of operators to minimize cost and the free movement of selection predicates between inner and outer operators, which enables operators to be more selective.

Although our normalization algorithm (given in Section 13.2.1) removes many forms of query nesting, it does not remove nested queries in predicates and in query result constructions. In this section, we present a complete

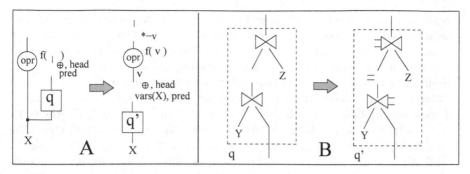

Fig. 13.2. Algebraic query unnesting.

algorithm that removes all the other forms of query nesting left out from normalization.

Our query unnesting algorithm is illustrated in Figure 13.2 (A): for each box, q, that corresponds to a nested query, it converts the reduction on top of q into a nest, and the joins/unnests that lay on the input–output path of the box q into outer-joins/outer-unnests in the box q' (as is shown in the example of Figure 13.2 (B)). At the same time, it embeds the resulting box q' at the point immediately before it is used. There is a very simple explanation why this algorithm is correct: the nested query, q, in Figure 13.2 (A), consumes the same input stream as that of the embedding operation, opr, and computes a value that is used in the component, f, of the embedding query. If we want to splice this box onto the stream of the embedding query we need to guarantee two things. First, q should not block the input stream by removing tuples from the stream. If the input of a join, for example, depends on the input stream, then the join will remove all tuples from the input stream that do not satisfy the join predicate. This join is called a blocking operation, since it removes data from the input stream, and henceforth, it blocks the stream. This problem can be fixed by converting the blocking joins into outer-joins and the blocking unnests into outer-unnests (box q'). Second, we need to extend the stream with the new value v of q before it is used in f. This extension can be achieved by converting the reduction (Δ) on top of q into a nest (Γ), since the main difference between nest and reduce is that, while the reduce returns a value (a reduction of a stream of values), nest embeds this value to the input stream. At the same time, the nest operator will convert null values to zeros (of the referred monoid) so that the stream that comes from the output of the spliced box q' will be exactly the same as it was before the splice.

Our unnesting algorithm is more concise, more uniform, and more general than earlier work, mostly due to the use of the monoid comprehension calculus as an intermediate form for OODB queries. The monoid comprehension calculus treats operations over multiple collection types, aggregates, and quantifiers in a similar way, resulting in a uniform way of unnesting queries, regardless of their type of nesting. In fact, many forms of nested queries can be unnested by the normalization algorithm for monoid comprehensions. The remaining forms require the introduction of outer-joins and grouping.

After normalization, all generator domains in comprehensions have been reduced to simple expression paths. Then, a comprehension $\oplus\{\, e \,\|\, \bar{r}\,\}$ is translated to an algebraic form by compiling the qualifiers in $\bar{r}$ from left to right. This is accomplished with the help of the function $[\![\oplus\{\, e \,\|\, \bar{r}\,\}]\!]^u_w E$, where the term E (the resulting algebraic tree) is a seed that grows at each step. The variables in w are the variables encountered so far during the translation while the variables in u are the group-by variables. When we have no variables in u, we are compiling an outermost comprehension (not a nested one). For nested queries, we have the rules

$$[\![\oplus\{\, e \,\|\, v \leftarrow X, \bar{r}\,\}]\!]^u_w E \;= [\![\oplus\{\, e \,\|\, \bar{r}\,\}]\!]^u_{(w,v)} \; (E \Join\!\!\!\!\!\to_{\lambda(w,v).true} X)$$

$$[\![\oplus\{\, e \,\|\, v \leftarrow path, \bar{r}\,\}]\!]^u_w E = [\![\oplus\{\, e \,\|\, \bar{r}\,\}]\!]^u_{(w,v)} \; (\not\!\!\mu^{\lambda w.path}_{\lambda(w,v).true}(E))$$

$$[\![\oplus\{\, e \,\|\, \,\}]\!]^u_w E \qquad\quad = \Gamma^{\oplus,\lambda w.e,\lambda w.u}_{\lambda w.true}(E)$$

Note that the predicates in the outer-joins and outer-unnests are set to true but they can easily become selective by moving the applicable predicates from $\bar{r}$ to these operators. For outermost comprehensions, we simply have join/unnest/reduce operations, rather than outer-join/outer-unnest/nest operations. Finally, correlated nested comprehensions are combined in a straightforward way:

$$[\![\oplus\{\, f(\otimes\{\, e \,\|\, \bar{r}\,\}) \,\|\, \,\}]\!]^u_w E = [\![\oplus\{\, f(v) \,\|\, \,\}]\!]^u_{(w,v)} \; ([\![\otimes\{\, e \,\|\, \bar{r}\,\}]\!]^w_w E)$$

where $f(\otimes\{\, e \,\|\, \bar{r}\,\})$ indicates a comprehension inside an arbitrary function f. The soundness of this algorithm has been proved elsewhere [13.18].

For example, the relational-style OQL query

```
        select distinct name: u.name,
                        descs: (select distinct i.description
                               from b in Bids, i in Items
                               where b.userid=u.userid
                               and i.itemno=b.itemno)
        from u in Users
```

which lists all users by name so that, for each user, it includes descriptions of all the items (if any) that were bid on by that user, is translated into the monoid comprehension

```
 ∪{ ⟨ name: u.name,
        descs: ∪{ i.description ‖ b ← Bids, i ← Items,
                                 b.userid=u.userid, i.itemno=b.itemno } ⟩
    ‖ u ← Users }
```

which, in turn, is unnested and translated to the algebraic tree shown in Figure 13.3. Here, the Box B, which represents the comprehension

∪{ i.description ∥ b ← Bids, i ← Items, b.userid=u.userid, i.itemno=b.itemno }

is embedded inside the Box A, which represents the comprehension

$$\cup\{\ \langle\ \text{name: u.name, descs: } \boxed{\text{B}}\ \rangle\ \|\ u \leftarrow \text{Users}\ \}$$

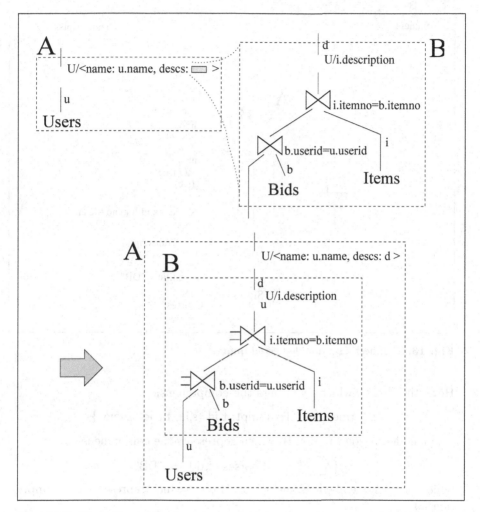

Fig. 13.3. Unnesting a simple query.

Another example, shown in Figure 13.4, represents the following double-nested comprehension that finds the students who have taken all database courses:

∪{ s ∥ s ← Students, ∧{ ∨{ true ∥ t ← Transcript, t.id=s.id, t.cno=c.cno }
∥ c ← Courses, c.title = "DB" } }

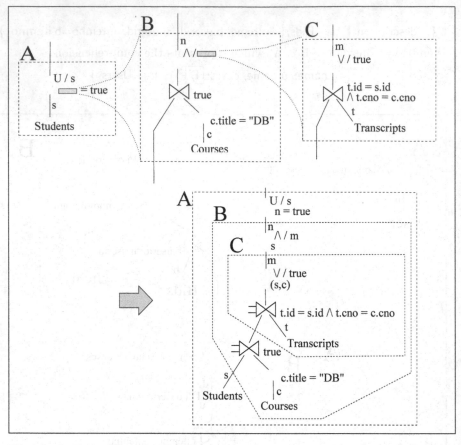

Fig. 13.4. Unnesting a double-nested query.

Here, the Box C, which represents the comprehension

$$\vee\{ \text{ true } \| \text{ t} \leftarrow \text{Transcript, t.id=s.id, t.cno=c.cno } \}$$

is embedded inside the Box B, which represents the comprehension

$$\wedge\{ \boxed{C} \| \text{ c} \leftarrow \text{Courses, c.title} = \text{"DB"} \}$$

which in turn is embedded inside the Box A, which represents the comprehension

$$\cup\{ \text{ s} \| \text{ s} \leftarrow \text{Students, } \boxed{B} \}$$

The resulting algebraic tree can be evaluated more efficiently if we switch Courses with Transcripts and move the join predicates. In that case, the resulting outer-joins are both assigned equality predicates, thus making them more efficient. Optimizations such as this justify query unnesting.

13.3 A Purely Functional Stream-Based Execution Engine

Algebraic operators, such as $R \bowtie_{R.A=S.B} S$, are intrinsically higher-order. That is, they are parametrized by pieces of code (i.e., functions) that specify some of the operation details. For the above join, the piece of code is the predicate $R.A = S.B$. Most commercial DBMSs evaluate query plans using a plan interpreter, rather than compiling the plans into executable code. In this section, we are presenting an interface to a stream-based execution engine that is purely functional. By expressing the evaluation algorithms as higher-order functions, we were able to build a complete library of evaluation algorithms, suitable for our monoid algebra.

If a query is to be compiled into execution code with no run-time interpretation of predicates, it should make use of higher-order evaluation algorithms. The alternative would be to define the evaluation algorithms as kinds of macros to be macroexpanded and individually tailored for each different instance of the evaluation operator in the query plan. This approach is clumsy and non-modular, and makes the development and extension of the evaluation algorithms very tedious and error prone. For example, a generic evaluation algorithm for a relational join may be defined as a higher-order function with signature

(x: Relation, y: Relation, pred: (tuple,tuple)→bool) → Relation

where pred is the join predicate function, or, more generally

(x: Set(a), y: Set(b), concat: (a,b)→c, pred: (a,b)→bool) → Set(c)

where a, b, and c are type parameters bound to tuple types, Set(a) is a parametric type that represents sets of elements of type a, and concat merges an a and a b element into a c element.

One very important issue to consider when writing high-performance evaluation algorithms for database queries is stream-based processing of data (sometimes called iterator-based processing or pipelining). It is highly desirable to avoid materializing the intermediate data in memory (or in secondary storage, when large) whenever possible. Our system pipelines all evaluation algorithms. Instead of using threads to implement pipelining, as is traditionally done in most systems, we developed a special technique borrowed from the area of lazy functional languages. Each of our evaluation algorithms is written in such a way that it returns a piece of data (one tuple) as soon as it constructs one. To retrieve all the tuples, the algorithm must be called multiple times. For example, the pipeline version of the nested-loop join has the signature

(sx: Stream, sy: Stream, pred: (tuple,tuple)→bool) → tuple

where Stream is an abstract data type that captures a stream of tuples and is equipped with standard stream operations, such as first and next. In contrast to the standard nested-loop algorithm, this algorithm returns the first qualified tuple that satisfies pred. To pipeline an evaluation algorithm, we construct a *suspended stream*, which is a structure with just one component: an embedded function, which, when invoked, calls the evaluation algorithm to construct one tuple. For example, to pipeline our nested-loop algorithm, we construct a suspended stream whose embedded function, F, is defined as

$$F() = \mathsf{nested\_loop(s1,s2,pred)}$$

where s1 and s2 are the streams that correspond to the join inputs and pred is the predicate function. When a tuple is needed from a suspended stream, its embedded function is called with no arguments to return the next tuple. This approach is a clean and efficient way of implementing pipelining and it resembles lazy evaluation in functional programming languages. Here, though, we provide an explicit control over the lazy execution, which gives a better handle for controlling the data materialization in the secondary storage.

13.4 Application: Processing Stored XML Data

We have chosen XML query processing as a realistic domain to demonstrate the effectiveness of our system. In this section, we present a framework for storing XML data in λ-DB and for translating XML queries into OQL queries. This framework does not require any fundamental change to the query optimizer and evaluator of an OODB system, since XML queries are translated into OQL code after type checking but before optimization.

XML [13.32] has emerged as the leading textual language for representing and exchanging data on the Web. Even though HTML is still the dominant format for publishing documents on the Web, XML has become the prevalent exchange format for business-to-business transactions and for enterprise Intranets. It is expected that in the near future the Internet will be populated with a vast number of web-accessible XML files. One of the reasons for its popularity is that, by supporting simple nested structures of tagged elements, the XML format is able to represent both the structure and the content of complex data very effectively. To take advantage of the structure of XML documents, new query languages had to be invented that go beyond the simple keyword-based boolean formulas supported by current web search engines, which are based on document indexing techniques, such as inverted indexes [13.3].

Our XML query language is an extension of standard OQL [13.6]. It captures all the important features found in most recent XML query languages, including XQuery [13.7] and Quilt [13.8]. It is not difficult to extend the OQL syntax with special constructs to handle XML data because this data has a tree-like structure that can be naturally mapped to linked objects. In fact there are several proposals for such extensions, such as POQL [13.9], Ozone [13.24], Lorel [13.21], WebOQL [13.2], and X-OQL [13.1]. XML-OQL is essentially OQL extended with XML path expressions and XML data constructions. For example, the following XML-OQL query

> **select list** $<$ bib $>$ $<$ author $>$ b.author.lastname $</$ author $>$,
>> $<$ title $>$ b.title $</$ title $>$,
>> $<$ related $>$ **select list** $<$ title $>$ r.title $</$ title $>$
>>> **from** r **in** b.@related_to
>>
>> $</$ related $>$
>
> $</$ bib $>$
>
> **from** bs **in** retrieve("bibliography").bib.vendor.book,
>> b **in** bs
>
> **where** b.year $>$ 1995 **and** count(b.author) $>$ 2
>> **and** b.title **like** "% computer %"

retrieves information about books written by more than two authors, published after 1995, and containing the word "computer" in their title, along with the titles of their related documents. It conforms to the following partial DTD:

> $<$!ELEMENT bib (vendor*) $>$
> $<$!ELEMENT vendor (name, email, book*) $>$
> $<$!ATTLIST vendor id ID #REQUIRED $>$
> $<$!ELEMENT book (title, publisher?, year?, price, author+) $>$
> $<$!ATTLIST book ISBN ID #REQUIRED $>$
> $<$!ATTLIST book related_to IDrefs $>$
> $<$!ELEMENT author (firstname?, lastname) $>$

where the rest of the elements are #PCDATA.

XML elements are constructed using the following syntax in XML-OQL:

$$< \text{tag } a_1 = u_1 \ldots a_m = u_m > e_1, \ldots, e_n </ \text{tag} >$$

for $m, n \geq 0$. This expression constructs an XML element with name, "tag", attributes $a_1, \ldots, a_m$, and subelements $e_1, \ldots, e_n$ for content. Each attribute a_i is bound to the result of the expression u_i. XML data can be accessed directly from a database by name, retrieve("bibliography"), or can be downloaded from a local file or from the Web using a URL address, such as document("http://www.acm.org/xml/journals.xml"). The tree structure of XML data can be traversed using path expressions of the form

$e.A$	projection over the tag name A
$e._$	projection over any tag
$e.*$	all subelements of e at any depth
$e.@A$	projection over the attribute A of e
$e[\backslash v \to e']$	the subelements of e that satisfy e'
$e[e']$	the subelement of e at position e'

where e and e' are XML-OQL expressions, A is a tag or an attribute name, and v is a variable. Filtering is an unambiguous version of XPath's element filtering: For each subelement v of e, it binds the variable v to the subelement and evaluates the predicate e'. The result is all subelements of e that satisfy e'. The scope of variable v is within the expression e' only. Note that $e.A$ is slightly different from the path expression e/A found in languages based on XPath, since $e.A$ strips out the outer tag names $< A > \ldots < / A >$ from e. Note also that our syntax allows IDref dereferencing, as is done for r.title in the inner *select*-statement of our example query, since variable r is an IDref that references a book element.

XML data may contain nested elements in many levels, and thus they closely resemble nested collections of elements, rather than flat relational tables. Schema-based approaches based on the relational database technology, such as the Niagara project [13.28], have had moderate success so far, mostly due to the normalization of the nested XML structures into flat tables, which may require many joins for reconstructing the original XML data. Tree-structured data is more naturally mapped to nested objects than to flat relations, while navigations along XML paths are more easily expressible in terms of OODB path expressions than in terms of joins. Consequently, we believe that the OODB technology has a better potential than the relational technology to become a good basis for storing and handling XML data.

```
enum attribute_kind { CDATA, IDref, ID, IDrefs };
enum element_kind { TAG, PCDATA };
union attribute_type switch (attribute_kind)
{   case CDATA:   string          value;
    case IDref:   string          id_ref;
    case IDrefs:  list< string >  id_refs;
    case ID:      string          id;
};
struct attribute_binding
{   string          name;
    attribute_type  value;
};
struct node_type {
    string                          name;
    list< attribute_binding >       attributes;
    list< XML_element >             content;
};
union element_type switch (element_kind)
{   case TAG:     node_type tag;
    case PCDATA:  string    data;
};
class XML_element ( extent Elements )
{   attribute element_type   element; };
```

Fig. 13.5. The ODL schema for storing XML data.

We present a framework for storing and querying XML data using the OODB λ-DB . Figure 13.5 shows a possible ODL schema for storing XML data. An element projection *e.A*, where *e* is an expression of type list⟨ XML_element ⟩, can be translated into the OQL expression

$$\text{tag\_projection(e, "A")}$$

of type list⟨ XML_element ⟩, defined as follows in OQL:

> **define** tag_projection (e: list⟨ XML_element ⟩, tag_name: string)
> : list⟨ XML_element ⟩ **as**
> **select list** y
> **from** x **in** e,
>   y **in** (**case** x.element **of**
>   PCDATA: list(),
>   TAG: **if** x.element.tag.name = tag_name
>   **then** x.element.tag.content
>   **else** list()
>   **end**);

where the **select list** syntax is an extension to standard OQL that allows the construction of list collections by a select–from–where query, much like the **select distinct** allows the construction of sets rather than bags. The **case** expression is another extension to OQL that allows the decomposition of union values. The above query scans the list of subelements of all elements in **e** to find those that have the tag name **tag_name**. Since there may be several elements with the same tag name, or no elements at all, it returns a list of elements. For non-matching elements, the empty list, list(), is returned.

Projections of the form *e._* are translated into any_projection(e), which is similar to **tag_projection** but with a true if–then–else condition. Wildcard projections, *e.**, require a transitive closure, which is not supported directly in OQL but can be simulated with a recursive function. More specifically, *e.** is translated into wildcard_projection(*e*), defined as follows:

> **define** wildcard_projection (e: list⟨ XML_element ⟩)
> : list⟨ XML_element ⟩ **as**
> e + (**select list** y
>   **from** x **in** e,
>   y **in** (**case** x.element **of**
>   PCDATA: list(),
>   TAG: wildcard_projection
>   (x.element.tag.content)
>   **end**));

where + is list concatenation. An attribute projection *e.@A* is translated into attribute_projection(e, "A"), defined as follows:

```
define attribute_projection ( e: list⟨ XML_element ⟩, aname: string )
                            : list⟨ attribute_type ⟩ as
select list y
from x in e,
     y in ( case x.element of
            PCDATA: list(),
            TAG: select a.value
                 from a in x.element.tag.attributes
                 where a.name = aname
            end );
```

Dereferencing an IDref attribute is expensive for schema-less XML data because it requires the scanning of the class extent, Elements, to find the XML element whose ID is equal to the IDref value. It is defined as follows:

```
define deref ( idrefs: list⟨ attribute_type ⟩ ) : list⟨ XML_element ⟩ as
       select list e
              from x in idrefs,
                   y in (case x of
                         IDref: list(x.id_ref),
                         IDrefs: x.id_refs,
                         default: list() end),
                   e in Elements
              where case e.element of
                    PCDATA: false,
                    TAG: exists a in e.element.tag.attributes:
                                 case a.value of
                                 ID: a.value.id=y,
                                 default: false end
              end;
```

The following translation rules map XML-OQL path expressions into OQL code:

$$e._ \; \rightarrow \; \text{any\_projection}(e) \tag{13.17}$$

$$e.* \; \rightarrow \; \text{wildcard\_projection}(e) \tag{13.18}$$

$$e.@A \; \rightarrow \; \text{attribute\_projection}(e, \text{``}A\text{''}) \tag{13.19}$$

$$\frac{e : \text{list}\langle \; \text{XML\_element} \; \rangle}{e.A \; \rightarrow \; \text{tag\_projection}(e, \text{``}A\text{''})} \tag{13.20}$$

$$\frac{e : \text{list}\langle \; \text{attribute\_type} \; \rangle, \; a \in \{A, @A, \_, *\}}{e.a \; \rightarrow \; \text{deref}(e).a} \tag{13.21}$$

$$\frac{e : \text{list}\langle \ \text{XML\_element} \ \rangle, \ e' : \text{integer}}{e[e'] \ \rightarrow \ \text{list}(e[e'])} \tag{13.22}$$

$$e[\backslash v \rightarrow e'] \ \rightarrow \ \textbf{select list} \ v \ \textbf{from} \ v \ \textbf{in} \ e \ \textbf{where} \ e' \tag{13.23}$$

The notation $e \rightarrow e'$ means that e is translated into e', the assertion $e : t$ means that expression e has type t, and a fraction is a conditional assertion. Rule (13.20) requires that the type of e is list$\langle$ XML_element $\rangle$, to distinguish a regular OQL projection from an XML projection. Rule (13.21) enforces an IDref dereferencing if e is the result of an attribute projection (which is indicated by the type of e). Rule (13.22) converts a path indexing into a list indexing (to differentiate them, bold-faced square brackets indicate list indexing while regular square brackets indicate path indexing). Finally, Rule (13.23) translates a path filtering into a select-list query.

An element construction of the form

$$< \text{tag} \ a_1 = u_1 \ldots a_m = u_m > e_1, \ldots, e_n </ \text{tag} >$$

allows expressions u_i of type string and expressions e_i of one of the following types: XML_element, list$\langle$ XML_element $\rangle$, string, or list$\langle$ string $\rangle$. It is translated into the OQL expression

XML_element(element: element_type(TAG: **struct**(
    name: tag, attributes: list($v_1, \ldots, v_m$),
    content: ($s_1 + s_2 + \cdots + s_n$))))

where v_i is attribute_type(CDATA: u_i) and s_i is the translation of e_i that depends on the type of e_i. That is, if e_i is of type string, then s_i is

list(XML_element(element: element_type(PC_DATA: e_i)))

while, if e_i is of type list$\langle$ string $\rangle$, then s_i is

select list XML_element(element: element_type(PC_DATA: v))
from v **in** e_i.

13.5 Conclusion

We have presented a uniform calculus based on comprehensions that captures many advanced features found in modern object-oriented and object–relational query languages. We showed that this calculus is easy to manipulate by presenting a normalization algorithm that unnests many forms of nested comprehensions. Queries in our framework are first translated into comprehensions and then into a lower-level algebra that reflects many relational DBMS physical algorithms. The algorithm that translates the calculus into the algebra performs query decorrelation by unnesting any form of nested comprehensions. We reported on an implementation of an ODMG-based DBMS based on our optimization framework. Finally, we have chosen XML query processing as a realistic domain to demonstrate the effectiveness of our system. We have presented a framework for storing XML data in our system and for translating XML queries into OQL queries. This framework does not require any fundamental change to the query optimizer and evaluator of an OODB system, since XML queries are translated into OQL code after type checking but before optimization.

We have already built a high-performance OODB management system based on our theoretical framework. It uses the SHORE [13.5] object store system as a back-end. The source programs of our system are available at http://lambda.uta.edu/ldb/doc/.

References

13.1 S. Abiteboul, et al.   XML Repository and Active Views Demonstration. In *Proceedings of 25th International Conference on Very Large Data Bases (VLDB'99), Edinburgh, Scotland*, pages 742–745, 1999.

13.2 G. Arocena and A. Mendelzon.   WebOQL: Restructuring Documents, Databases, and Webs. In *Proceedings of the Fourteenth International Conference on Data Engineering, Orlando, Florida*, pages 24–33, February 1998.

13.3 R. Baeza-Yates and B. Ribeiro-Neto.   *Modern Information Retrieval*. Addison-Wesley, 1999.

13.4 P. Buneman, L. Libkin, D. Suciu, V. Tannen, and L. Wong. Comprehension Syntax. *SIGMOD Record*, 23(1):87–96, March 1994.

13.5 M. Carey, D. DeWitt, M. Franklin, N. Hall, M. McAuliffe, J. Naughton, D. Schuh, M. Solomon, C. Tan, O. Tsatalos, S. White, and M. Zwilling. Shoring Up Persistent Applications. In *Proceedings of the 1994 ACM SIGMOD International Conference on Management of Data, Minneapolis, Minnesota*, pages 383–394, May 1994.

13.6 R. Cattell, editor.   *The Object Data Standard: ODMG 3.0*. Morgan Kaufmann, 2000.

13.7 D. Chamberlin, D. Florescu, J. Robie, J. Simeon, and M. Stefanescu. XQuery: A Query Language for XML. W3C Working Draft. Available at http://www.w3.org/TR/xquery/, 2000.

13.8 D. Chamberlin, J. Robie, and D. Florescu. Quilt: An XML Query Language for Heterogeneous Data Sources. In *ACM SIGMOD Workshop on The Web and Databases (WebDB'00), Dallas, Texas*, pages 53–62, May 2000.

13.9 V. Christophides, S. Abiteboul, S. Cluet, and M. Scholl. From Structured Documents to Novel Query Facilities. In *Proceedings of the 1994 ACM SIGMOD International Conference on Management of Data, Minneapolis, Minnesota*, pages 313–324, May 1994.

13.10 J. Claussen, A. Kemper, G. Moerkotte, and K. Peithner. Optimizing Queries with Universal Quantification in Object-Oriented and Object-Relational Databases. In *Proceedings of the 23th VLDB Conference, Athens, Greece*, pages 286–295, September 1997.

13.11 S. Cluet and C. Delobel. A General Framework for the Optimization of Object-Oriented Queries. In *Proceedings of the ACM SIGMOD International Conference on Management of Data, San Diego, California*, pages 383–392, June 1992.

13.12 S. Cluet and G. Moerkotte. Nested Queries in Object Bases. In *Fifth International Workshop on Database Programming Languages, Gubbio, Italy*, page 8, September 1995.

13.13 S. Cluet and G. Moerkotte. Efficient Evaluation of Aggregates on Bulk Types. Technical Report 95-05, Aachen University of Technology, October 1995.

13.14 L. S. Colby. A Recursive Algebra and Query Optimization for Nested Relations. In *Proceedings of the ACM SIGMOD International Conference on Management of Data, Portland, Oregon*, pages 273–283, 1989.

13.15 L. Fegaras. Query Unnesting in Object-Oriented Databases. In *ACM SIGMOD International Conference on Management of Data, Seattle, Washington*, pages 49–60, June 1998.

13.16 L. Fegaras and R. Elmasri. Query Engines for Web-Accessible XML Data. In *Very Large Data Bases (VLDB) Conference, Rome, Italy*, pages 251–260, 2001.

13.17 L. Fegaras and D. Maier. Towards an Effective Calculus for Object Query Languages. In *ACM SIGMOD International Conference on Management of Data, San Jose, California*, pages 47–58, May 1995.

13.18 L. Fegaras and D. Maier. Optimizing Object Queries Using an Effective Calculus. *ACM Transactions on Database Systems*, 25(4):457–516, December 2000.

13.19 L. Fegaras, C. Srinivasan, A. Rajendran, and D. Maier. λ-DB: An ODMG-Based Object-Oriented DBMS. In *Proceedings of the 2000 ACM SIGMOD International Conference on Management of Data, Dallas, Texas*, page 583, May 2000.

13.20 R. Ganski and H. Wong. Optimization of Nested SQL Queries Revisited. In *Proceedings of the ACM SIGMOD International Conference on Management of Data, San Francisco, California*, pages 23–33, May 1987.

13.21 R. Goldman, J. McHugh, and J. Widom. From Semistructured Data to XML: Migrating the Lore Data Model and Query Language. In *ACM SIGMOD Workshop on The Web and Databases (WebDB'99), Philadelphia, Pennsylvania*, pages 25–30, June 1999.

13.22 A. Kemper and G. Moerkotte. Advanced Query Processing in Object Bases Using Access Support Relations. In *Proceedings of the Sixteenth International Conference on Very Large Databases, Brisbane, Australia*, pages 290–301. Morgan Kaufmann, August 1990.

13.23 W. Kim. On Optimizing an SQL-like Nested Query. *ACM Transactions on Database Systems*, 7(3):443–469, September 1982.

13.24 T. Lahiri, S. Abiteboul, and J. Widom. Ozone: Integrating Structured and Semistructured Data. In *7th International Workshop on Database Programming Languages, DBPL'99, Kinloch Rannoch, Scotland, UK*, LNCS 1949, pages 297–323. Springer, September 1999.

13.25 M. Muralikrishna. Improved Unnesting Algorithms for Join Aggregate SQL Queries. In *Proceedings if the Eighteenth International Conference on Very Large Data Bases, Vancouver, Canada*, pages 91–102, August 1992.

13.26 Z. Ozsoyoglu and J. Wang. A Keying Method for a Nested Relational Database Management System. In *Proceedings of the IEEE International Conference on Data Engineering, Tempe, Arizona*, pages 438–446, February 1992.

13.27 P. Selinger, M. Astrahan, D. Chamberlin, R. Lorie, and T. Price. Access Path Selection in a Relational Database Management System. In *Proceedings of the ACM SIGMOD International Conference on Management of Data, Boston, Massachusetts*, pages 23–34, May 1979.

13.28 J. Shanmugasundaram, K. Tufte, C. Zhang, G. He, D. DeWitt, and J. Naughton. Relational Databases for Querying XML Documents: Limitations and Opportunities. In *Proceedings of 25th International Conference on Very Large Data Bases (VLDB'99), Edinburgh, Scotland*, pages 302–314, 1999.

13.29 H. Steenhagen, P. Apers, and H. Blanken. Optimization of Nested Queries in a Complex Object Model. In M. Jarke, J. Bubenko, and K. Jeffery, editors, *Advances in Database Technology – EDBT '94*, LNCS 779, pages 337–350. Springer, 1994.

13.30 S. Thompson. *Haskell: The Craft of Functional Programming*. Addison-Wesley, 1998.

13.31 P. Wadler. Deforestation: Transforming Programs to Eliminate Trees. In *Proceedings of the 2nd European Symposium on Programming, Nancy, France*, LNCS 760, pages 344–358. Springer, 1988.

13.32 World Wide Web Consortium (W3C). *Extensible Markup Language (XML)*. http://www.w3.org/XML/

14. A Structural Approach to Query Language Design

Peter Buneman[1] and Val Tannen[2]

[1] School of Informatics, University of Edinburgh, Edinburgh EH8 9YL
email: opb@inf.ed.ac.uk
[2] Department of Computer and Information Science, University of
Pennsylvania, Philadelphia, PA 19104-6389, USA
email: val@cis.upenn.edu

Summary.

This chapter is motivated by the question "are there any clean mathematical principles behind the design of query languages?" One can hardly blame the reader of various recent standards for asking this question. The authors try to sketch what such a mathematical framework could be. One of the classifying principles they use extensively is that of languages being organised around type systems, with language primitives corresponding to constructors and deconstructors for each type. There is some value in casting the concepts in as general a form as possible; hence the use of the language of category theory for describing them. Once the semantic framework is discussed, the chapter presents a calculus, itself a language, that could be (and was) used as an internal representation for various user languages. The discussion is relevant to all kinds of data models: relational, object–relational, object–oriented, and semi-structured.

14.1 Introduction

This chapter is a partial survey of a body of work [14.4, 14.7, 14.2, 14.3, 14.28, 14.33, 14.15] by the authors and their colleagues Limsoon Wong, Shamim Naqvi, Susan Davidson, Dan Suciu, Gerd Hillebrand, Kazem Lellahi, Lucian Popa, and Alin Deutsch who should be also credited for the concepts described here. Any defects in the present exposition are entirely the responsibility of the authors.

The story is about how simple syntactic and semantic principles can guide the design and implementation of database query languages. These principles have provided foundations for object-oriented query languages and also for the recent wave of languages for XML and semi-structured data.

To start, we begin with the account given in textbooks of the connection between the relational algebra and relational calculus. Relational algebra, as its name indicates, consists of a few simple operations on tables together with a well-understood *equational theory* — rewriting rules that allow us to turn one relational algebra expression into a more efficient one. Together with techniques for efficient implementation of these operations, such as join algorithms and indexing, this technology was responsible for the success of relational database management systems. Relational calculus on the other hand provides a syntactic basis for query languages that exploit Zermelo–Fraenkel set notation, or *comprehensions* as they are known in functional programming languages.

The connection between relational algebra and calculus was developed for "flat" (first normal form) tables: sets of tuples whose components are all of atomic type — integer, string etc. Througout the late 1970s and 1980s there were numerous attempts to stretch this connection. On the practical side, SQL, which never adhered precisely to the semantics of relational algebra, was extended to deal with grouping, recursive queries and mixed bag/set semantics, but still remaining within the confines of a "flat" model in which the components of tuples are always atomic. On the theoretical side, there were attempts to find algebras for dealing with "non-flat" tables in which the entries in a tuple could be "complex" types such as tuples or other tables. All these extensions were needed for query languages for object-oriented databases, which supported both a variety of collection types (sets, bags and lists) and also required the implementation of non-flat structures. In fact, it is a principle of object-oriented databases that all types, sets, bags, lists and tuples may be freely intermixed.

To provide a précis of the story, we start with the observation that each of these types has a set of natural operations associated with it. For a record type, these operations are simply the constructor and the selectors, which are in some sense "inverse" operations. For the collection types the situation is more complicated. For the special case of sets, assume that a set is built up from singletons using unions. The natural inverse of this operation is *structural recursion*, which not only allows us to express operations such as powerset that lie outside what is expressible in normal database query languages, but also allows us to write down operations that are not well-defined. However, a simple instance of structural recursion gives us a language which, we claim, is the "right" generalisation of relational algebra to complex types. The reason for this claim is a conservativity result: take any expression in this language whose input and output are "flat" (i.e. first-normal-form) tables. Then this expression is equivalent to a relational algebra expression. That is, the language when restricted to relational tables expresses precisely the relational algebra.

While it is always good to have a theoretical justification for a language, the practical consequences are equally convincing. First, the connection with relational algebra is more than a theoretical nicety; one can use it to generalise the well-understood optimisation techniques for relational algebra to those for nested relations. Second, we have a framework in which we can investigate optmisation techniques for other collection types such as bags and lists. Finally, the robustness of the approach has carried over into the realm of query languages for XML and semi-structured data.

14.2 Impact

One of the early uses of these ideas was the development of a system for the integration of heterogenous information called Kleisli [14.5, 14.14]. Kleisli's original user interface was CPL, a novel query language built around collection comprehensions. The *internal language*, in which queries are represented for optimisation, decomposition, etc., is based on the constructs discussed in [14.4, 14.7]. K2 [14.21, 14.13] is a successor to Kleisli whose user interface is based on the ODMG standards[14.10] and whose internal language is based on [14.28] plus the dictionaries of [14.33, 14.15]. The same internal language is used in the Chase&Backchase query optimiser [14.15].

The practical importance of these languages was the ease and efficiency with which they could query *structured text*. It is often forgotten by database researchers that until recently, surprisingly little scientific data was held in relational databases. Much of it was held in pre-XML data formats. These formats vary from being completely generic, such as ASN.1, to being specific to one collection of data. However, they mostly adhered to a nested relational model and in some cases had type systems which, in the authors' opinion, suited their purpose very much better that the quasi type systems of XML. In bioinformatics, where there are literally hundreds of data sources held both in conventional (relational and object-oriented) database systems and in a wide variety of data formats, the need to integrate these sources was a natural application for these ideas, and it was in bioinformatics that they found commercial application.

The language OQL [14.10] is an adaptation to commercial imperatives, by committee, of the influential O2SQL [14.12] . It bears some syntactic resemblance to SQL, but is simpler and semantically much cleaner. Moreover, since it allows nesting, it cannot be given a semantics based on relational algebra, which is how one normally explains SQL. OQL corresponds almost exactly to a fragment of *comprehension syntax* — a surface syntax developed for the language based on the principles described here. The monad algebras described in this chapter provided a semantics for OQL, as well as an equational theory that led to optimization techniques. In fact, this is how K2 was implemented.

The early papers in this work were also the starting point for *monoid comprehensions* [14.17, 14.18]. These were obtained by further restrictions of the semantics and the addition of specific monoids to handle aggregates. The approach described in Section 14.6 of this chapter places this work in a more general and powerful setting.

At the same time, these concepts pointed to natural extensions of the language for handling a wider variety of types and semi-structured data. UnQL [14.2] was a very early query language for semi-structured data, developed on the same principles espoused in this chapter. It was influential in the design of XML-QL, which in turn influenced XQuery, and it was in some senses more expressive than its successors, especially in its model of transformations of semi-structured data. The connection between comprehension syntax and monads, which was the basis for the syntax of practical query languages based on the formalisms in this chapter, was first observed by Wadler [14.40] who investigated them in the context of functional languages, and it is encouraging to see that he has picked up this thread in his work on typing and and optimising XQuery.

14.3 A Preliminary Description of Tuple, Variant and Set Operations

In this section we examine how some simple principles can be used to extract the natural operations with the types that we commonly use in database work.

14.3.1 Records and Tuples

Database people are used to switching between a labelled record notation such as $\langle$Name : "Joe", Age : 21$\rangle$ and a positional tuple notation such as $\langle$"Joe", 21$\rangle$. The distinction is practically important, especially for type checking. However, for simplicity we shall start by using the positional notation and assure the reader that everything can be worked out for labelled records. Worse, we shall deal only with pairs (2-tuples) observing that a triple, for example, can be uncomfortably encoded as a pair whose first component is also a pair.

The syntactic form $\langle e_1, e_2 \rangle$ is known as a *constructor*, in this case a constructor for pairs. In functional languages such as ML one can "decompose" the result of a constructor with pattern matching:

let $\langle x_1, x_2 \rangle = e$ **in** e'

Here, the $\langle x_1, x_2 \rangle$ is a *pattern* which binds the variables x_1, x_2 to the two components of the pair denoted by e. These bindings may then be used in the evaluation of e'. This form of variable binding is equivalent to using patterns as function parameters, and we may rewrite this expression as $F(e)$ where F is the function defined by

$$F\langle x_1, x_2 \rangle = e'$$

So, for example, the "projection" function, π_1, that extracts the first component of a pair, can be expressed as $\pi_1\langle x_1, x_2 \rangle = x_1$. In writing this, we do not argue that a database language should allow us to define arbitrary functions; we simply want to indicate the connection between pattern matching and function abstraction.

It is often useful to think of the constructor for pairs as a function. To this end, we introduce the notation $\langle \cdot\, f_1, f_2\, \cdot \rangle$ with the property that

$$\langle \cdot f_1, f_2 \cdot \rangle(e) = \langle f_1(e), f_2(e) \rangle$$

Using this, $\langle \cdot \pi_2, \pi_1 \cdot \rangle$ is a function that interchanges the two components of a tuple. Also, using $\circ$ for the composition of functions [$(f_1 \circ f_2)(e) = f_1(f2(e))$], a function that extracts the first and third components of a 3-tuple (encoded as a pair whose first component is a pair) is $\langle \cdot \pi_1 \circ \pi_1, \pi_2 \cdot \rangle$. These operations, $\pi_1, \pi_2, \langle \cdot ., . \cdot \rangle, \circ, \mathsf{id}$, where id is the identity function satisfy certain equations, for example, $\langle \cdot \pi_1, \pi_2 \cdot \rangle = \mathsf{id}$, $\pi_1 \circ \langle \cdot f_1, f_2 \cdot \rangle = f_1$ and $\langle \cdot f_1, f_2 \cdot \rangle \circ g = \langle \cdot f_1 \circ g, f_2 \circ g \cdot \rangle$. This is something that we could call an algebra of functions over pairs and is the starting point for a database query language. In category theory it also describes *categories with finite products* (see, for example, [14.29]).

14.3.2 Variants

Variant (tagged union) types are also common in programming languages. By the type $\mathsf{Int} + \mathsf{String}$ we mean a type that is either an integer or a string. Associated with this type are the constructors ι_1 and ι_2 that create values of this type, for example $\iota_1(3), \iota_2("\mathsf{cat}")$. Variant types can be decomposed by pattern matching by writing case expressions such as

case e **of** $\iota_1(x_1) \Rightarrow e_1 \mid \iota_2(x_2) \Rightarrow e_2$

in which the variable x_1 may occur in e_1 and x_2 may occur in e_2. Examples of the use of this: **case** e **of** $\iota_1(x) \Rightarrow x \mid \iota_2(x) \Rightarrow 0$ and **case** e **of** $\iota_1(x) \Rightarrow$ "left" $\mid \iota_2(x) \Rightarrow$ "right".

Once again, pattern matching is related to functional abstraction, if (as in ML) we are allowed to define functions by cases:

$$F(\iota_1(x_1)) = e_1$$

$$\mid F(\iota_1(x_2)) = e_2$$

Note that the definition of F consists of two functions, one for the first injection and one for the second. We can write this decomposition function as $[\cdot f1, f2 \cdot]$, and we expect equations such as $[\cdot \iota_1, \iota_2 \cdot] = \mathsf{id}$, $[\cdot f_1, f_2 \cdot] \circ inl_1 = \mathsf{id}$ and $g \circ \langle \cdot f_1, f_2 \cdot \rangle = \langle \cdot g \circ f_1, g \circ f_2 \cdot \rangle$. There is an obvious symmetry between the functional descriptions of product and variant types which is fundamental to category theory.

Before discussing constructors for sets, we should make a couple of remarks. The first concerns types, which we have mostly swept under the carpet. To indicate what we have omitted, our discussion of pairs suggested, for example, that there is one first projection function π_1. But this is incorrect. In fact there is one first projection function at each pair type such as $\mathsf{Int} \times \mathsf{String}$; similarly for variant types. Moreover, in a practical database setting we would be better off using *labelled types* such as $\langle \mathsf{name} : \mathsf{String}, \mathsf{age} : \mathsf{Int} \rangle$ and $[\mathsf{shortUSZip} : \mathsf{Int}, \mathsf{longUSZip} : \langle \mathsf{first} : \mathsf{Int}, \mathsf{last} : \mathsf{Int} \rangle, \mathsf{other} : \mathsf{String}]$. The distinction between positional and labelled notation is not trivial. Labelled record and variant types allow us to define subtyping.

Our second remark concerns the use of union types which is typically absent from databases. In relational databases, everything occurs within sets, and we can use the natural isomorphism between $\mathsf{Set}\ (\alpha + \beta)$ and $\mathsf{Set}\ \alpha \times \mathsf{Set}\ \beta$ ($\mathsf{Set} \ldots$ means "set of") to eliminate unions in favour of products. This idea can be extended to labelled sums and products. This elimination can cause an explosion in the number of products, which can happen in practice and cause a "blow up" in the size of a relational schema. This isomorphism does *not* hold for lists, and it is unfortunate that variant types are not built in to object-oriented databases. They can, however, be unpleasantly "fudged" through the use of inheritance.

14.3.3 Sets

The point of the foregoing is to show how, starting from the constructor for pairs, we can obtain a simple but natural functional algebra for operations on pairs and variants. Can we do the same for sets and other collection types? First we have to ask what are the constructors for sets? One choice, but not the only choice, is the singleton set constructor $\{.\}$, the union operation, $. \cup .$, and — since we cannot obtain it from these operations — the empty set, $\{\}$.

Following the idea we pursued for tuples and variants, we consider functions defined by pattern matching on these constructors. Because we have several constructors for sets, we have to use pattern matching by cases, and because a set may be constructed through an arbitrary number of unions, the form of our "deconstructing" function is going to be recursive. The accepted term for such definitions is *structural recursion*. The general form of a function defined by structural recursion on the empty–singleton–union presentation of finite sets is:

$$F(\{\}) \qquad = e$$
$$F(\{x\}) \qquad = s(x)$$
$$F(S_1 \cup S_2) = u\ \langle F(S_1), F(S_2) \rangle$$

Note that the function F is determined by our choice of e, s and u. For example, taking

$$e \qquad = \mathit{false}$$
$$s(x) \qquad = \mathit{true}$$
$$u(x, y) = x \vee y$$

we obtain a function that tests whether a set is non-empty. Using

$$e \quad = \{\}$$

$$s(x) \quad = \{\langle a, x \rangle\}$$

$$u(x, y) = x \cup y$$

we obtain a function that pairs the value a with every member of a set. Assuming some means of giving this function a name (again, we omit details), we call this function pairwith$\langle a, T \rangle$, which pairs its first argument a with every member of its second argument, a set T. We can use this function in a further instantiation of (e, s, u):

$$e \quad = \{\}$$

$$s(x) \quad = \mathsf{pairwith}(x, T)$$

$$u(x, y) = x \cup y$$

giving us a function cartprod$\langle S, T \rangle$ that yields the cartesian product of its two arguments. Moreover, assuming a conditional[1], from

$$e \quad = \{\}$$

$$s(x) \quad = \text{if } \mathrm{p(x)} \text{ then } \{x\} \text{ else } \{\}$$

$$u(x, y) = x \cup y$$

we obtain a function that selects only members of a set that satisfy the predicate p.

From this we can see can see that we can implement selection, cartesian product and projection. Also, union is assumed to be present so that we have gone some distance to implementing the operations of the relational algebra through structural recursion.

We can go further and define a function unionpairs that takes the union of each member of a set of pairs:

$$e \quad = \{\}$$

$$s(x) \quad = \pi_1(x) \cup \pi_2(x)$$

$$u(y, z) = y \cup z$$

(The only reason for writing $\pi_1(x) \cup \pi_2(x)$ rather than $\cup(x)$ is that we take $\cup$ as an infix operation.)

From these we can define a further function by taking

---

[1] In fact, taking $\{\}$ for *false* and any non-empty set as *true*, there is a trick that uses cartesian product to implement selection without using a conditional.

$$e \quad = \{\{\}\}$$

$$s(x) \quad = \{\{x\}\}$$

$$u(y,z) = unionpairs(cartprod(y,z))$$

It is easy to check that this last function defines a powerset operation, which is decidedly not in the relational algebra for two reasons. First, the result – a set of sets – is not in first normal form, but second it expresses an operation that is not computable in polynomial time.

Structural recursion of this form therefore appears to be too powerful. But there is worse news in that it is also ill-defined. Consider the obvious attempt to count the members of set by taking

$$e \quad = 0$$

$$s(x) \quad = 1$$

$$u(y,z) = y + z$$

This looks innocuous, but consider the set $\{1, 2, 3\}$ constructed by $(\{1\} \cup \{2\}) \cup (\{2\} \cup \{3\})$. The obvious application of structural recursion counts the number of elements as four rather than three. On the other hand, if the set had been defined by $(\{1\} \cup \{2\}) \cup \{3\}$ we would have obtained the expected answer. Even worse behavior is to be found if we take u as some non-commutative operation. One way out of this dilemma is to insist that the operations (u, e) form an associative, commutative, idempotent monoid with e as a unit. However, it has been shown that checking this property is undecidable [14.8, 14.34]. Therefore we have to cast around for restrictions of structural recursion that will yield well-defined languages of the appropriate expressive power.

14.3.4 Towards Monads and Comprehensions

Looking at most of the instances of structural recursion above, we see that a common pattern is:

$$e \quad = \{\}$$

$$s(x) \quad = \ldots$$

$$u(y,z) = y \cup z$$

What this function does is the "flatmap" operation known to many functional programmers. Applied to a set $\{x_1, x_2, \ldots, x_n\}$ it yields $s(x_1) \cup s(x_2) \cup \ldots \cup S(x_n)$. Functions defined in this way are clearly well-defined — $(\cup, \{\})$ is an associative, commutative, idempotent monoid. Moreover all the functions we used in our partial construction of the relational algebra are instances of this limited form of structural recursion.

In defining such instances, the only choice we have is that of $s(x)$, which must produce a set. Given such an s we refer to the function it defines as $\mathsf{ext}(s)$ and note that the familiar map function that applies a function f to each member of a set $\{x_1, x_2, \ldots, x_n\}$ in order to produce $\{f(x_1), f(x_2), \ldots, f(x_n)\}$ can be defined as $\mathsf{ext}(\mathsf{sng} \circ f)$ where sng is the singleton producing function defined by $\mathsf{sng}(x) = \{X\}$.

The operations $\mathsf{ext}(s)$ and sng are well-known in category theory. A category with these operations and the appropriate equational theory is called a *monad*. Monads are rather general structures and indicate how this approach to defining database query languages may be extended to other collection types. But there is also an important observation due to Wadler [14.40] that the evaluation of comprehensions can be explained through the use of monads.

We agree with Trinder [14.37] that comprehensions are the "abstract syntax" of database query languages. We shall use the form:

$$\{e \mid x_1 \leftarrow e_1, \ldots, x_n \leftarrow e_n, C\}$$

For example,

$$\{\langle \mathsf{Name} = x.\mathsf{Name},\ \mathsf{Addr} = x.\mathsf{Addr} \rangle \mid x \leftarrow \mathsf{Employee},\ x.\mathsf{Age} > 50\}$$

$$\{\langle \pi_1(x),\ \pi_2(y) \rangle \mid x \leftarrow S,\ y \leftarrow T,\ \pi_2(x) = \pi_1(y)\}$$

The first of these uses labelled tuples and shows the tight connection between comprehension syntax and OQL. The second expresses the composition of binary relations (a join) and uses the positional syntax of tuples used in this chapter. In a comprehension, the variables $x_1 \ldots x_n$ are all distinct. Each variable is introduced by a *generator* of the comprehension, $x_i \leftarrow e_i$, and may be used in its *head*, e, and its *condition* C. Moreover variable x_i may be used in the right hand side of any "downstream" generator, $x_j \leftarrow e_j$, $i < j \leq n$.

Wadler's observation was the rewriting

$$\{e \mid x_1 \leftarrow e_1, \ldots x_n \leftarrow e_n, C\} = \mathsf{ext}(F)(e_1)$$

$$\text{where } F(x_1) = \{e \mid x_2 \leftarrow e_2, \ldots, x_n \leftarrow e_n, C\}$$

Together with

$$\{e \mid C\} = \text{if } C \text{ then } \mathsf{sng}(e) \text{ else } \{\}$$

we have a simple evaluator for comprehensions using the operators of a monad.

14.4 Collections as Adjunctions

When we generalise from sets, wishing to deal also with other collection types, we encounter some beautiful abstractions. These are best explained in the language of *category theory*.

Collections, in this treatment, are data types such as homogeneous finite sets, bags, lists and trees with data on the leaves[2]. We always have collections of one element — *singletons*. We denote by Coll X the set of finite collections of a certain kind made out of elements in X. Examples: Set X (but recall that we denote by $\{\alpha\}$ the type of finite sets of α's) Bag X and List X.

A bit more formally, an *algebraic*[3] *collection type* is a parametrised type that admits an inductive definition of the following form (in ML-like syntax):

```
datatype 'a Coll = sng of 'a |
                   opcoll of 'a Coll * ...* 'a Coll |
                   ...
```

with one or more finitary algebraic operations of various arities (including nullary) on collections as constructors (in addition to singleton). Moreover, the meaning of such types can be further constrained by equations between the algebraic constructors (otherwise we would never get sets or bags).

An interesting example is the *Boom hierarchy* of types (see for instance [14.20]). These types have two algebraic constructors, one nullary, one binary, in addition to the singleton:

```
datatype 'a Coll = sng of 'a |
                   empty |
                   comb of 'a Coll * 'a Coll
```

The hierarchy is obtained by imposing progressively richer sets of equational constraints. With no constraints we get binary trees. When empty is a unit for comb$(\cdot, \cdot)$ we get binary trees with no empty subtree, and call them *compact* binary trees. If we add to this the associativity of comb we get lists (built with append, not with cons). Further adding the commutativity of comb gives bags and we get sets by also adding the idempotence of comb. Notice that lists have a monoid structure; for bags the monoid is commutative and for sets it is moreover idempotent.

The semantics of algebraic collection types can be formalised with the help of *algebras for an endofunctor*. Fix a category, Base . In all our examples, Base is the category of sets and functions, but there seem to be no drawbacks and there may be advantages to seeking more generality. Let E be an endofunctor E : Base $\rightarrow$ Base . As usual, we denote the action of E on an arrow f by E f.

---

[2] A treatment of trees with data on the nodes would be useful too.

[3] This is to distinguish from other types that people often call "collection" or "bulk" types, for example relations, finite mappings, queues or arrays.

Definition 14.4.1. *An* E-*algebra is a pair* $(A, \text{op} : \text{E}\,A \to A)$. *An* E-*algebra homomorphism between* (A, op) *and* (B, op') *is an arrow* $h : A \to B$ *such that* $h \circ \text{op} = \text{op}' \circ (\text{E}\,h)$. *We denote by* E-Alg *the category of* E*-algebras and their homomorphisms.*

For the semantics of algebraic collection types we require that Base have finite (including nullary) products and we take $\text{E}\,X = X \times \cdots \times X$. Then $\text{op} : A \times \cdots \times A \to A$ is just a finitary algebraic operation on A. Several operations can be postulated simultaneously when Base has sums (coproducts). For instance, the structures in the Boom hierarchy are B-algebras where $\text{B}\,X = \text{unit} + X \times X$ (where unit is the nullary product — a *terminator*). Monoids and similar structures are B-algebras.

Let V_C be the class (variety) of E-algebras satisfying a given set Eq of equational constraints. For each X, the semantics of the algebraic collection type $\text{Coll}\,X$ determined by V_C is the algebra $(\text{Coll}\,X, \text{opcoll})$ satisfying C *freely generated* by X via singletons. That is, for any other algebra A in V_C, and for any arrow $f : X \to A$, there is a unique homomorphism $h : \text{Coll}\,X \to A$ such that $h \circ \text{sng}_X = f$ (the semantics is a left *adjoint* to the forgetful functor $\text{V}_C \to \text{Base}$). We say that h is defined by *structural recursion*. For instance, it is easy to see that Set X is the commutative idempotent monoid freely generated by X via singletons and what we call here "structural recursion" corresponds to the same as defined for sets in Section 14.3.3.

This adjunction semantics suggests an immediate approach to designing query languages for algebraic collection types: give syntax for structural recursion. This works well in the absence of equational constraints and it would amount to special cases of the recursion on inductive data types found in languages like ML. But it is cumbersome when we have equational constraints, because they need to be verified for the structural recursion construct to have meaning [14.8]. Equations like associativity and even idempotence are powerful enough to encode undecidable, even non-r.e. properties [14.8, 14.34]. A more subtle objection is that the adjunction semantics in itself does not suggest directly a purely equational theory, rather it offers an induction principle. This principle likely proves all the desired program equivalences, but this leaves the discovery of these equivalences to an ad hoc process.

Instead, what we can do is extract out of the adjunction semantics constructs that are always defined, and characterise their properties through equations, which leads easily and directly to optimisations. As we suggested in Section 14.3.4 and as developed in detail in [14.4, 14.7] such a programme leads us naturally to consider the monads associated with the adjunctions. A calculus was proposed in these papers, called the Nested Relational Calculus (NRC). Algebraic constructor operators such as empty set or binary set union were considered in NRC but their equational axiomatisation was ad hoc. Important expressiveness results concerning the sommation aggregate were obtained in [14.27, 14.26]. The treatment that follows, from [14.28], unifies these aspects. It models collections through monads, aggregates through *monad algebras* and algebraic constructor operations *and* conversions between collections through *enrichments*.

14.5 Collections as Monads

We begin with the most commonly used definition of monads (often called *triples* [14.9, 14.25]) using, however, a notation inspired by our domain of application: collections.

Definition 14.5.1 ([14.29]). *A* monad *on* Base *is given by a functor* Base $\to$ Base *, whose action on objects we denote by* $X \mapsto$ Coll X *and whose action on morphisms we denote, instead of the usual* Coll f*, by* $f : X \to Y \mapsto$ map $f :$ Coll $X \to$ Coll Y *and two natural transformations* $\text{sng}_X : X \to$ Coll X *and* $\text{flatten}_X :$ Coll Coll $X \to$ Coll X *such that:*

$$\text{flatten}_X \circ (\text{map sng}_X) = \text{id}_{\text{Coll } X} \tag{14.1}$$

$$\text{flatten}_X \circ \text{sng}_{\text{Coll } X} = \text{id}_{\text{Coll } X} \tag{14.2}$$

$$\text{flatten}_X \circ (\text{map flatten}_X) = \text{flatten}_X \circ \text{flatten}_{\text{Coll } X} \tag{14.3}$$

Examples. Coll X is the set of finite sets (bags, lists, compact binary trees, binary trees, ternary trees, "2–3" trees, etc.) with elements from X. sng builds a singleton set (bag etc.), map f applies f to each element of a set, and flatten is the union of a set of sets. We denote the first three of these monads by Set , Bag , and List .

For applications to the theory of programming languages, Moggi [14.31] has found more suitable a succinct definition of monads formalised by Manes [14.30] and inspired by Kleisli's work [14.22]:

Definition 14.5.2 ([14.30]). *A* (Kleisli) monad *on* Base *is given by a function mapping any object* X *of* Base *to an object* Coll X *also of* Base *, a family of morphism* $\text{sng}_X : X \to$ Coll X*, and the "extension" operation on arrows* $p : X \to$ Coll $Y \mapsto$ ext $p :$ Coll $X \to$ Coll Y *such that* $(p : X \to$ Coll $Y, q : Y \to$ Coll $Z)$*:*

$$\text{ext sng}_X = \text{id}_{\text{Coll } X} \tag{14.4}$$

$$(\text{ext } p) \circ \text{sng}_X = p \tag{14.5}$$

$$(\text{ext } q) \circ (\text{ext } p) = \text{ext } ((\text{ext } q) \circ p) \tag{14.6}$$

The two definitions are equivalent via the transformations

$$\text{map } f \mapsto \text{ext } (\text{sng}_Y \circ f) \tag{14.7}$$

$$\text{flatten}_X \mapsto \text{ext id}_{\text{Coll } X} \tag{14.8}$$

$$\text{ext } p \mapsto \text{flatten}_Y \circ (\text{map } p) \tag{14.9}$$

In particular, the functoriality of map and the naturality of sng and flatten are all derivable from the three axioms of the Kleisli–Manes succinct presentation.

It is precisely the extension operation ext that arises naturally in the work on query languages mentioned above [14.4, 14.7]. It is shown there that together with sng, empty set, set union, pairing, projections, conditional and equality (what we called the Nested Relational Calculus) the ext operation can express many useful database operations (some examples were shown in Section 14.3), in particular the relational and the nested relational algebra[4].

14.6 Aggregates as Monad Algebras

Aggregates are operations of the form agg : Coll $A \to A$ which compute an element of A out of each collection of elements of A. The aggregate of a singleton must of course equal its only element. Examples of aggregates that fit in our treatment are agg_{or}, agg_{and} : Set bool $\to$ bool and agg_{max}, agg_{min} : Set num $\to$ num for the Set data type, agg_{sum} : Bag num $\to$ num for Bag and $\text{agg}_{\text{concat}}$: List string $\to$ string for List . (For agg_{max} and agg_{min} to be defined on the empty set, we assume that num has a least element $-\infty$, and a greatest element $+\infty$.)

On the other hand, not all functions Coll$A \to A$ are aggregates. We explain below why the obvious function addup : Set num $\to$ num does not fit in our treatment. Query language designers, however, have long remarked that this function is less than useful. For instance, $\text{agg}_{\text{sum}} \circ \text{map} \ (\lambda x \,.\, 1)$ computes the cardinality of bags while addup $\circ$ map $(\lambda x \,.\, 1)$ is always 1. That's why in practical query languages such as SQL and OQL the default semantics is bags, while sets can be requested explicitly using "select unique".

For the formal treatment, let (Coll , map , sng, flatten) be a monad. The following is due to Eilenberg and Moore:

Definition 14.6.1 ([14.29]). *A* monad algebra *for the monad* Coll *is a* Coll *-algebra (definition 14.4.1)* $(A, \ \text{agg}_A : \text{Coll} \ A \to A)$ *such that*

$$\text{agg}_A \circ \text{sng}_A = \text{id}_A \tag{14.10}$$

$$\text{agg}_A \circ (\text{map} \ \text{agg}_A) = \text{agg}_A \circ \text{flatten}_A \tag{14.11}$$

A homomorphism *of monad algebras is just a homomorphism of* Coll*-algebras. We denote by* MonAlg *the category of monad algebras and their homomorphisms.*

Note. Tagging agg with A only is an abuse of notation since one may have two different monad algebra structures on the same object A of Base . This will be corrected in the calculus (Section 14.9) while here we try to keep a simple and intuitive notation. In the same spirit we will sometimes refer here to the entire monad algebra as A.

---

[4] These formalisms, as well as the calculus developed in Section 14.9, correspond in fact to *strong* monads [14.31]

An immediate remark is that from (14.2) and (14.3) it follows that flatten is a particular case of agg, that is $(\mathsf{Coll} X, \mathsf{flatten}_X)$ is a monad algebra. In fact, it turns out that the forgetful functor from MonAlg to Base has a left adjoint, with $(\mathsf{Coll}\ X, \mathsf{flatten}_X)$ being the free monad algebra generated by X (via $\mathsf{sng}_X : X \to \mathsf{Coll}\ X$). The monad canonically associated to this adjunction is Coll again. This property is precisely why monad algebras were introduced, by Eilenberg and Moore [14.16] who managed thus to show that any monad comes out of an adjunction.

Another useful remark is that (14.11) states that $\mathsf{agg}_A : \mathsf{Coll}\ A \to A$ itself is a homomorphism.

Examples. For the monad Set , the aggregate operations $\mathsf{agg}_{\mathsf{or}}, \mathsf{agg}_{\mathsf{and}}$: Set bool $\to$ bool and $\mathsf{agg}_{\mathsf{max}}, \mathsf{agg}_{\mathsf{min}}$: Set num $\to$ num form monad algebras [5]. A monad algebra for Bag is given by $\mathsf{agg}_{\mathsf{sum}}$: Bag num $\to$ num and a monad algebra for List is given by $\mathsf{agg}_{\mathsf{concat}}$: List string $\to$ string .

Note that disjunction, conjunction, max and min aggregation are also monad algebras for Bag and List and sum aggregation is also a monad algebra for List (we explore inter collection relationships in Section 14.11) but sum aggregation is *not* a monad algebra for Set . Indeed, (14.11) fails: if we apply the left hand side to $\{\{1, 2\}, \{1, 3\}\}$ we get 7 while the right hand side produces 6. We see that the problem comes from the fact that addition is not an idempotent operation while union is.

A Kleisli-style Definition for Monad Algebras. We have already remarked that flatten is an instance of agg. We generalise the extension operation ext that produces collections, hence elements of *free* monad algebras, to an "aggregate extension" operation that produces elements of an arbitrary monad algebra:

Definition 14.6.2. *A* (Kleisli-style) *monad algebra for the monad* Coll *consists of an object A of* Base *and an operation on arrows* $r : X \to A \quad \mapsto$ agext $r : \mathsf{Coll}\ X \to A$ *such that* $(p : W \to \mathsf{Coll}\ X)$:

$$(\mathsf{agext}\ r) \circ \mathsf{sng}_X = r \tag{14.12}$$

$$(\mathsf{agext}\ r) \circ (\mathsf{ext}\ p) = \mathsf{agext}\ ((\mathsf{agext}\ r) \circ p) \tag{14.13}$$

Similar to an earlier remark, it follows from (14.5,14.6) that $(\mathsf{Coll}\ Y, \mathsf{ext}\ )$ is a monad algebra, that is ext is a particular case of agext .

The two definitions of monad algebras are equivalent via transformations that generalise (14.8) and (14.9):

$$\mathsf{agg}_A \mapsto \mathsf{agext}\ \mathsf{id}_A \tag{14.14}$$

$$\mathsf{agext}\ r \mapsto \mathsf{agg}_A \circ (\mathsf{map}\ r) \tag{14.15}$$

Homomorphisms of monad algebras can also be characterised in terms of the Kleisli-style definition:

---

[5] Yes, lattices come to mind and this is not accidental, given the correspondence between commutative idempotent monoids and semi-lattices.

Proposition 14.6.1. $h : A \rightarrow B$ *is a homomorphism of monad algebras if and only if:*

$$h \circ (\mathsf{agext}\ r) = \mathsf{agext}\ (h \circ r) \qquad \forall r : X \rightarrow A \tag{14.16}$$

It follows that for any $r : X \rightarrow A$, $\mathsf{agext}\ r : \mathsf{Coll}X \rightarrow A$ is a homomorphism of monad algebras, by (14.13). In particular, $\mathsf{ext}\ p$, $\mathsf{map}\ f$, agg and $\mathsf{flatten}$ are also homomorphisms. Moreover, the agext construct is intimately connected to the Eilenberg–Moore result. Indeed, let $r : X \rightarrow A$, and let $h : \mathsf{Coll}\ X \rightarrow A$ be a homomorphism such that $h \circ \mathsf{sng}_X = r$. By (14.16), $h \circ (\mathsf{ext}\ \mathsf{sng}_X) = \mathsf{agext}\ (h \circ \mathsf{sng}_X)$ hence $h = \mathsf{agext}\ r$. Therefore:

Theorem 14.6.1 (The Eilenberg–Moore Adjunction). *For any monad algebra, for any* $r : X \rightarrow A$, $\mathsf{agext}\ r : \mathsf{Coll}\ X \rightarrow A$ *is the only homomorphism of monad algebras such that* $(\mathsf{agext}\ r) \circ \mathsf{sng}_X = r$.

14.7 Adding Products

It is quite standard to add records or tuples, and variants to the setting we have so far. For simplicity we focus just on tuples, hence on *product types*.

The typed calculus that we introduce in Section 14.9 has terms that can have several free variables. Relating such a calculus to its categorical semantics usually requires that Base have finite products, an assumption that we now make. For simplicity, we only introduce notation for binary products, denoted $X \times Y$. Denote by $\pi_1 : X \times Y \rightarrow X, \pi_2 : X \times Y \rightarrow Y$ the two corresponding projections, and by $\langle f, g \rangle : Z \rightarrow X \times Y$ the pairing of arrows $f : Z \rightarrow X, g : Z \rightarrow Y$. It is straightforward to extend everything (including the calculus) assuming also a nullary products, i.e. a terminator.

Now this extension provides us with an interesting opportunity for modeling "horizontal fusion" of aggregates. Indeed, it is known that the category MonAlg is "as complete as" Base ; more precisely, the forgetful functor from MonAlg to Base creates limits [14.9] p117. Therefore, MonAlg has finite products too, and the product of (A, agext_A) and (B, agext_B) is $(A \times B, \mathsf{agext}_{A \times B})$ where $(s : X \rightarrow A \times B)$:

$$\mathsf{agext}_{A \times B}\ s = \langle \mathsf{agext}_A\ (\pi_1 \circ s), \mathsf{agext}_B\ (\pi_2 \circ s) \rangle \tag{14.17}$$

Therefore, to "product-aggregate" a collection of pairs, project on each component and aggregate separately the resulting collections. By the way, there may be other interesting aggregates (monad algebra structures) that one can define on $A \times B$, but they are not the categorical product. We are interested in fact in using this the other way: fusing different agext's over the same collection into one product agext .

Note. Equation (14.17) is equivalent, in terms of the original definition of monad algebras, to

$$\mathsf{agg}_{A \times B} = \langle \mathsf{agg}_A \circ (\mathsf{map}\ \pi_1), \mathsf{agg}_B \circ (\mathsf{map}\ \pi_2) \rangle \tag{14.18}$$

It will be useful to observe that this equation is in turn equivalent to the conjunction of

$$\pi_1 \circ \mathsf{agg}_{A \times B} = \mathsf{agg}_A \circ (\mathsf{map}\ \pi_1) \tag{14.19}$$

$$\pi_2 \circ \mathsf{agg}_{A \times B} = \mathsf{agg}_B \circ (\mathsf{map}\ \pi_2) \tag{14.20}$$

which state that the two projections are homomorphisms of monad algebras.

14.8 Collection Constructors: Enriched Monads

The general theory of monads accounts explicitly only for the singleton collection constructor. We wish now to formalise the presence of constructor operations such as binary union of sets or nullary empty set as well as corresponding finitary algebraic operations on monad algebras, such as binary disjunction and nullary false on bool or binary addition and nullary 0 on num among others. Surprisingly, we have found that with a little extra generality we can treat finitary algebraic operations and *conversions* between collection types (see Section 14.11) in the same semantic framework[6].

Assume an endofunctor E : Base $\to$ Base and denote by E-Alg the category of E-algebras and their homomorphisms. Our first example is when Base has finite (possibly nullary) products and $\mathsf{E}\,X = X \times \cdots \times X$. Then, E-algebras $\mathsf{E}\,A \to A$ are just finitary algebraic operations on A. Our second example assumes that E is another monad and uses its monad algebras (which are, in particular, E-algebras).

We present *three different ways* to *enrich* a monad Coll and its monad algebras with structure related to the endofunctor E. These three definitions turn out to be equivalent (theorem 14.8.1) which suggests that they capture a rather robust concept.

In the **first** kind of enrichment, we postulate an additional E-algebra structure on each monad algebra for the monad Coll. There are several possibilities for the accompanying *coherence* conditions but they can also be shown to be equivalent:

Definition 14.8.1. *An* E-algebra enrichment *of the monad* Coll *(and its monad algebras) is an* E-algebra *structure* $(A, \mathsf{op}_A : \mathsf{E}\,A \to A)$ *on each monad algebra* (A, agg_A) *such that any one of the following equivalent (Proposition!) coherence conditions hold:*

(i) *Any homomorphism of monad algebras is also a homomorphism for the corresponding* E-algebra *structures. In other words, the correspondence* $\mathsf{agg}_A \mapsto \mathsf{op}_A$ *is a functor* MonAlg $\to$ E-Alg *that commutes with the underlying forgetful functors* MonAlg $\to$ Base *and* E-Alg $\to$ Base .

---

[6] Although, as we explain later, it is impractical to try to achieve the same generality in the calculus.

(ii) map f and agg_A are homomorphisms for the corresponding E-algebra structures.

(iii) For each $r : X \to A$, $\text{agext}_A\, r$ is a homomorphism for the corresponding E-algebra structures.

Notes. Condition (i) is equivalent to asking that op be a natural transformation from $\mathsf{E} \circ \mathsf{B}$ to B where B is the forgetful functor from monad algebras to Base. In (ii), asking that map f be a homomorphism is the same as asking that $\text{op}_{\mathsf{Coll}\, X}$ be a natural transformation from $\mathsf{E} \circ \mathsf{Coll}$ to Coll.

The third coherence condition is the one we will use for our calculus. Let us give a special name to the E-algebra structure on the free monad algebras: $\text{opcoll}_X \overset{\text{def}}{=} \text{op}_{\mathsf{Coll}\, X}$ (we shall reuse this name below in a different but equivalent definition of enrichment). With this, condition (iii) becomes

$$(\text{agext } r) \circ \text{opcoll}_X = \text{op}_A \circ (\mathsf{E}\,(\text{agext } r)) \quad \text{where } r : X \to A \qquad (14.21)$$

Products. Like MonAlg, and with the same construction (minus checking the monad algebra laws), E-Alg has finite products when Base has them. Interestingly, it *already* follows from the its definition that the E-algebra enrichment functor MonAlg $\to$ E-Alg preserves products on the nose. Indeed, we have remarked that the projections are homomorphisms for the monad algebra structures, hence also for the corresponding E-algebra structure, which entails

$$\text{op}_{A \times B} = \langle \text{op}_A \circ (\mathsf{E}\,\pi_1), \text{op}_B \circ (\mathsf{E}\,\pi_2)\rangle \qquad (14.22)$$

The **second** kind of enrichment we consider is enriching as above but only the free monad algebras (for us, the collection structures); that is, postulating only opcoll instead of op. This generalises Wadler's notion of *ringad* [14.43].

The **third** kind of enrichment was considered in [14.23, 14.24] and it consists simply of a natural transformation $\text{tconv}_X : \mathsf{E}\,X \to \mathsf{Coll}\, X$. The intuition comes from our primary example: $\mathsf{E}\,X = X \times \cdots \times X$. In this case $\text{tconv}(x_1, \ldots, x_n)$ is the collection built out of the elements of the tuple $(x_1, \ldots, x_n)$ (e.g. if the monad is Set the ordering and the duplicates are lost).

We present the equivalence between the three kinds of enrichments in a slightly more general context, in which we postulate not only algebraic operations but also possible laws that such operations may obey (for instance, we may enrich Set monad algebras with commutative idempotent monoid structures). The intention again is to convince that the notions of enrichment we consider are quite robust. Such laws could be added to the equational theory of the calculus in Section 14.9, in conjunction with specifying particular collection types, such as Set.

Definition 14.8.2. An enriching variety *(for lack of a better name!) is a class $\mathcal{EV}$ of E-algebras that is closed under the following property: for any* *homomorphism of* E-*algebras* $h : A \to B$ *that has a right inverse in* Base *,* $h \circ g = \mathrm{id}_B$[7]*, if* A *is in* $\mathcal{EV}$ *then* B *is also in* $\mathcal{EV}$.

This is not an unfamiliar condition. Algebraic collection types (Section 14.4) arise in equationally defined varieties of algebraic structures and all such varieties have this property[8]. In addition, it is straightforward to verify the following (another robustness check, which will be useful in Section 14.11):

Proposition 14.8.1. *If* E *is a monad, then the class of* E-*algebras which are monad algebras is an enriching variety.*

The three enrichment definitions are equivalent:

Theorem 14.8.1. *Fix a monad and its monad algebras (notation as above). Let* $\mathcal{EV}$ *be an enriching variety (definition 14.8.2). The following three notions of* $\mathcal{EV}$-*enrichment are equivalent:*

(i) *An* E-*algebra enrichment (see definition 14.8.1) such that each* E-*algebra* (A, op_A) *belongs to* $\mathcal{EV}$.
(ii) *An* E-*algebra structure* $(\mathrm{Coll}\ X,\ \mathrm{opcoll}_X : \mathrm{E\,Coll}\ X \to \mathrm{Coll}\ X)$ *on each free monad algebra, belonging to* $\mathcal{EV}$ *and such that* map f *and* flatten *are homomorphisms of* E-*algebras (*map f *is a homomorphism also means that* opcoll_X *is a natural transformation).*
(iii) *A family of arrows* $\mathrm{tconv}_X : \mathrm{E}\,X \to \mathrm{Coll}\ X$ *which is a natural transformation, that is*

$$(\mathrm{map}\ f) \circ \mathrm{tconv}_X = \mathrm{tconv}_Y \circ (\mathrm{E}\,f) \qquad where \qquad f : X \to Y$$

and such that all E-*algebras of the form* $(\mathrm{Coll}\ X, \mathrm{flatten}_X \circ \mathrm{tconv}_{\mathrm{Coll}\ X})$ *belong to* $\mathcal{EV}$.

We omit the proof but we spell out the translations between different kinds of enrichments:

$$\mathrm{opcoll}_X \overset{\mathrm{def}}{=} \mathrm{op}_{\mathrm{Coll}\ X} \tag{14.23}$$

$$\mathrm{tconv}_X \overset{\mathrm{def}}{=} \mathrm{opcoll}_X \circ (\mathrm{E}\,\mathrm{sng}_X) \tag{14.24}$$

$$\mathrm{op}_A \overset{\mathrm{def}}{=} \mathrm{agg}_A \circ \mathrm{tconv}_A \tag{14.25}$$

14.9 The Calculus

Using the concept of enriched monad and its monad algebras as semantic foundation, we develop in this section a calculus of operations for *one* collection type and its aggregates. This calculus extends the NRC except for the

---

[7] Such an h is often called a *retract* or a *split epi*.
[8] In fact, this allows us to avoid the explicit use of coequalizers, which otherwise play a central role for monads, as Beck's theorem shows [14.29, 14.9].

conditional and equality, which can be easily added. Extensions to multiple collections and product aggregates are developed in Sections 14.11 and 14.7.

In the calculus we wish to avoid explicit higher-order functions, so all the expressions will denote "elements" of the objects of Base . This is in the spirit of [14.31, 14.7] and also of practical query languages. Expressions will have free variables, however, and we can bind variables in the principal construct (that corresponds to aggregate extension), so at least the intensional effect of functions as arguments is achieved.

This is a typed calculus and the types, in turn, are of two kinds, Base and MonAlg . We have *type constants* for each kind, such as or, and, max : MonAlg and bool , num : Base . We have the following constructions on types:

$$\frac{\sigma \; : \; \mathsf{Base}}{\mathsf{Coll}\,\sigma \; : \; \mathsf{Base}} \qquad\qquad \frac{\sigma \; : \; \mathsf{Base}}{\mathsf{W}\,\sigma \; : \; \mathsf{MonAlg}}$$

$$\frac{\sigma_1 : \mathsf{Base} \qquad \sigma_2 : \mathsf{Base}}{\sigma_1 \times \sigma_2 : \mathsf{Base}} \qquad\qquad \frac{\alpha_1 : \mathsf{MonAlg} \qquad \alpha_2 : \mathsf{MonAlg}}{\alpha_1 \times \alpha_2 : \mathsf{MonAlg}}$$

In order to state the typing rules, we *define* an auxiliary meta-function B from MonAlg to Base : $\mathsf{B}\,(\mathsf{W}\,\sigma) \stackrel{\mathrm{def}}{=} \mathsf{Coll}\,\sigma$, $\mathsf{B}\,(\alpha_1 \times \alpha_2) = \mathsf{B}\,\alpha_1 \times \mathsf{B}\,\alpha_2$ and, depending on the semantics, links between the MonAlg type constants and the Base type constants, for instance B or $=$ bool , B and $=$ bool or B max $=$ num .

The terms of the calculus are introduced together with their typing rules in Figure 14.1. We omit the explanation of the (standard) syntax for typing rules. By convention, $\sigma :$ Base and $\alpha :$ MonAlg . Note that the variables only range over Base types. Note also that in $\Theta_\alpha x \in e_1 . e_2$, x is a bound variable whose scope is e_2 (but *not* e_1). The usual conventions about bound variables apply.

The equational axioms are in Figure 14.2. The following abbreviations are used in the axioms:

$$\Theta\,x \in S . R \stackrel{\mathrm{def}}{=} \Theta_{\mathsf{W}\tau} x \in S . R \qquad\qquad \mathsf{opcoll}(S_1, \ldots, S_m) \stackrel{\mathrm{def}}{=} \mathsf{op}_{\mathsf{W}\sigma}(S_1, \ldots, S_m)$$

It is worth writing down the calculus version of (14.22):

$$\mathsf{op}_{\alpha_1 \times \alpha_2}((e_{11}, e_{21}), \ldots, (e_{1m}, e_{2m})) = (\mathsf{op}_{\alpha_1}(e_{11}, \ldots, e_{1m}), \mathsf{op}_{\alpha_2}(e_{21}, \ldots, e_{2m}))$$

and noting that, just as (14.22) holds in the enriched monad formalisation, this equation follows from the axioms in Figure 14.9.

One can give a formal semantics for this calculus in terms of the categorical constructs presented in Sections 14.5 and 14.8, along the lines of [14.31] or of [14.7], provided that Coll is a *strong* monad. This is well understood so we

$$\frac{}{\Gamma, x : \sigma \vdash x : \sigma} \qquad\qquad \frac{\Gamma \vdash e : \sigma}{\Gamma \vdash \mathsf{sng}(e) : \mathsf{Coll}\,\sigma}$$

$$\frac{\Gamma, x : \sigma \vdash e : \mathsf{B}\,\alpha \quad \Gamma \vdash S : \mathsf{Coll}\,\sigma}{\Gamma \vdash \Theta_\alpha x \in S . e : \mathsf{B}\,\alpha} \qquad\qquad \frac{\Gamma \vdash e_1, \ldots, e_m : \mathsf{B}\,\alpha}{\Gamma \vdash \mathsf{op}_\alpha(e_1, \ldots, e_m) : \mathsf{B}\,\alpha}$$

$$\frac{\Gamma \vdash e_1 : \sigma_1 \quad \Gamma \vdash e_2 : \sigma_2}{\Gamma \vdash (e_1, e_2) : \sigma_1 \times \sigma_2} \qquad\qquad \frac{\Gamma \vdash e : \sigma_1 \times \sigma_2}{\Gamma \vdash \pi_1 e : \sigma_1 \quad \Gamma \vdash \pi_2 e : \sigma_2}$$

Fig. 14.1. Typing rules.

omit the development. Not to lose sight of the intuition, we note that if **Base** is sets and functions then (confusing syntax and semantics for a moment):

$$\Theta_\alpha x \in S . e = (\mathsf{agext}\ (\lambda x.e)) S$$

where **agext** corresponds to the monad algebra denoted by α.

We also explain briefly the choice of syntax for representing enrichments (Section 14.8) in the calculus. The problem is that it is not clear how to express "elements" of type $\mathsf{E}\,X$ when E is an arbitrary endofunctor. So for the one-monad calculus presented in this section we have decided to consider only the particular case when the enrichments are finitary algebraic operations. We also consider without loss of generality only one algebraic operation, since for several operations the enrichments functor can be simply defined as a sum and the various laws can be just added up. In Section 14.11 we consider multiple monads and conversion enrichments, for whose calculus we provide a different kind of syntax. Finally, we have seen in theorem 14.8.1 that the enrichments of the free algebras can actually define the enrichments on any monad algebras. This seems to encumber the notation, however, so we found it more useful for understanding optimisations to postulate constructs and axioms for enrichments of arbitrary monad algebras.

We should also explain tagging the terms with types. Polymorphism and type inference for such calculi is an interesting topic but it is not addressed in this chapter. Instead, our goal is to provide just enough type annotation so that typable terms have unique types (and unique type derivations), modulo the simple equational constraints that link type constants. Hence the type tag in $\Theta_\alpha x \in S . e$. Notice, however, that we didn't tag the construct with σ, because it can be derived from the type of S. Similarly, when $\alpha = \mathsf{W}\,\tau$, we do not need to tag the construct at all because τ can be derived from the type of e. Similarly also for **opcoll** (except when $m = 0$!).

(proj$_i$)	$\pi_i(e_1, e_2) = e_i$
(surjprod)	$(\pi_1 e, \pi_2 e) = e$
(sng)	$\Theta\, x \in S \,.\, \mathsf{sng}(x) = S$
(β)	$\Theta_\alpha x \in \mathsf{sng}(e) \,.\, e' = e'[e/x]$
(assoc)	$\Theta_\alpha x \in (\Theta\, y \in R \,.\, S) \,.\, e = \Theta_\alpha y \in R \,.\, (\Theta_\alpha x \in S \,.\, e)$
(hom)	$\Theta_\alpha x \in \mathsf{opcoll}(S_1, \ldots, S_m) \,.\, e = \mathsf{op}_\alpha(\Theta_\alpha x \in S_1 \,.\, e, \ldots, \Theta_\alpha x \in S_m \,.\, e)$
(aggprod)	$\Theta_{\alpha_1 \times \alpha_2} x \in S \,.\, e = (\Theta_{\alpha_1} x \in S \,.\, \pi_1 e, \Theta_{\alpha_2} x \in S \,.\, \pi_2 e)$

Fig. 14.2. Axioms.

We emphasize that this calculus is not a presentation of *all* the monad algebras for Coll , just of the free ones and as many additional ones as we postulate through type constants. Indeed, including a mechanism for "user-defined" or "programmed" aggregates runs into the same problems as user-defined structural recursion on algebraic collection types with equational constraints [14.8, 14.34]: checking the axioms is undecidable, not even r.e.[9]

Finally, we point out that the equational laws shown above are true for any enriched monad, in particular for any data type defined by an algebraic signature and an equational axiomatisation. In databases the primary examples of collection types are sets, bags and lists. As we pointed out in Section 14.4 these have two algebraic constructors, a nullary and a binary operation, and we can instantiate the law (hom) for each of them. However, these specific collection types satisfy additional, special, laws [14.33] that are very important for query optimisation. To state them we introduce the notation null$_\alpha$ for the nullary operation on the (set-, bag- or list-)monad algebra α. Examples of null$_\alpha$ are the empty list, bag or set, boolean true or false, 0,

---

[9] This kind of extensibility may well be desirable, and could be present in practical languages (in fact, why not user-defined collection types?). But programmers must use it at their own risks: if the structure they programmed is not an aggregate or not a collection type then the optimiser may make mathematically invalid transformations.

the empty string, etc. We also introduce the notation ($\_ \bullet_\alpha \_$) for the binary operation on the (set-, bag- or list-)monad algebra α. Examples are set or bag union, list concatenation, boolean conjunction or disjunction, addition, string juxtaposition, etc.

The following law holds for any of the set, bag or list monads and for any of their algebras α (but fails for certain tree monads):

$$\text{(null)} \quad \Theta_\alpha x \in S . \mathsf{null}_\alpha = \mathsf{null}_\alpha$$

In addition, sets and bags satisfy two laws related to commutativity:

$$\text{(commute)} \quad \Theta_\alpha x \in R . \Theta_\alpha y \in S . e = \Theta_\alpha y \in S . \Theta_\alpha x \in R . e$$

$$\text{(bin)} \qquad \Theta_\alpha x \in S . (e_1 \bullet_\alpha e_2) = (\Theta_\alpha x \in S . e_1 \bullet_\alpha \Theta_\alpha x \in S . e_2)$$

where α is any algebra for the set monad or for the bag monad. It is not hard to see that these laws fail for the list monad.

Finally, the set monad satisfies a remarkable law related to the idempotence property of set union (for this law we shall also need a conditional, but adding it to the calculus is straightforward):

$$\text{(idemloop)} \quad \Theta_\alpha x \in S . \underline{\text{if }} b \underline{\text{ then }} e \underline{\text{ else }} \mathsf{null}_\alpha = \underline{\text{if }} \exists x \in S . b \underline{\text{ then }} e \underline{\text{ else }} \mathsf{null}_\alpha$$

where α is any algebra for the set monad and where x *may occur in b but not in e*. It is shown in [14.33] that (idemloop) is the core reason for the validity of the *chase* transformation on certain classes of queries. In general, when a distinction is being made in query manipulation between "set semantics" and "bag semantics", it is a good bet that the distinction can be traced to the (idemloop) law.

14.10 The Equational Laws Support Optimisations

We make this point mainly through examples. Consider the bag monad. To make the notation more suggestive, write $\uplus x \in S . R$ instead of $\Theta x \in S . R$.

Consider the type constants num : Base , sum : MonAlg with B sum $=$ num . Write $\sum x \in S \, . \, e$ instead of $\Theta_{\text{sum}} x \in S \, . \, e$. As is the case for all the collection types in the Boom hierarchy, the bag monad and its algebras can be enriched with two algebraic operations, one binary (ignored in these examples), and one nullary. Write empty for the nullary opcoll abbreviation and 0 for the nullary op$_{\text{sum}}$[10].

First we use a concrete query to show that (assoc) generalises the idea of *vertical loop fusion* [14.42]. Let B be a bag of pairs of numbers and suppose that we want the sum of all the first components of the pairs in the bag whose second components satisfy a given predicate $P(\cdot)$. An efficient answer to this problem is of course the expression $\sum z \in B \, . \, \underline{\text{if}} \, P(\pi_2 z) \, \underline{\text{then}} \, \pi_1 z \, \underline{\text{else}} \, 0$. But a more "modular" mind may well think as follows: first select the pairs whose second component satisfies the predicate, producing a bag B', and then add up the first components of the pairs in B':

$$\sum x \in (\uplus y \in B \, . \, \underline{\text{if}} \, P(\pi_2 y) \, \underline{\text{then}} \, \text{sng}(y) \, \underline{\text{else}} \, \text{empty}) \, . \, \pi_1 x$$

By applying the (assoc) axiom we obtain

$$\sum y \in B \, . \, \sum x \in \underline{\text{if}} \, P(\pi_2 y) \, \underline{\text{then}} \, \text{sng}(y) \, \underline{\text{else}} \, \text{empty} \, . \, \pi_1 x$$

After a standard transformation for conditionals:

$$\sum y \in B \, . \, \underline{\text{if}} \, P(\pi_2 y) \, \underline{\text{then}} \, \sum x \in \text{sng}(y) \, . \, \pi_1 x \, \underline{\text{else}} \, \sum x \in \text{empty} \, . \, \pi_1 x$$

Then, by (β) and (hom) we obtain

$$\sum y \in B \, . \, \underline{\text{if}} \, P(\pi_2 y) \, \underline{\text{then}} \, \pi_1 y \, \underline{\text{else}} \, 0$$

which is the desired efficient answer mentioned earlier.

Our second example shows that (aggprod) realises a form of *horizontal loop fusion*, quite a bit more general than that considered in [14.42]. Suppose we wish to compute the average of a bag of numbers. The immediate answer is

$$\text{div} \left(\sum x \in B \, . \, x, \sum x \in B \, . \, 1 \right)$$

A naive implementation would traverse B twice. If access to B is expensive, we are better off applying (aggprod) which produces

$$\text{div} \, \Theta_{\text{sum} \times \text{sum}} x \in B \, . \, (x, 1)$$

To make this truly useful in practice, one may have to detect, using a common subexpression algorithm, loops that iterate over the same collection in different positions in an expression and replace them with projections from the result of a product aggregate. While we can certainly do horizontal fusion without justifying it with products of monad algebras (!), the value of this formalisation lies in being able to mix this optimisation together with others, all based on rewriting modulo a uniform equational theory.

---

[10] We should have tagged empty with a type, but for these examples, the type is easily inferred from the mathematical context.

The equational laws we gave in Section 14.9 (including the special ones that hold only for sets and/or bags, and/or lists) validate not just vertical and horizontal loop fusion but in fact almost the entire variety of algebraic query optimisation transformations proposed in the literature. These transformations include the standard relational algebraic ones, such as selection and projection pushing or join reordering (which makes essential use of (commute)). It is shown in [14.33] that tableau minimisation and many semantic optimisation transformations are also validated (essentially with (idemloop)). These laws also validate the optimisations discussed in [14.35, 14.36, 14.11, 14.12, 14.17, 14.18] and in the very comprehensive work by Beeri and Kornatzky [14.6].

Interestingly, the equational characterisations of query lanaguages for nested data also provide the key to a nice proof that NRC is conservative over the relational algebra [14.41].

14.11 Multiple Collections and Conversion Enrichments

Query languages are seldom based on only one collection type. SQL works with both bags and sets, while object-oriented query languages can in addition manipulate lists. Moreover, these languages use explicit or implicit conversions from lists to bags (ordering removal) and from bags to sets (duplicate removal)[11].

We shall see that such conversions also behave like enrichments, although in this case we enrich a monad (and its algebras) with monad algebra structures corresponding to another monad! When we put the two monads together, the axioms satisfied by the conversions provide nice compatibility conditions between the corresponding constructs of the monads.

Moreover, each monad (sets, bags, etc.) is separately enriched by finitary algebraic operations. We look at the situation when these enrichments are compatible with each other modulo the conversions.

Definition 14.11.1 ([14.9]). *Let* Coll^1 *and* Coll^2 *be two monads on the same category* Base *(rest of the notation as in Section 14.5, with corresponding superscript 1 or 2). A* morphism of monads *is a family of arrows* $\mathsf{conv}_X :$ $\mathsf{Coll}^1 X \to \mathsf{Coll}^2 X$ *such that* $(f : X \to Y)$:

$$(\mathsf{map}^2 f) \circ \mathsf{conv}_X = \mathsf{conv}_Y \circ (\mathsf{map}^1 f) \qquad (14.26)$$

$$\mathsf{conv}_X \circ \mathsf{sng}^1_X = \mathsf{sng}^2_X \qquad (14.27)$$

$$\mathsf{conv}_X \circ \mathsf{flatten}^1_X = \mathsf{flatten}^2_X \circ (\mathsf{map}^2 \, \mathsf{conv}_X) \circ \mathsf{conv}_{\mathsf{Coll}^1 \, X} \qquad (14.28)$$

The first condition says that conv is a natural transformation and the third condition is clear when we notice that $(\mathsf{map}^2 \, \mathsf{conv}_X) \circ \mathsf{conv}_{\mathsf{Coll}^1 \, X}$ (by

---

[11] See the SQL and OQL "select unique" constructs.

naturality, the same as $\mathsf{conv}_{\mathsf{Coll}^2\,X} \circ (\mathsf{map}^1\,\mathsf{conv}_X))$ is the horizontal composition of conv with itself [14.29].

In the spirit of the succinct presentations of Section 14.5 and keeping in mind the intended formalisation for the calculus, we remark that (14.26) and (14.28) can be replaced by a single axiom $(p : X \to \mathsf{Coll}^1\,Y)$:

$$(\mathsf{ext}^2\,(\mathsf{conv}_Y \circ p)) \circ \mathsf{conv}_X = \mathsf{conv}_Y \circ (\mathsf{ext}^1\,p) \tag{14.29}$$

Proposition 14.11.1. *A natural transformation $\mathsf{Coll}^1 \to \mathsf{Coll}^2$ gives a MonAlg^1 -enrichment (as defined in theorem 14.8.1) of Coll^2 if and only if it is a morphism of monads.*

Now all the development in the proof of theorem 14.8.1 applies here. Given a monad algebra for Coll^2, $\mathsf{agg}_A^2 : \mathsf{Coll}^2\,A \to A$, we obtain a monad algebra for Coll^1 on the same Base object A: $\mathsf{agg}_A^1 \stackrel{\mathrm{def}}{=} \mathsf{agg}_A^2 \circ \mathsf{conv}_A : \mathsf{Coll}^1\,A \to A$, whose corresponding aggregate extension operation can be defined as $\mathsf{agext}^1\,r \stackrel{\mathrm{def}}{=} \mathsf{agext}^2 \circ \mathsf{conv}_X$.

Suppose now that we have an enriching variety $\mathcal{EV}$, an $\mathcal{EV}$-enrichment of Coll^1, $\mathsf{tconv}_X^1 : \mathsf{E}\,X \to \mathsf{Coll}^1\,X$, and a morphism of monads from Coll^1 to Coll^2, $\mathsf{conv}_X : \mathsf{Coll}^1\,X \to \mathsf{Coll}^2\,X$. It follows from theorem 14.8.1 that these two enrichments *compose*, yielding an $\mathcal{EV}$-enrichment of Coll^2, $\mathsf{tconv}_X^2 \stackrel{\mathrm{def}}{=} \mathsf{conv}_X \circ \mathsf{tconv}_X^1 : \mathsf{E}\,X \to \mathsf{Coll}^2\,X$. We shall assume that this is indeed the $\mathcal{EV}$-enrichment that we desire, as is the case, for instance, with the conversions from lists to bags, or from bags to sets. If (A, agg_A^2) is monad algebra for Coll^2 we can derive two E-algebra structures on the object A of Base : $\mathsf{op}_A^2 \stackrel{\mathrm{def}}{=} \mathsf{agg}_A^2 \circ \mathsf{tconv}_A^2$ corresponding to the Coll^2 monad algebra structure and $\mathsf{op}_A^1 \stackrel{\mathrm{def}}{=} \mathsf{agg}_A^1 \circ \mathsf{tconv}_A^1$ corresponding to the Coll^1 monad algebra structure $\mathsf{agg}_A^1 \stackrel{\mathrm{def}}{=} \mathsf{agg}_A^2 \circ \mathsf{conv}_A$. But $\mathsf{tconv}_X^2 = \mathsf{conv}_X \circ \mathsf{tconv}_X^1$ ensures that these are the same. Looking to extend our calculus, we will have to axiomatise this situation in terms of $\mathsf{opcoll}_X^1 : \mathsf{E}\,\mathsf{Coll}^1\,X \to \mathsf{Coll}^1\,X$ rather than in terms of tconv^1. Of course, opcoll^2 is expressible in terms of opcoll^1, but at the price of some lack of elegance:

$$\mathsf{opcoll}_X^2 \stackrel{\mathrm{def}}{=} \mathsf{flatten}_X^2 \circ \mathsf{conv}_{\mathsf{Coll}^2\,X} \circ \mathsf{opcoll}_{\mathsf{Coll}^2\,X}^1 \circ (\mathsf{E}\,\mathsf{sng}_{\mathsf{Coll}^2\,X}^1)$$

So we prefer to postulate both opcoll^2 and opcoll^1, and link them by observing that

$$\mathsf{conv}_X \circ \mathsf{tconv}_X^1 = \mathsf{tconv}_X^2 \quad \longleftrightarrow \quad \mathsf{conv}_X \circ \mathsf{opcoll}_X^1 = \mathsf{opcoll}_X^2 \circ (\mathsf{E}\,\mathsf{conv}_X)$$

To build a calculus for multiple collections, we put together the calculi for Coll^1 and Coll^2 as defined in Section 14.9 (keeping the same Base) and we add one term construct:

$$\frac{\sigma : \mathsf{Base} \qquad S : \mathsf{Coll}^1\,\sigma}{\mathsf{conv}(S) : \mathsf{Coll}^2\,\sigma}$$

as well as three new axioms, see Figure 14.3.

$$\mathsf{conv}(\mathsf{sng}^1(x)) = \mathsf{sng}^2(x)$$

$$\mathsf{conv}(\Theta^1\, x \in S\,.\,R) = \Theta^2\, x \in \mathsf{conv}(S)\,.\,\mathsf{conv}(R)$$

$$\mathsf{conv}(\mathsf{opcoll}^1(S_1,\ldots,S_m)) = \mathsf{opcoll}^2(\mathsf{conv}(S_1),\ldots,\mathsf{conv}(S_m))$$

Fig. 14.3. Conversion axioms.

According to the preceding discussion, the calculus behaves *as if* we had a new type construct that associates to each $\alpha : \mathsf{MonAlg}^2$ a $\mathsf{conv}(\alpha) : \mathsf{MonAlg}^1$ such that $\mathsf{B}^1\mathsf{conv}(\alpha) = \mathsf{B}^2\alpha$. But we do not need to add such a construct because the corresponding aggregate extension and algebraic enrichment operations are already definable, as we saw:

$$\Theta^1_{\mathsf{conv}(\alpha)}x \in S\,.\,e \overset{\mathrm{def}}{=} \Theta^2_{\alpha}x \in \mathsf{conv}(S)\,.\,e$$

and

$$\mathsf{op}^1_{\mathsf{conv}(\alpha)}(e_1,\ldots,e_m) \overset{\mathrm{def}}{=} \mathsf{op}^2_{\alpha}(e_1,\ldots,e_m)$$

However, during calculations it will be useful to keep these abbreviations in mind, knowing that the fact that they satisfy the axioms of the calculus as if they were among its primitives is provable from the axioms already given.

14.12 Object-Oriented Classes as Dictionaries

Dictionaries are just finite functions. It is customary to call the arguments of dictionaries "keys" and their values "entries". We add the basic operations for dictionaries to our calculus. We denote by $\sigma \gg \tau$ the type of dictionaries with keys of type σ and entries of type τ. We use the notation $\underline{\mathsf{dom}}\, M$ for the set of keys (the *domain*) of the dictionary M and the notation $K\,!\,M$ for the entry of M corresponding to the key K (the *lookup* operation). The lookup operation *fails* unless K is in $\underline{\mathsf{dom}}\, M$. When the entries of the dictionary have set, bag or list type, we often want to use a "non-failing" version of lookup which returns the empty set/bag/list for keys that are not in the domain.

Consider the following object-oriented schema consisting of a relation and a class expressed in ODL, the schema specification language of ODMG [14.10].

```
Proj : set<struct{              class Dept
   string PName;                   (extent depts){
   string CustName;                  attribute string DName;
   string PDept;}>                   attribute set<string> DProjs
                                     attribute string MgrName;}
```

We can model object-oriented classes with extents using dictionaries whose keys are the oids [14.28, 14.33, 14.15]. To maintain the abstract properties of oids we do not make any assumptions about their nature and we invent fresh new base types for them. Let us assume that Doid is the type of oids for the Dept class. Then, the type specifications of the schema above translate as

Proj : Set $\langle$ PName : string , CustName : string , PDept : string $\rangle$

Dept : Doid $\times\!\!>$ $\langle$ DName : string , DProjs : Set string , MgrName : string $\rangle$

When we translate queries into our calculus the extents become the domains of the dictionaries and the implicit oid dereferencing in OQL is translated by a lookup in the dictionary. For example, depts d and d.DProjs s become $d \in \underline{\text{dom}}\,\text{Dept}$ and $s \in d\,!\,\text{Dept.DProjs}$, and the query

```
define Q as select distinct  struct(PN: s, DN: d.DName)
              from  depts d, d.DProjs s, Proj p
              where  s = p.PName  and  p.CustName = "ABC"
```

translates as the expression

$\bigcup d \in \underline{\text{dom}}\,\text{Dept}\,.\,\bigcup s \in d\,!\,\text{Dept.DProjs}\,.\,\bigcup p \in \text{Proj}\,.$
$\quad \underline{\text{if}}\; s\; =\; p.\text{PName}\; \underline{\text{and}}\; p.\text{CustName}\; =\; \text{"ABC"}$
$\quad \underline{\text{then}}\; \text{sng}\langle \text{PN} : s, \text{DN} : d\,!\,\text{Dept.DName}\rangle$
$\quad \underline{\text{else}}\; \text{empty}$

We have used the more suggestive notation $\bigcup x \in S\,.\,R$ instead of the notation $\Theta\, x \in S\,.\,R$ for the set monad. Moreover, we use the conditional and we added equality to the calculus.

14.13 Indexes as Dictionaries

Another use for dictionaries is to represent physical data structures such as primary and secondary indexes [14.15].

Considering again the example from the previous section, we assume that certain indexes are maintained in conjunction with the relation Proj: specifically, a primary index I on the key PName and a secondary index SI on CustName. In our calculus, both indexes are represented by dictionaries:

Doid $\times\!\!>$ ⟨DName : string , DProjs : Set string , MgrName : string ⟩

I : string $\times\!\!>$ ⟨PName : string , CustName : string , PDept : string ⟩

SI : string $\times\!\!>$ Set ⟨PName : string , CustName : string , PDept : string ⟩

The first index associates each project name PName with its record in Proj while the second index associates each customer name CustName with the set of records in Proj that have CustName as customer. For example, s!I returns the record r in Proj such that r.PName $= s$. Similarly, c!SI gives back the set of records r in Proj such that r.CustName $= c$. Finally, here is an example of query that might be equivalent to the one we saw in the previous section, assuming a kind of "inverse relationship" between Proj and Dept:

$$\bigcup p \in \texttt{"ABC"!SI.sng}\langle \texttt{PN}: p.\texttt{PName}, \texttt{DN}: p.\texttt{PDept}\rangle$$

where we would probably want to use a non-failing lookup for "ABC"!SI; that is, returning the empty set when "ABC" is not in <u>dom</u> SI.

14.14 Structural Recursion and Semi-Structured Data

The development of query languages for semi-structured data preceded by a year or two, and guided, the development of XML query languages. UnQL [14.2, 14.3] (a query language for unstructured data) was one of the first such languages and was based on some of the ideas that we have already seen in this chapter. The starting point for semi-structured data is to use a labelled graph model. We have already introduced the notation $\langle l = v, \ldots, l = v \rangle$ for records. By relaxing the constraint that the labels are distinct, we can use the same notation to describe sets. For example, a simple relational table can be written

⟨Person=⟨Name="Jane", Age=21⟩, Person=⟨Name="Bill", Age=19⟩⟩

More generally, this syntax describes *edge-labelled trees*, for example

⟨Person=⟨Name=⟨First="Jane", Last="Dee"⟩,
        Email="jd@pqr.com"⟩,
  Person=⟨Name="John Doe",
        Tel=1234,
        Tel=7643⟩⟩

There are no typing constraints in this model. In conventional terms, attributes may be missing or occur many times, and the same attribute (e.g.

Name) is not constrained to have the same type. Internal nodes in the tree are simply sets of label/value pairs and may be built up with the usual constructors for sets: the empty set $\langle\rangle$, the singleton set $\langle l{=}v\rangle$, and set union $v \cup v$. To summarise the syntax for this basic form:

$$t ::= \langle\rangle \mid b \mid \langle l = t\rangle \mid t \cup t$$

where l ranges over edge labels and b over atomic values.

Following Section 14.3.3 we can write down a general form of structural recursion over labelled trees:

$$F(\langle\rangle) \quad = e$$

$$F(x) \quad = a(x) \qquad\qquad \text{for atomic values}$$

$$F(\langle l = t\rangle) = s(l, t, F(t))$$

$$F(S_1 \cup S_2) = u(F(S_1), F(S_2))$$

As before, this function is determined by our choice of e, a, s, u. Taking, for example, $e = \text{\textit{false}}$, $a(x) = (x = \text{"Jane"})$[12], $s(l, t, r) = r$ and $u(x_1, x_2) = x_1 \wedge x_2$, gives us a function that determines whether the value "Jane" occurs anywhere in the tree. Again, as before, following the direction of Section 14.3.4 we consider a restricted form of this structural recursion in which $e = \langle\rangle$ and $u(x_1, x_2) = x_1 \cup x_2$.

Example 14.14.1. With this restriction, taking

$$a(x) = x \quad \text{and} \quad s(l, t, r) = \text{if } l = \mathsf{Name} \text{ then } \langle\mathsf{Name} = t\rangle \cup r \text{ else } r$$

gives us a function that brings all Name *edges (and their subtrees) up to the top level.*

The ability of this generalised form of structural recursion arises from the recursive call to F in the third argument of s. It is possible, for example, express queries involving "regular path expressions" (cf. [14.39]). Note that instantiations of s that ignore the third argument leave us with functions that can explore the tree to a fixed depth — giving us essentially the same expressive power as the monad algebras explored in this chapter. If one makes the appropriate assumptions about the correspondence between typed and untyped representations of data, this equivalence of expressive power can be proved ([14.3]). However, the more general form of F allows us to write queries that work on both the "horizontal" and "vertical" structure of the tree and can represent a wide range of tree transformations.

Cyclic Structures. It is possible to extend the syntax for trees to rooted, directed, edge-labelled graphs. Consider Example 14.14.1. On trees the evaluation is straightforward; but on cyclic structures the recursive program that

---

[12] The unpleasant overloading of "=", inherited from standard programming language conventions, is partly alleviated in [14.3] by using $\{l : v, \ldots, l : v\}$ instead of $\langle l = v, \ldots, l = v\rangle$.

we would naturally associate with the definition does not terminate. Nevetheless, as a set of equations, there is a well-defined solution. A further restriction on the form of S which guarantees that a well-defined solution exists is given in [14.3]. However, this may not be the most general syntactic restriction; in fact it is likely that many useful questions concerning syntactic guarantees on well-definedness are undecidable.

Bisimulation Equivalence. The data model we have adopted generalises the relational data model to trees, and the appropriate definition of equality is tree equality. Thus $\langle a = \langle c = 4, c = 4 \rangle, b = false, a = \langle c = 4 \rangle \rangle$ and $\langle a = \langle c = 4 \rangle, b = false \rangle$ represent the same structure and UnQL queries generalise the relational algebra in computing results to within tree equality. When we generalise to cyclic structures the appropriate notion of equivalence is *bisimulation* [14.19]. This should be contrasted with the Object Exchange Model [14.32] in which equivalence is graph isomorphism. Although bisimulation is ostensibly more complex, it is nevertheless the right generalisation of the relational model, and it is computationally tractable (see [14.1] for a detailed discussion of semi-structured data models).

Query Languages. A comprehension-based query language was defined for UnQL whose abstract syntax is close to that of XML-QL and XQuery. Apart from its ability to deal with cyclic data, UnQL's advantages included arbitrary regular path expressions and pattern matching to bind variables. While we are on the topic of XML, it is worth making two remarks about the difference between models of XML and the model of semi-structured data we have used here. The first is that XML is generally taken to be a *node-labelled* model of data. This is a minor difference: with only minor complications, all the results for the edge-labelled model can be adjusted for a node-labelled model. The second, and important, distinction is that XML models are all for *ordered* trees. Modifying the languages associated with UnQL to deal with order (especially when combined with cyclic data) represents a major challenge. However, we note that most query languages associated with XML start from some unordered model and at best represent an uncomfortable compromise between ordered and unordered models.

Evaluation. The natural extension of structural recursion to deal with semi-structured data holds the promise that some uniform categorical account could generalise horizontal queries to the vertical. Unfortunately the authors know of no such generalisation, and were there no connection it would probably not be worth including any discussion of semi-structured data in this chapter. However, there is an engaging version — or "parody" — of ext(.) (Section 14.3.4) that works as a parallel graph transformation. The idea is simple. Replace each edge in the graph with a directed graph with n inputs and n outputs, where n is a constant for the whole graph. This is the "map" part of ext(.). Now glue the inputs and outputs of these graphs together as dictated by the connections between edges in the source graph. This is the "flattening" part of ext(.). For example, if we replace edges e_1 and e_2 with graphs G_1 and G_2 repsectively, and the output (target) of e_1 meets the input (source) of e_2, then the ith output of G_1 is connected with the ith input of G_2.

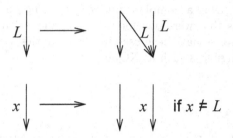

Fig. 14.4. An edge-to-graph mapping.

The details of this process are involved, but a simple example may show the general idea. Suppose we wish, following Example 14.14.1 to bring all edges labelled L, together with their associated subtrees, to the root. The mapping from labelled edges to graphs is shown in Figure 14.4, and the the application of the transformation in Figure 14.5.

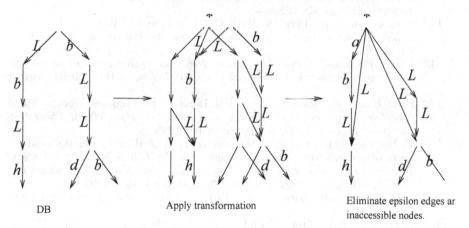

Fig. 14.5. Graph transformation.

As illustrated in this figure, the graphs that are produced by the mapping from edges may introduce "epsilon transitions" which may be eliminated in the final representation. Also, the transformation must specify a distinguished root (usually the first vertex) which is taken as the root of the final graph. Note that the resulting graph contains shared substructures, which should be duplicated if a tree-like representation is needed. This is one example of an optimisation that is immediate in this technique. Another arises from the pruning of inaccessible nodes, which can sometimes be determined statically. It should also be noted that the process lends itself naturally to parallel evaluation.

Although UnQL as a complete query system has not come to market, many of the ideas that were developed — together with many of the other ideas in this chapter — have been used in the semantics, typing and evaluation of XML query languages such as XQuery [14.38].

References

14.1 Serge Abiteboul, Peter Buneman, and Dan Suciu. *Data on the Web: From Relations to Semistructured Data and XML*. Morgan Kaufmann, 1999.

14.2 Peter Buneman, Susan Davidson, Gerd Hillebrand, and Dan Suciu. A query language and optimisation techniques for unstructured data . In *Proceedings of ACM SIGMOD International Conference on Management of Data*, 1996.

14.3 Peter Buneman, Mary Fernandez, and Dan Suciu. UnQL: A query language and algebra for semistructured data based on structural recursion. *VLDB Journal*, 9(1):75–110, 2000.

14.4 Val Breazu-Tannen, Peter Buneman, and Limsoon Wong. Naturally embedded query languages. In J. Biskup and R. Hull, editors, *LNCS 646: Proceedings of 4th International Conference on Database Theory, Berlin, Germany, October, 1992*, pages 140–154. Springer-Verlag, 1992. Available as UPenn Technical Report MS-CIS-92-47.

14.5 P. Buneman, S. Davidson, K. Hart, C. Overton, and L. Wong. A data transformation system for biological data sources. In *Proceedings of VLDB'95*, Zurich, 1995.

14.6 Catriel Beeri and Yoram Kornatzky. Algebraic optimisation of object oriented query languages. *Theoretical Computer Science*, 116(1):59–94, August 1993.

14.7 Peter Buneman, Shamim Naqvi, Val Tannen, and Limsoon Wong. Principles of programming with complex objects and collection types. *Theoretical Computer Science*, 149(1):3–48, September 1995.

14.8 V. Breazu-Tannen and R. Subrahmanyam. Logical and computational aspects of programming with sets/bags/lists. In *LNCS 510: Proceedings of 18th International Colloquium on Automata, Languages, and Programming, Madrid, Spain, July 1991*, pages 60–75. Springer-Verlag, 1991.

14.9 Michael Barr and Charles Wells. *Toposes, Triples, and Theories*. Springer-Verlag, 1985.

14.10 R. G. G. Cattell, editor. *The Object Database Standard: ODMG-93*. Morgan Kaufmann, 1996.

14.11 Sophie Cluet and Claude Delobel. A general framework for the optimisation of object oriented queries. In M. Stonebraker, editor, *Proceedings ACM SIGMOD International Conference on Management of Data*, pages 383–392, San Diego, California, June 1992.

14.12 Sophie Cluet. Langages et Optimisation de requetes pour Systemes de Gestion de Base de donnees oriente-objet. PhD thesis, Universite de Paris-Sud, 1991.

14.13 S.B. Davidson, S. Harker and V. Tannen. The information integration system K2. In T. Critchlow and Z. Lacroix, editors, *Bioinformatics: Managing Scientific Data*, Elsevier, 2003.

14.14 S. Davidson, C. Overton, V. Tannen, and L. Wong. BioKleisli: a digital library for biomedical researchers. *Journal of Digital Libraries*, 1997.

14.15 A. Deutsch, L. Popa, and V. Tannen. Physical data independence, constraints and optimization with universal plans. In *VLDB*, 1999.

14.16 S. Eilenberg and J.C. Moore. Adjoint functors and triples. *Illinois Journal of Mathematics*, 9:381–398, 1965.

14.17 L. Fegaras and D. Maier. Towards an effective calculus for object query languages. In *Proceedings of ACM SIGMOD International Conference on Management of Data*, pages 47–58, San Jose, California, May 1995.

14.18 L. Fegaras and D. Maier. An algebraic framework for physical oodb design. In *Proceedings of the 5th Internatinal Workshop on Database Programming Languages (DBPL95)*, Umbria, Italy, August 1995.

14.19 Monika Henzinger, Thomas Henzinger, and Peter Kopke. Computing simulations on finite and infinite graphs. In *Proceedings of 20th Symposium on Foundations of Computer Science*, pages 453–462, 1995.

14.20 P. Hoogendijk. Relational programming laws in the Boom hierarchy of types. Technical Report, Eindhoven University of Technology, The Netherlands, 1994.

14.21 http://db.cis.upenn.edu/K2

14.22 H. Kleisli. Every standard construction is induced by a pair of adjoint functors. *Proceedings of the American Mathematical Society*, 16:544–546, 1965.

14.23 K. Lellahi. Towards a characterization of bulk types. Technical Report 94-01, Université Paris 13, LIPN, 1994.

14.24 K. Lellahi. Type de collection et monades. In *Actes des Journées Cateégories, Algèbres, Esquisses et neo-esquisses*, Caen, 1994.

14.25 J. Lambek and P.J. Scott. *Introduction to Higher Order Categorical Logic*, volume 7 of *Cambridge Studies in Advanced Mathematics*. Cambridge University Press, 1986.

14.26 Leonid Libkin and Limsoon Wong. Aggregate functions, conservative extension, and linear orders. In Catriel Beeri, Atsushi Ohori, and Dennis E. Shasha, editors, *Proceedings of 4th International Workshop on Database Programming Languages, New York, August 1993*, pages 282–294. Springer-Verlag, 1994. See also UPenn Technical Report MS-CIS-93-36.

14.27 Leonid Libkin and Limsoon Wong. Some properties of query languages for bags. In Catriel Beeri, Atsushi Ohori, and Dennis E. Shasha, editors, *Proceedings of 4th International Workshop on Database Programming Languages, New York, August 1993*, pages 97–114. Springer-Verlag, 1994. See also UPenn Technical Report MS-CIS-93-36.

14.28 Kazem Lellahi and Val Tannen. A calculus for collections and aggregates. In E. Moggi and G. Rosolini, editors, *LNCS 1290: Category Theory and Computer Science, Proceedings of the 7th International Conference, CTCS'97*, Santa Margherita Ligure, September 1997, pages 261–280.

14.29 S. MacLane. *Categories for the Working Mathematician*. Springer-Verlag, 1971.

14.30 Ernest G. Manes. *Algebraic Theories*, volume 26 of Graduate Texts in Mathematics. Springer-Verlag, Berlin, 1976.

14.31 Eugenio Moggi. Notions of computation and monads. *Information and Computation*, 93:55–92, 1991.

14.32 Yannis Papakonstantinou, Hector Garcia-Molina, and Jennifer Widom. Object Exchange across Heterogeneous Information Sources *Proceedings of the 11th International Conference on Data Engineering*, pages 251–260, 1995.

14.33 Lucian Popa and Val Tannen. An equational chase for path-conjunctive queries, constraints, and views. In *Proceedings of ICDT*, Jerusalem, Israel, January 1999.

14.34 Dan Suciu and Val Breazu-Tannen. A query language for NC. In *Proceedings of 13th ACM Symposium on Principles of Database Systems*, pages 167–178, Minneapolis, Minnesota, May 1994. See also UPenn Technical Report MS-CIS-94-05.

14.35 G. Shaw and S. Zdonik. Object-oriented queries: Equivalence and optimization. In *Proceedings of International Conference on Deductive and Object-Oriented Databases*, 1989.

14.36 G. Shaw and S. Zdonik. An object-oriented query algebra. In *Proceedings of DBPL*, Salishan Lodge, Oregon, June 1989.

14.37 P.W. Trinder. Comprehensions, a query notation for DBPLs. In *Proceedings of 3rd International Workshop on Database Programming Languages, Nahplion, Greece*, pages 49–62. Morgan Kaufmann, August 1991.

14.38 http://www.w3.org/TR/xquery/

14.39 http://www.w3.org/TR/xpath

14.40 Philip Wadler. Comprehending monads. *Mathematical Structures in Computer Science*, 2:461–493, 1992.

14.41 Limsoon Wong. Normal forms and conservative properties for query languages over collection types. In *Proceedings of 12th ACM Symposium on Principles of Database Systems*, pages 26–36, Washington, DC, May 1993. See also UPenn Technical Report MS-CIS-92-59.

14.42 Limsoon Wong. Querying nested collections. PhD thesis, Department of Computer and Information Science, University of Pennsylvania, August 1994. Available as University of Pennsylvania IRCS Report 94-09.

14.43 David A. Watt and Phil Trinder. Towards a theory of bulk types. Fide Technical Report 91/26, Glasgow University, July 1991.

Section Editor's Preface

Introduction to Section IV:
Looking Forward to Functional Approaches for Semi-Structured Data
by Larry Kerschberg

This section of the book focuses on the use of the functional approach to manage semi-structured data, information and knowledge. The various chapters address the new and evolving applications that use both the Internet and Web as a platform for implementing distributed heterogeneous information systems.

The chapters share a common language for expressing semi-structured data, the eXtensible Markup Language (XML) together with the family of languages and open standards that are based on the XML infrastructure. XML enables this by serving as a meta-language that describes the *meta-data* associated with data, so that the schema information is closely associated with the data itself, thereby making the data *self-describing*.

Two important themes addressed in these chapters are the *integration* of information from multiple sources, and the *interoperation* of information among distributed heterogeneous information sources. Information integration is required when data from multiple heterogeneous sources is gathered together to form an integrated conceptual model of distributed resources. Enterprise application integration is important within the enterprise as a way to re-engineer business processes for Internet-based e-business.

Information interoperation is important to enable communities of interest to exchange information, understand its semantics, and take action based on that information. This is particularly the case in business-to-business e-commerce business partners wish to integrate order, supply, and production processes that span several organizations. The chapter authors show how the *functional approach* is a natural fit for modeling, implementing, managing and integrating such sytems.

Chapter 15 discusses how the functional approach can be used to enable applications such as the Semantic Web, web services for e-business and an agent-based approach to knowledge management. This chapter reviews several of the XML-based open standards for semantic markup, the role of ontology and intelligent thesauri to enable both intelligent search services and information integration services. The chapter also presents the Knowledge/Data Model, based on the functional data model, that incorporates constraints, rules and heuristics.

This chapter also explores the areas of e-business and knowledge management. With the advent of the Internet and XML-based open standards for documents and business processes, one can conceptualize that documents (entities) can travel from site-to-site, carrying their own *functional specification* of attributes, operations, and programs; this allows them to actively negotiate for services, and cooperate in multi-enterprise business processes.

Chapter 16 elaborates on the use of XML-based dynamic negotiation in e-business. XML-documents carry both a structural and a behavioral specification, so that negotiations among business partners may proceed automaically. The authors present an active negotiation architecture involving web services. As negotiations proceed the documents are updated and evolved, based on the current state of negotiations as well as on negotiation strategies. They show that data structure, business processes, and negotiation strategies can be expressed in XML-based documents. In order to reduce the size of files that are interchanged during negotiations, the XLink protocol is used because it sends only the changed portions of the document.

Chapter 17 presents a constraint-based functional approach to enabling Semantic Web applications. The functional data model (P/FDM) and associated constraint language Colan, are used to define a semantic data model. The authors then show that the model and constraints can be expressed in Resource Description Framework (RDF) and RDF Schema and a Constraint Interchange Format (CIF), allowing entities and constraints to be interchanged and fused. A knowledge-based constraint reasoner is used to perform constraint fusion.

Chapter 18 introduces RQL, a functional query language for RDF-based models. It is novel in the way it combines queries on the meta-data (schema) and the data (instances). The RDF is an activity coordinated by the World Wide Web Consortium (W3C) for specifying and managing *metadata about resources* on the Web. This metadata may be used to specify, configure and deploy Semantic Web applications. In order to do this, the authors argue that database concepts of *declarative access* and *logical/physical RDF data independence* are needed. A formal graph-theoretic data model for RDF and RDF Schema is presented, together with RQL, a functional query language that allows both RDF schema and resource descriptions be queried uniformly. RQL enables basic queries to be functionally composed into complex queries.

Chapter 19 shows how the functional approach can be used to *wrap* RDF descriptions of educational resources available on the Web. Schema definitions, expressed in RDF, are translated into a corresponding functional metadata schema consisting of a type hierarchy and a set of functions. This approach is used to create a *functional mediation system*, whereby users query a single functional semantic schema and receive query results showing diverse heterogeneous resources on the Web. A system call RDFAmos is described that provides mediation services for Edutella – a research project using peer-to-peer technology – to catalog educational resources which are available on the Web.

Table of Contents

15. Functional Approach in Internet-Based Applications: Enabling the Semantic Web, E-Business, Web Services and Agent-Based Knowledge Management

Larry Kerschberg[1]

[1]E-Center for E-Business, Department of Information and Software Engineering, George Mason University, Fairfax, Virginia, 22030-4444, USA
email: kersch@gmu.edu

Summary.

The functional approach to computing has an important role in enabling the Internet-based applications such as the Semantic Web, e-business, web services, and agents for managing the evolving distributed knowledge space. This chapter examines the research issues and trends in these areas, and focuses on how the Functional Data Model and a functional approach can contribute to solving some of the outstanding problems. Specifically, the chapter addresses the role of ontologies and the meta-tagging and indexing of resources; the role of search technologies; the Semantic Web and web services; intelligent agents; and knowledge management.

15.1 Introduction

The Functional Data Model, which was first introduced in 1976 [15.49-51, 15.83], has been used by researchers and practitioners for a variety of applications [15.10, 15.28, 15.29, 15.54, 15.82]. They include functional query and update languages, query optimization, functional programming, data semantics, active databases, constraint management, intelligent integration of information, and applications to bioinformatics.

This chapter focuses on the future of the Functional Data Model and, more generally, the functional approach to computing, as they relate to new frontiers and applications, especially those that use the Internet and World Wide Web, or, simply, the Web.

15.2   The Web and Internet as a Distributed Knowledge Space

The Web and Internet are transforming the way people, companies, organizations as well as computers interact, share data, create knowledge and transact business. The enabling technology is based on XML, the eXtensible Markup Language, and the various W3C (WWW Consortium) Working Groups that are defining the open XML-based standards that enable e-business processes, the Semantic Web, the semantic markup of documents and resources, security, trust, and computer-to-computer services, called web services.

The Web and the various XML-based markup languages allow us to posit a distributed information space consisting of resources that need to be managed. They include databases, knowledge bases, ontologies, programs, reasoning engines, business process templates and patterns, and web services. Whereas the first-generation Web was based on a client-server model wherein users used browsers to access information provided by servers, the next-generation Web will be based on open standards that implement a peer-to-peer architecture in which people, agents, and computers will interact, find useful information, and effect business transactions.

The challenge for the functional approach and the Functional Data Model is to show how functional concepts, structures, languages, and reasoning tools can be used to enable this next-generation distributed knowledge space.

15.3   Enabling the Distributed Knowledge Space

The functional approach is well suited to several emerging areas related to the distributed knowledge space. They include the semantic markup of resources, the integration of information from heterogeneous sources, the use of agents to enable web services for the creation of virtual enterprises, and a services-based knowledge management architecture.

In order to achieve the next-generation Semantic Web as a distributed knowledge space, we need to address problems in the areas of metadata management, semantic markup, intelligent search, web services, intelligent agents, and knowledge management. They will be discussed in the following sections.

15.3.1   Semantic Markup of Resources

The *Extensible Markup Language* (XML) [15.87] is a meta-language in which to define *applications* (languages) that specify the syntax of textual markup. XML is intended to be the *lingua franca* of the Internet. For example, the digital library community has proposed the Dublin Core markup language [15.16] for intellectual property. The Dublin Core metadata types cover Content (title, subject, description, type, source, relation, coverage); Intellectual Property (creator, publisher, contributor, rights, etc.); and Instantiation (date, format, identifier, language, etc.). Additionally, industry has adopted XML to develop a collection of open standards (ebXML and RosettaNet) for the exchange and interoperation of both data and process descriptions, for conducting e-business over the Internet.

The XML community, under the guidance of both the World Wide Web Consortium (W3C) (http://w3.org/) and OASIS (http://www.oasis-open.org), is developing a family of XML-application protocols to enable the concepts and potential of web services. These protocols include the Resource Description Framework (RDF), Security Assertion Markup Language (SAML), XML Schema, XForms, XML Query, Extensible Style Sheet Language (XSL), XML Signature, XML Encryption, etc.

The goal is to foster a set of open standards so that e-business activities can be conducted on the Internet under commonly understood semantics (an *ontology*), with negotiated commitments for quality of service and payments, and with the assurance that the documents that traverse the Internet are secure and cannot be repudiated.

15.3.2 Ontologies

The dictionary definition for *ontology* is the branch of metaphysics dealing with the nature of *being*. From the point of view of this research, the term ontology denotes a knowledge representation that can be used to express the definitions of objects, their relationships to other objects, and constraints governing their behavior.

Conceptual modeling techniques such as the Functional Data Model (FDM), Entity/Relationship Model, Unified Modeling Language, and the Relational Data Model may be thought of as very simple ontologies in that they provide constructs and a language in which to express schemas representing objects, attributes, relationships, operations, and constraints. Classification schemes such as taxonomies provide semantic rules in the form of transitive inheritance. Internet search engines such as Google and Yahoo! organize their web pages according to a taxonomy of concepts (cf. http://directory.google.com).

An ontology also lies at the core of WordNet [15.66] at Princeton University, a large online English thesaurus database. A large-scale ontology forms the basis of the National Library of Medicine's Unified Medical Language System (UMLS) [15.86]. UMLS consists of three knowledge sources: a meta-thesaurus, a semantic network, and a specialist lexicon. The meta-thesaurus contains information on biomedical concepts and terms culled from many sources including patient records, administrative health data, as well as bibliographic and full-text databases. Users and programs can access the thesaurus to refine queries, to search for the location of specific documents, and to mediate user terminology into terms used by the target data sources. The UMLS meta-thesaurus has more than 870,000 concepts and 2.1 million concept names in over 95 biomedical source vocabularies. The Semantic Net (ontology) consists of 134 semantic types that provide a consistent categorization of the meta-thesaurus concepts. There are 54 links among the semantic types. The primary link type is the "is-a" link used to create type hierarchies. Other links include "physically related to," "spatially related to", "temporally related to", "functionally related to", and "conceptually related to".

More sophisticated ontologies are being researched and proposed to form the basis for the Semantic Web [15.4, 15.20, 15.23, 15.24, 15.68]. These include constructs mentioned above, based on XML Schema together with limited reasoning capabilities. The goal is to consider the documents on the Web as objects in a semantic distributed information space.

Clearly the functional approach can be used in the specification and use of thesauri and ontologies. Kerschberg and Weishar [15.52] have explored the use of an intelligent thesaurus for a federated approach to integrate information from multiple sources. The meta-thesaurus is specified using the Knowledge/Data Model [15.41, 15.76], which extends the FDM by incorporating constraints, heuristics, and rules. These concepts are presented in the next few subsections.

The Knowledge Data Model (KDM). We present the KDM [15.76] and discuss its use in specifying the meta-schema for the Intelligent Thesaurus. The significant features of the KDM data model are:

- The incorporation of heuristics to model inferential relationships.
- The capability to organize these heuristics and to associate them with specific items involved in the inferential relationships.
- The capability to incorporate heuristics and constraints in a tightly coupled (unified) manner.
- The ability to define inferred (virtual) objects.
- A unified representational formalism for knowledge and data.
- A mechanism that allows for abstract knowledge typing; that is, handling rules and constraints as objects.

The following are the semantic primitives available in the KDM:

- Generalization: Generalization (the inverse of which is specialization) allows the KDM to abstract similar object-types into a more general object-type (an object-type is a collection of related objects). This is done by the "is-a" relationship (e.g., the object-types "student" and "soldier" are generalized to the "person" object-type).
- Aggregation: Aggregation (the inverse of which is decomposition) is an abstraction mechanism where an object is related to the components that constitute it via the "is-part-of" relationship.
- Classification: Classification (the inverse of which is instantiation) provides a means whereby specific object instances can be grouped together and considered to be an object-type.
- Membership: Membership is an abstraction mechanism that specifically supports the "is-a-member-of" relationship between objects or object-types.
- Constraint: This primitive is used to place a constraint on some aspect of an object, operation, or relationship via the "is-constraint-on" relationship.
- Heuristic: This primitive is used to attach an heuristic via the "is-heuristic-on" relationship. Heuristics are expressed in the form of rules.
- Method: This primitive is used to model the behavior of object-types and to manipulate object-types. For example, an object-type might invoke a "compute-pay" method in order to derive a person's pay.

- Temporal: The temporal relationship is used to model specific task- or event-oriented object-types that are related by synchronous or asynchronous characteristics. Synchronous objects are related to other synchronous objects by either the predecessor or successor relationship. Asynchronous objects are related to other asynchronous objects by a concurrent or parallel notion. Temporal primitives are also used for task planning and workflow analysis.

The Knowledge/Data Language (KDL). The most generic KDM construct is the object type, and the KDL template to specify an object-type is shown in Figure 15.1. KDL reserved words are shown in uppercase letters. Identifiers shown in lowercase are placeholders for user input. Optional items in the template are enclosed in square brackets, and at least one of each of the items contained in curly brackets must be part of the specification.

The optional characteristics of an object-type correspond to KDM modeling primitives while "class-name" uniquely identifies the object-type. Any object-type may be defined as a specialized (derived) form of one or more other object-types, called supertypes. Also, any object-type (or class) may be viewed as an encapsulation of the following KDL functions:

- Attributes are stored functions holding information or properties of an object.
- Members are multi-valued or association functions.
- Constraints are Boolean functions.
- Heuristics are functions or rules.

```
object-type ::=
    OBJECT-TYPE: class-name HAS
        [SUPERTYPES:              // Generalization
            class-name { , class-name};]
        [SUBTYPES:                // Specialization
            class-name { , class-name} [HIDING function-list];]
        [ATTRIBUTES:              // Aggregation
            {attribute-name: type-name
                [WITH CONSTRAINT: constraint ] ; }+ ]
        [MEMBERS:                 // Membership (Association)
            {member-name: [SET OF | LIST OF] class-name
                [INVERSE OF member-name [class-name)]]
                [WITH CONSTRAINT: constraint ] ; }+ ]
        [CONSTRAINTS: // Knowledge to enforce integrity
            { constraint; }+ ]
        [HEURISTICS:              // Knowledge to derive/infer information
            {heuristic}+ ]
        [METHODS:                 // Specifications of computations & behavior
            { method; }+ ]
    END class-name;
```

Fig. 15.1. KDM object-type specification in the KDL.

Methods are functions that are more general than heuristics in that they can take any number of parameters and allow limited side-effects (such as producing output) to occur.

The Intelligent Thesaurus. In this section we introduce the conceptual model for the Intelligent Thesaurus (IT) [15.52] and show the meta-schema for the IT as a KDM schema. The thesaurus consists of terms, relationships among terms, and their constraints, and is modeled after a library thesaurus. In addition, we can specify knowledge to be associated with the terms. The IT is an active data/knowledge dictionary capable of supporting multiple ontologies to allow users to browse the information space and to formulate and reformulate requests for information. The IT is similar to the thesaurus found in a library; it assists analysts in identifying similar, broader, or narrower terms related to a particular term, thereby increasing the likelihood of obtaining the desired information from the information sources. In addition, active rules and heuristics may be associated with object types as well as their attributes and functions.

Broader and narrower terms are depicted by object generalization and specialization hierarchies, respectively, and are normally formed using "is-a" relationships. Broader terms denote an expanded scope of the object-type's meaning. For example, an object-type "airplane" could have the broader term "aircraft". A broader term subsumes the object-type. Formally, a broader term B is a proper superset of a given object-type A (i.e., $A \subset B \Leftrightarrow$ for all $x[x \in A \Rightarrow x \in B]$ where $A \neq B$). Conversely, narrower terms restrict the scope of meaning. A narrower term "jet" could be specified for "airplane". Again, formally, a narrower term N is a proper subset of a given object-type A (i.e., $N \subset A \Leftrightarrow$ for all $x[x \in N \Rightarrow x \in A]$ where $N \neq A$).

Similar terms are depicted using "is-similar-to" relationships. The concept of similarity is not as formal as other concepts. Similar terms "resemble" or "approximate" the properties of the given object-type, i.e., they are alike but not identical.

Homonyms are treated as special cases of similar terms. Determining, for example, whether a car is an automobile or the first element of a Lisp list requires the attachment of context-sensitive heuristics to the object-type.

Synonyms and preferred terms (aliases) are denoted via the "is-eq-to" relationships. Two terms are synonymous if all of their attributes that are values are equal and all of their attributes that are objects are recursively value-equal. (Note that this definition is a less restrictive version of object value equality. Object identifiers do not have to be the same to establish synonymy.) Formally, a term S is equal to a given term A (i.e., $A = B \Leftrightarrow$ for all $x[x \in A \Rightarrow x \in B]$). **Antonyms**, which are opposites of synonyms, are depicted using "is-op-of" relationships.

Individual instances of the above categories can be shown in *classification hierarchies*, which are formed by applying "is-instance-of" relationships to class objects. Similarly, object-types grouped together to form higher-order object-types are organized into *aggregation hierarchies*, which are formed by applying "is-part-of" relationships to the group of class objects. Object-types that are part of a group of objects, each sharing common interests but neither changing individual attributes nor forming higher-order objects (e.g., showing student object–types as members of the computer-club object-type), are depicted using *membership hierarchies*. Membership hierarchies are formed by applying "is-member-of" relationships to the class-objects.

The Thesaurus Meta-Schema Specification

The Intelligent Thesaurus was designed to support database federations, and thus supports certain structures for schema integration: data source wrappers, the federated conceptual model, and different user views [15.88, 15.89].

Figure 15.2 depicts the KDM diagram for the THESAURUS_Object object-type specification that delineates object-type (class) inheritance through the SUPERTYPES and SUBTYPES slots. Note that inheritance within this context includes multiple inheritance. In this meta-object-type specification the DESCRIPTION attribute allows the object-type to be annotated in free text, a capability which can be useful to users browsing federation concepts. The boxes denote object-types and the double arrows denote multi-valued functions. The viewpoints object-type and its subtypes correspond to the various roles objects play at the data, wrapped, global, and external levels of the federation.

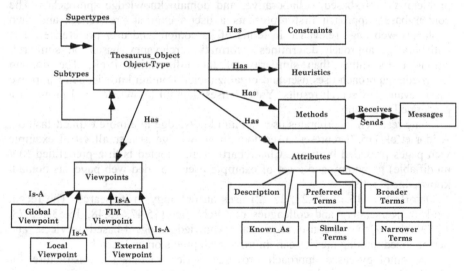

Fig. 15.2. KDM diagram of the Intelligent Thesaurus meta-schema.

The evolution of the FDM into the KDM was motivated by the need to incorporate constraints, rules, methods, and heuristics into data/knowledge models to address the requirements of federated information systems. The viewpoints allow an object's roles (views) to be characterized within a federation. Clearly, the Intelligent Thesaurus provides a mechanism to define metadata representing multiple views of the problem space, and the metadata can be used to formulate queries, and to generalize or specialize the terms used in a search. The temporal specifications of the KDM also allow the terms to evolve over time, and queries may undergo temporal mediation to find terms relevant to certain time periods, or to expand queries across epochs.

Weishar's doctoral thesis [15.88, 15.89] also introduced the notion of "data/knowledge packets", an encapsulation of thesaurus terms, relationships, constraints, and heuristics that could be shipped from one federation site to another, so that the receiving site would be able to understand the content and context of the message and act upon it accordingly. This approach to shipping constraints is also discussed by Gray et al. [15.27]. This concept also carries over to the Web in that agents may move from site to site and carry with them their "semantic provenance" by pointing to namespaces that define their ontologies, their tasks, the operations they have performed, and their role in a workflow specification [15.35].

15.3.3   Intelligent Search Services

Search is an important component of any system that uses web resources. One problem that everyone faces is the lack of precision in the results provided by search engines [15.57]. There are three major approaches to the precision problem: content-based, collaborative, and domain knowledge approaches. The content-based approach first represents a user's explicit preferences and then evaluates web page relevance in terms of its content and user preferences. The collaborative approach determines information relevancy based on similarity among users rather than similarity of the information itself. The domain knowledge approach uses user and organizational domain knowledge to improve the relevancy of search results. Yahoo! uses domain knowledge and provides a predefined taxonomy.

Some research incorporates user domain knowledge in a more explicit fashion. Aridor et al. [15.2] represent user domain knowledge as a small set of example web pages provided by users. Chakrabarti et al. adopted both a predefined (but modifiable) taxonomy and a set of example user-provided web pages as domain knowledge [15.13].

OntoBroker [15.17, 15.21, 15.22] uses an ontology in its search. The recent work of Kerschberg and colleagues on WebSifter [15.47, 15.48, 15.53, 15.78, 15.79] shows that the use of domain knowledge, agent-based services, and personalized ranking metrics can improve both precision and recall.

The ontology-based approach provides a rich metadata infrastructure for search. However, in order to make this approach viable, we must find ways to perform the markup of Web resources in a semi-automatic or completely automatic manner. Another important topic is the indexing [15.97] of large collections of XML-based documents for fast retrieval. Here functional tools would be quite useful.

One interesting approach that incorporates both peer-to-peer search and functional concepts is the EDUTELLA project [15.69, 15.93], an open-source collaboration to provide access to metadata on educational resources available over the Internet. The goal of EDUTELLA is to incorporate schemas expressed in the IEEE Learning Objects Metadata (LOM) [15.37], in IMS [15.38] and in Advanced Distributed Learning's Sharable Content Object Reference Model (SCORM) [15.1].

EDUTELLA uses the JXTA peer-to-peer search [15.40] to find resources defined using an RDF-based conceptual model. RQL and TRIPLE are the user query languages, and the RDF-QEL-i language serves as the standardized query exchange language format sent among peers. Query mediation is performed using the AMOS II system [15.39, 15.77], which accepts RDF-QEL-i language statements and translates them into AmosQL statements that use a *functional representation*. RDF Schema classes can be represented as AMOS II types.

This mediator-based approach allows distinct sites to maintain control over their resources and to use their preferred tagging language, while participating in a federation of systems that provides services for registration, subscription, query, and fulfillment. More will be said about this in later sections.

As the Semantic Web is deployed through the use of XML-based markup of web resources, more sophisticated search techniques must be developed to allow users, and their agents, to find relevant web services based on a suite of attributes including availability, cost, and quality of service; to rank them according to the requirements of the task at hand; to negotiate contracts and agreements for their use; and to include them in the problem workflow. The functional approach can be used to support these requirements, but research is needed in these areas.

15.3.4   E-Business and Web Services

As organizations move their operations to the Internet and establish partnerships, via portals and extranets, with both their customers and suppliers, the "data/knowledge" for the *e-enterprise* becomes distributed among many parties. While there is a need to share intellectual property among business partners, there is also the need to protect these strategic assets. Thus, organizations wish to: *own* their data, assume responsibility for the *curation* or *stewardship* of their data, and *share* their data according to well-defined sharing agreements.

The e-enterprise is based on inter-enterprise partnerships among customers and suppliers. These partnerships are predicated on the sharing of data, information, and knowledge through interoperable business processes, data sharing protocols, and open standards such as XML and its family of open standards including ebXML and RosettaNet.

E-enterprise strategic partnerships entail data that currently is distributed among specialized software-vendor-specific applications for Customer Relationship Management (CRM), Content Management (CM) for catalog integration and data meta-tagging, Enterprise Application Integration (EAI), Human Resources (HR), and back-end fulfillment systems such as Enterprise Resource Planning (ERP). Figure 15.3 depicts those relationships.

The dynamic nature of the inter-enterprise relationships and the distributed heterogeneous data contained in proprietary software systems requires new approaches to data sharing. The federated approach allows each application system to manage its data while sharing portions of its data with its partners.

There will have to be specific agreements with customers, vendors, and partners on how much of their data will be shared, the protocols and standards to be used to access and share data, the data security attributes and distribution permissions of shared data, as well as data quality standards to which these partners must adhere. The functional approach has been shown to be quite effective in handling the issues of data sharing in heterogeneous environments, and additional work is needed to support the evolving concept of the e-enterprise.

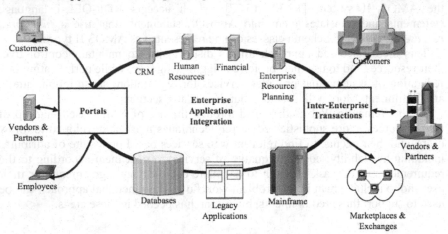

Fig. 15.3. E-enterprise heterogeneous distributed data/knowledge resources.

Another interesting development involves *web services* [15.14, 15.15]. This concept allows organizations to package their intellectual property, such as programs or methods, and publish them as Internet-based services that can be invoked by computers using standard protocols such as Universal Description, Discovery, and Integration (UDDI) [15.73], Simple Object Access Protocol (SOAP) [15.5], and Web Service Description Language (WSDL) [15.14].

An e-enterprise may define a stand-alone program as a web service and describe it using WSDL. Next, the web service is registered in a UDDI-compliant registry which may be searched by other enterprise programs. If the web service's attributes match certain search criteria, an enterprise may invoke the web service using SOAP.

Figure 15.4 shows two applications that are wrapped as separate web services, and have their respective WSDL and SOAP specifications. The numbered circles show the steps involved in registering, finding, and invoking the web services. First, both web services 1 and 2 are registered with a UDDI repository. A SOAP client can search the repository (step 3) for those web services satisfying desired criteria. Suppose that web service 2 is selected (step 4), in which case the SOAP client requests and receives the WSDL file that tells it how the web service is to be invoked via a SOAP command. The client sends the appropriate SOAP command as a message to the SOAP server, which in turn passes it to the application; the result of the computation is sent back to the client in a SOAP message in step 5.

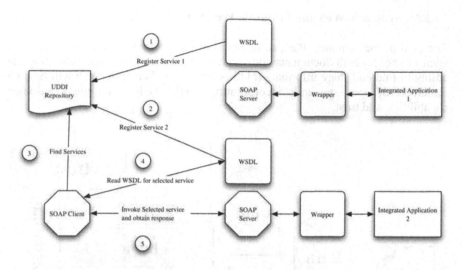

Fig. 15.4. Web services registration, search and invocation.

The web service concept is appealing in that one can wrap intellectual property and publish it via a web service. Users of these potential services can peruse UDDI repositories, select appropriate services, and dynamically configure them to form a virtual e-enterprise. Although this is a laudable goal, the reality is quite different. First, UDDI specifications are rather limited in their service description; in particular they lack attributes dealing with quality of service (QoS), service level agreements, scalability, and availability [15.60, 15.63, 15.64].

Second, the dynamic configuration of web services requires a workflow specification language and execution model. This is an area of intense research and development, led primarily by industry [15.11, 15.12, 15.36, 15.58, 15.65].

Third, the composition of web services to form a virtual enterprise is an active research topic [15.9, 15.61, 15.67, 15.75, 15.84, 15.85]; this work has focused primarily on the logical formalisms involved in reasoning about how to compose web services. Research is indicated for dynamically changing environments where QoS is crucial and web services may have to be dynamically deselected and replaced by more robust services. In addition, there are issues related to distributed transaction management for web services for long-running loosely coupled transactions. The Business Transaction Protocol [15.71] allows for two transaction types: ACID, called Atoms, and non-ACID, called Cohesions. IBM, Microsoft and BEA propose a framework called WS-Coordination [15.12] that provides protocols for distributed applications, while WS-Transaction [15.11], based on WS-Coordination, offers two types of transactions, Atomic (AT) and Business Activities (BA), which are useful for short-lived and long-lived transactions, respectively.

15.3.5   Semantic Web and Semantic Web Services

The goal of the *Semantic Web*, as depicted in Figure 15.5, is to allow intelligent agents to access both documents and services on behalf of humans, enhancing our ability to find and share information [15.3, 15.4]. The Semantic Web will be built on layers of open standards incorporating XML, RDF, ontologies, reasoning capabilities, and trust.

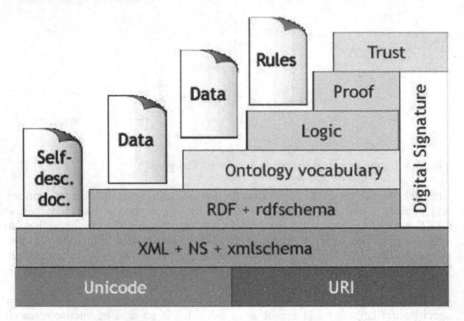

Fig. 15.5. The Semantic Web layers according to Berners-Lee.

At present, Semantic Web research focuses on designing languages embeddable into web pages and services to make them more accessible by computer agents as well as humans. Such languages are derivatives of the knowledge representation languages such as KL-ONE or KIF [15.6, 15.26]. Semantic Web languages range from binary relationship languages such as RDF [15.18, 15.56], to more expressive n-ary relationship languages with Horn clauses such as SHOE [15.31, 15.59].

DAML+OIL (DARPA Agent Markup Language and Ontology Inference Language) [15.24, 15.33] provides more sophisticated semantics as compared to XML/RDF [15.33, 15.34]. Related efforts include KQML, a generalized agent-communication language which enables the transmission of DAML+OIL, KIF, and other languages between agents or web services [15.25].

Part of the DAML+OIL [15.24] effort is DAML-S, extensions to DAML to specify and advertise web services. DAML-S consists of a *Service Profile Ontology* for advertising the capabilities and requirements of a web service; a *Service Model Ontology* to describe how a service operates; and a set of *Service Groundings* which specify how an atomic web service is accessed. These specifications are semantic extensions to UDDI, WSDL, and SOAP for web services. This is an excellent opportunity to investigate the functional approach in the context of web service description languages, and the ontologies needed for advertising, searching, negotiation, and composition of web services.

15.3.6 Agent-Based Web Services for E-Business

In this section we address the role that intelligent agents play in supporting web services for e-business. Agents may be thought of as software programs [15.94, 15.95] that act on behalf of humans, robots, or other programs, and exhibit autonomous, purposeful behavior. The goal is for the agent architecture to support dynamic discovery, negotiation, composition, configuration, workflow, and deployment of web services. In order to achieve this goal, the agents will have to be endowed with intelligence similar to the Semantic Web services [15.4, 15.30, 15.32, 15.62].

The architecture to be proposed, Functional Agent Services (FAS), is based on an agency-based approach in which agents are organized in agencies, similar to the Knowledge Rover Architecture [15.7, 15.43-15.45], developed to deal with the intelligent integration of information [15.90]. The goal is to motivate the use of the functional approach in conjunction with agents and web services.

The FAS architecture is a three-layer architecture depicted in Figure 15.6. There are *line* agents and *staff* agents to reflect that some agents are involved in work specifications while others play support roles. The User Layer is supported by the User Agency that coordinates a collection of services such as task specification, planning, user profile administration, and order tracking. The concept is that users would visit a portal of the e-enterprise, compose their request in terms of a high-level task, and interact with the planning agent to decompose the task into a plan that would be submitted to the next layer, Intelligent Middleware Services.

The Intelligent Middleware Services layer is supported by the Functional Services Agency whose agents include line agents for web service discovery, negotiation, contracting, and composition. These agents receive the task specification and plan from the User Agency, and search for appropriate Internet-based web services that can accomplish the tasks. Those web services may have already been vetted for use by the e-enterprise by the Services Coordination Agency residing at the Web Services Layer.

Staff agents include ontology, curation, and QoS monitoring, among others. For example, the ontology agent is responsible for maintaining the ontology of tasks and services provided by the e-enterprise. Curation agents are involved in identifying, storing, and evolving a repository of successful patterns of web services that have been successful in performing high-level user tasks.

The Web Services Layer is supported by the Services Coordination Agency whose agents support service mediation, workflow coordination, and transaction management.

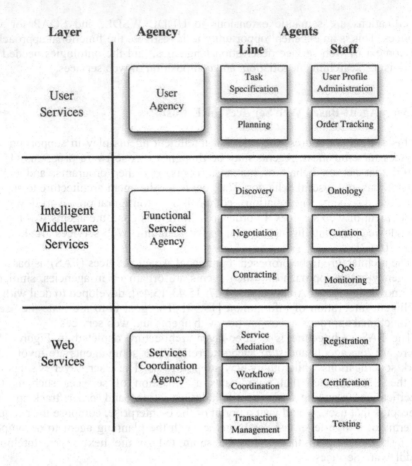

Fig. 15.6. Functional Agent Services (FAS) architecture.

The Functional Services Agency submits a web service configuration plan, and the Services Coordination Agency verifies that the services are available, schedules the various sub-transactions, and executes the plan on behalf of the Functional Services Agency. The Services Coordination Agency also monitors the progress of each transaction, maintains records of the transactions, their status, and QoS for future processing and reporting. In addition, several other agents reside at this layer and perform their collaborative functions to place new services in the service registry. This involves cooperation among the registration, certification, and testing agents. In order for a new service to be a candidate for inclusion into the e-enterprise repositories, it must be tested, annotated with QoS attributes, and certified to perform at advertised levels of service.

In order to realize the vision of an e-enterprise consisting of web services that can be composed dynamically, we need to bring together the concepts of the Semantic Web, multi-agent systems, workflow systems, and the functional approach.

15.3.7   Knowledge Management for E-Business

In an earlier section we posited that the Internet is evolving into a distributed knowledge space. Within the context of the e-enterprise, we need to manage enterprise knowledge resources that will be shared within the organization and with business partners.

In a manner similar to the FAS architecture for web services discussed in the previous section, we propose a knowledge management [15.42] architecture consisting of a collection of services organized into three layers: knowledge presentation and creation, knowledge management, and data source layers, as shown in Figure 15.7.

At the top layer, knowledge workers may create, communicate, collaborate, and share knowledge. They are provided information by means of a knowledge portal, which can be tailored to the profile of each knowledge worker. The portal also provides search services that combine internal searches on organizational holdings, as well as external Internet-based searches as discussed in section

The Knowledge Management Layer depicts the knowledge repository and the processes that are used to acquire, refine, store, retrieve, distribute, and present knowledge. These processes are used to create knowledge for the repository.

The Data Sources Layer consists of the organization's internal data sources including documents, electronic messages, web site repository, media repository of video, audio, and imagery, and the domain repository consisting of the domain model, ontology, etc. Also depicted are the external sources of data, including web services that can be used to augment the internal holdings.

The Knowledge Presentation and Creation Layer. The services provided at this layer enable knowledge workers to obtain personalized information, via portals, to perform specialized search for information, to collaborate in the creation of new knowledge, and to transform *tacit knowledge* into *explicit knowledge* [15.70] via discussion groups. Our work on WebSifter [15.47, 15.53, 15.78] indicates that personalized search preferences together with user-specified, ontology-directed search specification and results evaluation can enhance the precision of documents returned by search engines. Thus search services are an important component of knowledge management.

The knowledge creation services allow knowledge workers to create value-added knowledge by annotating existing knowledge, providing meta-tags, and aggregating heterogeneous documents into named collections for future use.

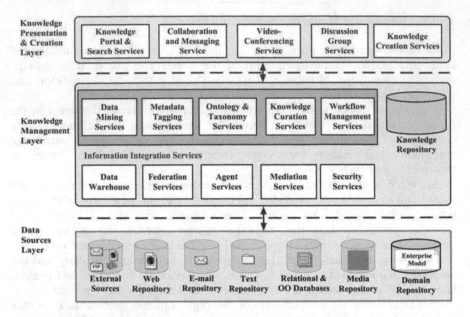

Fig. 15.7. Conceptual knowledge management system architecture.

Knowledge Management Layer. This layer provides middleware services associated with knowledge indexing and information integration services (IIS). Data warehouse services are listed among the IIS, together with federation, agent, security, and mediation services. Services such as data mining, metadata tagging, ontology and taxonomy, curation, and workflow services reside at this layer. We briefly discuss several of these services.

Data Mining Services. These services include tools for deducing rules from numeric data, as well as concept mining from text. This knowledge can be used to enhance the Knowledge Repository and to provide refined knowledge to decision-makers.

Meta-tagging Services. Appropriate indexing of knowledge assets is crucial as collections grow. As mentioned previously, XML and RDF are emerging as open standards for tagging and metadata descriptions. The Digital Library community has proposed the Dublin Core Metadata Initiative for tagging intellectual property. New metadata standards are being proposed for digital rights management and for security of XML documents [15.8, 15.72, 15.96].

Ontology and Taxonomy Services. The organization of enterprise knowledge is an area of ongoing research. Clearly, the construction of domain-specific ontologies is of utmost importance to providing consistent and reliable terminology across the enterprise. Hierarchical taxonomies are an important classification tool. Our research in this area includes the Intelligent Thesaurus [15.46, 15.52] and we have used user-specified taxonomies to guide the WebSifter meta-search engine. Content management in inter-enterprise environments can make use of ontologies, particularly in the area of catalog integration [15.19, 15.74].

Agent Services. As the e-enterprise forms strategic partnerships with customers, partners, and suppliers, we envision intelligent agents [15.35, 15.43, 15.45, 15.55] assisting in KM tasks such as: 1) monitoring e-enterprise business processes for performance information, 2) consulting authoritative external ontologies to obtain proper terminology for meta-tagging, 3) collecting metadata regarding objects that flow through enterprise processes, and 4) communicating with inter-enterprise processes and partners to coordinate information interoperability.

Mediation Services. Mediation refers to a broad class of services associated with the intelligent integration of information (I*3) [15.90-15.92]. Mediation services facilitate the extraction, matching, and integration of data from heterogeneous multi-media data sources such as maps, books, presentations, discussion threads, news reports, e-mail, etc.

15.4   Conclusions

The FDM has two basic constructs: entity sets and functions. There are other adornments to the model that allow for additional semantics to be specified. When I was researching and developing the FDM with João Pacheco, I found that there is a *duality* in the FDM schema constructs. At times it is important to focus on the entity sets and their instances, which constitute the database, but at other times, one focuses on the *functions*, as they carry and contain application knowledge regarding attributes, relationships, and constraints. It is precisely this duality that makes the functional approach to computing so *topical* and *compelling* to address the emerging challenges posed by subjects such as the Semantic Web, web services, information mediation, intelligent agents, and knowledge management.

In this chapter we have cast a wide net and have addressed open research in several important areas. It is our hope that others will join in this endeavor by researching how the functional approach can be used effectively in solving these problems. In order to realize the vision set forth for the semantic web, one needs to create ontologies, taxonomies, thesauri, indexes, and other knowledge representation schemes that define the knowledge resources. This involves the representation of these resources in XML, XML Schema, RDF, KIF, DAML+OIL, OWL, etc. Although we would like this to be done automatically, the reality is that this indexing and tagging is done semi-automatically at best. My view is that specialized communities, such as Intelligence and Bioinformatics, will develop tagging languages and interoperation standards for their communities. In order to gain widespread acceptance of the Semantic Web, we need indexing and tagging tools that are easy to use. The functional approach, with its simple structure, can be used to provide tools that assist in the creation of easy-to-understand structures that can be mapped to RDF. This is discussed in [15.35, 15.69] but more research is needed.

The web services area promotes the vision of agents that will search UDDI registries for services, then dynamically compose those services into a virtual enterprise, and finally coordinate workflow and transactions on behalf of the enterprise. The present-day reality is quite different. The UDDI directories provide only minimal information regarding service attributes. In addition, web services are cobbled together, requiring human intervention to make them work together. Workflow specification languages are beginning to appear, and more work is needed. Here again, the functional approach can make significant contributions to web services, particularly in the extensions to WSDL, XML Protocol, DAML-S service specifications, as well as languages for workflow specification and execution in the context of the e-enterprise.

Finally, the area of knowledge management can benefit from the functional approach by extending functional thinking to knowledge creation, curation, tagging, distribution, and sharing. The KM layer of Figure 15.7 shows many services to support the collection and curation of knowledge. In particular, agent services can make the KM architecture *active* and responsive to user needs. Agents can be used to search documents and Web sources for relevant information; they can cooperate in information integration [15.55]; they can monitor subscription services and update views [15.80, 15.81]; and they can roam the Internet to cooperate in executing workflow across multiple sites. The notion of agent mobility is based on moving programs (functions) to sites and executing those programs at remote sites. The functional approach, together with the web infrastructure, is well suited to mobile agents. For example, a *functional agent* could carry its functional specification in terms of its RDF schema, namespaces specifying the ontology and meta-tags it understands, and reasoning tools and protocols to negotiate with agents at a host site. This concept would be helpful in reducing the data traffic involved in exchanging verbose XML documents, when sending an agent would be more appropriate.

Acknowledgements

I would like to acknowledge discussions with Peter Gray, Sean Luke, Daniel Menascé, and Jongpil Yoon in the preparation of this chapter. This research was sponsored in part by the E-Center for E-Business and its sponsors, including the Virginia Center for Innovative Technology and webMethods.

References

15.1   ADL.   Sharable   Content   Object   Reference   Model   (SCORM) (http://www.adlnet.org/), Advanced Distributed Learning, 2002.

15.2 Aridor, Y., Carmel, D., Lempel, R., Soffer, A. and Maarek, Y.S. Knowledge Agent on the Web. In *Proceedings of the 4th International Workshop on Cooperative Information Agents IV*, (2000), 15-26.

15.3 Berners-Lee, T. Semantic Web Interest Group (http://www.w3.org/2001/sw/), World Wide Web Consortium, 2002.

15.4 Berners-Lee, T., Hendler, J. and Lassila, O. The Semantic Web: A new form of Web content that is meaningful to computers will unleash a revolution of new possibilities. *Scientific American*, 2001, 34-43.

15.5 Box, D., Ehnebuske, D., Kakivaya, G., Layman, A., Mendelsohn, N., Nielsen, H.F., Thatte, S. and Winer, D. Simple Object Access Protocol (SOAP) 1.1, 2000.

15.6 Brachman, R. and Schmolze, J. An Overview of the KL-ONE Knowledge Representation System. *Cognitive Science, 9*. 171-216.

15.7 Brodsky, A., Kerschberg, L. and Varas, S. Resource Management in Agent-based Distributed Environments. In Klusch, M., Shehory, O. and Weiss, G. eds. *Cooperative Information Agents III*, Springer-Verlag, 1999, 50-74.

15.8 Brown, A., Fox, B., Hada, S., LaMacchia, B. and Maruyama, H. SOAP Security Extensions: Digital Signature, W3C NOTE, 2001.

15.9 Bryson, J.J., Martin, D.L., McIlraith, S.A. and Stein, L.A. Toward Behavioral Intelligence in the Semantic Web. *IEEE Computer*, 2002, 48-55.

15.10 Buneman, P. and Frankel, R.E. FQL - A Functional Query Language. In *ACM SIGMOD Conference*, (Boston, Massachusetts, 1979), ACM Press, 52-58.

15.11 Cabrera, F., Copeland, G., Cox, B., Freund, T., Klein, J., Shewchuk, J., Storey, T. and Thatte, S. Web Services Transaction (WS-Transaction) (http://www.ibm.com/developerworks/library/ws-transpec), BEA, IBM, Microsoft, 2002.

15.12 Cabrera, F., Copeland, G., Freund, T., Klein, J., Langworthy, D., Orchard, D., Shewchuk, J. and Storey, T. Web Services Coordination (WS-Coordination) (http://www.ibm.com/developerworks/library/ws-coor/), BEA, IBM, Microsoft, 2002.

15.13 Chakrabarti, S., Berg, M.v.d. and Dom, B. Focused Crawling: A new approach to topic-specific web resource discovery. In *Proceedings of the Eighth International WWW Conference*, (1999), Elsevier, 545-562.

15.14 Chinnici, R., Gudgin, M., Moreau, J.-J. and Weerawarana, S. Web Services Description Language (WSDL) Version 1.2 (http://www.w3.org/TR/wsdl12/), W3C, 2002.

15.15 Curbera, F., Duftler, M., Khalaf, R., Nagy, W., Mukhi, N. and Weerawarana, S. Unraveling the Web Services Web: An introduction to SOAP, WSDL, and UDDI. *IEEE Internet Computing*, 2002.

15.16 DCMI. Dublin Core Metadata Initiative (http://dublincore.org/), 2002.

15.17 Decker, S., Erdmann, M., Fensel, D. and Studer, R. ONTOBROKER: Ontology Based Access to Distributed and Semi-Structured Information. In *Database Semantics: Semantic Issues in Multimedia Systems (Proceedings of the 8th Working Conference on Database Semantics)*, (New Zealand, 1999).

15.18   Decker, S., Melnik, S., van Harmelen, F., Fensel, D., Klein, M., Broekstra, J., Erdmann, M. and Horrocks, I. The Semantic Web: The roles of XML and RDF. *IEEE Internet Computing, 4* (5), 2002, 63-73.

15.19   Fensel, D. *Ontologies: Silver Bullet for Knowledge Management and Electronic Commerce.* Springer-Verlag, 2001.

15.20   Fensel, D. Ontology-Based Knowledge Management. *IEEE Computer,* 2002, 56-59.

15.21   Fensel, D., Angele, J., Decker, S., Erdmann, M., Schnurr, H.-P., Staab, S., Studer, R. and Witt, A. On2broker: Semantic-Based Access to Information Sources at the WWW. In *Proceedings of the World Conference on the WWW and Internet (WebNet 99),* (Honolulu, Hawaii, 1999), 25-30.

15.22   Fensel, D., Angele, J., Decker, S., Erdmann, M., Schnurr, H.-P., Studer, R. and Witt, A. On2broker: Lessons Learned from Applying AI to the Web, Institute AIFB, 1998.

15.23   Fensel, D. and Musen, M.A. The Semantic Web: A brain for humankind. *IEEE Intelligent Systems,* 2001, 24-25.

15.24   Fensel, D., van Harmelen, F., Horrocks, I., McGuinness, D.L. and Patel-Schneider, P.F. OIL: An ontology infrastructure for the Semantic Web. *IEEE Intelligent Systems,* 2001, 38-45.

15.25   Finin, T., Fritzson, R., McKay, D. and McEntire, R. KQML as an Agent Communication Language. In *International Conference on Information and Knowledge Management (CIKM-94),* (1994), ACM Press.

15.26   Genesereth, M. and Fikes, R. Knowledge Interchange Format, Version 3.0 Reference Manual (cf. http://logic.stanford.edu/kif/dpans.html), Computer Science Department, Stanford University, Palo Alto, California, 1991.

15.27   Gray, P.M.D., Embury, S.M. and Hui, K.Y. The Evolving Role of Constraints in the Functional Data Model. *Journal of Intelligent Information Systems, 12* (2/3), 1999, 113-137.

15.28   Gray, P.M.D., King, P.J.H. and Kerschberg, L. Guest Editor Introduction: Functional Approach to Intelligent Information Systems. *Journal of Intelligent Information Systems, 12* (2/3), 1999, 107-111.

15.29   Gray, P.M.D., Moffat, D.S. and Paton, N.W. A Prolog Interface to a Functional Data Model Database. In *Extending Database Technology Conference,* (1988), Springer-Verlag, 34-48.

15.30   Heflin, J. and Hendler, J. A Portrait of the Semantic Web in Action. *IEEE Intelligent Systems,* 2001, 54-59.

15.31   Heflin, J., Hendler, J. and Luke, S. Reading Between the Lines: Using SHOE to discover implicit knowledge from the web. In *Workshop on AI and Information Integration,* (1998), AAAI Press, 51-57.

15.32   Hendler, J. Agents and the Semantic Web. *IEEE Intelligent Systems, 16* (2). 2001, 30-37.

15.33   Hendler, J. DAML: DARPA Agent Markup Language effort (http://www.daml.org/), 2002.

15.34   Hendler, J. and McGuinness, D.L. DARPA Agent Markup Language. *IEEE Intelligent Systems,* 2001, 72-73.

15.35   Hui, K.Y., Chalmers, S., Gray, P.M.D. and Preece, A. Experience in Using RDF in Agent-mediated Knowledge Architectures. In *AAAI Workshop on*

Agent-Mediated Knowledge Management, (Stanford, CA, 2003), AAAI Press.

15.36   IBM. Web Services Architecture Directions (http://www.w3.org/2001/04/wsws-proceedings/rod_smith/rod.pdf), IBM, 2001.

15.37   IEEE-LOM. IEEE Learning Objects Metadata Standard 1484.12.1 (http://ltsc.ieee.org/wg12/), 2002.

15.38   IMS. IMS Global Learning Consortium Metadata Specification 1.2.2 (http://www.imsglobal.org/metadata/index.cfm), IMS, 2002.

15.39   Josifovski, V. and Risch, T. Functional Query Optimization over Object-Oriented Views for Data Integration. *Journal of Intelligent Information Systems, 12* (2/3), 1999, 165-190.

15.40   JXTA. JXTA Search Home Page (http://search.jxta.org/), 2002.

15.41   Kerschberg, L. Expert Database Systems: Knowledge/data management environments for intelligent information systems. *Information Systems, 15* (1), 1990, 151-160.

15.42   Kerschberg, L., Knowledge Management in Heterogeneous Data Warehouse Environments. In *International Conference on Data Warehousing and Knowledge Discovery*, (Munich, Germany, 2001), Springer-Verlag.

15.43   Kerschberg, L. Knowledge Rovers: Cooperative intelligent agent support for enterprise information architectures. In Kandzia, P. and Klusch, M. eds. *Cooperative Information Agents*, Springer-Verlag, Berlin, 1997, 79-100.

15.44   Kerschberg, L. The Role of Intelligent Agents in Advanced Information Systems. In Small, C., Douglas, P., Johnson, R., King, P. and Martin, N. eds. *Advances in Databases*, Springer-Verlag, 1997, 1-22.

15.45   Kerschberg, L. and Banerjee, S. An Agency-based Framework for Electronic Business. In Klusch, M., Shehory, O. and Weiss, G. eds. *Cooperative Information Agents III*, Springer-Verlag, Berlin, 1999, 254-279.

15.46   Kerschberg, L., Gomaa, H., Menascé, D.A. and Yoon, J.P. Data and Information Architectures for Large-Scale Distributed Data Intensive Information Systems. In *Proceedings of the Eighth IEEE International Conference on Scientific and Statistical Database Management*, (Stockholm, Sweden, 1996), IEEE Computer Society Press.

15.47   Kerschberg, L., Kim, W. and Scime, A. Intelligent Web Search via Personalizable Meta-Search Agents. In *International Conference on Ontologies, Databases and Applications of Semantics (ODBASE 2002)*, (Irvine, CA, 2002).

15.48   Kerschberg, L., Kim, W. and Scime, A. A Semantic Taxonomy-Based Personalizable Meta-Search Agent. In Truszkowski, W. ed. *Workshop on Radical Agent Concepts*, Springer-Verlag, 2002.

15.49   Kerschberg, L., Klug, A.C. and Tsichritzis, D. A Taxonomy of Data Models. in *Very Large Database Conference*, (1976).

15.50   Kerschberg, L., Ozkarahan, E.A. and Pacheco, J.E.S. A Synthetic English Query Language for a Relational Associative Processor. In *International Conference on Software Engineering*, (Los Angeles, 1976), 505-519.

15.51   Kerschberg, L. and Pacheco, J.E.S. A Functional Data Base Model, Department of Informatics, Catholic University of Rio de Janeiro, Rio de Janeiro, 1976, 23.

15.52   Kerschberg, L. and Weishar, D. Conceptual Models and Architectures for Advanced Information Systems. *Applied Intelligence, 13* (2), 2000, 149-164.

15.53   Kim, W., Kerschberg, L. and Scime, A. Learning for Automatic Personalization in a Semantic Taxonomy-Based Meta-Search Agent. *Electronic Commerce Research and Applications (ECRA), 1* (2), 2002.

15.54   King, P. and Poulovassilis, A. FDL: A language that integrates database and functional programming. In *Actes du Congres INFORSID 88*, (1988), 167-181.

15.55   Klusch, M. and Kerschberg, L. (eds.). *Cooperative Information Agents IV: The Future of Information Agents in Cyberspace, Fourth International Workshop*. Springer-Verlag, 2000.

15.56   Lassila, O. and Swick, R. Resource Description Framework (RDF) model and syntax specification (http://www.w3.org/RDF), World Wide Web Consortium, 1998.

15.57   Lawrence, S. and Giles, C.L. Context and Page Analysis for Improved Web Search. *IEEE Internet Computing, 2* (4). 1998, 38-46.

15.58   Leymann, F. Web Services Flow Language (WSFL 1.0), IBM, 2001.

15.59   Luke, S., Spector, L., Rager, D. and Hendler, J. Ontology-based Web Agents. In *First International Conference on Autonomous Agents (Autonomous Agents97)*, (1997), ACM Press, 59-66.

15.60   Mani, A. and Nagarajan, A. Understanding Quality of Services for Web Services (http://www-106.ibm.com/developerworks/library/ws-quality.html), IBM Developer Works, 2002.

15.61   McIlraith, S. and Son, T. Adapting Golog for Composition of Semantic Web Services. In *Eighth International Conference on Knowledge Representation and Reasoning (KR2002)*, (2002).

15.62   McIlraith, S.A., Son, T.C. and Zeng, H. Semantic Web Services. *IEEE Intelligent Systems*, 2001, 46-53.

15.63   Menascé, D.A. and Almeida, V.A. *Capacity Planning for Web Services: metrics, models, and methods*. Prentice Hall, 2002.

15.64   Menascé, D.A. and Almeida, V.A. *Scaling for E-business: technologies, models, performance, and capacity planning*. Prentice Hall, 2000.

15.65   Microsoft. .Net (http://www.microsoft.com/net/), 2002.

15.66   Miller, G.A. WordNet a Lexical Database for English. *Communications of the ACM, 38* (11), 1995, 39-41.

15.67   Miller, J.A., Palaniswami, D., Sheth, A.P., Kochut, K.J. and Singh, H. WebWork: METEOR2's Web-Based Workflow Management System. *Journal of Intelligent Information Systems, 10* (2), 1998, 185-215.

15.68   Missikoff, M., Navigli, R. and Velardi, P. Integrated Approach to Web Ontology Learning and Engineering. *IEEE Computer*, 2002, 60-63.

15.69   Nejdl, W., Wolf, B., Qu, C., Decker, S., Sintek, M., Naeve, A., Nilsson, M., Palmer, M. and Risch, T. EDUTELLA: A P2P Networking Infrastructure Based on RDF. In *World Wide Web Conference (WWW2002)*, (Honolulu, Hawaii, 2002), ACM Press.

15.70 Nonaka, I. and Takeuchi, H. *The Knowledge-Creating Company: How Japanese Companies Create the Dynamics of Innovation.* Oxford University Press, 1995.

15.71 OASIS. Business Transaction Protocol Primer, Version 1.0 (http://www.oasis-open.org/committees/business-transactions/#documents), OASIS, 2002.

15.72 OASIS. Security Assertion Markup Language (SAML) (http://www.oasis-open.org/committees/security), OASIS, 2002.

15.73 OASIS. Universal Description, Discovery and Integration (http://www.uddi.org/specification.html), OASIS, 2002.

15.74 Omelayenko, B. and Fensel, D. An Analysis of Integration Problems of XML-Based Catalogs fo B2B Electronic Commerce. In *IFIP 2.6 Working Conference on Data Semantics (DS-9)*, (Hong Kong, 2001), 232-246.

15.75 Piccinelli, G. and Mokrushin, L. Dynamic e-service Composition in DySCO. In *IEEE 21st International Conference on Distributed Computing Systems Workshops (ICDCSW'01)*, (2001).

15.76 Potter, W.D. and Kerschberg, L. The Knowledge/Data Model: An integrated approach to modeling knowledge and data. In Meersman, R.A. and Sernadas, A.C. eds. *Data and Knowledge (DS-2)*, North-Holland, 1988.

15.77 Risch, T. and Josifovski, V. Distributed Data Integration by Object-oriented Mediator Servers. *Concurrency and Computation: Practice and Experience, 13* (11), 2001, 933-953.

15.78 Scime, A. and Kerschberg, L. WebSifter: An ontological web-mining agent for e-business. In *Proceedings of the 9th IFIP 2.6 Working Conference on Database Semantics (DS-9): Semantic Issues in E-Commerce Systems*, (Hong Kong, 2001).

15.79 Scime, A. and Kerschberg, L. WebSifter: An ontology-based personalizable search agent for the Web. In *International Conference on Digital Libraries: Research and Practice*, (Kyoto, Japan, 2000), 493-446.

15.80 Seligman, L. and Kerschberg, L. Federated Knowledge and Database Systems: A new architecture for integrating AI and database systems. In Delcambre, L. and Petry, F. eds. *Advances in Databases and Artificial Intelligence, Vol. 1: The Landscape of Intelligence in Database and Information Systems*, JAI Press, 1995.

15.81 Seligman, L. and Kerschberg, L. A Mediator for Approximate Consistency: Supporting "Good Enough" materialized views. *Journal of Intelligent Information Systems, 8* (3), 1997 203-225.

15.82 Shipman, D.W. The Functional Data Model and the Data Language DAPLEX. *ACM Transactions on Database Systems, 6* (1), 1981, 140-173.

15.83 Sibley, E.H. and Kerschberg, L. Data Architecture and Data Model Considerations. In *AFIPS National Computer Conference*, (Dallas, Texas, 1977), AFIPS Press, 85-96.

15.84 Singh, M.P. Physics of Service Composition. *IEEE Internet Computing*, 2001.

15.85 Sycara, K., Lu, J., Klusch, M. and Widoff, S. Dynamic Service Matchmaking among Agents in Open Information Environments. In *ACM*

SIGMOD Record: Special Issue on Semantic Interoperability in Global Information Systems, (1999).

15.86   UMLS. United Medical Language System (http://www.nlm.nih.gov/research/umls/), National Library of Medicine, NIH, 2002.

15.87   W3C. Extensible Markup Language (XML) (http://www.w3.org/XML/), World Wide Web Consortium, 2002.

15.88   Weishar, D. A Knowledge-Based Architecture for Query Formulation and Processing in Federated Heterogeneous Databases. Ph.D. Dissertation in Information Technology, George Mason University, Fairfax, Virginia, 1993, 230.

15.89   Weishar, D. and Kerschberg, L. Data/Knowledge Packets as a Means of Supporting Semantic Heterogeneity in Multidatabase Systems. *SIGMOD Record*, 1991.

15.90   Wiederhold, G. Foreword to Special Issue on the Intelligent Integration of Information. *Journal of Intelligent Information Systems, 6, 2/3*, 1996 93-97.

15.91   Wiederhold, G. Mediators in the Architecture of Future Information Systems. *IEEE Computer, 25* (3), 1992, 38-49.

15.92   Wiederhold, G. The Roles of Artificial Intelligence in Information Systems. *Journal of Intelligent Information Systems, 1* (1), 1992, 35-56.

15.93   Wolf, B., Nejdl, W. and Decker, S. Edutella Home Page (http://edutella.jxta.org/), JXTA Project, 2002.

15.94   Wooldridge, M. Issues in Agent-Based Software Engineering. In Kandzia, P. and Klusch, M. eds. *Cooperative Information Agents*, Springer-Verlag, 1997, 1-18.

15.95   Wooldridge, M. and Jennings, N.R. Intelligent Agents: Theory and Practice. *The Knowledge Engineering Review, 10* (2), 1995, 115-152.

15.96   Xavier, E. XML based Security for E-Commerce Applications. In *Eighth Annual IEEE International Conference and Workshop on the Engineering of Computer Based Systems (ECBS '01)*, (2001), IEEE Press.

15.97   Yoon, J.P., Raghavan, V., Chakilam, V. and Kerschberg, L. BitCube: A Three-Dimensional Bitmap Indexing for XML Documents. *Journal of Intelligent Information Systems, 17* (2-3), 2001, 241-254.

16. A Functional Approach to XML-Based Dynamic Negotiation in E-Business

Jong P. Yoon[1] and Larry Kerschberg[2]

[1]Center for Advanced Computer Studies,
University of Louisiana, Lafayette, LA 70504-4330, USA
email: jyoon@cacs.louisiana.edu

[2]E-Center for E-Business
Department of Information and Software Engineering,
George Mason University, Fairfax, VA 22030-4444, USA
email: kersch@gmu.edu

Summary.

The Extensible Markup Language (XML) is a standard for information representation and exchange over the Internet. One of the applications where XML can be used is electronic business (e-business). E-business requires substantially large and frequent information exchanges among e-business parties. Such information exchange is required for search and discovery of services, automatic negotiation in sales/purchase activities, adaptive content management for multi-level users, and efficient follow-up services for terms-and-conditions and financial settlement. Many tasks can be automated through a functional approach to e-business negotiations. XML-based documents carry both a *structural specification* as well as a *behavioral specification* which are understood by e-business parties so that negotiations may proceed automatically.

This chapter presents a novel technique that enables XML documents to be active and to govern the e-business negotiations adaptively and efficiently. In order to perform an e-business negotiation, one or more document exchanges may be involved between business parties. During the negotiation, XML documents are updated, evolved, and exchanged. This evolution of XML documents in dynamic e-business negotiations should be managed in an adaptive fashion. Thus XML documents are *living* documents that evolve based on the current state of negotiation as well as the negotiation strategies defined by business policies.

The goal is to provide a functional approach and framework for XML-based web services to advertise, discover, negotiate, and collaborate in e-business. The contribution of this chapter is an architecture for the adaptive evolution of XML documents in response to the dynamic changes of e-business negotiations.

16.1   Introduction

The Extensible Markup Language (XML) is becoming a World Wide Web Consortium (W3C) standard for representing and exchanging information on the Internet. In recent years, documents in areas such as electronic business (e-business) have been increasingly represented in XML. XML data or documents are frequently exchanged among e-business parties.

One of the most important aspects of XML data is the ability to combine both data and metadata, allowing objects to be self-describing. The semantics of the Web is defined by using the Resource Description Framework (RDF), which can be expressed in terms of the Functional Data Model.

XML has become the lingua franca for data interchange in areas such as e-business, and many standards are being proposed, e.g., RosettaNet, ebXML, and web services using XML-based protocols such as SOAP (Simple Object Access Protocol), UDDI (Universal Description, Discovery and Integration standard), and WSDL (Web Service Description Language). Security is also an important concern in e-business and XML Signature is an important tool in signing portions of XML documents.

Our goal is to present a framework and functional approach for XML-based e-business, in which services can be discovered, negotiated, composed, organized and used to support e-business. The approach combines domain-independent policy and rules for search, negotiation, and composition, together with domain-specific XML documents containing data associated with e-business transactions.

In what follows, we describe some examples that motivate this approach:

1. Electronic business requires the exchange of negotiation documents in order to reach an agreement between two or more parties. A negotiating document is written by one party and transmitted to another party. The receiving party either revises it or accepts it. If revised, then a revised document is again transmitted to the originating party. Dynamic transactions and frequent transmissions of documents are increasing significantly as e-business becomes more popular. It is not unusual to find semantically sensitive and business-critical issues embedded within large collections of documents for an e-business negotiation.

2. If negotiations in e-business are made based on the business policies and strategies, those policies and strategies can be represented in XML. Although both negotiation strategies and organizational policies may be expressed in XML, it is not easy to counter-propose against the opponent proposal without having human intervention. However, if a negotiation document is *dynamic*, then it can be modified automatically in accordance with a negotiation strategy. Mundane issues are handled automatically by the documents themselves, and more important issues can then be handled through human intervention.

Although a negotiation document is dynamic, the number of document transmissions may increase until agreement is reached. This is inefficient in terms of performance due to transmission cost and time involved in sending XML documents which contain both data and metadata.. However, if a negotiating document is specified over Xlink [16.7], instead of transmitting the entire document, only modified portions of a document need be transmitted.

We are motivated by the functional approach to computing with data in that we view an XML document as having both a structural specification as well as a behavioral specification. The structural specification is provided by its DTD or XML Schema specification. The behavioral specification is determined by the constraints, operations, methods, etc., that define how the document can evolve. This evolution is also a function of the real-world state of the negotiations. The Internet and Web allow objects to refer to Uniform Resource Identifiers (URIs) that point to namespaces of definitions, standards, and protocols. Although a document may move from site to site during an e-business negotiation, its specification travels with it, thereby allowing a business partner to understand its real-world state, and the relevant and allowable operations that can be performed on it. This metaphor allows e-business parties to negotiate in confidence and trust.

16.2   Preliminaries

This section describes some notions about RDF and its representation in XML. It is required that web content and resources in general be marked up, or annotated, with some structured metadata that can be processed by machines. XML is the first layer of a framework that makes structured metadata possible, and the layers of meaning, c.g., XML Schema and XLink, are built on top of it.

Another layer of meaning is being exposed through the RDF. This is a framework that enables us to describe resources as structured metadata, and to exchange and reuse these resources in various possibly unrelated applications. It is built on three concepts:

1. *Resource*: that can be uniquely identified by a Uniform Resource Identifier (URI).
2. *Property*: that is, a resource having a name and that can be used to describe other resources. A property is defined as a property-type with a corresponding value. A collection of properties that refer to the same resource is called a description.
3. *Statement:* that is, a combination of a resource, a property-type, and a value.

For example, Figure 16.1 depicts a Functional Data Model-like instance diagram for a small application domain describing a negotiation document. There are six resource instances, related by the functions Property-Type. A property- type refers to another resource or a value. For example, the resource order_012 has the function item with the resource prod_112, which has in turn the function color with the resource rgb_32. The resource rgb_32 has a function with a value white. This diagram is represented in RDF as shown in Figure 16.2.

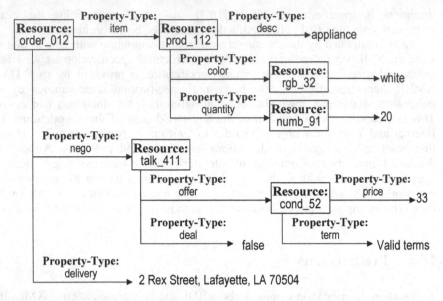

Fig. 16.1. Functional Data Model-like instance diagram for an RDF Schema.

XML provides a simple and general markup facility that is useful to represent complex multimedia data together with text data. An example of an XML document appears in Figure 16.3(a), which is an XML representation of the RDF diagram in Figure 16.1. The top element order has three subelements, item, nego, and delivery. Each such subelement may have other subelements or values (contents). For example, the element item contains subelements, desc, color, and quantity. However, the element delivery has a value, 2 Rex Street, Lafayette, LA 70504. The metadata specification for Figure 16.3(a) may be expressed as a Document Type Definition (DTD) or in XML Schema.

A DTD defines a class of XML elements using a language that is essentially a context-free grammar. As an example, the DTD of Figure 16.3(a) is shown in Figure 16.3(b). The first line of the DTD shows that the top element order has three subelements, item, nego, and delivery. In the second line the element item contains subelements, desc, color, and quantity, each of which is parsed character data (#PCDATA). XML Schemas are a vast improvement on the regular expressions of XPath over DTDs. Enhanced datatypes, e.g., sets or element repetitions, are provided, and more restrictive constraints, e.g., key constraints or null content, can be specified.

In this paper, we use XML and its related features to exemplify the concepts we propose. In addition to XML documents, our e-business model assumes there are at least two parties who participate in the negotiation process. Parties in e-business are specified in terms of subject profiles, based on the notion of authority. An authority is a quadruple (*subject, object, privilege, propagation*) as discussed in [16.1]. For example, the party who initially writes the XML document in Figure 16.3 is specified as a quadruple, (party1, XML_Instance_in_Figure_3.order, authoring, *), where * denotes that the propagation of authoring is maximum. Notice that the opposing party2can modify the XML_Instance_in_Figure_3 if that party has the authority, namely (party2, XML_Instance_in_Figure_3.order, authoring, *). If party2 has a viewing privilege, then that party can only read the document but cannot modify it. If party2 has 1 of propagation, then that party can modify only the content of the top element order and its subelements, item, nego, and delivery. In what follows, we will discuss the various documents required for e-business in XML.

16.3   XML Description

XML data for e-business applications will be defined and include: DTD, XML instances, XML schema, XML queries.

```
<?xml version="1.0" ?>
<rdf:RDF xmlns:rdf="URI://www.w3.org/199/02/22-rdf-syntax-ns#"
    xmlns:order="uri:X-louisiana.com/rdf/order/">
  <rdf:Description rdf:ID="order_012">
   <order:item rdf:URI="#prod_112" />
   <order:nego rdf:URI="#talk_411" />
   <order:delivery> 2 Rex St., Lafayette, LA 70504 </order:delivery>
  </rdf:Description>
  <rdf:Description rdf:ID="prod_112">
    <order:desc>appliance</order:desc>
    <order:color rdf:URI="#rgb32" />
    <order:quantity rdf:URI="#numb91" />
  </rdf:Description>
  <rdf:Description rdf:ID="rgb32">
    <order:color>white</order:color>
  </rdf:Description>
  <rdf:Description rdf:ID="numb91">
    <order:quantity>20</order:quantity>
  </rdf:Description>
  <rdf:Description rdf:ID="talk411">
    <order:offer rdf:URI="#cond52" />
    <order:deal>false</order:deal>
  </rdf:Description>
  <rdf:Description rdf:ID="cond52">
    <order:price>33</order:price>
    <order:term>Valid terms</order:term>
  </rdf:Description>
</rdf:RDF>
```

Fig. 16.2. XML specification of RDF for Figure 16.1.

16.3.1   Negotiating Documents in XML

In negotiations, each party of an e-business transaction may share offer documents until the deal is completed or fails. One example of an offer document is shown in Figure 16.3(a). The document describes item information that contains the description of an ordered item with color and quantity, together with negotiation information that can contain the negotiation price, terms and conditions, and delivery instructions.

This XML document conforms to the DTD in Figure 16.3(b). The DTD specifies that an order is a set of triples, (item, nego, delivery). Each element in an order can be further defined. For example, the element nego can be zero or more offers (e.g., a history of offers) followed by deal (i.e., finally a deal can be made to be either true or false). We assume that there could be numerous offers made by two parties before the deal is completed.

```
<?xml version="1.0" ?>
<order>
 <item>
  <desc>appliance</desc>
  <color>white</color>
  <quantity>20</quantity>
 </item>
 <nego>
  <offer>
   <price>33</price>
   <term>Valid terms</term>
  </offer>
  <deal>false</deal>
 </nego>
 <delivery>2 Rex St.,
Lafayette, LA 70504</delivery>
</order>
</xml>
```

```
<!ELEMENT order    (item, nego,delivery)+>
<!ELEMENT item     (desc,color,quantity)>
<!ELEMENT nego     (offer*, deal)>
<!ELEMENT delivery #PCDATA>
<!ELEMENT desc     #PCDATA>
<!ELEMENT color    #PCDATA>
<!ELEMENT quantity #PCDATA>
<!ELEMENT offer    (price, term)>
<!ELEMENT deal     #PCDATA>
<!ELEMENT price    #PCDATA>
<!ELEMENT term     #PCDATA>
```

(a) XML document   (b) DTD

Fig. 16.3. Example of a negotiating document.

The very same XML document may be modified by the two parties, and can be transmitted as a request and a response between them. The issue discussed in this section is how this type of XML document can be made *active* and can be transformed in reasonable ways during the negotiation process. We introduce two additional XML documents, called "negotiation strategy", and "domain data". This decouples the strategies used for negotiation from the actual state of negotiations, as reflected in the application domain data. These notions are described in the following subsection.

16.3.2   Negotiation Policy and Domain Data

Each e-business party may have a negotiation policy consisting of a collection of negotiating strategies that specify its negotiation terms, including under what conditions to end a negotiation or whether to continue until it concludes successfully. Each path in an XML document can describe a negotiation strategy for e-business. The *negotiation strategy* describes active bidding strategies and mechanisms for conflict resolution. An active bidding strategy is a conjunction of conditions to be satisfied and an action to be taken. This approach is comparable to production systems in artificial intelligence.

Each policy file describes the following:

- An input order file, which may be available from a remote site of the business partner.
- A variable bound to the domain data, which may be available from the local system. This domain data will be used to evaluate each strategy rule for those conditions which evaluate to true.
- A set of strategy rules: each rule has one or more conditions and an action. This rule is used to make a negotiation bid.
- A set of supporting rules: rules that are not directly used to reason about negotiation, but are useful to the negotiation process, e.g., an international currency conversion service.

A negotiation strategy rule can be reasoned about by means of the external files as described above: 1) input order file, and 2) domain data file. Those external files can be either explicitly specified or externally passed by a program. Figure 16.4(b) explicitly specifies the external file, http://www.your.com//order.xml, which is shown in Figure 16.3(a), and domain.data, which is depicted in Figure 16.4(a).

- Explicitly specified files. As seen in the element <using> of Figure 16.4(b), both a remote file and a local file are specified. The remote file is specified as an attribute value, while the local file is as an element value.
- Externally passed files. Unless the element <using> is specified in a negotiation strategy rule, the default domain data file predefined in the local system is used instead, while an input argument to a reasoning program is rather used. For example, the program in Figure 16.11 below can be activated with a remotely accessible file: java Negotiator http://www.you.com//order.xml. Internally, this argument is passed to the negotiation strategy rule and bound to the variable x.

The underlying goal of the separation of negotiation strategy rules from domain data is to facilitate the dynamic unification of the external files with the rules, while also allowing for the flexible modification of those external files. The next subsections describe in detail both negotiation strategy rules and domain data.

16.3.2.1   Negotiation Strategy Rules

An example of a negotiation strategy file is shown in Figure 16.4(b). In the figure, each rule is using the external file domain_data, which is in Figure 16.4(a), as well as the remotely accessible offer file, http://www.you.com//offer.xml. In the <using> element, there is an attribute variable with the value x, which is bound to the remote file order.xml in the http://www.you.com domain. The variable x can then be used throughout the strategy rules in that negotiation strategy file.

When the <using> element content is specified, several strategy rules can then be defined as shown in the figure. A strategy rule has its own label and priority. The first strategy has the label of "avg" with the priority of "2". If more than one strategy is evaluated and is applicable, then the strategy with the highest priority will be activated. The reasoning mechanism will be discussed in Section 16.5.2.

A strategy rule is specified with <condition> and <action> elements. The condition part in a strategy rule may consist of the conjunction of zero or more conditions denoted by the AND connector. The action part specifies what action is to be performed in response to the condition portion evaluating to true. In general there are two actions: an internal action and an external action. Internal actions are taken within a system, while external actions are performed outside a system. For example, in Figure 16.4(b), actions in all strategies but the last one are internal, and the action in the last strategy is an external alerter.

Each such negotiation strategy is evaluated in conjunction with the domain data which reflects the actual data instances. Unlike many other traditional rule-based systems, negotiation strategies (or rules) are separated from domain data. For example, the first rule in Figure 16.4(b), the condition part separates the condition from the domain data.

Assume that we want to specify a condition that the value associated with the element <order><nego><offer><price> is greater than 37:

If the data "http://www.you.com//order.xml/order.nego.offer.price" is greater than "37"

This hard-coded rule expression has some drawbacks. The negotiation strategy rule becomes dependent on one remote order file. To resolve this, a local variable x is used to bind the input file.

If the data x.price is greater than "37"

where x is bound to the external file, domain_data, and x.price is unified to be order.nego.price. The value associated with the element <offer><nego><price> is read to evaluate the condition, and the value 37 is preset by a rule designer.

The drawback in this specification is the inadaptability that the value 37 is preset to only one value until it is redefined. Although the real-world state is evolving, the condition specification above is fixed. However, in our approach, the condition may be specified as follows:

If the data x.price is greater than nego.give.avg_price

where nego.give.avg_price will be read from domain data, which is written in XML and generated directly from a real-world database.

In   Figure   16.4(a),   it   is   located   in   the   XML   path, <domain_data><nego><give><avg_price>.

```
<domain_data>
  <resolution>
    <contain>
      <container>maintenance</container>
      <contained>part order</contained>
      <contained>labor charge</contained>
    </contain>
    <synonym><item>price</item>
      <item>quote</item></synonym>
    <synonym><item>offer</item>
      <item>give</item></synonym>
    <synonym><item>electronic appliance</item>
      <item>home appliance</item>
    </synonym>
  </resolution>
  <nego>
    <give>
      <min_price>32</min_price>
      <avg_price>37</avg_price>
    </give>
    <take><margin>600</margin></take>
    <deal>4</deal>
    <intervene><name>Tom</name>
      <when><low>3.4</low><hi>4.5</hi></when>
      <issues>upfront cost deliverable price</issues>
      <done>upfront cost</done>
      <done>deliverable</done>
      <undone>price</undone></intervene>
    <completeness>.8</completeness>
    <ex_rate>0.9</ex_rate>
  </nego>
</domain_data>
```

```
<negotiation_policy>
  <using variable="x" file="http://www.you.com// order.xml">
    domain_data.xml</using>
  <strategy using="avg" priority="2">
    <condition>x.price > nego.give.avg_price</condition>
    <action>x.nego.deal = done</action>
  </strategy>
  <strategy using="min" priority="7">
    <condition>x.price > nego.give.min_price</condition>
    <action>x.nego.offer.price = (nego.give.avg_price+ x.price)/2
    </action></strategy>
  <strategy using="min" priority="5">
    <condition>x.price < nego.give.min_price</condition>
    <action>x.nego.deal = reject</action></strategy>
  <strategy using="margin" priority="3">
    <condition>x.nego.quantity*x.nego.price > nego.take.margin
    <action>x.nego.deal = done</action></strategy>
  <strategy using="freq" priority="6">
    <condition>nego.deal# > 4</condition>
    <condition>x.price > nego.give.min_price</condition>
    <action>x.nego.deal = done</action></strategy>
  <strategy using="intervene" priority="5">
    <condition>nego.deal > nego.intervene.when.low</condition>
    <condition>nego.deal < nego.intervene.when.hi</condition>
    <action><external>alert(nego.intervene.name, x)</external>
    </action>
  </strategy>
  <currency exchange_rate="x.ex_rate">
    <condition>x.ex_rate > nego.ex_rate</condition><action>USD</action>
    <condition>x.ex_rate <= nego.ex_rate</condition>
    <action>Euro</action></currency>
</negotiation_policy>
```

(a) Domain Data   (b) Negotiation Policy

Fig. 16.4. Domain-dependent and domain-independent e-business knowledge.

16.3.2.2   Domain Data

Domain data specifies alphanumeric values that reflect a real-world application domain. If such data is specified in a negotiation strategy rule, instead of having it in the rule, it may be represented separately in an XML file. We call that file Domain_Data. Domain data can contain two types of data: 1) resolution data, and 2) negotiation data.

- Resolution data. This data defines terms used in the negotiation strategy rules. Those terms are hierarchically defined, and the set of synonyms for are defined. Terms that reference the same orders but are specified differently are clarified and resolved in this XML file.

- Negotiation data. This data contains values that can be used to produce a counter-offer, to decide when to accept a proposed offer, and to suggest who may be involved in the negotiation, if necessary. It also contains some other bookkeeping data that can control the negotiation process, e.g., the number of negotiations and the currency exchange rate.

For example, in Figure 16.4(a), the concept "maintenance" subsumes the subconcepts "part orders" and "labor charge". The concept "price" is synonymous with "quote". This type of data will be used to resolve possible conflicts and ambiguities of terms used in strategies.

In contrast, negotiation data states the following:

- How to generate a counter-offer from either the content of the element <min_price> or <avg_price> in the <give> element.
- When to take, i.e., conclude, the negotiation with the content of the <margin> element of the <take> element.
- When to have a human involved as specified in the <intervene> element, which by the content of the <name> element specifies who should be involved for each type of intervention.
- How to determine when the negotiation is complete.

The time at which human intervention occurs is specified as the negotiation degree reaches below the content of the <low> element or above the content of the <hi> element. In case of intervention, it can issue as shown in the <issues> element. The history of an intervention is also maintained in the <done> element.

16.3.2.3   Hierarchical Structure of Negotiation Strategy and Domain Data

In addition to the separation of domain data from negotiation strategies, our approach is to represent both domain data and negotiation strategies hierarchically. Domain data is hierarchical with respect to components, while negotiation strategies are organized as generalization hierarchies. Figure 16.5 shows the hierarchy of the domain data. In the figure, personal_data and group_data compose domain_data. The XML element contents defined in domain_data are selectively chosen by personal_data and group_data. In practice, domain-dependent values in personal_data are more restricted than group_data. We will describe how they are related in the metadata in the next subsection. Only those elements that are allowed (or "restricted" in the XML Schema definition) for personal negotiation will appear in the XML document. Figure 16.6 shows the restricted version of the domain data. As can be seen, the elements <contain> and <nego><intervene> are dropped from Figure 16.4(a), making personal_data a specialization of domain_data.

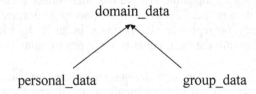

Fig. 16.5. Domain data hierarchy.

Such domain data sets can be logically equivalent to the following:

```
domain_data(d).
domain_data(d) <- personal_data(d).
domain_data(d) <- group_data(d)
```

This implies that domain_data is defined as shown in the DTD of Figure 16.3(b). domain_data can be defined by itself as shown in the first rule above. Also, since personal_data can be generalized to domain_data, it can be deduced from personal_data as shown in the second rule. Similarly, the third rule implies that group_data can be generalized to domain_data as well. It is defined if resolution and nego are defined. In turn, resolution is defined if contain or synonym is defined. Container is defined if all contained's are defined as follows:

container (c) <- ∀x contained (c, x) ∧ contained (x).
contained(x).
Synonym_term (s) <- term (t) ∧ term (s) ∧ synonym (t,s).

The container element is defined if all items x's are contained in a container c. Of course, contained of an item x is given from the domain_data file. Similarly, for item t, if there exists a synonym(t,s), then s can become a synonym term. As the functions defined above are applied to the domain_data file, they resolve conflicts by evaluating the appropriate synonyms.

Figure 16.7 shows the hierarchy of the negotiation strategies. Strategies in e_business can be classified into two types: business_strategy and management_strategy. Business_strategy is further decomposed into negotiation_strategy and business planning_strategy, while management_strategy is decomposed into control_strategy and security_strategy. Figure 16.4(b) shows an example of negotiation_strategy, which is a substrategy of business_strategy, which in turn is a substrategy of active_xml. The more specialized the strategy, the more XML elements can be specified.

```
<personal_data>
  <resolution>
    <synonym><item>price</item>
      <item>quotation</item></synonym>
    <synonym><item>offer</item>
      <item>give</item></synonym>
    <synonym><item>electronic appliance</item>
      <item>home appliance</item>
    </synonym>
  </resolution>
  <nego>
    <give>
      <min_price>32</min_price>
      <avg_price>37</avg_price>
    </give>
    <take><margin>600</margin></take>
    <deal>4</deal>
    <completeness>.8</completeness>
    <ex_rate>0.9</ex_rate>
  </nego>
</personal_data>
```

Fig. 16.6. Domain data specialized to personal data.

For example, in Figure 16.4(b), the contents of the element <currency> are available in negotiation_strategy, but not in active_xml nor in business_strategy. These hierarchical structures can be represented as follows:

negotiation_policy (n).   // e.g., given from the negotiation strategy file

planning_strategy (c).

business_strategy (n) <- negotiation_strategy (n).

business_strategy (n) <- planning_strategy (n).

active_xml (n) <- business_strategy(n).

active_xml (n) <- management_strategy (n).

Some of negotiation_policy in the negotiation strategy file of Figure 16.4(b) can be logically defined as follows:

price (n,p) <- NewOffer(n) $\wedge$ ReceivedOffer(x) $\wedge$ p = (a+c)/2 $\wedge$ avg_price(a) $\wedge$ price(x, c).

deal (n,F) <- NewOffer(n) $\wedge$ ReceivedOffer(x,p) $\wedge$ min_price(m) $\wedge$ (m > p).

deal (n,T) <- NewOffer(n) $\wedge$ ReceivedOffer(x,p,q) $\wedge$ margin(m) $\wedge$ (q*q> m).

alert (n) <- name(n) $\wedge$ deal(n,c) $\wedge$ intervene(n,l,h) $\wedge$ (c > l) $\wedge$ (c < h).

These rules will be evaluated as stated in Section 16.5.2. We will explain the metadata about the policies in the next subsection. Depending upon the ordered list of events, there may be an ordered collection of strategies. We call this collection a "chain" of strategies. A strategy chain can be optimized and simplified, and also verified for any redundancy and possible cycles.

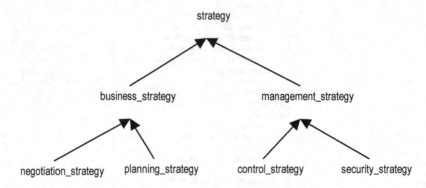

Fig. 16.7. Active strategy hierarchy.

16.3.3   Metadata for E-Business Knowledge

This subsection describes metadata about two types of e-business knowledge discussed in the previous subsection: domain data and strategy. For simplicity, we employ XML Schema to define metadata. Figure 16.8 shows the XML Schema definition for strategy, from which business_strategy and management_strategy are specialized. Further, negotiation_strategy and planning_strategy are specialized from business_strategy, while control_strategy and security_strategy are specialized from management_strategy. This generalization and specialization hierarchy appears in Figure 16.7. In the generalization hierarchy, the specialization is defined by a special element with attribute, e.g., <extension base= "super-document">. Based on a super document, a document in the specialized level is extended by adding more elements and attributes. For example, in Figure 16.8, strategy is a super document of the others. The document business_strategy is specialized (or extended) based on strategy by adding an additional element called "currency" with an attribute called "exchange_rate". The element currency may appear multiple times because of the unbounded maximum occurrence.

Correspondingly, the domain data is specified in XML Schema as shown in Figure 16.9. The XML instance shown in Figure 16.4(a) is the master domain data, called "domain_data". This master domain data is partially used to constitute a smaller data. In Figure 16.5, the documents personal_data and group_data are extracted from domain_data. This process of extraction is defined by using the element called "restriction" with an attribute "based". The metadata is shown in Figure 16.9. From domain_data in Figure 16.4(a), personal_data is extracted as shown in Figure 16.6 according to the XML Schema in Figure 16.9. The elements extension and restriction are part of the useful features provided by XML Schema. In this chapter, we utilize these features to organize both domain data and negotiation strategies in a hierarchy and to separate one from the other.

16.4   E-Business Active Negotiation Architecture

There are three document types in the active negotiation architecture: offer documents, negotiation policy documents, and domain data documents. An offer document is represented in XML and exchanged between the parties. Each party has its specific negotiation strategies and a domain data repository. Negotiation strategies are domain-independent rules, while the domain data repository is a data set that is domain-dependent. Reasoning logics are represented in a programming language. While negotiations are being conducted, reasoning logics are either generating another offer document or finalizing the negotiation deal.

The active negotiation architecture is shown in Figure 16.10. The documents to be given to users or to be received from users are written in XML. A user-provided XML request is modified based on the domain data and negotiation strategies. The modified XML document is then converted into a SOAP request message to be sent to an opposing party. A SOAP request message now invokes an object method. There are various object methods available to perform a particular task. An object method is executed and managed by a handler, and the handlers are chained in a specific order.

```
<?xml version="1.0"?>
<xsd:schema xmlns:xsd="http://www.w3.org/2001/XMLSchema"
            targetNamespace="http://party1.e-business.com"
            xmlns="http:// party1.e-business.com ">
  <xsd:complexType name="strategy">
    <xsd:sequence>
      <xsd:element name="using"/>
      <xsd:element ref="strategy" minOccurs="1" maxOccurs="unbounded"/>
    </xsd:sequence>
  </xsd:complexType>
  <xsd:element name="strategy">
    <xsd:complexType>
      <xsd:sequence>
        <xsd:element ref="condition" minOccurs="1" maxOccurs="unbound"/>
        <xsd:element ref="action" minOccurs="1" maxOccurs="1"/>
      </xsd:sequence>
      <xsd:attribute name="using" type="string" use="required"/>
      <xsd:attribute name="priority" type="integer" use="implied"/>
    </xsd:complexType>
  </xsd:element>
  <xsd:complexType name="business_strategy">
    <xsd:complexContent>
      <xsd:extension base="strategy">
        <xsd:sequence>
          <xsd:element name="currency" type="xsd:currency" maxOccurs="unbound"/>
            <xsd:complexContent>
              <xsd:sequence>
                <xsd:element ref="condition"/>
                <xsd:element ref="action"/>
              </xsd:sequence>
            </xsd:complexContent>
          <xsd:attribute name="exchange_rate" type="xsd:real" use="required"/>
        </xsd:sequence>
      </xsd:extension>
    </xsd:complexContent>
  </xsd:complexType>
  <xsd:complexType name="negotiation_strategy">
    <xsd:complexContent>
      <xsd:extension base="business_strategy">
        <xsd:sequence>
          <xsd:element name="margin" type="xsd:string"/>
        </xsd:sequence>
      </xsd:extension>
    </xsd:complexContent>
  </xsd:complexType>
  <xsd:complexType name="planning_strategy">
    <xsd:complexContent>
      <xsd:extension base="business_strategy">
        <xsd:sequence>
          <xsd:element name="discontinued" type="xsd:boolean"/>
        </xsd:sequence>
      </xsd:extension>
    </xsd:complexContent>
  </xsd:complexType>
  <xsd:element name="condition" type="xsd:string"/>
```

Fig. 16.8. XML Schema specification of strategy hierarchy.

```xml
<?xml version="1.0"?>
<xsd:schema
xmlns:xsd="http://www.w3.org/2001/XMLSchema"
     targetNamespace="http://party1.e-
business.com"
     xmlns="http:// party1.e-business.com ">
  <xsd:complexType name="domain_data">
    <xsd:sequence>
      <xsd:complexType name="resolution"
maxOccurs="unbound">
        <xsd:sequence>
          <xsd:complexType name="contain"
maxOccurs="unbound">
            <xsd:sequence>
              <xsd:element name="container"
maxOccurs="1"/>
              <xsd:element name="contained"
maxOccurs="unbound"/>
            </xsd:sequence>
          </xsd:complexType>
          <xsd:complexType name="synonym">
            <xsd:sequence>
              <xsd:element name="item"
minOccurs="2" maxOccurs="unbound"/>
            </xsd:sequence>
          </xsd:complexType>
        </xsd:sequence>
      </xsd:complexType>
      <xsd:complexType name="nego"
maxOccurs="unbound">
        <xsd:sequence>
          <xsd:complexType name="give">
            <xsd:sequence>
              <xsd:element name="min_price"/>
              <xsd:element name="avg_price"/>
            </xsd:sequence>
          </xsd:complexType>
          <xsd:complexType name="take">
            <xsd:sequence>
              <xsd:element name="margin"/>
            </xsd:sequence>
          </xsd:complexType>
          <xsd:element name="deal"/>
          <xsd:complexType name="intervene">
            <xsd:sequence>
              <xsd:element name="name"/>
              <xsd:complexType name="when">
                <xsd:sequence>
                  <xsd:element name="low"
maxOccurs="1"/>
                  <xsd:element name="hi"
maxOccurs="1"/>
                </xsd:sequence>
```

```xml
              </xsd:complexType>
              <xsd:element name="issues"/>
              <xsd:element name="done"
maxOccurs="unbound"/>
              <xsd:element name="undone"
maxOccurs="1"/>
            </xsd:sequence>
          </xsd:complexType>
          <xsd:element name="completeness"/>
          <xsd:element name="ex_rate"/>
        </xsd:sequence>
      </xsd:complexType>
    </xsd:sequence>
  </xsd:complexType>
  <xsd:complexType name="personal_data">
    <xsd:complexContent>
      <xsd:restriction base="domain_data">
        <xsd:sequence>
          <xsd:complexType name="resolution"
maxOccurs="unbound">
            <xsd:complexType
name="synonym">
              <xsd:sequence>
                <xsd:element name="item"
minOccurs="2" maxOccurs="unbound"/>
              </xsd:sequence>
            </xsd:complexType>
          </xsd:complexType>
          <xsd:complexType name="nego"
maxOccurs="unbound">
            <xsd:sequence>
              <xsd:complexType name="give">
                <xsd:sequence>
                  <xsd:element
name="min_price"/>
                </xsd:sequence>
              </xsd:complexType>
              <xsd:complexType name="take">
                <xsd:sequence>
                  <xsd:element name="margin"/>
                </xsd:sequence>
              </xsd:complexType>
              <xsd:element name="deal"/>
              <xsd:element
name="completeness"/>
              <xsd:element name="ex_rate"/>
            </xsd:sequence>
          </xsd:complexType>
        </xsd:sequence>
      </xsd:restriction>
    </xsd:sequence>
  </xsd:complexType>
</xsd:schema>
```

Fig. 16.9. XML Schema for domain data.

These handlers are classified into three groups: handlers for request messages, handlers for response messages, and the pivot point handler. The pivot point handler switches the context from request handling to response handling.

Request handlers manage tasks such as: 1) converting the SOAP request message into SOAP request data, 2) understanding the documents, 3) finding similar documents dealt with in the past (cases), 4) searching for appropriate negotiation strategies and domain data, and 5) chaining, if needed, additional request handlers. There is a transport listener at each site that looks for incoming SOAP messages. If a message comes in, the transport listener uses it as the request message, consults the negotiation strategies on it, and then places any response back into an outgoing message. As an outgoing message is produced, the pivot point handler switches the context to a response handler. Outgoing messages are then taken care of by response handlers.

Response handlers manage tasks such as: 1) reasoning about the selected strategies in the context of domain data against the SOAP request data, 2) adapting a past case matched to apply to the current SOAP request data, 3) generating SOAP response data, 4) converting the SOAP response data into a SOAP response message, and 5) chaining, if needed, additional response handlers. Broadly speaking, there are three types of response messages: accepting the offer, rejecting it, or proposing a counter-offer. Each such response message will be generated by a chain of handlers.

The handlers for request and response messages manage all features that XML documents provide. The features of XML documents will be described in the next section.

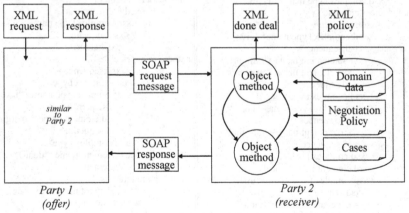

Fig. 16.10. The E-Business Active Negotiation Architecture

16.5   XML Active Features

This section describes XML functionalities that can govern the active features required for e-business. The technique proposed in this paper requires five steps: 1) select appropriate rules and policies from repositories; 2) those selected rules and policies are parsed to extract elements and attributes; 3) those extracted attributes and attributes of negotiation rules are applied to the proposed offer documents based on the strategy repository, 4) generate a new XML document, and 5) transmit the document to the negotiating party.

16.5.1   Selection of XML Rules and Strategies

In XML-based document processing for e-business, XML rules and strategies are to be selected. As popularly used in database management systems, XML policies and domain data can be indexed on one or more attributes that represent all document collections.

To improve the information retrieval and analysis performance, XML data can be indexed for its own special needs. Traditional database indexing schemes are B-trees and hash-indexing; inverted files are used by the information retrieval community. These techniques have been employed in XML data indexing [16.2, 16.3, 16.5, 16.6]. However, *such indexing techniques are not satisfactory because of the complexity of XML documents*. XML documents can contain less clearly defined, if not undefined (e.g., simply #PCDATA), types of elements and attributes, and the occurrence frequency of those elements is unpredictable (e.g., * or + for occurrence), their elements are inter- or hyper-linked to one another (e.g., XLink or Anchor A tag), and structurally different XML documents may be known to be semantically equivalent (e.g., although <e1>A B</e1> is structurally different from <e1>A <e2>B</e2> </e1>, they are semantically equivalent). Each aforementioned component may reference an external entity (e.g., <!ENTITY name SYSTEM "URI">), which is hard and uncontrollable information sources. These complexities are associated with XML documents, thus making them difficult to index.

To cope with all the useful features of XML, indexing schemes should be small and perform their operations quickly. In this chapter, we do not elaborate fully on the notion of XML indexing techniques, but our previous work is applicable [16.8]. Bitmap indexing reduces the size of indexes, while bit-wise operations speed up retrieval.

If XML documents are distributed without knowing site information in advance, then J2EE EJBs (Enterprise Java Beans) [16.4] can be used.

16.5.2   Reasoning about Negotiation

For a received order file, e.g., Figure 16.3(a), both a negotiation strategy (one of the strategy rules in Figure 16.7) and domain data (one of the domain data in Figure 16.6) are selected. Then a reasoning program, e.g., Figure 16.11, may be used to reason about e-business negotiations. This initialization is logically defined as follows:

Initialization ( ) <- negotiation_policy(n) ∧ domain_data (d) ∧ ReceivedOffer (r) ∧ ReasoningClass (c).

Once the reasoning system is initialized, the following functions can be evaluated. The main goal is to generate automatically a counter offer to the received offer or an order. The newly generated offer is also in XML, and it is obtained by the function NegotiationStrategy by taking as input a negotiation policy, reasoning class, received XML file, and domain data.

In what follows, we explain the mechanism of reasoning. Let's first consider the following.

generateCounterOffer (x) <- x = NegotiationStrategy (n, c, y, c) ∧
                negotiation_policy (n) ∧ ReasoningClass (c) ∧ receivedOrder (y)
                ∧ domain_data (d).

negotiationStrategy (n) <- negotiation_policy(n,u1,p1) ∧
                negotiation_policy(m,u2,p2) ∧ using(u1) ∧ using(u2) ∧ priority
                (p2) ∧ priority(p2) ∧ (u1=u2) ∧ (p1 >= p2).

negotiationStrategy (n) <- negotiation_policy(n,p1) ∧ negotiation_policy(m,p2)
                ∧ priority (p2) ∧ priority(p2) ∧ (p1 >= p2).

negotiation_policy (n).   // given from the negotiation strategy file

ReasoningClass (c).   // program class (e.g., Java class file)

ReasoningClass is a Java programming predicate that can be one or more class files. One of those class files is, for example, Negotiate.Class shown in Figure 16.11. Each class file specifies how to reason about offer XML files. So, there may be more than one class file c associated with the program ReasoningClass, and if there is a conflict, resolution rules need to be used. Note that resolution rules are not discussed in this chapter. However, for any two strategy rules with the conditions being satisfied, if the content of the <using> element is the same, then the rule with the higher priority will be fired first. This is stated in the first function negotiationStrategy ( ) above. The second function states that a negotiation strategy rule can be activated only if its priority is higher than any other candidate rules. The negotiation_policy contains a set of negotiation strategies, as discussed in Section 16.3.2.3.

16.5.3   Functional Generation of XML Documents

Using negotiation strategies and domain data, application logics written and implemented in the Java language can be executed to generate an offer document automatically. An example of e-business logic is depicted in Figure 16.11. This program receives a negotiating document, called "offerXML.xml" described in Figure 16.3(a), and parses the document to extract the offer price information. For this price information, the program reads the negotiation strategy file, called "negotiation_strategy.xml", from the local system. The program further extracts the conditions and actions from the local file "negotiation_strategy.xml" if they use an attribute "avg" in the "strategy" element.

```
package com.b2b.negotiation;
import java.io.InputStream;
import org.w3c.dom.*;
import javax.xml.parsers.DocumentBuilder;
import javax.xml.parsers.DocumentBuilderFactory;

public class Negotiate implements Negotiator {
  public void checkOffer (InputStream offerXML) throws Exception
  {
    DocumentBuilderFactory factory = DocumentBuilderFactory.newInstance();
    DocumentBuilder builder = factory.newDocumentBuilder();
    Document doc = builder.parse(offerXML);
    // Read offer from offerXML
    Node nodePricet = doc.getElementByTagName ("offer/price").item(0);
    // Obtain a strategy set from the active strategy file
    Document rdoc = builder.parse("activ_xml.xml");
    NodeList itemList = rdoc.getElementByTagName ("strategy");
    for (int i = 0; i < itemList.getLength(); i++) {
      Element item = (Element) itemList.item(i);
      if (Node) item.getAttribute ("using") == "avg" {
        Node nodeCond = item.getElementByTagName("condition");
        Node nodeAction = item.getElementByTagName("action");
      }
      optstrategy = optimizestrategy (nodeCond, nodeAction);
    }
    // Obtain an average from the policy file
    Document pdoc = builder.parse("policy.xml");
    Node nodeAvg = pdoc.getElementByTagName("nego/give/avg_price").item(0);
    doc.counterOffer (optstrategy, nodeAvg);
  }
}
```

Fig. 16.11. An application logic example.

Notice that the conditions and actions extracted by the application logic program may access the domain data as well. For example, assume that an application logic program uses the "min" attribute of the "strategy" element. Then, there are two rules applicable in Figure 16.4(b). The condition in the "negotiation_strategy.xml" file is evaluated by accessing the policy data, called "nego.give.min_price", from in the "domain_data.xml" file and by reading the x.price data from the "offerXML.xml" file. Notice that "x.price" is offered by one party, while "nego.give.min_price" is set locally in the strategy data file by another party. If the offered price x.price is greater than the local marginal price nego.give.min_price, then a new XML document is generated to make a counter-offer. Returning to our example in Figure 16.3(a) and Figure 16.4(a), the offered price is 33, which is greater than the preset minimum value, 32. The counter-offer specifies the new price by computing the action part of that rule. In this case, the x.nego.offer.price data in the new XML document is the average of the offered price, 33, and the locally preset average price, 37, i.e., 35. Taking this process into account, one possible new document is generated as shown in Figure 16.12.

This update processing continues until all possible strategies have been applied or a successful negotiation has occurred. One of those strategies is the termination strategy as shown in Figure 16.4(b). While executing this process, if the number of negotiations is 4, then the program should decide whether it accepts or rejects the offer, or asks for human intervention.

```
<?xml version="1.0" ?>
<order>
 <item>
  <desc>appliance</desc>
  <color>white</color>
  <quantity>20</quantity>
 </item>
 <nego>
  <offer>
   <price>35</price>
   <term>Valid terms</term>
  </offer>
  <deal>false</deal>
 </nego>
 <delivery>2 Rex St.,
Lafayette, LA 70504</delivery>
</order>
</xml>
```

Fig. 16.12. A newly generated document.

On the other hand, instead of using the domain_data (Figure 16.4(a)), if personal_data (Figure 16.6) were used, the negotiation result would be different. Depending upon the qualification of a person who participates in the negotiation, different personal data can be used. For example, those who do not need an intervention while negotiating will use the personal_data as shown in Figure 16.6. Notice that there is no description regarding the element <nego><intervene> in personal_data. In this case, even if the negotiation were not completed successfully by reasoning with negotiation strategies and external assistance were needed, no human intervention would be allowed. This is not the case when using domain_data shown in Figure 16.4(a).

16.5.4   XML Data Exchange

Negotiating XML documents generated by each e-business party are transmitted from one party to another. A negotiation takes place at one side and is sent to the opposing party for further processing. An example is depicted in Figure 16.13. A square bracket denotes a negotiation between the buyer's document (in a solid box) and the seller's document (in a dotted box). Initially, a seller's document is created in response to a buyer's document. It is the first negotiation. Then, the seller's document is transmitted back to the buyer's site. Another negotiation takes place. This process continues until agreement is reached, or the negotiation terminates.

A negotiating document will be transmitted back and forth until a deal is concluded. This can be costly, especially if negotiation requires additional information to be exchanged and retransmitted between the parties, or if the negotiation process is lengthy. We propose to use XLink, a proposed W3C standard, as a way to reduce the amount of XML data to be transmitted among the parties.

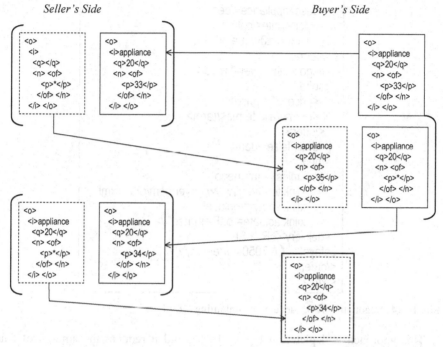

Fig. 16.13. Negotiation via Active XML documents.

XLink is a package that provides hyperlinking functionality that allows links required in negotiating XML documents to be represented. XLink specifies and governs how multiple interrelated resources are managed on the Internet. One well-known but simple example is the A tag in HTML that is a two-ended and unidirectional link. However, using XLink, the linking information can be specified over multiple resources, from sources to destinations, and it can be stored outside all the information that is to be linked, so that updates of such links are possible independent of the negotiating sites.

Instead of receiving the entire document back from a party, only the relevant portion of the document is transmitted back and the counter-offer is processed locally. To do so, we propose a negotiating XML document containing XLink as shown in Figure 16.14. We first level the portion of the document that we want to return. In the figure, that portion is <nego level= "nego">, which is used in the XLink element, <go>. The <go> element specifies the information about the portion to be transmitted as to where and when the transmission takes place, and what to do when it occurs. In this figure, the "nego" portion will be transmitted to the buyer's site when the new document is required. At the buyer's site, the old version will be updated with the appropriate revisions.

```
<?xml version="1.0" ?>
<order>
 <item>
   <desc>appliance</desc>
   <color>white</color>
   <quantity>20</quantity>
 </item>
 <nego xmlns:level="nego">
   <offer>
     <price>35</price>
     <term>Valid terms</term>
   </offer>
   <deal>false</deal>
 </nego>
 <go  xmlns:from="nego"
       xlink:to="http://www.buyer.com/order.xml"
       xlink:show="replace"
       xlink:actuate="onReturned" />
 <delivery>2 Rex St.,
Lafayette, LA 70504</delivery>
 </order>
 </xml>
```

Fig. 16.14. Negotiating XML document containing XLink.

This approach is depicted in Figure 16.15, and it reduces the amount of data transmitted in e-business transactions. Notice that a square bracket denotes a negotiation, and a document is denoted by a uniformly dashed box and one in a slide box denotes a seller's negotiating XML document and a buyer's document, respectively.

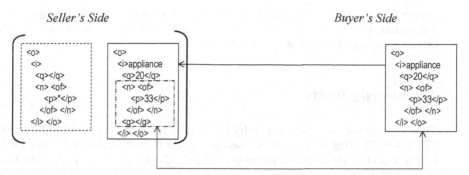

Fig. 16.15. Document transmission using XLink.

A portion of the buyer's document, which is in a dotted-dashed box, is transmitted back to the buyer's side. The benefits are as follows:

1. **Online Negotiation**. As shown in Figure 16.15, the negotiation takes place only on the seller's side. The negotiating XML document is therefore a negotiation proxy of one party. The seller can participate in the negotiation process face-to-face always at its own side as if it receives a proxy.
2. **Low Cost of Document Transmission**. As shown in the figure, only a portion of the negotiating document is transmitted. The seller's document does not need to be transmitted to the buyer's side. This saves computing resources.

16.6   Conclusions

This chapter presents a novel approach to e-business transactions by using XML-based documents to define business documents such as purchase orders as well as more complex documents to manage online negotiations. The approach uses a functional approach that combines documents representing domain data, negotiation strategies, active documents, and reasoning strategies that are used to facilitate negotiations among business partners. Thus each party may have separate negotiation strategies that dynamically modify XML documents as part of the negotiation process.

Rather than send entire XML documents during possibly prolonged negotiations, we propose to use XLink as a way to hyperlink portions of documents that are relevant to the negotiations, thereby reducing the amount of data and metadata transmitted during the entire negotiation process. We feel that the functional approach allows efficient specification of XML-based documents, together with domain data, negotiation strategies, and active rules that govern the bidding process.

This suggested approach is motivated by research in the use of XML-based documents for e-business, thereby enabling business processes. There are several ways in which to make the approach more *functional*. For example, as we gain further insight into the conceptual and architectural issues of the approach, we may move from an XML Schema specification to one in RDF/RDFS. In addition, the interpreted production rules used for negotiation could be couched as quantified constraints using functions. We feel the functional approach allows flexible information exchange and processing for e-business.

Acknowledgements

This research was supported in part by La LEQSF research grant No LEQSF(2000-03)-RD-A-42. This research was also sponsored in part by the E-Center for E-Business and its sponsors, including the Virginia Center for Innovative Technology and webMethods.

References

16.1   Bertino, E. and Ferrari, E. Secure and Selective Dissemination of XML Documents. *ACM Transactions on Information and Systems Security*, *5.*, 2002, 290-331.

16.2   Deutsch, A., Fernandez, M. and Suciu, D. Storing Semistructured Data with STORED. In *ACM SIGMOD International Conference on Management of Data*, (1999), ACM Press, 431-442.

16.3   Rizzolo, F. and Mendelzon, A. Indexing XML Data with ToXin. In *Fourth International Workshop on the Web and Databases (WebDB 2001)*, (Santa Barbara, California, 2001), 49-54.

16.4   SUN. Enterprise JavaBeans 2.1 Specification (http://java.sun.com/products/ejb/) , 2003.

16.5   Tian, F., DeWitt, D., Chen, J. and Zhang, C. The Design and Performance Evaluation of Alternative XML Storage Strategies. In *ACM SIGMOD Record*, (2002), ACM Press, 5-10.

16.6   Varlamis, I. and Vazirgiannis, M. Bridging XML-schema and Relational Databases: A System for Generating and Manipulating Relational Databases using Valid XML Documents. In *ACM Symposium on Document Engineering*, 2001, 105-114.

16.7   W3C. XML Linking Language (XLink) Version 1.0 http://www.w3.og/TR/xlink/) World Wide Web Consortium, 2001.

16.8   Yoon, J.P., Raghavan, V., Chakilam, V. and Kerschberg, L. BitCube: A Three-Dimensional Bitmap Indexing for XML Documents. *Journal of Intelligent Information Systems*, *17* (2-3), 2001, 241-254.

17. An FDM-Based Constraint Language for Semantic Web Applications

Alun Preece, Kit Hui,and Peter Gray

University of Aberdeen, Computing Science Department,
Aberdeen AB24 3UE, UK
email: {apreece|khui|pgray}@csd.abdn.ac.uk

Summary.
   The Semantic Web is a network of machine-processable resources existing in parallel with the traditional Web. Software systems can exploit the
resources available on the Semantic Web to automate tasks for users. A
variety of Semantic Web applications can be realised through constraint interchange and processing, including e-commerce and computer-supported
groupworking. In these kinds of application, users' requirements in the
form of constraints need to be brought together with data representing
parts of possible solutions, and constraint-solving techniques applied to
derive feasible solutions. Examples include the configuration of a custom-
designed product to meet some customers' requirements, or the scheduling of a project to satisfy co-workers' timetabling and task constraints. To
realise these applications, existing Semantic Web information representations need to be augmented with a formalism for expressing constraints,
and a problem-solving framework needs to be implemented to collect and
solve constraint satisfaction problems in a dynamic manner. This chapter
presents a Constraint Interchange Format (CIF) founded on a functional
data model (P/FDM), shows how this CIF can be used to augment the
Resource Description Framework (RDF) — the lower-level Semantic Web
data model — and outlines the components of an implemented constraint
interchange and processing system.

17.1 Introduction and Motivation

The *Semantic Web* vision is to enable rich machine processing of Web information sources, and thereby automate the carrying out of users' tasks on the
Web [17.3]. A broad range of potential Semantic Web applications involve
the exchange of constraints and data which are used to derive some solution or recommendation. For example, in an e-commerce scenario a customer
may specify a set of requirements as constraints; these would then need to be
reconciled with available products to identify possible recommendations to
the customer. The scenario is more interesting when the customer is looking
for a tailored product involving components from multiple vendors, where
compatibility constraints between components need to be factored-in also.
A second example involves the common problem of scheduling a project or
activity, where a number of people will have potentially conflicting timetable
and task constraints which must be reconciled. In these application scenarios,

constraints from various sources need to be brought together with data representing parts of possible solutions, and constraint-solving techniques applied to derive feasible solutions.

Most of the work done to date in building the Semantic Web has focused upon developing "Web-friendly" semantic data models, to allow structured information such as product catalogues and people's schedules to be made available on the Web. Building on the XML standard, a number of proposals for expressing data schemas have appeared, most notably RDF Schema and XML Schema [17.10]. These approaches support the representation and communication of entity–relational information in Web applications: for example, allowing a set of instances of some entity type to be gathered from several structured web pages, and transported for storage in a web-connected database.

The next significant stage in the realisation of the Semantic Web lies in extending the basic data schema representations with information on how the data can and should be used. This information can take various forms, including logical axioms, rules, constraints, or even functional and procedural representations. This work will create the *reasoning services* for the Semantic Web. Early work in this direction included inference engines for large-scale ontologies [17.9, 17.17], mechanisms for representing and reasoning with business rules [17.27], and mobile constraint languages and constraint-solving frameworks [17.29, 17.15]. Building on this early work, there is now a significant number of large-scale projects developing Semantic Web reasoning services, including AKT[1], DAML[2], IBROW[3], and Ontoknowledge[4].

In this chapter, we present a framework for Semantic Web applications based on constraint interchange and processing. At the core of our framework is a well-established semantic data model (P/FDM) with an associated expressive constraint language (Colan). To allow data instances to be transported across the Web, we map our data model to the RDF Schema specification. To allow constraints to be transported, we define a Constraint Interchange Format (CIF) in the form of an RDF Schema for Colan, allowing each constraint to be defined as a resource in its own right. We show that, because Colan is essentially a syntactically-sugared form of first-order logic, and P/FDM is based on the widely-used extended ER model, our CIF is actually very widely applicable and reusable. Finally, we outline a set of services for constraint fusion and solving, which are particularly applicable to business-to-business e-commerce applications [17.25]. We have also used them for Virtual Organisations involved in travel planning [17.4]. All of these services can be accessed using the CIF.

---

[1] www.aktors.org

[2] www.daml.org

[3] www.swi.psy.uva.nl/projects/ibrow/home.html

[4] www.ontoknowledge.com

The chapter is organised as follows: the next section introduces our constraint language, Colan, and the semantic data model upon which it operates; the following section describes the design of the RDF–CIF encoding of Colan expressions; the penultimate section gives an overview of the constraint-solving services already available for Semantic Web applications using the CIF; the final section concludes.

17.2 Colan: A Constraint Language Based on a Functional Data Model

In our previous work [17.2, 17.14] we showed how quantified constraints can be expressed in our Colan language, in a very readable form of first-order logic, including evaluable functions which can be computed over data values represented by a Functional Data Model (FDM). Our Constraint Interchange Format (CIF) is based on Colan, and has been developed as part of the AKT project, aimed specifically at business-to-business e-commerce applications on the Semantic Web. Colan is well-established, having evolved during the course of a number of previous projects, including the P/FDM[5] and KRAFT[6] projects. It has been used successfully in diverse and challenging application domains such as representing and reasoning about protein structures in biomedical applications [17.20], and configuring telecommunications network services [17.11]. Earlier versions of the CIF were based on Prolog term structures; this chapter presents an RDF encoding of the CIF, designed to be more open and less platform-dependent than its predecessor. The RDF–CIF has been modelled using the RDF Schema specification, so that constraints become web resources about which statements can be made (for example, statements about the authorship and context of a constraint). In addition, the CIF has been designed to refer to RDF Schema definitions so that the terms referred to in a constraint can have corresponding RDF Schema descriptions. Thus, any application making use of RDF Schema could incorporate RDF–CIF constraints and make use of our associated constraint-solving software services.

So, in defining our CIF, we were guided by the following design principles:

- the CIF should be serialisable in XML, to make it maximally portable and open;
- constraints should be represented as resources in RDF, to exploit RDF's widely used data model and readily available parsers, and so that RDF statements can be made about the constraints themselves;
- there must be no modification to the existing RDF and RDF Schema specifications, so that the CIF would be layered cleanly on top of RDF;

---

[5] www.csd.abdn.ac.uk/~pfdm
[6] www.csd.abdn.ac.uk/research/kraft.html

– it must be possible for constraints to refer to terms defined in any RDF Schema, with such references made explicit[7].

Note that our CIF work is related to the ongoing RuleML initiative[8] (positioned at the Semantic Web logic layer) and, while we would see our work coming into alignment with RuleML in the future, we note that currently RuleML is more concerned with traditional if–then rules rather than declarative constraints.

The remainder of this section introduces the salient features of Colan and its underlying P/FDM data model. The following section then describes the RDF–CIF formalism in detail.

17.2.1 Colan and the P/FDM Data Model

The semantics of the objects referred to in Colan constraints are described in terms of P/FDM, a semantic data model based on Shipman's original Daplex data model as introduced in Chapter 1. P/FDM can be thought of as an extended ER data model. Now, an ER diagram (or UML class diagram) is commonly thought of as being useful chiefly as a diagrammatic guide or visualisation of the types of entities and relationships in a database (or an object-oriented application) but we are using it as an operational basis for forming queries or for specifications which can be machine verified.

Two example Colan constraints are shown in Figure 17.1. The first example demonstrates how Colan [17.2] expresses a constraint on a university database containing student records. The same constraint language is applicable to the domain of protein structure modelling, as shown by the second example constraint restricting bond lengths. In the first example, a variable t ranges over an entity type `tutor` which is populated with stored object instances. Each of these instances may be related to instances of student entities through the relationship `advisee`, which delivers a set of related entities as in an object-oriented language. These entities can be restricted by the values of attributes such as `grade`. There are also other entity types such as `residue` (representing parts of protein chains) which have method functions for determining distances by computation. Thus functions may also represent a derived relationship, or method. The entity classes can form part of a subtype hierarchy, in which case all properties and methods on the superclass are inherited by each subclass. Method definitions may be overridden, but not constraints.

This is significant for Semantic Web applications, since it means that information represented in this way is not restricted to human inspection — it can be proof-checked mechanically, transformed by symbol manipulation,

---

[7] Essentially, we use RDF Schemas as a simple but practical form of ontology; previous work in the context of the KRAFT project [17.24] highlighted the importance of making explicit ontological mappings within knowledge resources.

[8] http://www.dfki.uni-kl.de/ruleml/

```
constrain each t in tutor
    such that astatus(t)="research"
no s in advisee(t) has grade(s) =< 30;
```

```
constrain each r in residue to have
    distance(atom(r,"sg"),
      atom(disulphide(r),"sg")) < 3.7;
```

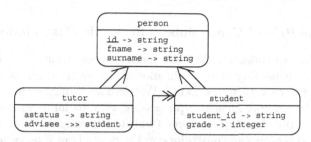

Fig. 17.1. Example Colan constraints from different application domains. The ER diagram models the relationships between entity classes in the first constraint.

or sent to a remote constraint solver. Moreover, given a standardised interchange format, data and attached constraints from multiple sources can be gathered together, checked for compatibility, and used to derive new information. Because our P/FDM data model is an extended ER model, it maps very easily onto the RDF Schema specification, as we shall show in the following section.

Colan is as expressive as the subset of first-order logic that is useful for expressing integrity constraints: namely, *range-restricted* constraints. This class of constraints includes those first-order logic expressions in which each variable is constrained to be a member of some finite set of values. Its use avoids the classic problem of safety of certain expressions [17.31].

Thus we have a formalism which gives us a precise denotation for constraints but it does not force us to evaluate them as integrity checks. The constraint expresses a formula of logic which is true when applied to all the instances in a database, but it is also applicable to instances in a solution database which is yet to be populated with constructed solutions by a solver process [17.14]. Here it is behaving more like a specification than as an integrity check. The power of this in the context of the Semantic Web is that constraints can be passed as a form of mobile knowledge between agents and processes; they are no longer tied to a piece of database software.

There is related work on OCL, which is a declarative expression language for annotating UML class diagrams with invariants, especially more complex cardinality constraints. It has been used to create formal models of configuration problems [17.8], although it is more concerned with formal specification correctness than with AI problem-solving. However, their logical formalism is very similar to ours, since a UML class diagram is basically just an ER diagram with methods, where we use functions.

In general, we believe that there is much to be gained from using the FDM as an intermediate representation of queries and constraints sent to remote sites, even when target databases use relational storage [17.20]. This is because FDM was originally devised for this purpose, in the Multibase heterogeneous distributed database project [17.23].

17.2.2 The Role of Constraints in Semantic Data Models

The original motivation for the introduction of constraints into P/FDM was to enrich the capability of the data model in capturing semantics, which is very much in line with the Semantic Web vision of making information self-describing for maximal machine processing without human mediation. Data models are more than type systems (which they resemble syntactically) because they also represent constraints on the data. Thus a powerful constraint language has enabled us to capture the semantic information that others have endeavoured to express by extending the diagrammatic notation of the ER model. Thus, although the original FDM was somewhat lacking in semantics, we have been able to more than make up for that by introducing constraints.

In doing this, we have capitalised on a cardinal virtue of the FDM, that it enables one to make well-formed mathematically precise computations over data stored as instances of entities related by an ER diagram. Thus we based the Colan formalism for constraints on just these well-formed computations, revising and extending it to use the full expression syntax of P/FDM's Daplex query language. Crucially, because the expressions are fully quantified and referentially transparent, it is straightforward to move them into other contexts and transform them in ways which preserve their semantics. This would not be so if our expression of data semantics had been confined to a diagrammatic notation.

Much early work on constraints, including deductive database approaches, used a predicate logic formalism. Closely related work by [17.30] led to ALICE which is a declarative language for the expression of complex logic-based constraints in an OODB environment, also using a semantic data model. An early example of representing semantic constraints in a functional syntax was in the Extended Functional Data Model project [17.22, 17.16]. Other proposals for functional constraint languages include PRISM [17.28], ADAPLAN (the Applicative Data Programming Language) [17.7] and PFL (Persistent Functional Language) [17.26].

Figure 17.2 shows the same constraint in three representations: ALICE, Colan, and first-order logic.

Note that, in Colan, the phrase so that is optional preceding a quantifier, and that has can be replaced by to have. These small changes do not affect the mathematical meaning, but they do help to make the functional style of Colan more readable to a non-mathematician than the predicate logic

ALICE version:

```
all T in tutor (where S.astatus="research")
  implies: (all S1 in S.studadvised implies:
  (S1.grade > 60))
```

Colan version:

```
constrain each t in tutor
  such that astatus(t)="research"
  so that each s in
    advisee(t) has grade(s) > 60;
```

First-order logic version:

$(\forall t,s,g)\ tutor(t) \wedge astatus(t, 'research') \wedge advisee(t,s) \wedge grade(s,g) \Rightarrow g > 60$

Fig. 17.2. Example constraint shown in ALICE, Colan, and first-order logic versions.

version. Thus, when following a universal quantifier in functional form, the keyword **has** behaves like an implication. However, following an existential quantifier, **has** behaves like a conjunction (possibly with an implied **true**). Further details, showing how universal quantifiers have a weak translation while existential quantifiers have a strong one, are given in [17.6].

In summary, we have introduced our constraint language, Colan, and the semantic data model upon which it operates, and we have argued for the applicability of this language and data model to Semantic Web applications. The following section describes our new XML encoding of Colan in the form of a CIF based on the RDF Schema specification.

17.3 XML Constraint Interchange Format

As we showed in the previous section, the entity-relational basis of both our P/FDM data model and RDF made it relatively straightforward to map from the former to the latter. In building the RDF Schema for our CIF we were guided by the existing grammar for Colan [17.14] which relates constraints to entities, attributes, and relationships present in the ER model. This grammar serves as a *metaschema* for the Colan constraints (such metaschemas are very common in relational and object database systems). A number of issues arose in developing the RDF Schema for CIF, discussed in the following subsections.

17.3.1 Metaclasses for Entities and Relations

In our P/FDM implementation, the metaschema is fully queryable, employing an **entmeta** class that holds information on all *entity* classes, and a **propmeta** class that holds information on relationships (functions), both stored and

```
% objmet - superclass of entity and property metaclasses
declare objmet ->> entity
declare oname(objmet) -> string

% entmeta - the metaclass of all entity classes
declare entmeta ->> objmet
declare super(entmeta) -> entmeta
declare rdfname(entmeta) -> string % link to RDF Schema

% propmeta - the metaclass of all properties (functions)
declare propmeta ->> objmet
declare fname(propmeta) -> string
declare firstargtype(propmeta) -> entmeta
declare resulttype(propmeta) -> entmeta
declare has_inv(propmeta) -> boolean
declare rdfname(propmeta) -> string % link to RDF Schema
```

Fig. 17.3. P/FDM Daplex definitions for entity and property metaclasses.

derived [17.6]. To support querying of the metaschema, the property values of members of these metaclasses are all held as strings (as is common in data dictionaries), so that the answer to a query on them returns the name of an entity or relation and not the contents of the entity or relation. The P/FDM Daplex definitions of the **entmeta** and **propmeta** classes are shown in Figure 17.3, together with their superclass, **objmet**.

The property **rdfname** on the **entmeta** and **propmeta** classes holds the unique URI for an RDF resource, and thus provides an explicit link to the RDF Schema definition for the corresponding RDF Schema class or property. Thus, constraints carry explicit relationships to the domain ontology (as represented by an RDF Schema) for the terminology to which they refer. We chose to employ our existing **entmeta** and **propmeta** classes rather than use the RDF **Class** and **Property** classes directly, in order to maintain close compatibility with our original Colan metaschema, and support extensibility in the CIF (for example, Figure 17.3 shows that **propmeta** has additional properties not required by the RDF **Property** class).

In the RDF Schema we introduce the corresponding metaclasses, **entmeta** and **propmeta**, which will record the graph of classes and properties. Thus there will be one instance of the **entmeta** class for each actual class representing a real-world entity in the instance-level RDF Schema for a given application domain. These metaclasses then provide the natural result types for properties used in constraints. Thus, for example, we can use them to say that an atomic boolean value in a predicate in a constraint can be derived by comparing the property value of a variable which holds an entity identifier with another value given by an expression. This entity and property must be known. We could even write a metalevel constraint to require their consistency, as checked by a type checker.

Figure 17.4 shows the RDF Schema definitions corresponding to the Daplex definitions of the `objmet` and `entmeta` classes from Figure 17.3. It is worth noting that, because properties in RDF are global, some of the original local P/FDM property names must be renamed (for example, `entmeta_rdfname` in Figure 17.4, renamed from `rdfname` in Figure 17.3).

```
<rdf:RDF
  xmlns:rdf="http://www.w3.org/1999/02/22-rdf-syntax-ns#"
  xmlns:rdfs="http://www.w3.org/2000/01/rdf-schema#">

<rdfs:Class rdf:ID="objmet">
  <rdfs:subClassOf rdf:resource=
  "http://www.w3.org/2000/01/rdf-schema#Resource"/>
</rdfs:Class>

<rdf:Property rdf:ID="oname">
  <rdfs:domain rdf:resource="#objmet"/>
  <rdfs:range rdf:resource=
  "http://www.w3.org/2000/01/rdf-schema#Literal"/>
</rdf:Property>

<rdfs:Class rdf:ID="entmeta">
  <rdfs:subClassOf rdf:resource="#objmet"/>
</rdfs:Class>

<rdf:Property rdf:ID="super">
  <rdfs:domain rdf:resource="#entmeta"/>
  <rdfs:range rdf:resource="#entmeta"/>
</rdf:Property>

<rdf:Property rdf:ID="entmeta_rdfname">
  <rdfs:domain rdf:resource="#entmeta"/>
  <rdfs:range rdf:resource=
  "http://www.w3.org/2000/01/rdf-schema#Literal"/>
</rdf:Property>
...
</rdf:RDF>
```

Fig. 17.4. RDF Schema definitions for the `objmet` and `entmeta` classes.

The rules we used when mapping the P/FDM declarations to RDF Schema are as follows:

- a P/FDM class c defined as an `entity` (declared as c ->> `entity`) maps to an RDF resource of type `rdfs:Class` (where `rdfs` is the namespace prefix for the RDF Schema descriptions);
- a P/FDM class c declared to be a subtype of another class s (declared as c ->> s) maps to an RDF resource of type `rdfs:Class`, with an `rdfs:subClassOf` property the value of which is the class named s;

− a P/FDM function f declared on entities of class c, with result type r (declared as $f(c) \rightarrow r$), maps to an RDF resource of type rdf:Property with an rdfs:domain of c and an rdfs:range of r.

17.3.2 Representation of Variables in Constraints

Any variable in Colan is always introduced in relation to a set that it ranges over. Thus terms such as (p in pc) and (e in employee) are common, as in the example expressions:

```
(p in pc) such that name (p) = "xxx"
(e in employee) such that  salary(e) > 5000 and age(e) < 50
```

This is represented in the syntax by the setmem metaclass, while variables themselves are described by the variable class, both defined as shown in Figure 17.5. An instance of the variable class is a legal instance of an expr class (representing an expression) by virtue of a series of subclass relationships. There is also a semantic constraint that such an instance must already have been introduced with a quantifier; this is not currently captured in the RDF Schema but could possibly be represented using the RDF Schema ConstraintResource extension mechanism. An example RDF–CIF fragment corresponding to the Colan fragment (p in pc) is shown in Figure 17.6.

```
<rdfs:Class rdf:ID="variable">
  <rdfs:subClassOf rdf:resource="#operand"/>
</rdfs:Class>

<rdf:Property rdf:ID="varname">
  <rdfs:domain rdf:resource="#variable"/>
  <rdfs:range rdf:resource=
  "http://www.w3.org/2000/01/rdf-schema#Literal"/>
</rdf:Property>

<rdfs:Class rdf:ID="setmem">
  <rdfs:subClassOf rdf:resource="#boolprim"/>
</rdfs:Class>

<rdf:Property rdf:ID="var">
  <rdfs:domain rdf:resource="#setmem"/>
  <rdfs:range rdf:resource="#variable"/>
</rdf:Property>

<rdf:Property rdf:ID="set">
  <rdfs:domain rdf:resource="#setmem"/>
  <rdfs:range rdf:resource="#setexpr"/>
</rdf:Property>
```

Fig. 17.5. RDF Schema definitions relating to the setmem metaclass.

In summary, our CIF RDF Schema[9] serves the purpose of describing what are valid constraints, themselves expressed at an instance level in RDF. It combines the information in a grammar, which is normally used by a syntax checker or a parser, with information normally held in a database schema and used to validate database queries. The interesting thing is that the P/FDM data description language is expressive enough to capture this, especially cardinality constraints. RDF is not so expressive, although it does provide for schema constraints such as cardinality through the `ConstraintResource` extension mechanism.

Thus our metaclasses in RDFS gain us *extensibility* by allowing us to add extra properties, such as *key*, to the metaobjects in `entmeta` or in `propmeta`. There is, of course, some redundancy, as where we record subclass information both in `entmeta` and by using `rdfs:subClassOf`. However, it is kept consistent, and provides a clean layering of extra semantic information to be used by enabled reasoners.

```
<cif:setmem>
  <cif:var>
    <cif:variable ID="#p">
      <cif:varname>p</cif:varname>
    </cif:variable>
  </cif:var>
  <cif:set>
    <cif:entset>
      <cif:entclass>
        <cif:entmeta>
          <cif:entmeta_rdfname>
            http://www.aktors.org/domain/pc_config#pc
          </cif:entmeta_rdfname>
        </cif:entmeta>
      </cif:entclass>
    </cif:entset>
  </cif:set>
</cif:setmem>
```

Fig. 17.6. RDF–CIF fragment corresponding to the Colan fragment (`p in pc`).

It should be noted that the metaschema makes a clean separation between the description of *constraints* (both universal and existential) and *expressions*. Constraints and their boolean components are a representation of first-order logic, with the usual connectives. Any knowledge source that uses FOL should be able to understand this. Expressions refer to facts about entities, their subtypes, attributes, and relationships, and is based on the concepts of an ER model, which are very widely used. The ER model abstracts over relational

---

[9] Space prohibits us from including the full CIF RDF Schema here, but both it and the P/FDM schema are available at: www.csd.abdn.ac.uk/research/akt/cif/.

storage, flat files, and object-oriented storage, following the principle of data independence. It does not tie one to any particular system, such as Oracle or P/FDM.

The following section describes our existing framework for using CIF constraints, as originally developed in the KRAFT project [17.24] for supporting virtual organisations in which communication and coordination are achieved by the exchange and fusion of constraint knowledge.

17.4 Fusion of Constraints from Different Sources

Having a semantic data model (P/FDM) extended with constraints (Colan) and mapped into an open interchange format (RDF Schema and RDF–CIF) supports a range of applications in which information needs to be moved across a network with rich metalevel information describing how the information can be used. An example application common in business-to-business e-commerce involves the composition of a package product from components selected from multiple vendors' catalogues (for example, consumer electronic equipment, package holidays, fitted kitchens, or financial products). In each case, there are various kinds of constraints which must be aggregated and solved over the available component instances: constraints representing customer requirements ("I want a PC with a colour printer"), constraints representing rules for what constitutes an acceptable package ("any printer must have a driver that is compatible with the PC's OS"), and constraints representing restrictions on the use of particular components ("this printer has drivers only for Windows OSs").

In this last case, the ability to store constraints together with data in P/FDM allows instructions to be attached to the class descriptor for data objects in a product catalogue database. When a data object is retrieved, these attached instructions must also be extracted to ensure that the data is properly used. Thus the attached constraint becomes mobile knowledge which is transported, transformed, and processed in a distributed environment. This approach used in the KRAFT project [17.24] differs from a conventional distributed database system where only database queries and data objects are shipped.

Since constraint processing is a more general formalism, it can also be used to represent user specifications on the required solutions. Here, the user–agent (Figure 17.7) serves as another information source feeding user requirement knowledge into the system in the form of constraints.

In general, there are three different ways to utilise the fused constraints:

1. We can check the constraints against sets of objects retrieved by a distributed database query across the network, so as to reject any not satisfying the conditions.

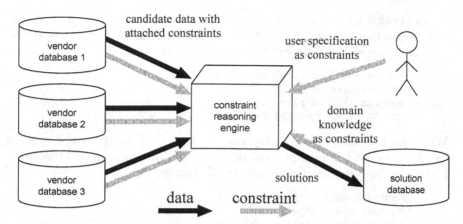

Fig. 17.7. KRAFT utilises both data and constraints which are mobile in the KRAFT domain; constraint knowledge flow is shown as grey arrows while data flow is in black.

2. We can use some combination of selection information in the constraint to refine the distributed database query, and thus do it more efficiently. This could also use the principles of semantic query optimisation.
3. We can use constraint logic solving techniques to see if a complex set of constraints, whose form is not known until run time, does have a solution.

17.4.1 A Constraint Fusion Example

To demonstrate constraint fusion from different sources, consider a configuration problem where a PC is built by combining components from vendors. All of the constraints below are expressed in Colan and so would be exchanged using the RDF–CIF representation described in the previous section.

The user specifies their requirement in the form of a constraint through the user–agent. In this example, the user specifies that the PC must use a "pentium3" processor but not the "win98" OS:

```
constrain each p in pc
  to have cpu(p)="pentium3"
  and name(has_os(p)) <> "win98"
```

For the components to fit together, they must satisfy certain constraints imposed by the solution database. For example, the size of the OS must be smaller or equal to the hard disk space for a proper installation:

```
constrain each p in pc
  to have size(has_os(p))
     =< size(has_disk(p))
```

Now the candidate components from different vendors may have instructions attached to them as constraints. In the vendor database of operating systems, "win2000" requires a memory of at least 64 megabytes:

```
constrain each p in pc such that
 manufacturer(p) = "MS"
 and name(has_os(p))="win2000"
    to have memory(p) >= 64
```

When we fuse all constraints together so that they apply to the solution database, we get the description of an equivalent constraint satisfaction problem (note the *conditional constraint* in the last line):

```
constrain each p in pc
 to have cpu(p)="pentium3"
 and name(has_os(p)) <> "win98"
 and size(has_os(p)) =< size(has_disk(p))
 and if manufacturer(p) = "MS"
     and  name(has_os(p))="win2000"
     then memory(p)) >= 64 else true
```

The process of solving the application problem, therefore, is to retrieve data from other databases and populate the solution database while satisfying (i) all the integrity constraints attached to the solution database, (ii) constraints on data objects, and (iii) user requirement constraints. This process corresponds to a generate-and-test approach where invalid candidates are rejected by database integrity constraints. A more efficient prune-and-search approach can be achieved by exporting constraint fragments to a constraint fusing mediator which composes the overall description as a constraint satisfaction problem (CSP) for a configuration task [17.13] so that it may plan the solution. The CSP is then analysed and decomposed into database queries and constraint logic programs which are fed across to distributed databases and constraint solvers, under the control of a mediator [17.19, 17.18].

17.5 Discussion and Conclusion

In this chapter, we have presented a framework for Semantic Web applications based on constraint interchange and processing. At the core of the framework is a well-established semantic data model (P/FDM) with an associated expressive constraint language (Colan). P/FDM can map to the extended ER as well as object data models, and coupled with the constraint language Colan, and the constraint reasoning engine of Figure 17.7, provides the basis of a framework for business-to-business e-commerce and other novel applications on the Semantic Web. To allow data instances to be transported across a network, we have mapped our data model to the less expressive (but adequate) RDF Schema. To allow constraints to be transported, we have provided a Constraint Interchange Format (CIF) in the form of an RDF Schema for Colan, allowing each constraint to be defined as a resource in its own right. From the KRAFT project, we have implemented a set of services for constraint fusion and solving, which are particularly applicable to business-to-business e-commerce applications. All of these services can be accessed using the CIF.

We targeted our approach for use with RDF Schema, and in particular the XML encoding of RDF Schema, in an effort to maximise the applicability of our work. RDF Schema is the simplest and most universal of the proposed Semantic Web data representations, while still being adequately expressive for our purposes. In linking Colan to RDF Schema, we also intend to make our RDF–CIF compatible with more expressive ontology representation languages being built on top of RDF Schema, including OIL[10], DAML+OIL[11], and OWL[12]. Moreover, a basic requirement of our approach in defining the RDF Schema for Colan expressions was that it should in no way require modification to the underlying RDF definitions (this is in contrast to the OIL and DAML approaches, which modify or override the RDF layer in order to capture certain kinds of expression [17.5]). Thus, we view RDF and RDFS as sufficiently useful and extensible in itself; in defence of this position, we have shown that the RDF data model is adequately expressive to transport data originally stored against the P/FDM semantic data model.

Other work within the AKT project further supports this position, where RDF is used to represent a large repository of information on the research activities of UK universities, and to draw inferences from this information [17.1]. Further evidence for the utility of RDF in knowledge management applications is provided by the EU COMMA project [17.12]. In all of these approaches, the sufficiency of RDF and RDFS to represent and communicate both ontological (schema) information and individual instances is demonstrated.

However, we have yet to integrate our constraint-solving mechanisms with the reasoning facilities available for these higher-level ontology representation languages, which typically offer terminological subsumption for automatic classification. Our current infrastructure can only deal with the RDF-compatible aspects of the ontology representation languages (corresponding to the extended ER model).

Our constraint interchange and solving services are being incorporated into the AKT infrastructure, as one of the basic knowledge reuse mechanisms in the AKT service layer. Further information on this work can be found at: www.aktors.org

---

[10] www.ontoknowledge.com/oil

[11] www.daml.org

[12] www.w3.org/sw

Acknowledgements

This work is supported under the Advanced Knowledge Technologies (AKT) Interdisciplinary Research Collaboration (IRC), which is sponsored by the UK Engineering and Physical Sciences Research Council (EPSRC) under grant number GR/N15764/01. The AKT IRC comprises the Universities of Aberdeen, Edinburgh, Sheffield, Southampton, and the Open University. The constraint fusion services were developed in the context of the KRAFT project, funded by the EPSRC and British Telecom. An earlier version of this chapter appeared in workshop proceedings edited by Preece, A., and O'Leary, D., (2001) *E-Business and the Intelligent Web: Papers from the IJCAI-01 Workshop*, AAAI Press, pp46–53.

References

17.1 H. Alani, K. O'Hara, and N. Shadbolt. Ontocopi: Methods and tools for identifying communities of practice. In M. Musen, B. Neumann, and R. Studer, editors, *Intelligent Information Processing*, pages 225–236. Kluwer Academic Press, 2002.

17.2 N. Bassiliades and P.M.D Gray. CoLan: a Functional Constraint Language and Its Implementation. *Data and Knowledge Engineering*, 14:203–249, 1995.

17.3 Tim Berners-Lee, editor. *Weaving the Web*. Orion, 1999.

17.4 S. Chalmers, P.M.D. Gray, and A. Preece. Supporting virtual organisations using BDI agents and constraints. In Klusch et al. [17.21], pages 226–240.

17.5 Stefan Decker, Sergey Melnik, Frank van Harmelen, Dieter Fensel, Michel Klein, Jeen Broekstra, Michael Erdmann, and Ian Horrocks. The semantic web: The roles of XML and RDF. *IEEE Internet Computing*, Sept–Oct:63–74, 2000.

17.6 S.M. Embury and P.M.D. Gray. The Declarative Expression of Semantic Integrity in a Database of Protein Structure. In A. Illaramendi and O. Díaz, editors, *Data Management Systems: Proceedings of the Basque International Workshop on Information Technology (BIWIT 95), San Sebastían, Spain*, pages 216–224, IEEE Computer Society Press. 1995.

17.7 M. Erwig and U.W. Lipeck. A Functional DBPL Revealing High Level Optimizations. In P. Kanellakis and J.W. Schmidt, editors, *Proceedings of the Third International Workshop on Database Programming Languages – Bulk Types and Persistent Data*, pages 306–321, Nafplion, Greece, Morgan Kaufmann, 1991.

17.8 A. Felfernig, G. Friedrich, and D. Jannach. Conceptual modeling for configuration of mass-customizable products. *Artificial Intelligence in Engineering*, 15(2):165–176, 2001.

17.9 Dieter Fensel, Jürgen Angele, Stefan Decker, Michael Erdmann, Hans-Peter Schnurr, Rudi Studer, and Andreas Witt. Lessons learned from applying AI to the Web. *International Journal of Cooperative Information Systems*, 9(4):361–382, 2000.

17.10 Dieter Fensel, Ora Lassila, Frank van Harmelen, Ian Horrocks, James Hendler, and Deborah L. McGuinness. The semantic web and its languages. *IEEE Intelligent Systems*, November/December 2000.

17.11 N.J. Fiddian, P. Marti, J.-C. Pazzaglia, K. Hui, A. Preece, D.M. Jones, and Z. Cui. A knowledge processing system for data service network design. *BT Technical Journal*, 17(4):117–130, October 1999.

17.12 F. Gandon and R. Dieng-Kuntz. Distributed artificial intelligence for distributed corporate knowledge management. In Klusch et al. [17.21], pages 202–217.

17.13 P.M.D. Gray, Z. Cui, S.M. Embury, W.A. Gray, K. Hui, and A.D. Preece. An Agent-Based System for Handling Distributed Design Constraints. In M. Boddy and M. Gini, editors, *Proceedings of Agents'98 Workshop on Agent-Based Manufacturing, Minneapolis, USA*, Dept. of Comp. Science and Eng., Univ. of Minnesota. 1998.

17.14 P.M.D. Gray, S.M. Embury, K. Hui, and G.J.L. Kemp. The evolving role of constraints in the functional data model. *Journal of Intelligent Information Systems*, 12:113–137, 1999.

17.15 P.M.D. Gray, K. Hui, and A.D. Preece. Finding and moving constraints in cyberspace. In *Intelligent Agents in Cyberspace*, pages 121–127. AAAI Press, 1999. Papers from the 1999 AAAI Spring Symposium Report SS-99-03.

17.16 P.M.D. Gray, K.G. Kulkarni, and N.W. Paton. *Object-Oriented Databases: a Semantic Data Model Approach*. Prentice Hall Series in Computer Science. Prentice Hall International, 1992.

17.17 Jeff Heflin and James Hendler. Dynamic ontologies on the web. In *Proceedings of the Seventeenth National Conference on Artificial Intelligence (AAAI-2000), Menlo Park, California*, AAAI Press. 443–449, 2000.

17.18 Kit-ying Hui. *Knowledge Fusion and Constraint Solving in a Distributed Environment*. PhD thesis, University of Aberdeen, 2000.

17.19 Kit-ying Hui and Peter M. D. Gray. Developing finite domain constraints – a data model approach. In *Proceedings of the 1st Internatinal Conference on Computational Logic (CL2000)*, pages 448–462. Springer-Verlag, 2000.

17.20 G.J.L. Kemp, C.J. Robertson, P.M.D. Gray, and N. Angelopoulos. CORBA and XML: Design Choices for Database Federations. In B. Lings and K. Jeffery, editors, *Advances in Databases: Proc. BNCOD17 Conference*, (LNCS1832), pages 191–208, Springer-Verlag, 2000.

17.21 M. Klusch, S. Ossowski, and O. Shehory, editors. *Proceedings of the 6th International Workshop on Cooperative Information Agents (CIA 2002), Madrid, Spain*, (LNAI 2446), Springer Verlag. 2002.

17.22 K.G. Kulkarni and M.P. Atkinson. EFDM: Extended Functional Data Model. *The Computer Journal*, 29(1):38–46, 1986.

17.23 T. Landers and R.L. Rosenberg. An Overview of MULTIBASE. In H.-J. Schneider, editor, *Distributed Data Bases*. North-Holland, 1982.

17.24 A. Preece, K. Hui, A. Gray, P. Marti, T. Bench-Capon, Z. Cui, and D. Jones. KRAFT: An agent architecture for knowledge fusion. *International Journal of Cooperative Information Systems*, 10(1 & 2):171–195, 2001.

17.25 Alun D. Preece, Kit-ying Hui, and Peter M.D. Gray. KRAFT: Supporting virtual organisations through knowledge fusion. In T. Finin and B. Grosof, editors, *Artificial Intelligence for Electronic Commerce*, pages 33–38. AAAI Press, 1999.

17.26 S. Reddi. Integrity Constraint Enforcement in the Functional Database Language PFL. In M. Worboys and A.F. Grundy, editors, *Proceedings of the 11th British National Conference on Databases, Keele, UK*, pages 238–257, Springer-Verlag. 1993.

17.27 D. Reeves, B. Grosof, M. Wellman, and H. Chan. Toward a declarative language for negotiating executable contracts. In *Artificial Intelligence for*

Electronic Commerce: Papers from the AAAI-99 Workshop, Menlo Park, California, AAAI Press. 1999.

17.28 A. Shepherd and L. Kerschberg. Prism: A knowledge based system for semantic integrity specification and enforcement in database systems. In B. Yormark, editor, *SIGMOD 84 Conference, Boston*, pages 307–315, ACM Press. 1984.

17.29 M. Torrens and B. Faltings. Smart clients: constraint satisfaction as a paradigm for scaleable intelligent information systems. In *Artificial Intelligence for Electronic Commerce: Papers from the AAAI-99 Workshop*, Menlo Park, California, AAAI Press. 1999.

17.30 S.D. Urban. ALICE: An Assertion Language for Integrity Constraint Expression. In *Proceedings of Conference on Computer Software Applications*, September 1989.

17.31 A. Van Gelder and R.W. Topor. Safety and translation of relational calculus queries. *ACM Transactions on Database Systems*, 16:235–278, 1991.

18. RQL: A Functional Query Language for RDF

Gregory Karvounarakis[1], Aimilia Magkanaraki[1], Sophia Alexaki[1], Vassilis Christophides[1], Dimitris Plexousakis[1], Michel Scholl[2], and Karsten Tolle[3]

[1] Institute of Computer Science, FORTH,
   PO Box 1385, GR 71110, Heraklion, Greece
   email: {gregkar, aimilia, alexaki, christop, dp}@ics.forth.gr
[2] INRIA-Rocquencourt, 78153 Le Chesnay Cedex, France
   email: scholl@cnam.fr
[3] Johann Wolfgang Goethe-University, Frankfurt, Germany
   email: tolle@dbis.informatik.uni-frankfurt.de

Summary.

Although real-scale Semantic Web applications, such as Knowledge Portals and E-Marketplaces, require the management of voluminous resource metadata, sufficiently expressive declarative languages for metadata created according to the W3C RDF/S standard[1] are still missing. In answer to this need, we have designed a typed, functional query language, called *RQL*, whose novelty lies in its ability to smoothly combine schema and data querying. The purpose of this chapter is to present *RQL*'s formal data model and type system and illustrate its expressiveness by means of exemplary queries. *RQL*'s formal foundations capture the RDF/S modeling primitives and provide a well-founded semantics for a declarative query language involving recursion and functional composition over complex description graphs.

18.1 Introduction

In the next evolutionary step of the Web, termed the *Semantic Web* [18.5], vast amounts of information resources (data, documents, programs, etc.) will be made available along with various kinds of descriptive information, i.e., *metadata*. The **Resource Description Framework** (RDF) [18.20, 18.8] constitutes part of the activity coordinated by the World Wide Web Consortium (W3C) for the management (encoding, exchange and process) of metadata as any other web data. The objective of RDF is to enable the definition of resource descriptions in a formal, interoperable and humanly readable way via appropriate languages, without making any assumption about the application domain or the structure of the described information resources. More precisely, RDF provides: (a) a *Standard Representation Language* [18.20] for metadata based on *directed labeled graphs*, in which nodes are called *resources* (or *literals*) and edges are called *properties*; (b) a *Schema Definition Language*

---

[1] For brevity, we denote as *RDF/S* the whole of the RDF Model and Syntax and Schema Specifications.

(RDFS) [18.8] for creating vocabularies of labels for these graph nodes (called *classes*) and edges (called *property types*); and (c) an *XML* [18.7] *syntax* for expressing metadata and schemas in a form that is both humanly readable and machine understandable. The most distinctive feature of RDF is its ability to *superimpose* several descriptions for the same information resources in a variety of application contexts (e.g., advertisements, recommendations, copyrights, content rating, push channels, etc.). Furthermore, metadata definitions can be exchanged, reused and extended, thus facilitating the automatic processing of resource descriptions on the Web.

Yet, the representation alone of resource metadata is not enough. Human information consumers as well as Semantic Web-aware agents have to use and query them. It becomes evident that managing voluminous *RDF description bases* and *schemas* with existing low-level APIs[2] (mostly file-based) does not ensure fast deployment and easy maintenance of Semantic Web applications [18.3]. Still, we want to benefit from database technology in order to support *declarative access* and *logical/physical RDF data independence*. In this way, Semantic Web applications have to specify in a high-level language only *which* resources need to be accessed, leaving the task of determining *how* to efficiently store or access the descriptions to the underlying *RDF database engine*.

The design of *RQL* [18.19, 18.18] has been motivated by the above issues. Based on the formal graph data model presented in Section 18.2.2 and on the type system presented in Section 18.2.3, *RQL* defines a set of basic queries and iterators, which can be used to build new complex queries, as demonstrated in Section 18.3. The smooth combination of *RQL* schema and data path expressions is a key feature for satisfying the needs of a wide spectrum of Semantic Web applications.

18.2 The *RQL* Data Model

The RDF/S data model is based on the notion of "resource". Everything, concept or object, available on the Web or not, can be modeled as a resource uniquely identified by a *Universal Resource Identifier* (URI) [18.4]. In general, we can distinguish resources into *tokens*, *classes* and *metaclasses* by taking into account the abstraction layer to which they belong, i.e., their ability to contain members. More specifically, we can distinguish three abstraction layers. In the lower abstraction layer, the *data layer*, we have the descriptions of individual information resources. These descriptions can be stated in XML [18.7]. For instance, lines 24–28 of the example below illustrate how one can state in RDF that (a) the resource with URI &r1 is both

---

[2] For example, **GINF** (www-db.stanford.edu/~melnik/rdf/api.html), **RADIX** (www.mailbase.ac.uk/lists/rdf-dev/1999-06/0002.html) and **Jena** (www-uk.hpl.hp.com/people/bwm/RDF/jena).

(i.e., *multiple classification*) a *Cubist* (lines 24–27) and *Sculptor* (line 28) and (b) it has two properties (i.e., *attribution*) *paints* with values the resources &r2 and &r3, which are instances of *Painting* (lines 25 and 26). It should be stressed that the same RDF resource description can be expressed in a variety of equivalent syntactic forms using, for instance, XML attributes (like *paints*) instead of XML elements, flat (as *Sculptor*) versus nested XML elements (as *Cubist*), etc. This fact motivates further the need for an RDF/S query language abstracting the various XML syntactic variations of resource descriptions.

```
1  <rdfs:Class rdf:ID="Artist"/>
2  <rdfs:Class rdf:ID="Artifact"/>
3  <rdf:Property rdf:ID="creates">
4  <rdfs:domain rdf:resource="#Artist"/>
5  <rdfs:range rdf:resource="#Artifact"/>
6  </rdf:Property>
7  <rdfs:Class rdf:ID="Painter"/>
8  <rdfs:subClassOf rdf:resource="#Artist"/></rdfs:Class>
9  <rdfs:Class rdf:ID="Painting">
10 <rdfs:subClassOf rdf:resource="#Artifact"/></rdfs:Class>
11 <rdf:Property rdf:ID="paints">
12 <rdfs:subPropertyOf rdf:resource="#creates"/>
13 <rdfs:domain rdf:resource="#Painter"/>
14 <rdfs:range rdf:resource="#Painting"/>
15 </rdf:Property>
16 <rdfs:Class rdf:ID="Sculptor">
17 <rdfs:subClassOf rdf:resource="#Artist"/></rdfs:Class>
18 <rdfs:Class rdf:ID="Sculpture">
19 <rdfs:subClassOf rdf:resource="#Artifact"/></rdfs:Class>
20 <rdf:Property rdf:ID="technique">
21 <rdfs:domain rdf:resource="#Painting"/>
22 <rdfs:range rdf:resource=
           "http://www.w3.org/2001/XMLSchema#string"/>
23 </rdf:Property>
24 <Cubist rdf:about="&r1">
25 <paints><Painting rdf:about="&r2"/></paints>
26 <paints><Painting rdf:about="&r3"/></paints>
27 </Cubist>
28 <Sculptor rdf:about="&r1"/>
```

To accommodate the definition of valid description labels, RDF is enhanced with a Schema Definition Language (RDFS) [18.8] at a higher abstraction layer which can also be expressed in XML. At the *schema layer*, *classes* represent abstract entities referring collectively to sets of similar tokens and *properties* represent attributes or relationships among classes. In lines 3–6 of the above example, we can see the declaration of the property (*rdf:Property*) *creates*, having the classes (*rdfs:Class*) *Artist* (line 1) and *Artifact* (line 2) as its domain (*rdfs:domain*) and range (*rdfs:range*) respectively. Furthermore, using the core RDF/S property *rdfs:subClassOf* (or *rdfs:subPropertyOf*), labels can be organized into taxonomies carrying inclusion semantics. Note that, in contrast to object-oriented data models [18.10], properties can also be organized into subsumption hierarchies. For example, class *Painter* is a subclass of class *Artist* (lines 7–8), while property *paints* refines the property *creates* (lines 11–15). Although not illustrated in our example, *multiple specialization* is also possible.

In a nutshell, properties can be *inherited* (e.g., the property *creates* can be used for the description of resource &r1), are *unordered* and *optional* (e.g., the property *technique* is not used) and they can be *multi-valued* (e.g., we have two *paints* properties). Moreover, resources can be *multiply classified* under different schema constructs using the basic RDF property *rdf:type* (e.g., &r1). Due to this mechanism, we can describe a resource using properties from several classes not necessarily related through a subsumption relationship. This way, a resource can be described from many "viewpoints".

The upper abstraction layer, the *RDF/S layer* or *metaschema layer*, is used to group schema entities into semantic units called *metaclasses*. We can distinguish between the *metaclasses of classes* (e.g., *rdfs:Class*) and *metaclasses of properties* (*rdf:Property*). As we will see later in Figure 18.1, in order to introduce *user-defined* metaclasses, the core RDF/S metaclasses can also be refined using the RDF/S property *rdfs:subClassOf*.

Finally, the uniqueness of (meta)schema labels and the ability to reuse labels from several schemas is ensured by the XML namespace facility [18.6][3]. With the use of an XML namespace, descriptive terms (i.e., (meta)class or property names) are uniquely identified as normal web resources by a URI composed from their names prefixed with the namespace of their schema (e.g., *ns1#Artifact*).

18.2.1 Triple vs. Graph-Based RDF/S Representation

Choosing a good data model to represent RDF/S descriptions and schemas is a core choice in order to design and formally define an RDF/S manipulation language. In particular, a query language describes in a declarative fashion the mapping from an input instance of the data model to an output instance of the data model. In the previous section, we have seen that a direct usage of the XML syntax (and its underlying tree data model) in order to represent RDF/S (meta)data is not appropriate, since semantically equivalent descriptions may have several XML serializations. In this section, we compare two candidate RDF/S representations based on *triple* and *graph* models.

The *triple*-based model provides a flat relational representation of RDF/S schemas and resource descriptions. More precisely, each RDF/S graph (i.e., a *data* or *schema description*) is represented as a set of edges, called *statements*. A *statement* is composed of a named edge (a property) and two end nodes (a resource and a value). Each statement can be represented by

---

[3] The prefixes *rdf* and *rdfs* are used to denote the namespaces where the basic RDF and RDFS modeling constructs (either at the schema or metaschema layers) are respectively defined

a *triple* having a *subject* (e.g., &r1), a *predicate* (e.g., fname), and an *object* (e.g., "Pablo"). The set of all statements referring to the same subject (i.e., the same URI) constitutes its corresponding *description*. For instance, the description of the resource &r1 (lines 24–28) under the form of triples (<subject, predicate, object>) is given below:

```
<&r1 rdf:type Cubist>
<&r1 paints &r2>
<&r1 paints &r3>
<&r2 rdf:type Painting>
<&r3 rdf:type Painting>
<&r1 rdf:type Sculptor>
```

Moreover, triples can also be used to represent RDF schemas. For example, the description of the classes *Artist* and *Artifact* as well as that of the property *creates* (line 1–6) is represented by the following triples:

```
<Artist rdf:type rdfs:Class>
<Artifact rdf:type rdfs:Class>
<creates rdf:type rdf:Property>
<creates rdfs:domain Artist>
<creates rdfs:range Artifact>
```

An alternative RDF/S representation is based on *directed graphs with labels on nodes and edges*. This representation extends well-known semistructured data models [18.2] by taking into account the peculiarities of RDF/S: (meta)schema (or data) graph nodes are labeled with (meta)class names (or resource URIs) while edges defined between these nodes are labeled with property names. Classes and properties can also be related at the (meta)schema layer through additional *subsumption* edges while nodes at the various abstraction layers are connected through *instantiation* edges. Figure 18.1 presents visually the graph representation of a cultural portal catalog, a small part of which was represented previously in the RDF/XML syntax.

The upper part of Figure 18.1 refers to the metaschema layer employed by our application example and consists of the metaclasses of classes *RealWorldObject* and *WebResource* and the metaclass of properties *SchemaProperty*, whose instances are the properties *related* and *maxCardinality*. The middle part of Figure 18.1 refers to the schema layer of our application example and essentially comprises two schemas. The schema on the left defines basic cultural entities, such as *Artist* and *Artifact*, and related properties, such as *technique*, *creates* and *exhibited*. The schema on the right provides the concepts needed by the application to describe the resources according to the administrative information they contain, e.g., the title (*title*), the date of last modification (*last_modified*) and the size (*file_size*) of each resource. Both classes and properties are further refined, forming subsumption hierarchies. The lower part of Figure 18.1 represents the resources descriptions created according to these schemas. As previously stated, properties can be inherited (e.g., the subclass *Sculptor* also has the property *lname* and therefore this property can be used in the description of resource &r12), they can be

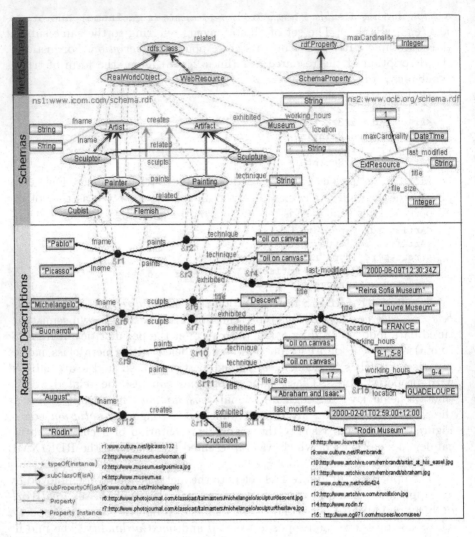

Fig. 18.1. An example cultural portal.

attached more than once to a resource (e.g., the property *paints* to resource &r1), they are unordered (e.g., the properties *fname* and *lname* of &r1 may occur in any order) and optional (e.g., the property *lname* is not used by the resource &r9). Note that due to *multiple classification*, the resource &r11 is classified under the classes *Painting* and *ExtResource* (not pairwise related with a subsumption relationship) and therefore &r1 can be described using properties attributed to both classes.

Compared to the *triple*-based representation, the *graph*-based representation of RDF/S schema and resource descriptions provides a number of significant advantages. End users are liberated from the arduous task of expressing joins over individual triples (i.e., edges) in order to navigate/filter complex description graphs. Developers can more easily understand the semantics of the created and queried description graphs, especially when classes or properties are related through subsumption relationships and therefore additional triples can be inferred from the original descriptions. Finally, database engines have more optimization opportunities in terms of storage volumes and query execution times compared to a monolithic RDF/S representation by a flat and untyped triple-table. Readers are referred to [18.3, 18.14] for further details and experimental results on the efficient processing of RDF/S graphs.

18.2.2 A Formal Data Model for RDF

In this section we introduce a formal data model for RQL bridging and reconciling W3C RDF Model & Syntax with Schema specifications [18.20, 18.8], which is based on directed labeled graphs. Compared to the RDF/S specifications, the main contribution of the RQL model is the introduction of a semistructured type system for RDF schemas, as well as the representation of RDF descriptions as atomic or complex data values. The connection between the two worlds is ensured by a type interpretation function, which (a) does not impose a strict typing on the descriptions (e.g., a resource may be liberally described using optional and repeated properties which are loosely coupled with classes); (b) permits superimposed descriptions of the same resources (e.g., by classifying resources under multiple classes which are not necessarily related by subsumption relationships); and (c) allows for a flexible schema refinement (e.g., through specialization of both entity classes and properties).

RDF resource descriptions [18.20] are represented as *directed labeled graphs*, whose nodes are called *resources* (or *literal* and *container values*) and edges are called *properties*. RDFS schemas [18.8] are also represented as directed acyclic labeled graphs and essentially define vocabularies of labels for graph nodes, called *classes* (or *literal* and *container types*) and edges called *property types*.

More formally, we initially assume the existence of the following countably infinite and disjoint sets of symbols:

- $\mathcal{M} = \{m_1, m_2 \ldots\}$: metaclass names
- $\mathcal{C} = \{c_1, c_2 \ldots\}$: class names
- $\mathcal{P} = \{p_1, p_2 \ldots\}$: property names
- $\mathcal{U} = \{u_1, u_2 \ldots\}$: resource URIs
- $\mathcal{O} = \{o_1, o_2 \ldots\}$: container values
- $\mathcal{L}$: literals, strings, integers, dates, etc.

These sets of symbols are used to label the nodes and edges of an RDF/S graph (at the data, schema and metaschema abstraction layers). More specifically, $\mathcal{M}$ represents the set of metaclass names. Metaclasses can be distinguished into metaclasses of classes, denoted by $\mathcal{M}_c$, and metaclasses of properties, denoted by $\mathcal{M}_p$ ($\mathcal{M} = \mathcal{M}_c \cup \mathcal{M}_p$). The former includes also the default RDF/S name *rdfs:Class* and the latter the default RDF/S name *rdf:Property*, representing respectively the root of the subsumption hierarchy of meta-classes of classes and properties. The set $\mathcal{C}$ contains also the default RDF/S name *rdfs:Resource* representing the root of the user-defined class hierarchy (schema layer).

Although not illustrated in Figure 18.1, RDF/S also supports structured values called *containers* (data layer). The set $\mathcal{P}$, apart from property names, includes also the arithmetic labels $\{1,2,3,\dots\}$ used as property names for the members of container values. The set of all container values is denoted as $\mathcal{O}$. Each RDF/S container value can be uniquely identified by a URI and can be an instance of one and only one bulk type in *Bt*, namely, *rdf:Bag*, *rdf:Seq* and *rdf:Alt*. Furthermore, the domain of every literal type *t* in *Lt* (e.g., string, integer, date, etc.) is denoted as $\mathtt{dom(t)}$, while $\mathcal{L}$ represents the set $\cup_{t\in Lt}dom(t)$, i.e., the definition of the default RDF/S name *rdfs:Literal*. As a matter of fact, *Lt* represents the set of all XML basic datatypes that can be used by an RDF/S schema [18.22].

Each RDF schema uses a finite number of metaclass names $M \subseteq \mathcal{M}$, class names $C \subseteq \mathcal{C}$, and property names $P \subseteq \mathcal{P}$, as well as the sets of type names *Lt* and *Bt*. The property names are defined using metaclass, class, literal or container type names, such that for every $p \in P$, $domain(p) \in M \cup C$ and $range(p) \in M \cup C \cup Bt \cup Lt$ **(1.1)**.

Definition 1 *An **RDF/S schema graph** RS is a 6-tuple RS $= (V_S, E_S, \psi, \lambda, \prec, N)$, where $N = M \cup C \cup P \cup Bt \cup Lt$ and*

- *V_S is a set of nodes and E_S is a set of edges, where $V_S = M \cup C \cup Bt \cup Lt$ and $E_S = P$ (1.1)*
- *ψ is an incidence function $\psi : E_S \to V_S \times V_S$ (1.2)*
- *λ is a labeling function $\lambda : V_S \cup E_S \to 2^M$ (1.3)*
- *$\prec$ is a subsumption relation, such that:*
  - ◇ *`rdfs:Class` is the root of the hierarchy of metaclasses of classes*
  - ◇ *`rdf:Property` is the root of the hierarchy of metaclasses of properties*
  - ◇ *`rdfs:Resource` is the root of the class hierarchy (1.4)* □

The *incidence function* ψ represents the domain (*rdfs:domain*) and range (*rdfs:range*) of properties and imposes the restriction that the domain and range of a property must be unique **(1.2)**. Using the example of Figure 18.1, the property edge *creates* connects the class nodes *Artist* and *Artifact*. The *labeling function* λ captures the *rdf:type* edges connecting the names of the schema layer with those of the metaschema **(1.3)**. In particular, applied to the nodes of an RDF/S schema graph, λ returns the names of one or more metaclasses of classes while, applied on edges, it returns the names of one or more metaclasses of properties. For instance, the schema class *Artist* has an *rdf:type* edge to the metaclass of classes *RealWorldObject*. The incidence function ψ and the labeling function λ are *total* on the sets E_S and $V_S \cup E_S$ respectively. This fact does not exclude the case of nodes not related with a schema property edge. Furthermore, we assume that the node and edge labels of an RDF/S schema graph are unique, i.e., we adopt a *unique name assumption* in N (possibly using namespace URIs for disambiguation). (Meta)schema names are finally organized in subsumption hierarchies through the relation "$\prec$", capturing the *rdfs:subClassOf* and *rdfs:subPropertyOf* edges (1.4).

In order to provide a crystal-clear definition of the RDF/S data model semantics, we introduce the notion of a *valid RDF/S schema graph* imposing adequate restrictions on the formed RDF/S schema graphs.

Definition 2 *An RDF/S schema graph* $RS = (V_S, E_S, \psi, \lambda, \prec, N)$ *is* **valid** *if and only if:*

- *For the labeling function λ, it holds that:*
  - ⋄ *if $c \in C$ and $\lambda(c) = \{m_1, \ldots, m_n\}$, for every $i \in [1 \ldots n]$, $m_i \in M_c$ (2.1)*
  - ⋄ *if $p \in P$ and $\lambda(p) = \{m_1, \ldots, m_n\}$, for every $i \in [1 \ldots n]$, $m_i \in M_p$ (2.2)*
- *For the subsumption relation $\prec$, it holds that:*
  - ⋄ *the relation $\prec$ is a strict partial order (irreflexive, antisymmetric and transitive relation)* [4] *(2.3)*
  - ⋄ *if $p_1, p_2 \in P$ and $p_1 \prec p_2$, then $domain(p_1) \preceq domain(p_2)$ and $range(p_1) \preceq range(p_2)$ (2.4)*
  - ⋄ *for every $n \prec n', n, n' \in C$ or $n, n' \in P$ or $n, n' \in M_c$ or $n, n' \in M_p$ (2.5)*
  - □

Condition *(2.1)* states that every class must be an instance only of meta-classes of classes. Condition *(2.2)* states that a property must be an instance only of metaclasses of properties. Condition *(2.3)* imposes that the subsumption relation is essentially an *acyclic, binary order relation*, so that RDF/S schema or metaschema hierarchies form a *directed acyclic graph* (DAG). As a matter of fact, RDF/S subsumption hierarchies are essentially semi-lattices. Condition *(2.4)* imposes that the domain and range of a subproperty must be subsumed by the domain and range of its super properties. Condition *(2.5)* restricts the application of the subsumption relation between (meta)schema names of the same kind (e.g., hierarchies between metaclasses and classes are not allowed). The above constraints guarantee that the *union of two valid RDF schema graphs is always valid* w.r.t. the inclusion semantics of (meta)class and property subsumption.

Resource descriptions are defined using a finite set of resource URIs $U \subseteq \mathcal{U}$, literal $L \subseteq \mathcal{L}$ or container values $O \subseteq \mathcal{O}$ and property names P, such that every $p \in P$ emanates from a node in U and ends on a node in $U \cup L \cup O$ (3.1).

---

[4] A relation R is *irreflexive* when it does not hold that iRi. In the case of class/metaclass and property hierarchies, it means that i$\not\prec$i. A relation R is *antisymmetric* when: if iRj, then it does not hold that jRi. A relation R is *transitive* when: if iRj and jRk, then iRk. The symbol $\preceq$ extends $\prec$ with equality (thus, the reflexive property holds).

Definition 3 *An **RDF** resource description RD, an instance of an RDF/S schema graph $RS = (V_S, E_S, \psi, \lambda, \prec, N)$, is a quintuple $RD = (RS, V_D, E_D, \psi, \lambda)$, such that:*
- *V_D is a set of nodes and E_D is a set of edges, where $V_D = U \cup L \cup O$ and $E_D = P$ (3.1)*
- *ψ is an incidence function $\psi : E_D \to V_D \times V_D$ (3.2)*
- *λ is a labeling function $\lambda : V_D \to 2^C \cup Lt \cup Bt$ (3.3)* □

The *incidence function* ψ represents the set of relationships and attributes attached to resources (3.2). The *labeling function* λ captures essentially the rdf:type edges, connecting the RDF data graph with an RDF/S schema graph (3.3). In particular, when applied to resource nodes λ returns the names of one or more classes, but when applied to value nodes it returns either a literal or a bulk type name. The incidence function ψ and the labeling function λ are *total* on the sets E_D and V_D respectively.

As in the case of RDF/S schemas, we introduce in the sequel the notion of a *valid RDF resource description*.

Definition 4 *An RDF resource description $RD = (RS, V_D, E_D, \psi, \lambda)$ is **valid** if and only if RS is a valid RDF/S schema and:*

- *for every node $n \in V_D$:*
  - ⋄ *if $n \in U \Rightarrow \lambda(n) \subseteq C$ (4.1)*
  - ⋄ *if $n \in L \Rightarrow \lambda(n) \in Lt$ (4.2)*
  - ⋄ *if $n \in O \Rightarrow \lambda(n) \in Bt$ (4.3)*
- *for every $p \in E_D$ from node n to node n':*
  - ⋄ *$\exists c \in \lambda(n), c \preceq domain(p) \wedge \exists c' \in \lambda(n'), c' \preceq range(p)$ (4.4)* □

Condition *(4.1)* states that a data resource is an instance only of classes. Condition *(4.2)* (like *(4.3)*) states that a literal (container) value is an instance of one and only one literal (bulk) type. Condition *(4.4)* imposes that a data resource (or literal, container value) to which a property is applied (ends), must be an instance of the class (or type) constituting the domain (range) of the property. The above constraints guarantee that the *union of two valid RDF resource descriptions is always valid* w.r.t. the inclusion semantics of class and property subsumption.

18.2.3 A Type System for RDF

Schemas or types have been traditionally exploited in the database world by query languages, such as OQL [18.10], for several reasons:

Clear data interpretation: a type system provides an unambiguous *understanding of the nature of RDF/S data* returned by a query. For example, we can understand that a URI identifies uniquely a data resource and not a class or property.

Error detection and safety: due to typing rules, we can—on the one hand—*ensure the safety of operations* and—on the other hand—*check the validity of their compositions*. For instance, arithmetic operations on class names are meaningless.

Better performance: a type system can provide valuable clues for designing a better storage for RDF/S graphs, while it can facilitate the efficient processing of queries (e.g., rewriting path expressions).

In order to introduce a type system for the RDF/S data model, a number of requirements must be taken into consideration. Firstly, in contrast to object-oriented schemas, RDF/S properties (i.e., attributes and relationships) are self-existent. For instance, one can query the property *creates* regardless of whether it emanates from resources that are instances of the class *Artist* or its subclass *Painter*. Secondly, due to the existence of the data–schema–metaschema abstraction layers, the instances of a type could be data of another type. For example, instances of the metaclass *rdf:Property* are schema properties like *creates*, while instances of this property are (binary) sequences. Lastly, container values may have heterogeneous contents, e.g., literal or other container values, resource URIs or (meta)class and property names. The type system foreseen by *RQL* is given below:

$$\tau = \tau_{M_c} \mid \tau_{M_p} \mid \tau_C \mid \tau_P[\tau, \tau] \mid \tau_U \mid \tau_L \mid \{\tau\} \mid [1 : \tau_1, 2 : \tau_2, \ldots, n : \tau_n] \mid$$
$$(1 : \tau_1 + 2 : \tau_2 + \ldots + n : \tau_n)$$

where τ_{M_c} is a **metaclass of classes** type, τ_{M_p} is a **metaclass of properties** type, τ_C is a **class** type, $\tau_P[\tau, \tau]$ is a **property** type, τ_U is the type of **resource URIs** (including the URIs of namespaces), τ_L is a **literal** type in *Lt*, {.} is a **bag** type, [.] is a **sequence** type and (.) is the **alternative** type. Alternatives in our model capture the semantics of union (or variant) types [18.9] and they are also ordered (i.e., integer labels play the role of union member markers). Since there exists a predefined ordering of labels for sequences and alternatives, labels can be omitted (for bags, labels are meaningless). Furthermore, no subtyping relation is defined in RDF/S. The set of all types one can construct from the (meta)class or property names, the resource URIs and the literal or container types is denoted as **T**.

The *RQL* type system provides all the components we need to capture collections with homogeneous and heterogeneous contents, as well as to uniformly interpret metaclasses, classes and properties. Thus, classes and metaclasses can be interpreted as unary relations (i.e., bags) of type $\{\tau_U\}$ (data layer) and $\{\tau\} : \tau \in \{\tau_C, \tau_P\}$ (schema layer) respectively, while properties can be interpreted (data layer) as binary relations (i.e., bag of sequences) of type $\{[\tau_U, \tau_U]\}$ for relationships and $\{[\tau_U, \tau_L]\}$ for atomic attributes. When the property range is a bulk type then the corresponding interpretation involves container values of an appropriate **bag** or **sequence** or **alternative** type. The notation $\tau_P[\tau, \tau]$ for property types indicates the exact type of its domain and range (first and second position in the sequence). Properties whose domain and range are metaclasses are interpreted (schema layer) as

$\{[\tau_1, \tau_2]\}$: $\tau_1, \tau_2 \in \{\tau_C, \tau_P\}$ depending on whether the domain (range) of the property is a metaclass of classes or of properties. Generally speaking, (meta)schema names in RDF/S play a dual role, both as *labels* and *containers* (disambiguation depends on the operation context). For instance, the name *Artist* refers to the schema graph node with the same label (class label), but also to the resource URIs which are direct and indirect instances of this class. The instantiation of (meta)schema names with a finite set of resource URIs (or schema names) is captured by appropriate *population functions*.

Definition 5 *A class population function,* $\pi_c : C \to 2^U$, *assigns a finite set of resource URIs to a schema class such that:*
– for every $c, c' \in C, c \preceq c', v \in \pi_c \Rightarrow v \notin \pi_{c'}$ *(5.1)* $\square$

In order to capture instantiation of metaclasses of classes and properties we also define the *population functions* $\pi_{M_c} : M_c \to 2^C$ and $\pi_{M_p} : M_p \to 2^P$. Note that the population functions are the inverse of the labeling functions λ employed at each abstraction layer (definitions 1 and 3). These functions are *partial*, due to the fact that there may be (meta)classes without population. Furthermore, since we can multiply classify resources (or class, property names) under several (meta)classes, π_c (or π_{M_c}, π_{M_p}) is *non-disjoint*. However, condition *(5.1)* imposes that a resource URI (or class, property name) appears only once in the extension of a (meta)class even though it can be classified more than once in its subclasses (i.e., it belongs to its "closest" class w.r.t. the defined subsumption hierarchy). It should be stressed that, by default, we use an *extended* (meta)class interpretation, denoted by π^*, including both the proper instances of a (meta)class and the instances of its subclasses:
$$\pi^*(n) = \pi(n) \cup \{\pi(n')|n' \prec n\}$$

The set of all values one can construct from the class or property names, the resource URIs and the literal and container values using the *RQL* type system is denoted as V and the *interpretation* function $[.]$ of *RQL* types is defined as follows:

Definition 6 *Given a population function* π *of (meta)schema names, the* *interpretation function* $[.]$ *is defined as follows:*
– literal types: $[\tau_L] = dom(\tau_L)$
– resource types: $[\tau_U] = u \in U$
– metaclass types: $[\tau_m] = \{v|v \in \pi_M^*(m)\}$
– class types: $[\tau_c] = \{v|v \in \pi_c^*(c)\}$
– property types: $[\tau_p[\tau_1, \tau_2]] = \{[v_1, v_2]|v_1 \in [\tau_1], v_2 \in [\tau_2]\} \cup$
$\{[v_1', v_2']|\tau_{p'}[\tau_1', \tau_2'], v_1' \in [\tau_1'], v_2' \in [\tau_2'], p' \prec p\}$
– bag types: $[\{\tau\}] = \{\{v_1, \ldots, v_j\}|j > 0, \forall i \in [1..j], v_i \in [\tau]\}$
– sequence types: $[[\tau]] = \{[1 : v_1, 2 : v_2, \ldots, n : v_n]|n > 0, \forall i \in [1..n], v_i \in [\tau_i]\}$
– alternative types: $[(1 : \tau_1 + 2 : \tau_2 + \ldots + n : \tau_n)] = \{i : v_i | \forall i \in [1 \ldots n], v_i \in [\tau_i]\}$ $\square$

In order to ensure a *set-based* interpretation of *RQL* types, restriction (5.1) on (meta)class population is also applied to the interpretation of sub-

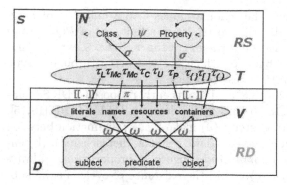

Fig. 18.2. The RQL formal data model

properties. In the rest of the chapter, we use the terms *class* and *property extent* to denote their corresponding interpretations.

On the whole, taking advantage of the *RQL* types T and values V, we introduce formally the notions of a *description schema* and *base*.

Definition 7 *A description schema S is a tuple* $S = (RS, \sigma)$, *where* $RS = (V_S, E_S, \psi, \lambda, \prec, N)$ *is a valid RDF/S schema graph and* σ *is a type function* $\sigma : N \to T$ □

The *typing function* σ, which is *total* on N, relates (meta)class names with (meta)class types and property names with property types. In addition, it relates the basic XML Schema or RDF/S container type names with the *RQL* literal or bulk types.

Definition 8 *A description base D, an instance of a description schema* $S = (RS, \sigma)$, *is a tuple* $D = (RD, \omega)$, *where* $RD = (RS, V_D, E_D, \psi, \lambda)$ *is a set of valid RDF resource descriptions and* ω *is a valuation function* $\omega : V_D \cup E_D \to V$, *such that:*
- *for every* $n \in V_D$, $\omega(n) \in [\![\sigma(\lambda(n))]\!]$ *(8.1)*
- *for every* $p \in E_D$, *from node n to node n'*, $[\omega(n), \omega(n')] \in [\![\sigma(p)]\!]$ *(8.2)* □

The *valuation function* ω relates the nodes and edges of RDF resource descriptions with one of the values in V. Conditions *(8.1)* and *(8.2)* impose that the value of a node (edge) belongs to the interpretation of the type attached to the label of that node (edge). Finally, atomic nodes valuated with literals belong to the interpretation of concrete types like *string, integer, date*, etc.

In Figure 18.2.3 we summarize graphically the formal definitions introduced in this section. An RDF schema graph RS consists of a set of names N, connected through subsumption ($\prec$) and property edges (ψ). An RDF resource description RD is also a graph comprising a set of resource URIs and literal (or container) values which are connected through property edges. Both graphs can be represented using triples of the form <subject, predicate, object>. Then, when RS and RD satisfy appropriate validity

constraints we are able to map the schema names N to a finite set of *RQL*
types T (function σ) and the description triples to a finite set of *RQL* values
V (function ω). RS and T constitute a `description schema` S, while V and
RD constitute a `description base` D, which are connected through a type
interpretation $[\![.]\!]$ mapping *RQL* types to values.

Compared to RDF/S [18.20, 18.8] and the recently proposed RDF Semantics [18.17], as well as *OWL* [18.16] and its predecessor *DAML+OIL* [18.15],
the *RQL* data model and type system: (a) make a clear distinction between
the different RDF/S abstraction layers (data, schema, metaschema); (b) enforce the constraint that *the domain and range of a property must always
be defined and be unique*; and (c) forbid the existence of cycles in the subsumption hierarchies. The first constraint allows the unambiguous definition
of appropriate interpretation functions to pass from one layer to another.
Regarding the domain and range of properties, permitting an optional declaration of multiple domains and ranges, as RDF Semantics [18.17] does, results
in properties whose semantics are completely unclear and whose values may
be both resources and literals. This freedom leads to semantic inconsistencies:
resources should be uniquely identified by their URIs, and literals by their
values. Moreover, this constraint ensures that specialized properties preserve
set inclusion semantics of their domain and range. Finally, the introduction
of cycles may considerably affect the semantics of already created RDF/S
schemas and resource descriptions, especially when the subclass declarations
are provided in many, different namespaces, while class equivalence relationships may still be expressed explicitly, using properties as *equivalentTo*—
defined by *OWL* [18.16]—that have as domain and range metaclasses.

18.3 The RDF Query Language: *RQL*

The data model and type system previously presented enable the definition
of a well-founded semantics of a declarative RDF/S query language involving recursion and functional composition. Exploiting its formal background,
RQL constitutes a typed, declarative query language for uniformly navigating
RDF/S graphs at all abstraction layers.

In the next sections, we are going to illustrate *RQL*'s expressiveness by
means of queries of increasing complexity, while showing how this querying
flexibility is accomplished due to the type system used (for an exhaustive
comparison of *RQL* with other RDF query languages, readers are referred to
[18.21]). The example of Figure 18.1 is employed as a running example for all
the *RQL* queries presented in this section. Readers can explore the expressive
power of *RQL* with the *RQL* online demo[5], where they can experiment with
queries and see the results either in RDF/XML syntax or in HTML produced
after appropriate XSLT processing.

---

[5] http://139.91.183.30:9090/RDF/RQL/

18.3.1 Basic Querying Functionality

Due to its functional nature, RQL can compose basic queries and iterators into complex queries. The basic RQL queries essentially constitute a simple browsing interface with minimal knowledge of the employed schema(s) for RDF description bases. For instance, in knowledge portals for each topic (i.e., class), one can navigate to its subtopics (i.e., subclasses) and eventually discover the resources (or their total number) which are directly classified under them. Similar needs are exhibited for the classification schemas used in E-Marketplace registries. To accommodate these needs, RQL provides appropriate functions for traversing recursively the class/property hierarchies defined in a (meta)schema, such as `subClassOf/subPropertyOf` and `superClassOf/superPropertyOf`. In order to retrieve the direct subclasses or superclasses of a (meta)class, these query expressions can be used with the operator "^" (respectively for properties). For example, the query

    subClassOf^(Artist)

returns a bag with the class names *Painter* and *Sculptor*. These functions may also be used with a second integer parameter, in order to return, for example, subclasses of *Artist* up to depth 2:

    subClassOf(Artist, 2)

Furthermore, to retrieve root and leaf nodes of the subclass/subproperty hierarchies at the schema layer, RQL provides predefined functions with no arguments, namely `topclass(topproperty)` and `leafclass(leafproperty)`. To query the metaschema these functions have overloaded signatures so they can be applied on metaclasses, e.g.,

    subClassOf(Class)

will return the metaclasses (of type τ_{M_c}) `RealWorldObject` and `WebResource`. In order to find the definition of a specific property one can use the functions `domain` and `range`. For instance,

    domain(creates)
    range(creates)

retrieve the domain and range of property *creates*, thus returning the class names   *Artist*   and   *Artifact*   respectively.   On   the   other   hand, `domain(maxCardinality)` will return the metaclass *Property*.

RQL's ability to functionally compose basic query expressions into more complex ones is ensured by the type system presented in section 18.2.3. For instance,

If e is an expression of type class (or metaclass), then `subClassOf(e)` (or `superClassOf(e)`) is a valid expression of type bag of classes (or metaclasses). Otherwise a type error is returned.

Query Expression	Typing Rules	
sub/superClassOf(1)	$\dfrac{e:\tau,\tau\in\{\tau_C,\tau_M\},\ e'\in\{subClassOf,superClassOf\}}{e'(e):\{\tau\}}$	(1)
sub/superClassOf(2)	$\dfrac{e_1:\tau,\tau\in\{\tau_C,\tau_M\},e_2:integer,\ e'\in\{subClassOf,superClassOf\}}{e'(e_1,e_2):\{\tau\}}$	(2)
sub/superPropertyOf(1)	$\dfrac{e:\tau_P[\tau_1,\tau_2],\ e'\in\{subPropertyOf,superPropertyOf\}}{e'(e):\{\tau_P[\tau_1,\tau_2]\}}$	(3)
sub/superPropertyOf(2)	$\dfrac{e_1:\tau_P[\tau_1,\tau_2],e_2:integer,\ e'\in\{subPropertyOf,superPropertyOf\}}{e'(e_1,e_2):\{\tau_P[\tau_1,\tau_2]\}}$	(4)
top/leafclass	$\dfrac{e\in\{topclass,leafclass\}}{e:\{\tau_C\}}$	(5)
top/leafproperty	$\dfrac{e\in\{topproperty,leafproperty\}}{e:\{\tau_P[\tau_1,\tau_2]\}}$	(6)
domain	$\dfrac{e:\tau_P[\tau_1,\tau_2],\tau_1\in\{\tau_C,\tau_M\}}{domain(e):\tau_1}$	(7)
range	$\dfrac{e:\tau_P[\tau_1,\tau_2],\tau_2\in\{\tau_C,\tau_M,\tau_L\}}{range(e):\tau_2}$	(8)
typeof	$\dfrac{e:\tau,(\tau=\tau_U\mid\tau\in\{\tau_C,\tau_P[\tau_1,\tau_2]\})}{typeof(e):(\{\tau_C\}\mid\{\tau_M\})}$	(9)
namespace	$\dfrac{e:\tau,\tau\in\{\tau_C,\tau_M,\tau_P[\tau_1,\tau_2],\tau_L\}}{namespace(e):\{\tau_U\}}$	(10)

Table 18.1. Schema operations

These kinds of restrictions and inferences are captured by the typing rules of basic data and schema queries illustrated in Tables 18.1 and 18.2. Each rule represents the drawing of a conclusion (the part below the horizontal line) on the basis of a premise (the part above the horizontal line); static type checking is based on the validity of this premise for the corresponding *RQL* expression. For example, the expression range(Artist) will return a type error at compile time since the function range() takes as operand only expressions (including names) of type property (rule (8) of Table 18.1).

More generally, since we are placed in a semistructured context, the whole RDF/S description graph can be viewed as a collection of nodes/edges. Then, schema nodes and edges can be queried as normal data using metaclass names, which serve essentially as entry points to the corresponding graph (rule (10) of Table 18.2). Using, for instance, the core RDF metaclasses Class and Property (of type τ_M) as basic *RQL* queries, we obtain in our example

Query Expression	Typing Rules	
count	$$\dfrac{e : \{\tau\}}{count(e) : integer}$$	(1)
min, max	$$\dfrac{e : \{\tau\}, \tau \in \{integer, float, date\}, e' \in \{min, max\}}{e'(e) : \tau}$$	(2)
avg, sum	$$\dfrac{e : \{\tau\}, \tau \in \{integer, float\}, e' \in \{avg, sum\}}{e'(e) : \tau}$$	(3)
bag	$$\dfrac{e_1 : \tau, e_2 : \tau, \ldots, e_n : \tau}{bag(e_1, e_2, \ldots, e_n) : \{\tau\}}$$	(4)
seq	$$\dfrac{e_1 : \tau_1, e_2 : \tau_2, \ldots, e_n : \tau_n}{seq(e_1, e_2, \ldots, e_n) : [\tau_1, \tau_2, \ldots, \tau_n]}$$	(5)
ith	$$\dfrac{e : [\tau_1, \tau_2, \ldots, \tau_n], i : integer, i \in [1..n]}{(e[i]) : \tau_i}$$	(6)
in	$$\dfrac{e : \tau, e' : \{\tau\}}{(e\ in\ e') : boolean}$$	(7)
set operations	$$\dfrac{e_1 : \{\tau\}, e_2 : \{\tau'\}, \tau = \tau', \ \theta = \{intersect, union, minus\}}{(e_1\ \theta\ e_2) : \{\tau\}}$$	(8)
comp	$$\dfrac{e : \tau, e' : \tau', \tau = \tau', \theta \in (=, ! =, <, >, \leq, \geq, like)}{(e\ \theta\ e') : boolean}$$	(9)
^name	$$\dfrac{e : \tau, \tau \in \{\tau_C, \tau_M, \tau_P[\tau_1, \tau_2]\}}{\verb|^|e : \{cval(\tau)\}}$$	(10)

Table 18.2. Data Operations

the names of all classes (of type τ_C) and properties (of type τ_P) illustrated in Figure 18.1. Of course, user-defined metaclasses (e.g., RealWorldObject or SchemaProperty) can also be used as basic queries to retrieve the schema classes or properties defined as their instances. In addition, to retrieve only the schema properties representing relationships or attributes of resources at the schema layer (e.g., all the properties of Figure 18.1 except *maxCardinality* and *related*), one can use the built-in *RQL* metaclass DProperty.

In the same style, we can access any RDF graph nodes and edges at the data layer, by just writing the appropriate schema names. For instance, the query

Artist

returns a bag containing the URIs (i.e., $\{\tau_U\}$) &r1, &r5, &r9 and &r12, since these resources belong to the extent of *Artist*. By considering properties as binary relations, the basic query

creates

returns the bag of ordered pairs of resources (i.e., $\{[\tau_U, \tau_U]\}$) belonging to the extended interpretation of *creates*.

In order to obtain only the proper instances of a class/property (i.e., only the nodes/edges labeled with the class/property name), one can use the restricting operator "^". In our example, the result of query ^Artist is the empty bag, since no resource has been directly classified as an instance of *Artist*. Due to the dual nature of RDF (meta)schema names both as labels and collections, we use in rule (10) of Table 18.2 an *eval* function, such that:
$eval(\tau) = \tau'$ iff $\forall d \in [\![\tau]\!], d : \tau'$
This function returns the type of the instances of an RDF (meta)schema name, depending on its type; for example, instances of an RDF class are resources (of type τ_U). More precisely

- $eval(\tau_M) = (\tau_C \mid \tau_P)$
- $eval(\tau_C) = \tau_U$
- $eval(\tau_P[\tau_1, \tau_2]) = [eval(\tau_1), eval(\tau_2)]$
- $eval(\tau_L) = \tau_L$
- $eval(\{\tau\}) = \{\tau\}$
- $eval([\tau_1, \tau_2, \ldots, \tau_n]) = [\tau_1, \tau_2, \ldots, \tau_n]$
- $eval((\tau_1 + \tau_2 + \ldots + \tau_n)) = \tau : \exists i[1 \ldots n], \tau = \tau_i$

For cases where several schemas are used at the same time, *RQL* provides the function namespace, in order to retrieve the (meta)schema namespace where a name is defined (rule (10), Table 18.1). For example, the query:

```
namespace(Artist)
```

returns the URI http://www.icom.com/schema.rdf. In cases where the same names are defined in different schemas, one can use the *RQL* using namespace clause, in order to resolve such naming conflicts explicitly, e.g.,

```
ns:Artist
USING NAMESPACE ns=&http://www.icom.com/schema.rdf#
```

Furthermore, using the *RQL* function typeof (rule (9), Table 18.1), one can find all classes (or metaclasses) under which a given resource (or class/property name) is classified. For example, the query

```
typeof(&http://www.artchive.com/crucifixion.jpg)
```

returns a bag consisting of the class names *ExtResource* and *Sculpture*.

Apart from the basic querying functionality presented above, there are several other query facilities that add to the expressiveness of *RQL*. One of the additional querying facilities is the support of *set-based queries* and *container queries*. In particular, *RQL* supports common set operators (union, intersect, minus), which can be applied on collections of the same type (rule (8), Table 18.1). For example, the *RQL* expression:

```
Sculpture intersect ExtResource
```

returns a bag with the URIs of all resources which are classified under both *Sculpture* and *ExtResource*. According to our example, only the resources &r6 and &r13 are classified under both classes.

As we can observe from the above query, *RQL* also permits the manipulation of RDF container values. More precisely, we can explicitly construct bags and sequences using the basic *RQL* queries bag and seq (rules (4) and (5), Table 18.2). To access a member of a sequence we can use the operator "[ ]" with an appropriate position index (rule (6)). If the specified member element does not exist, a run-time error is returned. Furthermore, the Boolean operator in can be used to test membership in bags (rule (7)). For example, the query

    seq(domain(creates), range(creates))[0]

returns the first element of the sequence, while

    &www.culture.net/picasso132 in Painter

is true, since the resource www.culture.net/picasso132 belongs to the extent of Painter.

For data filtering, *RQL* relies on standard Boolean predicates, such as =, <, > and like (for string pattern matching). All operators can be applied on literal values (i.e., strings, integers, reals, dates) or resource URIs (rule (9)). For example, the expression "$X=\&www.museum.es$" is an equality condition between resource URIs. It should be stressed that this also covers comparisons between (meta)class or property names. In this case, the application of these predicates corresponds to a subsumption test. For instance, the condition "*Painter < Artist*" returns true, since the first operand is a subclass of the second. Disambiguation is performed in each case by examining the type of operands (e.g., literal values vs. URI equality, lexicographical vs. class ordering, etc.).

Lastly, *RQL* is also equipped with a complete set of aggregate functions (min, max, avg, sum and count). For instance, we can inspect the cardinality of class extents (or of bags) using the count function, e.g.,

    count(Painting)

Note that the parameter of aggregate functions may be any query returning a collection of a proper type (rules (1–3)).

18.3.2 *RQL* Filters

RQL supports SQL-like filters, which use *generalized path expressions* [18.1, 18.12, 18.13] with variables on nodes and edges to traverse RDF/S description graphs at arbitrary depths.

Thus, the SELECT-FROM-WHERE filters provide a powerful tool to iterate over collections with RDF data or schema information of any kind. The result of an *RQL* filter is represented by an RDF bag container value, on which

		Path Expression	Interpretation
Data Path	1.	$c\{X\}$	$\{v \mid v \in [\![\tau_c]\!]\}$
	2.	$\{X\}p\{Y\}$	$\{[v_1, v_2] \mid [v_1, v_2] \in [\![\tau_p[\tau_1, \tau_2]]\!]\}$
	3.	$\{X\}@P\{Y\}$	$\{[v_1, p, v_2] \mid p \in [\![\tau_{M_p}]\!], [v_1, v_2] \in [\![\hat{\ }\tau_p[\tau_1, \tau_2]]\!]\}$
	4.	$\$X\{Y\}$	$\{[c, v] \mid c \in [\![\tau_{M_c}]\!], v \in [\![\hat{\ }\tau_c]\!]\}$
Schema Path	5.	$Class\{X\}$	$\{c \mid c \in [\![\tau_{M_c}]\!]\}$
	6.	$\$X$	$\{c \mid c \in [\![\tau_{M_c}]\!]\}$
	7.	$Property\{P\}$	$\{p \mid p \in [\![\tau_{M_p}]\!]\}$
	8.	$@P$	$\{p \mid p \in [\![\tau_{M_p}]\!]\}$
	9.	$c\{\$C\}$	$\{c' \mid c' \in [\![\tau_{M_c}]\!], c' \preceq c\}$
	10.	$\{\$X\}p\{\$Y\}$	$\{[c_1, c_2] \mid c_1, c_2 \in [\![\tau_{M_c}]\!],$ $c_1 \preceq domain(p), c_2 \preceq range(p)\}$
	11.	$\$X\{\$Y\}$	$\{[c_1, c_2] \mid c_1, c_2 \in [\![\tau_{M_c}]\!], c_2 \preceq c_1\}$
	12.	$\{\$X\}@P\{\$Y\}$	$\{[c_1, p, c_2] \mid p \in [\![\tau_{M_P}]\!], c_1, c_2 \in [\![\tau_{M_c}]\!],$ $c_1 \preceq domain(p), c_2 \preceq range(p)\}$
Mixed Path	13.	$c\{X; \$C\}$	$\{[v, c'] \mid c' \in [\![\tau_{M_c}]\!], c' \preceq c, v \in [\![\hat{\ }\tau_{c'}]\!]\}$
	14.	$\{X; \$Z\}p\{Y; \$W\}$	$\{[v_1, c_1, v_2, c_2] \mid c_1, c_2 \in [\![\tau_{M_C}]\!], c_1 \preceq domain(p),$ $v_1 \in [\![\hat{\ }\tau_{c_1}]\!], c_2 \preceq range(p),$ $v_2 \in [\![\hat{\ }\tau_{c_2}]\!], [v_1, v_2] \in [\![\tau_p[\tau_1, \tau_2]]\!]\}$
	15.	$p\{Y; \$W\}$	$\{[v_2, c_2] \mid c_2 \in [\![\tau_{M_c}]\!], c_2 \preceq range(p),$ $v_2 \in [\![\hat{\ }\tau_{c_2}]\!], [v_1, v_2] \in [\![\tau_p[\tau_1, \tau_2]]\!]\}$
	16.	$\{X\}p\{Y; \$W\}$	$\{[v_1, v_2, c_2] \mid c_2 \in [\![\tau_{M_c}]\!], c_2 \preceq range(p),$ $v_2 \in [\![\hat{\ }\tau_{c_2}]\!], [v_1, v_2] \in [\![\tau_p[\tau_1, \tau_2]]\!]\}$
	17.	$\{X\}p\{\$W\}$	$\{[v_1, c_2] \mid c_2 \in [\![\tau_{M_c}]\!], c_2 \preceq range(p),$ $v_2 \in [\![\hat{\ }\tau_{c_2}]\!], [v_1, v_2] \in [\![\tau_p[\tau_1, \tau_2]]\!]\}$
	18.	$\{\$Z\}p\{Y; \$W\}$	$\{[c_1, v_2, c_2] \mid c_1, c_2 \in [\![\tau_{M_C}]\!], c_1 \preceq domain(p),$ $v_1 \in [\![\hat{\ }\tau_{c_1}]\!], c_2 \preceq range(p),$ $v_2 \in [\![\hat{\ }\tau_{c_2}]\!], [v_1, v_2] \in [\![\tau_p[\tau_1, \tau_2]]\!]\}$
	19.	$\{X; \$Z\}@P\{Y; \$W\}$	$\{[v_1, c_1, p, v_2, c_2] \mid p \in [\![\tau_{M_p}]\!], c_1, c_2 \in [\![\tau_{M_c}]\!],$ $c_1 \preceq domain(p), v_1 \in [\![\hat{\ }\tau_{c_1}]\!],$ $c_2 \preceq range(p), v_2 \in [\![\hat{\ }\tau_{c_2}]\!],$ $[v_1, v_2] \in [\![\hat{\ }\tau_p[\tau_1, \tau_2]]\!]\}$

Table 18.3. Formal interpretation of the basic *RQL* path expressions

we can define iterators using nested queries, while ordered tuples can be represented by RDF sequences and, as we have already seen, they can be accessed through a position index (rule (6)). In particular, the SELECT clause defines—as usual—a projection over the variables whose values participate in the result. Moreover, we can use "SELECT *" to include in the result the values of all variables. This clause constructs an ordered tuple, whose arity depends on the number of projection variables. The FROM clause hosts the defined path expressions, which essentially define the part of the RDF/S graph that will participate in the evaluation of the query. In fact, a path expression consists of a series of steps. Each step represents movement in a particular direction by identifying node labels, and each step can apply one or more predicates to eliminate nodes that fail to satisfy a given condition. These filtering conditions are declared at the (optional) WHERE clause. The result of each step is a list of nodes that serves as a starting point for the next step. Table 18.3 presents the formal interpretation of the basic kinds of *RQL* path expressions. Furthermore, we can use the (optional) clause USING NAMESPACE for the definition of namespace prefixes as explained previously.

RQL filters are used in a variety of contexts and application cases. The next sections illustrate how *RQL* exploits their presence to provide sophisticated querying functionality.

18.3.3 Schema Navigation

RQL extends the notion of generalized path expressions to entire class (or property) inheritance paths in order to implement *schema browsing or filtering* using appropriate conditions. This declarative query support for navigating through taxonomies of classes and properties is especially useful for real-scale applications, such as Portal catalogs, which employ large description schemas. Consider for instance the following query, where given a specific schema property we want to find all related schema classes:

```
SELECT $C1, $C2
FROM {$C1}creates{$C2}
```

The result of this query is a bag of type $\{[\tau_C, \tau_C]\}$ and is depicted in a tabular form as:

$C1	$C2		Painter	Painting
Artist	Artifact		Painter	Sculpture
Artist	Painting		Cubist	Artifact
Artist	Sculpture		Cubist	Painting
Sculptor	Artifact		Cubist	Sculpture
Sculptor	Painting		Flemish	Artifact
Sculptor	Sculpture		Flemish	Painting
Painter	Artifact		Flemish	Sculpture

As in the case of core schema and data operations, the validity of operations is ensured by means of appropriate type inference rules. Table 18.4 presents the typing rules used for *RQL* basic filters and rule (4) is applicable in this query. In particular, the FROM clause of this filter uses a basic *schema path expression* composed of the property name *creates* and two class variables *$C1* and *$C2* (Schema Path 10, Table 18.3), with "{ }" used to introduce appropriate schema (or data) variables. In general, class variables are prefixed by "$" in order to be disambiguated syntactically from data variables and schema names.

Since RDF properties can be applied to any subclass of their domain and range (because of inclusion polymorphism), the path expression "{$C1}creates{$C2}" simply denotes that $C1 and $C2 iterate over subClassOf(domain(creates)) and subClassOf(range(creates)) respectively (including the hierarchy roots). We can observe that the above path expression essentially traverses the rdfs:subClassOf links in the schema

Path Expression	Typing Rules	
Data Paths	$\dfrac{e : \tau, \tau \in \{\tau_C, \tau_M\}, eval(e) : \tau'}{(\text{select } x \text{ from } e\{x\}) : \{\tau'\}, x : \tau'}$	(1)
	$\dfrac{e : \tau_P[\tau_1, \tau_2], eval(\tau_1) : \tau_1', eval(\tau_2) : \tau_2'}{(\text{select } x, y \text{ from } \{x\}e\{y\}) : \{[\tau_1', \tau_2']\},\ x : \tau_1', y : \tau_2'}$	(2)
	$\dfrac{e : \{\tau\}}{(\text{select } x \text{ from } e\{x\}) : \{\tau\}, x : \tau}$	(3)
Schema Paths	$\dfrac{e : \tau_P[\tau_C, \tau_C]}{(\text{select } \$c_1, \$c_2 \text{ from } \{\$c_1\}e\{\$c_2\}) : \{[\tau_C, \tau_C]\},\ \$c_1 : \tau_C, \$c_2 : \tau_C}$	(4)
	$\dfrac{e : \tau_P[\tau_1, \tau_2]}{(\text{select } \$\$c_1, \$\$c_2 \text{ from } \{\$\$c_1\}e\{\$\$c_2\}) : \{[\tau_1, \tau_2]\},\ \$\$c_1 : \tau_1, \$\$c_2 : \tau_2}$	(5)
Mixed Paths	$\dfrac{e : \tau_P[\tau_C, \tau_C]}{(\text{select } \$c_1, x, \$c_2, y \text{ from } \{x; \$c_1\}e\{y; \$c_2\}) :\ \{[\tau_C, \tau_U, \tau_C, \tau_U]\}, \$c_1 : \tau_C, x : \tau_U, \$c_2 : \tau_C, y : \tau_U}$	(6)
	$\dfrac{e : \tau_P[\tau_1, \tau_2], eval(\tau_1) : \tau_1', eval(\tau_2) : \tau_2'}{(\text{select } \$\$c_1, x, \$\$c_2, y \text{ from } \{x; \$\$c_1\}e\{y; \$\$c_2\}) :\ \{[\tau_1, \tau_1', \tau_2, \tau_2']\}, \$\$c_1 : \tau_1, x : \tau_1', \$\$c_2 : \tau_2, y : \tau_2'}$	(7)

Table 18.4. Basic filters

graph. It should be stressed that such *RQL* path expressions can be composed not only of edge labels like *creates*, but also of node labels like *Artist*. For instance, "*Artist{$C}*" is a shortcut for subClassOf(Artist){C} (including the root class *Artist*) (Schema Path 9, Table 18.3).

Let us now see how we can retrieve all related schema properties for a specific class:

```
SELECT  @P, range(@P)
FROM    {$C}@P
WHERE $C=Painter
```

The result of the above query contains all properties that may be applied on Painters, either because they are directly defined on class *Painter* or because they are inherited from a superclass of *Painter*. In the FROM clause of this query, we use another *schema path expression* composed of a class variable $C and a property variable @P. In general, property variables (of type τ_P) are prefixed by "@" and are implicitly range-restricted on the set of all data properties (i.e., *DProperty*). Then, for each valuation p of @P, the class variable $C ranges over subClassOf(domain(p)). The condition in the WHERE clause filters @P valuations to keep only those properties for which class *Painter* is equal to their domain (e.g., *paints*) or is a valid subclass of their domain (e.g., *creates*, *lname*, *fname*). In other words, the query is equivalent to the filtering condition "*domain(P)>=Painter*" evaluated over *DProperty* (i.e., DProperty{P}). We can observe that the above path expression traverses the rdfs:domain and rdfs:range links in conjunction with the rdfs:subClassOf links in the schema graph. Note that in the result, range(P) is of type union ($\tau_C + \tau_L$), since data properties may range over classes and literal types.

In cases where we only want to find the relationships that can be applied on *Painter*, i.e., only properties with class range, and iterate on their subclasses (i.e., get all possible range classes), we can use the query:

```
SELECT @P, $Y
FROM   {;Painter}@P{$Y}
```

In this case, "{;*Painter*}" simply denotes a filtering condition of schema nodes identified by the name *Painter* and taking into account the rdfs:subClassOf links. The symbol ";" is used as a syntactic way to disambiguate data variables from constant names, and determine the kind of the path (data vs. schema path) accordingly. Thus, in the expression "{;*Painter*}@P", the domain of @P is denoted to be *Painter* or any of its superclasses and it implies the filtering condition "*Painter>=domain(@P)*". The use of a schema variable restricts the result to the properties with class range. More specifically, it implies the condition "*range(@P) in Class*". In order to also include properties with literal or metaclass range, we use the prefix "$$" instead of "$". Furthermore, similar to the use of class names in path extremities, we can also use literal type names, where applicable, e.g., use the path expression "@P{; *string*}" to find all string-valued properties. Note, however, that such a restriction, if imposed on the domain of a property, would produce a compile-time type error.

To illustrate the *RQL* schema querying capabilities combined with its functional semantics, consider the query which retrieves all information related to class *Painter* (superclasses as well as direct or inherited properties):

```
seq( Painter,
       superClassOf(Painter),
       ( SELECT @P, domain(@P), range(@P)
         FROM {;Painter}@P ) )
```

To collect all relevant information we explicitly construct a sequence with three elements. The first element is a constant (*Painter*) interpreted by the *RQL* type system as a class name (i.e., of type τ_C). The second element is a bag containing the names of the superclasses of *Painter* (i.e., of type {τ_C}). The third element, which corresponds to the *RQL* filter, is a bag of sequences with three elements: the first of type property names (τ_P), the second of type class (τ_C), since a property domain is always a class, and the third of type union (i.e., Alternative) of class and literal type names. The result of the query in HTML form is presented in Figure 18.3.

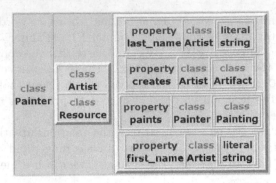

Fig. 18.3. HTML form of result.

We conclude this subsection with a query illustrating how *RQL* schema paths can be composed to perform more complex schema navigation. For instance, the following query retrieves the properties that can be reached (in one step) from the range classes of property *creates*:

```
SELECT $Y, @P, range(@P)
FROM   creates{$Y}.@P
```

The result of this query is depicted in a tabular form as:

$Y	@P	range($@P$)
Artifact	exhibited	Museum
Painting	exhibited	Museum
Sculpture	exhibited	Museum
Painting	technique	string
Sculpture	material	string

In the above query, the "." notation implies a join condition between the range classes of the property *creates* and the domain of @P valuations: for each class name Y in the range of creates, we look for all properties whose domain is $Y or a superclass, i.e., "$Y <= domain(@P) and $Y <= range(creates)". This join condition enables us to follow properties which can be applied to range classes of *creates* (i.e., either because they are directly defined or because they are inherited) to any subclass of the range of *creates*. Schema path expressions may also be exclusively composed of property variables (with or without variables on domains and ranges). For instance, @P.@Q will retrieve all two-step schema paths emanating from the subclasses of the domain of @P and whose second part is either inherited from or defined on superclasses/subclasses of the domain of @Q.

18.3.4 Data Navigation

The *RQL* generalized path expressions can also be used to *navigate/filter RDF description bases* without taking into account the (domain and range) restrictions implied by the properties in an RDF/S schema. This is quite useful since resources can be multiply classified and several properties coming from different class hierarchies may be used to describe the same resources. In this context, path expressions may be liberally composed from node and edge labels featuring both data or schema variables. In this case, the "." notation is used to introduce appropriate join conditions between the left and the right part of the expression, depending on the kind of Z each path component and the specific operations defined by them (i.e., node vs. edge labels, data vs. schema variables). Consider, for example, the following query:

```
SELECT X, Y
FROM Museum{X}.last_modified{Y}
WHERE Y>=2000-01-01
```

In the FROM clause we use a *data path expression* with the class name *Museum* and the property name *last_modified*. The introduced data variables X and Y range respectively over the extent of class *Museum* (i.e., traversing the rdf:type links connecting schema and data graphs) and the *target* values of the extent of property *last_modified* (i.e., traversing properties in the RDF data graph). The "." used to concatenate the two path components implies a join condition between the *source* values of the extent of *last_modified* and X. Hence, this query is equivalent to the expression "*Museum{X}*, *{Z}last_modified{Y}* *whereX = Z*". As we can see in Figure 18.1, the *last_modified* property has been defined with *domain* the class *ExtResource* but, due to multiple classification, X may be valuated with resources also labeled with any other class name (e.g., *Museum*, *Artifact*, etc.). The composition of the two paths is valid in terms of typing since both X and the implied Z are of type τ_U. Thus, due to multiple classification of nodes, we can query paths in a data graph that are not explicitly declared in the schema. For instance, "*creates.exhibited.title*" is not foreseen in any RDF schema, since the *domain* of the *title* property is the class *ExtResource* and not *Museum*. Yet, in our model X has the unique type τ_U, Y has type the literal type *date*, the implied join conditions are comparisons between values of type τ_U and the result of the above query is of type $\{[\tau_U, date]\}$. According to our example, this query returns the sites www.museum.es (&r4) with last modification date 2000-06-09 and www.rodin.fr (&r14) with date 2000-02-01.

More complex forms of navigation through RDF description bases are possible, using several data path expressions. For instance, to find the names of Artists whose Artifacts are exhibited in museums, along with the related Museum titles, we issue the query:

```
SELECT V, R, Y, Z
FROM    {X}creates.exhibited{Y}.title{Z},
        {X}fname{V}, {X}lname{R}
```

In the FROM clause we use three data path expressions. Variable X (Y) ranges over the *source* (*target*) values of the *creates* (*exhibited*) property. Then, the reuse of variable X in the other two path expressions simply introduces implicit (equi-)joins between the extents of the properties *fname*/*lname* and *creates* on their *source* values. Since the *range* of property *exhibited* is the class *Museum* we do not need to further restrict the labels for the Y values in this query.

18.3.5 Combining Schema and Data Navigation

Up to now we have seen how we can query and navigate in schemas, as well as how we can query and navigate in description graphs **regardless** of the underlying schema(s). *RQL* allows the combination of schema and data filtering and navigation, through the use of *mixed path expressions* that enable us to *turn on* or *off* schema information during data filtering with the use of appropriate class and property variables. This functionality is illustrated in the following query, which finds the source and target values of properties emanating from ExtResources (similar to Mixed Path 19, Table 18.3):

```
SELECT X, Y
FROM    {X;ExtResource}@P{Y}
```

The mixed path expression in the above query, features both data (X, Y) and schema variables on graph edges (@P). The notation "{$X;ExtResource$}" denotes a restriction on X to the resources that are (transitive) instances of class *ExtResource*. @P is of type τ_P and is valuated to all properties having as a domain *ExtResource* or one of its superclasses. Finally, Y is range-restricted, for each successful binding of @P, to the corresponding target values. X is of type τ_U, while the type of Y is a union of all the range types of ExtResource properties. According to the schema of Figure 18.1, @P is valuated to *file_size*, *title* and *last_modified*, while Y will be of type (*integer* + *string* + *date*). Note that this mixed path expression is not equivalent to the data path expression "*ExtResource*{X}.@P{Y}", which returns as a result not only the values of the properties having as a domain *ExtResource* but also those with domain any class under which instances of *ExtResource* are multiply classified (e.g., *exhibited*, *technique*). Note that, when using constant class or property names as the path's elements (e.g., *Museum*, *last_modified*), path components are automatically considered as data paths if no variables are defined on their extremities. On the other hand, paths containing property (@P) or class (X) variables as their elements are treated as schema paths (i.e., their domain or range is used to infer the implied condition).

The previous query introduced union type values in its result. The *RQL* type system is equipped with rules allowing us to infer appropriate union types, whenever it is required for query evaluation. Table 18.5 presents the typing rules applicable in cases of union type coercions. In these rules we use the **coerce** function, which returns the types of the given expression for which

Union Type Expression	Typing Rules	
sub/super ClassOfU	$$\dfrac{e:(\tau_1+\tau_2+\cdots+\tau_n), \exists i \in [1\ldots n], \tau_i \in \{\tau_C, \tau_M\} \quad e' \in \{subClassOf, superClassOf\},}{e'(e):\{\Sigma_i(\tau_i)\}, coerce(e):\Sigma_i(\tau_i)}$$	(1)
inbagU	$$\dfrac{e:\tau, e':\{(\tau_1'+\tau_2'+\cdots+\tau_n')\}, \exists i \in [1\ldots n], \tau_i' = \tau}{(e\ in\ e'):boolean, coerce(e'):\{\tau\}}$$	(2)
Uinbag	$$\dfrac{e:(\tau_1+\tau_2+\cdots+\tau_n), e':\{\tau'\}, \exists i \in [1\ldots n], \tau_i = \tau'}{(e\ in\ e'):boolean, coerce(e):\tau'}$$	(3)
UinbagU	$$\dfrac{e:(\tau_1+\tau_2+\cdots+\tau_n), e':\{(\tau_1'+\tau_2'+\cdots+\tau_m')\}, \quad \exists i \in [1\ldots n],\ j \in [1\ldots m],\ k \in [1\ldots l], \tau_i = \tau_j'(=\tau_k'')}{(e\ in\ e'):boolean, \quad coerce(e):\Sigma_k(\tau_k''), coerce(e'):\{\Sigma_k(\tau_k'')\}}$$	(4)
Uintersect	$$\dfrac{e:\{(\tau_1+\tau_2+\cdots+\tau_n)\}, e':\{\tau'\}, \exists i \in [1\ldots n], \tau_i = \tau'}{(e\ intersect\ e'):\{\tau'\}, coerce(e):\{\tau'\}}$$	(5)
UintersectU	$$\dfrac{e:\{(\tau_1+\tau_2+\cdots+\tau_n)\}, e':\{(\tau_1'+\tau_2'+\cdots+\tau_m')\}, \quad \exists i \in [1\ldots n],\ j \in [1\ldots m],\ k \in [1\ldots l], \tau_i = \tau_j'(=\tau_k'')}{(e\ intersect\ e'):\{\Sigma_k(\tau_k'')\}, \quad coerce(e):\{\Sigma_k(\tau_k'')\}, coerce(e'):\{\Sigma_k(\tau_k'')\}}$$	(6)
Uminus	$$\dfrac{e:\{(\tau_1+\tau_2+\cdots+\tau_n)\}, e':\{\tau'\}, \exists i \in [1\ldots n], \tau_i = \tau'}{(e\ minus\ e'):\{(\tau_1+\tau_2+\cdots+\tau_n)\}}$$	(7)
minusU	$$\dfrac{e:\{\tau\}, e':\{(\tau_1'+\tau_2'+\cdots+\tau_n')\}, \exists i \in [1\ldots n], \tau_i' = \tau}{(e\ minus\ e'):\{\tau\}, coerce(e'):\{\tau\}}$$	(8)
UminusU	$$\dfrac{e:\{(\tau_1+\tau_2+\cdots+\tau_n)\}, e':\{(\tau_1'+\tau_2'+\cdots+\tau_m')\}, \quad \exists i \in [1\ldots n],\ j \in [1\ldots m],\ k \in [1\ldots m], \tau_i - \tau_j'(=\tau_k'')}{(e\ minus\ e'):\{(\tau_1+\tau_2+\cdots+\tau_n)\}}$$	(9)
Uunion	$$\dfrac{e:\{(\tau_1+\tau_2+\cdots+\tau_n)\}, e':\{\tau'\}}{(e\ union\ e'):\{(\Sigma_i(\tau_i)+\tau')\}}$$	(10)
UunionU	$$\dfrac{e:\{(\tau_1+\tau_2+\cdots+\tau_n)\}, e':\{(\tau_1'+\tau_2'+\cdots+\tau_m')\}}{(e\ union\ e'):\{(\Sigma_i(\tau_i)+\Sigma_j(\tau_j'))\}}$$	(11)
Ucomp	$$\dfrac{e:(\tau_1+\tau_2+\cdots+\tau_n), e':\tau', \quad \theta \in \{=, !=, <, >, \le, \ge, like\}, \exists i \in [1\ldots n], \tau_i = \tau'}{(e\ \theta\ e'):boolean, coerce(e):\tau'}$$	(12)
UcompU	$$\dfrac{e:(\tau_1+\tau_2+\cdots+\tau_n), e':(\tau_1'+\tau_2'+\cdots+\tau_m'), \quad \exists i \in [1\ldots n],\ j \in [1\ldots m],\ k \in [1\ldots m], \tau_i = \tau_j'(=\tau_k''), \quad \theta \in (=, !=, <, >, \le, \ge, like)}{(e\ \theta\ e'):boolean, coerce(e):\Sigma_k(\tau_k''), coerce(e'):\Sigma_k(\tau_k'')}$$	(13)

Table 18.5. Union type coercions

the corresponding operation is defined. The value of union type coercions is more obvious in the following query:

```
SELECT X, @P, Y
```

```
FROM {X}@P{Y}
WHERE Y >= 2000-01-01
```

In this query, Y is initially bound to a collection of type $(\tau_U + string + float + integer + date)$. Then, the condition in the WHERE clause imposes an additional implicit type condition: Y values should be of type $date$ (rule "Ucomp" in Table 18.5). As a consequence, the result of the query is of type $([\tau_U, \tau_P, date])$.

Using RQL's mixed path expressions, one can start querying resources according to one schema, while discovering in the sequel how the same resources are described using another schema. To our knowledge, none of the existing query languages has the power of RQL path expressions. Consider, for example, the following query that finds related data and schema information of resources, whose URI matches "www.museum.es":

```
SELECT X, ( SELECT $W, ( SELECT @P, Y
                                FROM {X;$W}@P{Y} )
                FROM $W{X} )
FROM Resource{X}
WHERE X like ''www.museum.es''
```

In the above query, we are interested to discover, for each matching resource, the classes under which it is classified and then, for each class, the properties which are used along with their respective values. This grouping functionality is captured by the two nested queries in the SELECT clause of the external query. Note the use of string predicates such as like on resource URIs. Then for each successful valuation of X (of type τ_U), in the outer query, variable $\$W$ iterates over the classes (type τ_C) having X in their extent. Finally, for each successful valuation of X and $\$W$ in the inner query, variable $@P$ iterates over the properties which may have $\$W$ as domain and X as source value in their extent, by defining appropriate implicit filtering conditions on $@P$. According to the example of Figure 18.1, the type of Y is the union $(\tau_U + string + date)$. The final result of the query in HTML form is presented in Figure 18.4.

In cases where a grouped form of results is not desirable, we can easily generate a flat triple-based representation (i.e., subject, predicate, object) of resource descriptions. For instance, to retrieve the description of resources, excluding properties related to the class $ExtResource$, we issue the query:

```
( ( SELECT X, @P, Y FROM {X}@P{Y} )
  union
  ( SELECT X, type, $W FROM $W{X} ) )
minus
( ( SELECT X, @P, Y FROM {X;ExtResource}@P{Y} )
  union
  ( SELECT X, type, ExtResource FROM ExtResource{X} ) )
```

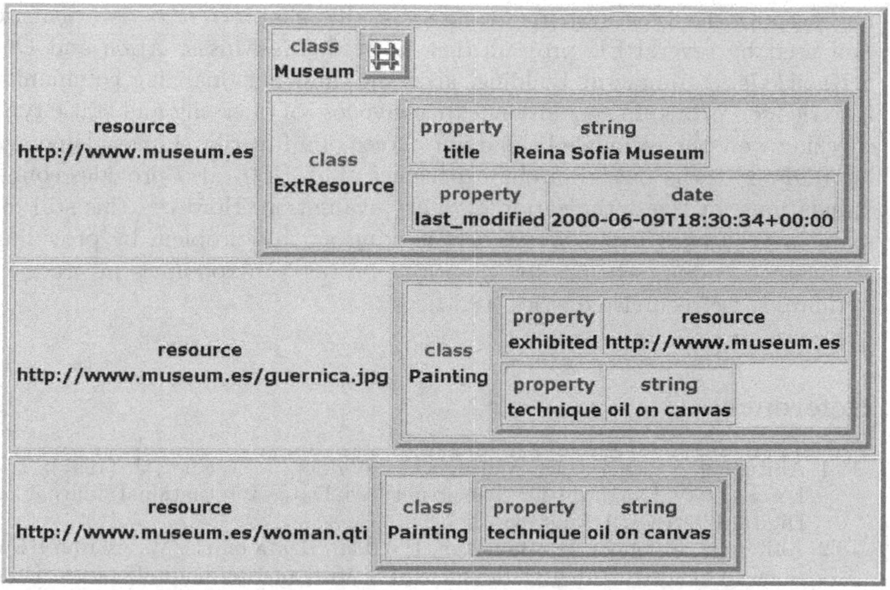

Fig. 18.4. HTML form of result

In the above query, we essentially perform a set difference between the entire set of resource descriptions (i.e., the attributed properties and their values, as well as the class instantiation properties) and the descriptions of resources which are instances of class *ExtResource*. Note that, since *RQL* query results are also typed collections, we are able to perform static type checking when they are used (nested) in other queries (e.g., set operations, scans on nested queries). Regarding the typing of the two union query results, which contain union type values, rules (9) and (11) of Table 18.5 hold. Firstly, the inferred type for the constants **type** and *ExtResource* (in the SELECT clause of the two union subqueries) is τ_P (i.e., a property name) and τ_C (i.e., class name). Secondly, variables Y and $\$W$ (in the SELECT clause of the first union) is of type $(\tau_U + string + float + integer + date)$ and τ_C. In this case, the union operation is performed between subqueries of different types.

18.4 Summary and Conclusions

In this chapter, we have presented a formal graph data model capturing the most salient features of RDF and a functional query language, *RQL*, for uniformly querying both RDF schema and resource descriptions. There currently exist two distinct implementations of *RQL*, one by ICS-FORTH (*139.91.183.30:9090/RDF/RQL*) and the other by Aidministrator (*sesame.aidministrator.nl/rql/*). The latter implementation, however, does not support the type system presented in this chapter. *RQL* is a generic tool used by several EU projects (i.e., *C-Web*, *MesMuses*, *Arion* and *OntoKnowledge*[6]) aiming at building, accessing and personalizing community Knowledge Portals. In conclusion, expressiveness of querying and static type checking were the rationale behind our choice of a functional query language for RDF. It turns out from our experience that *RQL* also provides sound foundations for the optimization of query evaluation. However, this still remains a very hard issue. We started looking at this problem by providing adequate encoding schemes for class and property taxonomies in order to optimize some recursive queries [18.14].

References

18.1 Abiteboul, S., Quass, D., McHugh, J., Widom, J., Wiener, J. (1997): The Lorel Query Language for Semistructured Data. International Journal on Digital Libraries, 1(1):68–88

18.2 Abiteboul, S., Suciu, D., Buneman, P. (1999): Data on the Web: From Relations to Semistructured Data and XML. Morgan Kaufmann Series in Data Management Systems

18.3 Alexaki, S., Christophides, V., Karvounarakis, G., Plexousakis, D. (2001): On Storing Voluminous RDF Descriptions: The case of Web Portal Catalogs. In Proceedings of the 4th International Workshop on the Web and Databases (WebDB'01) - In conjunction with ACM SIGMOD/PODS, Santa Barbara, CA

18.4 Berners-Lee, T., Fielding, R., Masinter, L. (1998): Uniform Resource Identifiers (URI): Generic Syntax. RFC 2396. Available at: http://www.ietf.org/rfc/rfc2396.txt

18.5 Berners-Lee, T., Hendler, J., Lassila, O. (2001): The Semantic Web. Scientific American.
Available at: http://www.sciam.com/2001/0501issue/0501berners-lee.html

18.6 Bray, T., Hollander, D., Layman, A. (1999): Namespaces in XML. W3C Recommendation

18.7 Bray, T., Paoli, J., Sperberg-McQueen, C.M., Maler, E. (2000): Extensible Markup Language (XML) 1.0 (Second Edition). W3C Recommendation

18.8 Brickley, D., Guha, R.V. (2000): Resource Description Framework Schema (RDF/S) Specification 1.0. W3C Candidate Recommendation

18.9 Cardelli, L. (1988): A Semantics of Multiple Inheritance. Information and Computation, 76(2/3):138–164

18.10 Cattell, R.G.G., Barry, D.K., Berler, M., Eastman, J., Jordan, D., Russell, C., Schadow, C., Stanienda, T., Velez, F. (2000): The Object Database Standard: ODMG 3.0. Morgan Kaufmann Publishers

18.11 Chamberlin, D., Florescu, D., Robie, J., Simeon, J., Stefanescu, M. (2001): XQuery: A Query Language for XML. W3C Working Draft.
Available at: http://www.w3.org/TR/xquery/

18.12 Christophides, V., Abiteboul, S., Cluet, S., Scholl, M. (1994): From Structured Documents to Novel Query Facilities. In Proceedings of ACM SIGMOD Conference on Management of Data, Minneapolis, Minnesota (pp.313–324)

---

[6] See cweb.inria.fr, cweb.inria.fr/mesmuses, dlforum.external.forth.gr:8080, and www.ontoknowledge.org respectively.

18.13 Christophides, V., Cluet, S., Moerkotte, G. (1996): Evaluating Queries with Generalized Path Expressions. In Proceedings of ACM SIGMOD Conference on Management of Data (pp.413–422)

18.14 Christophides, V., Plexousakis, D., Scholl, M., Tourtounis, S. (2003): On Labeling Schemes for the Semantic Web, The Twelfth International World Wide Web Conference (WWW'03), Budapest, Hungary

18.15 Connolly, D., Van Harmelen, F., Horrocks, I., McGuinness, D., Patel-Schneider, P., Stein, L.A. (2001): DAML+OIL (March 2001) Reference Description. W3C Note

18.16 Dean, M., Connolly, D., Van Harmelen, F., Hendler, J., Horrocks, I., McGuinness, D., Patel-Schneider, P., Stein, L.A., (2002): OWL Web Ontology Language 1.0 Reference. W3C Working Draft

18.17 Hayes, P. (2002): RDF Semantics. W3C Working Draft

18.18 Karvounarakis, G., Alexaki, S., Christophides, V., Plexousakis, D. (2001): Querying RDF Descriptions for Community Web Portals. In Proc. of BDA'2001 (the French Conference on Databases), Agadir, Morocco (pp.133–144)

18.19 Karvounarakis, G., Alexaki, S., Christophides, V., Plexousakis, D., Scholl, M. (2002): RQL: A Declarative Query Language for RDF. In Proc. of Eleventh International World Wide Web Conference (WWW'02), Honolulu, Hawaii, USA (pp.592–603)

18.20 Lassila, O., Swick, R. (1999): Resource Description Framework (RDF) Model and Syntax Specification. W3C Recommendation

18.21 Magkanaraki, A., Karvounarakis, G., Tuan Anh, T., Christophides, V., Plexousakis, D. (2002): Ontology Storage and Querying. Technical Report 308, ICS-FORTH, Heraklion, Crete, Greece

18.22 Maloney, M., Malhotra, A. (2000): XML Schema part 2: Datatypes. W3C Candidate Recommendation

19. Functional Queries to Wrapped Educational Semantic Web Meta-Data

Tore Risch

Dept. of Information Technology, Uppsala University, SE-751 05 Uppsala, Sweden
email: Tore.Risch@it.uu.se

Summary.

The aim of the Edutella project is to provide a peer-to-peer infrastructure for educational material retrieval using semantic web meta-data descriptions of educational resources. Edutella uses the semantic web meta-data description languages RDF and RDF-Schema for describing web resources. The aim of this work is to wrap the Edutella infrastructure with a functional mediator system. This makes it possible to define general functional queries and views over educational and other material described using RDF and RDF-Schema. It is based on the observation that RDF-Schema definitions are easily mapped into a functional data model. This allows any RDF-Schema file to be wrapped by a functional mediator system. The RDF-Schema definitions are translated into a corresponding functional meta-data schema consisting of a type hierarchy and a set of functions. Queries then can be expressed in terms of the translated semantic functional schema. Since meta-data descriptions can contain both RDF and RDF-Schema definitions, the system allows both to co-exist with the difference that queries over basic RDF meta-data are expressed on a lower level in terms of a generic functional schema representing all RDF structures.

19.1 Introduction

In most query languages the queries are expressed against a *schema* that provides a meta-data description of the data to be queried. Not only does the schema provide for efficient data management but also, very importantly, it provides also a map for the user of the structure of the data to be queried. A well known example of queries without schemas are free text searches in web search engines, e.g., where most users have been frustrated by the lack of guidance on how to find the information relevant for a subject. By contrast, SQL databases always have a detailed database schema for efficient access, documentation, and user guidance. The goal of this chapter is to show how web search can be enhanced by means of a schema.

RDF (Resource Description Framework) [19.9] is an XML-based notation for associating arbitrary properties with any web resource (URI). However, there is no real schema description in RDF since there are no restrictions on the kinds of properties a given class of web resources can have. In contrast, RDF-Schema [19.2] extends RDF with schema definition capabilities. For example, for a particular class of web resources an RDF-Schema provides a description of allowed properties along with an inheritance mechanism.

The observation of this work is that the semantic data model of RDF-Schema can be regarded as a functional data model as well. Given that observation, we show how RDF-Schema definitions can be mapped to typed functions. We then develop a wrapper for RDF-Schema definitions allowing a functional mediator engine, Amos II [19.14], to import RDF-Schema definitions. The imported RDF-Schema definitions are translated to the functional data model used in Amos II. The user can then specify high-level functional queries in the query language AmosQL [19.14] of data described by the translated schema.

A particular problem in the semantic web environment is that RDF and RDF-Schema descriptions can be freely mixed. Thus, some web resources for a subject may be described only though RDF while others have RDF-Schema descriptions. Furthermore, a class of resources described through RDF-Schema may have additional RDF properties not included in the schema. Therefore, it is important to be able to transparently query both RDF and RDF-Schema meta-data.

Edutella [19.11] provides a peer-to-peer standardized interface and infrastructure for searching and accessing educational material known to Edutella. Web sources described by RDF or RDF-Schema are accessed through Edutella and can be queried through a family of RDF-based query languages, $QELi$, of increasing expressibility. In this way the data and knowledge in educational sources provided through Edutella can be queried.

The system presented here, RDFAmos, can directly wrap any RDF- or RDF-Schema-based data source on the Web. Its mediator functionality allows reconciliation of differences and similarities between different kinds of wrapped sources, e.g., different RDF-Schema views, RDF-standards such as Dublin Core [19.5], relational databases, etc. General functional queries of mediated views over different sources are then allowed [19.14].

RDFAmos provides mediation services for Edutella. This means that RDF-Amos peers are made accessible through Edutella's JXTA-based [19.13] peer-to-peer (P2P) infrastructure. Through the infrastructure RDFAmos receives QEL3 queries for execution. The query result is delivered back to Edutella through the same infrastructure.

Edutella-based sources can be wrapped as well. A wrapper including a QEL3 query generator is being developed. It can generate QEL3 query expressions executed through Edutella's distributed P2P search facilities. This allows mediating functional views to be defined that combine heterogeneous learning material from Edutella with data from other sources.

The next section presents an overview of the RDFAmos system, followed by a description of how it is being integrated into the Edutella P2P infrastructure. Two subsequent sections show how RDF-Schema and basic RDF meta-data descriptions are translated.

19.2 Architecture

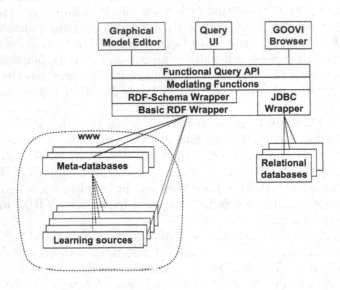

Fig. 19.1. RDFAmos architecture.

Figure 19.1 illustrates the architecture of RDFAmos, and how it accesses various data sources, including RDF and RDF-Schema meta-data definitions describing web resources. The meta-data definitions of each source are imported to the mediator where they are represented using the Amos II functional data model. Users and applications can formulate queries over the imported meta-data in terms of a functional schema automatically created in the mediator from the imported meta-data definitions. In Figure 19.1 there are examples of three kinds of applications: the *GOOVI Browser* is a general browser of functional Amos II databases [19.4], the *Query API* is a query executor for ad hoc functional queries, and the *Graphical Model Editor* is a system for editing meta-data structures and graphically specifying RDF-based queries [19.12].

The *Mediating Functions* of RDFAmos define functional views over combinations of data from different sources. Applications and users may specify arbitrary queries and views in terms of the mediated sources and combinations of them.

In Figure 19.1 there are examples of three kinds of data sources: relational databases, RDF-Schema, and basic RDF web sources. For each kind of data source the mediator needs a *wrapper*, which is a program module to import any schema definition for that kind of data source and translate it to functions and types in the functional data model. Once a particular schema is imported, the wrapper can translate queries in terms of the translated functional schema into accesses to the source. For example, relational databases can be accessed through JDBC and there is a *JDBC Wrapper* that imports relational schema descriptions through the standard JDBC relational database API and translates functional queries to SQL.

For RDF-based sources the *Basic RDF Wrapper* allows the import of any RDF meta-data description. All imported RDF objects are represented in the mediator using a simple functional schema, the *basic functional RDF representation*. It can represent any RDF-based meta-data. An RDF parser [19.3] translates RDF statements to corresponding binary relationships (triples) imported to the mediator. Once imported to the mediator, the RDF structures can be analyzed through queries to the basic functional RDF representation. Such queries are relatively primitive with little user guidance on what properties are available for a resource, its classifications, etc.

On top of the basic RDF wrapper the *RDF-Schema Wrapper* translates the RDF-Schema meta-data definitions expressed in RDF to a functional representation called *a functional RDFS view*. Since RDF-Schema provides schema information for RDF sources, unlike basic RDF, RDF-Schema definitions can be translated to data-source-specific function and type definitions in the mediator. Once a functional RDFS view for a web source has been imported by the wrapper it can be queried. Thus location-independent queries utilizing the full power of the semantic functional data model can be specified and executed. In particular, web sources describing learning material can be imported and queried. The result of such a query is a set of web resources that can be browsed by the user using a web browser or GOOVI [19.4].

In contrast to basic RDF, RDF-Schema requires further processing to semantically enrich the basic functional RDF representation to include the data-source-specific functions (properties), types (classes), and inheritance. Therefore, after an RDF meta-data document is loaded using the basic RDF wrapper, the system goes through the loaded binary RDF relationships (triples) to find the RDF-Schema type, inheritance, and property definitions. From these definitions the corresponding meta-definitions in RDFAmos are automatically generated as a set of type and derived function definitions. The function definitions are defined in terms of the basic RDF binary relationships as views. In this way we maintain both the basic functional RDF representation of meta-data along with semantic views that access it, thus making it possible to query the data using different models with different semantic expressiveness.

One difference between relational database sources and web sources is that in RDF-Schema there is no clear distinction between schema and data definitions, and RDF-Schema and RDF definitions can be freely mixed. This requires a system that can dynamically extend the schema at run time.

The RDFAmos architecture allows functional queries and views over any web source described by RDF or RDF-Schema alone, or combined with any other wrapped data source. Applications can be written in C, C++, Java, or Lisp. The applications do not have to know any details of the data sources, but need only see mediated data. For Java there is a "bean" package [19.1] that generates transparent Java interface class definitions from the mediator schema. This allows navigation through the mediated structures as regular Java classes, while at the same time being able to dynamically execute from Java functional queries over the mediated structures.

An RDFAmos peer can be also a data source for other RDFAmos peers [19.14]. There is thus a special wrapper for interfacing other RDFAmos peers. This mechanism allows modularization of mediators for scalable mediation [19.7, 19.8].

19.3 Mediating Edutella Peers

Figure 19.2 illustrates how RDAmos is interfaced with the Edutella infrastructure for P2P access to educational material. Edutella uses QEL3 as its query language. QEL3 is a Datalog-based query language for basic RDF data. RDFAmos is made available as a peer to Edutella by being able to execute queries in QEL3 (see top of the Figure). Our approach thus accepts basic RDF queries in QEL3 to RDFAmos which processed the query over mediated data sources.

A special property of QELi is that the general structure of, for example QEL3 queries, is described by a special RDF-Schema, the *query schema* for QEL3, which is imported to RDFAmos through the RDF-Schema wrapper as other schemas. Once the QEL3 schema is imported the system can import any QEL3 query as data producing a functional representation of the query itself in the mediator. Thus queries are regarded as yet another RDF-Schema data source. The functional representation of QEL3 query structures can be queried as other data.

In order not only to represent but also to execute QEL3 queries, we have created a query building AmosQL function that produces an AmosQL query string from an imported QEL3 query description. The query generation itself is implemented as query functions concatenating query elements retrieved from the imported query structure[1]. The query string is then evaluated using a system function **eval** and the result is converted and delivered back to Edutella as a QEL3 result structure in RDF. This makes RDFAmos an

---

[1] AmosQL has string construction and concatenation functions.

Edutella peer capable of executing arbitrary QEL3 queries over its mediated data.

Some wrapped sources may be interfaced from mediators using the regular web-based wrapper interfaces of Figure 19.1. In Figure 19.2 wrapper *W3* illustrates this. In this way, for instance, relational databases and RDF-Schema web sources are mediated and made available to Edutella.

A wrapper is also being developed for treating Edutella as a QEL3-based source, as illustrated by *W1* in Figure 19.2. This wrapper will allow mediation of data from Edutella-based QEL3-compliant peers. As is done for SQL [19.6], the wrapper will generate QEL3 query specifications in RDF to the wrapped Edutella source. After the query has been processed by some peers managed by Edutella, the result is delivered back to the mediator as RDF structures. Some of the processing peers might be other RDFAmos mediators.

One limitation of the current implementation is that it is based on using QEL3 as the query language when interfacing with Edutella. QEL3 is equivalent to basic Datalog over RDF statement without recursion. Rules allow named and disjunctive queries. Even though QEL3 itself is described through RDF-Schema, the QEL3 queries range only over basic RDF statements. It supports object abstraction only through explicit predicates over the RDF-Schema type system. Thus the QEL3 queries must be specified over the basic functional RDF representation which has little semantics.

In order to fully utilize the functional data model, a next step is to define a QELf for functional queries and support these in RDFAmos. An Edutella-based wrapper for RDFAmos data sources can then be defined, illustrated by *W2* in Figure 19.2). In order to allow one mediator to access mediator definitions from other mediators through Edutella, the mediator definitions of RDFAmos should be exportable as RDF-Schema.

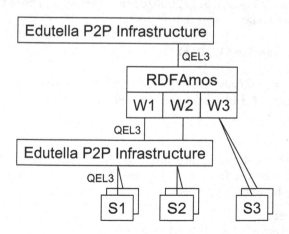

Fig. 19.2. Edutella interfaces.

19.4 Functional Wrapping of RDF-Schema Definitions

The RDF-Schema wrapper can import any RDF-Schema meta-data description document from the Web. The RDF-Schema definitions are thereby translated into corresponding function and type definitions. Data described by the RDF-Schema definitions is translated into object instances.

Types in RDFAmos are equivalent to *classes* in RDF-Schema. Both RDFAmos and RDF-Schema use extent-subset semantics [19.14] for inheritance. Only stored functions [19.14] have correspondence in RDF-Schema and they correspond to *properties* there. Meta-objects (schema elements) in RDFAmos mediators, such as types and function, are first class and can be queried as any other objects, as in RDF-Schema.

For example, assume the following RDF-Schema definition of learning materials [19.11]:

```
<rdf:Description ID="Book">
 <rdf:type resource=
        "http://www.w3.org/2000/01/rdf-schema#Class"/>
 <rdfs:subClassOf rdf:resource=
        "http://www.w3.org/2000/01/rdf-schema#Resource"/>
</rdf:Description>

<rdf:Description ID="Title">
 <rdf:type resource=
        "http://www.w3.org/2000/01/rdf-schema#Property"/>
 <rdfs:domain rdf:resource="#Book"/>
 <rdfs:range rdf:resource=
        "http://www.w3.org/2000/01/rdf-schema#Literal"/>
</rdf:Description>

<rdf:Description ID="AI_Book">
 <rdf:type
  resource="http://www.w3.org/2000/01/rdf-schema#Class"/>
 <rdfs:subClassOf rdf:resource="#Book"/>
</rdf:Description>
```

The RDF-Schema definitions are imported into the mediator and automatically translated to the following type and function definitions, as illustrated graphically by Figure 19.3.

```
create type Book;
create function title(Book b)->Literal as
        select getprop(b,"Title");
create type AI_Book under Book;
```

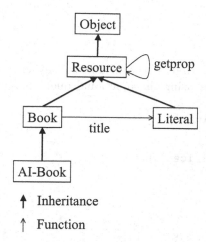

Fig. 19.3. Functional schema.

Notice that short, readable type and function *nicknames* are constructed from the URIs. For example, the nickname of
`http://www.edutella.org/edutella#Title` is `Title`. The nick names allow readable query statements without having to specify full URIs as function and type names. The function `getprop` is a function accessing properties of objects stored using the basic functional RDF representation.

The following database instances satisfy the above RDF-Schema definitions:

```
<rdf:RDF xml:lang="en"
  xmlns:rdf="http://www.w3.org/1999/02/22-rdf-syntax-ns#"
  xmlns:rdfs="http://www.w3.org/2000/01/rdf-schema#"
  xmlns:sch="http://user.it.uu.se/~torer/rdf/schema#"
  >
```

```
<sch:Book about="http://www.xyz.com/sw.html">
  <sch:Title>Software Engineering</sch:Title>
</sch:Book>
```

```
<sch:Book about="http://www.xyz.com/ai.html">
  <sch:Title>Artificial Intelligence</sch:Title>
</sch:Book>
```

```
<sch:AI_Book about="http://www.xyz.com/pl.html">
  <sch:Title>Prolog</sch:Title>
```

```
</sch:AI_Book>

</rdf:RDF>
```

Once the instances are imported to the mediator they can be queried in terms of functions and types using the functional query language AmosQL of RDFAmos.

The general syntax for AmosQL queries is:

```
select <result>
    from <domain specifications>
    where <condition>
```

For example,

```
select distinct X
    from Book X, AI_Book Y
    where title(X) = 'Artificial Intelligence' or
        X = Y;
```

The query searches for AI books by looking for books where either the title is "Artificial Intelligence" or the book is an instance of type AI-book. It is an example of a query to a functional RDFS view where the types Book and AI-Book are defined as RDF-Schema classes and the function title is a property. Each *domain specification* associates a query variable with a type where the variable is universally quantified over the extent of the type.

19.5 Basic Functional RDF Representation

The schema used in basic RDF descriptions (http://www.w3.org/TR/rdf-mt/) is rudimentary and provides little guidance at all for the user. In general one may associate freely chosen properties about any web resource, e.g.:

```
<edu:Book about="http://www.xyz.com/sw.html">
    <edu:Title>Software Engineering</edu:Title>
</edu:Book>
```

The above states that the Edutella registered book in http://www.xyz.com/sw.html has the title Software Engineering. In basic RDF the user can choose any property for the annotation (here Title), while RDF-Schema allows one to restrict the allowable properties.

The basic functional RDF representation is described by the following functional schema:

```
create type Resource;
create function uri(Resource) -> String as stored;
create function rl(String u)  -> Resource r
```

```
           as select r
              where uri(r)=u;
  create function name(Resource) -> String as stored;
  create type Statement under Resource;
  create function triple(Statement s) -> <Resource subject,
                                          Resource predicate,
                                          Resource object>
           as stored;
  create function stmt(Resource s, Resource p, Resource o)
                   -> Boolean
           as select true
              from Statement st
              where triple(st)= <s,p,o>;
  create function getprop(Resource r, String propname)
                   -> Resource v
           as select v
              from Resource p
              where stmt(r,p,v) and
                    name(p)=propname;
```

When RDF data is imported, the wrapper creates Resource and Statement objects and adds instances to the functions uri (resources) and triple (statements). The RDF statements always have an OID in the wrapper. In RDF only *reified statements* have URIs. By treating all statements as objects we are able to easily reason about statements and treat reified statements as a subtype of type Statement.

The function getprop is a convenience function for accessing properties of objects without having to specify long and complex URIs. Examples of queries are as follows:

```
getprop(uri("http://www.xyz.com/sw.html"),"Title")

Answer: "Artificial Intelligence"

select r
from Resource r
where "Artificial Intelligence" = getprop(r,"Title");

Answer: uri("http://www.xyz.com/sw.html")
```

Further abstractions can be made manually by defining functions accessing properties such as title above. Such property function are automatically generated by the wrapper for RDF-Schema properties.

It would be possible to automatically define the property functions from basic RDF definitions as the triples were asserted. However, this might generate very many functions and would not really guide the user further. The

RDF-Schema provides a better solution by explicitly specifying allowable properties.

19.6 Summary

RDFAmos extends Amos II [19.14] by providing transparent functional mediation over RDF- and RDF-Schema-based meta-data descriptions of web sources. Wrappers are defined for other sources too, e.g., relational databases [19.6] or engineering systems [19.10]. Applications can access mediated data using an API based on functional queries. The RDF and RDF-Schema wrappers can import any RDF(-Schema) definition and make it available for functional queries. The data model of RDF-Schema is very similar to a subset of the functional data model used in Amos II which makes it particularly straightforward to mediate RDF-Schema described web sources.

The Edutella P2P infrastructure allows queries over distributed educational material. RDFAmos can run as an Edutella peer thus providing general mediation services. In Edutella schema, data, and queries are represented using a mixture of RDF and RDF-Schema. Since the approach makes no clear distinction between data, schema, and query definitions, the mediator engine treats all three kinds of data in a uniform way as wrapped data. Edutella queries in the Datalog-based query language QEL3 are transformed by RDFAmos queries to functional query strings for evaluation.

This work shows that the functional data model is very well suited for managing and mediating RDF and RDF-Schema based data.

References

19.1 M. Bendtsen and M. Björknert: Transparent Java Access to Mediated Database Objects, *http://user.it.uu.se/~udbl/publ/ace.pdf*, 2001
19.2 D. Brickley and R.V. Guha: RDF Vocabulary Description Language 1.0: RDF-Schema, WC3 Working Draft, *http://www.w3.org/TR/rdf-schema*, 2003.
19.3 J. Carroll: ARP: Another RDF Parser, *http://www-uk.hpl.hp.com/people/jjc/arp/*, 2001.
19.4 K. Cassel and T. Risch: An Object-Oriented Multi-Mediator Browser. *2nd International Workshop on User Interfaces to Data Intensive Systems*, Zürich, Switzerland, 2001.
19.5 Dublin Core Metadata Initiative, *http://dublincore.org/*, 2003.
19.6 G. Fahl and T. Risch: Query Processing over Object Views of Relational Data. *The VLDB Journal*, 6(4), 261-281, 1997.
19.7 V.Josifovski, T. Katchaounov, and T. Risch: Optimizing Queries in Distributed and Composable Mediators. *4th Conference on Cooperative Information Systems CoopIS'99*, 291-302, 1999.
19.8 T. Katchaounov, V. Josifovski, and T. Risch: Scalable View Expansion in a Peer Mediator System, *Proc. 8th International Conference on Database Systems for Advanced Applications (DASFAA 2003)*, Kyoto, Japan, 2003.

19.9 G. Klyne and J.J. Carroll: Resource Description Framework (RDF): Concepts and Abstract Syntax, W3C Working Draft, *http://www.w3.org/TR/rdf-concepts/*, 2003.

19.10 M. Koparanova and T. Risch: Completing CAD Data Queries for Visualization, *International Database Engineering and Applications Symposium (IDEAS 2002)*, Edmonton, Alberta, Canada, July 17-19, 2002.

19.11 W. Neidl, B. Wolf, C. Qu, S. Decker, M. Sinek, A. Naeve, M. Nilsson, M. Palmèr, and T. Risch: EDUTELLA: A P2P Networking Infrastructure Based on RDF. *11th International World Wide Web Conference (WWW2002)*, Honolulu, Hawaii, USA, 2002.

19.12 M. Nilsson, M. Palmèr, A. Naeve: Semantic Web Meta-data for e-Learning - Some Architectural Guidelines, *11th World Wide Web Conference (WWW2002)*, Hawaii, USA, 2002.

19.13 S. Oaks, B. Traversat, and L. Gong: *JXTA in a Nutshell*, ISBN 0-596-00236-X, O'Reilley, 2002.

19.14 T. Risch, V. Josifovski, T. Katchaounov: Functional Data Integration in a Distributed Mediator System, in P. Gray, L. Kerschberg, P. King (eds.): *Functional Approach to Computing with Data*, Springer, 2003.

Author Index

Subject Index